MW01698559

# Ethics

PHI 2600

Edison State College

Denise | White | Peterfreund | James E. White

CENGAGE Learning™

Australia • Brazil • Japan • Korea • Mexico • Singapore • Spain • United Kingdom • United States

CENGAGE Learning™

**Ethics: PHI 2600, Edison State College**

Executive Editors:
Maureen Staudt
Michael Stranz

Senior Project Development Manager:
Linda deStefano

Marketing Specialist:
Courtney Sheldon

Senior Production/
Manufacturing Manager:
Donna M. Brown

PreMedia Manager:
Joel Brennecke

Sr. Rights Acquisition Account Manager:
Todd Osborne

Cover Image:
Getty Images*

*Unless otherwise noted, all cover images used by Custom Solutions, a part of Cengage Learning, have been supplied courtesy of Getty Images with the exception of the Earthview cover image, which has been supplied by the National Aeronautics and Space Administration (NASA).

Printed in the United States of America

Great Traditions in Ethics, 12th Edition
Denise | White | Peterfreund


Contemporary Moral Problems, 10th Edition
James E. White


ISBN-13: 978-1-133-23464-7

ISBN-10: 1-133-23464-X

**Cengage Learning**
5191 Natorp Boulevard
Mason, Ohio 45040
USA

Cengage Learning is a leading provider of customized learning solutions with office locations around the globe, including Singapore, the United Kingdom, Australia, Mexico, Brazil, and Japan. Locate your local office at: **international.cengage.com/region.**
Cengage Learning products are represented in Canada by Nelson Education, Ltd.
For your lifelong learning solutions, visit **www.cengage.com /custom.**
Visit our corporate website at **www.cengage.com.**

C O N T E N T S

# AUTHORS

**SAINT THOMAS AQUINAS** Selections from the *Summa Contra Gentiles,* Book iii, and the *Summa Theologica,* Articles i–iii and v–viii

**ARISTOTLE** Selections from the *Nicomachean Ethics,* Books i–ii, vi, and x

**SAINT AUGUSTINE** Selections from the *Enchiridion,* Chapters xi–xii, xcvi, and c–ci, and *The City of God,* Books v, xii, xiv, and xix–xxii

**A. J. AYER AND C. L. STEVENSON** Selections from Ayer's *Language, Truth and Logic,* Chapter vi, and Stevenson's "The Nature of Ethical Disagreement"

**ANNETTE BAIER** Selections from "Trust and Antitrust"

**KURT BAIER** Selections from *The Moral Point of View*

**JOSEPH BUTLER** Selections from *Sermons* i–iii and xi and the *Preface*

**JOHN DEWEY** Selections from *The Quest for Certainty,* Chapter x

**EPICTETUS** Selections from *The Discourses,* Books i–iv, the *Enchiridion,* and the *Fragments*

**EPICURUS** Selections from the letters *To Herodotus* and *To Menoeceus,* the *Principal Doctrines,* and the *Fragments*

**PHILIPPA FOOT** Selections from *Virtues and Vices and Other Essays in Moral Philosophy*

**THOMAS HOBBES** Selections from the *Leviathan,* Chapters vi, xiii–xv, and xxix–xxx, and *Philosophical Rudiments,* Chapter i

**DAVID HUME** Selections from *An Enquiry Concerning the Principles of Morals*

**IMMANUEL KANT** Selections from *Fundamental Principles of the Metaphysic of Morals,* First and Second Sections

**SØREN KIERKEGAARD** Selections from *Either/Or, Fear and Trembling,* and *Concluding Unscientific Postscript*

**J. L. MACKIE** Selections from *Inventing Right and Wrong*

**KARL MARX** Selections from *Karl Marx: Selected Writings*

**JOHN STUART MILL** Selections from *Utilitarianism,* Chapters ii–iii

**G. E. MOORE** Selections from *Principia Ethica*

**FRIEDRICH NIETZSCHE** Selections from *The Will to Power, The Genealogy of Morals* (First Essay), and *Beyond Good and Evil*

**PLATO** Selections from the *Gorgias* and the *Republic,* Books i–ii, iv, vi–vii, and ix

**JOHN RAWLS** Selections from "Justice as Reciprocity"

**W. D. ROSS** Selections from *The Right and the Good*

**JEAN-PAUL SARTRE** Selections from *Existentialism and Human Emotions*

**HENRY SIDGWICK** Selections from *The Methods of Ethics*

**BENEDICT DE SPINOZA** Selections from *On the Improvement of the Understanding* and the *Ethics,* Chapters i–v

**BERNARD WILLIAMS** Selections from *Morality: An Introduction to Ethics and the Limits of Philosophy*

# PREFACE

WITH GREAT SADNESS WE record the death of Theodore C. Denise, one of the moving spirits responsible for *Great Traditions in Ethics.* Ted was a fine philosopher and a fine man. He was a devoted contributor to philosophy and to the teaching of it. *Great Traditions* is but one testimonial to his contribution.

The new edition contains a much expanded Appendix on applied ethics, and a selection of earlier material has been redesigned to prepare for it. The Appendix discusses ways in which some of the ethical positions presented in earlier chapters—those of Aristotle, Epicurus, the Stoics, Mill, Kant, and Rawls—can be applied to concrete large-scale ethical problems.

These are only examples of how this can be done. Applied ethics is nothing new. Virtually all of the ethical ideas in this book were meant to be brought to bear on concrete problems.

Applied ethics is an extremely complex matter, or rather an extremely complex array of extremely complex discussions. The Appendix suggests several different applications that traditions of ethics have made possible. The Appendix does not aim at completeness. The applications described in it are intended as examples, and as encouragement to students to think of further ways in which ethical thinking can be applied.

*Great Traditions in Ethics* has always been true to its title and to the original plan laid out by Ted Denise and his original co-editors. It presents traditional philosophical ethics, some recent developments of them, and some skeptical philosophical reactions to them. The book is based on the conviction, supported by the many teachers who have used the book and contributed to it by their comments and criticisms, that traditions of philosophical ethics are as indispensable as they ever were to human ethical thinking.

I am, as always, thankful to the reviewers of this edition and others who have made suggestions that have both led to improvements and minimized mistakes. In particular these are Edwin E. Crawford, Jr., Northwest Nazarene University; Daniel Frank, Purdue University; William Isanhart, Oakland Community College, Auburn Hills; Mary Kay Klein, Bridgewater State College; Hans-Herbert Kögler, University of North Florida; Mark Packer, University of South Carolina, Upstate; and Duff R. Waring, York University.

# Great Traditions in Ethics

PART ONE

# Classic Ethical Traditions

CHAPTER ONE

# Introduction

## *The Unexamined Life Is Not Worth Living*

"THE UNEXAMINED LIFE is not worth living." In these terms, Socrates—the first great moral philosopher of Western civilization—stated the creed of reflective individuals and set the task of ethical theory. To seek, with the aid of reason, a consistent and correct ideal of life is the traditional goal of moral philosophers. Yet to search for basic moral principles and to attempt to solve problems concerning the good and the bad, the right and the wrong, is not the exclusive province of philosophers. Writers, government leaders, historians, and ordinary citizens also conduct ethical inquiry, although they may not call it that. Aristotle's *Nicomachean Ethics,* Shakespeare's *Hamlet,* Lincoln's *Gettysburg Address,* and Adam Smith's *Wealth of Nations,* as well as discussions at the bridge table and in college dormitories, exemplify at various levels the same questing spirit and desire for wisdom.

Flowing beneath every human action is the current of ethical significance, and in all ages and places, questions about moral conduct and moral principles are posed and answers attempted. "To be or not to be?" is at its heart a question of ethics. And "Whether 'tis nobler in the mind to suffer the slings and arrows of outrageous fortune, or to take arms against a sea of troubles, and by opposing end them"—this is, indeed, a difficult decision. In this, Hamlet's dilemma is typical of the problems that confront the ethical theorist and the sensitive lay person alike. They are among the most subtle and pressing problems of life.

The answers to ethical questions, whether as momentous as the agonized query of Hamlet or as trivial as the smallest matter of conformity to convention, are not to be found at the back of the book. The various means that have been devised to deal with ethical problems range from the mute acceptance of authority, through the poet's inspiration and the gambler's hunch, to the moral philosopher's direct and systematic analysis of the foundations of morality. Admittedly, the philosopher's commitment "to seek the truth, and to follow it wherever it leads" involves a harsh discipline. To earn the title of "rational animal," we are not obligated to think through every moral situation to its very roots; but once we go beyond immediate action to a consideration of the reasons for our actions, we are in reason's territory, and there, logic rules. In truth, we have only two alternatives: to reflect on moral matters or to remain silent. We would have to use reason even to argue for the soundness of refraining from rational discussion. The philosopher Epictetus, confronted by a skeptic, made plain the inescapability of committing ourselves to the use of logic:

> When one of the company said, "Convince me that logic is necessary," Epictetus asked: "Do you wish me to demonstrate this to you?" "Yes." "Then must I use a demonstrative form of argument?" And when this was admitted: "Then how will you know whether I argue fallaciously?" And as the man was silent: "Don't you see," said Epictetus, "how even you yourself acknowledge that *logic is necessary, since without its assistance you cannot so much as know whether it is necessary or not?*"

## PRINCIPLES AND PRACTICES

To think about morality, deeply and honestly, is the main business of ethical theorists, and in this, we can all participate to some degree. But more often than not, it is an instructive and chastening experience to seek out the theory that lies beneath actual practice, for we can then see the inconsistencies of ordinary moral thought and practice. We condemn as lazy the person who chooses the life of a beachcomber, yet we envy and admire those who are sufficiently wealthy to spend their time doing nothing. We disapprove of the "climber" who is someone we dislike, yet we praise the same quality when it appears in a "go-getter" who is our friend. We say that "honesty is the best policy" and yet acknowledge in our actions and words the good taste and practicality of telling white, gray, and black lies. It would be difficult to reconcile the principles underlying such judgments, and we can see why systematic ethical theorists usually distrust common-sense morality. On examination, it proves to be a murky and illogical collection of rules bound together only by the slender threads of chance and custom.

When observation and experience reveal to us how great the distance is between the high-flown ideals to which people give lip service and the down-to-earth expediency of the morality they practice, we may lose confidence in the efficacy of moral principles and theories. But moral principles cannot be escaped. Even the most cynical moral opportunists, in their recommendation that we act in each case only to promote our best interests, are setting up a principle to govern behavior. It is different *in content* but not *in kind* from the Socratic ideal of the life of reason or the Utilitarian goal of "the greatest good of the greatest number." Our moral integrity suffers when our principles are allowed to remain underground or when they are inconsistent with each other or with our actions.

We all have beliefs in accordance with which we judge actions and characters, our own and those of others, to be right or wrong, good or bad; we have aspirations that we strive to realize; and we have a conception, dim or clear, of the best way to live. When we endeavor to fill in the blank places in our moral theory, to eliminate as far as possible contradictory directives for behavior; when we endeavor to know what principles we act upon and how these are related to the principles to which we give intellectual assent; and when we endeavor to know *why* we think an ideal or moral judgment is correct, we have made a good beginning in our effort to apply reason to the moral life—to seek an ethical theory.

## REASON AND MORALITY

Reason is applied to moral situations and problems in different ways, depending on the purposes of the investigator. *Social scientists* undertake to describe how we actually behave, and they may or may not draw conclusions from their inquiry as to how we ought to act. *Casuists,* drawing on moral principles, law, religion, and related areas, attempt to decide concrete cases of morality. *Moralists,* whether literary lights or religious leaders, tell us what they think we ought to do and exhort us to follow the right way. Finally, *ethical theorists* undertake the systematic questioning and critical examination of the underlying principles of morality. These ways of dealing with morality are not mutually exclusive, and it is not uncommon for an individual to combine all four in an approach to morality.

For social scientists, the examination of moral behavior entails the processes of definition, classification, and generalization. They observe and compare the mores, customs, traditions, morals, and laws of different societies and formulate theories about the role of morals in society; or they may study the relationship between technological and moral-cultural change; or they may report the facts, points of view, and actions taken in specific cases of moral conduct. Although their findings are relevant to conclusions reached by others interested in morality, social scientists as such are essentially engaged in *descriptive* activity.

Casuistry—applied ethics—deals with individual moral problems, such as matters of conscience and conflicts of obligation. Casuists act on some occasions in an *advisory* capacity, guiding individuals in their choice of actions; for example, they may attempt to resolve the conflicting duties of the father of a starving family who has no other course than to steal. They also have an *adjudicative* function, for they must bring to bear various principles that they regard as relevant to a particular case and judge the guilt and responsibility of the offender by weighing the various circumstances of the case. Confronted with the problem of being both just and merciful to a hungry man who has stolen bread, a judge in a court of law would be engaged in casuistry in order to balance the principle of justice and the principle of mercy to meet the demands of a practical situation.

Moralists want to keep alive the values they consider worthwhile and to improve the moral quality of their community. Seeking to win others over to their ethical convictions and to exhort such others to act in accordance with these beliefs, they act in a manner that is primarily *persuasive* and *prescriptive.* To them, such actions as the stealing of bread provide the impetus and occasion to warn people away from what is wrong and to guide them toward what is right.

Ethical theorists, were they to examine the case of the hungry thief, would be interested in it chiefly as an illustration of a more general problem: whether it is possible to reconcile the principle of justice—which demands that all people be given what is due them—with the principle of mercy—which requires that extenuating circumstances be taken into account. In dealing with principles that establish standards for action, ethical theorists have in common with casuists and moralists an interest in the normative—that is, the *regulative*—phase of ethics. Their distinctive function, however, is a *deliberative* one, for they are interested in the examination of underlying assumptions and the critical evaluation of principles.

## HISTORY AND ETHICAL THEORY

The development of ethical theory in Western civilization has been by the gradual accretion of insights, rather than by a systematic evolution in a straight line of progress. Two principal influences, divergent in origin and direction, have provided most of the concepts with which ethical theorists in the Western world deal. In the Greek tradition, ethics was conceived as relating to the "good life." Inquiry was directed toward discovering the nature of happiness; differences of opinion regarding the characteristics of the happiest life and the means for achieving it enliven the writings of the ancient philosophers. A quite different orientation was introduced by the Judeo-Christian ethic. In this tradition, the ideals of righteousness before God and the love of God and neighbor, not the happy or pleasant life, constitute the substance of morality. These two influences reflect a major cleavage between those theorists who regard duty and the right as the primary ethical concepts and those who view happiness and the good life as the fundamental concerns of ethics. If we make an effort to reconcile these diverse views, we are faced with the difficult task of defining the relationship between "doing what is right" and "being happy."

The diverse traditions of the Greek and Judeo-Christian ethics, in combination with the many other historical and cultural factors operative in the formation of ideas, produce a multiplicity of systems in ethics. To the extent that ethical theory addresses itself to the problems current in the time of its formulation, it necessarily manifests this variety. History does not follow an orderly course in which one set of problematic situations is neatly solved and filed away before a new set of problems arises. The content of ethical theories, as a consequence, is largely a series of problems posed, solutions tendered, objections made, and replies attempted. The problems that occupy a generation may not be solved, yet fresh difficulties may demand to be treated; a German sage is reported to have observed that problems are never solved but are merely superseded by new ones. Even so, the very issues that have been put aside in favor of more pressing matters may reappear generations, or even centuries, later, to be considered afresh. Within any one ethical theory, there is system, rational structure, and a high degree of definiteness, but the history of ethical theory in the heterogeneous Western tradition is markedly irregular, unsystematic, and unsettled. Ethics is, in consequence, all the richer and the more challenging.

## THE NATURE OF ETHICAL THEORY

The initial problem of ethical theory is that of defining the nature of ethics. Any definition of a discipline so long in tradition and so rich in variety is made vague by the demands of inclusiveness. Broadly conceived, ethical theorizing is concerned with the construction of a rational system of moral principles and, as we have seen, with the direct and more systematic examination of the underlying assumptions of morality. More specifically, we find among the enterprises attempted by ethical theorists (1) the analysis and explanation of moral judgments and behavior, (2) the investigation and clarification of the meanings of moral terms and statements, and (3) the establishment of the validity of a set of norms or standards for the governing of behavior, an ideal of human character to be achieved, or ultimate goals to be striven for. We may still call people ethical theorists even if they do not attempt all these tasks.[1]

The more specific our statement of what ethical theory is, the more we find ourselves committed to a particular ethical theory. To define ethics as the study of the conditions for human happiness would provide an appropriate description of ethics as it was conceived by Aristotle, but not as it was understood by Immanuel Kant. Or, conversely, if we portray ethics as the study of humanity's irrevocable duties, we will be characterizing Kant's theory adequately, but we would have a completely misleading notion of the ethics of Aristotle. Further, although the classical ethical theorists attempt to present systems of moral principles and the reasons why they are valid, there are ethical theorists—the positivists, in particular—who deny the logical defensibility of such systems. Again, there are theorists who insist that those who attach great importance to the factual aspect of morality should be classified as social scientists and not as ethical theorists at all. And even on a point of general agreement, diversity may nevertheless persist. For example, although many ethical theorists agree that it is necessary to analyze the meaning of the language of morality, they use methods that vary so greatly as to produce strikingly different results.

In regard to the definition of ethics, as for the many other unresolved problems of ethical theory, the best appreciation of the meaning and importance of a problem comes from an examination of the various solutions that have been attempted. Each ethical theorist conceives of ethics in a personal way, and to obtain a truly meaningful conception of ethics, there is no substitute for acquaintance with the ethical theories themselves. From participating in the clashes of opinion, we shall discover that the challenge of ethics consists in the stimulation of its questions rather than in the finality of its answers. There is, moreover, the promise of the essential benefits of all philosophical controversy—the achievement of a measure of intellectual independence and maturity and a sense of security in dealing with abstract concepts. And for those who enter into the spirit of the philosophic enterprise, the traditions of ethics provide an adventure into a whole new range of ideas.

---

[1] *A note on terminology:* The term *moral* is essentially equivalent to the term *ethical.* Etymologically, these terms are identical, the former being derived from the Latin word *mores,* the latter from the Greek word *ethos,* both words referring to customary behavior. Both terms may be used with two different antonyms. Ordinarily, the opposite of *moral* is taken to be *immoral,* so that we mean by a "moral person" one who is good and does what is right, and by an "immoral person" one who is bad and does what is wrong. However, *moral* may also be used in a wider sense to refer simultaneously to right and wrong. In this case, its antonym is *amoral.* In this usage, people are moral in the sense that certain of their actions—for example, the way parents treat their children, the way we handle our obligations, the ideals by which we live, and so on—are subject to judgments of right and wrong. By contrast, the functioning of the digestive system, like the operation of a machine or the flavor of an apple, are considered amoral; that is, they are objects to which moral judgments are irrelevant. The same analysis may be made of the term *ethical.* Its antonym may be either *unethical*—that is, it may refer to what is wrong—or it may have as an antonym *nonethical,* in which case it applies to objects that are not subject to moral or ethical evaluation.

CHAPTER TWO

# Knowledge and Virtue

© North Wind Picture Archives

PLATO

THE LIFETIME OF PLATO (427–347 B.C.E.) covers a period of social, political, and intellectual change in both the city-state of Athens and Greece as a whole. From approximately 600 B.C.E., an expansion of trade had occurred between the Greeks and the peoples of other parts of the Mediterranean Sea. One by-product of this contact had been an increased awareness of various different social systems and ways of life besides their own.

This awareness encouraged two tendencies against which Plato's philosophy was a complex reaction. The first was a widespread tendency to question the validity of traditional Greek customs and ways of life. The second was an increasingly *relativistic* attitude toward ethical standards, traditional Greek polytheistic religion, and many other beliefs as well. This relativism held that what each individual or society believes may be true only "*for*" that individual or society. It denied that any belief is ever simply true or false objectively. In such a view, there would never be any point in trying to ask which of two seemingly opposed beliefs is in fact correct. Each belief would be correct *for* the person who held it and false *for* the person who rejected it. Beyond that there would be no objective matter of fact. All facts would exist only relative to the particular person(s) who believed them to hold.

This relativist viewpoint is often associated with the so-called Sophists in general, but it was advanced primarily by the Sophist named Protagoras (481?–411? B.C.E.) Protagoras's famous slogan, "Man is the measure of all things," was interpreted by Plato as an expression of a relativist viewpoint, and so Protagoras became one of Plato's principal opponents. Plato also opposed the doctrine of *hedonism*—the thesis that pleasure is the good—because it seemed to him to imply a relativistic view according to which a person should approve of any activity that gives him or her pleasure.

The Sophists were a varied and unorganized collection of teachers and thinkers who traveled from place to place in Greece, especially after about 450 B.C.E., offering lectures and lessons in all sort of subjects, from wrestling to political rhetoric to what we now call philosophy. Athens was the main center of their activity. There they were much in demand as teachers and even as celebrities, though more traditional-minded Athenian citizens were highly suspicious of them and regarded them as a threat to civic order and tradition. Many Sophists were actively sought as advisers on how, for instance, a citizen might win a case in a law court by giving an effective and eloquent speech. A Sophist known as Gorgias (485?–380? B.C.E.) offered to teach anyone who paid the appropriate fee to speak convincingly about any subject whatever. Even though not all Sophists were relativists, this kind of activity, along with Protagoras's slogan as Plato interpreted it, combined to give all of the Sophists the reputation of being self-seeking tricksters who believed in no objective values and used clever language to manipulate others to their own advantage.

Plato's teacher Socrates (470–399 B.C.E.) was sometimes called a Sophist, but Plato presents him in a completely different light. Socrates often insisted on how difficult it is for anyone to attain knowledge of the real truth about difficult questions, especially concerning ethics. He was for the most part an exploratory rather than a dogmatic philosopher. However, he never abandoned the conviction that there is, even about controversial ethical issues, an objective truth that is not simply relative to an individual's beliefs. Some beliefs, Socrates held, are objectively true and others are objectively false. His philosophical mission was to find out which are which. Like the Sophists, however, Socrates often offended Athenian traditionalists. Indeed, he was put to death in 399 B.C.E. on charges of impiety and of corrupting the youth of Athens with his ideas.

Socrates influenced Plato greatly, not through writing (Socrates wrote nothing) but through personal acquaintance and through the intelligent and courageous manner both of Socrates' response to the charges against him and of his death, which Plato describes in his *Apology of Socrates, Crito,* and *Phaedo.* These experiences, reinforced by the failure of Plato's attempt to persuade the dictator of the Sicilian city of Syracuse to accept his ethical ideas, left Plato disillusioned with political activity and turned him toward a life mainly of philosophizing—always with practical aims and implications. At some time between 387 and 367 he founded a school in the district of Athens known as the Academy. This school continued to exist for more than 800 years.

Plato presents Socrates' way of thinking in his own works, most of which are dialogues in which Socrates plays the leading role. Some of these dialogues are searches for definitions of important ethical concepts: the *Charmides* concerning temperance, for instance, the *Laches* concerning courage, and the *Euthyphro* concerning piety. These works probably reflect closely the conversational style of philosophy that Socrates practiced, especially in that they reach few firm conclusions and confine themselves mainly to exploring philosophical problems and disagreements. However, in other works, though Socrates often appears in them as a character, Plato sets forth his own philosophical doctrines in a much more definite way. In the *Symposium* and the *Phaedrus* he discusses love. In the *Gorgias* he investigates various ethical issues and vigorously attacks hedonism. The *Theaetetus* deals with questions about knowledge, and the *Sophist* attacks problems about the notion of being. The *Timaeus* presents an account of the structure of the universe.

The *Republic,* Plato's best-known work, explores the concept of justice, largely by giving parallel descriptions of both human society and the human soul or personality. As contrasted with relativist thinkers like Protagoras, Plato believes that there is both an objectively correct answer to questions like "What is justice?" and objectively correct beliefs about which sorts of personality, institutions, and actions are just. He also believes, and argues in the *Republic,* that among all of the virtues that a person may have, justice is the most important, especially because it brings about happiness in the just person, who is far happier than an unjust one.

Justice in anything, according to Plato, is a special sort of balance, order, or harmony among its components. In an individual person, this harmony is established and governed by reason, and in a political community it is maintained by the wise philosopher-rulers. In a just individual soul or personality, harmony obtains among the person's desires for various different things and among the satisfactions that result from fulfilling those desires. Plato divides these desires into three groups: (1) the desire of reason for knowledge and orderliness, (2) the desire of "spirit" (*thymos*) for self-defense, and (3) the bodily appetites. In a just political community—Plato focuses on the city-state, or *polis,* into which Greeks typically organized themselves—harmony obtains among the three main classes of people: (1) the philosopher-rulers, (2) the military, and (3) the artisans and farmers. Within such a society each individual has his or her own naturally established role or function, serving to maintain the stability and unity of the community as a whole. At the personal level, analogously, each desire, so long as it is governed by reason, has a role in the individual's overall life.

The idea of objective correctness enters into Plato's doctrine in his view that justice is, emphatically, *not* established merely by convention or the laws or customs that may happen to be observed in one place or another. Rather, he holds, a certain kind of order or harmony among groups in society is what social justice really is, even though this harmony is only very imperfectly exemplified in actual societies in the world. Analogously, Plato also holds that individual justice consists in one particular kind of reason-governed balance among a person's desires and satisfactions, even though different actual societies may regard various different kinds of behavior as just and lawful. Moreover, Plato holds both that the individual who is the most just in this way is also the most happy and that the most just society is likewise the happiest one. These two facts obtain objectively, Plato maintains against the relativist, and are not dependent on the particular desires, preferences, or tastes that an individual may have or that a society may approve of.

Plato attempts to provide a theoretical basis for these claims in his theory of "Forms" or "Ideas." These entities, according to him, exist neither in an individual's private consciousness nor in space and time, but rather timelessly and objectively so that they are accessible to any wise person's reason when it operates independently of the senses and of the person's accidental tastes and pleasures.

Plato holds that the nature and structure of these entities—which include the Form of Justice and the Form of the Good—determine the objective facts that exist to be known. He seems to have derived this scheme from mathematics, especially geometry. For instance, a sensible figure drawn in the sand would be a circle, he thinks, insofar as it perfectly exemplifies the Form of Circle, which is an ideal pattern of circularity. Plato carries this analogy over into the discussion of all concepts, including virtue, justice, and happiness. Facts about the sensible world—such as which individuals and communities are just or unjust—are determined by which souls and cities most closely resemble the Form of Justice. The full understanding of this difficult scheme (which Plato does not claim to be able to present fully in the *Republic* nor in any other of his writings) is the goal of the education of the rulers in Plato's ideal city-state. The ultimate goal is the understanding of the Good (which Plato explicitly refuses to identify with pleasure):

> In the world of knowledge [the Form or Idea of the Good] appears last of all, and is seen only with an effort; and, when seen, is also inferred to be the universal author of all things beautiful and right, parent of light and of the lord of light [i.e., the sun] in this visible world, and the immediate source of reason and truth in the intellectual [world]; and this is the power upon which he who would act rationally either in public or private life must have his eye fixed.[a]

The understanding of the Good, Plato thus contends, will enable the philosopher-rulers to organize their community so that it and its inhabitants are virtuous and happy.

---

**1.** Plato gives an account of the manner in which his philosophical opponents, the Sophists, answer the question "Why should men be morally virtuous?" They maintain that the weak value justice only because it restrains the strong. Most people would take advantage of their neighbors if they were certain that they would not be apprehended and punished, for they are interested only in their own welfare. Injustice is more profitable than justice, provided that it is possible to escape detection. This conception of human nature is presented by Glaucon [a brother of Plato] in the following story of Gyges' ring.

Now that those who practice justice do so involuntarily and because they have not the power to be unjust will best appear if we imagine something of this kind: having given both to the just and the unjust power to do what they will, let us watch and see whither desire will lead them; then we shall discover in the very act the just and unjust man to be proceeding along the same road, following their interest, which all natures deem to be their good, and are only diverted into the path of justice by the force of law. The liberty which we are supposing may be most completely given to them in the form of such a power as is said to have been possessed by Gyges, the ancestor of Croesus the Lydian. According to the tradition, Gyges was a shepherd in the service of the king of Lydia; there was a great storm, and an earthquake made an opening in the earth at the place where he was feeding his flock. Amazed at the sight, he descended into the opening, where, among other marvels, he beheld a hollow brazen horse, having doors, at which he stooping and looking in saw a dead body of stature, as appeared to him, more than human, and having nothing on but a gold ring; this he took from the finger of the dead and reascended. Now the shepherds met together, according to custom, that they might send their monthly report about the flocks to the king; into their assembly he came having the ring on his finger, and as he was sitting among them he chanced to turn the collet of the ring inside his hand, when instantly he became invisible to the rest of the company and they began to speak of him as if he were no longer present. He was astonished at this, and again touching the ring he turned the collet outwards and reappeared; he made several trials of the ring, and always with the same result—when he turned the collet inwards he became invisible, when outwards he reappeared. Whereupon he contrived to be chosen one of the messengers who were sent to the court; where as soon as he arrived he seduced the queen, and with her help conspired against the king and slew him, and took the kingdom. Suppose now that there were two such magic rings, and the just put on one of them and the unjust the other; no man can be imagined to be of such an iron nature that he would stand fast in justice. No man would keep his hands off what was not his own when he could safely take what he liked out of the market, or go into houses and lie with any one at his pleasure, or kill or release from prison whom he would, and in all respects be like a god among men. Then the actions of the just would be as the actions of the unjust; they would both come at last to the same point. And this we may truly affirm to be a great proof that a man is just, not willingly or because he thinks that justice is any good to him individually, but of necessity, for wherever anyone thinks that he can safely be unjust, there he is unjust. For all men believe in their hearts that injustice is far more profitable to the individual than justice, and he who argues as I have been supposing, will say that they are right. If you could imagine anyone obtaining this power of becoming invisible, and never doing any wrong or touching what was another's, he would be thought by the lookers-on to be a most wretched idiot, although they would praise him to one another's faces, and keep up appearances with one another from a fear that they too might suffer injustice.[b]

**2.** Thrasymachus, the celebrated Sophist, elaborates the advantages of injustice in political and economic affairs. He contends that injustice is rewarding particularly when it is conducted on a large scale. Happiness, he concludes, comes from injustice and not from justice.

So entirely astray are you in your ideas about the just and unjust as not even to know that justice and the just are in reality another's good; that is to say, the interest of the ruler and stronger, and the loss of the subject and servant; and injustice the opposite; for the unjust is lord over the truly simple and just: he is the stronger, and his subjects do what is for his interest, and minister to his happiness, which is very far from being their own. Consider further, most foolish Socrates, that the just is always a loser in comparison with the unjust. First of all, in private contracts: wherever the unjust is the partner of the just you will find that, when the partnership is dissolved, the unjust man has always more and the just less. Secondly, in their dealings with the State: when there is an income tax, the just man will pay more and the unjust less on the same amount of income; and when there is anything to be received the one gains nothing and the other much. Observe also what happens when they take an office; there is the just man neglecting his affairs and perhaps suffering other losses, and getting nothing out of the public, because he is just; moreover he is hated by his friends and acquaintances for refusing to serve them in unlawful ways.

But all this is reversed in the case of the unjust man. I am speaking, as before, of injustice on a large scale in which the advantage of the unjust is most apparent; and my meaning will be most clearly seen if we turn to that highest form of injustice in which the criminal is the happiest of men, and the sufferers or those who refuse to do injustice are the most miserable—that is to say tyranny, which by fraud and force takes away the property of others, not little by little but wholesale, comprehending in one, things sacred as well as profane, private and public; for which acts of wrong, if he were detected perpetrating any one of them singly, he would be punished and incur great disgrace—they who do such wrong in particular cases are called robbers of temples, and man-stealers and burglars and swindlers and thieves. But when a man besides taking away the money of the citizens has made slaves of them, then, instead of these names of reproach, he is termed happy and blessed, not only by the citizens but by all who hear of his having achieved the consummation of injustice. For mankind censure injustice, fearing that they may be the victims of it and not because they shrink from committing it. And thus, as I have shown, Socrates, injustice, when on a sufficient scale, has more strength and freedom and mastery than justice; and, as I said at first, justice is the interest of the stronger, whereas injustice is a man's own profit and interest.[c]

**3.** But constant discussion does not terminate the disagreement between Plato and the Sophists in regard to the value of justice. Underlying many Sophists' rejection of the just life is their contention that pleasure is the supreme good and that injustice is better than justice because it brings more pleasure. In the dialogue *Gorgias*, Plato attempts to refute this doctrine by focusing attention on the logical inadequacy of identifying pleasure with the good. Callicles, an admirer of the Sophist Gorgias, is Socrates' opponent.

*Soc:* Well, then, let us remember that Callicles, the Acharnian, says that pleasure and good are the same, but that knowledge and courage [as examples of virtue] are not the same, either with one another, or with the good.

*Cal:* And what does our friend Socrates, of Foxton, say—does he assent to this, or not?

*Soc:* He does not assent; neither will Callicles, when he sees himself truly. You will admit, I suppose, that good and evil fortune are opposed to each other?

*Cal:* Yes.

*Soc:* And if they are opposed to each other, then, like health and disease, they exclude one another; a man cannot have them both, or be without them both, at the same time?

*Cal:* What do you mean?

*Soc:* Take the case of any bodily affection:—a man may have the complaint in his eyes which is called ophthalmia?

*Cal:* To be sure.

*Soc:* But he surely cannot have the same eyes well and sound at the same time?

*Cal:* Certainly not.

*Soc:* And when he has got rid of his ophthalmia, has he got rid of the health of his eyes too? Is the final result, that he gets rid of them both together?

*Cal:* Certainly not.

*Soc:* That would surely be marvelous and absurd?

*Cal:* Very.

*Soc:* I suppose that he is affected by them, and gets rid of them in turns?

*Cal:* Yes.

*Soc:* And he may have strength and weakness in the same way, by fits?

*Cal:* Yes.

*Soc:* Or swiftness and slowness?

*Cal:* Certainly.

*Soc:* And does he have and not have good and happiness, and their opposites, evil and misery, in a similar alternation?

*Cal:* Certainly he has.

*Soc:* If then there be anything which a man has and has not at the same time, clearly that cannot be good and evil—do we agree? Please not to answer without consideration.

*Cal:* I entirely agree.

*Soc:* Go back now to our former admissions.—Did you say that no hunger, I mean the mere state of hunger, was pleasant or painful?

*Cal:* I said painful, but that to eat when you are hungry is pleasant.

*Soc:* I know; but still the actual hunger is painful: am I not right?

*Cal:* Yes.

*Soc:* And thirst, too, is painful?

*Cal:* Yes, very.

*Soc:* Need I adduce any more instances, or would you agree that all wants or desires are painful?

*Cal:* I agree, and therefore you need not adduce any more instances.

*Soc:* Very good. And you would admit that to drink, when you are thirsty, is pleasant?

*Cal:* Yes.

*Soc:* And in the sentence which you have just uttered, the word "thirsty" implies pain?

*Cal:* Yes.

*Soc:* And the word "drinking" is expressive of pleasure, and of the satisfaction of the want?

*Cal:* Yes.

*Soc:* There is pleasure in drinking?
*Cal:* Certainly.
*Soc:* When you are thirsty?
*Cal:* Yes.
*Soc:* And in pain?
*Cal:* Yes.[d]

**4.** The first phase of Socrates' argument is now completed: It is granted that good and evil are contradictories—that is, mutually exclusive in one person at one time—whereas pleasure and pain may occur simultaneously. If one may have pleasure and pain at the same time, but not good and evil, then there is a contradiction in identifying "good" with "pleasure" and "evil" with "pain." Socrates continues in the same vein, after summarizing his argument to this point. He is aided in this debate by Gorgias, a teacher of rhetoric.

*Soc:* Do you see the inference:—that pleasure and pain are simultaneous, when you say that being thirsty, you drink? For are they not simultaneous, and do they not affect at the same time the same part, whether of the soul or the body?—which of them is affected cannot be supposed to be of any consequence: Is not this true?
*Cal:* It is.
*Soc:* You said also, that no man could have good and evil fortune at the same time?
*Cal:* Yes, I did.
*Soc:* But you admitted, that when in pain a man might also have pleasure?
*Cal:* Clearly.
*Soc:* Then pleasure is not the same as good fortune, or pain the same as evil fortune, and therefore the good is not the same as the pleasant?
*Cal:* I wish I knew, Socrates, what your quibbling means.
*Soc:* You know, Callicles, but you affect not to know.
*Cal:* Well, get on, and don't keep fooling: then you will know what a wiseacre you are in your admonition of me.
*Soc:* Does not a man cease from his thirst and from his pleasure in drinking at the same time?
*Cal:* I do not understand what you are saying.
*Gor:* Nay, Callicles, answer, if only for our sakes;—we should like to hear the argument out.
*Cal:* Yes, Gorgias, but I must complain of the habitual trifling of Socrates; he is always arguing about little and unworthy questions.
*Gor:* What matter? Your reputation, Callicles, is not at stake. Let Socrates argue in his own fashion.
*Cal:* Well, then, Socrates, you shall ask these little piddling questions, since Gorgias wishes to have them.
*Soc:* I envy you, Callicles, for having been initiated into the great mysteries before you were initiated into the lesser. I thought that this was not allowable. But to return to our argument:—Does not a man cease from thirsting and from the pleasure of drinking at the same moment?
*Cal:* True.
*Soc:* And if he is hungry, or has any other desire, does he not cease from the desire and the pleasure at the same moment?
*Cal:* Very true.
*Soc:* Then he ceases from pain and pleasure at the same moment?
*Cal:* Yes.
*Soc:* But he does not cease from good and evil at the same moment, as you have admitted:—do you still adhere to what you said?
*Cal:* Yes, I do; but what is the inference?
*Soc:* Why, my friend, the inference is that the good is not the same as the pleasant, or the evil the same as the painful; there is a cessation of pleasure and pain at the same moment; but not of good and evil, for they are different. How then can pleasure be the same as good, or pain as evil? And I would have you look at the matter in another light, which could hardly, I think, have been considered by you when you identified them: Are not the good good because they have good [that is, the Idea of the Good] present

with them, as the beautiful are those who have beauty present with them?[e]

**5.** Plato's ethics rests upon two major points of this psychology. (1) The souls of all individuals consist of three basic elements or faculties: reason, spirit (passion), and appetite (desire). (2) An individual's character depends on the comparative development of the three elements and the dominance of one faculty over the others.

Each of the three elements of the soul (psyche) is involved in moral behavior, and each, when it carries out its proper function, is characterized by an appropriate virtue: Governing the soul by reason constitutes *wisdom*; rational regulation of desire constitutes *temperance*; the support of reason by the passions constitutes *courage;* the harmony of the three faculties constitutes *justice*, which is the overarching virtue. The same kind of analysis applies to the functioning of society, because for Plato, the state is the "individual writ large." Socrates and Glaucon, discussing the virtues, agree that "the same principles which exist in the state exist also in the individual, and that they are three in number." The exposition of the several virtues continues:

He is to be deemed courageous whose spirit retains in pleasure and in pain the commands of reason about what he ought or ought not to fear.... And him we call wise who has in him that little part which rules, and which proclaims these commands; that part too being supposed to have a knowledge of what is for the interest of each of the three parts and of the whole....

And would you not say that he is temperate who has these same elements in friendly harmony, in whom the one ruling principle of reason, and the two subject ones of spirit and desire are equally agreed that reason ought to rule, and do not rebel?

Certainly, he said, that is the true account of temperance whether in the State or individual.

And surely, I said, we have explained again and again how and by virtue of what quality a man will be just.

That is very certain.

And is justice dimmer in the individual, and is her form different, or is she the same which we found her to be in the State?

There is no difference in my opinion, he said.

Because, if any doubt is still lingering in our minds, a few commonplace instances will satisfy us of the truth of what I am saying.

What sort of instances do you mean?

If the case is put to us, must we not admit that the just State, or the man who is trained in the principles of such a State, will be less likely than the unjust to make away with a deposit of gold or silver? Would anyone deny this?

No one, he replied.

Will the just man or citizen ever be guilty of sacrilege or theft, or treachery either to his friends or to his country?

Never.

Neither will he ever break faith where there have been oaths or agreements?

Impossible.

No one will be less likely to commit adultery, or to dishonor his father and mother, or to fail in his religious duties.... And the reason is that each part of him is doing its own business, whether in ruling or being ruled.... Are you satisfied then that the quality which makes such men and such states is justice, or do you hope to discover some other?

Not I, indeed.

Then our dream has been realized; and the suspicion which we entertained at the beginning of our work of construction, that some divine power must have conducted us to a primary form of justice, has now been verified.... And the division of labor which required the carpenter and the shoemaker and the rest of the citizens to be doing each his own business, and not another's, was a shadow of justice, and for that reason it was of use....

But in reality justice was such as we were describing, being concerned however, not with the outward man, but with the inward, which is the true self and concernment of man: for the just man does not permit the several elements within him to interfere with one another, or any of them to do the work of others,—he sets in order his own inner life, and is his own master and his own law, and at peace with himself; and when he has bound together the three principles within him, which may be compared to the higher, lower, and middle notes of the scale, and the intermediate intervals—when he has bound all these together, and is no longer many, but has become one entirely temperate and perfectly adjusted nature, then he proceeds to act, if he has to act, whether in a matter of property, or in the treatment of the body, or in some affair of politics or private business; always thinking and calling that which preserves and cooperates with this harmonious condition, just and good action, and the knowledge which presides over it, wisdom and that which at any time impairs this condition, he will call unjust action, and the opinion which presides over it ignorance.

You have said the exact truth, Socrates.

Very good; and if we were to affirm that we had discovered the just man and the just State, and the nature of justice in each of them, we should not be telling a falsehood?

Most certainly not.[f]

**6.** Just people, then, are "integrated"—reason, emotion, and desire function harmoniously within them. On the other hand, unjust individuals are beset by inner "rebellion"—there is disorder within their souls. For injustice destroys the natural order of the personality, as disease detracts from bodily health. Accordingly, those actions that preserve a harmonious state in humans will be deemed good and those that diminish it will be termed bad. Plato is now in a position to answer the original question, "Why should any person be morally virtuous, or just?" Once the nature of justice is clearly understood, its practical superiority over injustice is manifest.

And now, I said, injustice has to be considered.... Must not injustice be a strife which arises among the three principles—a meddlesomeness, and interference, and rising up of a part of the soul against the whole, an assertion of unlawful authority, which is made by a rebellious subject against a true prince, of whom he is the natural vassal,—what is all this confusion and delusion but injustice, and intemperance and cowardice and ignorance, and every form of vice?

Exactly so.

And if the nature of justice and injustice be known, then the meaning of acting unjustly and being unjust, or, again, of acting justly, will also be perfectly clear.... They are like disease and health; being in the soul just what disease and health are in the body.... That which is healthy causes health, and that which is unhealthy causes disease.... And just actions cause justice, and unjust actions cause injustice.... And the creation of health is the institution of a natural order and government of one by another in the parts of the body; and the creation of disease is the production of a state of things at variance with this natural order....

And is not the creation of justice the institution of a natural order and government of one by another in the parts of the soul, and the creation of injustice the production of a state of things at variance with the natural order?

Exactly so, he said.

Then virtue is the health and beauty and well-being of the soul, and vice the disease and weakness and deformity of the same.... Do not good practices lead to virtue, and evil practices to vice?

Assuredly.

Still our old question of the comparative advantage of justice and injustice has not been answered: Which is the more profitable, to be just and act justly and practice virtue, whether seen or unseen of gods and men, or to be unjust and act unjustly, if only unpunished and unreformed?

In my judgment, Socrates, the question has now become ridiculous. We know that, when the bodily constitution is gone, life is no longer endurable, though pampered with all kinds of meats and drinks, and having all wealth and all power; and shall we be told that when the very essence of the vital principle is undermined and corrupted, life is still worth having to a man, if only he be allowed to do whatever he likes with the single exception that he is not to acquire justice and virtue, or to escape from injustice and vice; assuming them both to be such as we have described?

Yes, I said, the question is, as you say, ridiculous.[g]

**7.** Having expounded the nature of justice in detail, Socrates takes his listeners by surprise with his assertion that there is something higher than justice—namely, the Idea of the Good. Adeimantus, another brother of Plato, presses Socrates for an explanation.

What, he said, is there a knowledge still higher than this—higher than justice and the other virtues?

Yes, I said, there is. And of the virtues too we must behold not the outline merely, as at present—nothing short of the most finished picture should satisfy us. When little things are elaborated with an infinity of pains, in order that they may appear in their full beauty and utmost clearness, how ridiculous that we should not think the highest truths worthy of attaining the highest accuracy!

A right noble thought; but do you suppose that we shall refrain from asking you what is this highest knowledge?

Nay, I said, ask if you will; but I am certain that you have heard the answer many times, and now you either do not understand me or, as I rather think, you are disposed to be troublesome; for you have often been told that the idea of good is the highest knowledge, and that all other things become useful and advantageous only by their use of this. You can hardly be ignorant that of this I was about to speak, concerning which, as you have often heard me say, we know so little; and, without which, any other knowledge or possession of any kind will profit us nothing. Do you think that the possession of all other things is of any value if we do not possess the good? Or the knowledge of all other things if we have no knowledge of beauty and goodness?

Assuredly not.[h]

**8.** Plato now argues that neither knowledge nor pleasure is the Good itself but that the Good must be something different from both of them. Everyone, he says, acknowledges a difference between what really is good and what merely seems good. True rulers of a city should know what the Good really is. He will not, however, give a definition of the Good, but will try to explain it by analogy to its "child," the sun.

You are further aware that most people affirm pleasure to be the good, but the finer sort of wits say it is knowledge?

Yes.

And you are aware too that the latter cannot explain what they mean by knowledge, but are obliged after all to say knowledge of the good?

How ridiculous!

Yes, I said, that they should begin by reproaching us with our ignorance of the good, and then presume our knowledge of it—for the good they define to be knowledge of the good, just as if we understood them when they use the term 'good'—this is of course ridiculous.

Most true, he said.

And those who make pleasure their good are in equal perplexity; for they are compelled to admit that there are bad pleasures as well as good.

Certainly.

And therefore to acknowledge that bad and good are the same?

True.

There can be no doubt about the numerous difficulties in which this question is involved.

There can be none.

Further, do we not see that many are willing to do or to have or to seem to be what is just and honourable without the reality; but no one is satisfied with the appearance of good, appearance is despised by every one.

Very true, he said.

Of this then, which every soul of man pursues and makes the end of all his actions, having a presentiment that there is such an end, and yet hesitating because neither knowing the nature nor having the same assurance of this as of other things, and therefore losing whatever good there is in other things,—of a principle such and so great as this ought the best man in our State, to whom everything is entrusted, to be in the darkness of ignorance?

Certainly not, he said.

I am sure, I said, that he who does not know how the beautiful and the just are likewise good will be but a sorry guardian of them; and I suspect that no one who is ignorant of the good will have a true knowledge of them.

That, he said, is a shrewd suspicion of yours.

And if we only have a guardian who has this knowledge our State will be perfectly ordered?

Of course, he replied; but I wish that you would tell me whether you conceive this supreme principle of the good to be knowledge or pleasure, or different from either?

Aye, I said, I knew all along that a fastidious gentleman like you would not be contented with the thoughts of other people about these matters.

True, Socrates; but I must say that one who like you has passed a lifetime in the study of philosophy should not be always repeating the opinions of others, and never telling his own.

Well, but has any one a right to say positively what he does not know?

Not, he said, with the assurance of positive certainty; he has no right to do that: but he may say what he thinks, as a matter of opinion.

And did you not know, I said, that all mere opinions are bad, and the best of them blind? You would not deny that those who have any true notion without intelligence are only like blind men who feel their way along the road?

Very true.

And do you wish to behold what is blind and crooked and base, when others will tell you of brightness and beauty?

Still, I must implore you, Socrates, said Glaucon, not to turn away just as you are reaching the goal; if you will only give such an explanation of the good as you have already given of justice and temperance and the other virtues, we shall be satisfied.

Yes, my friend, and I shall be at least equally satisfied, but I cannot help fearing that I shall fail, and that my indiscreet zeal will bring ridicule upon me. No, sweet sirs, let us not at present ask what is the actual nature of the good, for to reach what is now in my thoughts would be an effort too great for me. But of the child of the good who is likest him, I would fain speak, if I could be sure that you wished to hear—otherwise, not.

By all means, he said, tell us about the child, and you shall remain in our debt for the account of the parent.[i]

–**9.** Plato, then, has answered the question "What is the ultimate knowledge upon which moral virtue is based?" It is the knowledge of the Good. However, the ultimate and supreme Good is too exalted an idea to be grasped fully by the human mind. Because the Idea of the Good defies direct statement, Plato's presentation of it must take the form of an analogy. Thus sight requires not only the eye and the object of sight but also the sun, which is the source of light. In the same way, understanding requires not only the mind and the objects of understanding but also the Good, which is the source of intelligibility. In short, visible objects can be seen only when the sun shines on them, and truth can be known only when illuminated by the Good. Socrates spells out this analogy in conversation with Glaucon.

Why, you know, I said, that the eyes, when a person directs them towards objects on which the light of day is no longer shining, but the moon and stars only, see dimly, and are nearly blind; they seem to have no clearness of vision in them.... But when they are directed towards objects on which the sun shines, they see clearly and there is sight in them.... And the soul is like the eye: when resting upon that on which truth and being shine, the soul perceives and understands and is radiant with intelligence; but when turned towards the twilight of becoming and perishing, then she has opinion only, and goes blinking about, and is first of one opinion and then of another, and seems to have no intelligence.... Now, that which imparts truth to the known and the power of knowing to the knower is what I would have you term the idea of good, and this you will deem to be the cause of science, and of truth in so far as the latter becomes the subject of knowledge; beautiful too, as are both truth and knowledge, you will be right in esteeming this other nature as more beautiful than either; and, as in the previous instance, light and sight may be truly said to be like the sun, and yet not to be the sun, so in this other sphere, science and truth may be deemed to be like the good, but not the good; the good has a place of honor yet higher.

What a wonder of beauty that must be, he said, which is the author of science and truth, and yet surpasses them in beauty; for you surely cannot mean to say that pleasure is the good?

God forbid, I replied; but may I ask you to consider the image in another point of view? . . . You would say, would you not, that the sun is not only the author of visibility in all visible things, but of generation and nourishment and growth, though he himself is not generation?

Certainly.

In like manner the good may be said to be not only the author of knowledge to all things known, but of their being and essence, and yet the good is not essence, but far exceeds essence in dignity and power.[j]

**10.** Making use of the analogy between the eye's vision and the soul's vision, Plato goes on to discuss the conditions and circumstances of our knowledge of the Good.

My opinion is that in the world of knowledge the idea of good appears last of all, and is seen only with an effort; and, when seen, is also inferred to be the universal author of all things beautiful and right, parent of light and of the lord of light in this visible world, and the immediate source of reason and truth in the intellectual; and that this is the power upon which he who would act rationally either in public or private life must have his eye fixed. [It is my further conviction] that the power and capacity of learning exists in the soul already; and that just as the eye [is] unable to turn from darkness to light without the whole body, so too the instrument of knowledge can only by the movement of the whole soul be turned from the world of becoming [—the changing world of experience—] into that of being [—the world of permanent reality—], and learn by degrees to endure the sight of being, and of the brightest and best of being, or in other words, of the good. . . .

And must there not be some art which will effect conversion in the easiest and quickest manner; not implanting the faculty of sight, for that exists already, but has been turned in the wrong direction, and is looking away from the truth?

Yes, [Glaucon] said, such an art may be presumed.

And whereas the other so-called virtues of the soul seem to be akin to bodily qualities, for even when they are not originally innate they can be implanted later by habit and exercise, the virtue of wisdom more than anything else contains a divine element which always remains, and by this conversion is rendered useful and profitable.[k]

**11.** Convinced that "the philosopher holding converse with the divine order, becomes orderly and divine, as far as the nature of man allows," Plato summarizes his case against those who believe that injustice is more profitable than justice. Philosophers, properly trained, can model their lives after the ideal of perfection that reason discloses to them.

[Glaucon asked:] From what point of view, then, and on what ground can we say that a man is profited by injustice or intemperance or other baseness, which will make him a worse man, even though he acquire money or power by his wickedness?

From no point of view at all.

What shall he profit, if his injustice be undetected and unpunished? He who is undetected only gets worse, whereas he who is detected and punished has the brutal part of his nature silenced and humanized; the gentler element in him is liberated, and his whole soul is perfected and ennobled by the acquirement of justice and temperance and wisdom, more than the body ever is by receiving gifts of beauty, strength and health, in proportion as the soul is more honorable than the body....

To this nobler purpose the man of understanding will devote the energies of his life. And in the first place, he will honor studies which impress these qualities on his soul, and will disregard others.... In the next place, he will regulate his bodily habit and training, and so far will he be from yielding to brutal and irrational pleasures, that he will regard even health as quite a secondary matter; his first object will be not that he may be fair or strong or well, unless he is likely thereby to gain temperance, but he will always desire so to attemper the body as to preserve the harmony of the soul.... And in the acquisition of wealth there is a principle of order and harmony which he will also observe; he will not allow himself to be dazzled by the foolish applause of the world, and heap up riches to his own infinite harm....

He will look at the city which is within him, and take heed that no disorder occur in it, such as might arise either from superfluity or from want; and upon his principle he will regulate his property and gain or spend according to his means.... And, for the same reason, he will gladly accept and enjoy such honors as he deems likely to make him a better man; but those, whether private or public, which are likely to disorder his life, he will avoid....

Then, if that is his motive, he will not be a statesman.

By the dog of Egypt, he will! in the city which is his own he certainly will, though in the land of his birth perhaps not, unless he have a divine call.

I understand; you mean that he will be a ruler in the city of which we are the founders, and which exists in idea only; for I do not believe that there is such a one anywhere on earth?

In heaven, I replied, there is laid up a pattern of it, methinks, which he who desires may behold, and beholding, may set his own house in order. But whether such a one exists, or ever will exist in fact, is no matter; for he will live after the manner of that city, having nothing to do with any other.[1]

## QUESTIONS

1. "Everything in the universe has a purpose or proper function within a harmonious hierarchy of purposes." In Plato's ethics, what is an individual's proper function, and how is it related to one's moral worth?
2. What is the connection between *knowledge* and *moral conduct* in Plato's moral theory? What arguments can be put forward to support his view, and what can be said against it?
3. Describe Socrates' "dialectical," or conversational, method of philosophical discussion. Does it provide an effective way of combating relativism?
4. Reconstruct the Sophists' conception of human motivation, and develop its implications for their definition of *justice*.
5. What are Plato's objections to the hedonism of the Sophists? How does he support the view that reason is indispensable even to hedonists?
6. Explain the concept of *harmony* in Plato's ethical theory, and relate it to his definition of the cardinal virtues.
7. Against the Sophists' argument that injustice is more profitable than justice, Socrates holds the belief that it is better to be done an injustice than to commit one. What arguments are offered by both parties to the debate, in defense and in attack? Evaluate the short-term and long-run practicality of these conflicting moral theories.
8. Describe the psychological theory underlying Plato's ethics. How is it related to his conception of the state?
9. What is the place of the "Idea of the Good" in Plato's general philosophical position? In his ethical theory?
10. Plato expounds his ethical views by describing *ideals* of a person and of a society. Do you think that using ideals in ethics is reasonable, or does it create unreasonably high expectations?
11. Plato argues that the Good is neither knowledge nor pleasure. Do you have any criticisms to bring against either of his arguments on these points?

## KEY TO SELECTIONS

Plato, *The Dialogues of Plato*, tr. B. Jowett, 3rd ed., New York, Oxford University Press, 1892.

[a]*Republic*, Bk. VII, pp. 517.
[b]____, Bk. II, pp. 359–360.
[c]____, Bk. I, pp. 343–344.
[d]*Gorgias*, pp. 495–496.
[e]____, pp. 496–497.
[f]*Republic*, Bk. IV, pp. 442–444.
[g]____, Bk. IV, pp. 444–445.
[h]____, Bk. VI, pp. 504–505.
[i]____, Bk. VI, pp. 505–507.
[j]____, Bk. VI, pp. 508–509.
[k]____, Bk. VII, pp. 517–519.
[l]____, Bk. IX, pp. 591–592.

## GUIDE TO ADDITIONAL READING


### PRIMARY SOURCES

Plato, *The Collected Dialogues of Plato*, ed. E. Hamilton and H. Cairns, Princeton, Princeton University Press, 1961.

____, *The Dialogues of Plato*, tr. B. Jowett, 3rd ed., New York, Oxford University Press, 1892.

### DISCUSSION AND COMMENTARY

Annas, J., *An Introduction to Plato's Republic*, Oxford, Clarendon Press, 1981.

Annas, Julia, *Platonic Ethics, Old and New*, Ithaca, Cornell University Press, 1999.

Irwin, T., *Plato's Ethics*, Oxford, Oxford University Press, 1995.

Jaeger, W. W., *Paideia: The Ideals of Greek Culture*, vol. 3, Oxford, Basil Blackwell and Mott, 1944.

Kraut, Richard (ed.), *The Cambridge Companion to Plato*, Cambridge, Cambridge University Press, 1992.

Shorey, P., *What Plato Said*, Chicago, University of Chicago Press, 1933.

Taylor, A. E., *Plato: The Man and His Works*, London, Methuen, 1926.

White, N., *A Companion to Plato's Republic*, Indianapolis, Hackett, 1979.

CHAPTER THREE

# Moral Character

© Bettmann/CORBIS

ARISTOTLE

ARISTOTLE (384–322 B.C.E.), the philosopher with whom only Plato compares in influence on the history of Western thought, was born in the Greek colony of Stagira in Macedonia. His father, Nicomachus, a student of natural history and an eminent physician, held the post of physician to Amnytas II, King of Macedonia, father of Philip the Great, until his death in Aristotle's eighteenth year. At his father's death, Aristotle, who had been brought up in an atmosphere of science and scholarship, went to Athens to study philosophy under Plato, and he remained at the Academy until Plato's death in 347 B.C.E.

Though Aristotle was unquestionably Plato's most talented student, he was by no means his most devoted disciple: "Dear is Plato, but dearer still is truth." It has been suggested that his refusal to defer to the master cost him the nomination to succeed Plato as the head of the Academy. In any event, Aristotle was passed over in favor of Speusippus, a man who did not approach him in intellectual stature. In 343 B.C.E. Aristotle was selected as tutor to Alexander, the thirteen-year-old son of King Philip of Macedonia. It was Philip who planned and began the world conquest that Alexander the Great so nearly fulfilled. There is no evidence that Aristotle, in his three years as tutor, modified the influence of father on son or in any way affected the subsequent thoughts and deeds of Alexander; neither is there evidence that Aristotle ever recognized the significance of Alexander's goal of political unity. A bond of friendship was formed between teacher and pupil, however, and it is reported that Alexander later subsidized some of Aristotle's researches in the natural sciences.

At the age of forty-nine, Aristotle returned to Athens and founded the Lyceum, the second of the four great schools of antiquity. An immediate success as a lecturer, he entered into the enormously productive period of his life: combining the roles of encyclopedist, scientist, and philosopher, he is reputed to have written over four hundred works, to have conducted and directed prodigious researches in botany and zoology, and to have amassed one of the great libraries of the Greek world. As the result of an anti-Macedonian uprising after the death of Alexander in 323 B.C.E., Aristotle left Athens. It is said by some authorities that he was accused of dangerous teachings and indicted by the Athenian citizens, just as Socrates had been seventy-six years earlier, but that he, in contrast to Socrates, accepted the option of exile. Aristotle died at Chalcis on the island of Euboea in the next year.

According to Aristotle's own classification, his works deal with the theoretical sciences, as in *Metaphysics, Physics, De Caelo* (astronomy), *De Generatione et Corruptione* (biology), *De Anima* (psychology); the practical sciences, as in *Nicomachean Ethics, Eudemian Ethics, Politics;* the productive or poetical sciences *(Rhetoric, Poetics);* and logic *(Organon)*. On such impressive evidence, it is said of Aristotle that for his time he knew all that was to be known.

Historically, Aristotle's *Nicomachean Ethics* is the first systematic treatment of ethics in Western civilization. It belongs in the tradition begun by Socrates and advanced by Plato, a tradition that stresses both the supremacy of our rational nature and the purposive nature of the universe. Nevertheless, within this broad framework, the ethical theories of Aristotle and those of his teacher, Plato, stand in sharp contrast. This difference stems from conflicting conceptions of the nature of the ultimate moral principle and is a consequence of different metaphysical positions. Aristotle takes issue with Plato's thesis that individual objects are intelligible only in terms of immutable forms or ideas that exist in and of themselves. According to Aristotle's doctrine, the forms that make objects understandable cannot exist apart from particular objects. That is, individual objects, for Aristotle, are a *unity* of a universal, repeatable form and a unique content or matter: "no form without matter, no matter with form." Consequently, Aristotle rejects the Platonic view that the moral evaluations of daily life presuppose a "good" that is independent of experience, personality, and circumstances. Rather, he insists that the basic moral principle is immanent in the activities of our daily lives and can be discovered only through a study of them.

In keeping with his general position, Aristotle begins his ethical inquiry with an empirical investigation of what it is that people fundamentally desire. In his search, he finds such goals as wealth and honors inadequate. He points out that an ultimate end for people must be one that is, first, *self-sufficient*—"that which [even] when isolated makes life desirable and lacking in nothing"—second, *final*—"that which is always desirable in itself and never for the sake of something else"—and third, *attainable.* People are agreed, Aristotle maintains, that happiness alone is the goal that meets these requirements. However, he recognizes that this is no more than a preliminary agreement about what it is that we should investigate in ethics. More specifically, we want to know the nature of happiness and the conditions of its attainment.

Following Plato, Aristotle tells us that happiness must be explained in terms of reason, a human being's distinctive function or activity. In his philosophical system, however, this view is significantly modified by the doctrine of *potentiality* and *actuality.* Just as the acorn actualizes its unique potentiality by becoming an oak, people actualize their distinctive or defining potentiality by living the life of reason. To Aristotle, this means that happiness depends on the actualization—the full realization—of one's rationality.

Consideration of the conditions requisite to the attainment of happiness leads Aristotle into a discussion of virtue. For him, as for other Greek philosophers, *virtue* refers to the excellence of a thing and hence to the disposition to perform effectively its proper function. For example, a "virtuous" knife cuts well, and a "virtuous" physician successfully restores patients to health. By the same token, Aristotle argues, a virtuous person lives according to reason, thus realizing his or her distinctive potentiality. However, he subdivides human virtue into two types, the *moral* and the *intellectual.* The moral virtues concern the habitual choice of actions in accordance with rational principles. The contemplation of theoretical truths and the discovery of the rational principles that ought to control everyday actions give rise to the intellectual virtues. But whereas contemplation, that activity by which people may attain the highest human happiness, is limited to the divinely gifted few, the practical virtues, with their lesser degrees of happiness, are within reach of the ordinary person.

Aristotle, then, in harmony with the Greek tradition, stresses the value of contemplation but, withal, is much impressed with the fact that people live for the most part at the level of practical decision and routine behavior. The good habits necessary to moral virtue are not strictly personal matters but can best be formed in a sound social and legal structure:

> It is difficult to get from youth up a right training for virtue if one has not been brought up under right laws; for to live temperately and hardily is not pleasant to most people, especially when they are young. For this reason their nurture and occupations should be fixed by law; for they will not be painful when they have become customary. But it is surely not enough that when they are young they should get the right nurture and attention; since they must, even when they are grown up, practice and be habituated to them, we shall need laws for this as well, and generally speaking to cover the whole life; for most people obey necessity rather than argument, and punishments rather than the sense of what is noble.[a]

---

> **1.** Aristotle assumes that any investigation, practical or theoretical, has a teleological basis—that is, it aims at some end or good. By using examples from ordinary experience, he attempts to show that ends or goods form a hierarchy.

Every art and every inquiry, and similarly every action and pursuit, is thought to aim at some good; and for this reason the good has rightly been declared to be that at which all things aim. But a certain difference is found among ends; some are activities, others are products apart from the activities that produce them. Where there are ends apart from the actions, it is the nature of the products to be better than the activities. Now, as there are many actions, arts, and sciences, their ends also are many; the end of the medical art is health, that of shipbuilding a vessel, that of strategy victory, that of economics wealth. But where such arts fall under a single capacity—as bridle making and the other arts concerned with the equipment of horses fall under the art of riding, and this and every military action under strategy, in the same way other arts fall under yet others—in all of these the ends of the master arts are to be preferred to all the subordinate ends; for it is for the sake of the former that the latter are pursued. It makes no difference whether the activities themselves are the ends of the actions, or something else apart from the activities, as in the case of the sciences just mentioned.[b]

**2.** Analogously, each theoretical pursuit has its appropriate end, but the science of politics—ethics and social philosophy—includes all the others in the sense that it determines their roles and directs their development. For this reason, the science of politics can have as its proper end nothing less than "the good for man."

If, then, there is some end of the things we do, which we desire for its own sake (everything else being desired for the sake of this), and if we do not choose everything for the sake of something else (for at that rate the process would go on to infinity, so that our desire would be empty and vain), clearly this must be the good and the chief good. Will not the knowledge of it, then, have a great influence on life? Shall we not, like archers who have a mark to aim at, be more likely to hit upon what is right? If so, we must try, in outline at least to determine what it is, and of which of the sciences or capacities it is the object. It would seem to belong to the most authoritative art and that which is most truly the master art. And politics appears to be of this nature; for it is this that ordains which of the sciences should be studied in a state, and which each class of citizens should learn and up to what point they should learn them; and we can see even the most highly esteemed of capacities to fall under this, for example, strategy, economics, rhetoric; now, since politics uses the rest of the sciences, and since, again, it legislates as to what we are to do and what we are to abstain from, the end of this science must include those of the others, so that this end must be the good for man. For even if the end is the same for a single man and for a state, that of the state seems at all events something greater and more complete whether to attain or to preserve; though it is worthwhile to attain the end merely for one man, it is finer and more godlike to attain it for a nation or for city-states.[c]

**3.** Aristotle warns us against expecting a high degree of precision in our study of political science, because it deals with the human variable. As such, it is a subject best handled by those of experience.

Our discussion will be adequate if it has as much clearness as the subject matter admits of, for precision is not to be sought for alike in all discussions, any more than in all the products of the crafts. Now fine and just actions, which political science investigates, admit of much variety and fluctuation of opinion, so that they may be thought to exist only by convention, and not by nature. And goods also give rise to a similar fluctuation because they bring harm to many people; for before now men have been undone by reason of their wealth, and others by reason of their courage. We must be content, then, in speaking of such subjects and with such premises to indicate the truth roughly and in outline, and in speaking about things which are only for the most part true and with premises of the same kind to reach conclusions that are no better. In the same spirit, therefore, should each type of statement be *received;* for it is the mark of an educated man to look for precision in each class of things just so far as the nature of the subject admits; it is evidently equally foolish to accept probable reasoning from a mathematician and to demand from a rhetorician scientific proofs.

Now each man judges well the things he knows, and of these he is a good judge. And so the man who has been educated in a subject is a good judge of that subject, and the man who has received an all-round education is a good judge in general. Hence a young man is not a proper hearer of lectures on political science; for he is inexperienced in the actions that occur in life, but its discussions start from these and are about these; and, further, since he tends to follow his passions, his study will be in vain and unprofitable, because the end aimed at is not knowledge but action. And it makes no difference whether he is young in years or youthful in character; the defect does not depend on time, but on his living, and pursuing each successive object, as passion directs. For to such persons, as to the incontinent, knowledge brings no profit; but to those who desire and act in accordance with a rational principle knowledge about such matters will be of great benefit.[d]

**4.** Among those who are sufficiently mature to discuss ethics, there is verbal agreement that the ultimate human good is happiness, but opinions about its precise nature vary.

Let us resume our inquiry and state, in view of the fact that all knowledge and every pursuit aims at some good, what it is that we say political science aims at and what is the highest of all goods achievable by action. Verbally there is very general agreement; for both the general run of men and people of superior refinement say that it is happiness, and identify living well and doing well with being happy; but with regard to what happiness is they differ, and the many do not give the same account as the wise. For the former think it is some plain and obvious thing, like pleasure, wealth, or honor; they differ, however, from one another—and often even the same man identifies it with different things, with health when he is ill, with wealth when he is poor; but, conscious of their ignorance, they admire those who proclaim some great ideal that is above their comprehension. Now some thought [for example, Plato] that apart from these many goods there is another which is self-subsistent and causes the goodness of all these as well. To examine all the opinions that have been held were perhaps somewhat fruitless; enough to examine those that are most prevalent or that seem to be arguable.[e]

**5.** Aristotle then proceeds to discuss the general criteria that make possible the identification of a human being's chief good.

Let us again return to the good we are seeking, and ask what it can be. It seems different in different actions and arts; it is different in medicine, in strategy, and in the other arts likewise. What then is the good of each? Surely that for whose sake everything else is done. In medicine this is health, in strategy victory, in architecture a house, in any other sphere something else, and in every action and pursuit the end; for it is for the sake of this that all men do whatever else they do. Therefore, if there is an end for all that we do, this will be the good achievable by action, and if there are more than one, these will be the goods achievable by action.

So the argument has by a different course reached the same point; but we must try to state this even more clearly. Since there are evidently more than one end, and we choose some of these (for example, wealth, flutes, and in general instruments) for the sake of something else, clearly not all ends are final ends; but the chief good is evidently something final. Therefore, if there is only one final end, this will be what we are seeking, and if there are more than one, the most final of these will be what we are seeking. Now we call that which is in itself worthy of pursuit more final than that which is worthy of pursuit for the sake of something else, and that which is never desirable for the sake of something else more final than the things that are desirable both in themselves and for the sake of that other thing, and therefore we call final without qualification that which is always desirable in itself and never for the sake of something else.

Now such a thing happiness, above all else, is held to be; for this we choose always for itself and never for the sake of something else, but honor, pleasure, reason, and every virtue we choose indeed for themselves (for if nothing resulted from them we should still choose each of them), but we choose them also for the sake of happiness, judging that by means of them we shall be happy. Happiness, on the other hand, no one chooses for the sake of these, nor, in general, for anything other than itself.

From the point of view of self-sufficiency the same result seems to follow; for the final good is thought to be self-sufficient. Now by self-sufficient we do not mean that which is sufficient for a man by himself, for one who lives a solitary life, but also for parents, children, wife, and in general for his friends and fellow citizens, since man is born for citizenship. But some limit must be set to this; for if we extend our requirement to ancestors and descendants and friends' friends we are in for an indefinite series. Let us examine this question, however, on another occasion; the self-sufficient we now define as that which when isolated makes life desirable and lacking in nothing; and such we think happiness to be; and further we think it most desirable of all things, without being counted as one good thing among others—if it were so counted it would clearly be made more desirable by the addition of even the least of goods; for that which is added becomes an excess of goods, and of goods the greater is always more desirable. Happiness, then, is something final and self-sufficient, and is the end of action.[f]

**6.** Although it is agreed that happiness meets these criteria, Aristotle recognizes that the precise nature of happiness still remains to be explained. His definition of happiness contains two vital concepts: "Activity of soul," which means the exercise of reason, and "in accordance with virtue," which describes the quality of the performance.

Presumably, however, to say that happiness is the chief good seems a platitude, and a clearer account of what it is is still desired. This might perhaps be given, if we could first ascertain the function of man. For just as for a flute player, a sculptor, or any artist, and, in general, for all things that have a function of activity, the good and the "well" is thought to reside in the function, so would it seem to be for man, if he has a function. Have the carpenter, then, and the tanner certain functions or activities, and has man none? Is he born without a function? Or as eye, hand, foot, and in general each of the parts evidently has function, may one lay it down that man similarly has a function apart from all these? What then can this be? Life seems to be common even to plants, but we are seeking what is peculiar to man. Let us exclude, therefore, the life of nutrition and growth. Next there would be a life of perception, but *it* also seems to be common even to the horse, the ox, and every animal. There remains, then, an active life of the element that has a rational principle; of this, one part has such a principle in the sense of being obedient to one, the other in the sense of possessing one and exercising thought. And, as "life of the rational element" also has two meanings, we must state that life in the sense of activity is what we mean; for this seems to be the more proper sense of the term. Now if the function of man is an activity of soul which follows or implies a rational principle, and if we say "a so-and-so" and "a good so-and-so" have a function which is the same in kind, for example, a lyre player and a good lyre player, and so without qualification in all cases, eminence in respect of goodness being added to the name of the function (for the function of a lyre player is to play the lyre, and that of a good lyre player is to do so well): if this is the case, [and we state the function of man to be a certain kind of life, and this to be an activity or actions of the soul implying a rational principle, and the function of a good man to be the good and noble performance of these, and if any action is well performed when it is performed in accordance with the appropriate excellence: if this is the case,] human good turns out to be activity of soul in accordance with virtue, and if there are more than one virtue, in accordance with the best and most complete.

But we must add "in a complete life." For one swallow does not make a summer, nor does one day; and so too one day, or a short time, does not make a man blessed and happy.... [Also, a happy man] needs the external goods as well; for it is impossible, or not easy, to do noble acts without the proper equipment. In many actions we use friends and riches and political power as instruments; and there are some things the lack of which takes the luster from happiness, as good birth, goodly children, beauty; for the man who is very ugly in appearance or ill born or solitary and childless is not very likely to be happy, and perhaps a man would be still less likely if he had thoroughly bad children or friends or had lost good children or friends by death.[g]

**7.** Aristotle's definition of happiness cannot be fully understood until the nature of virtue has been thoroughly examined. But the nature of virtue, in turn, depends on the structure of the soul, which contains both rational and irrational components. Two functions fall to the rational part: the control of a human being's irrational propensities and the exercise of reason for its own sake.

Since happiness is an activity of soul in accordance with perfect virtue, we must consider the nature of virtue; for perhaps we shall thus see better the nature of happiness. The true student of politics, too, is thought to have studied virtue above all things; for he wishes to make his fellow citizens good and obedient to the laws. As an example of this we have the lawgivers of the Cretans, the Spartans, and any others of the kind that there may have been. And if this inquiry belongs to political science, clearly the pursuit of it will be in accordance with our original plan. But clearly the virtue we must study is human virtue; for the good we were seeking was human good and the happiness human happiness. By human virtue we mean not that of the body but that of the soul; and happiness also we call an activity of soul. But if this is so, clearly the student of politics must know somehow the facts about soul, as the man who is to heal the eyes or the body as a whole must know about the eyes or the body; and all the more since politics is more prized and better than medicine; but even among doctors the best educated spend much labor on acquiring knowledge of the body. The student of politics, then, must study the soul, and must study it with these objects in view, and do so just to the extent which is sufficient for the questions we are discussing; for further precision is perhaps something more laborious than our purposes require.

Some things are said about it, adequately enough, even in the discussions outside our school, and we must use these; e.g., that one element in the soul is irrational and one has a rational principle. Whether these are separated as the parts of the body or of anything divisible are, or are distinct by definition but by nature inseparable, like convex and concave in the circumference of a circle, does not affect the present question.

Of the irrational element one division seems to be widely distributed, and vegetative in its nature, I mean that which causes nutrition and growth; for it is this kind of power of the soul that one must assign to all nurslings and to embryos, and this same power to full-grown creatures; this is more reasonable than to assign some different power to them. Now the excellence of this seems to be common to all species and not specifically human . . . let us leave the nutritive faculty alone, since it has by its nature no share in human excellence.

There seems to be also another irrational element in the soul—one which in a sense, however, shares in a rational principle. For we praise the rational principle of the continent man and of the incontinent, and the part of their soul that has such a principle, since it urges them aright and towards the best objects; but there is found in them also another element naturally opposed to the rational principle, which fights against and resists that principle. For exactly as paralyzed limbs when we intend to move them to the right turn on the contrary to the left, so is it with the soul; the impulses of incontinent people move in contrary directions. But while in the body we see that which moves astray, in the soul we do not. No doubt, however, we must none the less suppose that in the soul too there is something contrary to the rational principle, resisting and opposing it. In what sense it is distinct from the other elements does not concern us. Now even this seems to have a share in a rational principle, as we said, at any rate in the continent man it obeys the rational principle—and presumably in the temperate and brave man it is still more obedient; for in him it speaks, on all matters, with the same voice as the rational principle.

Therefore the irrational element also appears to be twofold. For the vegetative element in no way shares in a rational principle, but the appetitive, and in general the desiring element in a sense shares in it, insofar as it listens to and obeys it; this is the sense in which we speak of "taking account" of one's father or one's friends, not that in which we speak of "accounting" for a mathematical property. That the irrational element is in some sense persuaded by a rational principle is indicated also by the giving of advice and by all reproof and exhortation. And if this element also must be said to have a rational principle, that which has a rational principle (as well as that which has not) will be twofold, one subdivision having it in the strict sense and in itself, and the other having a tendency to obey as one does one's father.[h]

**8.** The virtues corresponding to the two functions of reason are the intellectual and the moral. The wise individual personifies the intellectual virtues, whereas the continent person typifies the moral virtues. The former's excellence is attained through instruction and evidenced by knowledge. The excellence of the latter is produced by habits of choice and expressed in practical actions tempered by both the circumstance and the individual.

Virtue too is distinguished into kinds in accordance with this difference; for we say that some of the virtues are intellectual and others moral, philosophic wisdom and understanding and practical wisdom being intellectual, liberality and temperance moral. For in speaking about a man's character we do not say that he is wise or has understanding but that he is good tempered or temperate; yet we praise the wise man also with respect to his state of mind; and of states of mind we call those which merit praise virtues.

Virtue, then, being of two kinds, intellectual and moral, intellectual virtue in the main owes both its birth and its growth to teaching (for which reason it requires experience and time), while moral virtue comes about as a result of habit, whence also its name *ethike* is one that is formed by a slight variation from the word *ethos* (habit). From this it is also plain that none of the moral virtues arises in us by nature; for nothing that exists by nature can form a habit contrary to its nature. For instance the stone which by nature moves downwards cannot be habituated to move upwards, not even if one tries to train it by throwing it up ten thousand times; nor can fire be habituated to move downwards, nor can anything else that by nature behaves in one way be trained to behave in another. Neither by nature, then, nor contrary to nature do the virtues arise in us; rather we are adapted by nature to receive them, and are made perfect by habit.

Again, of all the things that come to us by nature we first acquire the potentiality and later exhibit the activity (this is plain in the case of the senses; for it was not by often seeing or often hearing that we got these senses, but on the contrary we had them before we used them, and did not come to have them by using them); but the virtues we get by first exercising them, as also happens in the case of the arts as well. For the things we have to learn before we can do them, we learn by doing them, e.g., men become builders by building and lyre players by playing the lyre; so too we become just by doing just acts, temperate by doing temperate acts, brave by doing brave acts.[i]

**9.** Aristotle turns his attention to the task of explaining moral virtue. He analyzes human personality into three elements: "passions, faculties, and states of character." Because passions (for example, anger and fear) and faculties (for example, the ability to feel anger and fear) are not in and of themselves blameworthy or praiseworthy, virtue must be a state of character. Experience shows that the states of character that enable a person to fulfill his or her proper function aim at an intermediary point between the opposing extremes of excess and deficiency. The morally virtuous person, then, always chooses to act according to the "golden mean," but, Aristotle points out, the mean is not the same for all individuals.

We must . . . not only describe [moral] virtue as a state of character, but also say what sort of state it is. We may remark, then, that every virtue or excellence both brings into good condition the thing of which it is the excellence and makes the work of that thing be done well; e.g., the excellence of the eye makes both the eye and its work good; for it is by the excellence of the eye that we see well. Similarly the excellence of the horse makes a horse both good in itself and good at running and at carrying its rider and at awaiting the attack of the enemy. Therefore, if this is true in every case, the virtue of man also will be the state of character which makes a man good and which makes him do his own work well.

How this is to happen we have stated already, but it will be made plain also by the following consideration of the specific nature of virtue. In everything that is continuous and divisible it is possible to take more, less, or an equal amount, and that either in terms of the thing itself or relatively to us; and the equal is an intermediate between excess and defect. By the intermediate in the object I mean that which is equidistant from each of the extremes, which is one and the same for all men; by the intermediate relatively to us that which is neither too much nor too little—and this is not one, nor the same for all. For instance, if ten is many and two is few, six is the intermediate, taken in terms of the object; for it exceeds and is exceeded by an equal amount; this is intermediate according to arithmetical proportion. But the intermediate relatively to us is not to be taken so; if ten pounds are too much for a particular person to eat and two too little, it does not follow that the trainer will order six pounds; for this also is perhaps too much for the person who is to take it, or too little—too little for Milo [a famous Greek athlete], too much for the beginner in athletic exercises. The same is true of running and wrestling. Thus a master of any art avoids excess and defect, but seeks the intermediate and chooses this—the intermediate not in the object but relatively to us.[j]

**10.** Aristotle is now ready to assemble the results of his investigation into a definition of moral virtue.

Virtue, then, is a state of character concerned with choice, lying in a mean, i.e., the mean relative to us, this being determined by a rational principle, and by that principle by which the man of practical wisdom would determine it. Now it is a mean between two vices, that which depends on excess and that which depends on defect; and again it is a mean because the vices respectively fall short of or exceed what is right in both passions and actions, while virtue both finds and chooses that which is intermediate. Hence in respect of its substance and the definition which states its essence virtue is a mean, with regard to what is best and right an extreme.

But not every action nor every passion admits of a mean; for some have names that already imply badness, e.g., spite, shamelessness, envy, and in the case of actions adultery, theft, murder; for all of these and suchlike things imply by their names that they are themselves bad, and not the excesses or deficiencies of them. It is not possible, then, ever to be right with regard to them; one must always be wrong. Nor does goodness or badness with regard to such things depend on committing adultery with the right woman, at the right time, and in the right way, but simply to do any of them is to go wrong. It would be equally absurd, then, to expect that in unjust, cowardly, and voluptuous action there should be a mean, an excess, and a deficiency; for at that rate there would be a mean of excess and of deficiency, an excess of excess, and a deficiency of deficiency. But as there is no excess and deficiency of temperance and courage because what is intermediate is in a sense an extreme, so too of the actions we have mentioned there is no mean nor any excess and deficiency, but however they are done they are wrong; for in general there is neither a mean of excess and deficiency, nor excess and deficiency of a mean.[k]

**11.** His general formulation of moral virtue completed, Aristotle proceeds to a direct examination of specific moral virtues.

We must, however, not only make this general statement, but also apply it to the individual facts. For among statements about conduct those which are general apply more widely, but those which are particular are more genuine, since conduct has to do with individual cases, and our statements must harmonize with the facts in these cases. We may take these cases from our table. With regard to feelings of fear and confidence courage is the mean; of the people who exceed, he who exceeds in fearlessness has no name (many of the states have no name), while the man who exceeds in confidence is rash, and he who exceeds in fear and falls short in confidence is a coward. With regard to pleasures and pains—not all of them, and not so much with regard to the pains—the mean is temperance, the excess self-indulgence. Persons deficient with regard to the pleasures are not often found; hence such persons also have received no name. But let us call them "insensible."

With regard to giving and taking of money the mean is liberality, the excess and the defect prodigality and meanness. In these actions people exceed and fall short in contrary ways; the prodigal exceeds in spending and falls short in taking, while the mean man exceeds in taking and falls short in spending.... With regard to money there are also other dispositions—a mean, magnificence (for the magnificent man differs from the liberal man; the former deals with large sums, the latter with small ones), an excess, tastelessness and vulgarity, and a deficiency, niggardliness....

With regard to honor and dishonor the mean is proper pride, the excess is known as a sort of "empty vanity," and the deficiency is undue humility; and as we said liberality was related to magnificence, differing from it by dealing with small sums, so there is a state similarly related to proper pride, being concerned with small honors while that is concerned with great. For it is possible to desire honor as one ought, and more than one ought, and less, and the man who exceeds in his desires is called ambitious, the man who falls short unambitious, while the intermediate person has no name. The dispositions also are nameless, except that that of the ambitious man is called ambition. Hence the people who are at the extremes lay claim to the middle place; and we ourselves sometimes call the intermediate person ambitious and sometimes unambitious, and sometimes praise the ambitious man and sometimes the unambitious. The reason of our doing this will be stated in what follows; but now let us speak of the remaining states according to the method which has been indicated.

With regard to anger also there is an excess, a deficiency, and a mean. Although they can scarcely be said to have names, yet since we call the intermediate person good tempered let us call the mean good temper; of the persons at the extremes let the one who exceeds be called irascible, and his vice irascibility, and the man who falls short an inirascible sort of person, and the deficiency inirascibility.[1]

**12.** Next, Aristotle investigates the intellectual virtues—that is, the virtues that accompany the proper exercise of reason in its various functions. The primary tasks of intellect are first, to give us knowledge of invariable and fixed principles and second, to provide a rational guide for action in daily life. The pursuit and discovery of truth is the aim of *philosophical wisdom,* whereas the purpose of *practical wisdom* is intelligent conduct. The basis for intelligent conduct is the union of true knowledge of what we ought to do and the desire to do it. Aristotle contrasts his view with that of Socrates on this point. He holds that Socrates was correct in associating virtue with principles discovered by reason but was wrong in assuming that knowledge of the good is necessarily accompanied by a desire to act on this knowledge.

We divided the virtues of the soul and said that some are virtues of character and others of intellect. Now we have discussed in detail the moral virtues; with regard to the others let us express our view as follows, beginning with some remarks about the soul. We said before that there are two parts of the soul—that which grasps a rule or rational principle, and the irrational; let us now draw a similar distinction within the part which grasps a rational principle. And let it be assumed that there are two parts which grasp a rational principle—one by which we contemplate the kind of things whose originative causes are invariable, and one by which we contemplate variable things; for where objects differ in kind the part of the soul answering to each of the two is different in kind, since it is in virtue of a certain likeness and kinship with their objects that they have the knowledge they have.

...The virtue of a thing is relative to its proper work. Now there are three things in the soul which control action and truth—sensation, reason, desire.

Of these sensation originates no [moral] action; this is plain from the fact that the lower animals have sensation but no share in [such] action.[1]

What affirmation and negation are in thinking, pursuit and avoidance are in desire; so that since moral virtue is a state of character concerned with choice, and choice is deliberate desire, therefore both the reasoning must be true and the desire right, if the choice is to be good, and the latter must pursue just what the former asserts. Now this kind of intellect and of truth is practical; of the intellect which is contemplative, not practical nor productive, the good and the bad state are truth and falsity respectively (for this is the work of everything intellectual); while of the part which is practical and intellectual the good state is truth in agreement with right desire.

The origin of [moral] action—its efficient, not its final cause[2]—is choice, and that of choice is desire and reasoning with a view to an end. This is why choice cannot exist either without reason and intellect or without a moral state; for good action and its opposite cannot exist without a combination of intellect and character. Intellect itself, however, moves nothing, but only the intellect which aims at an end and is practical; for this rules the productive intellect as well, since everyone who makes makes for an end, and that which is made is not an end in the unqualified sense (but only an end in a particular relation, and the end of a particular operation)—only that which is *done* is that; for good action is an end, and desire aims at this. Hence choice is either desiderative reason or ratiocinative desire, and such an origin of action is a man.

...This is why some say that all the virtues are forms of practical wisdom.... Socrates in one respect was on the right track while in another he went astray; in thinking that all the virtues were forms of practical wisdom he was wrong, but in saying they implied practical wisdom he was right. This is confirmed by the fact that even now all men, when they define virtue, after naming the state of character and its objects add "that (state) which is in accordance with the right rule"; now the right rule is that which is in accordance with practical wisdom. All men, then, seem somehow to divine that this kind of state is virtue, viz., that which is in accordance with practical wisdom. But we must go a little further. For it is not merely the state in accordance with the right rule, but the state that implies the *presence* of the right rule, that is virtue; and practical wisdom is a right rule about such matters. Socrates, then, thought the virtues were rules or rational principles (for he thought they were, all of them, forms of scientific knowledge), while we think they *involve* a rational principle.[m]

**13.** Aristotle maintains that we should not choose activities by how pleasant they are. Rather, although good activities are pleasant, and are choiceworthy because they are pleasant, their pleasantness is a function of their goodness, not vice versa.

Now the activities of thought differ from those of the senses, and both differ among themselves,

[1]Aristotle's analysis in this passage is directed toward those actions of people of which it may be said, in some sense, that their "moving principle is in the agent himself, he being aware of the particular circumstances of the action"—that is, *voluntary actions.* He ascribes no moral significance to *involuntary actions*—that is, actions for which people are not responsible (for example, actions resulting from external forces, those arising "by reason of ignorance" of the particular circumstances, and those done because of excessive pain or the fear of excessive pain).

[2]Aristotle distinguishes the *efficient cause*, the agent or force that produces an effect, from the *final cause*, the end or purpose "for the sake of which a thing is done." For example, the efficient cause of the mural on the wall of an auditorium is the painter, whereas its final cause is the decoration of the room.

in kind; so, therefore, do the pleasures that complete them.

This may be seen, too, from the fact that each of the pleasures is bound up with the activity it completes. For an activity is intensified by its proper pleasure, since each class of things is better judged of and brought to precision by those who engage in the activity with pleasure; e.g., it is those who enjoy geometrical thinking that become geometers and grasp the various propositions better, and, similarly, those who are fond of music or of building, and so on, make progress in their proper function by enjoying it; so the pleasures intensify the activities, and what intensifies a thing is proper to it, but things different in kind have properties different in kind.

This will be even more apparent from the fact that activities are hindered by pleasures arising from other sources. For people who are fond of playing the flute are incapable of attending to arguments if they overhear some one playing the flute, since they enjoy flute-playing more than the activity in hand; so the pleasure connected with flute-playing destroys the activity concerned with argument. This happens, similarly, in all other cases, when one is active about two things at once; the more pleasant activity drives out the other, and if it is much more pleasant does so all the more, so that one even ceases from the other. This is why when we enjoy anything very much we do not throw ourselves into anything else, and do one thing only when we are not much pleased by another; e.g., in the theatre the people who eat sweets do so most when the actors are poor. Now since activities are made precise and more enduring and better by their proper pleasure, and injured by alien pleasures, evidently the two kinds of pleasure are far apart. For alien pleasures do pretty much what proper pains do, since activities are destroyed by their proper pains; e.g., if a man finds writing or doing sums unpleasant and painful, he does not write, or does not do sums, because the activity is painful. So an activity suffers contrary effects from its proper pleasures and pains, i.e., from those that supervene on it in virtue of its own nature. And alien pleasures have been stated to do much the same as pain; they destroy the activity, only not to the same degree.

Now since activities differ in respect of goodness and badness, and some are worthy to be chosen, others to be avoided, and other neutral, so, too, are the pleasures; for to each activity there is a proper pleasure. The pleasure proper to a worthy activity is good and that proper to an unworthy activity bad; just as the appetites for noble objects are laudable, those for base objects culpable. But the pleasures involved in activities are more proper to them than the desires; for the latter are separated both in time and in nature, while the former are close to the activities, and so hard to distinguish from them that it admits of dispute whether the activity is not the same as the pleasure.... As activities are different, then, so are the corresponding pleasures. Now sight is superior to touch in purity, and hearing and smell to taste; the pleasures, therefore, are similarly superior, and those of thought superior to these, and within each of the two kinds some are superior to other.[n]

**14.** Although Aristotle acknowledges the importance of reason as a guide to moral action, he maintains that philosophic wisdom is superior even to practical wisdom. He defends his esteem for contemplation by showing that the life of contemplation comes closest to meeting the conditions for happiness.

If happiness is activity in accordance with virtue, it is reasonable that it should be in accordance with the highest virtue; and this will be that of the best thing in us. Whether it be reason or something else that is this element which is thought to be our natural ruler and guide and to take thought of things noble and divine, whether it be itself also divine or only the most divine element in us, the activity of this in accordance with its proper virtue will be perfect happiness. That this activity is contemplative we have already said.

Now this would seem to be in agreement both with what we said before and with the truth. For, firstly, this activity is the best (since not only is reason the best thing in us, but the objects of reason are the best of knowable objects); and, secondly, it is the most continuous, since we can contemplate truth more continuously than we can *do* anything. And we think happiness has pleasure mingled with it, but the activity of philosophic wisdom is admittedly the pleasantest of virtuous activities; at all events the pursuit of it is thought to offer pleasures marvelous for their purity and their enduringness, and it is to be expected that those who know will pass their time more pleasantly than those who inquire. And the self-sufficiency that is spoken of must belong most to the contemplative activity. For while a philosopher, as well as a just man or one possessing any other virtue, needs the necessaries of life, when they are sufficiently equipped with things of that sort the just man needs people towards whom and with whom he shall act justly, and the temperate man, the brave man, and each of the others is in the same case, but the philosopher, even when by himself, can contemplate truth, and the better the wiser he is; he can perhaps do so better if he has fellow workers, but still he is the most self-sufficient. And this activity alone would seem to be loved for its own sake; for nothing arises from it apart from the contemplating, while from practical activities we gain more or less apart from the action. And happiness is thought to depend on leisure; for we are busy that we may have leisure, and make war that we may live in peace. Now the activity of the practical virtues is exhibited in political or military affairs, but the actions concerned with these seem to be unleisurely. Warlike actions are completely so (for no one chooses to be at war, or provokes war, for the sake of being at war; anyone would seem absolutely murderous if he were to make enemies of his friends in order to bring about battle and slaughter); but the action of the statesman is also unleisurely, and—apart from the political action itself—aims at despotic power and honors, or at all events happiness, for him and his fellow citizens—a happiness different from political action, and evidently sought as being different. So if among virtuous actions political and military actions are distinguished by nobility and greatness, and these are unleisurely and aim at an end and are not desirable for their sake, but the activity of reason, which is contemplative, seems both to be superior in serious worth and to aim at no end beyond itself, and to have its pleasure proper to itself (and this augments the activity), and the self-sufficiency, leisureliness, unweariedness (so far as this is possible for man), and all the other attributes ascribed to the supremely happy man are evidently those connected with this activity, it follows that this will be the complete happiness of man, if it be allowed a complete term of life (for none of the attributes of happiness is *in*complete).

But such a life would be too high for man; for it is not insofar as he is man that he will live so, but insofar as something divine is present in him; and by so much as this is superior to our composite nature is its activity superior to that which is the exercise of the other kind of virtue. If reason is divine, then, in comparison with man, the life according to it is divine in comparison with human life. But we must not follow those who advise us, being men, to think of human things, and, being mortal, of mortal things, but must, so far as we can, make ourselves immortal, and strain every nerve to live in accordance with the best thing in us; for even if it be small in bulk, much more does it in power and worth surpass everything. This would seem, too, to be each man himself, since it is the authoritative and better part of him. It would be strange, then, if he were to choose not the life of his self but that of something else. And what we said before will apply now; that which is proper to each thing is by nature best and most pleasant for each thing; for man, therefore, the life according to reason is best and pleasantest, since reason more than anything else *is* man. This life therefore is also the happiest.°

## QUESTIONS

1. In the context of Greek philosophy, what is virtue?
2. What are the essential features of a suitable goal for humanity, in Aristotle's view?
3. "Happiness is an activity of soul in accordance with virtue." Explain and expand this definition, and show how it leads to the conclusion that the contemplative life is the happiest.
4. Outline Aristotle's psychological theory. How does it bear on his ethical theory?
5. What arguments can you offer either for or against Aristotle's contention that not all studies admit of the same degree of precision?
6. What differences exist between Aristotle's "golden mean" and an "absolute mean"? Provide illustrations that make the contrast clear.
7. Distinguish between the *moral* and *intellectual* virtues, defining and illustrating each type. What are the means by which they are acquired?
8. In what respects do the ethical theories of Plato and Aristotle stand in sharp contrast? In what respects are they alike?
9. What is Aristotle's judgment of the Socratic thesis "virtue is knowledge"? How does Aristotle conceive the relationship between virtue and knowledge?
10. Do you regard the ideal of the "life of reason" as out of date? Discuss.

## KEY TO SELECTIONS

Aristotle, *Nicomachean Ethics,* tr. W. D. Ross, from *The Works of Aristotle*, vol. IX, W. D. Ross, ed., Oxford, Clarendon Press, 1925. With the kind permission of the publishers.

[a]Bk. X, pp. 1179b31–1180a4.
[b]Bk. I, pp. 1094a1–18.
[c]Bk. I, pp. 1094a18–1094b10.
[d]Bk. I, pp. 1094b12–1095a11.
[e]Bk. I, pp. 1095a13–29.
[f]Bk. I, pp. 1097a15–1097b22.
[g]Bk. I, pp. 1097b23–1098a19, 1099a31–1099b6.
[h]Bk. 1, pp. 1102a5–1103a3.
[i]Bks. I & II, pp. 1103a4–1103b2.
[j]Bk. II, pp. 1106a14–1106b8.
[k]Bk. II, pp. 1106b36–1107a26.
[l]Bk. II, pp. 1107a27–1108a8.
[m]Bk.VI, pp. 1138b35–1139b5, 1144b17–29.
[n]Bk. X, pp. 1175a27–1176a2.
[o]Bk. X, pp. 1177a12–1178a8.

## GUIDE TO ADDITIONAL READING


### PRIMARY SOURCES

*The Basic Works of Aristotle*, ed. R. McKeon, New York, Random House, 1941.

*The Complete Works of Aristotle*, ed. Jonathan Barnes, Princeton, Princeton University Press, 1984.

Aristotle, *Nicomachean Ethics*, tr. Terence Irwin, Indianapolis, Hackett, 1985.

### DISCUSSION AND COMMENTARY

J. L. Ackrill, *Aristotle the Philosopher*, Oxford, Oxford University Press, 1981, chs. 2 and 10.

Hardie, W., *Aristotle's Ethical Theory*, New York, Oxford University Press, 1980.

Joachim, H. H., *Aristotle: The Nicomachean Ethics*, London, Oxford University Press, 1954.

Kraut, R., *Aristotle on the Human Good*, Princeton, Princeton University Press, 1989.

Reeve, C. D. C., *Practices of Reason: Aristotle's Nicomachean Ethics*, Oxford, Clarendon Press, 1992.

Rorty, A. (ed.), *Essays on Aristotle's Ethics*, Berkeley, University of California Press, 1980.

Ross, W. D., *Aristotle*, New York, Methuen, 1923.

Urmson, J. O., *Aristotle's Ethics*, Oxford, Blackwell, 1988.

CHAPTER FOUR

# The Pleasant Life

EPICURUS

EPICUREANISM WAS ONE OF THE philosophies that arose during the decline of ancient Greece as a source of relief from increasing social disorganization. Of these "salvation philosophies," which flourished until the Greco-Roman culture was superseded by the Christian, Epicureanism was distinguished for the constancy of its doctrine. Epicurus teaches us that happiness involves serenity and is achieved through the simple pleasures that preserve bodily health and peace of mind. To realize their ideal, the members of the Epicurean community refrained, insofar as possible, from participation in the affairs of the troubled world, spending their time in philosophical conversation.

Epicurus (342 or 341–270 B.C.E.), inheriting Athenian citizenship from his parents, was born and educated on the island of Samos in the Aegean Sea, where he spent the first two decades of his life. When, following the death of Alexander the Great in 323 B.C.E., the Athenians were driven out of Samos, Epicurus went to Asia Minor. After teaching there for several years, he moved to Athens (306 B.C.E.) and until his death taught in his famous garden. The Garden of Epicurus served as a sanctuary from the turmoil of the outer world for a select group of men who applied in their daily lives the precepts of their mentor. Epicurus's Garden ranked as one of the great schools of antiquity, along with Plato's Academy, Aristotle's Lyceum, and Zeno's Stoa.

It is a prank of history that the word *epicure* is frequently used to denote a gourmet or a fastidious voluptuary. Epicurus's enemies in fact accused him of sensualism, but his philosophical teachings and the frugality and simplicity of his life effectively refuted their charge. It was the nobility of his character that accounted for his great popularity. Indeed, the biographer of ancient philosophers,

Diogenes Laertius (third century after the birth of Christ), eulogized him in the following manner:

> Epicurus has witnesses enough and to spare of his unsurpassed kindness to all men. There is his country which honored him with bronze statues, his friends so numerous they could not even be reckoned by entire cities, and his disciples who all remained bound for ever by the charm of his teaching, except Metrodorus . . . overweighted perhaps by Epicurus's excessive goodness. There is also the permanent continuance of the school after almost all the others had come to an end, and that though it had a countless succession of heads from among the disciples. There is again his grateful devotion to his parents, his generosity to his brothers, and his gentleness towards his servants. . . . In short there is his benevolence to all.[1]

Although Epicurus was a very prolific writer, only a few letters and fragments of his writings are extant. They give little more than a summary of his theories of physics and astronomy, his theory of knowledge, and his ethics. However, a fuller view of his doctrines is provided by the works of his disciples, of whom the most distinguished is the Roman Lucretius Carus (94–55? B.C.E.). Lucretius's *De Rerum Natura (On the Nature of Things)* is both fine poetry and an excellent statement of Epicureanism; in it, he says of Epicurus,

> When human life to view lay foully prostrate upon earth crushed down under the weight of religion . . . a man of Greece ventured first to lift up his mortal eyes to her face and first to withstand her to her face. Him neither story of gods nor thunderbolts nor heaven with threatening roar could quell: they only chafed the more the eager courage of his soul, filling him with desire to be the first to burst the fast bars of nature's portals. [Book I.]

The ethical theory of Epicurus stems from the Cyrenaic doctrine formulated by Aristippus (*c.* 435–356 B.C.E.), who, even though he was a student of Socrates, advocates the hedonistic principle that pleasure is the supreme good. Epicurus and the Cyrenaics have widely different conceptions of the pleasant life, the former stressing peace of mind and the latter sensual pleasures, but they concur with respect to general principles. Both maintain that human nature is so constituted that people always seek what they believe will give them pleasure and avoid what they believe will give them pain and that pleasure is the only intrinsic good and pain the only intrinsic evil. Again, both are agreed that "no pleasure is a bad thing in itself." Yet they enjoin us to choose our pleasures judiciously, for "the means which produce some pleasures bring with them disturbances many times greater than the pleasures." Aristippus and Epicurus teach that the person who wishes to be happy must cultivate an ability to choose the right pleasures; and, they assert, only those actions that further individuals' enjoyment can have moral significance for them. Beyond this point, however, Epicureanism and Cyrenaicism diverge.

In opposition to Aristippus, Epicurus maintains that the *duration of pleasures is more important than their intensity* in achieving happiness. Consequently, he argues that the mental pleasures are in general superior to the physical, because they are longer-lasting, albeit less intense. Although he finds the physical pleasures unobjectionable in themselves, he contends that the pursuit of them for their own sake leads not to happiness but to its opposite. Experience shows us that the desire for a life

[1]Diogenes Laertius, *Lives of Eminent Philosophers* (New York: G. P. Putnam's, 1925), pp. 537–538.

filled with intense pleasures will be frustrated, because there are not enough of them in the ordinary course of events. What is more, the pleasures derived from such objectives as fame, wealth, and the like are usually outweighed by the pains necessary to procure them, and the pains consequent upon such activities as feasting, drinking, and merrymaking either cancel the pleasures or leave a balance of pain. From these considerations, Epicurus can only conclude that Aristippus' standard of judging what is good—that is, "the most intense sensual pleasure of the moment"—is entirely self-defeating.

The chief difference between Cyrenaicism and Epicureanism lies in their divergent conception of the nature of true pleasure. Fundamental to their disagreement is the distinction between *active* or *positive* pleasure, which comes from the gratification of specific wants and desires, and *passive* or *negative* pleasure, which is the absence of pain. Aristippus sets as the goal of life a constant round of active pleasures, whereas Epicurus maintains that the active pleasures are important only insofar as they terminate the pain of unfulfilled desires. For Epicurus, the passive pleasures are more fundamental than the active, because it is through them that happiness is gained. A human being's ultimate goal is not a constant succession of intense sensual pleasures, but is rather the state of serenity, *ataraxia,* characterized by "freedom from trouble in the mind and pain in the body."

Epicurus assures us that the calm and repose of the good life are within the reach of all. It is necessary that we keep our desires at a minimum, however, and distinguish the natural and necessary desires from those that are artificial—for example, longings for wealth, excitement, fame, and power. The latter are not merely unnecessary to health and tranquility but are in fact destructive of them. By contrast, the satisfaction of the natural desires (the desires that must be fulfilled to preserve bodily health and mental peace) and the freedom from pain that accompanies such satisfaction lead to happiness.

Without being entirely clear about the matter, Epicurus seems to say that we should assess an action by the amount or *quantity* of pleasure that the action brings about. To the extent that this is so, it makes Epicurus a close ancestor of certain later philosophical views, including especially the Utilitarianism of Jeremy Bentham and John Stuart Mill (to be presented in Ch. 13).

Epicurus's ethical view can accordingly be called *consequentialist,* as can Mill's. That is to say, Epicurus's view advocates judging actions by their consequences, by features of the things that they cause or bring about. (By contrast Kant's view, to be discussed in Ch. 13, is anti-consequentialist: It tries to judge actions not by their consequences, but by other features of them.)

As just noted, Epicurus's view appears to be *quantitative,* though not in a very precise way. It is quantitative in the sense that when it speaks of duration and intensity of pleasures, it holds that the evaluation of actions depends in some way on measurements of the quantities of pleasure they bring about. It thus invites us to think that the determination of these quantities is accomplished by some kind of calculation. The calculation would take account of both intensity and duration, and perhaps other quantitative variables as well.

On the other hand, it cannot be said that the method of calculation that Epicurus has in mind is fully clear in what he says, nor very precise. He does not explain exactly how one is supposed to measure or calculate the amount of pleasure that results from a particular action. This absence of a clear method of measurement or calculation has led some people to believe that Epicurus's view is not in fact quantitative, in spite of the quantitative language he often uses.

Epicurus tells us that our good can be realized through philosophy, the quest for knowledge. It must be understood, however, that the function of philosophy is preeminently practical:

> Vain is the word of a philosopher which does not heal any suffering of man. For just as there is no profit in medicine if it does not expel the diseases of the body, so there is no profit in philosophy either, if it does not expel the suffering of the mind.[a]

By nature men seek pleasure, but by knowledge they are guided to the choice of the true pleasures. Without deliberation, we cannot hope either to forestall needless and artificial desires or to secure the pleasures required for happiness. In addition, without knowledge of the nature of things, we cannot rid ourselves of the fears and superstitions that destroy tranquility.

Epicurus undertakes to demonstrate the groundlessness of the two overwhelming fears that troubled his contemporaries: the *fear of death* and the *fear of divine retribution*. The philosophy of nature that he finds best suited to the task of destroying these terrifying chimeras is the "atomism" of Democritus (fifth century B.C.E.), in which the universeis explained wholly in terms of "atoms in motion in the void." Arguing that Democritus's mechanistic account of the universe is adequate to explain all that occurs, Epicurus holds that it is superfluous to postulate the interference of the gods in human affairs.[2] Moreover, the Democritean theory of the soul supports his arguments against the fear of death: The soul is no more than a collection of small atoms within the body, and death is only the dispersal of the soul-atoms. In any case, we need not fear death, "since as long as we exist, death is not with us; but when death comes, then we do not exist."

Despite the general suitability of Democritean atomism as an account of nature, its theory of motion is said by Epicurus to be incomplete in a way that has serious consequences for ethics. In dealing with the motion of atoms, he observes that if their original motion is only a uniform downward fall, it is impossible to account for the collisions of atoms necessary to form complex bodies. Hence he assumes that atoms deviate spontaneously, or "swerve," in their course. But this kind of motion, being irregular and unpredictable, introduces an element of freedom or indeterminacy into the universe that is excluded by the absolute determinism of Democritus. The advantage of the Epicurean interpretation for ethics becomes evident when it is realized that men fear, more than the hand of the gods, the control of an inexorable fate or necessity of the kind implied by Democritus' deterministic atomism. However, because his theory of motion leaves a margin of indeterminacy, Epicurus believes it admits of the possibility that men can to some extent influence and control the course of their lives. He therefore exhorts us to realize

---

[2]Epicurus does not deny that there are gods. However, he argues that it does not follow logically from the existence of gods, nor does experience testify, that "the greatest misfortunes befall the wicked and the greatest blessings the good by the gift of the gods."(*Principal Doctrines,* I.) He also says on the subject: "If God listened to the prayers of men, all men would quickly have perished: for they are forever praying for evil against one another." (*Fragments,* no 58.)

A further argument against divine causation of human good or evil is presented in a paradox attributed to Epicurus by Lactantius, in which the logical difficulties of the conception of an all-powerful and all-good deity are treated. For a statement of this paradox, see Chapter 6, no. 1, of this book.

that although "necessity is an evil . . . there is no necessity to live under the control of necessity."

Through the true philosophy, Epicurus tells us, we can see that the fear of death, of the interference of the gods, and of the hard grip of necessity are without foundation in reality. Philosophy serves us well—it is not only an indispensable tool for the good life but also the most pleasant of activities: "in all other occupations the fruit comes painfully after completion, but in philosophy pleasure goes hand in hand with knowledge. . . . " Wherefore, Epicurus admonishes: "Let no one when young delay to study philosophy, nor when he is old, grow weary of his study. For no one can come too early or too late to secure the health of his soul."

**1.** In setting forth the nature of the universe, Epicurus lays down the fundamental principles "nothing is created out of nothing" and "nothing is destroyed into nothing." Moreover, he reaffirms the Democritean doctrine that nature consists solely of atoms in motion in empty space. Together, these tenets support his argument that only natural causes operate in the world, and they also provide a reassuring stability and permanence in the basic stuff of the universe.

Nothing is created out of that which does not exist: for if it were, everything would be created out of everything with no need of seeds. And again, if that which disappears were destroyed into that which did not exist, all things would have perished, since that into which they were dissolved would not exist. Furthermore, the universe always was such as it is now, and always will be the same. For there is nothing into which it changes: for outside the universe there is nothing which could come into it and bring about the change.

Moreover, the universe is bodies and space: for that bodies exist, sense itself witnesses in the experience of all men. . . . And if there were not that which we term void and place and intangible existence, bodies would have nowhere to exist and nothing through which to move, as they are seen to move. And besides these two nothing can even be thought of. . . . Furthermore, among bodies some are compounds, and others those of which compounds are formed. And these latter are indivisible and unalterable if, that is, all things are not to be destroyed into the nonexistent, but something permanent is to remain behind at the dissolution of compounds: they are completely solid in nature, and can by no means be dissolved in any part. So it must needs be that the first beginnings are indivisible corporeal existences. . . .

Moreover, we must suppose that the atoms do not possess any of the qualities belonging to perceptible things, except shape, weight, and size, and all that necessarily goes with shape. For every quality changes; but the atoms do not change at all, since there must needs be something which remains solid and indissoluble at the dissolution of compounds, which can cause changes; not changes into the nonexistent or from the nonexistent, but changes effected by the shifting of position of some particles, and by the addition or departure of others. For this reason it is essential that the bodies which shift their position should be imperishable and should not possess the nature of what changes, but parts and configuration of their own. For thus much must needs remain constant. . . .

And the atoms move continuously for all time, some of them falling straight down, others swerving, and other recoiling from their collisions. And of the latter, some are borne on separating to a long distance from one another, while others again recoil and recoil, whenever they chance to be checked by the interlacing with others, or else shut in by atoms interlaced around them. For on the one hand the nature of the void which separates each atom by itself brings this about, as it is not able to afford resistance, and on the other hand the hardness which belongs to the atoms makes them recoil after collision to as great a distance as the interlacing permits separation after the collision. And these motions have no beginning, since the atoms and the void are the cause.[b]

**2.** The doctrine that everything is made up of material atoms applies not only to inanimate and living bodies but also to the soul. The atoms of the soul are exceedingly fine; enclosed within the body, they are the means by which sensations occur in us. With this theory, Epicurus is well situated to attack the fear of what comes after death. When, in death, the atoms of the soul leave the body, we become incapable of sensation, and it is therefore impossible for us to experience painful punishments after we die. Yet we should be comforted by the knowledge that the atoms that compose our soul are in themselves indestructible. Furthermore, Epicurus attempts to prove that those who argue that the soul is immortal because it is incorporeal are reasoning from a false premise.

Next, referring always to the sensations and the feelings, for in this way you will obtain the most trustworthy ground of belief, you must consider that the soul is a body of fine particles distributed throughout the whole structure, and most resembling wind with a certain admixture of heat, and in some respects like to one of these and in some to the other. There is also the part which is many degrees more advanced even than these in fineness of composition, and for this reason is more capable of feeling in harmony with the rest of the structure as well. Now all this is made manifest by the activities of the soul and the feelings and the readiness of its movements and its processes of thought and by what we lose at the moment of death. Further, you must grasp that the soul possesses the chief cause of sensation: yet it could not have acquired sensation, unless it were in some way enclosed by the rest of the structure. And this in its turn having afforded the soul this cause of sensation acquires itself too a share in this contingent capacity from the soul. Yet it does not acquire all the capacities which the soul possesses: and therefore when the soul is released from the body, the body no longer has sensation. For it never possessed this power in itself, but used to afford opportunity for it to another existence, brought into being at the same time with itself: and this existence, owing to the power now consummated within itself as a result of motion, used spontaneously to produce for itself the capacity of sensation and then to communicate it to the body as well, in virtue of its contact and correspondence of movement, as I have already said. Therefore, so long as the soul remains in the body, even though some other part of the body be lost, it will never lose sensation; any more, whatever portions of the soul may perish too, when that which enclosed it is removed either in whole or in part, if the soul continues to exist at all, it will retain sensation. On the other hand, the rest of the structure, though it continues to exist either as a whole or in part, does not retain sensation, if it has once lost that sum of atoms, however small it be, which together goes to produce the nature of the soul. Moreover, if the whole structure is dissolved, the soul is dispersed and no longer has the same powers nor performs its movements, so that it does not possess sensation either. For it is impossible to imagine it with sensation, if it is not in this organism and cannot effect these movements, when what encloses and surrounds it is no longer the same as the surroundings in which it now exists and performs these movements. Furthermore, we must clearly comprehend as well, that the incorporeal in the general acceptation of the term is applied to that which could be thought of as much as an independent existence. Now it is impossible to conceive the incorporeal as a separate existence, except the void: and the void can neither act nor be acted upon, but only provides opportunity of motion through itself to bodies. So that those who say that the soul is incorporeal are talking idly. For it would not be able to act or be acted on in any respect, if it were of this nature. But as it is, both these occurrences are clearly distinguished in respect of the soul.[c]

**3.** Although Epicurus does not deny the existence of divine beings, he is much concerned to dispel the notion that the gods interfere in any way with the events of nature. He opposes as impious the belief of many of his contemporaries that the heavenly bodies are gods or are under the control of gods. On the contrary, he maintains that the heavenly bodies are natural phenomena and that accurate knowledge of at least the general principles of their motions is requisite to happiness. Freedom from the fear of punishment or of annihilation after death and from the fear of the gods can be achieved only when we understand the true nature of things.

Furthermore, the motions of the heavenly bodies and their turnings and eclipses and risings and settings, and kindred phenomena to these, must not be thought to be due to any being who controls and ordains or has ordained them and at the same time enjoys perfect bliss together with immortality (for trouble and care and anger and kindness are not consistent with a life of blessedness, but these things come to pass where there is weakness and fear and dependence on neighbors). Nor again must we believe that they, which are but fire agglomerated in a mass, possess blessedness, and voluntarily take upon themselves these movements. But we must preserve their full majestic significance in all expressions which we apply to such conceptions, in order that there may not arise out of them opinions contrary to this notion of majesty. Otherwise this very contradiction will cause the greatest disturbance in men's souls. Therefore we must believe that it is due to the original inclusion of matter in such agglomerations during the birth-process of the world that this law of regular succession is also brought about.

Furthermore, we must believe that to discover accurately the cause of the most essential facts is the function of the science of nature, and that blessedness for us in the knowledge of celestial phenomena lies in this and in the understanding of the nature of the existences seen in these celestial phenomena, and of all else that is akin to the exact knowledge requisite for our happiness . . . nothing which suggests doubt or alarm can be included at all in that which is naturally immortal and blessed. Now this we can ascertain by our mind is absolutely the case. . . .

And besides all these matters in general we must grasp this point, that the principal disturbance in the minds of men arises because they think that these celestial bodies are blessed and immortal, and yet have wills and actions and motives inconsistent with these attributes; and because they are always expecting or imagining some everlasting misery, such as is depicted in legends, or even fear the loss of feeling in death as though it would concern them themselves; and, again, because they are brought to this pass not by reasoned opinion, but rather by some irrational presentiment, and therefore, as they do not know the limits of pain, they suffer a disturbance equally great or even more extensive than if they had reached this belief by opinion. But peace of mind is being delivered from all this, and having a constant memory of the general and most essential principles.

Wherefore we must pay attention to internal feelings and to external sensations in general and in particular, according as the subject is general or particular, and to every immediate intuition in accordance with each of the standards of judgment. For if we pay attention to these, we shall rightly trace the causes whence arose our mental disturbance and fear, and, by learning the true causes of celestial phenomena and all other occurrences that come to pass from time to time, we shall free ourselves from all which produces the utmost fear in other men.[d]

**4.** In setting forth the principles of the good life, Epicurus recommends that we keep always before us the two fundamental beliefs for which he has provided the metaphysical basis: First, God is truly blessed—and therefore above dealing in rewards and punishments for humans—and second, "death is nothing to us." Fortified with these ideas, we can hope to live a pleasant life, and a pleasant life is more to be desired than a long one.

First of all believe that God is a being immortal and blessed, even as the common idea of a god is engraved on men's minds, and do not assign to him anything alien to his immortality or ill-suited to his blessedness: but believe about him everything that can uphold his blessedness and immortality. For gods there are, since the knowledge of them is by clear vision. But they are not such as the many believe them to be: for indeed they do not consistently represent them as they believe them to be. And the impious man is not he who denies the gods of the many, but he who attaches to the gods the beliefs of the many. For the statements of the many about the gods are not conceptions derived fromsensation, but false suppositions, according to which the greatest misfortunes befall the wicked and the greatest blessings the good by the gift of the gods. For men being accustomed always to their own virtues welcome those like themselves, but regard all that is not of their nature as alien. . . .

The blessed and immortal nature knows no trouble itself nor causes trouble to any other, so that it is never constrained by anger or favor. For all such things exist only in the weak. . . .

Become accustomed to the belief that death is nothing to us. For all good and evil consists in sensation, but death is deprivation of sensation. And therefore a right understanding that death is nothing to us makes the mortality of life enjoyable, not because it adds to it an infinite span of time, but because it takes away the craving for immortality. For there is nothing terrible in life for the man who has truly comprehended that there is nothing terrible in not living. So that the man speaks but idly who says that he fears death not because it will be painful when it comes, but because it is painful in anticipation. For that which gives no trouble when it comes is but an empty pain in anticipation. So death, the most terrifying of ills, is nothing to us, since so long as we exist, death is not with us; but when death comes, then we do not exist. It does not then concern either the living or the dead, since for the former it is not, and the latter are no more.

But the many at one moment shun death as the greatest of evils, at another yearn for it as a respite from the evils in life. But the wise man neither seeks to escape life nor fears the cessation of life, for neither does life offend him nor does the absence of life seem to be any evil. And just as with food he does not seek simply the larger share and nothing else, but rather the most pleasant, so he seeks to enjoy not the longest period of time, but the most pleasant.[e]

**5.** In Epicurus's view, all our actions are directed toward bodily and mental pleasures. Although pleasure is intrinsically good, we will find that the most pleasant life sometimes requires us to undergo pain for the sake of greater pleasure.

Since pleasure is the first good and natural to us, for this very reason we do not choose every pleasure, but sometimes we pass over many pleasures, when greater discomfort accrues to us as the result of them: and similarly we think many pains better than pleasures, since a greater pleasure comes to us when we have endured pains for a long time. Every pleasure then because of its natural kinship to us is good, yet not every pleasure is to be chosen: even as every pain also is an evil, yet not all are always of a nature to be avoided. Yet by a scale of comparison and by the consideration of advantages and disadvantages we must form our judgment on all these matters. For the good on certain occasions we treat as bad, and conversely the bad as good. . . .

No one when he sees evil deliberately chooses it, but is enticed by it as being good in comparison with a greater evil and so pursues it.[f]

**6.** To understand how we should live in order to enjoy the most pleasant and serene existence, Epicurus tells us, we must know the nature of the various desires and the different pleasures that come from their satisfaction.

We must consider that of desires some are natural, others vain, and of the natural some are necessary and others merely natural; and of the necessary some are necessary for happiness, others for the repose of the body, and others for very life. . . .

Unhappiness comes either through fear or through vain and unbridled desire: but if a man curbs these, he can win for himself the blessedness of understanding.... Of desires, all that do not lead to a sense of pain, if they are not satisfied, are not necessary, but involve a craving which is easily dispelled, when the object is hard to procure or they seem likely to produce harm.... Wherever in the case of desires which are physical [natural], but do not lead to a sense of pain, if they are not fulfilled, the effort is intense, such pleasures are due to idle imagination, and it is not owing to their own nature that they fail to be dispelled, but owing to be empty imaginings of the man....

The disturbance of the soul cannot be ended nor true joy created either by the possession of the greatest wealth or by honor and respect in the eyes of the mob or by anything else that is associated with causes of unlimited desires.... We must not violate nature, but obey her; and we shall obey her if we fulfill the necessary desires and also the physical [natural], if they bring no harm to us, but sternly reject the harmful.... The man who follows nature and not vain opinions is independent in all things. For in reference to what is enough for nature every possession is riches, but in reference to unlimited desires even the greatest wealth is not riches but poverty.

Insofar as you are in difficulties, it is because you forget nature; for you create for yourself unlimited fears and desires. It is better for you to be free of fear lying upon a pallet, than to have a golden couch and a rich table and be full of trouble.... Thanks be to blessed Nature because she has made what is necessary easy to supply, and what is not easy unnecessary.... The right understanding of these facts enables us to refer all choice and avoidance to the health of the body and the soul's freedom from disturbance, since this is the aim of the life of blessedness. For it is to obtain this end that we always act, namely, to avoid pain and fear. And when this is once secured for us, all the tempest of the soul is dispersed, since the living creature has not to wander as though in search of something that is missing, and to look for some other thing by which he can fulfill the good of the soul and the good of the body. For it is then that we have need of pleasure, when we feel pain owing to the absence of pleasure; but when we do not feel pain, we no longer need pleasure. And for this cause we call pleasure the beginning and end of the blessed life. For we recognize pleasure as the first good innate in us, and from pleasure we begin every act of choice and avoidance, and to pleasure we return again, using the feeling as the standard by which we judge every good.[g]

**7.** Epicurus describes the prudent person as one who knows that the truly good things are easy to obtain and that evils are either short-lived or slight. Prudent people also know that they themselves, not destiny, control the factors that decide their happiness, and they have the power to turn chance occurrences to good account. Moreover, the wise decision rather than the fortunate outcome is the prudent individual's choice.

[The prudent person] understands that the limit of good things is easy to fulfill and easy to attain, whereas the course of ills is either short in time or slight in pain.

Pain does not last continuously in the flesh, but the acutest pain is there for a very short time, and even that which just exceeds the pleasure in the flesh does not continue for many days at once....

He laughs at destiny, whom some have introduced as the mistress of all things. He thinks that with us lies the chief power in determining events, some of which happen by necessity and some by chance, and some are within our control; for while necessity cannot be called to account, he sees that chance is inconstant, but that which is in our control is subject to no master, and to it are naturally attached praise and blame. For, indeed, it were better to follow the myths about the gods than to become a slave to the destiny of the natural philosophers: for the former suggests a hope of placating the gods by worship, whereas the latter involves a necessity which knows no placation. As to chance, he does not regard it as a god as most men do (for in a god's acts there is no disorder), nor as an uncertain cause of all things: for he does not believe that good and evil are given by chance to man for the framing of a blessed life, but that opportunities for great good and great evil are afforded by it. He therefore thinks it better to be unfortunate in reasonable action than to prosper in unreason. For it is better in a man's actions that whatis well chosen should fail, rather than that what is ill chosen should be successful owing to chance.[h]

**8.** When he turns his attention to the nature of community life, Epicurus finds that the principle of justice is required to assure mutual help among people and to prevent them from injuring one another. To these ends, individuals form a social compact, with justice governing their interrelations. Epicurus points out that although justice is the same for all when it is considered as a general principle, it manifests variations when it is applied in specific situations.

The justice which arises from nature is a pledge of mutual advantage to restrain men from harming one another and save them from being harmed.

For all living things which have not been able to make compacts not to harm one another or be harmed, nothing ever is either just or unjust; and likewise too for all tribes of men which have been unable or unwilling to make compacts not to harm or be harmed.

Justice never is anything in itself, but the dealings of men with one another in any place whatever and at any time it is a kind of compact not to harm or be harmed.

Injustice is not an evil in itself, but only in consequence of the fear which attaches to the apprehension of being unable to escape those appointed to punish such actions.

It is not possible for one who acts in secret contravention of the terms of the compact not to harm or be harmed, to be confident that he will escape detection, even if at present he escapes a thousand times. For up to the time of death it cannot be certain that he will indeed escape.

In its general aspect justice is the same for all, for it is a kind of mutual advantage in the dealings of men with one another: but with reference to the individual peculiarities of a country or any other circumstances the same thing does not turn out to be just for all.

Among actions which are sanctioned as just by law, that which is proved on examination to be of advantage in the requirements of men's dealings with one another, has the guarantee of justice, whether it is the same for all or not. But if a man makes a law and it does not turn out to lead to advantage in men's dealings with each other, then it no longer has the essential nature of justice. And even if the advantage in the matter of justice shifts from one side to the other, but for a while accords with the general concept, it is none the less just for that period in the eyes of those who do not confound themselves with empty sounds but look to the actual facts.

Where, provided the circumstances have not been altered, actions which were considered just have been shown not to accord with the general concept in actual practice, then they are not just. But where, when circumstances have changed, the same actions which were sanctioned as just no longer lead to advantage, there they were just at the time when they were of advantage for the dealings of fellow citizens with one another; but subsequently they are no longer just, when no longer of advantage.[i]

**9.** In our concern for our safety, Epicurus tells us, we are likely to be misled by seeing protections against the misdeeds of our neighbors. He recommends as the surest protection that we "release ourselves from the prison of affairs and politics" and withdraw into the company of a few select friends. In this, he is in effect referring to the ideal Epicurean community, of which the Garden of Epicurus was the actual embodiment.

To secure protection from men anything is a natural good, by which you may be able to attain this end.

Some men wished to become famous and conspicuous, thinking that they would thus win for themselves safety from other men. Wherefore if the life of such men is safe, they have obtained the good which nature craves; but if it is not safe, they do not possess that for which they strove at first by the instinct of nature....

The most unalloyed source of protection from men, which is secured to some extent by a certain force of expulsion, is in fact the immunity which results from a quiet life and the retirement from the world....

Of all the things which wisdom acquires to produce the blessedness of the complete life, far the greatest is the possession of friendship.

The same conviction which has given us confidence that there is nothing terrible that lasts forever or even for long, has also seen the protection of friendship most fully completed in the limited evils of this life....

As many as possess the power to procure complete immunity from their neighbors, these also live most pleasantly with one another, since they have the most certain pledge of security.[j]

**10.** From his own diligent application of his ethical theory, Epicurus draws confidence to assure those who follow his teachings that they may expect more than ordinary mortal blessedness.

Some men throughout their lives gather together the means of life, for they do not see that the draught swallowed by all of us at birth is a draught of death. Against all else it is possible to provide security, but as against death all of us mortals alike dwell in an unfortified city....

[But] I have anticipated thee, Fortune, and entrenched myself against all thy secret attacks. And we will not give ourselves up as captives to thee or to any other circumstance; but when it is time for us to go, spitting contempt on life and on those who here vainly cling to it, we will leave life crying aloud in a glorious triumph-song that we have lived well. We must try to make the end of the journey better than the beginning, as long as we are journeying; but when we come to the end, we must be happy and content....

Meditate therefore on these things and things akin to them night and day by yourself, and with a companion like to yourself, and never shall you be disturbed waking or asleep, but you shall live like a god among men. For a man who lives among immortal blessings is not like to a mortal being.[k]

## QUESTIONS

1. Although Epicurus is a hedonist, he is opposed to the philosophy that teaches, "Eat, drink, and be merry, for tomorrow you die." Reconstruct Epicurus's theory of pleasure to account for his opposition to this view. Can you find additional arguments for or against the theory of the sensualistic hedonists?
2. Outline the view of nature that Epicurus adopted from Democritus, stating its premises and noting the changes he made in the original doctrine. How does the atomistic metaphysic fit into Epicurus's ethical theory?
3. What is *ataraxia?* What is its role in the Epicurean ethic, and how is it achieved?
4. Freedom from the fear of death and of the heavy hand of the gods is one of the chief benefits promised by Epicurus's ethics. What conception of death and of the nature of the gods does he offer in order to bring about release from these fears? Do you think Epicurus's arguments are effective?
5. Discuss the role of the study of philosophy in Epicureanism.
6. What is the significance of Epicurus's assertion that "prudence is more precious than philosophy"?
7. What does Epicurus attempt to accomplish by calling attention to the differences between "natural" and "unnatural" desires? What are the chief differences? How is this distinction related to the contrast between the duration and the intensity of pleasures and between active and passive pleasures?
8. Discuss the role of freedom in Epicurus's ethical theory, especially as an antidote to fatalism.
9. Describe and discuss Epicurus's conception of justice. Is it satisfactory for the organization of an ordinary social group? Why is it unnecessary

in the Garden of Epicurus? What activities and values distinguish the Epicurean community from ordinary communities?

10. Draw up a panel of arguments for and against hedonism as an ethical theory, utilizng the ideas of Epicurus for the affirmative and the ideas of Plato and Aristotle for the negative.

## KEY TO SELECTIONS

Epicurus, *Epicurus: The Extant Remains,* tr. Cyril Bailey, Oxford, Clarendon Press, 1926. With the kind permission of the publishers.

The following abbreviations are used:

Her. —the letter of *Epicurus to Herodotus;*
Men. —the letter of *Epicurus to Menoeceus;*
P.D. —*Principal Doctrines;*
Frag. —*Fragments.* (Roman numerals refer to the Vatican collection, Arabic numerals to remains assigned to certain books.)

[a]Frag. p. 54
[b]Her. pp. 39–41, 54, 43–44.
[c]Her. pp. 63–67.
[d]Her. pp. 77–78, 81–82.
[e]Men. pp. 123–124, P.D. pp. I, Men. pp. 125–126.
[f]Men. pp. 129–130, Frag. p. XVI.
[g]Men. p. 127, Frag. p. 74, P.D. p. XXVI, P.D. p. XXX, Frag. p. LXXXI, Frag. p. XXI, Frag. pp. 45–46, 48, Frag. p. 67, Men. p. 128.
[h]Men. p. 133, P.D. p. IV, Men. pp. 133–135.
[i]P.D. pp. XXXI–XXXVIII.
[j]P.D. pp. VI–VII, XIV, XXVII–XXVIII, XL.
[k]Frag. pp. XXX–XXXI, XLVII–XLVIII, Men. p. 135.

## GUIDE TO ADDITIONAL READING


### PRIMARY SOURCES

Diogenes Laertius, *Lives of Eminent Philosophers,* Cambridge, Mass., Harvard University Press.

Lucretius, *Of the Nature of Things,* Everyman's Library (Dutton).

———, *On the Nature of Things* (Books I–IV), Great Books Foundation (Regnery).

### DISCUSSION AND COMMENTARY

Annas, Julia, *The Morality of Happiness,* Oxford, Oxford University Press, 1993, Chs. 7 and 16.

Hicks, R. D., *Stoic and Epicurean,* New York, Charles Scribner's 1910.

Long, A. A., *Hellenistic Philosophy,* 2nd ed., Ithaca, Cornell University Press, 1986.

Long, A. A., and Sedley, D. N., *The Hellenistic Philosophers,* Cambridge, Cambridge University Press, 1987.

Mitsis, P., *Epicurus' Ethical Theory,* Ithaca, Cornell University Press, 1988.

Rist, J. M., *Epicurus: An Introduction*, Cambridge, Cambridge University Press, 1972.

Zeller, E., *Stoics, Epicureans and Sceptics,* London, Longmans, Green, 1892.

CHAPTER FIVE

# Self-Discipline

EPICTETUS

THE PHILOSOPHY OF EPICTETUS, a Roman Stoic, developed from the teachings of Zeno (336–264 B.C.E.), who founded the *Stoa Poikile* (Painted Porch), the last of the four most famous schools of ancient Athens. Dependence on Greek thought is typical of Roman philosophy; in the long history of the Roman Empire, no indigenous philosophies of merit were produced. Of all the Greek philosophical systems transplanted to Rome, Stoicism was probably the most successful. By the close of the second century B.C.E., the Stoic philosophy was firmly rooted in its new environment, and in the succeeding four centuries, it was accepted by members of both the lower and the upper strata of society. It became extremely popular with the Roman soldiery as a philosophy of manly indifference to hardship, and it also appealed as a "citadel of the soul" to such outstanding intellectuals as Cicero, Seneca, Emperor Marcus Aurelius, and Epictetus. The pressing need for the prophylactic powers of the Stoic philosophy was generated by the sordidness and debauchery of the era, for which one of Epictetus's observations serves well as a description: "[Men] bite and vilify each other, and take possession of public assemblies, as wild beasts do of solitudes and mountains; and convert courts of justice into dens of robbers. [They] are intemperate, adulterers, seducers."

There is little information about the personal history of Epictetus. The precise date and location of his birth are unknown, but what evidence exists indicates that he was born in the Greek city of Hierapolis in Phrygia about 50 C.E. It is reported that as a child he was sold into slavery by his parents, and he became part of the household of a profligate Roman soldier. An apt characterization of Epictetus, even as a young man, is given in an anecdote narrated by Origen: Upon one occasion in which his angry master was twisting his leg, Epictetus commented, "You will break my leg," whereupon the master twisted harder and broke the leg. To this, Epictetus rejoined with utter calm, "Did I not tell you so?" In keeping with Roman practice, Epictetus was allowed to attend the lectures of a contemporary teacher of Stoic philosophy, because he showed great intellectual ability. When his master died, he gained his freedom. By this time, he had already achieved some fame as a philosopher and chose to remain in Rome as a teacher. When, in 89 C.E., the despotic emperor Domitian forced all philosophers to leave Rome, Epictetus went to Nicopolis. There he started another school, in which he taught until his death (*c.* 130 C.E.).

Epictetus was more distinguished as a lecturer than as a writer. Nothing has been preserved of his original writings, but Arrian, one of his ciples, transcribed his lectures on ethics and had them edited in eight volumes. The most important of these works are the *Discourses of Epictetus* and the *Enchiridion*, or *Manual.* Epictetus's aim was "to excite his hearers to virtue," and when he gave his lectures, we have it from Arrian that "his audience could not help being affected in the very manner he intended they should."

The Stoics identify as moral people those who live in accordance with the dictates of reason, and they portray them as self-sufficient individuals capable of disciplining their desires and of remaining supremely indifferent to life's vicissitudes. By virtue of their moral principles and their conception of the good life, the Stoics regard themselves as belonging in the Socratic tradition. They maintain, as do their forerunners, the Cynics,[1] that the lesson to be drawn from the life and teachings of Socrates is that human virtue and happiness depend not on material success but on the formation of character that is true to one's essential nature, one's *rationality.* Furthermore, the Stoics contend, it is through conduct in conformity with their rational nature that people are united with each other and with the universe. The meaning of the Socratic exhortation "Know thyself" is then clear, for it is only through self-knowledge that people can participate in the moral community and fulfill their functions in the grand design of the universe.

The Stoic view of the universe, compounded from among a wide range of Greek theories by the founder of the Stoa, Zeno, and his brilliant successors, Cleanthes (*c.* 310–230 B.C.E.) and Chrysippus (280–209 B.C.E.), lends support to the Stoic ethic. Drawing chiefly from the doctrines of the early physical philosopher Heraclitus (*c.* 500 B.C.E.),[2] they depict the universe as an organic unity in which the form and

---

[1]Led by Antisthenes of Athens (*c.* 444–358 B.C.E.), a disciple of Socrates, the Cynic school subscribed to a doctrine that emphasized self-discipline and stressed virtue for its own sake. The Cynics were convinced of the intrinsic worthlessness of our ordinary desires and objectives and of the lack of relevance of the dictates of custom and convention to our well-being.

The negative aspect of the Cynic teachings has been recorded indelibly in the stories about Diogenes of Sinope (*c.* 412–323 B.C.E.). Diogenes is reputed to have lived in a tub, ignoring all the social amenities, and to have carried a lighted lantern day and night, looking for an honest man. Legend has it that when Alexander the Great rode up to the old Cynic while he was basking in the sun and offered to grant him any favor, Diogenes responded, "Only stand out of my light."

[2]According to Heraclitus, the underlying material of the universe is "ever-living Fire," from which everything comes and to which everything strives to return. However, notwithstanding the fact that the physical universe at any instant is basically nothing but "fire" in constant flux, the cosmic process of transformation is ordered and intelligible, because it conforms to an immutable law of necessity, the *Logos.*

purpose of each part is determined by God, who is thought of as a rational principle immanent in the whole. The Stoics understand God as both the vital force that creates all things in this internally connected universe and as the cosmic intelligence that governs it from within. This conception of God—called pantheism—serves as a basis for the ethical insights of the Stoics, because an individual, as a rational being, is a "fragment torn from God." All people possess the ability to comprehend the divine nature, and the good life consists in living in conformity with it. For, as Epictetus says, "Where the essence of God is, there too is the essence of good. What is the essence of God? . . . Right Reason? Certainly. Here, then, without more ado, seek the essence of good."

Epictetus is more interested than other Roman Stoics in metaphysics and remains more loyal than they to the original position of the Stoa. Nevertheless, his attitude toward speculation about the nature of things is more pious than probing, more religious than philosophical, more practical than theoretical. For Epictetus, the indisputable facts to which philosophers should direct their attention are humanity's inherent value, its kinship to God, and its duty to be worthy of God, as well as the hindrances that people encounter in their attempts to live nobly. The conditions and limitations of the moral life are already given in human nature:

> But what says Zeus? "Epictetus, if it were possible I would have made your body and your possessions (those trifles that you prize) free and untrammelled. But as things are—never forget this—this body is not yours, it is but a clever mixture of clay. But since I could not make it free, I gave you a portion of our divinity, this faculty of impulse to act and not to act, of will to get and will to avoid."[3]

The mission of the sage is to urge people to examine themselves and to discipline their will to conform to reason.

According to Epictetus, the person who *values virtue for its own sake* is happy. Virtue, he tell us, is a condition of the will wherein it is governed by reason, with the result that the virtuous person seeks only those things that are within reach and avoids those things that are beyond it. Unhappiness is the inevitable lot of those who desire what they cannot obtain. Wise individuals, then, resign themselves to limiting desires to matters within their control. With respect to desires that cannot be satisfied, they are literally *apathetic*, that is, they have no feelings about them. In addition, they know that *whatever is beyond an individual's control is irrelevant to ethics.* Virtuous persons find within themselves all that is necessary to achieve happiness—morally, they are entirely self-sufficient.

In answering the question "What is within our power?" Epictetus reaffirms one of the distinctive doctrines of Stoicism: It is our *attitudes* toward events, not events themselves, that we can control. Nothing is by its own nature calamitous—even death is terrible only if we fear it. Again, although one may fail to carry out the actions prescribed by divine providence—that is, in the execution of one's duties, circumstances may prevent a successful outcome—one should remain unconcerned. For example, if because of poverty parents are unable to feed their children, they should not be disturbed as long as they sincerely make the effort to provide for them. If they *will* to do their duty, they are fulfilling their obligation, for only this

[3] *The Discourses of Epictetus with the Enchiridion and Fragments*, tr. G.Long (London: George Bell, 1877), bk. 1, ch. 1.

much lies within their power. Moreover, they may be sure that all that happens comes about by divine necessity and that whatever God does is for the best.

Epictetus, as a moral adviser, counsels us to cultivate an attitude of indifference to good and bad fortune alike, because external events are beyond our control. Therefore, prudent individuals do not allow themselves to be enslaved by the demands of their bodies or to become emotionally attached to persons or objects. But we are warned that happiness requires unremitting self-discipline:

> Practice yourself, for heaven's sake, in little things; and thence proceed to greater. "I have a pain in my head." Do not lament. "I have a pain in my ear." Do not lament. I do not say you may never groan; but do not groan in spirit; or, if your servant be a long while in bringing you something to bind your head, do not croak and go into hysterics, and say, "Everybody hates me." For, who would not hate such a one? . . . Relying for the future on these principles, walk erect and free.[a]

---

**1.** Epictetus maintains that proper perspective in ethics requires us to understand the metaphysical conception of *divine providence:* cosmic reason, rather than chance, is the governing principle of all things. The universe operates according to laws with which human reason is in harmony and that we should strive to understand.

What then, after all, is the world? Who governs it? Has it no governor? How is it possible, when neither a city nor a house can remain, ever so short a time, without someone to govern and take care of it, that this vast and beautiful system should be administered in a fortuitous and disorderly manner? . . . The philosophers say, that we are first to learn that there is a god; and that his providence directs the whole; and that it is not merely impossible to conceal from him our actions, but even our thoughts and emotions. . . .

He then . . . understands the administration of the universe, and has learned that the principal and greatest and most comprehensive of all things is this vast system, extending from men to God; and that from Him the seeds of being are descended, not only to one's father or grandfather, but to all things that are produced and born on earth; and especially to rational natures, as they alone are qualified to partake of a communication with the Deity, being connected with him by reason. . . . All things serve and obey the [laws of the] universe; the earth, the sea, the sun, the stars, and the plants and animals of the earth. Our body likewise obeys the same, in being sick and well, young and old, and passing through the other changes decreed. It is therefore reasonable that what depends on ourselves, that is, our own understanding, should not be the only rebel. For the universe is powerful and superior, and consults the best for us by governing us in conjunction with the whole. And further; opposition, besides that it is unreasonable, and produces nothing except a vain struggle, throws us into pain and sorrows.[b]

**2.** Because all things are in harmony under divine supervision, it is essential that a person, as a "fragment of God," should recognize his or her proper place and status in the scheme of things.

A person asked him, how anyone might be convinced that his every act is under the supervision of God? Do not you think, said Epictetus, that all things are mutually connected and united?

"I do."

Well; and do not you think, that things on earth feel the influence of the heavenly powers?

"Yes."

Else how is it that in their season, as if by express command, God bids the plants to blossom and they blossom, to bud and they bud, to bear fruit and they bear it, to ripen it and they ripen;—and when again he bids them drop their leaves and withdrawing into themselves to rest and wait, they rest and wait? Whence again are there seen, on the increase and decrease of the moon, and the approach and departure of the sun, so great changes and transformations in earthly things? Have then the very leaves, and our own bodies, this connection and sympathy with the whole; and have not our souls much more? But our souls are thus connected and intimately joined to God, as being indeed members and distinct portions of his essence; and must not he be sensible of every movement of them, as belonging and connatural to himself? Can even you think of the divine administration, and every other divine subject, and together with these of human affairs also; can you at once receive impressions on your senses and your understanding, from a thousand objects; at once assent to some things, deny or suspend your judgment concerning others, and preserve in your mind impressions from so many and various objects, by whose aid you can revert to ideas similar to those which first impressed you? Can you retain a variety of arts and the memorials of ten thousand things? And is not God capable of surveying all things, and being present with all, and in communication with all? Is the sun capable of illuminating so great a portion of the universe, and of leaving only that small part of it unilluminated, which is covered by the shadow of the earth,—and cannot He who made and moves the sun, a small part of himself, if compared with the whole,—cannot he perceive all things?

"But I cannot," say you, "attend to all things at once."

Who asserts that you have equal power with Zeus? Nevertheless he has assigned to each man a director, his own good [spirit], and committed him to that guardianship; a director sleepless and not to be deceived. To what better and more careful guardian could he have committed each one of us? So that when you have shut your doors, and darkened your room, remember, never to say that you are alone; for you are not alone; but God is within.... You are a primary existence. You are a distinct portion of the essence of God; and contain a certain part of him in yourself. Why then are you ignorant of your noble birth? Why do not you consider whence you came? Why do not you remember, when you are eating, who you are who eat; and whom you feed? When you are in the company of women; when you are conversing; when you are exercising; when you are disputing; do not you know, that it is the Divine you feed; the Divine you exercise? You carry a god about with you, poor wretch, and know nothing of it. Do you suppose I mean some god without you of gold or silver? It is with yourself that you carry him; and you do not observe that you profane him by impure thoughts and unclean actions. If the mere external image of God were present, you would not dare to act as you do; and when God himself is within you, and hears and sees all, are not you ashamed to think and act thus; insensible of your own nature, and at enmity with God?[c]

**3.** Through his pantheism, Epictetus introduces into his ethical theory a cosmopolitan strain: He maintains that because humans, as rational beings, are part of the universal city of God, or cosmic reason, each individual is a part of the whole and as such should recognize his or her duty to all other individuals.

We should reason in some such manner concerning ourselves. Who are you? A man. If then, indeed, you consider yourself isolatedly, it is natural that you should live to old age, should be prosperous and healthy; but if you consider yourself as a man, and as a part of the whole, it will be fit, in view of that whole, that you should at one time be sick; at another, take a voyage, and be exposed to danger; sometimes be in want; and possibly die before your time. Why, then, are you displeased? Do not you know, that otherwise...you are no longer a man? For what is a man? A part of a commonwealth; first and chiefly of that which includes both gods and men; and next, of that to which you immediately belong, which is a miniature of the universal city.... You are a citizen of the universe, and a part of it; not a subordinate, but a principal part. You are capable of comprehending the Divine economy; and of considering the connections of things. What then does the character of a citizen imply? To hold no private interest; to deliberate of nothing as a separate individual, but rather like the hand or the foot, which, if they had reason, and comprehended the constitution of nature, would never pursue, or desire, but with a reference to the whole. Hence the philosophers rightly say, that, if it were possible for a wise and good man to foresee what was to happen, he might cooperate in bringing on himself sickness, and death, and mutilation, being sensible that these things are appointed in the order of the universe; and that the whole is superior to a part, and the city to the citizen. But, since we do not foreknow what is to happen, it becomes our duty to hold to what is more agreeable to our choice, for this too is a part of our birthright.[d]

**4.** In order to live in a manner befitting our rational nature, we must "make the best of what is in our power, and take the rest as it occurs." For Epictetus, the faculty of will *is within our control and constitutes the ultimate source of ethical behavior.*

Man, be not ungrateful, nor, on the other hand, unmindful of your superior advantages; but for sight, and hearing, and indeed for life itself, and the supports of it, as fruits, and wine, and oil, be thankful to God; but remember that He hath given you another thing, superior to them all, which uses them, proves them, estimates the value of each. For what is it that pronounces upon the value of each of these faculties? Is it the faculty itself? Did you ever perceive the faculty of sight or hearing, to say anything concerning itself? Or wheat, or barley, or horses, or dogs? No. These things are appointed as instruments and servants, to obey that which is capable of using things as they appear. If you inquire the value of anything; of what do you inquire? What is the faculty that answers you? How then can any faculty be superior to this, which uses all the rest as instruments, and tries and pronounces concerning each of them? For which of them knows what itself is; and what is its own value? Which of them knows, when it is to be used, and when not? Which is it, that opens and shuts the eyes, and turns them away from improper objects? Is it the faculty of sight? No; but that of Will. Which is it, that opens and shuts the ears? Which is it, by which they are made curious and inquisitive; or on the contrary deaf, and unaffected by what is said? Is it the faculty of hearing? No; but that of Will. This, then, recognizing itself to exist amidst other faculties, all blind and deaf, and unable to discern anything but those offices, in which they are appointed to minister and serve; itself alone sees clearly, and distinguishes the value of each of the rest. Will this, I say, inform us, that anything is supreme, but itself? What can the eye, when it is opened, do more than see? But whether we ought to look upon the wife of any one, and in what manner, what is it that decides us? The faculty of Will. Whether we ought to believe, or disbelieve what is said; or whether, if we do believe, we ought to be moved by it, or not; what is it that decides us? Is it not the faculty of Will? Again; the very faculty of eloquence, and that which ornaments discourse, if any such peculiar faculty there be, what does it more than merely ornament and arrange expressions, as curlers do the hair? But whether it be better to speak, or to be silent; or better to speak in this, or in that manner; whether this be decent, or indecent; and the season and use of each; what is it that decides for us, but the faculty of Will? What then, would you have it appear, and bear testimony against itself? What means this? If the case be thus, then that which serves may be superior to that to which it is subservient; the horse to the rider; the dog to the hunter; the instrument to the musician; or servants to the king. What is it that makes use of all the rest? The Will. What takes care of all? The Will. What destroys the whole man, at one time, by hunger; at another, by a rope, or a precipice? The Will. Has man, then, anything stronger than this? And how is it possible, that what is liable to restraint should be stronger than what is not? What has a natural power to restrain the faculty of sight? The Will and its workings. And it is the same with the faculties of hearing and of speech. And what has a natural power of retraining the Will? Nothing beyond itself, only its own perversion. Therefore in the Will alone is vice: in the Will alone is virtue.[e]

> **5.** In establishing the metaphysical and moral primacy of the will, Epictetus believes that he undermines the philosophy of Epicurus. The doctrine that matter is the most excellent and real thing, he points out, could have been asserted only if its author had the *will* to do so.

Since, then, the Will is such a faculty, and placed in authority over all the rest, suppose it to come forth and say to us, that the body, is, of all things, the most excellent! If even the body itself pronounced itself to be the most excellent, it could not be borne. But now, what is it, Epicurus, that pronounces all this? What was it, that composed volumes concerning "the End," "the Nature of things," "the Rule"; that assumed a philosophic beard; that, as it was dying, wrote, that it was "then spending its last and happiest day"? Was this the body, or was it the faculty of Will? And can you, then, without madness, admit anything to be superior to this? Are you in reality so deaf and blind? What, then, does any one dishonor the other faculties? Heaven forbid! Does anyone assert that there is no use or excellence in the faculty of sight? Heaven forbid! It would be stupid, impious, and ungrateful to God. But we render to each its due. There is some use in an ass, though not so much as in an ox; and in a dog, though not so much as in a servant: and in a servant, though not so much as in the citizens; and in the citizens, though not so much as in the magistrates. And though some are more excellent than others, those uses, which the last afford, are not to be despised. The faculty of eloquence has thus its value, though not equal to that of the Will. When therefore I talk thus, let not anyone suppose, that I would have you neglect eloquence, any more than your eyes, or ears, or hands, or feet, or clothes, or shoes. But if you ask me what is the most excellent of things, what shall I say? I cannot say, eloquence, but a right. Will; for it is this which makes use of that, and of all the other faculties, whether great or small. If this be set right, a bad man becomes good; if it be wrong, a good man becomes wicked. By this we are unfortunate or fortunate; we disapprove or approve each other. In a word, it is this which, neglected, forms unhappiness; and, well cultivated, happiness.[f]

> **6.** The avoidance of frustration and disappointment requires both the *control of those things that are in our power* (our attitudes and reactions to things) and *indifference to those things that are beyond our control* (externals such as wealth and fame). Epictetus explains frustration as the consequence of false judgments of things, by which we are led to attempt to control what is actually uncontrollable by us.

There are things which are within our power, and there are things which are beyond our power. Within our power are opinion, aim, desire, aversion, and, in one word, whatever affairs are our own. Beyond our power are body, property, reputation, office, and, in one word, whatever are not properly our own affairs.

Now the things within our power are by nature free, unrestricted, unhindered; but those beyond our power are weak, dependent, restricted, alien. Remember then, that, if you attribute freedom to things by nature dependent, and take what belongs to others for your own, you will be hindered, you will lament, you will be disturbed, you will find fault both with gods and men. But if you take for your own only that which is your own, and view what belongs to others just as it really is, then no one will ever compel you, no one will restrict you, you will find fault with no one, you will accuse no one, you will do nothing against your will; no one will hurt you, you will not have an enemy, nor will you suffer any harm.

Aiming therefore at such great things, remember that you must not allow yourself any inclination, however slight, towards the attainment of the others; but that you must entirely quit some of them, and for the present postpone the rest. But if you would have these, and possess power and wealth likewise, you may miss the latter in seeking the former; and you will certainly fail of that, by which along happiness and freedom are procured.

Seek at once, therefore, to be able to say to every unpleasing semblance, "You are but a semblance and by no means the real thing." And then examine it by those rules which you have; and first and chiefly, by this: whether it concerns the things which are within our own power, or those which are not; and if it concerns anything beyond our power, be prepared to say that it is nothing to you.

Remember that desire demands the attainment of that of which you are desirous; and aversion demands the avoidance of that to which you are averse; that he who fails ofthe object of his desires, is disappointed; andhe who incurs the object of his aversion, is wretched. If, then, you shun only those undesirable things which you can control, you will never incur anything which you shun. But if you shun sickness, or death, or poverty, you will run the risk of wretchedness. Remove aversion, then, from all things that are not within our power, and transfer it to things undesirable, which are within our power. But for the present altogether restrain desire; for if you desire any of the things not within our own power, you must necessarily be disappointed; and you are not yet secure of those which are within our power, and so are legitimate objects of desire. Where it is practically necessary for you to pursue or avoid anything, do even this with discretion, and gentleness, and moderation.[g]

**7.** If free, happy individuals confine their desires to those things that depend on their own will and are thus in harmony with God's will, then even death will appear trivial. For the proper attitude toward such events will be one of apathy—indifference, imperturbability. After all, Epictetus argues, every external event follows from the divine nature with logical necessity, and therefore, only individuals' judgments of things cause distress. One should accept with equanimity what is inevitable; no event is terrible when viewed by the disciplined mind.

[Remember] that such is, and was, and will be, the nature of the world, nor is it possible that things should be otherwise than they now are; and that not only men and other creatures upon earth partake of this change and transformation, but diviner things also. For indeed even the four elements are transformed and metamorphosed; and earth becomes water, and water air, and this again is transformed into other things. And the same manner of transformation happens from things above to those below. Whoever endeavors to turn his mind towards these points, and persuade himself to receive with willingness what cannot be avoided, will pass his life in moderation and harmony.... Remember that you are an actor in a drama of such sort as the author chooses. If short, then in a short one; if long, then in a long one. If it be his pleasure that you should act a poor man, see that you act it well; or a cripple, or a ruler, or a private citizen. For this is your business, to act well the given part; but to choose it, belongs to another....

You hear the vulgar say, "Such a one, poor soul! is dead." Well, his father died: his mother died. "Ay, but he was cut off in the flower of his age, and in a foreign land." Observe these contrary ways of speaking; and abandon such expressions. Oppose to one custom, a contrary custom; to sophistry, the art of reasoning, and the frequent use and exercise of it. Against specious appearances we must set clear convictions, bright and ready for use. When death appears as an evil, we ought immediately to remember, that evils are things to be avoided, but death is inevitable. For what can I do, or where can I fly from it? ... Whither shall I fly from death? Show me the place, show me the people, to whom I may have recourse, whom death does not overtake. Show me the charm to avoid it. If there be none, what would you have me do? I cannot escape death; but cannot I escape the dread of it? Must I die trembling, and lamenting? For the very origin of the disease lies in wishing for something that is not obtained. Under the influence of this, if I can make outward things conform to my own inclination, I do it; if not, I feel inclined to tear out the eyes of whoever hinders me. For it is the nature of man not to endure the being deprived of good; not to endure the falling into evil. And so, at last, when I can neither control events, nor tear out the eyes of him who hinders me, I sit down, and groan, and revile him whom I can; Zeus, and the rest of the gods. For what are they to me, if they take no care of me? . . .

Men are disturbed not by things, but by the views which they take of things. Thus death is nothing terrible.... But the terror consists in our notion of death, that it is terrible. When, therefore, we are hindered, or disturbed, or grieved, let us never impute it to others, but to ourselves; that is, to our own views. It is the action of an uninstructed person to reproach others for his own misfortunes; of one entering upon instruction, to reproach himself; and of one perfectly instructed, to reproach neither others nor himself.... Demand not that events should happen as you wish; but wish them to happen as they do happen, and you will go on well.[h]

**8.** Epictetus observes that persons who are resigned to the limitations of human power and the inevitability of all that occurs will not give way to sorrow at their own misfortunes or those of others.

The only real thing is, to study how to rid life of lamentation, and complaint, and *Alas!* And *I am undone,* and misfortune, and failure; and to learn what death, what exile, what a prison, what poison is; that he may be able to say in a prison, like Socrates, "My dear Crito, if it thus pleases the gods thus let it be"; and not, "Wretched old man, have I kept my gray hairs for this!" [Do you ask] who speaks thus? Do you think I quote some mean and despicable person? Is it not Priam who says it? Is it not Oedipus? Nay, how many kings say it? For what else is tragedy, but the dramatized sufferings of men, bewildered by an admiration of externals? If one were to be taught by fictions, that things beyond our will are nothing to us, I should rejoice in such a fiction, by which I might live prosperous and serene.... When you see anyone weeping for grief, either that his son has gone abroad, or that he has suffered in his affairs; take care not to be overcome by the apparent evil. But discriminate, and be ready to say, "What hurts this man is not this occurrence itself, for another man might not be hurt by it;—but the view he chooses to take of it." As far as conversation goes, however, do not disdain to accommodate yourself to him, and if need be, to groan with him. Take heed, however, not to groan inwardly too.[i]

**9.** Epictetus advocates the life of self-control—that is, mastery of one's desires—and the possession of a virtuous disposition. "It is not poverty that causes sorrow, but covetous desires.... Nothing is meaner than the love of pleasure, the love of gain, and indolence. Nothing is nobler than magnanimity, meekness, and philanthropy." Primarily he is warning us against being victimized by the pleasures of life.

[We represent] those intractable philosophers who do not think pleasure to be in itself the natural state of man; but merely an incident of those things in which his natural state consists,—justice, moderation, and freedom. Why, then, should the soul rejoice and be glad in the minor blessings of the body, as Epicurus says, and not be pleased with its own good, which is the very greatest? And yet Nature has given me likewise a sense of shame; and I am covered with blushes when I think I have uttered any indecent expression. This emotion will not suffer me to recognize pleasure as a good and the end of life.... If you are dazzled by the semblance of any promised pleasure, guard yourself against being bewildered by it; but let the affair wait your leisure, and procure yourself some delay. Then bring to your mind both points of time; that in which you shall enjoy the pleasure, and that in which you will repent and reproach yourself, after you have enjoyed it; and set before you, in opposition to these, how you will rejoice and applaud yourself, if you abstain. And even though it should appear to you a seasonable gratification, take heed that its enticements and allurements and seductions may not subdue you; but set in opposition to this, how much better it is to be conscious of having gained so great a victory.... Chastise your passions, that they may not chastise you.... It belongs to a wise man to resist pleasure; and to a fool to be enslaved by it.[j]

**10.** Having given warning that hedonism is a false doctrine, Epictetus tells us that "two rules we should have always ready—that there is nothing good or evil save in the will; and, that we are not to lead events, but to follow them." Employing these rules, wise individuals will guard the virtues that are their only true possessions and the source of their serenity, and they will avoid the disappointments and disturbances that plague those who pursue externals such as fame, honors, and wealth.

When you have lost anything external, have always at hand the consideration of what you have got instead of it; and if that be of more value, do not by any means call yourself a loser; whether it be a horse for an ass; an ox for a sheep; a good action for a piece of money; a due composure of mind for a dull jest; or modesty for indecent talk. By continually remembering this, you will preserve your character such as it ought to be. Otherwise, consider that you are spending your time in vain; and all that to which you are now applying your mind, you are about to spill and overturn. And there needs but little, merely a small deviation from reason, to destroy and overset all. A pilot does not need so much apparatus to overturn a ship as to save it; but if he exposes it a little too much to the wind, it is lost; even if he should not do it by design, but only for a moment be thinking of something else, it is lost. Such is the case here, too. If you do but nod a little, all that you have hitherto accomplished is gone. Take heed, then, to the appearances of things. Keep yourself watchful over them. It is no inconsiderable matter that you have to guard; but modesty, fidelity, constancy, docility, innocence, fearlessness, serenity; in short, freedom. For what will you sell these? Consider what the purchase is worth. "But shall I not get such a thing instead of it?" Consider, if you do not get it, what it is that you have instead. Suppose I have decency, and another the office of tribune; I have modesty, and he the praetorship? But I do not applaud where it is unbecoming; I will pay no undeserved honor; for I am free, and the friend of God, so as to obey him willingly; but I must not value anything else, neither body, nor possessions, nor fame; in short, nothing. For it is not His will that I should value them. For if this had been His pleasure, He would have placed in them my good, which now He hath not done; therefore I cannot transgress his commands. Seek in all things your own highest good,—and for other aims, recognize them as far as the case requires, and in accordance with reason, contented with this alone. Otherwise you will be unfortunate, disappointed, restrained, hindered. These are the established laws, these the statutes. Of these one ought to be an expositor, and to these obedient.[k]

**11.** Epictetus outlines the proper subject matter of philosophy and emphasizes the importance of the application of ethical theory to actual behavior: "It is not reasonings that are wanted now, for there are books stuffed full of stoical reasonings. 'What is wanted, then?' The man who shall apply them; whose actions may bear testimony to his doctrines."

There are three topics in philosophy, in which he who would be wise and good must be exercised. That of the *desires* and *aversions,* that he may not be disappointed of the one, nor incur the other. That of the *pursuits* and *avoidances,* and, in general, the duties of life; that he may act with order and consideration, and not carelessly. The third includes integrity of mind and prudence, and, in general, whatever belongs to the judgment.

Of these points, the principal and most urgent is that which reaches the passions; for passion is produced no otherwise than by a disappointment of one's desires and an incurring of one's aversions. It is this which introduces perturbations, tumults, misfortunates, and calamities; this is the spring of sorrow, lamentation, and envy; this renders us envious and emulous, and incapable of hearing reason.

The next topic regards the duties of life. For I am not to be undisturbed by passions, in the same sense as a statue is; but as one who preserves the natural and acquired relations; as a pious person, as a son, as a brother, as a father, as a citizen.

The third topic belongs to those scholars who are now somewhat advanced; and is a security to the other two, that no bewildering semblance may surprise us, either in sleep, or wine, or in depression....

[But]—Philosophy . . . doth not promise to procure any outward good for man; otherwise it would admit something beyond its proper theme. For as the material of a carpenter is wood; of a statuary, brass; so of the art of living, the material is each man own life.

"What, then, is my brother's life?"

That, again, is matter for his own art, but is external to you; like property, health, or reputation. Philosophy promises none of these.... The beginning of philosophy, at least to such as enter upon it in a proper way, and by the door, is a consciousness of our own weakness and inability in necessary things. For we came into the world without any natural idea of a right-angled triangle; of a diesis, or a semitone, in music; but we learn each of these things by some artistic instruction. Hence, they who do not understand them, do not assume to understand them. But who ever came into the world without an innate idea of good and evil; fair and base; becoming and unbecoming; happiness and misery; proper and improper; what ought to be done, and what not to be done? Hence we all make use of the terms, and endeavor to apply our impressions to particular cases. "Such a one hath acted well, not well; right, not right; is unhappy, is happy; is just, is unjust." Which of us refrains from these terms? Who defers the use of them, till he has learnt it; as those do, who are ignorant of lines and sounds? The reason of this is, that we come instructed, in some degree, by nature, upon these subjects; and from this beginning, we go on to add self-conceit. "For why," say you, "should I not know what fair or base is? Have I not the idea of it?" You have. "Do I not apply this idea to the particular instance?" You do. "Do I not apply it rightly then?" Here lies the whole question; and here arises the self-conceit. Beginning from these acknowledged points, men proceed, by applying them improperly, to reach the very position most questionable. For, if they knew how to apply them also, they would be all but perfect.... What seems to each man, is not sufficient to determine the reality of a thing. For even in weights and measures we are not satisfied with the bare appearance; but for everything we find some rule. And is there then, in the present case, no rule preferable to what seems? Is it possible, that what is of the greatest necessity in human life, should be left incapable of determination and discovery?

There must be some rule. And why do we not seek and discover it, and, when we have discovered, ever after make use of it, without fail, so as not even to move a finger without it. For this, I conceive, is what, when found, will cure those of their madness, who make use of no other measure, but their own perverted way of thinking. Afterwards, beginning from certain known and determinate points, we may make use of general principles, properly applied to particulars.

Thus, what is the subject that falls under our inquiry? Pleasure. Bring it to the rule. Throw it into the scale. Must good be something in which it is fit to confide, and to which we may trust? Yes. Is it fit to trust to anything unstable? No. Is pleasure, then, a stable thing? No. Take it, then, and throw it out of the scale, and drive it far distant from the place of good things.

But, if you are not quick-sighted, and one balance is insufficient, bring another. Is it fit to be elated by good? Yes. Is it fit, then, to be elated by a present pleasure? See that you do not say it is; otherwise I shall not think you so much as worthy to use a scale. Thus are things judged, and weighed, when we have the rules ready. This is the part of philosophy, to examine, and fix the rules; and to make use of them, when they are known, is the business of a wise and good man.[1]

## QUESTIONS

1. Outline the most important features of the Stoic ethic. Do these factors account for the fact that a slave and an emperor could both be Stoics?
2. What is the relationship between Stoic metaphysics and Stoic ethics? Do you think that rationalism and pantheism necessarily result in an ethical theory that values "virtue for its own sake"?
3. Explain and discuss the Stoic doctrine that virtue consists in living "according to nature." Can you define *nature* in such a way that this doctrine would no longer be acceptable?
4. Discuss critically Epictetus's recommendation that we "make the best of what is in our power, and take the rest as it occurs." What things are within our control, according to the Stoics?
5. Describe in detail what the Stoics mean by *apathy*. Do you believe this is the most satisfactory state we can achieve?
6. If a debate between Epictetus and Epicurus could be arranged, what arguments would each put forward against the moral philosophy of the other? Could they agree on any major issues of theory? Could they agree on any major principles of conduct?
7. How does Epictetus conceive of the proper subject matter of philosophy? Which is more important to him, the activity of reasoning or acting according to reason? Would he, accordingly, agree or disagree with Plato's tenet "virtue is knowledge"?
8. How true to the original doctrines of the Stoics is the term *stoic* as it is commonly used today?
9. The Stoics are credited with influencing considerably the development of international law. Examine their ethical doctrines for the principles that account for this contribution. Can you find further political implications of the Stoic ethic?
10. (a) Do you think the Stoics influenced the thinking of the early Christians? (b) Do you think that a revival of stoicism in our times is a reasonable possibility? Justify your answers by referring to specific Stoic doctrines.

## KEY TO SELECTIONS

Epictetus, *The Works of Epictetus,* tr. T. W. Higginson, Boston, Little, Brown, 1866.

The following abbreviations are used:

Dis. —*The Discourses;*
Ench. —*Enchiridion;*
Frag. —*Fragments.*

[a]Dis. Bk. I, Ch. XVIII.
[b]Dis. Bk. II, Ch. XIV, Bk. I, Ch. IX, Frag. CXXXI.
[c]Dis. Bk. I, Ch. XIV, Bk. II, Ch. VIII.
[d]Dis. Bk. II, Ch. V, Bk. II, Ch. X.
[e]Dis. Bk. II, Ch. XXIII.
[f]Dis. Bk. II, Ch. XXIII.
[g]Ench. I, II.
[h]Frag. CXXIX, Ench. XVII, Dis. Bk. I, Ch. XXVII, Ench. V, VIII.
[i]Dis. Bk. 1, Ch. IV, Ench. XVI.
[j]Frag. XLVII, Ench. XXXIV, Frag. IV, CVI.
[k]Dis. Bk. IV, Ch. III.
[l]Dis. Bk. III, Ch. II, Bk. I, Ch. XV, Bk. II, Ch. XI.

## GUIDE TO ADDITIONAL READING


**PRIMARY SOURCES**

Diogenes Laertius, *Lives of Eminent Philosophers,* Cambridge, Mass., Harvard University Press.
Epictetus, *Handbook,* Indianapolis, Hackett, 1983.
_____, *Moral Discourses,* Everyman's Library (Dutton).
Marcus Aurelius, *Meditations,* Everyman's Library (Dutton).
_____, _____, Great Books Foundation (Regnery).
_____, _____, Masterpieces of Literature (Collins).
_____, _____, World's Classics (Oxford University Press).

**DISCUSSION AND COMMENTARY**

Julia Annas, *The Morality of Happiness,* Oxford, Oxford University Press, 1993, ch. 5.
Long, A. A., *Hellenistic Philosophy,* Ithaca, Cornell University Press, 2nd ed., 1986.
Long, A. A., and Sedley, D. N., *The Hellenistic Philosophers,* Cambridge, Cambridge University Press, 1987.
Zeller, E., *Stoics, Epicureans and Sceptics,* London, Longmans, Green, 1892.

CHAPTER SIX

# The Love of God

SAINT AUGUSTINE

SAINT AUGUSTINE (354–430) lived in a crucial period in the history of Christianity. In 313 the emperor Constantine granted liberty of worship to Christians, and in 325 the Council of Nicaea defined basic Christian doctrine, declaring all other interpretations heretical. In the attempt to put down heresies, Saint Augustine was a powerful influence. He was born in Tagaste, a small town in North Africa. His mother, though not his father, was a Christian, and until Augustine's conversion to Christianity in his thirty-second year, his life followed the pattern typical of the young Roman provincial of the times. However, his boyhood pranks, his pride in his proficiency in the schools of the Roman rhetoricians, and his indulgence in sensual pleasure became a source of self-reproach when he viewed them in retrospect as a mature man and a pious Christian.

Before his conversion, Augustine was a highly successful teacher of rhetoric. During this phase of his career, his philosophical position shifted several times in his search for a satisfactory set of beliefs. He joined for a time the sect of Manichaeans, who explained the universe through the dualistic doctrine of God and Satan engaged in a struggle to dominate the world. Dissatisfied with their answers to the questions that troubled him, he turned to Greek philosophy and in particular to Neo-Platonism. Here he met with no better success, although the Neo-Platonic teachings later stood him in good stead. He rejected the pantheistic conception that the human soul is part of the World-Soul but incorporated in his own theory of knowledge the Neo-Platonic doctrine that the ultimate in knowledge is a mystical intuition of the Supreme Reality, which only a few can experience. Augustine came at last under the influence of Saint Ambrose, Bishop of Milan, who reinforced the efforts of the young man's mother, Monica, to turn him to Christianity. A decisive inner experience resulted in his conversion in 386, and he was baptized by Saint Ambrose the following year.

Augustine entered the priesthood in 391, rising in the course of time to become Bishop of Hippo. He applied his great talent as a thinker and writer and his knowledge of philosophy to the study of the Holy Scriptures and other teachings of his new religion, producing numerous works on Christian doctrine. His *Confessions,* although they contain abundant autobiographical detail, are primarily a eulogy of God and a declaration of devotion and love for Him. *The City of God,* on the other hand, is an extensive philosophy of history in the framework of the Christian religion, and it functions as an elaborate theodicy—a justification of the ways of God to humans. The *Enchiridion*, a work of his later years, is a manual in which he sets forth the meaning of the virtues of faith, hope, and love. The clearest expression of Augustine's theory of knowledge is to be found in the work *De Musica*. His other contributions to Christian philosophy and theology include the treatises *On the Nature of God, On Free Will, On the Immortality of the Soul, On Nature and Grace, On the Trinity,* and *On Christian Doctrine.*

The teachings of Augustine dominated Christian belief almost exclusively for more than nine centuries, after which the scholastic philosophy of Saint Thomas Aquinas (1225–1274) shared dominion with them.

Augustine is the first Christian philosopher to formulate the doctrines of his religion in a comprehensive and enduring world view. In elaborating the Christian revelation, he dedicates himself to the task of showing the way to the spiritual safety and happiness of salvation. Consequently, he carries on an unrelenting campaign to root out the heretical beliefs that mislead human beings in their search for the true religion. In addition, Augustine undertakes the construction of a reasoned defense against charges of paradoxes, contradictions, and absurdities in Christian doctrine. The accomplishment of his task is facilitated by an effective assimilation of Greek philosophy into Christian belief.[1]

The Christian creed that is the basis of Augustine's writings is contained in God's revelation as set forth in the Old and New Testaments of the Bible. Its metaphysical and ethical focus is God, the omnipotent, omniscient, and benevolent Creator of man and the universe. Human beings, created only "a little lower than the angels," were endowed with free will and were therefore able to choose between good and evil. Adam, the first man, chose evil, thus falling from God's favor, and his original sin is inherited by all humans. The punishment for sin is eternal death, but God in His mercy provides the possibility of redemption through union with His Son, Jesus Christ, our Savior. Jesus assumes the burden of the original sin of those who have faith in Him, but people must also follow His example of humility, respect, and obedience to God's commandments. The reward of those who are infused with the Holy Spirit of God is eternal life.

The works of Augustine are permeated by the gospel of love that unifies and illuminates the Christian religion. The personal, passional aspect of his love of God finds

---

[1]Three important examples of Augustine's adaptation of concepts from Greek philosophy are (1) the incorporation of Plato's conception of the "Good" in the characterization of God, (2) the use of the Neo-Platonic idea of the mediating function of the *Logos* (the Cosmic Reason or Divine Word) in interpreting the role of Jesus Christ in the Holy Trinity, and (3) the use of the Neo-Platonic definition of evil as the absence of good in the resolution of the "problem of evil."

frequent expression in the *Confessions:* "Thou hast stricken my heart with Thy word, and I loved Thee. And also the heaven and earth, and all that is therein, behold, on every side, they say that I should love Thee." And, as an article of faith, the love of God and the related love of our neighbor is treated by Augustine as an indispensable constituent of Christian doctrine:

> All the commandments of God, then, are embraced in love, of which the apostle says: "Now the end of the commandment is charity, out of a pure heart, and of a good conscience, and of faith unfeigned." Thus the end of every commandment is charity, that is, every commandment has love for its aim.... This love embraces both the love of God and the love of our neighbor, and "on these two commandments hang all the law and the prophets," we may add the Gospel and the apostles. For it is from these that we hear this voice: The end of the commandment is charity, and God is love.[a]

In loving God, Augustine tells us, we love truth. On the attainment of true knowledge, people will discover, as he did, that "where I found truth, there I found my God, who is truth itself." Individuals come to know truth through inner experience and conviction. Moreover, they must make an effort of will to prepare the mind to receive truth. Augustine maintains that one cannot obtain true knowledge without faith: One should first believe in order to understand. The intellectual knowledge of God, however, does not by itself suffice for the perfect and ultimate comprehension of God that is our happiness. For this, one must go beyond reason to mystical vision, the spiritual seeing of God that transcends reason. Faith, knowledge, and mystical vision may be conceived as progressive steps on the way to the transcendental understanding of God, who is the essence of all truth.

Knowledge of God is indispensable to our blessedness, but, Augustine holds, it is false pride for people to believe that they can know God by their own efforts. Only when God by His grace illuminates the mind can it grasp the truth. Similarly, salvation can be achieved only through God's grace. In the Augustinian theology, each person is predestined by God either to salvation or to damnation. Because all people are stained with original sin, they deserve only punishment. Consequently, salvation is a free gift of God bestowed on the chosen few. Without divine grace, neither faith nor good works can ensure salvation. No human mind can penetrate the mystery of God's wisdom in electing some but not others to be saved. Trusting in God's goodness, and despite the fact that we cannot judge whether we will be saved, we are obligated to seek God and to live according to His commandments.[2]

The human struggle to turn away from evil and seek the good is described by Augustine in *The City of God*. The whole history of humanity from the fall of Adam and Eve to the Last Judgment is depicted as a conflict between the "City of God" and the "City of Man." Those who live in the earthly city pursue material interests and carnal pleasures. They not only suffer the frustrations brought about by their false beliefs while on earth but also endure the everlasting alienation from God that is the punishment of the sinful. By contrast, the citizens of the City of God form a "mystical and unanimous society of saints in heaven and believers on Earth." Through the redemptive mission of Jesus Christ, God's True Word, they

---

[2]There seems to be an unreconciled conflict between Augustine's theological doctrine of divine predestination, with its implication of human impotency, and his philosophical defense of human freedom of will, with its implication of moral responsibility.

enjoy both spiritual peace on earth and the eternal blessedness of the vision of God that is humanity's true happiness.

---

**1.** In the support and defense of Christian doctrine, Augustine is obliged to resolve some of the most troublesome metaphysical problems of ethics. Among these, perhaps the most crucial challenge to the effectiveness of his ethical theory and a natural point of entry into his entire moral philosophy is the so-called problem of evil—namely, how to reconcile the existence of evil in the world with the omnipotence and benevolence of God. The paradoxical nature of this problem is clearly evident from the formulation of it attributed to the Greek philosopher Epicurus:

> Either God would remove evil out of this world, and cannot: or He can, and will not; or, He has not the power nor will; or, lastly, He has both the power and will. If He has the will, and not the power, this shows weakness, which is contrary to the nature of God. If He has the power, and not the will, it is malignity, and this is no less contrary to His nature. If He is neither able nor willing, He is both impotent and malignant, and consequently cannot be God. If He be both willing and able (which alone is consonant to the nature of God), whence comes evil, or why does He not prevent it?[3]

[3]Various answers to the paradoxical problem of evil have been given in its long and controversial history: (1) If the reality of evil is denied, it follows that there is no paradox—as, for example, when it is argued that what appears evil to people is really good in the overall view of the universe. (2) If it is conceded that God's power is finite, then the existence of evil is not paradoxical. (3) If it is held that our limited intellect cannot grasp the mystery, then we must trust in God's goodness and accept the paradox unresolved. (4) If, as Augustine asserts, God is both supremely good and all-powerful, and yet evil is not illusory, then the paradox can be attacked by defining evil as nothing more than the absence of good.

As a starting point for his treatment of the problem of evil, Augustine insists that God is perfectly good and that all things come from Him. Because God in His goodness cannot create anything evil, it follows that evil cannot be a positive characteristic of things. However, the things that God creates are less than wholly good, and they are evil only insofar as they lack goodness.

*What is called evil in the universe is but the absence of good:* . . . In the bodies of animals, disease and wounds mean nothing but the absence of health; for when a cure is effected, that does not mean that the evils which were present—namely, the diseases and wounds—go away from the body and dwell elsewhere: they altogether cease to exist; for the wound or disease is not a substance, but a defect in the fleshly substance—the flesh itself being a substance, and therefore something good, of which those evils—that is, privations of the good which we call health—are accidents. Just in the same way, what are called vices in the soul are nothing but privations of natural good. And when they are cured, they are not transferred elsewhere: when they cease to exist in the healthy soul, they cannot exist anywhere else.

*All beings were made good, but not being made perfectly good, are liable to corruption:* All things that exist, therefore, seeing that the Creator of them all is supremely good, are themselves good. But because they are not, like their Creator, supremely and unchangeably good, their good may be diminished and increased. But for good to be diminished is an evil, although, however much it may be diminished, it is necessary, if the being is to continue, that some good should remain to constitute the being. For however small or of whatever kind the being may be, the good which makes it a being cannot be destroyed without destroying the being itself. An uncorrupted nature is justly held in esteem. But if, still further, it be incorruptible, it is undoubtedly considered of still higher value. When it is corrupted, however, its corruption is an evil, because it is deprived of some sort of good. For if it be deprived of no good, it receives no injury; but it does receive injury, therefore it is deprived of good. Therefore, so long as a being is in process of corruption, there is in it some good of which it is being deprived; and if a part of the being should remain which cannot be corrupted, this will certainly be an incorruptible being, and accordingly the process of corruption will result in the manifestation of this great good. But if it does not cease to be corrupted, neither can it cease to possess good of which corruption may deprive it. But if it should be thoroughly and completely consumed by corruption, there will then be no good left, because there will be no being. Wherefore corruption can consume the good only by consuming the being. Every being, therefore, is a good; a great good, if it cannot be corrupted; a little good, if it can: but in any case, only the foolish or ignorant will deny that it is a good. And if it be wholly consumed by corruption, then the corruption itself must cease to exist, as there is no being left in which it can dwell.[b]

**2.** Nevertheless, it still remains to resolve another part of the problem of evil. If God is able to do all things, why does He permit us to choose evil? Or, if God is free to do whatsoever He will, why should He will evil? Augustine argues that because God is all-powerful, He can prevent evil if He so wills, so that His permitting evil must reflect His goodness in some way. He explains that God's mercy and justice are served by presenting individuals with a choice between good and evil. Whichever we choose, God's will ultimately is fulfilled, and even evil choices are turned to good account by Him. In our present imperfect state, we cannot always perceive the wisdom of God's ways, but Augustine is confident that in the fullness of faith, all will become clear.

*The omnipotent God does well even in the permission of evil:* Nor can we doubt that God does well even in the permission of what is evil. For He permits it only in the justice of His judgment. And surely all that is just is good. Although, therefore, evil, insofar as it is evil, is not a good; yet the fact that evil as well as good exists, is a good. For if it were not a good that evil should exist, its existence would not be permitted by the omnipotent God, who without doubt can as easily refuse to permit what He does not wish, as bring about what He does wish. And if we do not believe this, the very first sentence of our creed is endangered, wherein we profess to believe in God the Father Almighty. For He is not truly called Almighty if He cannot do whatsoever He pleases, or if the power of His almighty will is hindered by the will of any creature whatsoever. . . .

*The will of God is never defeated, though much is done that is contrary to His will:* These are the great works of the Lord, sought out according to all His pleasure, and so wisely sought out, that when the intelligent creation, both angelic and human, sinned, doing not His will but their own, He used the very will of the creature which was working in opposition to the Creator's will as an instrument for carrying out His will, the supremely Good thus turning to good account even what is evil, to the condemnation of those whom in His justice He has predestined to punishment, and to the salvation of those whom in His mercy He has predestined to grace. For, as far as relates to their own consciousness, these creatures did what God wished not to be done: but in view of God's omnipotence, they could in no wise effect their purpose. For in the very fact that they acted in opposition to His will, His will concerning them was fulfilled. And hence it is that "the works of the Lord are great, sought out according to all His pleasure," because in a way unspeakably strange and wonderful, even what is done in opposition to His will does not defeat His will. For it would not be done did He not permit it (and of course His permission is not unwilling, but willing); nor would a Good Being permit evil to be done that in His omnipotence He can turn evil into good.

*The will of God, which is always good, is sometimes fulfilled through the evil will of man:*

Sometimes, however, a man in the goodness of his will desires something that God does not desire, even though God's will is also good, nay, much more fully and more surely good (for His will never can be evil): for example, if a good son is anxious that his father should live, when it is God's goodwill that he should die. Again, it is possible for a man with evil will to desire what God wills in His goodness: for example, if a bad son wishes his father to die, when this is also the will of God. It is plain that the former wishes what God does not wish, and that the latter wishes what God does wish; and yet the filial love of the former is more in harmony with the goodwill of God, though its desire is different from God's, than the want of filial affection of the latter, though its desire is the same as God's. So necessary is it, in determining whether a man's desire is one to be approved or disapproved, to consider what it is proper for man, and what it is proper for God, to desire, and what is in each case the real motive of the will. For God accomplishes some of His purposes, which of course are all good, through the evil desires of wicked men.[c]

**3.** Although Augustine has resolved here and elsewhere the problem of evil to his satisfaction, another traditional paradox arises when it is considered that God knows in advance what choices we will make. Divine foreknowledge must be reconciled with our freedom to choose good or evil. Because all things have causes, it would appear that if God knows in advance what is to happen, all that happens is determined, and individuals cannot have free will. Then, if we are not free, punishment and reward are both unjust and ineffective. On the other hand, if we are free to choose our own courses of action, God cannot have foreknowledge of human behavior and consequently cannot be omniscient.

Augustine sets about the task of showing how it is possible to retain the belief in both divine prescience and human free will. Granting that every event has a cause, he points out that human will is one of the causes of its actions. Hence the causal power of the will is part of the overall causal order of events foreknown by God. The paradox is effectively resolved by the distinction between the knowledge of a cause and the cause itself: God's knowing in advance that an event will necessarily occur is not the same as His causing it to occur.

But it does not follow that, though there is for God a certain order of all causes, there must therefore be nothing depending on the free exercise of our own wills, for our wills themselves are included in that order of causes which is certain to God, and is embraced by His foreknowledge, for human wills are also causes of human actions; and He who foreknew all the causes of things would certainly among those causes not have been ignorant of our wills. . . .

If that is to be called *our necessity* which is not in our power, but even though we be unwilling, effects what it can effect,—as, for instance, the necessity of death,—it is manifest that our wills by which we live uprightly or wickedly are not under such a necessity; for we do many things which, if we were not willing, we should certainly not do. This is primarily true of the act of willing itself,—for if we will, it *is*; if we will not, it *is* not,—for we should not will if we were unwilling. But if we define necessity to be that according to which we say that it is necessary that anything be of such or such a nature, or be done in such and such a manner, I know not why we should have any dread of that necessity taking away the freedom of our will. For we do not put the life of God or the foreknowledge of God under necessity if we should say that it is necessary that God should live forever, and foreknow all things; as neither is His power diminished when we say that He cannot die or fall into error,—for this is in such a way impossible to Him, that if it were possible for Him, He would be of less power. But assuredly He is rightly called omnipotent, though He can neither die nor fall into error. For He is called omnipotent on account of His doing what He wills, not on account of His suffering what He wills not; for if that should befall Him, He would by no means be omnipotent. Wherefore,

He cannot do some things for the very reason that He is omnipotent.[d]

**4.** It follows, then, that people are themselves responsible for their misfortunes; they are free to choose, and they choose evil. For Augustine, however, an evil will itself is a defective one. Just as he defines evil as the absence of good, so too he characterizes an evil will as one that fails to choose the good.

Let no one, therefore, look for an efficient cause of the evil will; for it is not efficient, but deficient, as the will itself is not an effecting of something, but a defect. For defection from that which supremely is, to that which has less of being,—this is to begin to have an evil will. Now, to seek to discover the causes of these defections,—causes, as I have said, not efficient, but deficient,—is as if someone sought to see darkness, or hear silence. Yet both of these are known by us, and the former by means only of the eye, the latter only by the ear; but not by their positive actuality, but by their want of it. Let no one, then, seek to know from me what I know that I do not know; unless he perhaps wishes to learn to be ignorant of that of which all we know is, that it cannot be known.... For when the eyesight surveys objects that strike the sense, it nowhere sees darkness but where it begins not to see. And so no other sense but the ear can perceive silence, and yet it is only perceived by not hearing. Thus, too, our mind perceives intelligible forms by understanding them; but when they are deficient, it knows them by not knowing them; for who can understand defects?

... And I know likewise, that the will could not become evil, were it unwilling to become so; and therefore its failings are justly punished, being not necessary, but voluntary. For its defections are not to evil things, but are themselves evil; that is to say, are not towards things that are naturally and in themselves evil, but the defection of the will is evil, because it is contrary to the order of nature, and an abandonment of that which has supreme being for that which has less. For avarice is not a fault inherent in gold, but in the man who inordinately loves gold, to the detriment of justice, which ought to be held in incomparably higher regard than gold. Neither is luxury the fault of lovely and charming objects, but of the heart that inordinately loves sensual pleasures, to the neglect of temperance, which attaches us to objects more lovely in their spirituality, and more delectable by their incorruptibility. Nor yet is boasting the fault of human praise, but of the soul that is inordinately fond of the applause of men, and that makes light of the voice of conscience. Pride, too, is not the fault of him who delegates power, nor of power itself, but of the soul that is inordinately enamored of its own power, and despises the more just dominion of a higher authority. Consequently he who inordinately loves the good which any nature possesses, even though he obtain it, himself becomes evil in the good, and wretched because deprived of a greater good.[e]

**5.** Augustine's rational justification of the Christian belief in an individual's moral responsibility and the presence of moral evil in the world constitutes a philosophical background for his description of the City of God and the City of Man. Those who choose good he calls citizens of the City of God, and those who choose evil are called citizens of the City of Man. To live in the heavenly city, one must follow the spirit as well as the letter of the teachings of Jesus; those who pursue the pleasures of the body or accept idolatrous or heretical beliefs must be said to "live after the flesh" in the earthly city.

Though there are very many and great nations all over the earth, whose rites and customs, speech, arms, and dress, are distinguished by marked differences, yet there are no more than two kinds of human society, which we may justly call two cities, according to the language of our Scriptures. The one consists of those who wish to live after the flesh, the other of those who wish to live after the spirit; and when they severally achieve what they wish, they live in peace, each after their kind....

If we are to ascertain what it is to live after the flesh (which is certainly evil, though the nature of flesh is not itself evil), we must carefully examine that passage of the epistle which the Apostle Paul wrote to the Galatians, in which he says, "Now the works of the flesh are manifest, which are these: adultery, fornication, uncleanness, lasciviousness, idolatry, witchcraft, hatred, variance, emulations, wrath, strife, seditions, heresies, envyings, murders, drunkenness, revelings, and such like: of the which I tell you before, as I have also told you in time past, that they which do such things shall not inherit the kingdom of God." This whole passage of the apostolic epistle being considered, so far as it bears on the matter in hand, will be sufficient to answer the question, what it is to live after the flesh. For among the works of the flesh which he said were manifest, and which he cited for condemnation, we find not only those which concern the pleasure of the flesh, as fornications, uncleanness, lasciviousness, drunkenness, revelings, but also those which, though they be remote from fleshly pleasure, reveal the vices of the soul. For who does not see that idolatries, witchcrafts, hatreds, variance, emulations, wrath, strife, heresies, envyings, are vices rather of the soul than of the flesh? For it is quite possible for a man to abstain from fleshly pleasures for the sake of idolatry or some heretical error; and yet, even when he does so, he is proved by this apostolic authority to be living after the flesh; and in abstaining from fleshly pleasure, he is proved to be practicing damnable works of the flesh. Who that has enmity has it not in his soul? or would say to his enemy, or to the man he thinks his enemy, You have a bad flesh towards me, and not rather, You have a bad spirit towards me? In fine, if anyone heard of what I may call "carnalities," he would not fail to attribute them to the carnal part of man; so no one doubts that animosities[4] belong to the soul of man.[f]

**6.** It must be realized, Augustine points out, that supreme good and evil refer to eternity, not to the brief moment of this life. Those who seek happiness in this world and through their own efforts cannot be either truly happy or truly moral. Not only those who pursue the carnal pleasures, but also those who rely on reason as the foundation of mortality, are in error. Unaided by divine guidance, reason cannot provide a cure for the evils of life.

*What the Christians believe regarding the supreme good and evil, in opposition to the philosophers, who have maintained that the supreme good is in themselves:* If, then, we be asked what the city of God has to say upon these points, and, in the first place, what its opinion regarding the supreme good and evil is, it will reply that life eternal is the supreme good, death eternal the supreme evil, and that to obtain the one and escape the other we must live rightly. And thus it is written, "The just lives by faith," for we do not as yet see our good, and must therefore live by faith; neither have we in ourselves power to live rightly, but can do so only if He who has given us faith to believe in His help does help us when we believe and pray. As for those who have supposed that the sovereign good and evil are to be found in this life . . . all these have, with a marvelous shallowness, sought to find their blessedness in this life and in themselves. Contempt has been poured upon such ideas by the Truth, saying by the prophet, "The Lord knoweth the thoughts of men" (or, as the Apostle Paul cites the passage, "The Lord knoweth the thoughts of the *wise*") "that they are vain."

For what flood of eloquence can suffice to detail the miseries of this life? . . . For when, where, how, in this life can these primary objects of nature be possessed so that they may not be assailed by unforeseen accidents? Is the body of the wise man exempt from any pain which may dispel pleasure, from any disquietude which may banish repose? The amputation or decay of the members of the body puts an end to its integrity, deformity blights its beauty, weakness its health, lassitude its vigor, sleepiness or sluggishness its activity,—and which of these is it that may not assail the flesh of the wise man? Comely and fitting attitudes and movements of the body are numbered among the prime natural

[4] *Anima* is the Latin word for *soul.*

blessings; but what if some sickness makes the members tremble? what if a man suffers from curvature of the spine to such an extent that his hands reach the ground, and he goes upon all fours like a quadruped? Does not this destroy all beauty and grace in the body, whether at rest or in motion? What shall I say of the fundamental blessings of the soul, sense and intellect, of which the one is given for the perception, and the other for the comprehension of truth? But what kind of sense is it that remains when a man becomes deaf and blind? Where are reason and intellect when disease makes a man delirious? We can scarcely, or not at all, refrain from tears, when we think of or see the actions and words of such frantic persons, and consider how different from and even opposed to their own sober judgment and ordinary conduct their present demeanor is. And what shall I say of those who suffer from demoniacal possession? Where is their own intelligence hidden and buried while the malignant spirit is using their body and soul according to his own will? And who is quite sure that no such thing can happen to the wise man in this life? Then, as to the perception of truth, what can we hope for even in this way while in the body, as we read in the true book of Wisdom, "The corruptible body weigheth down the soul, and the earthly tabernacle presseth down the mind that museth upon many things?" And eagerness or desire of action . . . is also reckoned among the primary advantages of nature; and yet is it not this which produces those pitiable movements of the insane, and those actions which we shudder to see, when sense is deceived and reason deranged?[g]

**7.** When we appreciate the feebleness of unaided human reason, we see that faith, hope, and love are the fundamental virtues of the true Christian, who seeks peace and happiness through God. The virtues of prudence, temperance, justice, and fortitude that the rationalistic Greek philosophers value so highly are nothing more than prideful vices unless they are used in the service of the true religion.

What shall I say of that virtue which is called *prudence?* Is not all its vigilance spent in the discernment of good from evil things, so that no mistake may be admitted about what we should desire and what avoid? And thus it is itself a proof that we are in the midst of evils, or that evils are in us; for it teaches us that it is an evil to consent to sin, and a good to refuse this consent. And yet this evil, to which prudence teaches and *temperance* enables us not to consent, is removed from this life neither by prudence nor by temperance. And *justice,* whose office it is to render to every man his due, whereby there is in man himself a certain just order of nature, so that the soul is subjected to God, and the flesh to the soul, and consequently both soul and flesh to God,—does not this virtue demonstrate that it is as yet rather laboring towards its end than resting in its finished work? For the soul is so much the less subjected to God as it is less occupied with the thought of God; and the flesh is so much the less subjected to the spirit as it lusts more vehemently against the spirit. So long, therefore, as we are beset by this weakness, this plague, this disease, how shall we dare to say that we are safe? and if not safe, then how can we be already enjoying our final beatitude? Then that virtue which goes by the name of *fortitude* is the plainest proof of the ills of life, for it is these ills which it is compelled to bear patiently. And this holds good, no matter though the ripest wisdom coexists with it. . . .

Therefore the Apostle Paul, speaking not of men without prudence, temperance, fortitude, and justice, but of those whose lives were regulated by true piety, and whose virtues were therefore true, says, "For we are saved by hope: now hope which is seen is not hope; for what a man seeth, why doth he yet hope for? But if we hope for that we see not, then do we with patience wait for it." As, therefore, we are saved, so we are made happy by hope. And as we do not as yet possess a present, but look for a future salvation, so is it with our happiness, and this "with patience"; for we are encompassed with evils, which we ought patiently to endure, until we come to the ineffable enjoyment of unmixed good; for there shall be no longer anything to endure. Salvation, such as it shall be in the world to come, shall itself be our final happiness. And this happiness these philosophers refuse to believe in, because they do not see it, and attempt to fabricate for themselves a happiness in this life, based upon a virtue which is as deceitful as it is proud. . . .

*That where there is no true religion there are no true virtues:* For though the soul may seem to rule the body admirably, and the reason the vices, if the soul and reason do not themselves obey God, as God has commanded them to serve Him, they have no proper authority over the body and the vices. For what kind of mistress of the body and the vices can that mind be which is ignorant of the true God, and which, instead of being subject to His authority, is prostituted to the corrupting influences of the most vicious demons? It is for this reason that the virtues which it seems to itself to possess, and by which it restrains the body and the vices that it may obtain and keep what it desires, are rather vices than virtues so long as there is no reference to God in the matter. For although some suppose that virtues which have a reference only to themselves, and are desired only on their own account, are yet true and genuine virtues, the fact is that even then they are inflated with pride, and are therefore to be reckoned vices rather than virtues. For as that which gives life to the flesh is not derived from flesh, but is above it, so that which gives blessed life to man is not derived from man, but is something above him; and what I say of man is true of every celestial power and virtue whatsoever.[h]

**8.** Everyone earnestly desires peace, but the misdirected methods of the City of Man fail to achieve it. Those who dwell in God's city know that peace is achieved not by war but by love. Hence everyone should obey and teach the precepts of Jesus, "Love God" and "Love thy neighbor as thyself."

The whole use, then, of things temporal has a reference to this result of earthly peace in the earthly community, while in the city of God it is connected with eternal peace. And therefore, if we were irrational animals, we should desire nothing beyond the proper arrangement of the parts of the body and the satisfaction of the appetites—nothing, therefore, but bodily comfort and abundance of pleasures, that the peace of the body might contribute to the peace of the soul. For if bodily peace be awanting, a bar is put to the peace even of the irrational soul, since it cannot obtain the gratification of its appetites. And these two together help out the mutual peace of soul and body, the peace of harmonious life and health. For as animals, by shunning pain, show that they love bodily peace, and, by pursuing pleasure to gratify their appetites, show that they love peace of soul, so their shrinking from death is a sufficient indication of their intense love of that peace which binds soul and body in close alliance. But, as man has a rational soul, he subordinates all this which he has in common with the beasts to the peace of his rational soul, that his intellect may have free play and may regulate his actions, and that he may thus enjoy the well-ordered harmony of knowledge and action which constitutes, as we have said, the peace of the rational soul. And for this purpose he must desire to be neither molested by pain, nor disturbed by desire, nor extinguished by death, that he may arrive at some useful knowledge by which he may regulate his life and manners. But, owing to the liability of the human mind to fall into mistakes, this very pursuit of knowledge may be a snare to him unless he has a divine Master, whom he may obey without misgiving, and who may at the same time give him such help as to preserve his own freedom. And because so long as he is in this mortal body, he is a stranger to God, he walks by faith, not by sight; and he therefore refers all peace, bodily or spiritual or both, to that peace which mortal man has with the immortal God, so that he exhibits the well-ordered obedience of faith to eternal law. But as this divine Master inculcates two precepts,—the love of God and the love of our neighbor,—and as in these precepts a man finds three things he has to love,—God, himself, and his neighbor,—and that he who loves God loves himself thereby, it follows that he must endeavor to get his neighbor to love God, since he is ordered to love his neighbor as himself. He ought to make this endeavor in behalf of his wife, his children, his household, all within his reach, even as he would wish his neighbor to do the same for him if he needed it; and consequently he will be at peace, or in well-ordered concord, with all men as far as in him lies. And this is the order of this concord, that a man, in the first place, injure no one, and, in the second, do good to everyone he can reach.[i]

**9.** It is not possible to judge from our earthly history whether we are blessed or not, for "in the mingled web of human affairs, God's judgment is present, though it cannot be discerned." We must accept without complaint the knowledge that the good may suffer earthly misfortunes and that the wicked may enjoy life.

In this present time we learn to bear with equanimity the ills to which even good men are subject, and to hold cheap the blessings which even the wicked enjoy. And consequently, even in those conditions of life in which the justice of God is not apparent, His teaching is salutary. For we do not know by what judgment of God this good man is poor and that bad man rich; why he who, in our opinion, ought to suffer acutely for his abandoned life enjoys himself, while sorrow pursues him whose praiseworthy life leads us to suppose he should be happy; why the innocent man is dismissed from the bar not only unavenged, but even condemned, being either wronged by the iniquity of the judge, or overwhelmed by false evidence, while his guilty adversary, on the other hand, is not only discharged with impunity, but even has his claims admitted; why the ungodly enjoys good health, while the godly pines in sickness; why ruffians are of the soundest constitution, while they who could not hurt anyone even with a word are from infancy afflicted with complicated disorders; why he who is useful to society is cut off by premature death, while those who, as it might seem, ought never to have been so much as born have lives of unusual length; why he who is full of crimes is crowned with honors, while the blameless man is buried in the darkness of neglect. But who can collect or enumerate all the contrasts of this kind? But if this anomalous state of things were uniform in this life, in which, as the sacred Psalmist says, "Man is like to vanity, his days as a shadow that passeth away,"—so uniform that none but wicked men won the transitory prosperity of earth, while only the good suffered its ills,—this could be referred to the just and even benign judgment of God. We might suppose that they who were not destined to obtain those everlasting benefits which constitute human blessedness were either deluded by transitory blessings as the just reward of their wickedness, or were, in God's mercy, consoled by them, and that they who were not destined to suffer eternal torments were afflicted with temporal chastisement for their sins, or were stimulated to greater attainment in virtue. But now, as it is, since we not only see good men involved in the ills of life, and bad men enjoying the good of it, which seems unjust, but also that evil often overtakes evil men, and good surprises the good, then rather on this account are God's judgments unsearchable, and His ways past finding out. Although, therefore, we do not know by what judgment these things are done or permitted to be done by God, with whom is the highest virtue, the highest wisdom, the highest justice, no infirmity, no rashness, no unrighteousness, yet it is salutary for us to learn to hold cheap such things, be they good or evil, as attach indifferently to good men and bad, and to covet those good things which belong only to good men, and flee those evils which belong only to evil men. But when we shall have come to that judgment, the date of which is called peculiarly the day of judgment, and sometimes the day of the Lord, we shall then recognize the justice of all God's judgments, not only of such as shall then be pronounced, but of all which take effect from the beginning, or may take effect before that time. And in that day we shall also recognize with what justice so many, or almost all, the just judgments of God in the present life defy the scrutiny of human sense or insight, though in this matter it is not concealed from pious minds that what is concealed is just.[j]

**10.** The Last Judgment will be a day of reckoning when virtue and vice will be clearly seen and just reward and punishment meted out. The City of Man will be dissolved and its citizens condemned to eternal death. This is not the ordinary death in which the soul leaves the body but a "second death," in which God abandons the soul. Although eternal punishment is a harsh judgment, the enormity of our sin merits it. But God in His goodness is not only just but also merciful, for He sent to us His only Son through whom the citizens of the City of God are saved.

*Of the greatness of the first transgression, on account of which eternal punishment is due to all who are not within the pale of the Savior's grace:* But eternal punishment seems hard and unjust to human perceptions, because in the weakness of our mortal condition there is wanting that highest and purest wisdom by which it can be perceived how great a wickedness was committed in that first transgression. The more enjoyment man found in God, the greater was his wickedness in abandoning Him; and he who destroyed in himself a good which might have been eternal, became worthy of eternal evil. Hence the whole mass of the human race is condemned; for he who at first gave entrance to sin has been punished with all his posterity who were in him as in a root, so that no one is exempt from this just and due punishment, unless delivered by mercy and undeserved grace; and the human race is so apportioned that in some is displayed the efficacy of merciful grace, in the rest the efficacy of just retribution. . . .

*That everything which the grace of God does in the way of rescuing us from the inveterate evils in which we are sunk, pertains to the future world, in which all things are made new:* Nevertheless, in the "heavy yoke that is laid upon the sons of Adam, from the day that they go out of their mother's womb to the day that they return to the mother of all things," there is found an admirable though painful monitor teaching us to be sober minded, and convincing us that this life has become penal in consequence of that outrageous wickedness which was perpetrated in Paradise, and that all to which the New Testament invites belongs to that future inheritance which awaits us in the world to come, and is offered for our acceptance, as the earnest that we may, in its own due time, obtain that of which it is the pledge. Now, therefore, let us walk in hope, and let us by the spirit mortify the deeds of the flesh, and so make progress from day to day. For "the Lord knoweth them that are His"; and "as many as are led by the Spirit of God, they are sons of God," but by grace, not by nature. For there is but one Son of God by nature, who in His compassion became Son of man for our sakes, that we, by nature sons of men, might by grace become through Him sons of God. For He, abiding unchangeable, took upon Him our nature, that thereby He might take us to Himself; and, holding fast His own divinity, He became partaker of our infirmity, that we, being changed into some better thing, might, by participating in His righteousness and immortality, lose our own properties of sin and mortality, and preserve whatever good quality He had implanted in our nature, perfected now by sharing in the goodness of His nature. For as by the sin of one man we have fallen into a misery so deplorable, so by the righteousness of one Man, who also is God, shall we come to a blessedness inconceivably exalted. Nor ought anyone to trust that he has passed from the one man to the other until he shall have reached that place where there is no temptation, and have entered into the peace which he seeks in the many and various conflicts of this war, in which "the flesh lusteth against the spirit, and the spirit against the flesh."[k]

**11.** The final vision of God, permitted to those who have lived in righteousness and been blessed with God's grace, is "the reward of our faith."

*Of the beatific vision:* And now let us consider, with such ability as God may vouchsafe, how the saints shall be employed when they are clothed in immortal and spiritual bodies, and when the flesh shall live no longer in a fleshly but a spiritual fashion. And indeed, to tell the truth, I am at a loss to understand the nature of that employment, or shall I rather say, repose and ease, for it has never come within the range of my bodily senses. And if I should speak of my mind or understanding, what is our understanding in comparison of its excellence? For then shall be that "peace of God which," as the apostle says, "passeth all understanding,"—that is to say, all human, and perhaps all angelic understanding, but certainly not the divine. That it passeth ours there is no doubt; but if it passeth that of the angels,—and he who says "*all* understanding" seems to make no exception in their favor,—then we must understand him to mean that neither we nor the angels can understand, as God understands, the peace which God Himself enjoys. Doubtless this passeth all understanding but His own. But as we shall one day be made to participate, according to our slender capacity, in His peace, both in ourselves, and with our neighbor, and with God our chief good, in this respect the angels understand the peace of God in their own measure, and men too, though now far behind them, whatever spiritual advance they have made. For we must remember how great a man he [Saint Paul] was who said, "We know in part and we prophesy in part, until that which is perfect is come"; and "Now we see through a glass, darkly; but then face to face."

*Of the eternal felicity of the city of God, and of the perpetual Sabbath:* How great shall be that felicity, which shall be tainted with no evil, which shall lack no good, and which shall afford leisure for the praises of God, who shall be all in all! For I know not what other employment there can be where no lassitude shall slacken activity, nor any want stimulate to labor. I am admonished also by the sacred song, in which I read or hear the words, "Blessed are they that dwell in Thy house, O Lord; they will be still praising Thee." All the members and organs of the incorruptible body, which now we see to be suited to various necessary uses, shall contribute to the praises of God; for in that life necessity shall have no place, but full, certain, secure, everlasting felicity. For all those parts of the bodily harmony, which are distributed through the whole body, within and without, and of which I have just been saying that they at present elude our observation, shall then be discerned; and, along with the other great and marvelous discoveries which shall then kindle rational minds in praise of the great Artificer, there shall be the enjoyment of a beauty which appeals to the reason. What power of movement such bodies shall possess, I have not the audacity rashly to define, as I have not the ability to conceive. Nevertheless I will say that in any case, both in motion and at rest, they shall be, as in their appearance, seemly; for into that state nothing which is unseemly shall be admitted. One thing is certain, the body shall forthwith be wherever the spirit wills, and the spirit shall will nothing which is unbecoming either to the spirit or to the body. True honor shall be there, for it shall be denied to none who is worthy, nor yielded to any unworthy; neither shall any unworthy person so much as sue for it, for none but the worthy shall be there. True peace shall be there, where no one shall suffer opposition either from himself or any other. God Himself, who is the Author of virtue, shall there be its reward; for, as there is nothing greater or better, He has promised Himself. What else was meant by His word through the prophet, "I will be your God, and ye shall be my people," than, I shall be their satisfaction, I shall be all that men honorably desire,—life, and health, and nourishment, and plenty, and glory, and honor, and peace, and all good things? This, too, is the right interpretation of the saying of the apostle, "That God may be all in all." He shall be the end of our desires who shall be seen without end, loved without cloy, praised without weariness. This outgoing of affection, this employment, shall certainly be, like eternal life itself, common to all.

But who can conceive, not to say describe, what degrees of honor and glory shall be awarded to the various degrees of merit? Yet it cannot be doubted that there shall be degrees. And in that blessed city there shall be this great blessing, that no inferior shall envy any superior, as now the archangels are not envied by the angels, because no one will wish to be what he has not received, though bound in strictest concord with him who has received; as in the body the finger does not seek to be the eye, though both members are harmoniously included in the complete structure of the body. And thus, along with his gift, greater or less, each shall receive this further gift of contentment to desire no more than he has.[l]

**12.** His vast description of the cities of God and of Man completed, Augustine expresses the hope that he has communicated the meaning of the love of God through giving a true account of the true religion.

Since, then, the supreme good of the city of God is perfect and eternal peace, not such as mortals pass into and out of by birth and death, but the peace of freedom from all evil, in which the immortals ever abide, who can deny that that future life is most blessed, or that, in comparison with it, this life which now we live is most wretched, be it filled with all blessings of body and soul and external things? And yet, if any man uses this life with a reference to that other which he ardently loves and confidently hopes for, he may well be called even now blessed, though not in reality so much as in hope. But the actual possession of the happiness of this life, without the hope of what is beyond, is but a false happiness and profound misery. For the true blessings of the soul are not now enjoyed; for that is no true wisdom which does not direct all its prudent observations, manly actions, virtuous self-restraint, and just arrangements, to that end in which God shall be all and all in a secure eternity and perfect peace....

There we shall rest and see, see and love, love and praise. This is what shall be in the end without end. For what other end do we propose to ourselves than to attain to the kingdom of which there is no end?

I think I have now, by God's help, discharged my obligation in writing this large work. Let those who think I have said too little, or those who think I have said too much, forgive me; and let those who think I have said just enough join me in giving thanks to God. Amen.[m]

## QUESTIONS

1. Describe the Christian conception of God's nature and the nature of man. In Augustine's ethical theory, what can be done by God and what by individuals to realize the Christian ideal?
2. What does Augustine mean when he speaks of "the love of God"? What place does it occupy in his ethical theory?
3. What is the "problem of evil," and to what extent do Augustine's definitions of good and evil resolve the paradox?
4. Discuss the principal differences between citizens of the "City of God" and citizens of the "City of Man." What place, if any, may be assigned to time and space in distinguishing between the two cities?
5. How can knowledge help a person pass from the City of Man to the City of God? Is there any clear sign, in an individual's personal history, of future reward or punishment?
6. Why does Augustine reject the philosophic enterprise as an end in itself? What does he regard as the correct use of reason?
7. Compare the Christian virtues with the Greek virtues, and discuss Augustine's attitude toward the latter.
8. Explain the concept of "Judgment Day." How do God's grace and Jesus's role as humanity's Savior affect the outcome of the Last Judgment?
9. Discuss Augustine's conception of the "vision of God" as the ultimate reward of faith. Explain the significance, in this connection, of Saint Paul's phrase "Now we see through a glass darkly; but then face to face."
10. From a review of the principal elements of Augustine's ethical theory, reconstruct his theory of the relative roles of faith and knowledge in the achievement of the good life.

## KEY TO SELECTIONS

Saint Augustine, *Enchiridion,* tr. J. F. Shaw, from *The Works of Aurelius Augustine,* vol. IX, Rev. Marcus Dods, ed., Edinburgh, T. & T. Clark, 1892.
[a]Ch. CXXI.
[b]Chs. XI-XII.
[c]Chs. XCVI, C–CI.

Saint Augustine, *City of God,* vols I and II, tr. Rev. Marcus Dods, Edinburgh, T. & T. Clark, 1881.
[d]Bk. V: pp. 9–10.
[e]Bk. XII: pp. 7–8.
[f]Bk. XIV: pp. 1–2.
[g]Bk. XIX: p. 4.
[h]Bk. XIX: pp. 4, 25.
[i]Bk. XIX: p. 14.
[j]Bk. XX: p. 2.
[k]Bk. XXI: pp. 12, 15.
[l]Bk. XXII: pp. 29–30.
[m]Bk. XIX: p. 20, XXII: p. 30.

## GUIDE TO ADDITIONAL READING


**PRIMARY SOURCES**

Saint Augustine, *Confessions*, Black and Gold Library (Liveright).

_____, _____, Everyman's Library (Dutton) .

_____, _____, (Books I–VIII), Great Books Foundation (Regnery).

_____, _____, (Books IX–XIII), Great Books Foundation (Regnery).

_____, _____, Modern Library (Random House).

_____, *The City of God*, Everyman's Library (Dutton), 2 vols.

_____, _____, Hafner Library of Classics (Hafner), 2 vols.

_____, _____, Modern Library (Random House).

**DISCUSSION AND COMMENTARY**

Bourke, V. J., *Augustine's Quest of Wisdom*, Milwaukee, Bruce Publishing, 1945.

Cochrane, C. N., *Christianity and Classical Culture*, Oxford, Clarendon Press, 1940.

O'Donovan, O., *The Problem of Self-Love in St. Augustine*, New Haven, Yale University Press, 1980.

Tolley, W. P., *The Idea of God in the Philosophy of St. Augustine*, New York, R. R. Smith, 1930.

Vessey, M., Pollmann, K., and Fitzgerald, A. (eds.), *History, Apocalypse, and the Secular Imagination: New Essays on Augustine's City of God*, Bowling Green, Bowling Green State University Press, 1999.

Warfield, B., *Studies in Tertullian and Augustine*, New York, Oxford University Press, 1931.

CHAPTER SEVEN

# Morality and Natural Law

SAINT THOMAS AQUINAS

IT HAS OFTEN BEEN REMARKED that if Saint Augustine is the Plato of the Middle Ages, Saint Thomas Aquinas (1225–1274) is its Aristotle. The seventh son of the Count of Aquino, Thomas was born at the castle of Rocca Secca in the kingdom of Naples. His parents resolved that he was to be an ecclesiastical dignitary and, to this end, entrusted his education to his uncle, the wise and learned Abbot of Monte Cassino. Thomas showed great promise as a student and was sent to the University of Naples at the age of fourteen. While there he came to admire the religious sincerity and vitality of the Dominicans he chanced to meet on the streets; indeed, he was so impressed by the members of this newly formed evangelical order that embraced the ideals of chastity and poverty that he, without consulting his parents, became a Dominican in 1244. Distressed—the more so after his mother was forbidden by zealous monks to talk to him—his family took drastic action: Some of his brothers forcibly returned him to the castle of Rocca Secca. Aquinas was kept prisoner there for a year. Noting no diminution in his conviction, however, the family finally relented and allowed him to return to Naples.

In 1248, Aquinas went to Cologne to study with Albert of Bollstadt (1205–1280), an impressive scholar with a reputation for originality. Albert ("The Great") maintained that the theological difficulties besetting Christianity could be solved through a thorough understanding of the complete works of Aristotle. The master, recognizing that his pupil was a genius who would soon outdo him, openly shared his vision and knowledge. They became an academic team for several years and were sent to Paris to advance the viewpoint of the Dominican and other mendicant orders, a viewpoint to which they were contributing. In simple terms, the dominating clash of viewpoints at the time came to this: In the tradition of Augustine, the Franciscans held that there is no sharp distinction between revealed theology and philosophy, whereas the Dominicans held that there is.

Aquinas's reputation grew steadily. He became a master of theology at the University of Paris in 1256 and, throughout his remaining eighteen years, responded to invitations to lecture and instruct at many universities and to advise numerous kings, prelates, and scholars. In 1323 he was canonized.

Despite a life responsive to demands placed on him, Saint Thomas Aquinas wrote prodigiously. His best-known systematic treatises are the *Summa Contra Gentiles* (*A Summary Against the Gentiles*) and the *Summa Theologica* (*A Summary of Theology*). The former was composed to provide missionaries with the means to convert "pagans" as well as Moslems and Jews to Christianity; the latter was written in textbook form to give novices a systematic understanding of Christian theology. Both works go well beyond the original purposes and exhibit Aquinas's ability to use reason in dealing with such profound subjects as God's existence, the relation of soul to body, and the supreme good for humanity. His writings show that philosophy can provide a framework for theology.

It is a commonplace to observe that Saint Thomas Aquinas offers us a Christianized version of Aristotle's moral theory. This assessment is instructive in suggesting that Aristotle's ethics is a *sine qua non* for that of Aquinas. But to conclude from this that Aquinas's moral theory is merely a Christian reinterpretation of Aristotle is misleading. Even the more magnanimous historical depiction of Aquinas's moral philosophy as a synthesis of the humanistic tradition of Plato and Aristotle, the Christian tradition of Saint Paul, and the Greco-Roman tradition of natural law underplays its innovations.

Christianity is a revelatory religion, which accounts for one of its perennial and divisive problems. Throughout history, Christian thinkers have recognized that in accepting revelation—accepting that there are occasions when humans have extranatural access to genuine knowledge—they are reducing the authority of natural, reason-guided inquiry. A radical solution to this problem of two sources of knowledge was declared early on. The remark of Tertullian (*c.* 160–230), *"Credo quia absurdum est"* (I believe it because it is absurd), which refers to the Christian doctrine of God's sacrifice on the cross, is still echoed by many Christians. He warned that it is prideful to regard the world as ordered in accordance with our finite reason. Tertullian insisted that it is only through faith in Christian revelation (and immediate intuitions in religious experience) that we are afforded glimpses of ultimate truth; again, he stressed that such revelations are not subject to the logical norms governing mundane affairs; and finally, he maintained that the paradoxes and contradictions that finite reason finds in Christian articles of faith are positive signs of their truth.[1]

If Tertullian is at the extreme left of the faith-reason controversy, Aquinas is at center-right. He draws a sharp distinction between the domains of theology and philosophy. As Christians recognize, theology begins with the sacred principles that revelation provides, and, as Aristotelians recognize, philosophy begins with the subject matter that observation provides. But theology, no less than philosophy, uses reason

---

[1]This extreme but historically influential reading of Tertullian is not accepted by all scholars.

to develop its "given" into a clear and comprehensible body of knowledge.[2] Furthermore, according to Aquinas, the domains of theology and philosophy overlap. Thus, for example, not only theology but also philosophy includes the judgment that God exists.[3] That God is triune, however, is a distinctively theological thesis; that is, it is a revealed truth, the proof of which is beyond the resources of philosophy. The assertion that the sentient faculty never exists without the nutritive, on the other hand, is distinctively philosophical; that is, it is a philosophically disclosed truth that, as it happens, is not among the truths God has made available to human beings either by direct revelation or by the rational development of such revelations.

Aquinas preserves the pattern and most of the detail of Aristotle's ethics. He views Aristotle as having provided the proper philosophical foundation for the study of morality. But he maintains that Aristotle's theory is grievously incomplete; furthermore, he holds that Aristotle's theory cannot be completed without drawing on Christian insights. Thus, though it is thoroughly Aristotelian, Aquinas's theory adds the concept of the beatific vision of God as humanity's final goal, a special doctrine of free will, and a theory of natural law as the reflection of divine order.

In its briefest version, the Aristotelian theory, reasserted by Aquinas, is as follows: Human actions are directed toward ends, and such ends, when they are achieved, become means for attaining still other ends. On the basis of this teleological thesis, both argue not only that an individual's activities are related as a succession of ends becoming means to ends but also that such a succession can occur only if there is a final end. This latter proposition is what people are testifying to when they declare themselves to be seekers of happiness (well-being). But what of their different opinions about the nature of happiness? Aristotle (following Plato and followed by Aquinas) comes to grips with this problem by pointing out that because it is agreed that happiness, the final end, satisfies certain criteria, an analysis of proposed ends may settle the issue. These criteria for the final end are (1) being desirable to us for its own sake, (2) being sufficient of itself to satisfy us, and (3) being attainable by the wise among us. Aristotle's profound and extended analysis in this connection provides the answer that happiness, the final end, can only be the fulfillment of the highest potential of human nature under the direction of reason.

Aquinas maintains, however, that a secular reading restricts this account of happiness. We should understand it as telling us that there is a twofold perfection of the rational or intellectual nature—"that, along with natural happiness, there is a supernatural happiness of coming to 'see God as he is.'" To understand Aquinas's justification of this claim, consider the following: Non-Christians (including Aristotle, of course) have a tacit criterion—being attainable by humans through their natural power. Expressed in this way, our final end is related to our being the highest and

[2]"Sacred doctrine also makes use of human reason, not, indeed, to prove faith (for thereby the merit of faith would come to an end), but to make clear other things that are set forth in the doctrine. Since therefore grace does not destroy nature, but perfects it, natural reason should minister to faith." *Summa Theologica*, A. C. Pegis, ed., in *Basic Writings of Saint Thomas Aquinas* (New York: Random House, 1945), Pt. I, Quest. 1, Art. 8.

[3]Although it is loosely correct to say that theology and philosophy overlap, Aquinas points out that the occurrence of common judgments means only that there is theological and philosophical agreement about these propositions. It does not mean that, insofar as theology and philosophy overlap, they are identical systems.

only animals who can attain philosophical truth. But according to Aquinas, humans have two sources of truth rather than one: those that human faculties provide and those that God reveals. Furthermore, the proper activity of human reason is the development of both.

Aquinas contends, however, that our direct realization of natural and supernatural happiness in this earthly life is systematically limited, because few among us sustain the intellectual activity of philosophers or the spiritual intensity of saints. Moreover, he notes that good character is a necessary condition not only for the intellectual virtues but also for our social lives. Thus Aquinas's account of good character, of the moral virtues, is of major importance in his ethical theory.

Aquinas judges that Aristotle's account of the moral virtues—those virtues concerning our habitual choices of conduct—is correct in outline but incomplete in details. At its core, Aristotle's theory tells us that goodness involves choice and that choice includes both an appetitive and a deliberative element: The former focuses on what we seek, the latter on how we attain it. A good character is constituted by habits of choice that are in accordance with appropriate principles, such principles being those that a wise person would find to be self-evident after sifting through and analyzing all relevant facts and opinions. Aquinas supplements and refines this in two ways. In the first, he subsumes the Aristotelian analysis of choice under his own concept of free will. This includes Aristotle's basic corollary that people bear responsibility for their actions unless they are physically compelled to do them or are inadvertently ignorant about what they involve. In the second, he ascribes the source and authority of the principles determining proper choice to the natural laws God makes available to humans.

Identifying will as the agency of choice, Aquinas's analysis of the moral worth of voluntary action is more sharply delineated than Aristotle's. Three components of voluntary acts are morally relevant and, accordingly, bring about different measures of moral worth for nominally identical acts. The first and primary component of an act is the kind of overt act that it is, the second is the kind of motive that prompts it, and the third is its set of consequence-bearing circumstances. To understand fully what these components of a voluntary action are and how they contribute to its "measure of goodness," consider an act in terms of such factors.

Suppose in one case that A is submitting her first paper for publication and acknowledges the helpful comments provided by a relatively unknown colleague B. In this instance, one might describe the kind of overt act as being an author's *honest portrayal of her endeavors,* the kind of motive as being one of *gratitude,* and the set of circumstances as consisting of the author being unpublished and of her colleague being undistinguished. Suppose in a second case that A is submitting her first paper for publication and receives helpful comments from a distinguished colleague but this time does not acknowledge the aid. In this instance, the assessable features would be different. The act would be one of dishonest portrayal of the author's work, the motive would be one of self-promotion, and the circumstances would include a well-known colleague. The two acts would have different measures of goodness. The first act would be better than the second. Considering only the first component, clearly honest portrayal is superior to dishonest portrayal. Introducing the other two factors allows one to make an even more precise appraisal of both acts.

Aquinas traces the ultimate principles to which we refer in moral judgments back to our intuitive knowledge of the natural law. That is, he traces them back to our experience as rational creatures of the eternal law, which is God's plan for rationally ordered movements and actions in the created universe. Aquinas's ethical theory, however, gains strength from recognizing the gap between, on the one hand, knowing and assenting to the authority of the principles of the natural law and, on the other, interpreting and applying them to concrete situations. The practical wisdom by which a person's will is directed to its proper choice in a specific circumstance includes a resolution of the relevant problem of interpreting and applying such intuitive knowledge. The foregoing is a composite of the rational endeavors that constitute what Aquinas calls *conscience.* Although he insists on the moral authority of the dictates of conscience, he cannot, and does not, insist on their infallibility. Even as conscientious people, we are still vulnerable to mistakes in reasoning and to severely limited knowledge. Moreover, it is unfortunate that as willful individuals, we do not always abide by the dictates of our conscience.[4]

---

**1.** On the basis of his philosophy wherein God is seen to be both the creator of all things and the determiner of their purposes, Aquinas details our relationship to God.

We have shown in the preceding books that there is one First Being, possessing the full perfection of all being, Whom we call God, and Who, of the abundance of His Perfection, bestows being on all that exists, so that He is proved to be not only the first of beings, but also the beginning of all. Moreover He bestows being on others, not through natural necessity, but according to the decree of His will.... Hence it follows that He is the Lord of the things made by Him, since we are masters over those things that are subject to our will. Now it is a perfect dominion that He exercises over things made by Him, for in making them He needs neither the help of an extrinsic agent, nor matter as the foundation of His work. For He is the universal efficient cause of all being.

Now everything that is produced through the will of an agent is directed to an end by that agent, because the good and the end are the proper object of the will; and therefore whatever proceeds from a will must needs be directed to an end. But each thing attains its end by its own action, which action needs to be directed by him who endowed things with the principles whereby they act. Consequently God, Who in Himself is perfect in every way, and by His power endows all things with being, must needs be the Ruler of all, Himself ruled by none; nor is anything to be excepted from His ruling, as neither is there anything that does not owe its being to Him. Therefore, as He is perfect in being and causing, so He is perfect in ruling.

The effect of this ruling is seen to differ in different things, according to the difference of natures. For some things are so produced by God that, being intelligent, they bear a resemblance to Him and reflect His image. Hence, not only are they directed, but they direct themselves to their appointed end by their own actions. And if in thus directing themselves they be subject to the divine ruling, they are admitted by that divine ruling to the attainment of their

[4]Aquinas accepts the Christian doctrine of original sin. Until human nature is restored by the grace of God to the integrity of innocence it enjoyed before the fall, natural humans can only distantly approach natural happiness.

last end; but they are excluded therefrom if they direct themselves otherwise.[a]

**2.** Having emphasized that an individual, being made in God's image, has a free will that is directed to distinctive human ends, Aquinas begins with an analysis similar to Aristotle's. He stresses that in principle, all human ends can be attained.

We must first show that every agent, by its action, intends an end.

For in those things which clearly act for an end, we declare the end to be that towards which the movement of the agent tends; for when this is reached, the end is said to be reached, and to fail in this is to fail in the end intended. This may be seen in the physician who aims at health, and in a man who runs towards an appointed goal. Nor does it matter, as to this, whether that which tends to an end be endowed with knowledge or not; for just as the target is the end of the archer, so is it the end of the arrow's flight. Now the movement of every agent tends to something determinate, since it is not from any force that any action proceeds, but heating proceeds from heat, and cooling from cold; and therefore actions are differentiated by their active principles. Action sometimes terminates in something made, as for instance building terminates in a house, and healing in health; while sometimes it does not so terminate, as for instance, in the case of understanding and sensation. And if action terminates in something made, the movement of the agent tends by that action towards the thing made; while if it does not terminate in something made, the movement of the agent tends to the action itself. It follows therefore that every agent intends an end while acting, which end is sometimes the action itself, sometimes a thing made by the action.

Again. In all things that act for an end, that is said to be the last end beyond which the agent seeks nothing further; and thus the physician's action goes as far as health, and when this is attained, his efforts cease. But in the action of every agent, a point can be reached beyond which the agent does not desire to go; or else actions would tend to infinity, which is impossible, for since *it is not possible to pass through an infinite medium*, the agent would never begin to act, because nothing moves towards what it cannot reach. Therefore every agent acts for an end.[b]

**3.** Having analyzed the ends that are natural and fitting for an agent and having shown that these are good, Aquinas raises the following question: What constitutes our proper end and what determines our proper action? Note that in outline, his answer appears to be Aristotelian: The highest end for humanity is contemplation of the truth. However, in detail his answer diverges decisively. In brief, to say that our ultimate happiness depends on discerning the first principles of nature falls short. Humanity, being God's creation, requires contemplation of the divine.

We must go on to prove that every agent acts for a good.

For that every agent acts for an end clearly follows from the fact that every agent tends to something definite. Now that to which an agent tends definitely must needs be befitting to that agent, since the agent would not tend to it save because of some fittingness thereto. But that which is befitting to a thing is good for it. Therefore every agent acts for a good.

Further. The end is that wherein the appetite of the agent or mover comes to rest, as also the appetite of that which is moved. Now it is the very notion of good to be the term of appetite, since *good is the object of every appetite*. Therefore all action and movement is for a good.

Again. All action and movement would seem to be directed in some way to being, either for the preservation of being in the species or in the individual, or for the acquisition of being. Now this itself, namely, being, is a good; and for this reason all things desire being. Therefore all action and movement is for a good.

Furthermore. All action and movement is for some perfection. For if the action itself be the end, it is clearly a second perfection of the agent. And if the action consist in the transformation of external matter, clearly the mover intends to induce some perfection into the thing moved, towards which perfection the movable also tends, if the movement be natural. Now we say that this is to be good, namely, to be perfect. Therefore every action and movement is for a good.

Also. Every agent acts according as it is actual. Now by acting it tends to something similar to itself. Therefore it tends to an act. But an act has the nature of good, since evil is not found save in a potentiality lacking act. Therefore every action is for a good.

Moreover. The intellectual agent acts for an end, as determining for itself its end; whereas the natural agent, though it acts for an end . . . does not determine its end for itself, since it knows not the nature of end, but is moved to the end determined for it by another. Now an intellectual agent does not determine the end for itself except under the aspect of good; for the intelligible object does not move except it be considered as a good, which is the object of the will. Therefore the natural agent also is not moved, nor does it act for an end, except insofar as this end is a good, since the end is determined for the natural agent by some appetite. Therefore every agent acts for a good.

It is clear that all things are directed to one good as their last end.

For if nothing tends to something as its end, except insofar as this is good, it follows that good, as such, is an end. Consequently that which is the supreme good is supremely the end of all. Now there is but one supreme good, namely God. . . . Therefore all things are directed to the highest good, namely God, as their end.[c]

Besides, man is more self-sufficing for this operation, seeing that he stands in little need of the help of external things in order to perform it.

Further. All other human operations seem to be ordered to this as to their end. For perfect contemplation requires that the body should be disencumbered, and to this effect are directed all the products of art that are necessary for life. Moreover, it requires freedom from the disturbance caused by the passions, which is achieved by means of the moral virtues and of prudence; and freedom from external disturbance, to which the whole governance of the civil life is directed. So that, if we consider the matter rightly, we shall see that all human occupations appear to serve those who contemplate the truth.

Now, it is not possible that man's ultimate happiness consist in contemplation based on the understanding of first principles; for this is most imperfect, as being most universal, containing potentially the knowledge of things. Moreover, it is the beginning and not the end of human inquiry, and comes to us from nature, and not through the pursuit of the truth. Nor does it consist in contemplation based on the sciences that have the lowest things for their object, since happiness must consist in an operation of the intellect in relation to the most noble intelligible objects. It follows then that man's ultimate happiness consists in wisdom, based on the consideration of divine things.

It is therefore evident also by way of induction that man's ultimate happiness consists solely in the contemplation of God, which conclusion was proved above by arguments.[d]

**4.** Aquinas sees Aristotle's account of our quest for happiness as overly optimistic in two ways: In the first and less important way, our nature makes it difficult for us to achieve the moral and intellectual virtues while trying to avoid corruption; in the second way, the higher wisdom cannot be found within the confines of our natural life.

**5.** Aquinas provides people with moral guidance. We must recognize that God is the lawgiver and that humans, being in God's image, possess the rational and volitional capacities to comprehend and obey eternal law.

Augustine says: *That Law which is the Supreme Reason cannot be understood to be otherwise than unchangeable and eternal*.... [A] law is nothing else but a dictate of practical reason emanating from the ruler who governs a perfect community. Now it is evident, granted that the world is ruled by divine providence, as was stated in the First Part, that the whole community of the universe is governed by the divine reason. Therefore the very notion of the government of things in God, the ruler of the universe, has the nature of a law. And since the divine reason's conception of things is not subject to time, but is eternal, ... therefore it is that this kind of law must be called eternal.

Law, being a rule and measure, can be in a person in two ways: in one way, as in him that rules and measures; in another way, as in that which is ruled and measured, since a thing is ruled and measured insofar as it partakes of the rule or measure. Therefore, since all things subject to divine providence are ruled and measured by the eternal law, as was stated above, it is evident that all things partake in some way in the eternal law, insofar as, namely, from its being imprinted on them, they derive their respective inclinations to their proper acts and ends. Now among all others, the rational creature is subject to divine providence in a more excellent way, insofar as it itself partakes of a share of providence, by being provident both for itself and for others. Therefore it has a share of the eternal reason, whereby it has a natural inclination to its proper act and end; and this participation of the eternal law in the rational creature is called the natural law. Hence the Psalmist, after saying (Ps. 4:6): *Offer up the sacrifice of justice*, as though someone asked what the works of justice are, adds: *Many say, Who showeth us good things?* in answer to which question he says: *The light of Thy countenance, O Lord, is signed upon us.* He thus implies that the light of natural reason, whereby we discern what is good and what is evil, which is the function of the natural law, is nothing else than an imprint on us of the divine light. It is therefore evident that the natural law is nothing else than the rational creature's participation of the eternal law.[e]

**6.** The eternal law that represents God's idea of an ordered universe preexists and controls all animate and inanimate things in it. In turn, natural law represents "a rational creature's participation in the eternal law." Whereas inanimate objects are completely governed by natural inclinations and tendencies to act and react in certain ways, humans, though subject to natural tendencies to act and react in certain ways, possess a natural inclination to know and choose.

The precepts of the natural law in man stand in relation to operable matters as first principles do to matters of demonstration. But there are several first indemonstrable principles. Therefore there are also several precepts of the natural law.

*I answer that*, as was stated above, the precepts of the natural law are to the practical reason what the first principles of demonstrations are to the speculative reason, because both are self-evident principles. Now a thing is said to be self-evident in two ways: first, in itself; secondly, in relation to us. Any proposition is said to be self-evident in itself, if its predicate is contained in the notion of the subject; even though it may happen that to one who does not know the definition of the subject, such a proposition is not self-evident. For instance, this proposition, *Man is a rational being*, is, in its very nature, self-evident, since he who says *man*, says *a rational being;* and yet to one who does not know what a man is, this proposition is not self-evident....

Now a certain order is to be found in those things that are apprehended by men. For that which first falls under apprehension is *being*, the understanding of which is included in all things whatsoever a man apprehends. Therefore the first indemonstrable principle is that *the same thing cannot be affirmed and denied at the same time*, which is based on the notion of *being* and
*being:* and on this principle all others are
Now as *being* is the first thing th
apprehension absolutely, so
that falls under the apprehen
reason, which is directed to
agent acts for an end, which
good). Consequently, the first

practical reason is one founded on the nature of good, viz., that *good is that which all things seek after*. Hence this is the first precept of law, that *good is to be done and promoted, and evil is to be avoided*. All other precepts of the natural law are based upon this; so that all the things which the practical reason naturally apprehends as man's good belong to the precepts of the natural law under the form of things to be done or avoided.

Since, however, good has the nature of an end, and evil, the nature of the contrary, hence it is that all those things to which man has a natural inclination are naturally apprehended by reason as being good, and consequently as objects of pursuit, and their contraries as evil, and objects of avoidance. Therefore, the order of the precepts of the natural law is according to the order of natural inclinations. For there is in man, first of all, an inclination to good in accordance with the nature which he has in common with all substances, inasmuch, namely, as every substance seeks the preservation of its own being, according to its nature; and by reason of this inclination, whatever is a means of preserving human life, and of warding off its obstacles, belongs to the natural law. Secondly, there is in man an inclination to things that pertain to him more specially, according to that nature which he has in common with other animals; and in virtue of this inclination, those things are said to belong to the natural law *which nature has taught to all animals*, such as sexual intercourse, the education of offspring and so forth. Thirdly, there is in man an inclination to good according to the nature of his reason, which nature is proper to him. Thus man has a natural inclination to know the truth about God, and to live in society; and in this respect, whatever pertains to this inclination belongs to the natural law: *e.g.*, to shun ignorance, to avoid offending those among whom one has to live, and other such things regarding the above inclination.[f]

**7.** Aquinas's analysis of voluntary acts leads to is rejecting the common view that moral ponsibility is obviated when one is overcome by fear or overwhelmed by desire. The key features of a voluntary act are that (1) it is initiated by the agent and (2) it is done for a rationally ascertained end.

There must needs be something voluntary in human acts. In order to make this clear, we must take note that the principle of some acts is within the agent, or in that which is moved; whereas the principle of some movements or acts is outside. For when a stone is moved upwards, the principle of this movement is outside the stone; whereas, when it is moved downwards, the principle of this movement is in the stone. Now of those things that are moved by an intrinsic principle, some move themselves, some not. For since every agent or thing moved acts or is moved for an end . . . those are perfectly moved by an intrinsic principle whose intrinsic principle is one not only of movement but of movement for an end. Now in order that a thing be done for an end, some knowledge of the end is necessary. Therefore, whatever so acts or is so moved by an intrinsic principle that it has some knowledge of the end, has within itself the principle of its act, so that it not only acts, but acts for an end. On the other hand, if a thing has no knowledge of the end, even though it have an intrinsic principle of action or movement, nevertheless, the principle of acting or being moved for an end is not in that thing, but in something else, by which the principle of its action towards an end is imprinted on it. Therefore such things are not said to move themselves, but to be moved by others. But those things which have a knowledge of the end are said to move themselves because there is in them a principle by which they not only act but also act for an end. And, consequently, since both are from an intrinsic principle, *i.e.*, that they act and that they act for an end, the movements and acts of such things are said to be voluntary; for the term *voluntary* signifies that their movements and acts are from their own inclination.

Things done through fear and compulsion differ . . . in this, that the will does not consent, but is moved entirely counter to that which is done through compulsion; whereas what is done through fear becomes voluntary because the will is moved towards it, although not for its own sake, but because of something else, that is, in order to avoid an evil which is feared. For the conditions of a voluntary act are satisfied, if it be done because of something else voluntary; since the voluntary is not only what we will for its own sake as an end, but also what we will for the sake of something else as an end. It is clear therefore that in what is done from compulsion, the will does nothing inwardly, whereas in what is done through fear, the will does something.

Concupiscence does not cause involuntariness, but, on the contrary, makes something to be voluntary. For a thing is said to be voluntary from the fact that the will is moved to it. Now concupiscence inclines the will to desire the object of concupiscence. Therefore the effect of concupiscence is to make something to be voluntary rather than involuntary.

Fear has reference to evil, but concupiscence has reference to good. Now evil of itself is counter to the will, whereas good harmonizes with the will. Therefore fear has a greater tendency than concupiscence to cause involuntariness.

He who acts from fear retains the repugnance of the will to that which he does, considered in itself. But he that acts from concupiscence, *e.g.*, an incontinent man, does not retain his former will whereby he repudiated the object of his concupiscence; rather his will is changed so that he desires that which previously he repudiated. Accordingly, that which is done out of fear is involuntary, to a certain extent, but that which is done from concupiscence is in no way involuntary. For the man who yields to concupiscence acts counter to that which he purposed at first, but not counter to that which he desires now; whereas the timid man acts counter to that which in itself he desires now.

If concupiscence were to destroy knowledge altogether, as happens with those whom concupiscence has rendered mad, it would follow that concupiscence would take away voluntariness. And yet, properly speaking, it would not make the act involuntary, because in beings bereft of reason there is neither voluntary nor involuntary.[g]

**8.** In his continued discussion of the range of moral responsibility, Aquinas analyzes the circumstances under which one might or might not disclaim responsibility on grounds of ignorance.

If ignorance cause involuntariness, it is insofar as it deprives one of knowledge, which is a necessary condition of voluntariness, as was declared above. But it is not every ignorance that deprives one of this knowledge. Accordingly, we must take note that ignorance has a threefold relationship to the act of the will: in one way, *concomitantly;* in another, *consequently;* in a third way, *antecedently. Concomitantly*, when there is ignorance of what is done, but so that even if it were known, it would be done. For then ignorance does not induce one to will this to be done, but it just happens that a thing is at the same time done and not known. Thus, . . . [for] example, . . . a man did indeed will to kill his foe, but killed him in ignorance, thinking to kill a stag. And ignorance of this kind, as the philosopher states, does not cause involuntariness, since it is not the cause of anything that is repugnant to the will; but it causes *nonvoluntariness*, since that which is unknown cannot be actually willed.

Ignorance is *consequent* to the act of the will, insofar as ignorance itself is voluntary; and this happens in two ways in accordance with the two aforesaid modes of the voluntary. First, because the act of the will is brought to bear on the ignorance, as when a man wills not to know, that he may have an excuse for sin, or that he may not be withheld from sin, according to Job 21:14: *We desire not the knowledge of Thy ways.* And this is called *affected ignorance.*—Secondly, ignorance is said to be voluntary, when it regards that which one can and ought to know, for in this sense *not to act* and *not to will* are said to be voluntary, as was stated above. And ignorance of this kind happens either when one does not actually consider what one can and ought to consider (this is called *ignorance of evil choice*, and arises from some passion or habit), or when one does not take the trouble to acquire the knowledge which one ought to have; in which sense, ignorance of the general principles of law, which one ought to know, is voluntary, as being due to negligence.

Ignorance is *antecedent* to the act of the will when it is not voluntary, and yet is the cause of man's willing what he would not will otherwise. Thus a man may be ignorant of some circumstance of his act, which he was not bound to know, with the result that he does that which he would not do if he knew of that circumstance. For instance, a man, after taking proper precaution, may not know that someone is coming along the road, so that he shoots an arrow and slays a passer-by. Such ignorance causes what is involuntary absolutely.[h]

**9.** The difference between good acts of will and bad acts of will derives from the goodness or badness of the object to which reason directs the will.

Virtue is a habit through which men wish for good things. But a good will is one which is in accordance with virtue. Therefore the goodness of the will is from the fact that a man wills that which is good.

Good and evil are essential differences of the act of the will. For good and evil pertain essentially to the will; just as truth and falsehood pertain to the reason, the act of which is distinguished essentially by the difference of truth and falsehood.... The specific difference in acts is according to objects, as was stated above. Therefore good and evil in the acts of the will is derived properly from the objects.

The will is not always directed to what is truly good, but sometimes to the apparent good; and this has indeed some measure of good, but not of a good that is suitable absolutely to be desired. Hence it is that the act of the will is not always good, but sometimes evil.

Given that the act of the will is fixed on some good, no circumstance can make that act evil. Consequently, when it is said that a man wills a good when he ought not, or where he ought not, this can be understood in two ways. First, so that this circumstance is referred to the thing willed. According to this, the act of the will is not fixed on something good, since to will to do something when it ought not to be done is not to will something good. Secondly, so that the circumstance is referred to the act of willing. According to this, it is impossible to will something good when one ought not to, because one ought always to will what is good; except, perhaps, accidentally, insofar as a man, by willing some particular good, is prevented from willing at the same time another good which he ought to will at that time. And then evil results, not from his willing that particular good, but from his not willing the other. The same applies to the other circumstances.

The will's object is proposed to it by the reason. For the understood good is the proportioned object of the will, while the sensible or imaginary good is proportioned, not to the will, but to the sensitive appetite; for the will can tend to the universal good, which reason apprehends, whereas the sensitive appetite tends only to the particular good, apprehended by a sensitive power. Therefore the goodness of the will depends on the reason in the same way as it depends on its object.[i]

**10.** Aquinas next moves to undermine a grievous misconception of the relationship between reason (conscience) and will (power of choice). Some may find it plausible, for example, to deny that people are morally reprehensible whenever they willfully follow the dictate of conscience. Aquinas argues otherwise, however: If one's conscience is in fundamental error—that is, one's conscience is mistaken about a moral principle rather than being ignorant of specific facts in a situation—then the will in following errant conscience is evil. Aquinas does, however, distinguish between circumstances of the foregoing sort, which constitute only accidental evil, and circumstances in which the will is unresponsive to conscience and this is absolutely evil.

Since conscience is a kind of dictate of the reason (for it is an application of knowledge to action...) to inquire whether the will is evil when it is at variance with erring reason is the same as to inquire whether an erring conscience binds. On this matter, some distinguished three kinds of acts; for some are good of their nature, some are indifferent, some are evil of their nature. And they say that if reason or conscience tell us to do something which is of its nature good, there is no error; and the same thing is true, if it tell us not to do something which is evil of its nature, since it is the same reason that prescribes what is good and forbids what is evil. On the other hand, if a man's reason or conscience tell him that he is bound by precept to do what is in itself evil, or that what is in itself good is forbidden, then his reason or conscience errs. In like manner, if a man's reason or conscience tell him that what is in itself indifferent, for instance, to lift a straw from the ground, is forbidden or commanded, his reason or conscience errs. They say, therefore, that reason or conscience, when erring in matters of indifference, either by commanding or by forbidding them, binds; so that the will which is at variance with that erring reason is evil and sinful. But when reason or conscience errs in commanding what is evil in itself, or in forbidding what is good in itself and necessary for salvation, it does not bind; and so in such cases the will which is at variance with erring reason or conscience is not evil.

But this is unreasonable. For in matters of indifference, the will that is at variance with erring reason or conscience is evil in some way because of the object on which the goodness or malice of the will depends; not indeed because of the object according as it is in its own nature, but according as it is accidentally apprehended by reason as something evil to do or to avoid. And since the object of the will is that which is proposed by the reason, as we have stated above, from the very fact that a thing is proposed by the reason as being evil, the will by tending thereto becomes evil. And this is the case not only in indifferent matters, but also in those that are good or evil in themselves. For it is not only indifferent matters that can receive the character of goodness or malice accidentally; but likewise that which is good can receive the character of evil, or that which is evil can receive the character of goodness, because of the reason apprehending it as such. For instance, to refrain from fornication is good, and yet the will does not tend to this good except insofar as it is proposed by the reason. If, therefore, the erring reason propose it as an evil, the will tends to it as to something evil. Consequently, the will is evil because it wills evil, not indeed that which is evil in itself, but that which is evil accidentally, through being apprehended as such by the reason. In like manner, to believe in Christ is good in itself, and necessary for salvation; but the will does not tend thereto, except inasmuch as it is proposed by the reason. Consequently, if it be proposed by the reason as something evil, the will tends to it as to something evil; not as if it were evil in itself, but because it is evil accidentally, through the apprehension of the reason. Hence the philosopher says that, *properly speaking, the incontinent man is one who does not follow right reason; but accidentally, he is also one who does not follow false reason.* We must therefore conclude that, absolutely speaking, every will at variance with reason, whether right or erring, is always evil.

. . . Ignorance sometimes causes an act to be involuntary, and sometimes not. And since moral good and evil consist in an act insofar as it is voluntary, as was stated above, it is evident that when ignorance causes an act to be involuntary, it takes away the character of moral good and evil; but not, when it does not cause the act to be involuntary. Again, it has been stated above that when ignorance is in any way willed, either directly or indirectly, it does not cause the act to be involuntary. And I call that ignorance *directly* voluntary to which the act of the will tends, and that, *indirectly* voluntary, which is due to negligence, because a man does not wish to know what he ought to know, as we have stated above.

If, therefore, reason or conscience err with an error that is voluntary, either directly or through negligence, so that one errs about what one ought to know, then such an error of reason or conscience does not excuse the will, which abides by that erring reason or conscience, from being evil. But if the error arise from the ignorance of some circumstance, and without any negligence, so that it cause the act to be involuntary, then that error of reason or conscience excuses the will, which abides by that erring reason, from being evil. For instance, if erring reason tell a man that he should go to another man's wife, the will that abides by that erring reason is evil, since this error arises from ignorance of the divine law, which he is bound to know. But if a man's reason errs in mistaking another for his wife, and if he wish to give her her right when she asks for it, his will is excused from being evil; for this error arises from ignorance of a circumstance, which ignorance excuses, and causes the act to be involuntary.[j]

> **11.** As a Christian philosopher, Aquinas maintains that what is good or evil about an act is what the agent intends and not the consequences the act produces. Note, however, that intent does include consequences foreseeable by the agent. Aquinas is fully aware of human limitations. Thus those acts leading to consequences that the agent could not possibly foresee do not make the agent's will bad.

The consequences do not make an act that was evil, to be good; nor one that was good, to be evil. For instance, if a man give an alms to a poor man who makes bad use of the alms by committing a sin, this does not undo the good done by the giver; and, in like manner, if a man bear patiently a wrong done to him, the wrong-doer is not thereby excused. Therefore the consequences of an act do not increase its goodness or malice.

The consequences of an act are either foreseen or not. If they are foreseen, it is evident that they increase the goodness or malice. For when a man foresees that many evils may follow from his act, and yet does not therefore desist from it, this shows his will to be all the more inordinate.

But if the consequences are not foreseen, we must make a distinction. For if they follow from the nature of the action, and in the majority of cases, in this respect the consequences increase the goodness or malice of that action; for it is evident that an action is of its nature better, if better results can follow from it, and of its nature worse, if it is of a nature to produce worse results. On the other hand, if the consequences follow by accident and seldom, then they do not increase the goodness or malice of the act; for we do not judge of a thing according to that which belongs to it by accident, but only according to that which belongs to it essentially.[k]

## QUESTIONS

1. What does Aquinas mean by an *act?* How does he distinguish *acts* from *movements?*
2. Aquinas and Aristotle both insist that happiness consists in contemplation of the truth. Wherein do they differ and why?
3. Discuss the concepts of eternal and natural law and their significance in Aquinas's ethics.
4. Under what conditions can a human being be held morally responsible, according to Aquinas?
5. Some philosophers maintain that a person who follows his or her conscience is not blameworthy. How does Aquinas respond to this claim?
6. Many ethical theorists are convinced that Christian thinkers neglect the role of consequences in our moral actions. Does Aquinas escape their criticism? Discuss.
7. How does Aquinas's view of the relationship between reason and faith compare with that of Augustine?
8. If for Aquinas the natural law is found to be the same by everyone, how can he account for different people assenting to diverse and conflicting moral principles?
9. Many people speak of conscience as though it were an extra faculty of human nature. Try to formulate such a view and then criticize it in terms of Aquinas's account.

10. Admittedly, Aquinas's moral philosophy shows the influence of both Aristotle and Christianity, but this does not deny his originality and innovativeness. Defend this thesis.

## KEY TO SELECTIONS

Thomas Aquinas, *Basic Writings of St. Thomas Aquinas*, vol II, A. C. Pegis, ed., New York, Random House, 1945. With the kind permission of Richard J. Pegis.

From *Summa Contra Gentiles*

[a]Bk. III, Ch. I, pp. 3–4.

[b]Bk. III, Ch. II, p. 5.

[c]Bk. III, Ch. XXXVII, pp. 59–60.

[d]Bk. III, Ch. XLVIII, p. 85.

From *Summa Theologica*

[e]Question XCI, 1st and 2nd Articles, pp. 748–750.

[f]Question XCI, 2nd Articles, pp. 774–775.

[g]1st Pt. of 2nd Pt., Question 6, Articles I, VI, VII, pp. 226–227, 234–236.

[h]1st Pt. of 2nd Pt., Question 6, Article VIII, pp. 237–238.

[i]1st Pt. of 2nd Pt., Question 19, Articles I, II, III, pp. 335–337.

[j]1st Pt. of 2nd Pt., Question 19, Articles V, VI, pp. 339–342.

[k]1st Pt. of 2nd Pt., Question 20, Article V, pp. 356–357.

## GUIDE TO ADDITIONAL READING

### PRIMARY SOURCES

Gilby, T. (ed.), *St. Thomas Aquinas: Philosophical Texts*, New York, Oxford University Press, 1960.

Pegis, A. C. (ed.), *Introduction to St. Thomas Aquinas*, New York, Random House, 1948.

### DISCUSSION AND COMMENTARY

Bourke, V. J., *St. Thomas and the Greek Moralists*, Milwaukee, Marquette University Press, 1947.

Copleston, F. C., *Aquinas*, Harmondsworth, Penguin Books, 1954.

D'Arcy, M. C., *St. Thomas Aquinas*, Westminster, Newman Press, 1958.

Kenny, A., *Aquinas*, New York, Hill and Wang, 1980.

MacDonald, S., and Stump, E. (eds.), *Aquinas's Moral Theory*, Ithaca, Cornell University Press, 1999.

McInerny, R., *Ethica Thomistica: The Moral Philosophy of Thomas Aquinas*, Washington, D.C., Catholic University American Press, 1982.

O'Connor, D. J., *Aquinas and Natural Law*, London, Macmillan, 1968.

Redpath, P., *The Moral Wisdom of St. Thomas*, Lanham, University Press of America, 1983.

Steel, C., "Does Evil Have a Cause? Augustine's Perplexity and Thomas' Answer," *Review and Metaphysics*, December 1994, pp. 251–273.

CHAPTER EIGHT

# Social Contract Ethics

© Burghley House Collection/Lincolnshire, UK/The Bridgman Art Library

THOMAS HOBBES

THOMAS HOBBES (1588–1679) was born in Malmesbury, England, to poor and uneducated parents. Because he was precocious, however, his uncle provided the financial assistance needed to send him to Oxford University. There, finding the curriculum of scholastic logic boring and Aristotelian physics confusing and irksome, he devoted much of his time to independent reading of literary classics. Upon graduation in 1608, Hobbes was selected as a tutor for the young son of the Cavendish family, a family to which he was attached for almost the whole of his life. In this capacity, he had sufficient time to reflect, to travel, and to become acquainted with such outstanding contemporary philosophers and scientists as Galileo, Bacon, Kepler, and Descartes.

It is reported in John Aubrey's *Brief Lives* that at the age of forty, quite by chance, Hobbes became enamored of the deductive certainty of mathematics. "Being in a gentleman's library, Euclid's *Elements* lay open, and 'twas the forty-seventh [theorem of Book I]. He read the proposition. 'By God,' he said, 'this is impossible.' So he reads the demonstration of it which referred him back to such a proposition: which proposition he read. That referred him back to another, which he also read. [And so back to the self-evident axioms, when] at last he was demonstratively convinced of that truth. This made him in love with geometry." Presumably, at about the same time, he read Galileo's *Dialogues* and became firmly convinced that a systematic philosophy must be based on the physical principle that every change is a change in motion. The deductive form of geometry and the materialism of physics became essential features of his philosophy, which was then in its formative stage.

During the period of Hobbes's intellectual development, the English political scene was one of constant crisis and turbulence. While the tension between Parliament and King Charles I was at its peak, Hobbes wrote a political treatise defending the doctrine of absolute sovereignty. He believed that absolute sovereignty was the necessary condition of a secure and peaceful society, arguing that if supreme authority were to be divided and limited, as, for example, between the King and Parliament, only chaos could result. Though he made no explicit reference to the current situation, Hobbes imagined that he was in danger of reprisal from Parliament and fled to France. During this self-imposed and unnecessary exile (1640–1651), he engaged in philosophical inquiry, tutored the future Charles II, and wrote the important political treatise, *De Cive (On the State)* in 1642 and his major philosophical work, *Leviathan,* in 1651.

Upon his return to England, Hobbes remained aloof from the political scene but continued to write. The most significant work of this period was *De Homine (On Man),* published in 1658. Although Hobbes's writings exhibit fine scholarship, they are particularly distinguished by their penetration and originality.

Historically, Thomas Hobbes is the first philosopher to apply systematically the basic assumptions of seventeenth-century science to human behavior. Impressed with the advance in "natural philosophy" achieved by Copernicus in astronomy, Galileo in physics, and Harvey in physiology, Hobbes attempts to obtain comparable results in the other divisions of philosophy.[1] He envisions a unification of all the branches of philosophy, the study of physical bodies, the study of living bodies, and the study of political bodies. Convinced that the key to the success of physics resided in its underlying assumption of *mechanistic materialism*—the view that everything is ultimately reducible to material bodies in motion—Hobbes extends this doctrine to psychology and to political and moral philosophy. He insists that although the several sciences investigate different subject matter, the basic laws of each describe the motions of bodies.

Hobbes's moral philosophy is directly related to his psychological theory, in which he constructs his mechanistic conception of motivation. He opposes the prevailing notion of his time that the mind and body are different substances, maintaining that *mental phenomena are nothing but physiological motions.* The thoroughgoing nature of his psychology comes out most forcibly in his mechanistic analysis of voluntary actions. These he traces to a variety of "animal motions," which he calls *endeavors*—that is, predispositions to act in a certain direction. Endeavors are mechanically initiated by sensory stimuli, augmented by the action of imagination and memory, and guided by a calculated appraisal of the situation. The most important kinds of endeavors are *desires* and *aversions.* Desires move one to pursue objects, and aversions move one to avoid objects. Endeavors are not only the chief determinants of behavior but also the basis of evaluations.

Evaluating objects or actions as good or evil depends, Hobbes insists, on no other basis than desires and aversions. No objects or actions are intrinsically

---

[1] *Philosophy* was for some time used interchangeably with *knowledge* and *science.* For example, physics was referred to as one of the branches of natural philosophy and ethics were included under moral philosophy.

good—that is, good by their very nature. Rather, people call *good* the objects of their desires, whereas they call *evil* the objects of their aversions. Therefore, evaluations are *transient* and *relative to the individual.* Values are transient, because the desire for an object may change to indifference or even to aversion: What is good on one occasion may on another be ethically neutral or even evil. Values are relative to the individual, because one person may love an object to which a second is indifferent and that a third may hate: The same object is then simultaneously good, neutral, and evil.

Another feature of Hobbes's psychological theory is his conception of human nature as completely and exclusively egoistic. He depicts people as being by nature entirely selfish and devoid of any genuine feelings of sympathy, benevolence, or sociability. Each individual is preoccupied exclusively with the gratification of personal desires, and one's success in maintaining a continuous flow of gratifications is the measure of one's happiness. The means for attaining the objects of desire Hobbes calls *power.* He maintains that in a natural state, individuals are approximately equal in their mental and physical powers. Under these conditions, intense competition eliminates virtually all chances for individuals to achieve happiness and, what is more serious, threatens their very survival.

Hobbes believes that reason points to voluntary collective organization as the most effective way for individuals to utilize their powers. When our rights to do whatever will satisfy our desires are deputed to a central governing authority, the conditions requisite to our survival and happiness are provided. Each individual asserts in effect, "I authorize, and give up my right of governing myself, to this man or to this assembly of men, on this condition, that thou give up thy right and authorize all his actions in a like manner." It is through a "social contract" that the state of nature is transformed into a civil society:

> A *commonwealth* is said to be *instituted* when a *multitude* of men do agree, and *covenant, every one, with everyone,* that to whatsoever *man,* or *assembly of men,* shall be given by the major part, the *right* to *present* the person of them all, that is to say, to be their *representative;* everyone, as well he that *voted for it,* as he that *voted against it,* shall *authorize* all the actions and judgments, of that man, or assembly of men, in the same manner, as if they were his own, to the end, to live peaceably amongst themselves, and be protected against other men.[a]

With the establishment of the commonwealth through the social contract, Hobbes tells us, the necessary and sufficient condition for morality is present. Whatever is in accordance with the law of the sovereign is *right,* whereas that which deviates from it is *wrong.* Hobbes thus establishes *civil authority and law as the foundation of morality.* He is arguing that morality requires social authority, which must be in the hands of the sovereign. The will of a sovereign power whose authority is absolute and indivisible constitutes the only law by which human behavior can be properly regulated. Morality, then, is based on law—the law of the absolute sovereign. Only with the institution of a government that can reward right action and punish wrongdoing is moral conduct possible. Without a civil authority, it would be foolish and dangerous to follow the precepts of morality, whereas with it, morality turns out to be the "dictate of reason." In the last analysis, we are moral only because it is conducive to individual security, and the prime condition of security is absolute civil power.

**1.** The elements of Hobbes's psychological theory are presented in a set of principles that govern the various "motions" of the human mind.

There be in animals, two sorts of *motions* peculiar to them: one called *vital;* begun in generation, and continued without interruption through their whole life; such as are the *course* of the *blood,* the *pulse,* the *breathing,* the *concoction, nutrition, excretion,* etc., to which motions there needs no help of imagination; the other is *animal motion,* otherwise called *voluntary motion;* as to *go,* to *speak,* to *move* any of our limbs, in such manner as is first fancied in our minds. That sense of motion in the organs and interior parts of man's body, caused by the action of the things we see, hear, etc.; and that fancy is but the relics of the same motion, remaining after sense, has been already said in the first and second chapters. And because *going, speaking,* and the like voluntary motions, depend always upon a precedent thought of *whither, which way,* and *what;* it is evident, that the imagination is the first internal beginning of all voluntary motion. And although unstudied men do not conceive any motion at all to be there, where the thing moved is invisible; or the space it is moved in is, for the shortness of it, insensible; yet that doth not hinder, but that such motions are. For let a space be never so little, that which is moved over a greater space, whereof that little one is part, must first be moved over that. These small beginnings of motion, within the body of man, before they appear in walking, speaking, striking, and other visible actions, are commonly called ENDEAVOR.

This endeavor, when it is toward something which causes it, is called APPETITE, or DESIRE; the latter, being the general name; and the other oftentimes restrained to signify the desire of food, namely *hunger* and *thirst.* And when the endeavor is fromward something, it is generally called AVERSION. These words, *appetite* and *aversion,* we have from the Latins; and they both of them signify the motions, one of approaching, the other of retiring. . . . For nature itself does often press upon men those truths, which afterwards, when they look for somewhat beyond nature, they stumble at. For the schools find in mere appetite to go, or move, no actual motion at all: but because some motion they must acknowledge, they call it metaphorical motion; which is but an absurd speech: for though words may be called metaphorical; bodies and motions cannot.

That which men desire, they are also said to LOVE: and to HATE those things for which they have aversion. So that desire and love are the same thing; save that by desire, we always signify the absence of the object; by love, most commonly the presence of the same. So also by aversion, we signify the absence; and by hate, the presence of the object.

Of appetites and aversions, some are born with men; as appetite of food, appetite of excretion, and exoneration, which may also and more properly be called aversions, from somewhat they feel in their bodies; and some other appetites, not many. The rest, which are appetites of particular things, proceed from experience, and trial of their effects upon themselves or other men. For of things we know not at all, or believe not to be, we can have no further desire, than to taste and try. But aversion we have for things, not only which we know have hurt us, but also that we do not know whether they will hurt us, nor not.

Those things which we neither desire nor hate, we are said to *contemn;* CONTEMPT being nothing else but an immobility, or contumacy of the heart, in resisting the action of certain things; and proceeding from that the heart is already moved otherwise, by other more potent objects; or from want of experience of them.

And because the constitution of a man's body is in continual mutation, it is impossible that all the same things should always cause in him the same appetites, and aversions: much less can call men consent, in the desire of almost any one and the same object.[b]

**2.** Hobbes interprets the traditional ethical concepts, "good" and "evil," in terms of this mechanistic psychological theory.

But whatsoever is the object of any man's appetite or desire, that is it which he for his part calleth *good:* and the object of his hate and aversion, *evil;* and of his contempt, *vile* and *inconsiderable.* For these words of good, evil, and contemptible, are ever used with relation to the person that useth them: there being nothing simply and absolutely so; nor any common rule of good and evil, to be taken from the nature of the objects themselves.[c]

**3.** For people in a presocial state, the desires and aversions that underlie their judgments of good and evil are directed toward their primary objective, self-preservation. Hobbes terms continual success in preserving oneself *felicity* or *happiness.* Various objects of desire—that is, goods such as friendship, riches, and intelligence—promote this felicity. Friends are good because they come to our defense when we are in difficulties; riches are good because they buy the allies we need for our security; intelligence is good because it alerts us to danger.

When the objects of desire are examined from the point of view of effectiveness in promoting felicity, they are termed powers. Hobbes ascribes to humans in their natural state a general tendency to "a perpetual and restless desire of power after power that ceaseth only in death." When several persons desire the same object, enmity arises; and because nature endows them equally with the various mental and physical powers, the personal confidence that each one feels intensifies the likelihood of conflict.

Nature hath made men so equal, in the faculties of the body, and mind; as that though there be found one man sometimes manifestly stronger in body, or of quicker mind than another; yet when all is reckoned together, the difference between man, and man, is not so considerable, as that one man can thereupon claim to himself any benefit, to which another may not pretend, as well as he. For as to the strength of body, the weakest has strength enough to kill the strongest, either by secret machination, or by confederacy with others, that are in the same danger with himself.

And as to the faculties of the mind, setting aside the arts grounded upon words, and especially that skill of proceeding upon general, and infallible rules, called science; which very few have, and but in few things; as being not a native faculty, born with us; nor attained, as prudence, while we look after somewhat else, I find yet a greater equality amongst men, than that of strength. For prudence, is but experience; which equal time, equally bestows on all men, in those things they equally apply themselves unto. That which may perhaps make such equality incredible, is but a vain conceit of one's own wisdom, which almost all men think they have in a greater degree, than the vulgar; that is, than all men but themselves, and a few others, whom by fame, or for concurring with themselves, they approve. For such is the nature of men, that howsoever they may acknowledge many others to be more witty, or more eloquent, or more learned; yet they will hardly believe there be many so wise as themselves; for they see their own wit at hand, and other men's at a distance. But this proveth rather that men are in that point equal, than unequal. For there is not ordinarily a greater sign of the equal distribution of any thing, than that every man is contented with his share.

From this equality of ability, ariseth equality of hope in the attaining of our ends. And therefore if any two men desire the same thing, which nevertheless they cannot both enjoy, they become enemies; and in the way to their end, which is principally their own conservation, and sometimes their delectation only, endeavor to destroy, or subdue one another. And from hence it comes to pass, that where an invader hath no more to fear, than another man's single power; if one plant, sow, built, or possess a convenient seat, others may probably be expected to come prepared with forces united, to dispossess, and deprive him, not only of the fruit of his labor, but also of his life, or liberty. And the invader again is in the like danger of another.

And from this diffidence of one another, there is no way for any man to secure himself, so reasonable, as anticipation; that is, for force, or wiles, to master the persons of all men he can, so long, till he see no other power great enough to endanger him: and this is no more than his own conservation requireth, and is generally allowed. Also because there be some, that taking pleasure in contemplating their own power in the acts of conquest, which they pursue farther than their security requires; if others, that otherwise would be glad to be at ease within modest bounds, should not by invasion increase their power, they would not be able, long time, by standing only on their defense, to subsist. And by consequence, such augmentation of dominion over men being necessary to a man's conservation, it ought to be allowed him.

Again, men have no pleasure, but on the contrary a great deal of grief, in keeping company, where there is no power able to overawe them all. For every man looketh that his companion should value him, at the same rate he sets upon himself: and upon all signs of contempt, or undervaluing, naturally endeavors, as far as he dares, (which amongst them that have no common power to keep them in quiet, is far enough to make them destroy each other), to extort a greater value from his contemners, by damage; and from others, by the example.[d]

**4.** From his examination of the contentiousness of people in the absence of political organization, Hobbes discovers three sources of controversy in human nature. The natural condition of human beings, he says, is universal war. He does not claim that the "state of nature" actually existed historically; rather, it exists in any time or place where civil society is not functioning.

So that in the nature of man, we find three principal causes of quarrel. First, competition; secondly, diffidence; thirdly, glory.

The first, maketh men invade for gain; the second, for safety, and the third, for reputation. The first use violence, to make themselves masters of other men's persons, wives, children, and cattle; the second, to defend them; the third, for trifles, as a word, a smile, a different opinion, and any other sign of undervalue, either direct in their persons, or by reflection in their kindred, their friends, their nation, their profession, or their name.

Hereby it is manifest, that during the time men live without a common power to keep them all in awe, they are in that condition which is called war; and such a war, as is of every man, against every man. For WAR, consisteth not in battle only, or act of fighting; but in a tract of time, wherein the will to contend by battle is sufficiently known: and therefore the notion of *time,* is to be considered in the nature of war; as it is in the nature of weather. For as the nature of foul weather, lieth not in a shower or two of rain; but in an inclination thereto of many days together: so the nature of war, consisteth not in actual fighting; but in the known disposition thereto, during all the time there is no assurance to the contrary. All other time is PEACE.

Whatsoever therefore is consequent to a time of war, where every man is enemy to every man; the same is consequent to the time, wherein men live without other security, than what their own strength, and their own invention shall furnish them withal. In such condition, there is no place for industry; because the fruit thereof is uncertain: and consequently no culture of the earth; no navigation, nor use of the commodities that may be imported by sea; no commodious building; no instruments of moving, and removing, such things as require much force; no knowledge of the face of the earth; no account of time; no arts; no letters; no society; and which is worst of all, continual fear, and danger of violent death; and the life of man, solitary, poor, nasty, brutish, and short. . . .

It may peradventure be thought, there was never such a time, nor condition of war as this; and I believe it was never generally so, over all the world: but there are many places, where they live so now. For the savage people in many places of America, except the government of small families, the concord whereof dependeth on natural lust, have no government at all; and live at this day in that brutish manner, as I said before. Howsoever, it may be perceived what manner of life there would be, where there were no common power to fear, by the manner of life, which men that have formerly lived under a peaceful government, use to degenerate into, in a civil war.

But though there had never been any time, wherein particular men were in a condition of war one against another; yet in all times, kings, and persons of sovereign authority, because of the independency, are in continual jealousies, and in the state and posture of gladiators; having their weapons pointing, and their eyes fixed on one another; that is, their forts, garrisons, and guns upon the frontiers of their kingdoms; and continual spies upon their neighbors; which is a posture of war. But because they uphold thereby, the industry of their subjects; there does not follow from it, that misery, which accompanies the liberty of particular men.[e]

**5.** Hobbes argues that society originates out of self-interest and fear, not out of natural feeling for other people. He defends as natural and reasonable the interest one takes in one's own welfare and happiness. In a state of nature, the first and only rule of life is self-protection, and human beings have a natural right to do anything that serves this end.

All society therefore is either for gain, or for glory; that is, not so much for love of our fellows, as for the love of ourselves. But no society can be great or lasting, which begins from vain glory. Because that glory is like honor; if all men have it no man hath it, for they consist in comparison and precellence. Neither doth the society of others advance any whit the cause of my glorying in myself; for every man must account himself, such as he can make himself without the help of others. But though the benefits of this life may be much furthered by mutual help; since yet those may be better attained to by dominion than by the society of others, I hope no body will doubt, but that men would much more greedily be carried by nature, if all fear were removed, to obtain dominion, than to gain society. We must therefore resolve, that the original of all great and lasting societies consisted not in the mutual goodwill men had towards each other, but in the mutual fear they had of each other.

The cause of mutual fear consists partly in the natural equality of men, partly in their mutual will of hurting: whence it comes to pass, that we can neither expect from others, nor promise to ourselves the least security. For if we look on men full grown, and consider how brittle the frame of our human body is, which perishing, all its strength, vigor, and wisdom itself perisheth with it; and how easy a matter it is, even for the weakest man to kill the strongest: there is no reason why any man, trusting to his own strength, should conceive himself made by nature above others. They are equals, who can do equal things one against the other; but they who can do the greatest things, namely, kill, can do equal things. All men therefore among themselves are by nature equal; the inequality we now discern, hath its spring from the civil law....

Among so many dangers therefore, as the natural lusts of men do daily threaten each other withal, to have a care of one's self is so far from being a matter scornfully to be looked upon, that one has neither the power nor wish to have done otherwise. For every man is desirous of what is good for him, and shuns what is evil, but chiefly the chiefest of natural evils, which is death; and this he doth by a certain impulsion of nature, no less than that whereby a stone moves downward. It is therefore neither absurd nor reprehensible, neither against the dictates of true reason, for a man to use all his endeavors to preserve and defend his body and the members thereof from death and sorrows. But that which is not contrary to right reason, that all men account to be done justly, and with right. Neither by the word *right* is anything else signified, than that liberty which every man hath to make use of his natural faculties according to right reason. Therefore the first foundation of natural right is this, that *every man as much as in him lies endeavor to protect his life and members.*

But because it is in vain for a man to have a right to the end, if the right to the necessary means be denied him, it follows, that since every man hath a right to preserve himself, he must also be allowed a right *to use all the means, and do all the actions, without which he cannot preserve himself.*

Now whether the means which he is about to use, and the action he is performing, be necessary to the preservation of his life and members or not, he himself, by the right of nature, must be judge. For if it be contrary to right reason that I should judge of mine own peril, say that another man is judge. Why now, because he judgeth of what concerns me, by the same reason, because we are equal by nature, will I judge also of things which do belong to him. Therefore it agrees with right reason, that is, it is the right of nature that I judge of his opinion, that is, whether it conduce to my preservation or not.

Nature hath given to *everyone a right to all;* that is, it was lawful for every man, in the bare state of nature, or before such time as men had engaged themselves by any covenants or bonds, to do what he would, and against whom he thought fit, and to possess, use, and enjoy all what he would, or could get. Now because whatsoever a man would, it therefore seems good to him because he wills it, and either it really doth, or at least seems to him to contribute towards his preservation, (but we have already allowed him to be judge, in the foregoing article, whether it doth or not, insomuch as we are to hold all for necessary whatsoever he shall esteem so), and . . . it appears that by the right of nature those things may be done, and must be had, which necessarily conduce to the protection of life and members, it follows, that in the state of nature, to have all, and do all, is lawful for all. And this is that which is meant by that common saying, *nature hath given all to all.* From whence we understand likewise, that in the state of nature profit is the measure of right.

But it was the least benefit for men thus to have a common right to all things. For the effects of this right are the same, almost, as if there had been no right at all. For although any man might say of every thing, *this is mine,* yet could he not enjoy it, by reason of his neighbor, who having equal right and equal power, would pretend the same thing to be his.

If now to this natural proclivity of men, to hurt each other, which they derive from their passions, but chiefly from a vain esteem of themselves, you add, the right of all to all, wherewith one by right invades, the other by right resists, and whence arise perpetual jealousies and suspicions on all hands, and how hard a thing it is to provide against an enemy invading us with an intention to oppress and ruin, though he come with a small number, and no great provision; it cannot be denied but that the natural state of men, before they entered into society, was a mere war, and that not simply, but a war of all men against all men. For what is WAR, but that same time in which the will of contesting by force is fully declared, either by words or deeds?[f]

**6.** Defending himself against the possible charge of cynicism, Hobbes shows that there are no grounds for objections against self-interested action in the natural state. Social relations are not derived from the original nature of humanity but rather are artificially created. In fact, society is only a means to the furthering of each individual's interests and happiness. Moreover, Hobbes maintains, the concept of moral obligation has neither meaning nor application in the state of nature. Rather, the basic moral concepts, right and wrong, just and unjust, arise concomitantly with the establishment of a civil society.

It may seem strange to some man, that has not well weighed these things; that nature should thus dissociate, and render man apt to invade, and destroy one another: and he may therefore, not trusting to this inference, made from the passions, desire perhaps to have the same confirmed by experience. Let him therefore consider with himself, when taking a journey, he arms himself, and seeks to go well accompanied; when going to sleep, he locks his doors; when even in his house he locks his chests; and this when he knows there be laws, and public officers, armed, to revenge all injuries shall be done him; what opinion he has of his fellow subjects, when he rides armed; of his fellow citizens, when he locks his doors; and of his children, and servants, when he locks his chests. Does he not there as much accuse mankind by his actions, as I do by my words? But neither of us accuse man's nature in it. The desires, and other passions of man, are in themselves no sin. No more are the actions, that proceed from those passions, till they know a law that forbids them: which till laws be made they cannot know: nor can any law be made, till they have agreed upon the person that shall make it. . . .

To this war of every man, against every man, this also is consequent; that nothing can be unjust. The notions of right and wrong, justice and injustice have there no place. Where there is no common power, there is no law: where no law, no injustice. Force, and fraud, are in war the two cardinal virtues. Justice, and injustice are none of the faculties neither of the body, nor mind. If they were, they might be in a man that were alone in the world, as well as his senses, and passions. They are qualities, that relate to men in society, not in solitude. It is consequent also to the same condition, that there be no propriety, no dominion, no *mine* and *thine* distinct; but only that to be every man's, that he can get; and for so long, as he can keep it. And thus much for the ill condition, which man by mere nature is actually placed in; though with a possibility to come out of it, consisting partly in the passions, partly in his reason.

The passions that incline men to peace, are fear of death; desire of such things as are necessary to commodious living; and a hope by their industry to obtain them. And reason suggesteth convenient articles of peace, upon which men may be drawn to agreement. These articles, are they, which otherwise are called the Laws of Nature.[g]

> **7.** The termination of the perpetual warfare of the state of nature is brought about through the instrumentality of reason. First, an individual becomes aware, through rational deliberation, of the need for security. Second, reason discovers those precepts, or "laws of nature," by which peace may be realized.

A LAW OF NATURE, *lex naturalis,* is a precept or general rule, found out by reason, by which a man is forbidden to do that, which is destructive of his life, or taketh away the means of preserving the same; and to omit that, by which he thinketh it may be best preserved. For though they that speak of this subject, use to confound *jus,* and *lex, right* and *law:* yet they ought to be distinguished; because RIGHT, consisteth in liberty to do, or to forbear; whereas LAW, determineth, and bindeth to one of them: so that law, and right, differ as much, as obligation, and liberty; which in one and the same matter are inconsistent.

And because the condition of man, as hath been declared in the precedent chapter, is a condition of war of everyone against everyone: in which case everyone is governed by his own reason; and there is nothing he can make use of, that may not be a help unto him, in preserving his life against his enemies; it followeth, that in such a condition, every man has a right to every thing; even to one another's body. And therefore, as long as this natural right of every man to every thing endureth, there can be no security to any man, how strong or wise soever he be, of living out the time, which nature ordinarily alloweth men to live. And consequently it is a precept, or general rule of reason, *that every man, ought to endeavor peace, as far as he has hope of obtaining it; and when he cannot obtain it, that he may seek, and use, all helps, and advantages of war.* The first branch of which rule, containeth the first, and fundamental law of nature; which is *to seek peace, and follow it.* The second, the sum of the right of nature; which is, *by all means we can, to defend ourselves.*

From this fundamental law of nature, by which men are commanded to endeavor peace, is derived this second law; that *a man be willing, when others are so too, as farforth, as for peace, and defense of himself he shall think it necessary, to lay down this right to all things; and be contented with so much liberty against other men, as he would allow other men against himself.* For as long as every man holdeth this right, of doing any thing he liketh; so long are all men in the condition of war. But if other men will not lay down their right, as well as he; then there is no reason for anyone, to divest himself of his: for that were to expose himself to prey, which no man is bound to, rather than to dispose himself to peace.

Right is laid aside, either by simply renouncing it; or by transferring it to another. By *simply* RENOUNCING; when he cares not to whom the benefit thereof redoundeth. By TRANSFERRING; when he intendeth the benefit thereof to some certain person, or persons. And when a man hath in either manner abandoned, or granted away his right; then is he said to be OBLIGED, or BOUND, not to hinder those, to whom such right is granted, or abandoned, from the benefit of it: and that he *ought,* and it is his DUTY, not make void that voluntary act of his own: and that such hindrance is INJUSTICE, and INJURY, as being *sine jure;* the right being before renounced, or transferred. So that *injury,* or *injustice,* in the controversies of the world, is somewhat like to that, which in the disputations of scholars is called *absurdity.* For as it is there called an absurdity, to contradict what one maintained in the beginning: so in the world, it is called injustice, and injury, voluntarily to undo that, which from the beginning he had voluntarily done. . . .

Whensoever a man transferreth his right, or renounceth it; it is either in consideration of some right reciprocally transferred to himself; or for some other good he hopeth for thereby. For it is a voluntary act: and of the voluntary acts of every man, the object is some *good to himself.* And therefore there be some rights, which no man can be understood by and words, or other signs, to have abandoned, or transferred. As first a man cannot lay down the right of resisting them, that assault him by force, to take away his life; because he cannot be understood to aim thereby, at any good to himself. The same may be said of wounds, and chains, and imprisonment; both because there is no benefit consequent to such patience; as there is to the patience of suffering another to be wounded, or imprisoned: as also because a man cannot tell, when he seeth men proceed against him by violence, whether they intend his death or not. And lastly the motive, and end for which this renouncing, and transferring of right is introduced, is nothing else but the security of a man's person, in his life, and in the means of so preserving life, as not to be weary of it. And therefore if a man by words, or other signs, seem to despoil himself of the end, for which those signs were intended; he is not to be understood as if he meant it, or that it was his will; but that he was ignorant of how such words and actions were to be interpreted.[h]

**8.** When the egoistic nature of humans is taken into account, it is manifest that the first two laws of nature, in and of themselves, are not binding on the individual. Consequently, another law is necessary to make the first two effective.

From that law of nature, by which we are obliged to transfer to another, such rights, as being retained, hinder the peace of mankind, there followeth a third; which is this, *that men perform their covenants made:* without which, covenants are in vain, and by empty words; and the right of all men to all things remaining, we are still in the condition of war.

And in this law of nature, consisteth the fountain and original of JUSTICE. For where no covenant hath preceded, there hath no right been transferred, and every man has right to everything; and consequently, no action can be unjust. But when a covenant is made, then to break it is *unjust:* and the definition of INJUSTICE, is no other than *the not performance of covenant.* And whatsoever is not unjust, is *just.*

But because covenants of mutual trust, where there is a fear of not performance on either part . . . are invalid; though the original of justice be the making of covenants; yet injustice actually there can be none, till the cause of such fear be taken away; which while men are in the natural condition of war, cannot be done. Therefore before the names of just, and unjust can have place, there must be some coercive power, to compel men equally to the performance of their covenants, by the terror of some punishment, greater than the benefit they expect by the breach of their covenant; and to make good that propriety, which by mutual contract men acquire, in recompense of the universal right they abandon: and such power there is none before the erection of a commonwealth. And this is also to be gathered out of the ordinary definition of justice in the schools: for they say, that *justice is the constant will of giving to every man his own.* And therefore where there is no *own,* that is no propriety, there is no injustice; and where there is no coercive power erected, that is, where there is no commonwealth, there is no propriety; all men having right to all things: therefore where there is not commonwealth, there nothing is unjust. So that the nature of justice, consisteth in keeping of valid covenants: but the validity of covenants begins not but with the constitution of a civil power, sufficient to compel men to keep them: and then it is also that propriety begins.[i]

**9.** Hobbes concludes that the laws of nature may be summed up in a rule that everyone accepts, the Golden Rule.

These are the laws of nature, dictating peace, for a means of the conservation of men in multitudes; and which only concern the doctrine of civil society. There be other things tending to the destruction of particular men; as drunkenness, and all other parts of intemperance; which may therefore also be reckoned amongst those things which the law of nature hath forbidden; but are not necessary to be mentioned, nor are pertinent enough to this place.

And though this may seem too subtle a deduction of the laws of nature, to be taken notice of by all men; whereof the most part are too busy in getting food, and the rest too negligent to understand; yet to leave all men inexcusable, they have been contracted into one easy sum, intelligible even to the meanest capacity; and that is, *Do not that to another, which thou wouldest not have done to thyself;* which showeth him, that he has no more to do in learning the laws of nature, but, when weighing the actions of other men with his own, they seem too heavy, to put them into the center part of the balance, and his own into their place, that his own passions, and self-love, may add nothing to the weight; and then there is none of these laws of nature that will appear unto him very reasonable.[j]

**10.** Reason not only dictates peace and security in society but also prescribes the means by which they can be ensured: a commonwealth instituted by covenant. It was apparent to Hobbes that there must be some civil power to determine and interpret what is right and what wrong, what is good and what bad, in society. Such authority must be vested in a single sovereign power—either an individual or an assembly—to prevent the occurrence of jurisdictional disputes between one authority and another.

From this institution of a commonwealth are derived all the *rights,* and *faculties* of him, or them, on whom sovereign power is conferred by the consent of the people assembled. . . .

First, because they covenant, it is to be understood, they are not obliged by former covenant to anything repugnant hereunto. And consequently they that have already instituted a commonwealth, being thereby bound by covenant, to own the actions, and judgments of one, cannot lawfully make a new covenant, amongst themselves, to be obedient to any other, in any thing whatsoever, without his permission. And therefore, they that are subjects to a monarch, cannot without his leave cast off monarchy, and return to the confusion of a disunited multitude; nor transfer their person from him that beareth it, to another man, or other assembly of men: for they are bound, every man to every man, to own, and be reputed author of all, that he that already is their sovereign, shall do, and judge fit to be done: so that any one man dissenting, all the rest should break their covenant made to that man, which is injustice: and they have also every man given the sovereignty to him that beareth their person; and therefore if they depose him, they take from him that which is his own, and so again it is injustice. . . .

Secondly, because the right of bearing the person of them all, is given to him they make sovereign, by covenant only of one to another, and not of him to any of them; there can happen no breach of covenant on the part of the sovereign; and consequently none of his subjects, by any pretense of forfeiture, can be freed from his subjection. . . .

Thirdly, because the major part hath by consenting voices declared a sovereign; he that dissented must now consent with the rest; that is, be contented to avow all the actions he shall do, or else justly be destroyed by the rest. For if he voluntarily entered into the congregation of them that were assembled, he sufficiently declared thereby his will, and therefore tacitly covenanted, to stand to what the major part should ordain....

Fourthly, because every subject is by this institution author of all the actions, and judgments of the sovereign instituted; it follows, that whatsoever he doth, it can be no injury to any of his subjects; nor ought he to be by any of them accused of injustice. For he that doth anything by authority from another, doth therein no injury to him by whose authority he acteth: but by this institution of a commonwealth, every particular man is author of all the sovereign doth: and consequently he that complaineth of injury from his sovereign, complaineth of that whereof he himself is author; and therefore ought not to accuse any man but himself; no nor himself or injury; because to do injury to one's self, is impossible. It is true that they that have sovereign power may commit iniquity; but not injustice, or injury in the proper signification....

Sixthly, it is annexed to the sovereignty, to be judge of what opinions and doctrines are averse, and what conducing to peace; and consequently, on what occasions, how far, and what men are to be trusted withal, in speaking to multitudes of people; and who shall examine the doctrines of all books before they be published. For the actions of men proceed from their opinions; and in the well-governing of opinions, consisteth the well-governing of men's actions, in order to their peace, and concord. And though in matter of doctrine, nothing ought to be regarded but the truth; yet this is not repugnant to regulating the same by peace. For doctrine repugnant to peace, can no more be true, than peace and concord can be against the law of nature....

Seventhly, is annexed to the sovereignty, the whole power of prescribing the rules, whereby every man may know, what goods he may enjoy, and what actions he may do, without being molested by any of his fellow-subjects; and this is it men call *propriety*. For before constitution of sovereign power, as hath already been shown, all men had right to all things; which necessarily causeth war: and therefore this propriety, being necessary to peace, and depending on sovereign power, is the act of that power, in order to the public peace. These rules of propriety, or *meum* and *tuum*, and of *good, evil, lawful*, and *unlawful* in the actions of subjects, are the civil laws; that is to say, the laws of each commonwealth in particular.[k]

**11.** Hobbes believes that matters of conscience, for example, must be controlled entirely by the sovereign. Thus even church affairs should be dominated by the secular rules, "God's lieutenant on earth."

I observe the *diseases* of a commonwealth, that proceed from the poison of seditious doctrines, whereof one is, *That every private man is judge of good and evil actions.* This is true in the condition of mere nature, where there are no civil laws; and also under civil government, in such cases as are not determined by the law. But otherwise, it is manifest, that the measure of good and evil actions, is the civil law; and the judge the legislator, who is always representative of the commonwealth. From this false doctrine, men are disposed to debate with themselves, and dispute the commands of the commonwealth; and afterwards to obey, or disobey them, as in their private judgments they shall think fit; whereby the commonwealth is distracted and *weakened*.

Another doctrine repugnant to civil society, is, that *whatsoever a man does against his conscience, is sin;* and it dependeth on the presumption of making himself judge of good and evil. For a man's conscience, and his judgment is the same thing, and as the judgment, so also the conscience may be erroneous. Therefore, though he that is subject to no civil law, sinneth in all he does against his conscience, because he has no other rule to follow but his own reason; yet it is not so with him that lives in a commonwealth; because the law is the public conscience, by which he hath already undertaken to be guided. Otherwise in such diversity, as there is of private consciences, which are but private opinions, the commonwealth must needs be distracted, and no man dare to obey the sovereign power, further than it shall seem good in his own eyes.... There is [another] doctrine, plainly, and directly against the essence of a commonwealth; and it is this, *that the sovereign power may be divided.* For what is it to divide the power of a commonwealth, but to dissolve it; for powers divided mutually destroy each other. And for these doctrines, men are chiefly beholding to some of those, that making profession of the laws, endeavor to make them depend upon their own learning, and not upon the legislative power.[l]

**12.** In its ultimate consequences, then, Hobbes's ethical theory leads to the political doctrine of absolute sovereignty, designed to end the natural war of every person with every other person.

To the care of the sovereign, belongeth the making of good laws. But what is a good law? By a good law, I mean not a just law: for no law can be unjust. The law is made by the sovereign power, and all that is done by such power, is warranted, and owned by every one of the people; and that which every man will have so, no man can say is unjust. It is in the laws of the commonwealth, as in the laws of gaming: whatsoever the gamesters all agree on, is injustice to none of them. A good law is that, which is *needful,* for the *good of the people,* and withal *perspicuous.*

For the use of laws, which are but rules authorized, is not to bind the people from all voluntary actions; but to direct and keep them in such a motion, as not to hurt themselves by their own impetuous desires, rashness or indiscretion; as hedges are set, not to stop travelers, but to keep them in their way. And therefore a law that is not needful, having not the true end of the law, is not good. A law may be conceived to be good, when it is for the benefit of the sovereign; though it be not necessary for the people; but it is not so. For the good of the sovereign and people, cannot be separated. It is a weak sovereign, that has weak subjects; and a weak people, whose sovereign wanteth power to rule them at his will. Unnecessary laws are not good laws; but traps for money; which where the right of sovereign power is acknowledged, are superfluous; and where it is not acknowledged, insufficient to defend the people....

The office of the sovereign, be it a monarch or an assembly, consisteth in the end, for which he was trusted with the sovereign power, namely the procuration of *the safety of the people;* to which he is obliged by the law of nature, and to render an account thereof to God, the author of that law, and to none but him. But by safety here, is not meant a bare preservation, but also all other contentments of life, which every man by lawful industry, without danger, or hurt to the commonwealth, shall acquire to himself.

And this is intended should be done, not by care applied to individuals, further than their protection from injuries, when they shall complain; but by a general providence, contained in public instruction, both of doctrine, and example; and in the making and executing of good laws, to which individual persons may apply their own cases.

And because, if the essential rights of sovereignty ... be taken away the commonwealth is thereby dissolved, and every man returneth into the condition, and calamity of a war with every other man, which is the greatest evil that can happen in this life; it is the office of the sovereign, to maintain those rights entire.[m]

## QUESTIONS

1. Outline Hobbes's psychological theory. What effect does it have on his definitions of *good* and *evil?* On his moral philosophy in general?
2. In Hobbes's view, what is the "natural state" of humanity? To what political theory does this lead him?
3. How does Hobbes define *happiness?* Why can it not be achieved in a state of nature?
4. Discuss Hobbes's theory of the formation of society. How would he deal with the thesis that "man is by nature a social animal"?

5. What arguments does Hobbes offer in defense of his egoistic theory of human relations? Can you find arguments or evidence against his view?
6. What does Hobbes mean by "laws of nature"? Where do they originate? Do you agree that they are really laws of nature?
7. What use does Hobbes make of the doctrines of materialism and mechanism? Are these doctrines essential to his ethical theory?
8. In Hobbes's ethical theory, what is the basis of morality? Do the same moral principles apply in a state of war and in a civil society?
9. Explain and discuss Hobbes's claim that the laws of nature imply, as we say, the Golden Rule.
10. Are there some situations in which you would not prefer peace and security? Relate your answer to Hobbes's ethical theory.

## KEY TO SELECTIONS

Thomas Hobbes, *Leviathan* and *Philosophical Rudiments*, from *The English Works of Thomas Hobbes*, vols. II and III, Sir William Molesworth, ed., London, John Bohn, 1839.

From *Leviathan*

[a]Ch. XVIII, p. 159.
[b]Ch. VI, pp. 38–41.
[c]Ch. VI, p. 41.
[d]Ch. XIII, pp. 110–112.
[e]Ch. XIII, pp. 112–113, pp. 114–115.
[g]Ch. XIII, pp. 113–114, pp. 114–116.
[h]Ch. XIV, pp. 116–118, pp. 118–119, pp. 119–120.
[i]Ch. XV, pp. 130–131.
[j]Ch. XV, pp. 144–145.
[k]Ch. XVIII, p. 159, p. 160, p. 161, p. 162, p. 163, p. 164, p. 165.
[l]Ch. XXIX, pp. 310–311, p. 313.
[m]Ch. XXX, pp. 335–336, pp. 332–333.

From *Philosophical Rudiments*

[f]Ch. I, pp. 5–7, pp. 8–11.

## GUIDE TO ADDITIONAL READING


### PRIMARY SOURCES

Hobbes, T., Leviathan, Everyman's Library (Dutton).

____, ____ (Selections), Great Books Foundation (Regnery).

*English Philosophers from Bacon to Mill*, Modern Library (Random House).

*Hobbes Selections*, Modern Student's Library (Scribner's).

### DISCUSSION AND COMMENTARY

Farrell, D., "Hobbes as Moralist," *Philosophical Studies*, September 1985, pp. 257–284.

Gauthier, D., *The Logic of Leviathan*, Oxford, Clarendon Press, 1969.

Gooch, G. P., *Hobbes*, London, Humphrey, Milford, 1940.

Hampton, Jean, *Hobbes and the Social Contract Tradition*, Cambridge, Cambridge University Press, 1988.

Kavka, C., "Hobbes' War of All Against All," *Ethics*, January 1983, pp. 291–310.

____, "Right Reason and Natural Law in Hobbes' Ethics," *Monist*, January 1983, pp. 120–133.

Kidder, J., "Acknowledgment of Equals: Hobbes' Ninth Law of Nature," *Philosophical Quarterly*, April 1983, pp. 133–146.

Kymlicka, W., "The Social Contract Tradition," in *A Companion to Ethics*, ed. P. Singer, Cambridge, Blackwell, 1993, pp. 186–198.

Warrender, H., *The Political Philosophy of Hobbes*, Oxford, Clarendon Press, 1957.

C H A P T E R N I N E

# Nature and Reason

BENEDICT DE SPINOZA

AN UNCOMMON DEVOTION to intellectual independence and integrity is exemplified in the personal history of Spinoza (1632–1677). He was born a Jew whose paternal grandparents had sought refuge, first in Nantes, and then in Amsterdam, from Portuguese persecution. From the scholars of the Synagogue, Spinoza acquired a thorough knowledge of the Old Testament, such Hebrew religious classics as the Talmud and the mystical Kabbala, and the teachings of noted Jewish theologians. In addition, he mastered the works of Christian philosophers and the secular writings that marked the beginnings of the modern scientific era.

An early tendency to rebel against the narrow formalism and orthodoxy of his religion reached a critical point when Spinoza was twenty-four years old. His disregard of entreaties, bribes, and threats to his life intended to force him to at least outward conformity to Judaism resulted in his excommunication, in 1656, from the Jewish community. Changing his Hebrew name, Baruch, to its Latin equivalent, Benedict, he pursued his nonconformist views as a philosopher in the Christian world, but he did not become a Christian. In fact, his position in regard to religious matters has, since his lifetime, been a subject of debate. Although there is virtual unanimity in placing him in the first rank of the philosophers, there has never been agreement as to whether he was a "God-intoxicated man" or an atheist who made frequent use of the word *God* when he meant nothing more than *Nature.*

Following his excommunication, Spinoza withdrew from Amsterdam, living first in Voorburg, then in Rijnsburg, and finally in The Hague, where he spent the last seven years of his life. Supporting himself by the humble occupation of lens grinding, he devoted his evenings to philosophical composition. He enjoyed the loyalty of a few friends and disciples and maintained a learned correspondence with such distinguished men of the times as Henry Oldenburg, of the Royal Society of England; Christian Huygens, the physicist; and Gottfried Leibniz, the philosopher.

Through his commentary on the writings of the philosopher Descartes, Spinoza proved himself a competent scholar. His *Tractatus Theologico-Politicus* (Theologico-Political Treatise) (1670) raised a storm of protest by its strong plea for freedom of thought and criticism, a radical idea in the seventeenth century. Moreover, the criticisms of traditional religion contained in the work alienated religious leaders and some of his own friends. For the sake of peace, Spinoza kept his subsequent writings from public view, and they were not published until the year of his death. These comprised chiefly a political treatise, an incomplete essay, "On the Improvement of the Understanding," and his main work, *Ethics, Demonstrated in Geometrical Order*. The latter, composed mainly of definitions, axioms, and propositions with their proofs, testifies to Spinoza's conviction that the rigorous method of mathematics is the appropriate method for philosophy.

Spinoza's reputation among the scholars of the day as a learned and profound thinker brought him, in 1673, an offer of a professorship in philosophy at the great University of Heidelberg. His explanation for refusing this honorable post bespeaks his dedication to the contemplative way of life: He did not wish to take time away from philosophical reflection for the training of disciples, nor did he wish to teach in public, where he would almost certainly suffer from the disturbance of religious quarrels through his persistence in his own way of understanding God.

Spinoza's ethical theory is the culmination of a complex philosophical system that involves not only our nature, but also the nature of God and our relation to God. For Spinoza, the key to ethics lies in the proposition "All things . . . are in God, and all things which come to pass, come to pass solely through the laws of the infinite nature of God, and follow . . . from the necessity of his essence." He thus equates God with Nature, or Reality, or the Universe, and characterizes the complex totality as a rational unity in which everything follows with logical necessity from the nature of the whole.[1] Because they share in the rationality of the divine order, human minds are able to know God, or Nature. Wise people, aware that moral excellence and the happiness it brings are proportionate to their knowledge of God, devote themselves to the cultivation of reason.

Although men and women are essentially rational beings in a rational universe, their intellects are imperfect and limited. They have natural tendency to view events in relation to themselves and therefore can form only confused and inadequate ideas of reality. In such a state, the mind projects upon the external world its judgments of what is good or evil to us, thus fostering the illusion that good and evil exist as objective realities in the universe. But in the Spinozistic view, the distinction between good and evil is not applicable to the universe as such, for the universe is God,

[1]From Spinoza's pantheism—his identification of God with Nature—and his characterization of God as a fixed rational order, it is evident that his conception of the divine being is markedly different from that of the Judeo-Christian religious tradition. Spinoza dismisses as superstition the belief that God transcends nature and is a merciful and just Person who acts with free will. Moreover, miracles, acts of divine providence, prayer, and the working of divine power are rejected as inconsistent with the logical necessity of events.

and God is necessarily perfect. Hence, uneducated people are mentally and morally weak. In their ignorance of the order of Nature they are subject to what appears to them to be the whim of events. In these circumstances, they are beset by the uncontrolled and conflicting emotions that cause their unhappiness. In contrast:

> . . . the strong man has ever first in his thoughts, that all things follow from the necessity of the divine nature; so that whatsoever he deems to be hurtful and evil, and whatsoever, accordingly, seems to him impious, horrible, unjust, and base, assumes that appearance owing to his own disordered, fragmentary, and confused view of the universe. Wherefore he strives before all things to conceive things as they really are, and to remove the hindrances to true knowledge, such as are hatred, anger, envy, derision, pride, and similar emotions.[a]

The removal of the ills that destroy happiness, therefore, can be accomplished only by freeing the mind from its bondage to the emotions that becloud it: How to do this is the basic ethical problem for humanity.

To free themselves from bondage, rational individuals attack the difficulty at its source. They seek knowledge of the causes of things, accepting without protest the unchangeable order of events. At the zenith of their intellectual power, they rise far above the limited perspective of personal interests to the view of all things "under the aspect of eternity." The pursuit and possession of objective knowledge free their minds from error, and emotional conflict, which Spinoza always correlates with intellectual confusion, gives way to emotional stability. When they understand that each object and each event has a fixed place in the rational order of Nature, reflective people are well on their way to felicity.

In Spinoza's ethical theory, human effort to acquire knowledge and virtue is accounted for by a striving (*conatus*) for self-preservation. In human beings, whose essential nature is rational, this striving is directed toward the perfection of the intellect. The happiness enjoyed by rational individuals accompanies their "knowledge of the union existing between the mind and the whole of nature." The contemplation of reality under the aspect of eternity leads people to their highest good, the "intellectual love of God," which is the understanding of God as the eternal Being in whose rational order each of us has a proper place. In this way, human beings proceed from the state of human bondage to the state of human freedom—from the wretchedness of an unstable emotional existence to the happiness of the tranquil life of reason.

---

**1.** In his essay "On the Improvement of the Understanding," Spinoza examines the false values that arise out of misunderstandings of the nature of the true good for humans. He concludes that it is necessary to surrender the pursuit of such goals as riches, fame, and pleasure because they consume mental energy and time that should be given to meditation.

After experience had taught me that all the usual surroundings of social life are vain and futile; seeing that none of the objects of my fears contained in themselves anything either good or bad, except insofar as the mind is affected by them, I finally resolved to inquire whether there might be some real good having power to communicate itself, which would affect the mind singly, to the exclusion of all else: whether, in fact, there might be anything of which the discovery and attainment would enable me to enjoy continuous, supreme, and unending happiness. I say "I *finally* resolved," for at first sight it seemed unwise willingly to lose hold on what was sure for the sake of something then uncertain. I could see the benefits which are acquired through fame and riches, and that I should be obliged to abandon the quest of such objects, if I seriously devoted myself to the search for something different and new. I perceived that if true happiness chanced to be placed in the former I should necessarily miss it; while if, on the other hand, it were not so placed, and I gave them my whole attention, I should equally fail.

I therefore debated whether it would not be possible to arrive at the new principle, or at any rate at a certainty concerning its existence, without changing the conduct and usual plan of my life; with this end in view I made many efforts, but in vain. For the ordinary surroundings of life which are esteemed by men (as their actions testify) to be the highest good, may be classed under the three heads—Riches, Fame, and the Pleasures of Sense: with these three the mind is so absorbed that it has little power to reflect on any different good. By sensual pleasure the mind is enthralled to the extent of quiescence, as if the supreme good were actually attained, so that it is quite incapable of thinking of any other object; when such pleasure has been gratified it is followed by extreme melancholy, whereby the mind, though not enthralled, is disturbed and dulled.

The pursuit of honors and riches is likewise very absorbing, especially if such objects be sought simply for their own sake, inasmuch as they are then supposed to constitute the highest good. In the case of fame the mind is still more absorbed, for fame is conceived as always good for its own sake, and as the ultimate end to which all actions are directed. Further, the attainment of riches and fame is not followed as in the case of sensual pleasures by repentance, but, the more we acquire, the greater is our delight, and, consequently, the more are we incited to increase both the one and the other; on the other hand, if our hopes happen to be frustrated we are plunged into the deepest sadness. Fame has the further drawback that it compels its votaries to order their lives according to the opinions of their fellow men, shunning what they usually shun, and seeking what they usually seek.[b]

**2.** Spinoza argues that the things most people value are evil, rather than good, and only unhappiness can follow from "the love of what is perishable." He is in quest of a good that cannot be destroyed by external causes. Because the process of inquiry itself allays the anxieties that usually accompany the pursuit of material objectives, he has an indication of the direction in which he must look for true happiness.

When I saw that all these ordinary objects of desire would be obstacles in the way of a search for something different and new—nay, that they were so opposed thereto, that either they or it would have to be abandoned, I was forced to inquire which would prove the most useful to me: for, as I say, I seemed to be willingly losing hold on a sure good for the sake of something uncertain. However, after I had reflected on the matter, I came in the first place to the conclusion that by abandoning the ordinary objects of pursuit, and betaking myself to a new quest, I should be leaving a good, uncertain by reason of its own nature, as may be gathered from what has been said, for the sake of a good not uncertain in its nature (for I sought for a fixed good), but only in the possibility of its attainment.

Further reflection convinced me, that if I could really get to the root of the matter I should be leaving certain evils for a certain good. I thus perceived that I was in a state of great peril, and I compelled myself to seek with all my strength for a remedy, however uncertain it might be; as a sick man struggling with a deadly disease, when he sees that death will surely be upon him unless a remedy be found, is compelled to seek such a remedy with all his strength, inasmuch as his whole hope lies therein. All the objects pursued by the multitude not only bring no remedy that tends to preserve our being, but even act as hindrances, causing the death not seldom of those who possess them, and always of those who are possessed by them. There are many examples of men who have suffered persecution even to death for the sake of their riches, and of men who in pursuit of wealth have exposed themselves to so many dangers, that they have paid away their life as a penalty for their folly. Examples are no less numerous of men, who have endured the utmost wretchedness for the sake of gaining or preserving their reputation. Lastly, there are innumerable cases of men, who have hastened their death through overindulgence in sensual pleasure. All these evils seem to have arisen from the fact, that happiness or unhappiness is made wholly to depend on the quality of the object which we love. When a thing is not loved, no quarrels will arise concerning it—no sadness will be felt if it perishes—no envy if it is possessed by another—no fear, no hatred, in short no disturbances of the mind. All these arise from the love of what is perishable, such as the objects already mentioned. But love towards a thing eternal and infinite feeds the mind wholly with joy, and is itself unmingled with any sadness, wherefore it is greatly to be desired and sought for with all our strength. Yet it was not at random that I used the words, "If I could go to the root of the matter," for, though what I have urged was perfectly clear to my mind, I could not forthwith lay aside all love of riches, sensual enjoyment, and fame. One thing was evident, namely, that while my mind was employed with these thoughts it turned away from its former objects of desire, and seriously considered the search for a new principle; this state of things was a great comfort to me, for I perceived that the evils were not such as to resist all remedies. Although these intervals were at first rare, and of very short duration, yet afterwards, as the true good became more and more discernible to me, they became more frequent and more lasting; especially after I had recognized that the acquisition of wealth, sensual pleasure, or fame, is only a hindrance, so long as they are sought as ends not as means; if they be sought as means, they will be under restraint, and, far from being hindrances, will further not a little the end for which they are sought, as I will show in due time.[c]

**3.** Spinoza concludes from this inquiry that although individuals' capabilities are limited, they can aspire to a greater perfection both for themselves and for others.

Man conceives a human character much more stable than his own, and sees that there is no reason why he should not himself acquire such a character. Thus he is led to seek for means which will bring him to this pitch of perfection, and calls everything which will serve as such means a true good. The chief good is that he should arrive, together with other individuals if possible, at the possession of the aforesaid character. What that character is we shall show in due time, namely, that it is the knowledge of the union existing between the mind and the whole of nature. This, then, is the end for which I strive, to attain to such a character myself, and to endeavor that many should attain to it with me. In other words, it is part of my happiness to lend a helping hand, that many others may understand even as I do, so that their understanding and desire may entirely agree with my own. In order to bring this about, it is necessary to understand as much of nature as will enable us to attain to the aforesaid character, and also to form a social order such as is most conducive to the attainment of this character by the greatest number with the least difficulty and danger.[d]

**4.** In the essay "On the Improvement of the Understanding," Spinoza cautions us that "before all things, a means must be devised for improving the understanding and purifying it, as far as may be at the outset, so that it may apprehend things without error, and in the best possible way." Therefore, in his detailed and systematic work, the *Ethics,* he both presents his positive theory and exposes the conceptual errors that mislead individuals in their search for happiness. One of the common misconceptions results from viewing the world as God's purposive scheme. Because of this mistake, people are misled into believing that objects and events in nature are either inherently good or inherently bad.

There remain misconceptions not a few, which might and may prove very grave hindrances to the understanding of the concatenation of things.... I have therefore thought it worthwhile to bring these misconceptions before the bar of reason.

All such opinions spring from the notion commonly entertained, that all things in nature act as men themselves act, namely, with an end in view. It is accepted as certain, that God himself directs all things to a definite goal (for it is said that God made all things for man, and man that he might worship him). I will, therefore, consider this opinion, asking first, why it obtains general credence, and why men are naturally so prone to adopt it? Secondly, I will point out its falsity; and, lastly, I will show how it has given rise to prejudices about good and bad, right and wrong, praise and blame, order and confusion, beauty and ugliness, and the like. However, this is not the place to deduce these misconceptions from the nature of the human mind. It will be sufficient here, if I assume as a starting point, what ought to be universally admitted, namely, that all men are born ignorant of the causes of things, that all have the desire to seek what is useful to them, and that they are conscious of such desire. Herefrom it follows, first, that men think themselves free inasmuch as they are conscious of their volitions and desires, and never even dream, in their ignorance, of the causes which have disposed them so to wish and desire. Secondly, that men do all things for an end, namely, for that which is useful to them, and which they seek. Thus it comes to pass that they only look for a knowledge of the final causes of events, and when these are learned, they are content, as having no cause for further doubt. If they cannot learn such causes from external sources, they are compelled to turn to considering themselves, and reflecting what end would have induced them personally to bring about the given event, and thus they necessarily judge other natures by their own. Further, as they find in themselves and outside themselves many means which assist them not a little in their search for what is useful, for instance, eyes for seeing, teeth for chewing, herbs and animals for yielding food, the sun for giving light, the sea for breeding fish, &c., they come to look on the whole of nature as a means for obtaining such conveniences. Now as they are aware, that they found these conveniences and did not make them, they think they have cause for believing, that some other being has made them for their use....

Consider, I pray you, the result: among the many helps of nature they were bound to find some hindrances, such as storms, earthquakes, diseases, &c.: so they declared that such things happen, because the gods are angry at some wrong done them by men, or at some fault committed in their worship. Experience day by day protested and showed by infinite examples, that good and evil fortunes fall to the lot of pious and impious alike; still they would not abandon their inveterate prejudice, for it was more easy for them to class such contradictions among other unknown things of whose use they were ignorant, and thus to retain their actual and innate condition of ignorance, than to destroy the whole fabric of their reasoning and start afresh....

We must not omit to notice that the followers of this doctrine, anxious to display their talent in assigning final causes, have imported a new method of argument in proof of their theory—namely, a reduction, not to the impossible, but to ignorance; thus showing that they have no other method of exhibiting their doctrine. For example, if a stone falls from a roof on to someone's head, and kills him, they will demonstrate by their new method, that the stone fell in order to kill the man; for, if it had not by God's will fallen with that object, how could so many circumstances (and there are often many concurrent circumstances) have all happened together by chance? Perhaps you will answer that the event is due to the facts that the wind was blowing, and the man was walking that way. "But why," they will insist, "was the wind blowing and why was the man at that very time walking that way?" If you again answer, that the wind had then sprung up because the sea had begun to be agitated the day before, the weather being previously calm, and that the man had been invited by a friend, they will again insist: "But why was the sea agitated, and why was the man invited at that time?" So they will pursue their questions from cause to cause, till at last you take refuge in the will of God—in other words, the sanctuary of ignorance....

After men persuaded themselves, that everything which is created is created for their sake, they are bound to consider as the chief quality in everything that which is most useful to themselves, and to account those things the best of all which have the most beneficial effect on mankind. Further, they were bound to form abstract notions for the explanation of the nature of things, such as *goodness, badness, order, confusion, warmth, cold, beauty, deformity,* and so on....

Everything which conduces to health and the worship of God they have called *good,* everything which hinders these objects they have styled *bad;* and inasmuch as those who do not understand the nature of things do not verify phenomena in any way, but merely imagine them after a fashion, and mistake their imagination for understanding, such persons firmly believe that there is an *order* in things, being really ignorant both of things and their own nature.[e]

**5.** Spinoza finds the doctrine of free will to be particularly pernicious. In his judgment, it is from ignorance of the true causes of our actions that we come to believe that anything we do can possibly be otherwise than it actually is. The will is nothing but a form of the intellect, he argues, and as such can act only according to the fixed laws that govern all thought.

Thus an infant believes that of its own free will it desires milk, an angry child believes that it freely desires vengeance, a timid child believes that it freely desires to run away; further, a drunken man believes that he utters from the free decision of his mind words which, when he is sober, he would willingly have withheld: thus, too, a delirious man, a garrulous woman, a child, and others of like complexion, believe that they speak from the free decision of their mind, when they are in reality unable to restrain their impulse to talk. Experience teaches us no less clearly than reason, that men believe themselves to be free, simply because they are conscious of their actions, and unconscious of the causes whereby those actions are determined; and, further, it is plain that the dictates of the mind are but another name for the appetites, and therefore vary according to the varying state of the body. Everyone shapes his actions according to his emotion, those who are assailed by conflicting emotions know not what they wish; those who are not attacked by any emotion are readily swayed this way or that. All these considerations clearly show that a mental decision and a bodily appetite, or determined state, are simultaneous, or rather are one and the same thing, which we call decision, when it is regarded under and explained through the attribute of thought, and a conditioned state, when it is regarded under the attribute of extension, and deduced from the laws of motion and rest.... I wish to call attention to another point, namely, that we cannot act by the decision of the mind, unless we have a remembrance of having done so. For instance, we cannot say a word without remembering that we have done so. Again, it is not within the free power of the mind to remember or forget a thing at will. Therefore the freedom of the mind must in any case be limited to the power of uttering or not uttering something which it remembers. But when we dream that we speak, we believe that we speak from a free decision of the mind, yet we do not speak, or, if we do, it is by a spontaneous motion of the body. Again, we dream that we are concealing something, and we seem to act from the same decision of the mind as that, whereby we keep silence when awake concerning something we know. Lastly, we dream that from the free decision of our mind we do something, which we should not dare to do when awake.

Now I should like to know whether there be in the mind two sorts of decisions, one sort illusive, and the other sort free? If our folly does not carry us so far as this, we must necessarily admit, that the decision of the mind, which is believed to be free, is not distinguishable from the imagination or memory, and is nothing more than the affirmation, which an idea, by virtue of being an idea, necessarily involves. Wherefore these decisions of the mind arise in the mind by the same necessity, as the ideas of things actually existing. Therefore those who believe, that they speak or keep silence or act in any way from the free decision of their mind, do but dream with their eyes open.[f]

**6.** Belief in the freedom of the will is pernicious, Spinoza maintains, because it introduces an element of uncertainty into life. Furthermore, the delusion that we have the power and freedom to do whatever we wish raises false hopes. True freedom, he says, is action in accordance with the laws of our reason. In support of his position, Spinoza enumerates its beneficial effects on human conduct. His doctrine is good, he says:

1. Inasmuch as it teaches us to act solely according to the decree of God, and to be partakers in the Divine nature, and so much the more, as we perform more perfect actions and more and more understand God. Such a doctrine not only completely tranquilizes our spirit, but also shows us where our highest happiness and blessedness is, namely, solely in the knowledge of God, whereby we are led to act only as love and piety shall bid us. We may thus clearly understand, how far astray from a true estimate of virtue are those who expect to be decorated by God with high rewards for their virtue, and their best actions, as for having endured the direst slavery; as if virtue and the service of God were not in itself happiness and perfect freedom.

2. Inasmuch as it teaches us, how we ought to conduct ourselves with respect to the gifts of fortune, or matters which are not in our own power, and do not follow from our nature. For it shows us, that we should await and endure fortune's smiles or frowns with an equal mind, seeing that all things follow from the eternal decree of God by the same necessity, as it follows from the essence of a triangle, that the three angles are equal to two right angles.

3. This doctrine raises social life, inasmuch as it teaches us to hate no man, neither to despise, to deride, to envy, or to be angry with any. Further, as it tells us that each should be content with his own, and helpful to his neighbor, not from any womanish pity, favor, or superstition, but solely by the guidance of reason, according as the time and occasion demand....

4. Lastly, this doctrine confers no small advantage on the commonwealth; for it teaches how citizens should be governed and led, not so as to become slaves, but so that they may freely do whatsoever things are best.[g]

**7.** Spinoza's approach to psychology reflects his deterministic view of human behavior. He asserts that the emotions are natural phenomena, subject to definite laws, and should therefore be studied according to the same geometrical method as the rest of nature.

Most writers on the emotions and on human conduct seem to be treating rather of matters outside nature than of natural phenomena following nature's general laws. They appear to conceive man to be situated in nature as a kingdom within a kingdom: for they believe that he disturbs rather than follows nature's order, that he has absolute control over his actions, and that he is determined solely by himself. They attribute human infirmities and fickleness, not to the power of nature in general, but to some mysterious flaw in the nature of man, which accordingly they bemoan, deride, despise, or, as usually happens, abuse: he, who succeeds in hitting off the weakness of the human mind more eloquently or more acutely than his fellows, is looked upon as a seer. Still there has been no lack of very excellent men (to whose toil and industry I confess myself much indebted), who have written many noteworthy things concerning the right way of life, and have given much sage advice to mankind. But no one, so far as I know, has defined the nature and strength of the emotions, and the power of the mind against them for their restraint.

...Such persons will doubtless think it strange that I should attempt to treat of human vice and folly geometrically, and should wish to set forth with rigid reasoning those matters which they cry out against as repugnant to reason, frivolous, absurd, and dreadful. However, such is my plan. Nothing comes to pass in nature, which can be set down to a flaw therein; for nature is always the same, and everywhere one and the same in her efficacy and power of action; that is, nature's laws and ordinances, whereby all things come to pass and change from one form to another, are everywhere and always the same; so that there should be one and the same method of understanding the nature of all things whatsoever, namely, through nature's universal laws and rules. Thus the passions of hatred, anger, envy, and so on, considered in themselves, follow from this same necessity and efficacy of nature; they answer to certain definite causes, through which they are understood, and possess certain properties as worthy of being known as the properties of anything else, whereof the contemplation in itself affords us delight. I shall, therefore, treat of the nature and strength of the emotions according to the same method, as I employed heretofore in my investigations concerning God and the mind. I shall consider human actions and desires in exactly the same manner, as though I were concerned with lines, planes, and solids.[h]

**8.** The focal point of Spinoza's complex psychological theory is the concept of the striving (*conatus*) for self-preservation and self-perfection that characterizes all things. The drive to preserve our existence and perfect our essential nature is not only the basis of all behavior, but it is also the foundation of virtue. Because our essential nature is rational, the preservation of our being prescribes obedience to reason, and this constitutes virtue.

PROP. XX. The more every man endeavors, and is able to seek what is useful to him—in other words, to preserve his own being—the more is he endowed with virtue; on the contrary, in proportion as a man neglects to seek what is useful to him, that is, to preserve his own being, he is wanting in power....

PROP. XXI. No one can desire to be blessed, to act rightly, and to live rightly, without at the same time wishing to be, to act, and to live—in other words, to actually exist....

PROP. XXII. No virtue can be conceived as prior to this endeavor to preserve one's own being....

*Corollary.*—The effort for self-preservation is the first and only foundation of virtue. For prior to this principle, nothing can be conceived, and without it no virtue can be conceived....

PROP. XXIV. To act absolutely in obedience to virtue is in us the same thing as to act, to live, or to preserve one's being (these three terms are identical in meaning) in accordance with the dictates of reason on the basis of seeking what is useful to one's self....

PROP. XXVI. Whatsoever we endeavor in obedience to reason is nothing further than to understand; neither does the mind, insofar as it makes use of reason, judge anything to be useful to it, save such things as are conducive to understanding.

*Proof.*—The effort for self-preservation is nothing else but the essence of the thing in question, which, insofar as it exists such as it is, is conceived to have force for continuing in existence and doing such things as necessarily follow from its given nature. But the essence of reason is nought else but our mind, insofar as it clearly and distinctly understands; therefore whatsoever we endeavor in obedience to reason is nothing else but to understand. Again, since this effort of the mind wherewith the mind endeavors, insofar as it reasons, to preserve its own being is nothing else but understanding; this effort at understanding is the first and single basis of virtue, nor shall we endeavor to understand things for the sake of any ulterior object; on the other hand, the mind, insofar as it reasons, will not be able to conceive any good for itself, save such things as are conducive to understanding.[i]

**9.** The same striving for self-preservation that dictates conformity to reason generates the powerful emotions, *desire, pleasure,* and *pain,* from which all other emotions are derived. Even judgments of good and evil are decided by the emotions: People term *good* those things which give pleasure, that is, whatever they believe increases their perfection; they term *evil* those things which are painful, that is, whatever they believe diminishes their perfection.[2] That is to say:

We in no case desire a thing because we deem it good, but, contrariwise, we deem a thing good because we desire it: consequently we deem evil that which we shrink from; everyone, therefore, according to his particular emotions, judges or estimates what is good, what is bad, what is better, what is worse, lastly, what is best, and what is worst. Thus a miser thinks that abundance of money is the best, and want of money the worst; an ambitious man desires nothing so much as glory, and fears nothing so much as shame. To an envious man nothing is more delightful than another's misfortune, and nothing more painful than another's success. So every man, according to his emotions, judges a thing to be good or bad, useful or useless.[j]

**10.** Spinoza defines the knowledge of good and evil in terms of the emotions of pleasure and pain. Then, on the ground that "an emotion can only be controlled or destroyed by another emotion," not by a mere idea, he asserts that the effectiveness of the knowledge of good and evil is proportionate to its own emotive force, not to its truth. The emotions vary in their power, and the emotive strength of ordinary moral knowledge may easily be overwhelmed by baser emotions.

PROP. VIII. The knowledge of good and evil is nothing else but the emotions of pleasure or pain, insofar as we are conscious thereof.

*Proof.*—We call a thing good or evil, when it is of service or the reverse in preserving our being, that is, when it increases or diminishes, helps or hinders, our power of activity. Thus, insofar as we perceive that a thing affects us with pleasure or pain, we call it good or evil; wherefore the knowledge of good and evil is nothing else but the idea of the pleasure or pain, which necessarily follows from that pleasurable or painful emotion. . . .

PROP. XIV. A true knowledge of good and evil cannot check any emotion by virtue of being true, but only insofar as it is considered as an emotion.

*Proof.*—An emotion is an idea, whereby the mind affirms of its body a greater or less force of existing than before; therefore it has no positive quality, which can be destroyed by the presence of what is true; consequently the knowledge of good and evil cannot, by virtue of being true, restrain any emotion. But, insofar as such knowledge is an emotion if it have more strength for restraining emotion, it will to that extent be able to restrain the given emotion. Q.E.D.

PROP. XV. Desire arising from the knowledge of good and bad can be quenched or checked by many of the other desires arising from the emotions whereby we are assailed.

*Proof.*—From the true knowledge of good and evil, insofar as it is an emotion, necessarily arises desire, the strength of which is proportioned to the strength of the emotion wherefrom

---

[2]It follows from Spinoza's theory that judgments of good and evil are subject to three kinds of error: (1) people may judge as pleasant, that is, as good, things which do not actually conserve their rational nature, for example, fame, wealth, and sensual pleasures; (2) it may not be realized that good and evil do not belong to objects considered in themselves, but are only relative to the emotions of pleasure and pain; and (3) pleasure, the *criterion* of human good, may be mistaken for the *source* of the true good for humans, which is the knowledge of God.

it arises. But, inasmuch as this desire arises (by hypothesis) from the fact of our truly understanding anything, it follows that it is also present with us, insofar as we are active, and must therefore be understood through our essence only; consequently its force and increase can be defined solely by human power. Again, the desires arising from the emotions whereby we are assailed are stronger, in proportion as the said emotions are more vehement; wherefore their force and increase must be defined solely by the power of external causes, which, when compared with our own power, indefinitely surpass it; hence the desires arising from like emotions may be more vehement, than the desire which arises from a true knowledge of good and evil, and may, consequently, control or quench it. Q.E.D.

PROP. XVI. Desire arising from the knowledge of good and evil, insofar as such knowledge regards what is future, may be more easily controlled or quenched, than the desire for what is agreeable at the present moment.

*Proof.*—Emotion towards a thing, which we conceive as future, is fainter than emotion towards a thing that is present. But desire which arises from the true knowledge of good and evil, though it be concerned with things which are good at the moment, can be quenched or controlled by any headstrong desire (by the last Prop., the proof whereof is of universal application). Wherefore desire arising from such knowledge, when concerned with the future, can be more easily controlled or quenched, etc. Q.E.D.

PROP. XVII. Desire arising from the true knowledge of good and evil, insofar as such knowledge is concerned with what is contingent, can be controlled far more easily still, than desire for things that are present.

*Note.*—I think I have now shown the reason, why men are moved by opinion more readily than by true reason, why it is that the true knowledge of good and evil stirs up conflicts in the soul, and often yields to every kind of passion. This state of things gave rise to the exclamation of the poet:—

> "The better path I gaze at and approve,
> The worse—I follow."

Ecclesiastes seems to have had the same thought in his mind, when he says, "He who increaseth knowledge increaseth sorrow." I have not written the above with the object of drawing the conclusion, that ignorance is more excellent than knowledge, or that a wise man is on a par with a fool in controlling his emotions, but because it is necessary to know the power and the infirmity of our nature, before we can determine what reason can do in restraining the emotions, and what is beyond her power.[k]

> **11.** "Human infirmity in moderating and checking the emotions" Spinoza calls bondage, "for, when a man is a prey to his emotions he is not his own master, but lies at the mercy of fortune." By contrast, people are free when their actions are determined solely by the laws of their reason. The power of the mind to understand the emotions determines the extent to which freedom can be achieved. But it is particularly difficult to control the emotions, or passions, that arise when the mind is passive, that is, responsive to external causes rather than expressive of the inner activity of the mind. When human actions and judgments are dominated by such "passive" emotions as love and hate, hope and fear, envy and anger, the moral influence of the emotions associated with the *active* intellect is necessarily feeble by comparison. But, reaffirming his confidence in the power of reason, Spinoza assures us that with a sober appreciation of the strength of the emotions, we are able to pass from bondage to freedom.

PROP. III. An emotion which is a passion ceases to be a passion, as soon as we form a clear and distinct idea thereof.

*Proof.*—An emotion which is a passion is a confused idea. If, therefore, we form a clear and distinct idea of a given emotion, that idea will only be distinguished from the emotion, insofar as it is referred to the mind only, by reason; therefore, the emotion will cease to be a passion. Q.E.D.

*Corollary.*—An emotion therefore becomes more under our control, and the mind is less passive in respect to it, in proportion as it is more known to us.

. . . Everyone has the power of clearly and distinctly understanding himself and his emotions, if not absolutely, at any rate in part, and consequently of bringing it about, that he should become less subject to them. To attain this result, therefore, we must chiefly direct our efforts to acquiring, as far as possible, a clear and distinct knowledge of every emotion, in order that the mind may thus, through emotion, be determined to think of those things which it clearly and distinctly perceives, and wherein it fully acquiesces: and thus that the emotion itself may be separated from the thought of an external cause, and may be associated with true thoughts; whence it will come to pass, not only that love, hatred, etc., will be destroyed, but also that the appetites or desires, which are wont to arise from such emotion, will become incapable of being excessive.[l]

**12.** The contrast between those things which are known to occur necessarily and those things which it is believed may possibly have been otherwise is also relevant to the achievement of freedom. When reason governs, people understand that in this determinate universe, all things are as they must be and cannot be otherwise. As a consequence, they are better able to control the passions.

PROP. VI. The mind has greater power over the emotions and is less subject thereto, insofar as it understands all things as necessary.

*Proof.*—The mind understands all things to be necessary and to be determined to existence and operation by an infinite chain of causes; therefore, it thus far brings it about, that it is less subject to the emotions arising therefrom, and feels less emotion toward the things themselves. Q.E.D.

*Note.*—The more this knowledge, that things are necessary, is applied to particular things, which we conceive more distinctly and vividly, the greater is the power of the mind over the emotions, as experience also testifies. For we see, that the pain arising from the loss of any good is mitigated, as soon as the man who has lost it perceives, that it could not by any means have been preserved. So also we see that no one pities an infant, because it cannot speak, walk, or reason, or lastly, because it passes so many years, as it were, in unconsciousness. Whereas, if most people were born full-grown and only one here and there as an infant, everyone would pity the infants; because infancy would not then be looked on as a state natural and necessary, but as a fault or delinquency in Nature; and we may note several other instances of the same sort.[m]

**13.** It has now been made clear that the passage from the state of bondage to the state of freedom requires the assiduous application of reason. Not only the emotions, but also the whole order of Nature must be studied, and the continuous study of the casual order of Nature leads ultimately to the highest or "third" kind of knowledge.[3] At this level, the mind no longer views things merely as finite and temporal, but rather, it grasps their essential characteristics under the aspect of eternity. People come to understand themselves as part of God, or Nature, both bodily and mentally. By this means, it is possible to achieve the greatest good, namely, the intellectual love of God.

PROP. XXV. The highest endeavor of the mind, and the highest virtue is to understand things by the third kind of knowledge.

*Proof.*—The third kind of knowledge proceeds from an adequate idea of certain attributes of God to an adequate knowledge of the essence of things; and, in proportion as we understand things more in this way, we better understand God; therefore the highest virtue of the mind, that is the power, or nature, or highest endeavor of the mind, is to understand things by the third kind of knowledge. Q.E.D.

---

[3]Knowledge of the first kind is mere belief or imagination; knowledge of the second kind is scientific knowledge or knowledge of causes and effects; and knowledge of the third kind is "intuition," in which individual things are understood through a comprehension of God.

PROP. XXIX. Whatsoever the mind understands under the form of eternity, it does not understand by virtue of conceiving the present actual existence of the body, but by virtue of conceiving the essence of the body under the form of eternity.

PROP. XXX. Our mind, insofar as it knows itself and the body under the form of eternity, has to that extent necessarily a knowledge of God, and knows that it is in God, and is conceived through God.

*Proof.*—Eternity is the very essence of God, insofar as this involves necessary existence. Therefore to conceive things under the form of eternity, is to conceive things insofar as they are conceived through the essence of God as real entities, or insofar as they involve existence through the essence of God; wherefore our mind, insofar as it conceives itself and the body under the form of eternity, has to that extent necessarily a knowledge of God, and knows etc. Q.E.D.

PROP. XXXII. Whatsoever we understand by the third kind of knowledge, we take delight in, and our delight is accompanied by the idea of God as cause.

*Proof.*—From this kind of knowledge arises the highest possible mental acquiescence, that is, pleasure, and this acquiescence is accompanied by the idea of the mind itself, and consequently the idea of God as cause. Q.E.D.

*Corollary.*—From the third kind of knowledge necessarily arises the intellectual love of God. From this kind of knowledge arises pleasure accompanied by the idea of God as cause, that is, the love of God; not insofar as we imagine him as present, but insofar as we understand him to be eternal; this is what I call the intellectual love of God.

PROP. XXXIII. The intellectual love of God, which arises from the third kind of knowledge, is eternal.[n]

**14.** Spinoza reviews the findings of his ethical theory:

In order that this power of the mind over the emotions may be better understood, it should be specially observed that the emotions are called by us strong, when we compare the emotion of one man with the emotion of another, and see that one man is more troubled than another by the same emotion; or when we are comparing the various emotions of the same man one with another, and find that he is more affected or stirred by one emotion than by another. For the strength of every emotion is defined by a comparison of our own power with the power of an external cause. Now the power of the mind is defined by knowledge only, and its infirmity or passion is defined by the privation of knowledge only: it therefore follows, that the mind is most passive, whose greatest part is made up of inadequate ideas, so that it may be characterized more readily by its passive states than by its activities: on the other hand, that mind is most active, whose greatest part is made up of adequate ideas, so that, although it may contain as many inadequate ideas as the former mind, it may yet be more easily characterized by ideas attributable to human virtue, than by ideas which tell of human infirmity. Again, it must be observed, that spiritual unhealthiness and misfortunes can generally be traced to excessive love for something which is subject to many variations, and which we can never become masters of. For no one is solicitous or anxious about anything, unless he loves it; neither do wrongs, suspicions, enmities, etc., arise, except in regard to things whereof no one can be really master.

We may thus readily conceive the power which clear and distinct knowledge, and especially that third kind of knowledge, founded on the actual knowledge of God, possesses over the emotions: if it does not absolutely destroy them, insofar as they are passions; at any rate, it causes them to occupy a very small part of the mind. Further, it begets a love towards a thing immutable and eternal, whereof we may really enter into possession; neither can it be defiled with those faults which are inherent in ordinary love; but it may grow from strength to strength, and may engross the greater part of the mind, and deeply penetrate it.[o]

**15.** The closing of *The Ethics* is a final eulogy to the rational life.

*Note.*—I have thus completed all I wished to set forth touching the mind's power over the emotions and the mind's freedom. Whence it appears, how potent is the wise man, and how much he surpasses the ignorant man, who is driven only by his lusts. For the ignorant man is not only distracted in various ways by external causes without ever gaining the true acquiescence of his spirit, but moreover lives, as it were unwitting of himself, and of God, and of things, and as soon as he ceases to suffer, ceases also to be.

Whereas the wise man, insofar as he is regarded as such, is scarcely at all disturbed in spirit, but, being conscious of himself, and of God, and of things, by a certain eternal necessity, never ceases to be, but always possesses true acquiescence of his spirit.

If the way which I have pointed out as leading to this result seems exceedingly hard, it may nevertheless be discovered. Needs must it be hard, since it is so seldom found. How would it be possible, if salvation were ready to our hand, and could without great labor be found, that it should be by almost all men neglected? But all things excellent are as difficult as they are rare.[p]

## QUESTIONS

1. Discuss the significance for Spinoza's ethical theory of his statement, "Whatever is, is in God."
2. Explain Spinoza's belief that "the love of what is perishable" is incompatible with true happiness. Do you agree with his position?
3. Why does Spinoza attach great importance to "the improvement of the understanding"?
4. What difference to ethical theory does it make when one denies that the universe is a purposive scheme?
5. What reasons does Spinoza give for his belief that it is morally wrong to believe that people have free will? In what sense does he say we are "free"?
6. Discuss the ethical significance of Spinoza's doctrine of *conatus,* the striving for self-preservation and self-perfection.
7. How does Spinoza estimate the relative strength of emotion and reason? What method does he recommend for the study of the emotions?
8. What are the means by which people can escape from human bondage? Are there any external forces that can aid humans to pass from bondage to freedom?
9. Why does Spinoza devote himself to a detailed discussion of the emotions? What connection does he establish between emotion and error? What moral significance does he attach to intellectual error?
10. Explain what is meant by "the intellectual love of God." How does this enter into the moral life?

## KEY TO SELECTIONS

Benedict de Spinoza, *On the Improvement of the Understanding* and *The Ethics*, tr. R. H. M. Elwes, from *The Chief Works of Benedict Spinoza*, vol. II, London, George Bell, 1898. Proofs, corollaries, notes, and references to prior proofs have been omitted from selections from *The Ethics*, except where otherwise indicated.

From *On the Improvement of the Understanding*
[b]pp. 3–4.
[c]pp. 4–6.
[d]pp. 6–7.

From *Ethics*
[a]Part IV, Prop. LXXIII, Note.
[e]Part I, Appendix.
[f]Part III, Prop. II, Note.
[g]Part II, Prop. XLIX, Note.
[h]Part III, Introduction.
[i]Part IV.
[j]Part III, Prop. XXXIX, Note.
[k]Part IV.
[l–p]Part V.

## GUIDE TO ADDITIONAL READING


### PRIMARY SOURCES

Spinoza, B., *Ethics*, Hafner Library of Classics (Hafner).

———, *Ethics, On the Correction of the Understanding*, Everyman's Library (Dutton).

*Spinoza Selections*, Modern Student's Library (Scribner's).

*The Philosophy of Spinoza*, Modern Library (Random House).

### DISCUSSION AND COMMENTARY

Bennett, Jonathan, *A Study of Spinoza's Ethics*, Indianapolis, Hackett, 1984.

Broad, C. D., *Five Types of Ethical Theory*, New York, Harcourt, Brace, 1928, Ch. 2.

Curley, E. M., *Spinoza's Metaphysics: An Essay in Interpretation*, Cambridge, Mass., Harvard University Press, 1969.

Frankena, W. K., "Spinoza's New Morality: Notes on Book IV," in *Spinoza: Essays and Interpretations*, ed. E. Freeman and M. Mandelbaum, LaSalle, Open Court, 1975, pp. 85–100.

Garrett, Don (ed.), *Cambridge Companion to Spinoza*, Cambridge, Cambridge University Press, 1996.

Grene, Marjorie (ed.), *Spinoza: A Collection of Critical Essays*, Garden City, Doubleday, 1973.

Hampshire, S., *Spinoza*, Harmondsworth, Penguin Books, 1954.

Joachim, H. H., *A Study of the Ethics of Spinoza*, Oxford, Clarendon Press, 1901.

McKeon, R., *The Philosophy of Spinoza*, New York, Longmans, Green, 1928.

Wolfson, H. A., *The Philosophy of Spinoza*, Cambridge, Harvard University Press, 1948.

C H A P T E R T E N

# Conscience in Morality

JOSEPH BUTLER

JOSEPH BUTLER (1692–1752) is a splendid example of a Christian who was both sincere in his faith and reasonable in his judgment. The youngest of eight children, he was born at Wantage, England, just three years after passage of the Toleration Act that allowed all religious sects to worship freely. His father, a middle-class shopkeeper and a God-fearing member of the Protestant Dissenters (a Presbyterian group), recognized early that his son was intellectually gifted and determined that he should be trained for the ministry. Accordingly, Joseph was sent to a grammar school and then to Tewkesbury Academy, where he distinguished himself by his originality in theology. While he was at the Academy, however, he became convinced that the relatively liberal doctrine of the Dissenters was inferior to the conservative theology of the Church of England. In view of this challenge of allegiance, in 1714 he entered Oriel College, Oxford, where, despite his disappointment at finding the lectures "frivolous" and the disputations "unintelligible," he completed his theological training. Butler's ecclesiastical career, in which he made his reputation at once, began in 1719 when he was appointed preacher to the Rolls Chapel in London.

Butler's first published work was *Fifteen Sermons Preached at the Rolls Chapel* (1726). Although it has been said that these were wonderful sermons to sleep through, they contain his chief statement of ethical theory. He was assigned to the obscure parsonage of Stanhope the same year that his book appeared. When, in the year 1736, Queen Caroline asked whether the brilliant Butler were dead, she was told, "No, madam, he is not *dead*, but he is *buried*." Thereupon Butler was recalled to London to serve as a court chaplain. Almost immediately upon his arrival, *The Analogy of Religion, Natural and Revealed, to the Constitution and Course of*

*Nature* (1736) was published. This became one of the most influential books of the century, despite the uncompromising difficulty of its argument. In it, Butler comes to the defense of *Theism*—the traditional view that God, though a transcendent Being, is immanent in the universe and concerned with human affairs—against the doctrine of *Deism*—the view that because God is a transcendent Being, he can have no concern with or influence on human affairs.

His fame secure, Butler was elevated to the Deanery of St. Paul in 1740. King George II, however, was still not satisfied with the recognition accorded to him and opened the way to additional promotions and honors. At the time of his death, Butler occupied the important Bishopric of Durham. He remains the most capable defender of his faith against religious skepticism and the free thinking of the Age of Reason.

Bishop Joseph Butler is the most distinguished in a line of English and Scottish philosophers for whom the ground of morality is "conscience." In his ethical theory, conscience is conceived as a *reflective or rational faculty that discerns the moral characteristics of actions.* Consequently, he is not a defender of the popular, unsophisticated view that the conscience is like an additional eye that can perceive directly the rightness or wrongness of conduct. Nevertheless, his conception of it is closer to this view than to the one in which "conscience" is understood as a name for mere feelings of approval and disapproval due to psychological and social conditioning. For him, the judgments of conscience are based not on moral sense or feelings but on moral reason.

Although Butler was a devoutly religious clergyman, he studiously avoids basing his arguments on supernatural authority. The general goal of his philosophical inquiry is the substantiation of revealed Christianity by means of a reasoned study of human nature. For his purpose, it would be begging the question to argue from the same revelations that he intends to reinforce. Accordingly, he resolves to confirm the Christian principles through data that each person can find within. Against the contention of his educated contemporaries that reasoning conflicts with revealed religion and discredits it, Butler holds that the results of his rational method of introspection will be evidence for, rather than against, Christianity:

> It is come, I know not how, to be taken for granted by many persons that Christianity is not so much a subject of inquiry; but that it is, now at length, discovered to be fictitious. And accordingly they treat it as if, in the present age, this were an agreed point among all people of discernment; and nothing remained, but to set it up as a principal subject of mirth and ridicule, as it were by way of reprisals, for its having so long interrupted the pleasures of the world. On the contrary, thus much at least will be here found, not taken for granted, but proved, that any reasonable man, who will thoroughly consider the matter may be as much assured as he is of his own being, that it is not, however, so clear a case, that there is nothing in it. There is, I think, strong evidence of its truth; but it is certain no one can, upon principles of reason, be satisfied of the contrary.[1]

The intellectual basis for irreligion in the England of Butler's day consisted of a fusion of two assumptions: that people are exclusively egoistic (that is, they are

[1] J. Butler, "Advertisement" prefixed to *The Analogy of Religion, Natural and Revealed, to the Constitution and Course of Nature* (New York: Robert Carter, 1849).

committed solely to promoting their own good) and that no moral obligation is valid if it runs counter to the way people are by nature capable of acting. Butler rejects the first of these as bad psychology in general; and in particular, he criticizes Thomas Hobbes, the most influential exponent of the egoistic theory. According to Butler, Hobbes failed to detect the difference between the *immediate gratification of desire* and the *achievement of self-preservation*. The former, being merely a momentary satisfaction of a particular drive, may or may not serve a person's genuine self-interest. On the other hand, self-preservation, which is a form of self-love, represents a selection of desires that culminates in the individual's well-being. At the same time, Butler gives a classic refutation of psychological hedonism (the theory that pleasure is the motive of all conduct) by pointing out that although pleasure *accompanies* the satisfaction of desire, the desire is for a particular object, not for the pleasure that accompanies it. Otherwise, desires would be "objectless" and not directed to *specific* situations.

Butler accepts with reservations the second of the assumptions made by the antireligious thinkers of his day; that is, he grants that rules governing what people ought to do must be confined to what they can do within the limits of human nature. However, he insists that a clear understanding of what is meant by "human nature" is necessary. To begin with, the springs of all human actions are specific passions and appetites, but introspection reveals that we also have the means by which these impulses can be regulated: self-love, benevolence, and conscience. In and of themselves, the basic drives and the desire to satisfy them are ethically neutral. For example, when one is driven by thirst, one's only object is to find water. However, the moral element appears when the problem of *regulation* is considered. Private and public well-being depend on the proper choice and limitation of the desires to be satisfied.

*Self-love* is the effective regulative principle that operates when individuals organize their desires to promote their own best interests. When they control their appetites to further the public good, the operative principle is that of *benevolence*. Yet, Butler tells us, there is no guarantee that these regulative principles of self-love and benevolence will always reinforce and complement one another. Under these circumstances, conflicts between personal and social interests are frequently resolved by a regulative principle of a higher order—namely, the *conscience*. The conscience is reason functioning at times as the arbiter of conflicting interests of self-love and benevolence; it is the author of and the authority for our moral obligations; it prompts us to the performance of our duties. Thus the conscience is the "knowledge of right" within us that makes us moral agents. We are unconditionally obligated to follow the dictates of conscience, Butler explains, because the conscience carries with it the "light of self-attestment." In other words, the authority of conscience is self-evident, and there can be no appeal from it to any higher principle.

Butler concludes that the results of his rational investigation of human nature and morality strengthen faith in Christian ethics through confirming its underlying principle. This he draws from Romans (2:14–15): "For when the Gentiles, which have not the law, do by nature the things contained in the law, these, having not the law, are a law unto themselves: Which show the work of the law written in their hearts, their conscience also bearing witness." For Butler, this means that "everyone may find within himself the rule of right, and obligations to follow it."

**1.** Butler's ethical theory rests upon a teleological conception of humans. He is convinced that in order to understand the ethical concepts "virtue" and "vice," one must first study the appropriate design and intent of human nature.

There are two ways in which the subject of morals may be treated. One begins from inquiring into the abstract relations of things: the other from a matter of fact, namely, what the particular nature of man is, its several parts, their economy or constitution; from whence it proceeds to determine what course of life it is, which is correspondent to this whole nature. In the former method the conclusion is expressed thus, that vice is contrary to the nature and reason of things: in the latter, that it is a violation or breaking in upon our own nature. Thus they both lead us to the same thing, our obligations to the practice of virtue; and thus they exceedingly strengthen and enforce each other. The first seems the most direct formal proof, and in some respects the least liable to cavil and dispute: the latter is in a peculiar manner adapted to satisfy a fair mind; and is more easily applicable to the several particular relations and circumstances in life.

The following Discourses proceed chiefly in this latter method.... They were intended to explain what is meant by the nature of man, when it is said that virtue consists in following, and vice in deviating from it; and by explaining to show that the assertion is true....

Whoever thinks it worthwhile to consider this matter thoroughly, should begin with stating to himself exactly the idea of a system, economy, or constitution of any particular nature, or particular anything: and he will, I suppose, find, that it is a one or a whole, made up of several parts; but yet, that the several parts even considered as a whole do not complete the idea, unless in the notion of a whole you include the relations and respects which those parts have to each other. Every work both of nature and of art is a system: and as every particular thing, both natural and artificial, is for some use or purpose out of and beyond itself, one may add, to what has been already brought into the idea of a system, its conduciveness to this one or more ends. Let us instance in a watch—Suppose the several parts of it taken to pieces, and placed apart from each other; let a man have ever so exact a notion of these several parts, unless he considers the respects and relations which they have to each other, he will not have anything like the idea of a watch. Suppose these several parts brought together and any how united: neither will he yet, be the union ever so close, have an idea which will bear any resemblance to that of a watch. But let him view those several parts put together, or consider them as to be put together in the manner of a watch; let him form a notion of the relations which those several parts have to each other—all conducive in their respective ways to this purpose, showing the hour of the day; and then he has the idea of a watch. Thus it is with regard to the inward frame of man.[a]

**2.** For Butler, then, human nature is a system whose constituent elements are harmoniously ordered. He examines several other meanings of the term *nature* and concludes that if they are employed, no ethical distinctions can be made.

If by following nature were meant only acting as we please, it would indeed be ridiculous to speak of nature as any guide in morals: nay the very mention of deviating from nature would be absurd; and the mention of following it, when spoken by way of distinction, would absolutely have no meaning. For did ever anyone act otherwise than as he pleased? And yet the ancients speak of deviating from nature as vice; and of following nature so much as a distinction, that according to them the perfection of virtue consists therein. So that language itself should teach people another sense to the words *following nature*, than barely acting as we please.

...By nature is often meant no more than some principle in man, without regard either to the kind or degree of it. Thus the passion of anger, and the affection of parents to their children, would be called equally *natural*. And as the same person hath often contrary principles, which at the same time draw contrary ways, he may by the same action both follow and contradict his nature in this sense of the word; he may follow one passion and contradict another.

. . . *Nature* is frequently spoken of as consisting in those passions which are strongest, and most influence the actions; which being vicious ones, mankind is in this sense naturally vicious, or vicious by nature. Thus Saint Paul says of the Gentiles, *who were dead in trespasses and sins, and walked according to the spirit of disobedience, that they were by nature the children of wrath.* They could be no otherwise *children of wrath*, by nature, than they were vicious by nature.[b]

**3.** Butler proceeds to a careful analysis of human nature as he understands it, to establish "that there are as real and the same kind of indications in human nature, that we were made for society and to do good to our fellow creatures, as that we were intended to take care of our own life and health and private good." He presents a detailed discussion of the appetites and passions and of two of the principles that regulate behavior: benevolence and self-love. Butler cautions against supposing that these principles are in natural opposition.

First, there is a natural principle of *benevolence* in man; which is in some degree to *society*, what *self-love* is to the *individual.* And if there be in mankind any disposition to friendship, if there be any such thing as compassion, for compassion is momentary love; if there be any such thing as the paternal or filial affections; if there be any affection in human nature, the object and end of which is the good of another, this is itself benevolence, or the love of another. Be it ever so short, be it in ever so low a degree, or ever so unhappily confined; it proves the assertion, and points out what we were designed for, as really as though it were in a higher degree and more extensive. I must, however, remind you that though benevolence and self-love are different; though the former tends most directly to public good, and the latter to private: yet they are so perfectly coincident that the greatest satisfactions to ourselves depend upon our having benevolence in a due degree; and that self-love is one chief security of our right behavior towards society. It may be added, that their mutual coinciding, so that we can scarce promote one without the other, is equally a proof that we were made for both.

Secondly, this will further appear, from observing that the *several passions* and *affections*, which are distinct, both from benevolence and self-love, do in general contribute and lead us to *public* good as really as to *private.* It might be thought too minute and particular, and would carry us too great a length, to distinguish between and compare together the several passions or appetites distinct from benevolence, whose primary use and intention is the security and good of society; and the passions distinct from self-love, whose primary intention and design is the security and good of the individual. It is enough to the present argument, that desire of esteem from others, contempt and esteem of them, love of society as distinct from affection to the good of it, indignation against successful vice, that these are public affections or passions; have an immediate respect to others, naturally lead us to regulate our behavior in such a manner as will be of service to our fellow creatures. If any or all of these may be considered likewise as private affections, as tending to private good; this does not hinder them from being public affections too, or destroy the good influence of them upon society, and their tendency to public good. It may be added, that as persons without any conviction from reason of the desirableness of life, would yet of course preserve it merely from the appetite of hunger; so by acting merely from regard (suppose) to reputation, without any consideration of the good of others, men often contribute to public good. In both these instances they are plainly instruments in the hands of another, in the hands of Providence, to carry on ends, the preservation of the individual and good of society, which they themselves have not in their view or intention. The sum is, men have various appetites, passions, and particular affections, quite distinct both from self-love and from benevolence: all of these have a tendency to promote both public and private good, and may be considered as respecting others and ourselves equally and in common: but some of them seem most immediately to respect others, or tend to public good; others of them most immediately to respect self, or tend to private good: as the former are not benevolence, so the latter are not self-love: neither sort are instances of our love either to ourselves or others; but only instances of our Maker's care and love both of the individual and the species, and proofs that he intended we should be instruments of good to each other, as well as that we should be so to ourselves.[c]

**4.** Butler criticizes further the erroneous but popular notion that there is a natural opposition between self-love and benevolence.

There seems no other reason to suspect that there is any such peculiar contrariety, but only that the courses of action which benevolence leads to, has a more direct tendency to promote the good of others, than that course of action, which love of reputation suppose, or any other particular affection leads to. But that any affection tends to the happiness of another, does not hinder its tending to one's own happiness too. That others enjoy the benefit of the air and the light of the sun, does not hinder but that these are as much one's own private advantage now, as they would be if we had the property of them exclusive of all others. So a pursuit which tends to promote the good of another, yet may have as great tendency to promote private interest, as a pursuit which does not tend to the good of another at all, or which is mischievous to him. All particular affections whatever, resentment, benevolence, love of arts, equally lead to a course of action for their own gratification, *i.e.*, the gratification of ourselves; and the gratification of each gives delight: so far then it is manifest they have all the same respect to private interest. Now take into consideration further, concerning these three pursuits, that the end of the first is the harm, of the second, the good of another, of the last, somewhat indifferent; and is there any necessity, that these additional considerations should alter the respect, which we before saw these three pursuits, had to private interest; or render any one of them less conducive to it, than any other? Thus one man's affection is to honor as his end; in order to obtain which he thinks no pains too great. Suppose another, with such a singularity of mind, as to have the same affection to public good as his end, which he endeavors with the same labor to obtain. In case of success, surely the man of benevolence hath as great enjoyment as the man of ambition; they both equally having the end of their affections, in the same degree, tended to: but in case of disappointment, the benevolent man has clearly the advantage; since endeavoring to do good considered as a virtuous pursuit, is gratified by its own consciousness, *i.e.*, is in a degree its own reward.[d]

**5.** After differentiating between self-love and benevolence, Butler turns to the task of refuting the popular belief that self-love is reducible to the unrestrained gratifications of impulses. He points out that any such reduction fails to take into account an important distinction: The object of self-love is general and internal (that is, the individual is concerned to achieve a lifetime of happiness), but the object of an impulse is particular and external (for example, the object of hunger is food, not the pleasure that arises from eating, and the object of revenge is to inflict pain, not the satisfaction of being avenged). Clearly, then, because impulses are specific and external, they can be in conflict with the long-term objective of self-love.

Every man hath a general desire of his own happiness; and likewise a variety of particular affections, passions, and appetites to particular external objects. The former proceeds from, or is self-love; and seems inseparable from all sensible creatures, who can reflect upon themselves and their own interest or happiness, so as to have that interest an object to their minds: what is to be said of the latter is, that they proceed from, or together make up that particular nature, according to which man is made. The object the former pursues is somewhat internal, our own happiness, enjoyment, satisfaction; whether we have, or have not, a distinct particular perception what it is, or wherein it consists: the objects of the latter are this or that particular external thing, which the affections tend towards, and of which it hath always a particular idea or perception. The principle we call self-love never seeks any thing external for the sake of the thing, but only as a means of happiness or good: particular affections rest in the external things themselves. One belongs to man as a reasonable creature reflecting upon his own interest or happiness. The other, though quite distinct from reason, are as much a part of human nature.

That all particular appetites and passions are towards *external things themselves*, distinct from the *pleasure arising from them*, is manifested from hence; that there could not be this pleasure, were it not for that prior suitableness between the object and the passion: there could be no enjoyment or delight from one thing more than another, from eating food more than from swallowing a stone, if there were not an affection or appetite to one thing more than another.

Every particular affection, even the love of our neighbor, is as really our own affection, as self-love; and the pleasure arising from its gratification is as much my own pleasure, as the pleasure self-love would have, from knowing I myself should be happy some time hence, would be my own pleasure. And if, because every particular affection is a man's own, and the pleasure arising from its gratification his own pleasure, or pleasure to himself, such particular affection must be called self-love; according to this way of speaking, no creature whatever can possibly act but merely from self-love; and every action and every affection whatever is to be resolved up into this one principle. But then this is not the language of mankind: if it were, we should want words to express the difference, between the principle of an action, proceeding from cool consideration that it will be to my own advantage; and an action, suppose of revenge, or of friendship, by which a man runs upon certain ruin, to do evil or good to another. It is manifest the principles of these actions are totally different, and so want different words to be distinguished by: all that they agree in is, that they both proceed from, and are done to gratify an inclination in a man's self. But the principle or inclination in one case is self-love: in the other, hatred or love of another. There is then a distinction between the cool principle of self-love, or general desire of our own happiness, as one part of our nature, and one principle of action; and the particular affections towards particular external objects, as another part of our nature, and another principle of action. How much soever therefore is to be allowed to self-love, yet it cannot be allowed to be the whole of our inward constitution; because, you see, there are other parts or principles which come into it.[e]

**6.** Through illustration, Butler strengthens the distinction between a governing principle and a particular impulse. He makes manifest the natural superiority of the one over the other.

Man may act according to that principle or inclination which for the present happens to be strongest, and yet act in a way disproportionate to, and violate his real proper nature. Suppose a brute creature by any bait to be allured into a snare, by which he is destroyed. He plainly followed the bent of his nature, leading him to gratify his appetite: there is an entire correspondence between his whole nature and such an action: such action therefore is natural. But suppose a man, foreseeing the same danger of certain ruin, should rush into it for the sake of a present gratification; he in this instance would follow his strongest desire, as did the brute creature: but there would be as manifest a disproportion, between the nature of a man and such an action, as between the meanest work of art and the skill of the greatest master in that art: which disproportion arises, not from considering the action singly in *itself*, or in its *consequences;* but from *comparison* of it with the nature of the agent. And since such an action is utterly disproportionate to the nature of man, it is in the strictest and most proper sense unnatural; this word expressing that disproportion. Therefore instead of the word *disproportionate to his nature*, the word *unnatural* may now be put; this being more familiar to us: but let it be observed, that it stands for the same thing precisely.

Now what is it which renders such a rash action unnatural? Is it that he went against the principle of reasonable and cool self-love, considered *merely* as a part of his nature? No: for if he had acted the contrary way, he would equally have gone against a principle, or part of his nature, namely, passion or appetite. But to deny a present appetite, from foresight that the gratification of it would end in immediate ruin or extreme misery, is by no means an unnatural action; whereas to contradict or go against cool self-love for the sake of such gratification, is so in the instance before us. Such an action then being unnatural; and its being so not arising from a man's going against a principle or desire barely, nor in going against that principle or desire which happens for the present to be strongest; it necessarily follows that there must be some other difference or distinction to be made between these two principles, passion and cool self-love, than what I have yet taken notice of. And this difference, not being a difference in strength or degree, I call a difference in *nature* and in *kind*. And since, in the instance still before us, if passion prevails over self-love, the consequent action is unnatural; but if self-love prevails over passion, the action is natural: it is manifest that self-love is in human nature a superior principle to passion. This may be contradicted without violating that nature; but the former cannot. So that, if we will act conformably to the economy of man's nature, reasonable self-love must govern. Thus, without particular consideration of conscience, we may have a clear conception of the *superior nature* of one inward principle to another; and see that there really is this natural superiority, quite distinct from degrees of strength and prevalency.[f]

> **7.** The highest of the governing principles is the reflective principle of conscience. It both influences and evaluates behavior by means of approval and disapproval.

There is a principle of reflection in men, by which they distinguish between, approve and disapprove their own actions. We are plainly constituted such sort of creatures as to reflect upon our own nature. The mind can take a view of what passes within itself, its propensions, aversions, passions, affections, as respecting such objects, and in such degrees; and of the several actions consequent thereupon. In this survey it approves of one, disapproves of another, and towards a third is affected in neither of these ways, but is quite indifferent. This principle in man, by which he approves or disapproves his heart, temper, and actions, is conscience; for this is the strict sense of the word, though sometimes it is used so as to take in more. And that this faculty tends to restrain men from doing mischief to each other, and leads them to do good, is too manifest to need being insisted upon. Thus a parent has the affection of love to his children: this leads him to take care of, to educate, to make due provision for them; the natural affection leads to this: but the reflection that it is his proper business, what belongs to him, that it is right and commendable so to do; this added to the affection becomes a much more settled principle, and carries him on through more labor and difficulties for the sake of his children, then he would undergo from that affection alone, if he thought it, and the course of action it led to, either indifferent or criminal. This indeed is impossible, to do that which is good and not to approve of it; for which reason they are frequently not considered as distinct, though they really are: for men often approve of the actions of others, which they will not imitate, and likewise do that which they approve not. It cannot possibly be denied that there is this principle of reflection or conscience in human nature. Suppose a man to relieve an innocent person in great distress; suppose the same man afterwards, in the fury of anger, to do the greatest mischief to a person who had given no just cause of offense; to aggravate the injury, add the circumstances of former friendship and obligation from the injured person; let the man who is supposed to have done these two different actions, coolly reflect upon them afterwards, without regard to their consequences to himself: to assert that any common man would be affected in the same way towards these different actions, that he would make no distinction between them, but approve or disapprove them equally, is too glaring a falsity to need being confuted. There is therefore this principle of reflection or conscience in mankind. It is needless to compare the respect it has to public; since it plainly tends as much to the latter as to the former, and is commonly thought to tend chiefly to the latter.[g]

**8.** It has already been pointed out that although benevolence and self-love may not always prevail over desire, their lack of power does not reduce their proper authority. The same contrast between actual power and natural authority is seen to apply to conscience. Even if conscience should fail to control conduct, it possesses its natural authority undiminished.

Let us now take a view of the nature of man, as consisting partly of various appetites, passions, affections, and partly of the principle of reflection or conscience; leaving quite out all consideration of the different degrees of strength, in which either of them prevail, and it will further appear that there is this natural superiority of one inward principle to another, and that it is even part of the idea of reflection or conscience.

Passion or appetite implies a direct simple tendency towards such and such objects, without distinction of the means by which they are to be obtained. Consequently it will often happen there will be a desire of particular objects, in cases where they cannot be obtained without manifest injury to others. Reflection or conscience comes in, and disapproves the pursuit of them in these circumstances; but the desire remains. Which is to be obeyed, appetite or reflection? Cannot this question be answered, from the economy and constitution of human nature merely, without saying which is strongest? Or need this at all come into consideration? Would not the question be *intelligibly* and fully answered by saying, that the principle of reflection or conscience being compared with the various appetites, passions, and affections in men, the former is manifestly superior and chief, without regard to strength? And how often soever the latter happens to prevail, it is mere *usurpation:* the former remains in nature and in kind its superior; and every instance of such prevalence of the latter is an instance of breaking in upon and violation of the constitution of man.

All this is no more than the distinction, which everybody is acquainted with, between *mere power* and *authority:* only instead of being intended to express the difference between what is possible, and what is lawful in civil government; here it has been shown applicable to the several principles in the mind of man. Thus that principle, by which we survey, and either approve or disapprove our own heart, temper, and actions, is not only to be considered as what is in its turn to have some influence; which may be said of every passion, of the lowest appetites: but likewise as being superior; as from its very nature manifestly claiming superiority over all others; insomuch that you cannot form a notion of this faculty, conscience, without taking in judgment, direction, super-intendency. This is a constituent part of the idea, that is, of the faculty itself: and, to preside and govern, from the very economy and constitution of man, belongs to it. Had it strength, as it had right; had it power, as it had manifest authority, it would absolutely govern the world.

This gives us a further view of the nature of man; shows us what course of life we were made for: not only that our real nature leads us to be influenced in some degree by reflection and conscience; but likewise in what degree we are to be influenced by it, if we will fall in with, and act agreeably to the constitution of our nature: that this faculty was placed within to be our proper governor; to direct and regulate all under principles, passions, and motives of action. This is its right and office: thus sacred is its authority. And how often soever men violate and rebelliously refuse to submit to it, for supposed interest which they cannot otherwise obtain, or for the sake of passion which they cannot otherwise gratify; this makes no alteration as to the *natural right* and *office* of conscience.[h]

**9.** The basis for the authority of conscience does not arise from any external source. Rather, the very existence of conscience is its own sufficient justification.

The inquiries which have been made by men of leisure after some general rule, the conformity to, or disagreement from which, should denominate our actions good or evil, are in many respects of great service. Yet let any plain honest man, before he engages in any course of action, ask himself, Is this I am going about right, or is it wrong? Is it good, or is it evil? I do not in the least doubt, but that this question would be answered agreeably to truth and virtue, by almost any fair man in almost any circumstance. Neither do there appear any cases which look like exceptions to this; but those of superstition, and of partiality to ourselves. Superstition may perhaps be somewhat of an exception: but partiality to ourselves is not; this being itself dishonesty. For a man to judge that to be the equitable, the moderate, the right part for him to act, which he would see to be hard, unjust, oppressive in another; this is plain vice, and can proceed only from great unfairness of mind.

But allowing that mankind hath the rule of right within himself, yet it may be asked, "What obligations are we under to attend to and follow it?" I answer: it has been proved that man by his nature is a law to himself, without the particular distinct consideration of the positive sanctions of that law; the rewards and punishments which we feel, and those which from the light of reason we have ground to believe, are annexed to it. The question then carries its own answer along with it. Your obligation to obey this law, is its being the law of your nature. That your conscience approves of and attests to such a course of action, is itself alone an obligation. Conscience does not only offer itself to show us the way we should walk in, but it likewise carries its own authority with it, that it is our natural guide; the guide assigned us by the Author of our nature: it therefore belongs to our condition of being, it is our duty to walk in that path, and follow this guide, without looking about to see whether we may not possibly forsake them with impunity.[i]

**10.** Butler summarizes the basic points of his ethical theory in the following manner:

We may from it form a distinct notion of what is meant by *human nature*, when virtue is said to consist in following it, and vice in deviating from it.

As the idea of a civil constitution implies in it united strength, various subordinations, under one direction, that of the supreme authority; the different strength of each particular member of the society not coming into the idea; whereas, if you leave out the subordination, the union, and the one direction, you destroy and lose it: so reason, several appetites, passions, and affections, prevailing in different degrees of strength, is not *that* idea or notion of *human nature;* but *that nature* consists in these several principles considered as having a natural respect to each other, in the several passions being naturally subordinate to the one superior principle of reflection or conscience. Every bias, instinct, propension within, is a natural part of our nature, but not the whole: add to these the superior faculty, whose office it is to adjust, manage, and preside over them, and take in this its natural superiority, and you complete the idea of human nature. And as in civil government the constitution is broken in upon, and violated by power and strength prevailing over authority; so the constitution of man is broken in upon and violated by the lower faculties or principles within prevailing over that which is in its nature supreme over them all. Thus, when it is said by ancient writers, that tortures and death are not so contrary to human nature is injustice; by this to be sure is not meant, that the aversion to the former in mankind is less strong and prevalent than their aversion to the latter: but that the former is only contrary to our nature considered in a partial view, and which takes in only the lowest part of it, that which we have in common with the brutes; whereas the latter is contrary to our nature, considered in a higher sense, as a system and constitution contrary to the whole economy of man.

Every man, in his physical nature is one individual single agent. He has likewise properties and principles, each of which may be considered separately, and without regard to the respects which they have to each other. Neither of these are the nature we are taking a view of. But it is the inward frame of man considered as a *system* or *constitution:* whose several parts are united, not by a physical principle of individuation, but by the respects they have to each other; the chief of which is the subjection which the appetites, passions, and particular affections have to the one supreme principle of reflection or conscience. The system or constitution is formed by and consists in these respects and this subjection. Thus, the body is a *system* or *constitution:* so is a tree: so is every machine. Consider all the several parts of a tree, without the natural respects they have to each other, and you have not at all the idea of a tree; but add these respects, and this gives you the idea. The body may be impaired by sickness, a tree may decay, a machine be out of order, and yet the system and constitution of them not totally dissolved. There is plainly somewhat which answers to all this in the moral constitution of man. Whoever will consider his own nature, will see that the several appetites, passions, and particular affections, have different respects amongst themselves. They are restraints upon, and are in proportion to each other. This proportion is just and perfect, when all those under principles are perfectly coincident with conscience, so far as their nature permits, and in all cases, under its absolute and entire direction. The least excess or defect, the least alteration of the due proportions amongst themselves, or of their coincidence with conscience, though not proceeding into action, is some degree of disorder in the moral constitution. But perfection, though plainly intelligible and unsupposable, was never attained by any man. If the higher principle of reflection maintains its place, and as much as it can corrects that disorder, and hinders it from breaking out into action, this is all that can be expected from such a creature as man. And though the appetites and passions have not their exact due proportion to each other; though they often strive for mastery with judgment or reflection: yet, since the superiority of this principle to all others is the chief respect which forms the constitution, so far as this superiority is maintained, the character, the man, is good, worthy, virtuous.[j]

## QUESTIONS

1. What does Butler mean when he says that *virtue* consists in "acting according to nature" and *vice* consists in "acting contrary to nature"?
2. Discuss Butler's conception of "nature" and "human nature." To what difficulties do the popular misconceptions of human nature lead?
3. Reconstruct Butler's argument against the belief that self-love and benevolence are naturally opposed. Do you regard his position as a sound one?
4. How does Butler refute the Hobbesian doctrine that self-love is nothing but the unlimited gratification of impulses?
5. List Butler's "governing principles" in human nature. How is "conscience" related to the other principles?
6. Discuss Butler's contention that the authority of conscience does not arise from any external source.
7. Explain what Butler means when he asserts that "every man is naturally a law to himself."
8. In which respects is Butler's conception of "conscience" different from popular conceptions? In what respects is it similar?
9. How do you think Butler would respond to the objection that the consciences of people are not all the same?
10. What is Butler's attitude toward the antireligious sentiments of his contemporaries? To what extent, if any, does he employ theological arguments to support his ethical theory?

## KEY TO SELECTIONS

Joseph Butler, *Sermons*, New York, Robert Carter, 1873.

[a]Preface, pp. vi–viii.
[b]Sermon II, pp. 40–41.
[c]Sermon I, pp. 27–30.
[d]Sermon XI, pp. 132–133.
[e]Sermon XI, pp. 126–128.
[f]Sermon II, pp. 43–44.
[g]Sermon I, pp. 30–32.
[h]Sermon II, pp. 44–46.
[i]Sermon II, pp. 48–49.
[j]Sermon III, pp. 47–48, fn. p. 48.

## GUIDE TO ADDITIONAL READING


**PRIMARY SOURCES**

Butler, J., *Five Sermons*, Indianapolis, Hackett Publishing Co., 1983.

**DISCUSSION AND COMMENTARY**

Broad, C. D., *Five Types of Ethical Theory*, New York, Harcourt, Brace, 1930, Ch. 3.

Duncan-Jones, A., *Butler's Moral Philosophy*, Harmondsworth, Penguin Books, 1952.

James, E., "Butler, Fanaticism and Conscience," *Philosophy*, October 1981, pp. 517–532.

Raphael, D. D., *The Moral Sense*, London, Oxford University Press, 1947.

Rorty, A., "Butler on Benevolence and Conscience," *Philosophy*, April 1978, pp. 171–184.

Sturgeon, N., "Nature and Conscience in Butler's Ethics," *Philosophical Review*, July 1976, pp. 316–356.

CHAPTER ELEVEN

# Morality and Sentiment

DAVID HUME

DAVID HUME (1711–1776) is undoubtedly one of the most influential figures in the history of thought. In 1739, however, when Hume's *A Treatise of Human Nature* was published anonymously, there was little prospect that such a statement would ever be made. This first and (some would say) most important of his philosophical publications—involving a devastating attack on speculative metaphysics—received virtually no notice from his contemporaries. A revised and popularized version of the arguments in Book I of the *Treatise* appeared in 1748 as *Philosophical Essays Concerning Human Understanding* (later retitled *An Enquiry Concerning Human Understanding*) and marked the beginning of the modest philosophical reputation he enjoyed for the rest of his life.

In 1751, Hume published *An Enquiry Concerning the Principles of Morals*, an amplification of the theory of morality that he had outlined in Book III of the *Treatise*. Hume later said of this work that it was "of all my writings, historical, philosophical, or literary, incomparably the best." Another of his philosophical works, *Dialogues Concerning Natural Religion*, written in the early 1750s but published posthumously, deserves special mention. In it Hume sets forth his skepticism regarding proofs of God's existence and the possibility of describing His nature. It is ironic that even after his death, many people dismissed Hume as an annoying atheist and failed to recognize that he was a first-rate philosopher.

Oddly enough, however, Hume's fame during his life rested largely on his literary and historical, rather than his philosophical, writings. His six-volume *History of England* (1754–1762) became a classic in its field and influenced subsequent historians to include social and literary events as well as political developments in their accounts. The illustrious historian Edward Gibbon (1737–1794) acknowledged his debt to Hume.

As might be expected from someone born of an aristocratic family in Edinburgh, Scotland, Hume attended Edinburgh University. As might not be expected, however, his efforts at obtaining a Chair of Philosophy at both Edinburgh and Glasgow universities were unsuccessful; as a result, he spent five years as librarian to the Edinburgh Faculty of Law and once served as secretary to the British embassy in Paris.

A brilliant but modest man, Hume commented about himself shortly before his death, "I was, I say, a man of mild dispositions, of command of temper, of an open, social, and cheerful humor, capable of attachment, but little susceptible of enmity, and of great moderation in all my passions."

Attributing the successes of natural philosophy (that is, physical science) to the empirical, experimental method of inquiry, Hume is convinced that such inquiry can and must be employed in other domains of philosophical investigation. For Hume, this method proves that nothing is present to the mind except its perceptions, which are either sense impressions or ideas based on sense impressions; hence all knowledge consists in judgments about either matters of fact or relations between ideas. It is therefore a central thesis of Hume's understanding of the empirical method that factual knowledge arises solely from the data supplied by the senses and is extended in usefulness by means of inferences based on a belief in cause-and-effect relations. To Hume, the idea of causation is rooted in belief, which is a lively idea associated with a present impression. Regarded very loosely, the thesis that factual knowledge is sense knowledge would have been acceptable to many scientists and philosophers of the Newtonian era, but strictly speaking, it constituted a radical departure from their thinking and from the thinking of their predecessors.

Hume's most striking and innovative departure concerns the "traditionalist" view of causality. According to this view, a necessary connection exists between a cause (A) and its effect (B). Factual knowledge of this relationship involves not only the constant conjunction in time and place of events like A and events like B—provided by the senses—but also a necessary, real relation between these types of events—contributed by reason. Hume attacks the idea of such a necessity connection and argues that the traditionalist confuses a mental habit with an alleged real relation—expecting, because in the past every B event followed every A event, that A is the "metaphysical" cause of B.

Certain results of Hume's investigation of moral philosophy by his empirical method of inquiry are sufficiently foreshadowed by the account of causality embedded in that method to suggest (1) a similarity, (2) a contrast, and (3) a comparison between causative explanations of moral issues and empirical matters of fact. First, there is a generic similarity between moral assertions—for example, "Helping the injured is good"—and scientific assertions—for example, "Acid causes litmus paper to turn red." Both assertions deal with matters of fact and, like all other factual judgments, are only contingently true and not *necessarily* true. Furthermore, the matters of fact of scientific assertions lie in the object, whereas the matters of fact of moral assertions are rooted in human feelings or human nature. Next, Hume argues that a distinction must be made. The justification of a causal statement is based on the conjunction of two kinds of experiential events, which may both be regarded as *external*. But the basis of a moral assertion is the experienced conjunction, not of two external events, but of an external behavioral event and an internal mental event; more specifically, one event consists of ***voluntary actions*** and the other of ***feelings of approval*** or ***disapproval.*** And finally, Hume suggests a plausible comparison: Just as we are psychologically constituted to attribute causal necessity to the constant conjunction of two kinds of empirical events, we are also psychologically constituted to attribute a moral quality or property to an external action constantly conjoined with our feelings of approval or disapproval.

A great deal of the foregoing is captured in Hume's summary of his discussion of moral theory in the *Treatise:*

> Take any action allowed to be vicious: willful murder, for instance. Examine it in all its lights, and see if you can find that matter of fact, or real existence, which you call *vice*.... You never can find it, till you turn your affection into your own breast, and find a sentiment of disapprobation, which arises in you, towards this action. Here is a matter of fact; but it is the object of feeling, not of reason. It lies in your self, not in the object. So that when you pronounce any action or character to be vicious, you mean nothing, but that from the constitution of your nature you have a feeling or sentiment of blame from the contemplation of it.[1]

One cannot reflect on this quotation without asking whether Hume reduces ethics to a mere matter of taste. Indeed, some philosophers who have been much influenced by Hume insist on an interpretation of this sort.[2] Hume himself recognizes that if he fails to establish that our feelings of approval and disapproval are more than idiosyncratic responses, there cannot be a morality that is in any sense objective and public. He feels, however, that in turning from reason to sentiment, he has avoided radical relativism or mere subjectivism. Because people have the same psychological makeup, says Hume, their moral responses for the most part will be comparable. Of course, he is not saying that all people will agree about the moral worth of every particular action. Rather, he is underscoring the fact that if they are provided with the same data, they will *tend* to respond similarly. Thus, for example, in ordinary circumstances, people believe that the sun rises in the east and sets in the west because their common natures are exposed to the same matters of fact. Likewise, they are similar in their cognitive and passional[3] natures; therefore, when two people come to a full understanding of the same set of facts and the accompanying consequences, they tend to make the same moral judgment. In brief, Hume relies heavily on the observation that ethical disagreements generally stem not from differences in our passional nature but from misunderstandings about the actual circumstances surrounding a given act or from incomplete analyses of the consequences accruing from that act.

Hume further insists that the study of individuals' moral assessments reveals that socially useful acts are approved whereas those that are socially detrimental are disapproved. And from this he argues that because we judge acts generally by their conformity to social utility, rather than by immediate, personal preferences, there is strong indication that impartiality prevails when we make moral judgments.[4]

---

[1]David Hume, *A Treatise of Human Nature*, Everyman's Library (New York: E. P. Dutton , 1956), vol. 2, p. 177.

[2]See Chapter 21 of this book.

[3]Passional, i.e., affective, nature.

[4]Moreover, in his later essay "The Standard of Taste"(1757), Hume argues against relativistic morality by reminding us that we are usually willing to assimilate, as our very own, judgments of the fully informed, impartial observer.

Some critics have objected that Hume's empirical claim about social utility cannot provide an adequate basis for our moral obligations. One line of criticism, for example, begins with the observation that the concept of justice must be an integral part of any moral theory. The basic feature of that concept consists of an obligation to act in conformity with an inflexible set of rules; it does not, however, appear to include the idea of promoting social utility. Hume's rebuttal takes this into account. It is, indeed, obligatory to be just, he points out, but the reason we adopt the concept of justice and guide our actions in conformity with it is precisely that it is socially useful to do so. Hume does not deny that a specific instance of injustice could be more beneficial to society than its corresponding instance of justice (for example, if a poor person with a large family were awarded by the courts the disputed title to an estate that belongs to a dissolute, rich bachelor). But upon reflection, we see that such cases are not really exceptions. In becoming aware of the complications of circumstances and the unending consequences of our actions, we discover that only by strictly conforming to the rule of justice can humanity be served.

**1.** Hume raises the question of whether the source of morality resides solely in our rational nature or solely in our passional nature. Initially, he finds convincing features on each side.

There has been a controversy started of late, much better worth examination, concerning the general foundation of Morals; whether they be derived from Reason, or from Sentiment; whether we attain the knowledge of them by a chain of argument and induction, or by an immediate feeling and finer internal sense; whether, like all sound judgment of truth and falsehood, they should be the same to every rational intelligent being; or whether, like the perception of beauty and deformity, they be founded entirely on the particular fabric and constitution of the human species.

The ancient philosophers, though they often affirm that virtue is nothing but conformity to reason, yet, in general, seem to consider morals as deriving their existence from taste and sentiment. On the other hand, our modern enquirers, though they also talk much of the beauty of virtue, and deformity of vice, yet have commonly endeavored to account for these distinctions by metaphysical reasonings, and by deductions from the most abstract principles of the understanding. Such confusion reigned in these subjects, that an opposition of the greatest consequence could prevail between one system and another, and even in the parts of almost each individual system. . . .

It must be acknowledged, that both sides of the question are susceptible of specious arguments. Moral distinctions, it may be said, are discernible by pure *reason:* else, whence the many disputes that reign in common life, as well as in philosophy, with regard to this subject: the long chain of proofs often produced on both sides; the examples cited, the authorities appealed to, the analogies employed, the fallacies detected, the inferences drawn, and the several conclusions adjusted to their proper principles. Truth is disputable; not taste: what exists in the nature of things is the standard of our judgment; what each man feels within himself is the standard of sentiment. Propositions in geometry may be proved, systems in physics may be controverted; but the harmony of verse, the tenderness of passion, the brilliancy of wit, must give immediate pleasure. No man reasons concerning another's beauty; but frequently concerning the justice or injustice of his actions. In every criminal trial the first object of the prisoner is to disprove the facts alleged, and deny the actions imputed to him: the second to prove, that, even if these actions were real, they might be justified, as innocent and lawful. It is confessedly by deductions of the understanding, that the first point is ascertained: how can we suppose that a different faculty of the mind is employed in fixing the other?

On the other hand, those who would resolve all moral determinations into *sentiment*, may endeavor to show, that it is impossible for reason ever to draw conclusions of this nature. To virtue, say they, it belongs to be *amiable*, and vice *odious*. This forms their very nature or essence. But can reason or argumentation distribute these different epithets to any subjects, and pronounce beforehand, that this must produce love, and that hatred? Or what other reason can we ever assign for these affections, but the original fabric and formation of the human mind, which is naturally adapted to receive them?[a]

**2.** Hume suggests that finding a way of blending both positions would be attractive.

These arguments on each side (and many more might be produced) are so plausible, that I am apt to suspect, they may, the one as well as the other, be solid and satisfactory, and that *reason* and *sentiment* concur in almost all moral determinations and conclusions. The final sentence, it is probable, which pronounces characters and actions amiable or odious, praiseworthy or blameable; that which stamps on them the mark of honor or infamy, approbation or censure; that which renders morality an active principle and constitutes virtue our happiness, and vice our misery; it is probable, I say, that this final sentence depends on some internal sense or feeling, which nature has made universal in the whole species. For what else can have an influence of this nature? But in order to pave the way for such a sentiment, and give a proper discernment of its object, it is often necessary, we find, that much reasoning should precede, that nice distinctions be made, just conclusions drawn, distant comparisons formed, complicated relations examined, and general facts fixed and ascertained. Some species of beauty, especially the natural kinds, on their first appearance, command our affection and approbation; and where they fail of this effect, it is impossible for any reasoning to redress their influence, or adapt them better to our taste and sentiment. But in many orders of beauty, particularly those of the finer arts, it is requisite to employ much reasoning, in order to feel the proper sentiment; and a false relish may frequently be corrected by argument and reflection. There are just grounds to conclude, that moral beauty partakes much of this latter species, and demands the assistance of our intellectual faculties, in order to give it a suitable influence on the human mind.[b]

**3.** According to Hume, however, there can be no compromise about which of the two, reason or sentiment, is the ultimate source of morality. Two decisive arguments against reason are offered. The first is simply that morality is practical—that is, it influences or regulates our conduct. But the fact that reason in itself does not provide a spring of action forces us to conclude that it cannot be the source of moral conduct.

The end of all moral speculations is to teach us our duty; and, by proper representations of the deformity of vice and beauty of virtue, beget correspondent habits, and engage us to avoid the one, and embrace the other. But is this ever to be expected from inferences and conclusions of the understanding, which of themselves have no hold of the affections or set in motion the active powers of men? They discover truths: but where the truths which they discover are indifferent, and beget no desire or aversion, they can have no influence on conduct and behavior. What is honorable, what is fair, what is becoming, what is noble, what is generous, takes possession of the heart, and animates us to embrace and maintain it. What is intelligible, what is evident, what is probable, what is true, procures only the cool assent of the understanding; and gratifying a speculative curiosity, puts an end to our researches.

Extinguish all the warm feelings and prepossessions in favor of virtue, and all disgust or aversion to vice: render men totally indifferent towards these distinctions; and morality is no longer a practical study, nor has any tendency to regulate our lives and actions.[c]

**4.** The second argument against reason is subtle and distinctively Humean. Although we are aware of all the objective facts in a given immoral situation (such as A promised to repay a debt to B on a certain day, A has sufficient funds to repay his or her debt on that day, A refuses to do so, and so on) the wrongness of A's action cannot be found as an item in a complex list of facts on which we reflect in arriving at a moral judgment. Hume argues further that the rightness or wrongness is not to be discerned in relationships between any of these facts or even between A's action and a rule about one's being expected to pay one's debts.

Reason judges either of *matter of fact* or of *relations.* Enquire then, *first*, where is that matter of fact which we here call *crime;* point it out; determine the time of its existence; describe its essence or nature; explain the sense or faculty to which it discovers itself. It resides in the mind of the person who is ungrateful. He must, therefore, feel it, and be conscious of it. But nothing is there, except the passion of ill will or absolute indifference. You cannot say that these, of themselves, always, and in all circumstances, are crimes. No, they are only crimes when directed towards persons who have before expressed and displayed good will towards us. Consequently, we may infer, that the crime of ingratitude is not any particular individual *fact;* but arises from a complication of circumstances, which, being presented to the spectator, excites the *sentiment* of blame, by the particular structure and fabric of his mind.

This representation, you say, is false. Crime, indeed, consists not in a particular *fact*, of whose reality we are assured by *reason;* but it consists in certain *moral relations* discovered by reason, in the same manner as we discover by reason the truths of geometry or algebra. But what are the relations, I ask, of which you here talk? In the case stated above, I see, first, goodwill and good offices in one person; then, ill will and ill offices in the other. Between these there is the relation of *contrariety.* Does the crime consist in that relation? But suppose a person bore me ill will or did me ill offices, and I, in return, were indifferent toward him, or did him good offices—here is the same relation of *contrariety;* and yet my conduct is often highly laudable. Twist and turn this matter as much as you will, you can never rest the morality on relation, but must have recourse to the decisions of sentiment.

When it is affirmed that two and three are equal to the half of ten, this relation of equality I understand perfectly. I conceive, that if ten be divided into two parts, of which one has as many units as the other; and if any of these parts be compared to two added to three, it will contain as many units as that compound number. But when you draw thence a comparison to moral relations, I own that I am altogether at a loss to understand you. A moral action, a crime, such as ingratitude, is a complicated object. Does the morality consist in the relation of its parts to each other? How? After what manner? Specify the relation: be more particular and explicit in your propositions, and you will easily see their falsehood.

No, say you, the morality consists in the relation of actions to the rule of right; and they are denominated good or ill, according as they agree or disagree with it. What then is this rule of right? In what does it consist? How is it determined? By reason, you say, which examines the moral relations of actions. So that moral relations are determined by the comparison of action to a rule. And that rule is determined by considering the moral relations of objects. Is not this fine reasoning?[d]

**5.** Having examined the overwhelming case against reason, Hume comes down squarely on the side of sentiment as the source of morality.

The hypothesis which we embrace is plain. It maintains that morality is determined by sentiment. It defines virtue to be *whatever mental action or quality gives to a spectator the pleasing sentiment of approbation;* and vice the contrary.

We then proceed to examine a plain matter of fact, to wit, what actions have this influence. We consider all the circumstances in which these actions agree, and thence endeavor to extract some general observations with regard to these sentiments.[e]

**6.** Even though reason is incapable of being the source of morality, it plays an essential role in rendering moral decisions.

When a man, at any time, deliberates concerning his own conduct (as, whether he had better, in a particular emergency, assist a brother or a benefactor), he must consider these separate relations, with all the circumstances and situations of the persons, in order to determine the superior duty and obligation; and in order to determine the proportion of lines in any triangle, it is necessary to examine the nature of that figure, and the relation which its several parts bear to each other. But notwithstanding this appearing similarity in the two cases, there is, at bottom, an extreme difference between them. A speculative reasoner concerning triangles or circles considers the several known and given relations of the parts of these figures; and thence infers some unknown relation, which is dependent on the former. But in moral deliberations we must be acquainted beforehand with all the objects, and all their relations to each other and from a comparison of the whole, fix our choice or approbation. No new fact to be ascertained; no new relation to be discovered. All the circumstances of the case are supposed to be laid before us, ere we can fix any sentence of blame or approbation. If any material circumstance be yet unknown or doubtful, we must first employ our inquiry or intellectual faculties to assure us of it; and must suspend for a time all moral decision or sentiment. While we are ignorant whether a man were aggressor or not, how can we determine whether the person who killed him be criminal or innocent? But after every circumstance, every relation is known, the understanding has no further room to operate, nor any object on which it could employ itself. The approbation or blame which then ensues, cannot be the work of the judgment, but of the heart; and is not a speculative proposition or affirmation, but an active feeling or sentiment. In the disquisitions of the understanding, from known circumstances and relations, we infer some new and unknown. In moral decisions, all the circumstances and relations must be previously known; and the mind, from the contemplation of the whole, feels some new impression of affection or disgust, esteem or contempt, approbation or blame.

Hence the great difference between a mistake of *fact* and one of *right;* and hence the reason why the one is commonly criminal and not the other. When Oedipus killed Laius, he was ignorant of the relation, and from circumstances, innocent and involuntary, formed erroneous opinions concerning the action which he committed. But when Nero killed Agrippina, all the relations between himself and the person, and all the circumstances of the fact, were previously known to him; but the motive of revenge, or fear, or interest, prevailed in his savage heart over the sentiments of duty and humanity. And when we express that detestation against him to which he himself, in a little time, became insensible, it is not that we see any relations, of which he was ignorant; but that, for the rectitude of our disposition, we feel sentiments against which he was hardened from flattery and a long perseverance in the most enormous crimes. In these sentiments then, not in a discovery of relations of any kind, do all moral determinations consist. Before we can pretend to form any decision of this kind, everything must be known and ascertained on the side of the object or action. Nothing remains but to fell, on our part, some sentiment of blame or approbation; whence we pronounce the action criminal or virtuous.[f]

**7.** Hume discusses the two great social virtues, benevolence and justice, extensively. He observes that the first of these is universally esteemed.

It may be esteemed, perhaps, a superfluous task to prove, that the benevolent or softer affections are estimable; and wherever they appear, engage the approbation and good will of mankind. The epithets *sociable, good-natured, humane, merciful, grateful, friendly, generous, beneficent*, or their equivalents, are known in all languages, and universally express the highest merit, which *human nature* is capable of attaining. Where these amiable qualities are attended with birth and power and eminent abilities, and display themselves in the good government or useful instruction of mankind, they seem even to raise the possessors of them above the rank of *human nature*, and make them approach in some measure to the divine. Exalted capacity, undaunted courage, prosperous success; these may only expose a hero or politician to the envy and ill will of the public: but as soon as the praises are added of humane and beneficent; when instances are displayed of lenity, tenderness or friendship; envy itself is silent, or joins the general voice of approbation and applause.... No qualities are more entitled to the general goodwill and approbation of mankind than beneficence and humanity, friendship and gratitude, natural affection and public spirit, or whatever proceeds from a tender sympathy with others, and a generous concern for our kind and species. These wherever they appear seem to transfuse themselves, in a manner, into each beholder, and to call forth, in their own behalf, the same favorable and affectionate sentiments, which they exert on all around.

We may observe that, in displaying the praises of any humane, beneficent man, there is one circumstance which never fails to be amply insisted on, namely, the happiness and satisfaction, derived to society from his intercourse and good offices.[g]

**8.** With respect to the virtue justice, Hume argues that its sole source is utility. He arrives at this conclusion by asking us to imagine several sets of social and human circumstances and to note that in these circumstances, the virtue would be idle, in the sense that it would be either superfluous or unworkable.

That Justice is useful to society, and consequently that *part* of its merit, at least, must arise from that consideration, it would be superfluous undertaking to prove. That public utility is the *sole* origin of justice, and that reflections on the beneficial consequences of this virtue are the *sole* foundation of its merit; this proposition, being more curious and important, will better deserve our examination and enquiry.

Let us suppose that nature has bestowed on the human race such profuse *abundance* of all *external* conveniences, that, without any uncertainty in the event, without any care or industry on our part, every individual finds himself fully provided with whatever his most voracious appetites can want, or luxurious imagination wish or desire. His natural beauty, we shall suppose, surpasses all acquired ornaments: the perpetual clemency of the seasons renders useless all clothes or covering: the raw herbage affords him the most delicious fare; the clear fountain, the richest beverage. No laborious occupation required: no tillage: no navigation. Music, poetry, and contemplation form his sole business: conversation, mirth, and friendship his sole amusement.

It seems evident that, in such a happy state, every other social virtue would flourish and receive tenfold increase; but the cautious, jealous virtue of justice would never once have been dreamed of. For what purpose make a partition of goods, where everyone has already more than enough? Why give rise to property, where there cannot possibly be any injury? Why call this object *mine*, when upon the seizing of it by another, I need but stretch out my hand to possess myself to what is equally valuable? Justice, in that case, being totally useless, would be an idle ceremonial, and could never possibly have place in the catalogue of virtues....

Again; suppose, that, though the necessities of human race continue the same as at present, yet the mind is so enlarged, and so replete with friendship and generosity, that every man has the utmost tenderness for every man, and feels no more concern for his own interest than for that of his fellows; it seems evident, that the use of justice would, in this case, be suspended by such an extensive benevolence, nor would the divisions and barriers of property and obligation have ever been thought of. Why should I bind another, by a deed or promise, to do me any good office, when I know that he is already prompted, by the strongest inclination, to seek my happiness, and would, of himself, perform the desired service; except the hurt, he thereby receives, be greater than the benefit accruing to me? in which case, he knows that, from my innate humanity and friendship, I should be the first to oppose myself to his imprudent generosity. Why raise landmarks between my neighbor's field and mine, when my heart has made no division between our interests; but shares all his joys and sorrows with the same force and vivacity as if originally my own? Every man, upon this supposition, being a second self to another, would trust all his interests to the discretion of every man; without jealousy, without partition, without distinction. And the whole human race would form only one family; where all would lie in common, and be used freely, without regard to property; but cautiously too, with as entire regard to the necessities of each individual, as if our own interests were most intimately concerned. . . .

To make this truth more evident, let us reverse the foregoing suppositions; and carrying everything to the opposite extreme, consider what would be the effect of these new situations. Suppose a society to fall into such want of all common necessaries, that the utmost frugality and industry cannot preserve the greater number from perishing, and the whole from extreme misery; it will readily, I believe, be admitted, that the strict laws of justice are suspended, in such a pressing emergency, and give place to the stronger motives of necessity and self-preservation. Is it any crime, after a shipwreck, to seize whatever means or instrument of safety one can lay hold of, without regard to former limitations of property? Or if a city besieged were perishing with hunger; can we imagine, that men will see any means of preservation before them, and lose their lives, from a scrupulous regard to what, in other situations, would be the rules of equity and justice? The use and tendency of that virtue is to procure happiness and security, by preserving order in society: but where the society is ready to perish from extreme necessity, no greater evil can be dreaded from violence and injustice; and every man may now provide for himself by all the means, which prudence can dictate, or humanity permit. The public, even in less urgent necessities, opens granaries, without the consent of proprietors, as justly supposing, that the authority or magistracy may, consistent with equity, extend so far: but were any number of men to assemble, without the tie of laws or civil jurisdiction; would an equal partition of bread in a famine, though effected by power and even violence, be regarded as criminal or injurious?

Suppose likewise, that it should be a virtuous man's fate to fall into the society of ruffians, remote from the protection of laws and government; what conduct must he embrace in that melancholy situation? He sees such a desperate rapaciousness prevail; such a disregard to equity, such contempt of order, such stupid blindness to future consequences, as must immediately have the most tragical conclusion, and must terminate in destruction to the greater number, and in a total dissolution of society to the rest. He, meanwhile, can have no other expedient than to arm himself, to whomever the sword he seizes, or the buckler, may belong: To make provision of all means of defense and security: And his particular regard to justice being no longer of use to his own safety or that of others, he must consult the dictates of self-preservation alone, without concern for those who no longer merit his care and attention.[h]

**9.** Hume summarizes the foregoing argument.

Thus, the rules of equity or justice depend entirely on the particular state and condition in which men are placed, and owe their origin and existence to that utility, which results to the public from their strict and regular observance. Reverse, in any considerable circumstance, the condition of men: Produce extreme abundance or extreme necessity: Implant in the human breast perfect moderation and humanity, or perfect rapaciousness and malice: By rendering justice totally *useless*, you thereby totally destroy its essence, and suspend its obligation upon mankind.

The common situation of society is a medium amidst all these extremes. We are naturally partial to ourselves, and to our friends; but are capable of learning the advantage resulting from a more equitable conduct. Few enjoyments are given us from the open and liberal hand of nature; but by art, labor, and industry, we can extract them in great abundance. Hence the ideas of property become necessary in all civil society: Hence justice derives its usefulness to the public: And hence alone arises its merits and moral obligation.[i]

> **10.** Hume is confident that anyone who looks will see that it is characteristic of items of *personal merit,*—of, that is, virtues (mental qualities that arouse the sentiment of approbation)—to be useful or agreeable to the person who possesses them or to others.

It may justly appear surprising that any man in so late an age, should find it requisite to prove, by elaborate reasoning, that Personal Merit consists altogether in the possession of mental qualities, *useful* or *agreeable* to the *person himself* or to *others.* It might be expected that this principle would have occurred even to the first rude, unpractised enquirers concerning morals, and been received from its own evidence, without any argument or disputation. Whatever is valuable in any kind, so naturally classes itself under the division of *useful* or *agreeable*, the *utile* or the *dulce*, that it is not easy to imagine why we should ever seek further.... What so natural, for instance, as the following dialogue? You are very happy, we shall suppose one to say, addressing himself to another, that you have given your daughter to Cleanthes. He is a man of honour and humanity. Every one, who has any intercourse with him, is sure of *fair* and *kind* treatment.[5] I congratulate you too, says another, on the promising expectations of this son-in-law; whose assiduous application to the study of the laws, whose quick penetration and early knowledge both of men and business, prognosticate the greatest honours and advancement.[6] You surprise me, replies a third, when you talk of Cleanthes as a man of business and application. I met him lately in a circle of the gayest company, and he was the very life and soul of our conversation: so much wit with good manners; so much gallantry without affectation; so much ingenious knowledge so genteelly delivered, I have never before observed in any one.[7] You would admire him still more, says a fourth, if you knew him more familiarly....[j]

> **11.** In the final analysis, Hume's moral theory presumes that some, at least, of any person's passions do not have their origin in personal concerns. Thus he insists that an individual's morality is based on sentiments having their origin in concern for others. Such sentiments are universally shared, because they are not affected by the relativism of any personal considerations.

It seems a happiness in the present theory; that it enters not into that vulgar dispute concerning the *degrees* of benevolence or self-love, which prevail in human nature; a dispute which is never likely to have an issue, both because men, who have taken part, are not easily convinced, and because the phenomena, which can be produced on either side, are so dispersed, so uncertain, and subject to so many interpretations, that it is scarcely possible accurately to compare them, or draw from them any determinate inference or conclusion. It is sufficient for our present purpose, if it be allowed, what surely, without the greatest absurdity cannot be disputed, that there is some benevolence, however small, infused into our bosom; some spark of friendship for humankind; some particle of the dove kneaded into our frame, along with the elements of the wolf and serpent. Let these generous sentiments be supposed ever so weak; let them be insufficient to move even a hand or finger of our body, they must still direct the determinations of our mind, and where everything else is equal,

[5]Qualities useful to others.

[6]Qualities useful to the person himself.

[7]Qualities immediately agreeable to others.

produce a cool preference of what is useful and serviceable to mankind, above what is pernicious and dangerous. A *moral distinction*, therefore, immediately arises....

The notion of morals implies some sentiment common to all mankind, which recommends the same object to general approbation, and makes every man, or most men, agree in the same opinion or decision concerning it. It also implies some sentiment, so universal and comprehensive as to extend to all mankind, and render the actions and conduct, even of the persons the most remote, an object of applause or censure, according as they agree or disagree with that rule of right which is established. These two requisite circumstances belong alone to the sentiment of humanity here insisted on. The other passions produce in every breast, many strong sentiments of desire and aversion, affection and hatred; but these neither are felt so much in common, nor are so comprehensive, as to be the foundation of any general system and established theory of blame or approbation.

When a man denominates another his *enemy*, his *vial*, his *antagonist*, his *adversary*, he is understood to speak the language of self-love, and to express sentiments, peculiar to himself, and arising from his particular circumstances and situation. But when he bestows on any man the epithets of *vicious* or *odious* or *depraved*, he then speaks another language, and expresses sentiments, in which he expects all his audience are to concur with him. He must here, therefore, depart from his private and particular situation, and must choose a point of view, common to him with others; he must move some universal principle of the human frame, and touch a string to which all mankind have an accord and symphony. If he mean, therefore, to express that this man possesses qualities, whose tendency is pernicious to society, he has chosen this common point of view, and has touched the principle of humanity, in which every man, in some degree, concurs. While the human heart is compounded of the same elements as at present, it will never be wholly indifferent to public good, nor entirely unaffected with the tendency of characters and manners. And though this affection of humanity may not generally be esteemed so strong as vanity or ambition, yet, being common to all men, it can alone be the foundation of morals, or of any general system of blame or praise. One man's ambition is not another's ambition, nor will the same event or object satisfy both; but the humanity of one man is the humanity of everyone, and the same object touches this passion in all human creatures.

Whatever conduct gains my approbation, by touching my humanity, procures also the applause of all mankind, by affecting the same principle in them; but what serves my avarice or ambition pleases these passions in me alone, and affects not the avarice and ambition of the rest of mankind. There is no circumstance of conduct in any man provided it have a beneficial tendency, that is not agreeable to my humanity, however remote the person.[k]

**12.** Hume returns finally to the topic of virtues—items of personal merit. He emphasizes and illustrates that it is manifest not only that virtues are mental qualities characterized as useful or agreeable to the person possessing them, or to others, but also that any mental quality so characterized is a virtue.

It must still be allowed that every quality of the mind, which is *useful* or *agreeable* to the *person himself* or to *others*, communicates a pleasure to the spectator, engages his esteem, and is admitted under the honourable denomination of virtue or merit. Are not justice, fidelity, honour, veracity, allegiance, chastity, esteemed solely on account of their tendency to promote the good of society? Is not that tendency inseparable from humanity, benevolence, lenity, generosity, gratitude, moderation, tenderness, friendship, and all the other social virtues? Can it possibly be doubted that industry, discretion, frugality, secrecy, order, perseverance, forethought, judgement, and this whole class of virtues and accomplishments, of which many pages would not contain the catalogue; can it be doubted, I say, that the tendency of these qualities to promote the interest and happiness of their possessor, is the sole foundation of their merit? Who can dispute that a mind, which supports a perpetual serenity and cheerfulness, a noble dignity and undaunted spirit, a tender affection and goodwill to all around: as it has more enjoyment within itself, is also a more animating and rejoicing spectacle, than if dejected with melancholy, tormented with anxiety, irritated with rage, or sunk into the most abject baseness and degeneracy? And as to the qualities, immediately *agreeable to others*, they speak sufficiently for themselves; and he must be unhappy, indeed, either in his own temper, or in his situation and company, who has never perceived the charms of a facetious wit or flowing affability, of a delicate modesty or decent genteelness of address and manner. . . .

I must confess, that this enumeration puts the matter in so strong a light, that I cannot, *at present*, be more assured of any truth, which I learn from reasoning and argument, than that personal merit consists entirely in the usefulness or agreeableness of qualities to the person himself possessed of them, or to others, who have any intercourse with him.[l]

## QUESTIONS

1. Do you agree with Hume's observation that if people did not experience feelings of approval or disapproval, they would not render moral judgments about actions?
2. Discuss Hume's arguments against reason as the basis of morality.
3. What is the role of reason in moral deliberation?
4. At the theoretical level, Hume's view of morality resembles his account of causality. In what ways are they similar and in what ways are they different?
5. Can Hume be defended against the charge of moral relativism if he bases morality on sentiment?
6. How does Hume's discussion of justice show that it is based on social utility?
7. Suggest that Hume is correct in insisting that references to sentiments of approval and blame are not reducible to references to likes and dislikes or to pleasures and displeasures by examples.
8. Adopting Hume's view, provide arguments against an ethical intuitionist who claims we know that certain actions are by their very nature right, and others wrong.
9. What are some of the features of the psychological theory that underlie Hume's ethics?
10. Hume believes that people who are not directly involved in a moral situation can nevertheless make moral judgments about it. Do you agree with him? Discuss.

## KEY TO SELECTIONS

David Hume, *An Enquiry Concerning the Principles of Morals*, Reprinted from the edition of 1777, LaSalle, Open Court, 1938.
[a]pp. 2–4.
[b]pp. 5–6.
[c]pp. 4–5.
[d]pp. 127–129.
[e]pp. 129–130.
[f]pp. 130–132.
[g]pp. 8–10.
[h]pp. 15–20.
[i]pp. 20–21.
[j]pp. 106–107.
[k]pp. 109–113.
[l]pp. 116–117.

## GUIDE TO ADDITIONAL READING

**PRIMARY SOURCES**

Hume, D., *An Inquiry Concerning the Principles of Morals* (Bobbs-Merrill).

———, *A Treatise of Human Nature*, Everyman's Library (Dutton), 2 vols.

Wolff, R. P. (ed.), *The Essential David Hume* (New American Library).

**DISCUSSION AND COMMENTARY**

Broad, C. D., *Five Types of Ethical Theory*, New York, Harcourt, Brace, 1930, Ch. 4.

Broiles, R. D., *The Moral Philosophy of David Hume*, The Hague, Martinus Nijhoff, 1964.

Chappell, V., *A Collection of Critical Essays*, Notre Dame, University of Notre Dame Press, 1968.

Mackie, J., *Hume's Moral Theory*, London, Routledge and Kegan Paul, 1980.

MacNabb, D. G. C., *David Hume: His Theory of Knowledge and Morality*, New York, Hutchinson's University Library, 1951.

Martin, Marie, "Hume as Classical Moralist," *International Philosophical Quarterly*, September 1994.

Reck, L. (ed.), *Studies in the Philosophy of David Hume*, New York, Garland, 1983.

Smith, N. K., *The Philosophy of David Hume*, London, Macmillan, 1941.

Stewart, J. B., *The Moral and Political Philosophy of David Hume*, New York, Columbia University Press, 1963.

CHAPTER TWELVE

# Duty and Reason

IMMANUEL KANT

IMMANUEL KANT (1724–1804), whose writings are required reading for all who desire to understand nineteenth- and twentieth-century thought, lived a life singularly without incident. Kant lived by routine, and, although he had many friends, he never married and never ventured more than forty miles from Königsberg, East Prussia, the city of his birth and death. The German writer Heine, though without doubt exercising some poetic license, has immortalized Kant as an automaton: "Rising, coffee drinking, writing, lecturing, dining, walking each had its set time. And when Immanuel Kant, in his gray coat, cane in hand, appeared at the door of his house, and strolled towards the small avenue of linden trees which is still called 'The Philosopher's Walk,' the neighbors knew it was exactly half-past-three by the clock."

The Kant family belonged to the lower middle class and was devoutly religious. In recognition of his son's academic ability and because of the family's religious persuasion, Immanuel's father sent him to the local Pietistic College to prepare for the ministry. Immanuel continued his studies at the University of Königsberg and became increasingly interested in natural science and philosophy. Between 1746 and 1755, he supported himself as a private teacher for various landed families in and around his native city. He was then appointed to an instructorship at his university and finally, in 1770, was promoted to a full professorship. Kant was a popular and successful teacher. Perhaps surprisingly for one who was so rigorous in his own thinking, he is reputed to have given the following advice in practical pedagogy: "Attend most to the student of middle ability, the dunces are beyond help, and the geniuses help themselves."

Kant's inner life was as dramatic as his outer life was drab: He renounced the external and emotional side of religion; he evolved from a man-of-letters philosopher with a free and flowing style of writing and thinking into a "critical" philosopher with a labored style of presenting uncompromisingly profound thoughts; he transformed a spontaneous scientific curiosity into an impulse to explore the foundations of science; at first a passive follower of an accepted school of philosophy, he became the innovator of an important school of thought. What is more, he took a passionate interest in the American and French revolutions. The conservative outer mien of Kant was a deceptive façade for the inner Kant.

The most important of Kant's scientific writings is his *General Natural History and Theory of the Heavens* (1755), in which he accounts for the origin of the solar system by formulating the nebular hypothesis. His revolutionary philosophical work is *Critique of Pure Reason* (1781), in which he is concerned to demonstrate that it is possible to have certain knowledge in the natural sciences and mathematics. In his *Critique of Judgment* (1790), he analyzes aesthetics and biology. Kant endeavors to show the foundations of genuine morality in *The Fundamental Principles of the Metaphysics of Morals* (1785) and the *Critique of Practical Reason* (1788); in the latter he investigates the implications of morality for religion.

The direction of Kant's philosophical interests is revealed in his reflection that "two things fill the mind with ever new and increasing admiration and awe . . . *the starry heavens above and the moral law within.*" His concern is with nature and morality. Against the background of eighteenth-century skepticism, which called into question the foundations of scientific knowledge and morality, he proposes a comprehensive system of the universe in which their certainty is guaranteed. According to Kant, skepticism results from the error of seeking a basis for certainty where it cannot be found, in the *content* of experience. The grounds of certainty, he asserts, are located in the *form* of reason itself. Accordingly, he undertakes an intensive examination of the nature of thought to show how we can have certain knowledge of both scientific facts and moral duties.

Kant demonstrates by an analysis of knowledge that the necessity and universality of scientific knowledge are guaranteed by the laws through which the categories (concepts) of the mind become effective.[1] They are the forms of all possible knowledge and are not limited to some specific content. For example, it is the nature of the mind to think in accordance with the principle that every event must have a cause. The concept of causality that enters into the principle is one of the categories of the understanding. Thus, despite our ignorance of the cause of a given disease, we are nevertheless certain that it has a cause, and this certainty is a product of mind, not of observation. Although it is generally held that nature itself provides the causal order of our experience, Kant reverses this position, insisting it is the mind that orders our experience causally. Otherwise, we could not be certain, as we are, of the causal interconnection of events; for, although experience teaches us what actually happens, it does not teach us what *necessarily* happens. The categories are

[1]What Kant opposes in skepticism is its theory that knowledge of experience or appearances (*phenomena*) cannot be certain. According to his theory, it is knowledge of ultimate reality or "things-in-themselves" (*noumena*) that is impossible.

*a priori*—that is, they are not derived from experience; they are universally applicable to experience; and they are the necessary preconditions of empirical knowledge. Furthermore, though all knowledge necessarily begins with experience, the *a priori* structure of it cannot be gotten by induction from experience but can be understood only through examining the presuppositions of our orderly experience of nature.

In his search for the grounds of the validity of ethics, Kant employs the same method by which he establishes the grounds of the certainty of science. A valid moral principle, he tells us, must be independent of the empirical data of morality if it is to be binding on all men. In short, a genuine morality—a morality that is objectively and universally binding—requires an *a priori* foundation. Kant believes that ordinary moral consciousness, or conscience, reveals to every person that moral precepts are universal and necessary—they are valid for all rational beings.

Universal obligation, according to Kant, cannot be discovered by studying such empirical data as human desires or inclinations, for these vary from one person to another. The universal basis of morality in people must lie in their rational nature; this alone is the same in everyone. No so-called moral law is valid if it is not rational—that is to say, if it cannot be applied to all rational beings without contradiction. Putting it another way, a moral principle must be such that one can will that all people, including oneself, should act on it. Kant uses the test of consistency as the core of the fundamental moral law, which he calls the *categorical imperative:* Those actions are right that conform to principles one can consistently will to be principles for everyone, and those actions are wrong that are based on maxims that a rational creature could not will that all persons should follow.

Because Kant rejects the idea of discovering our moral obligations empirically, he also rejects the idea of determining our moral obligations by discovering which states of affairs they cause or bring about. That is, he denies that we can determine whether an action is morally right by examining its *consequences.*

As a matter of standard terminology, Kant's view is accordingly *anti-consequentialist* or, as it is also put, *deontologist.* His view is opposed to the very widespread consequentialist Utilitarian view, which says that the test of right and wrong is whether an action has good consequences. This consequentialist idea will be presented in the next chapter (Ch. 13), but it has also appeared in, for example, the thinking of Epicurus (Ch. 4).

The categorical imperative, then, enables us to distinguish right from wrong actions. However, Kant tells us, it is not only the test but also the unconditional directive for behavior. It is binding on everyone because each rational being acknowledges an obligation to follow reason. The categorical imperative is, in fact, the only basis for determining our duties. Kant argues that the validity of the basic moral law would not be affected even if everyone were to violate it in actual conduct. Reason prescribes duty, and the moral law holds whether or not people actually follow it.

**1.** As a preliminary to his construction of a pure moral philosophy, Kant makes a critical analysis of the commonly accepted "good" things, such as health, wealth, and friendship. Asking under what conditions these may be considered good, he concludes that they are not good under all circumstances but only insofar as they are conjoined with something that is unqualifiedly good—a *good will.* To Kant, good will represents the effort of rational beings to do what they ought to do, rather than to act from inclination or self-interest.

Nothing can possibly be conceived in the world, or even out of it, which can be called good without qualification, except a Good Will. Intelligence, wit, judgment, and the other *talents* of the mind, however, they may be named, or courage, resolution, perseverance, as qualities of temperament, are undoubtedly good and desirable in many respects; but these gifts of nature may also become extremely bad and mischievous if the will which is to make use of them, and which, therefore, constitutes what is called *character,* is not good. It is the same with the *gifts of fortune.* Power, riches, honor, even health, and the general well-being and contentment with one's condition which is called *happiness,* inspire pride, and often presumption, if there is not a good will to correct the influence of these on the mind, and with this also to rectify the whole principle of acting, and adapt it to its end. The sight of a being who is not adorned with a single feature of a pure and good will, enjoying unbroken prosperity, can never give pleasure to an impartial rational spectator. Thus a good will appears to constitute the indispensable condition even of being worthy of happiness.

There are even some qualities which are of service to this good will itself, and may facilitate its action, yet which have no intrinsic unconditional value, but always presuppose a good will, and this qualifies the esteem that we justly have for them, and does not permit us to regard them as absolutely good. Moderation in the affections and passions, self-control and calm deliberation are not only good in many respects, but even seem to constitute part of the intrinsic worth of the person; but they are far from deserving to be called good without qualification, although they have been so unconditionally praised by the ancients. For without the principles of a good will, they may become extremely bad, and the coolness of a villain not only makes him far more dangerous, but also directly makes him more abominable in our eyes than he would have been without it.[a]

**2.** The good will is not good because it achieves good results. Even if it were unable to attain the ends it seeks, it would still be good in itself and have a higher worth than the superficial things gained by immoral actions.

A good will is good not because of what it performs or effects, not by its aptness for the attainment of some proposed end, but simply by virtue of the volition, that is, it is good in itself, and considered by itself is to be esteemed much higher than all that can be brought about by it in favor of any inclination, nay, even of the sum total of all inclinations. Even if it should happen that, owing to special disfavor of fortune, or the niggardly provision of a step-motherly nature, this will should wholly lack power to accomplish its purpose, if with its greatest efforts it should yet achieve nothing, and there should remain only the good will (not, to be sure, a mere wish, but the summoning of all means in our power), then, like a jewel, it would still shine by its own light, as a thing which has its whole value in itself. Its usefulness or fruitlessness can neither add to nor take away anything from this value. It would be, as it were, only the setting to enable us to handle it the more conveniently in common commerce, or to attract to it the attention of those who are not yet connoisseurs, but not to recommend it to true connoisseurs, or to determine its value.[b]

**3.** Experience shows that reason is a very inefficient instrument for the achievement of happiness. If nature intended humans to be happy, it would have provided an instinct to this end. What we observe is that the more people cultivate their reason, the less likely they are to find happiness. Kant concludes that reason is not intended to produce happiness but to produce a good will.[2]

There is, however, something so strange in this idea of the absolute value of the mere will, in which no account is taken of its utility, that notwithstanding the thorough assent of even common reason to the idea, yet a suspicion must arise that it may perhaps really be the product of mere high-flown fancy, and that we may have misunderstood the purpose of nature in assigning reason as the governor of our will. Therefore we will examine this idea from this point of view.

In the physical constitution of an organized being, that is, a being adapted suitably to the purposes of life, we assume it as a fundamental principle that no organ for any purpose will be found but what is also the fittest and best adapted for that purpose. Now in a being which has reason and a will, if the proper object of nature were its *conservation,* its *welfare,* in a word, its *happiness,* then nature would have hit upon a very bad arrangement in selecting the reason of the creature to carry out this purpose. For all the actions which the creature has to perform with a view to this purpose, and the whole rule of its conduct, would be far more surely prescribed to it by instinct, and that end would have been attained thereby much more certainly than it ever can be by reason. Should reason have been communicated to this favored creature over and above, it must only have served it to contemplate the happy constitution of its nature, to admire it, to congratulate itself thereon, and to feel thankful for it to the beneficent cause, but not that it should subject its desires to that weak and delusive guidance, and meddle bunglingly with the purpose of nature. In a word, nature would have taken care that reason should not break forth into *practical exercise,* nor have the presumption, with its weak insight, to think out for itself the plan of happiness, and of the means of attaining it. Nature would not only have taken on herself the choice of the ends, but also of the means, and with wise foresight would have entrusted both to instinct.

And, in fact, we find that the more a cultivated reason applies itself with deliberate purpose to the enjoyment of life and happiness, so much the more does the man fail of true satisfaction. And from this circumstance there arises in many, if they are candid enough to confess it, a certain degree of *misology,* that is, hatred of reason, especially in the case of those who are most experienced in the use of it, because after calculating all the advantages they derive, I do not say from the invention of all the arts of common luxury, but even from the sciences (which seem to them to be after all only a luxury of the understanding), they find that they have, in fact, only brought more trouble on their shoulders, rather than gained in happiness; and they end by envying, rather than despising, the more common stamp of men who keep closer to the guidance of mere instinct, and do not allow their reason much influence on their conduct. And this we must admit, that the judgment of those who would very much lower the lofty eulogies of the advantages which reason give us in regard to the happiness and satisfaction of life, or who would even reduce them below zero, is by no means morose or ungrateful to the goodness with which the world is governed, but that there lies at the root of these judgments the idea that our existence has a different and far nobler end, for which, and not for happiness, reason is properly intended, and which must, therefore, be regarded as the supreme condition to which the private ends of man must, for the most part, be postponed.

For as reason is not competent to guide the will with certainty in regard to its objects and

[2]Note that in emphasizing duty rather than happiness in his ethical theory, Kant does not deny that happiness is desirable for humans. Although he holds that the immediate object of reason is the production of a good will, which is the supreme good (*supremum bonum*), he acknowledges that a person of good will deserves happiness. The supreme good—that is, virtue—when conjoined with happiness in proportion to it, constitutes the greatest good (*summum bonum*).

the satisfaction of all our wants (which it to some extent even multiplies), this being an end to which an implanted instinct would have led with much greater certainty; and since, nevertheless, reason is imparted to us as a practical faculty, *i.e.*, as one which is to have influence on the *will*, therefore, admitting that nature generally in the distribution of her capacities has adapted the means to the end, its true destination must be to produce a *will*, not merely good as a *means* to something else, but *good in itself*, for which reason was absolutely necessary. This will then, though not indeed the sole and complete good, must be the supreme good and the condition of every other, even of the desire of happiness. Under these circumstances, there is nothing inconsistent with the wisdom of nature in the fact that the cultivation of the reason, which is requisite for the first and unconditional purpose, does in many ways interfere, at least in this life, with the attainment of the second, which is always conditional, namely, happiness. Nay, it may even reduce it to nothing, without nature thereby failing of her purpose. For reason recognizes the establishment of a good will as its highest practical destination, and in attaining this purpose is capable only of a satisfaction of its own proper kind, namely, that from the attainment of an end, which end again is determined by reason only, notwithstanding that this may involve many a disappointment to the ends of inclination.[c]

**4.** Kant then proceeds to explain the relationship between a good will and duty: A good will is one that acts for the sake of duty. Indeed, human actions have inner moral worth only if they are performed *from* duty. Actions that result from inclination or self-interest may be praiseworthy if they happen, for whatever reason, to accord with duty, but they have no inner worth. For example, a woman who preserves her life in routine conformity to duty is acting from an inclination that is *according* to duty, but not *from* duty. On the other hand, to preserve life when it has become a burden, only because duty requires it, is *morally* correct.

Kant does not mean that doing one's duty is always, or even generally, unpleasant. However, when our desires lead to actions that happen to conform to duty, we cannot be sure that the consciousness of duty, rather than inclination, was our motive. We can better discern the efficacy of dutifulness where it stands alone or in opposition to other motives. This, not disapproval of ordinary human motives, is what leads Kant to choose examples that are rather cold and unpleasant.

Kant warns that those who fail to understand properly the concept of duty may be tempted to act from motives that may be in accordance with duty or may be contrary to it. But even action in accordance with duty is not enough; only respect for duty gives an action inner moral worth.

We have then to develop the notion of a will which deserves to be highly esteemed for itself, and is good without a view to anything further, a notion which exists already in the sound natural understanding, requiring rather to be cleared up than to be taught, and which in estimating the value of our actions always takes the first place, and constitutes the condition of all the rest. In order to do this we will take the notion of duty, which includes that of a good will, although implying certain subjective restrictions and hindrances. These, however, far from concealing it, or rendering it unrecognizable, rather bring it out by contrast, and make it shine forth so much the brighter.

I omit here all actions which are already recognized as inconsistent with duty, although they may be useful for this or that purpose, for with these the question whether they are done *from duty* cannot arise at all, since they even conflict with it. I also set aside those actions which really conform to duty, but to which men have *no* direct *inclination*, performing them because they are impelled thereto by some other inclination. For in this case we can readily distinguish whether the action which agrees with duty is done *from duty*, or from a selfish view. It is much harder to make this distinction when the action accords with duty, and the subject has besides a *direct* inclination to it. For example, it is always a matter of duty that a dealer should not overcharge an inexperienced purchaser, and wherever there is much commerce the prudent tradesman does not overcharge, but keeps a fixed price for everyone, so that a child buys of him as well as any other. Men are thus *honestly* served; but this is not enough to make us believe that the tradesman has so acted from duty and from principles of honesty: his own advantage required it; it is out of the question in this case to suppose that he might besides have a direct inclination in favor of the buyers, so that as it were, from love he should give no advantage to one over another. Accordingly the action was done neither from duty nor from direct inclination, but merely with a selfish view.

On the other hand, it is a duty to maintain one's life; and, in addition, everyone has also a direct inclination to do so. But on this account the often anxious care which most men take for it has no intrinsic worth, and their maxim has no moral import. They preserve their life *as duty requires,* no doubt, but not *because duty requires.* On the other hand, if adversity and hopeless sorrow have completely taken away the relish for life; if the unfortunate one, strong in mind, indignant at his fate rather than desponding or dejected, wishes for death, and yet preserves his life without loving it—not from inclination or fear, but from duty—then his maxim has a moral worth.[d]

> **5.** By the use of an illustration, Kant differentiates merely praiseworthy behavior from moral action. Altruistic actions that result from feelings of sociability deserve praise and encouragement, but they cannot be classified as possessing strictly moral value.

To be beneficent when we can is a duty; and besides this, there are many minds so sympathetically constituted that, without any other motive of vanity or self-interest, they find a pleasure in spreading joy around them, and can take delight in the satisfaction of others so far as it is their own work. But I maintain that in such a case an action of this kind, however proper, however amiable it may be, has nevertheless no true moral worth, but is on a level with other inclinations, *e.g.*, the inclination to honor, which, if it is happily directed to that which is in fact of public utility and accordant with duty, and consequently honorable, deserves praise and encouragement, but not esteem. For the maxim lacks the moral import, namely, that such actions be done *from duty,* not from inclination. Put the case that the mind of that philanthropist were clouded by sorrow of his own, extinguishing all sympathy with the lot of others, and that while he still has the power to benefit others in distress, he is not touched by their trouble because he is absorbed with his own; and now suppose that he tears himself out of this dead insensibility, and performs the action without any inclination to it, but simply from duty, then first has his action its genuine moral worth. Further still; if nature has put little sympathy in the heart of this or that man; if he, supposed to be an upright man, is by temperament cold and indifferent to the sufferings of others, perhaps because in respect of his own he is provided with the special gift of patience and fortitude, and supposes, or even requires, that others should have the same—and such a man would certainly not be the meanest product of nature—but if nature had not specially framed him for a philanthropist, would he not still find in himself a source from whence to give himself a far higher worth than that of a good-natured temperament could be? Unquestionably. It is just in this that the moral worth of the character is brought out which is incomparably the highest of all, namely, that he is beneficent, not from inclination, but from duty.[e]

> **6.** Kant's first ethical proposition, then, is that an act must be done from duty in order to have inner moral worth. His second proposition is a development from the first: An act done from duty derives its moral value not from the results it produces but from the principle by which it is determined.

The second proposition is: That an action done from duty derives its moral worth, *not from the purpose* which is to be attained by it, but from the maxim by which it is determined, and therefore does not depend on the realization of the object of the action, but merely on the *principle of volition* by which the action has taken place, without regard to any object of desire. It is clear from what precedes that the purposes which we may have in view of our actions, or their effects regarded as ends and springs of the will, cannot give to actions any unconditional or moral worth. In what, then, can their worth lie, if it is not to consist in the will and in reference to its expected effect? It cannot lie anywhere but in the *principle of the will* without regard to the ends which can be attained by the action.[f]

**7.** The first two propositions lead Kant to a definition of duty. The morally right action is one done solely out of reverence for the law, and its unique and unconditioned worth is derived from this source.

The third proposition, which is a consequence of the two preceding, I would express thus: *Duty is the necessity of acting from respect for the law.* I may have *inclination* for an object as the effect of my proposed action, but I cannot have *respect* for it, just for this reason, that it is an effect and not an energy of will. Similarly, I cannot have respect for inclination, whether my own or another's; I can at most, if my own, approve it; if another's, sometimes even love it; *i.e.,* look on it as a favorable to my own interest. It is only what is connected with my will as a principle, by no means as an effect—what does not subserve my inclination, but overpowers it, or at least in case of choice excludes it from its calculation—in other words, simply the law of itself, which can be an object of respect, and hence a command. Now an action done from duty must wholly exclude the influence of inclination, and with it every object of the will, so that nothing remains which can determine the will except objectively the *law,* and subjectively *pure respect* for this practical law, and consequently the maxim that I should follow this law even to the thwarting of all my inclinations.

Thus the moral worth of an action does not lie in the effect expected from it, nor in any principle of action which requires to borrow its motive from this expected effect. For all these effects—agreeableness of one's condition, and even the promotion of the happiness of others—could have been also brought about by other causes, so that for this there would have been no need of the will of a rational being; whereas it is in this alone that the supreme and unconditional good can be found. This preeminent good which we call moral can therefore consist in nothing else than *the conception of law* in itself, *which certainly is only possible in a rational being,* insofar as this conception, and not the expected effect, determines the will. This is a good which is already present in the person who acts accordingly, and we have not to wait for it to appear first in the result.[g]

**8.** The supreme principle or law of morality that the good person must follow is the "categorical imperative." Rational beings, to the extent that they act rationally, will always be guided by ethical principles or maxims that can be adopted by everyone else without generating any contradiction.

But what sort of law can that be, the conception of which must determine the will, even without paying any regard to the effect expected from it, in order that this will may be called good absolutely and without qualification? As I have deprived the will of every impulse which could arise to it from obedience to any law, there remains nothing but the universal conformity of its actions to law in general, which alone is to serve the will as a principle, *i.e.,* I am never to act otherwise than so *that I could also will that my maxim should become a universal law.* Here now, it is the simple conformity to law in general, without assuming any particular law applicable to certain actions, that serves the will as its principle, and must so serve it, if duty is not to be a vain delusion and a chimerical notion. The common reason of men in its practical judgments perfectly coincides with this, and always has in view the principle here suggested. Let the question be, for example: May I when in distress make a promise with the intention not to keep it? I readily distinguish here between the two significations which the question may have: Whether it is prudent, or whether it is right, to make a false promise. The former may undoubtedly often be the case. I see clearly indeed that it is not enough to extricate myself from a present difficulty by means of this subterfuge, but it must be well considered whether there may not hereafter spring from this lie much greater inconvenience than that from which I now free myself, and as, with all my supposed *cunning*, the consequences cannot be so easily foreseen but that credit once lost may be much more injurious to me than any mischief which I seek to avoid at present, it should be considered whether it would not be more *prudent* to act herein according to a universal maxim, and to make it a habit to promise nothing except with the intention of keeping it. But it is soon clear to me that such a maxim will still only be based on the fear of consequences. Now it is a wholly different thing to be truthful from duty, and to be so from apprehension of injurious consequences. In the first case, the very notion of the action already implies a law for me; in the second case, I must first look about elsewhere to see what results may be combined with it which would affect myself. For to deviate from the principle of duty is beyond all doubt wicked; but to be unfaithful to my maxim of prudence may often be very advantageous to me, although to abide by it is certainly safer. The shortest way, however, and an unerring one, to discover the answer to this question whether a lying promise is consistent with duty, is to ask myself, Should I be content that my maxim (to extricate myself from difficulty by false promise) should hold good as a universal law, for myself as well as for others? and should I be able to say to myself, "Everyone may make a deceitful promise when he finds himself in a difficulty from which he cannot otherwise extricate himself"? Then I presently become aware that while I can will the lie, I can by no means will that lying should be a universal law. For with such a law there would be no promises at all, since it would be in vain to allege my intention in regard to my future actions to those who would not believe this allegation, or if they over-hastily did so, would pay me back in my own coin. Hence my maxim, as soon as it should be made a universal law, would necessarily destroy itself.[h]

> **9.** Kant distinguishes the *categorical* imperative from *hypothetical* imperatives. The former, an unconditional directive, prescribes actions to be done because of the moral worth of the maxim and not for the sake of some consequence that may result. By contrast, a hypothetical imperative is a conditional directive that advises us what ought to be done if a desired goal is to be achieved. For example, "One ought to tell the truth as a matter of principle" is a categorical imperative, whereas "*If* you want to avoid punishment, you ought to tell the truth" is a hypothetical imperative.

The conception of an objective principle, insofar as it is obligatory for a will, is called a command (of reason), and the formula of the command is called an imperative.

All imperatives are expressed by the word *ought* (or *shall*), and thereby indicate the relation of an objective law of reason to a will, which from its subjective constitution is not necessarily determined by it (an obligation). They say that something would be good to do or to forbear, but they say it to a will which does not always do a thing because it is conceived to be good to do it. That is practically *good*, however, which determines the will by means of the conceptions of reason, and consequently not from subjective causes, but objectively, that is on principles which are valid for every rational being as such. It is distinguished from the *pleasant*, as that which influences the will only by means of sensation from merely subjective causes, valid only for the sense of this or that one, and not as a principle of reason, which holds for everyone. . . .

Now all *imperatives* command either *hypothetically* or *categorically*. The former represent the practical necessity of a possible action as means to something else that is willed (or at least which one might possibly will). The categorical imperative would be that which represented an action as necessary of itself without reference to another end, *i.e.,* as objectively necessary.

Since every practical law represents a possible action as good, and on this account, for a subject who is practically determinable by reason, necessary, all imperatives are formulae determining an action which is necessary according to the principle of a will good in some respects. If now the action is good only as a means *to something else,* then the imperative is *hypothetical;* if it is conceived as good *in itself* and consequently as being necessarily the principle of a will which of itself conforms to reason, then it is *categorical.*[i]

**10.** His first explicit formulation of the categorical imperative requires an individual to obey a maxim that can, without contradiction, be willed to be a rule for everyone. This means the essence of morality lies in acting on the basis of an impersonal principle that is valid for everyone, including oneself.

When I conceive a hypothetical imperative in general I do not know beforehand what it will contain until I am given the condition [under which it is imperative, *viz.,* the desire which makes this imperative suitable to my purposes]. But when I conceive a categorical imperative I know at once what it contains. For as the imperative contains besides the law only the necessity that the maxims shall conform to this law, while the law contains no conditions restricting it, there remains nothing but the general statement that the maxim of the action should conform to a universal law, and it is this conformity alone that the imperative properly represents as necessary.

There is therefore but one categorical imperative, namely this: *Act only on that maxim whereby thou canst at the same time will that it should become a universal law.*

Now if all imperatives of duty can be deduced from this one imperative as from their principle, then, although it should remain undecided whether what is called duty is not merely a vain notion, yet at least we shall be able to show what we understand by it and what this notion means.

Since the universality of the law according to which effects are produced constitutes what is properly called *nature* in the most general sense (as to form), that is the existence of things as far as it is determined by general laws, the imperative of duty may be expressed thus: *Act as if the maxim of thy action were to become by thy will a Universal Law of Nature.*[j]

**11.** Kant conceives the categorical imperative to be a twofold test. It requires first, that maxims for moral action be universalized without logical contradiction, and second, that they be universal directives for action that do not bring the will into disharmony with itself by requiring it to will one thing for itself and another thing for others. Kant illustrates failure at the former level with the first two examples that follow and failure at the latter level with the third and fourth examples.

1. A man reduced to despair by a series of misfortunes feels wearied of life, but is still so far in possession of his reason that he can ask himself whether it would not be contrary to his duty to himself to take his own life. Now he inquires whether the maxim of his action could become a universal law of nature. His maxim is: From self-love I adopt it as a principle to shorten my life when its longer duration is likely to bring more evil than satisfaction. It is asked then simply whether this principle founded on self-love can become a universal law of nature. Now we see at once that a system of nature of which it should be a law to destroy life by means of the very feeling whose special nature it is to impel to the improvement of life would contradict itself, and therefore could not exist as a system of nature; hence that maxim cannot possibly exist as a universal law of nature, and consequently would be wholly inconsistent with the supreme principle of all duty.

2. Another finds himself forced by necessity to borrow money. He knows that he will not be

able to repay it, but sees also that nothing will be lent to him, unless he promises stoutly to repay it in a definite time. He desires to make this promise, but he has still so much conscience as to ask himself: Is it not unlawful and inconsistent with duty to get out of a difficulty in this way? Suppose, however, that he resolves to do so, then the maxim of his action would be expressed thus: When I think myself in want of money, I will borrow money and promise to repay it, although I know that I never can do so. Now this principle of self-love or of one's own advantage may perhaps be consistent with my whole future welfare; but the question now is, Is it right? I change then the suggestion of self-love into a universal law, and state the question thus: How would it be if my maxim were a universal law? Then I see at once that it could never hold as a universal law of nature, but would necessarily contradict itself. For supposing it to be a universal law that everyone when he thinks himself in a difficulty should be able to promise whatever he pleases, with the purpose of not keeping his promise, the promise itself would become impossible, as well as the end that one might have in view in it, since no one would consider that anything was promised to him, but would ridicule all such statements as vain pretenses.

3. A third finds in himself a talent which with the help of some culture might make him a useful man in many respects. But he finds himself in comfortable circumstances, and prefers to indulge in pleasure rather than to take pains in enlarging and improving his happy natural capacities. He asks, however, whether his maxim of neglect of his natural gifts, besides agreeing with his inclination to indulgence, agrees also with what is called duty. He sees then that a system of nature could indeed subsist with such a universal law although men (like the South Sea islanders) should let their talents rust, and resolve to devote their lives merely to idleness, amusement, and propagation of their species—in a word, to enjoyment; but he cannot possibly *will* that this should be a universal law of nature, or be implanted in us as such by a natural instinct. For, as a rational being, he necessarily wills that his faculties be developed, since they serve him and have been given him, for all sorts of possible purposes.

4. A fourth, who is in prosperity, while he sees that others have to contend with great wretchedness and that he could help them, thinks: What concern is it of mine? Let everyone be as happy as heaven pleases, or as he can make himself; I will take nothing from him nor even envy him, only I do not wish to contribute anything to his welfare or to his assistance in distress! Now no doubt if such a mode of thinking were a universal law, the human race might very well subsist, and doubtless even better than in a state in which everyone talks of sympathy and good will, or even takes care occasionally to put it into practice, but on the other side, also cheats when he can, betrays the rights of men, or otherwise violates them. But although it is possible that a universal law of nature might exist in accordance with that maxim, it is impossible to *will* that such a principle should have the universal validity of a law of nature. For a will which resolved this would contradict itself, inasmuch as many cases might occur in which one would have need of the love and sympathy of others, and in which, by such a law of nature, sprung from his own will, he would deprive himself of all hope of the aid he desires.

These are a few of the many actual duties, or at least what we regard as such, which obviously fall into two classes on the one principle that we have laid down. We must be *able to will* that a maxim of our action should be a universal law. This is the canon of the moral appreciation of the action generally. Some actions are of such a character that their maxim cannot without contradiction be even *conceived* as a universal law of nature, far from it being possible that we should *will* that it *should* be so. In others this intrinsic impossibility is not found, but still it is impossible to *will* that their maxim should be raised to the universality of a law of nature, since such a will would contradict itself. It is easily seen that the former violate strict or rigorous (inflexible) duty; the latter only laxer (meritorious) duty. Thus it has been completely shown by these examples how all duties depend as regards the nature of the obligation (not the object of the action) on the same principle.[k]

**12.** In one of Kant's formulations of the categorical imperative, we see more clearly its social implications. It requires us to *treat all human beings as ends in themselves and never as merely means to ends.* In brief, we should respect all human beings impartially and avoid exploiting anyone. Ends that are ends only because they are desired give us hypothetical imperatives, but if there is an *end in itself,* the imperative to seek it is independent of desire and is therefore a categorical imperative.

Supposing . . . that there were something *whose existence* has *in itself* an absolute worth, something which, being *an end in itself,* could be a source of definite laws, then in this and this alone would lie the source of a possible categorical imperative, *i.e.,* a practical law.

Now I say: man and generally any rational being *exists* as an end in himself, *not merely as a means* to be arbitrarily used by this or that will, but in all his actions, whether they concern himself or other rational beings, must be always regarded at the same time as an end. All objects of the inclinations have only a conditional worth, for if the inclinations and the wants founded on them did not exist, then their object would be without value. But the inclinations themselves being sources of want, are so far from having an absolute worth for which they should be desired, that on the contrary it must be the universal wish of every rational being to be wholly free from them. Thus the worth of any object which is *to be acquired* by our action is always conditional. Beings whose existence depends not on our will but on nature's, have nevertheless, if they are irrational beings, only a relative value as means, and are therefore called *things;* rational beings, on the contrary, are called *persons,* because their very nature points them out as ends in themselves, that is as something which must not be used merely as means, and so far therefore restricts freedom of action (and is an object of respect). These, therefore, are not merely subjective ends whose existence has a worth *for us* as an effect of our action, but *objective ends,* that is things whose existence is an end in itself: an end moreover for which no other can be substituted, which they should subserve *merely* as means, for otherwise nothing whatever would possess *absolute worth;* but if all worth were conditioned and therefore contingent, then there would be no supreme practical principle of reason whatever.

If then there is a supreme practical principle or, in respect of the human will, a categorical imperative, it must be one which, being drawn from the conception of that which is necessarily an end for everyone because it is *an end in itself,* constitutes an *objective* principle of will, and can therefore serve as a universal practical law. The foundation of this principle is: *rational nature exists as an end in itself.* Man necessarily conceives in his own existence as being so: so far then this is a *subjective* principle of human actions. But every other rational being regards its existence similarly, just on the same rational principle that holds for me: so that it is at the same time an objective principle, from which as a supreme practical law all laws of the will must be capable of being deduced. Accordingly the practical imperative will be as follows: *So act as to treat humanity, whether in thine own person or in that of any other, in every case as an end withal, never as means only.*[l]

**13.** Kant shows the basic identity of the first and second formulations of the categorical imperative. Those actions that, on the first formulation, cannot be universalized without contradiction (for example, committing suicide or refusing to help the needy) will be seen on the second formulation to be inconsistent with the idea of humanity as an end in itself.

The principle: So act in regard to every rational being (thyself and others), that he may always have place in thy maxim as an end in himself, is accordingly essentially identical with this other: Act upon a maxim which, at the same time, involves its own universal validity for every rational being. For that in using means for every end I should limit my maxim by the condition of its holding good as a law for every subject, this comes to the same thing as that the fundamental principle of all maxims of action must be that the subject of all ends, *i.e.*, the rational being himself, be never employed merely as means, but as the supreme condition restricting the use of all means, that is in every case as an end likewise.[m]

**14.** Having brought to light with logical rigor the implicit presuppositions of the common person's awareness of duty and shown it to be a universal categorical imperative, Kant gives eloquent praise to "pure moral philosophy" and a word of caution to those moralists who would allow reason to be corrupted by empirical considerations.

We see philosophy brought to a critical position, since it has to be firmly fixed, notwithstanding that it has nothing to support it either in heaven or earth. Here it must show its purity as absolute dictator of its own laws, not the herald of those which are whispered to it by an implanted sense or who knows what tutelary nature. Although these may be better than nothing, yet they can never afford principles dictated by reason, which must have their source wholly *a priori* and thence their commanding authority, expecting everything from the supremacy of the law and the due respect for it, nothing from inclination, or else condemning the man to self-contempt and inward abhorrence.

Thus every empirical element is not only quite incapable of being an aid to the principle of morality, but is even highly prejudicial to the purity of morals, for the proper and inestimable worth of an absolutely good will consists just in this, that the principle of action is free from all influence of contingent grounds, which alone experience can furnish. We cannot too much or too often repeat our warning against this lax and even mean habit of thought which seeks for its principle amongst empirical motives and laws; for human reason in its weariness is glad to rest on this pillow, and in a dream of sweet illusions (in which, instead of Juno, it embraces a cloud) it substitutes for morality a bastard patched up from limbs of various derivation, which looks like anything one chooses to see in it; only not like virtue to one who has once beheld her in her true form.

To behold virtue in her proper form is nothing else but to contemplate morality stripped of all admixture of sensible things and of every spurious ornament of reward or self-love. How much she then eclipses everything else that appears charming to the affections, everyone may readily perceive with the least exertion of his reason, if it be not wholly spoiled for abstraction.[n]

## QUESTIONS

1. In what ways does Kant's ethical theory discourage us from morally judging actions simply by the actual consequences that they have in the world? In what ways does his view insist that when we judge an action, we take into account the intentions with which it is performed?
2. Account for Kant's denial of the unqualified goodness of such commonly valued assets as friendship, health, wealth, and the like in terms of his interest in that which is good in itself. What does he regard as the only moral quality that is unqualifiedly good in itself?
3. What is the moral function of *reason* in Kant's philosophy? What is the relationship between reason and happiness?
4. Explain the relationship between *good will* and *duty* in Kant's ethics. Can you think of any alternative ways of relating them?
5. Why does Kant object to using "inclinations" or "feelings" as the basis of morality?
6. What criteria of the morality of actions does Kant establish? How would he evaluate an act of charity performed out of a natural sympathy for the sufferings of the poor?

7. State the "categorical imperative" in any of the forms Kant gives it, and use examples of moral acts to clarify its meaning. What is the basis of the moral law in Kant's system of ethics?
8. What is the role of "motives" in Kant's ethical theory?
9. What would Kant's position be as to moral values in the following situations? (a) A husband remains loyal to his wife because he loves her. (b) A husband recognizes loyalty to his wife as an obligation, although he finds it decidedly unpleasant.
10. If you look ahead to Chapter 13, you will see that according to Bentham and Mill, the moral value of an action depends solely on the happiness produced by it. Why and in what ways does Kant disagree with this view?

## KEY TO SELECTIONS

Immanuel Kant, *Fundamental Principles of the Metaphysic of Morals,* tr. T. K. Abbott, from *Kant's Critique of Practical Reason and Other Works on the Theory of Ethics,* London, Longmans, Green, 1898.

[a]1st. Sec., pp. 9–10.
[b]1st. Sec., p. 10.
[c]1st. Sec., pp. 10–12.
[d]1st. Sec., pp. 12–14.
[e]1st. Sec., pp. 14–15.
[f]1st. Sec., p. 16.
[g]1st. Sec., pp. 16–17.
[h]1st. Sec., pp. 17–19.
[i]2nd. Sec., pp. 30–31.
[j]2nd. Sec., pp. 38–39.
[k]2nd. Sec., pp. 39–42.
[l]2nd. Sec., pp. 46–47.
[m]2nd. Sec., p. 56.
[n]2nd. Sec., pp. 43–44, fn. p. 44.

## GUIDE TO ADDITIONAL READING


### PRIMARY SOURCES

Kant, I., *Foundations of the Metaphysic of Morals* (University of Chicago Press).

_____, *Fundamental Principles of the Metaphysics of Morals,* Appleton-Century Philosophy Source Books (Appleton-Century-Crofts).

_____, _____, Little Library of Liberal Arts (Liberal Arts Press).

_____, _____, Great Books Foundation (Regnery).

_____, _____, (Longmans, Green).

_____, *Groundwork of the Metaphysics of Morals,* Hutchinson's University Library (Hutchinson).

*Kant Selections,* Modern Students Library (Scribner's).

*The Philosophy of Kant,* Modern Library (Random House).

### DISCUSSION AND COMMENTARY

Baron, M., "The Alleged Moral Repugnance of Acting from Duty," *Journal of Philosophy,* April 1984, pp. 197–220.

Baron, Marcia W., *Kantian Ethics Almost without Apology,* Ithaca, Cornell University Press, 1999.

Beck, L. W., *A Commentary on Kant's Critique of Practical Reason,* Chicago, University of Chicago Press, 1960.

Broad, C. D., *Five Types of Ethical Theory,* New York, Harcourt, Brace, 1930, Ch. 5.

Herman, Barbara, *The Practice of Moral Judgment,* Cambridge, Harvard University Press, 1993.

Lindsay, A. D., *Kant,* London, Oxford University Press, 1934.

Nell, O., *Acting on Principle: An Essay on Kantian Ethics,* New York, Columbia University Press, 1975.

O'Neill, Onora, "Kantian Ethics," *A Companion to Ethics,* ed. P. Singer, Cambridge, Blackwell, 1993, pp. 175–185.

Paton, H. J., *The Categorical Imperative,* Chicago, University of Chicago Press, 1948.

Ross, W. D., *Kant's Ethical Theory,* Oxford, Oxford University Press, 1954.

Sen, S., "The Motive of Duty and Disinterestedness," *Indian Philosophical Quarterly,* January 1982, pp. 131–138.

Sullivan, R. J., *An Introduction to Kant's Ethics,* Cambridge, Cambridge University Press, 1994.

CHAPTER THIRTEEN

# The Greatest Happiness Principle

JOHN STUART MILL

JOHN STUART MILL (1806–1873), the intellectual heir of the Utilitarian movement in England, dedicated himself to clarifying the teachings of his father, James Mill, and those of Jeremy Bentham. In his *Autobiography*, a history of his "intellectual and moral development," John Stuart Mill describes the exacting "educational experiment" imposed on him from age three to age fourteen by his father. At the age of three, he studied Greek and arithmetic; at eight, he added Latin to his curriculum; and by the time he was twelve, Mill was reading extensively in logic, philosophy, and economic theory. His training, moreover, was never a mere exercise in memorization but was designed to produce an original thinker.

At the age of twenty-one, he reached an emotional crisis that he characterized as the result of a sudden loss of enthusiasm for the original goals of his life but that, in current parlance, might be called a nervous breakdown. However, after several years, with fresh stimulation of his emotions and feelings as well as his intellect, he resumed his career, fulfilling his early promise. When he was twenty-five, Mill met Mrs. Harriet Taylor, whom he later married. He believed that her character and ability wielded great influence in his life and helped to shape his thought. In 1823, after a brief period of legal study, Mill, on the advice of his father, accepted a position with the East India Company. For thirty years, he held this responsible post, while devoting his spare time to writing his books. Upon retirement, when he intended to devote himself exclusively to writing, Mill was proposed as a candidate for Parliament. Despite his refusal to campaign, he was elected to office. Of his political conduct, William Gladstone, British Prime Minister, said: "He had the good sense and practical tact of politics, together with the high independent thought of a recluse. He did us all good."

Mill's major works cover a variety of subjects, but his *System of Logic* (1843) is regarded as his most important philosophical contribution. In it he defends the inductive method of logic, showing that general laws or universal principles must be derived from empirical facts. Other outstanding works are his *Principles of Political Economy* (1848), which relates the application of Utilitarian principles to economics; his essays *On Liberty* (1859) and *Considerations on Representative Government* (1861), which are classical statements of his social and political philosophy; and the essay *Utilitarianism* (1861), his only explicit contribution to ethics. During the last few years in his life, he wrote the very distinctive *Autobiography* and *Three Essays on Religion*, both published after his death.

Unlike most philosophers, John Stuart Mill did not attempt to originate an ethical theory but rather defended the ethical theory to which he was born. However, his intellectual depth and his intense desire to find an ethics that fits the facts of life led him to modify and extend the Utilitarian doctrine as it was propounded by his father and Jeremy Bentham. Bentham based his Utilitarian philosophy on the principle that the object of morality is the promotion of the greatest happiness of the maximum number of members of society. He proceeded on the premise that the happiness of any individual consists in a favorable balance of pleasures over pains. Consequently, those actions that tend to increase pleasure are called good, and those that tend to increase pain are called bad. For Bentham, however, Utilitarianism was less important as an ethical system than as a philosophical support for much-needed social legislation.

Bentham was motivated by the idea that "the *Public Good* ought to be the object of the legislator: *General Utility* ought to be the foundation of his reasonings. To know the true good of the community is what constitutes the science of legislation; the art consists in finding the means to realize that good." To implement this social and political ideal, he constructed a "hedonistic calculus" by means of which pleasures and pains could be measured. In this way, good and bad acts, and consequently good and bad legislation, can be evaluated in terms of such factors as intensity, duration, and extent.[1]

It's important to remember that Mill's view, in contrast with Kant's (Ch. 12), is a *consequentialist* one. Mill thinks that the evaluation of an action or a policy has to be based on a judgment about its consequences. He even seems to think that the value of a motive or intention is determined by its consequences. Mill's view seems to tell you that to assess an action or a motive you must determine the happiness and unhappiness that result from it. (This is opposed to the deontologist or anti-consequentialist view of philosophers such as Kant, who deny that the value of an action or an intention or motive is a function of its consequences; cf. Ch. 12.)

---

[1]Bentham composed the following verse to help the student remember the criteria of hedonistic measurement:

> *Intense, long, certain, speedy, fruitful, pure—*
> Such marks in *pleasures* and *pains* endure.
> Such pleasures seek, if *private* be thy end:
> If it be *public*, wide let them *extend*.
> Such *pains* avoid, whichever be thy view:
> If pains *must* come, let them extend to few.

J. Bowring, ed., *The Works of Jeremy Bentham* (London: Simpkin, Marshall, 1838), vol. 1, p. 16, note.

In his essay, Mill is concerned less with the political implications of Bentham's doctrine than with the provision of a defensible statement of its underlying ethical principles. In addition to answering objections put forward by opponents of Utilitarianism and correcting misrepresentations of it, he also restates the doctrine. In his restatement, he goes beyond Bentham's contention that the essential differences among pleasures and pains are quantitative, maintaining that they are also subject to significant qualitative differentiation. For example, anyone who has experienced the pleasure attendant upon the resolution of an intellectual problem will, Mill believes, attest to the fact that it is superior in kind to the pleasure of eating a meal.

Although Mill departs from Bentham's conception that all the significant differences among pleasures are quantitative, he accepts in principle Bentham's doctrines regarding the basic role of pleasures and pains in morality: *individual psychological hedonism* and *universal ethical hedonism*. According to the former, the sole motive of an action *is* an individual's desire for happiness—that is, for a balance of pleasure over pain. According to the latter, the "greatest happiness of greatest number" *ought* to be the individual's goal and standard of conduct. Psychological hedonism is primarily a *descriptive* doctrine, because it purports to be an account of the actual motive of behavior. By contrast, universal ethical hedonism is a *normative* theory in that it stipulates what *ought* to be done. It is a principle by which actions are evaluated in terms of their *consequences*, irrespective of the nature of the motive.

However, there are two gaps between individual psychological hedonism and universal ethical hedonism: (1) If each individual is motivated solely by the desire for her or his own happiness, there is no reason to assume that personal actions will at the same time always promote the interests of society. (2) The descriptive fact that people do desire their own happiness does not imply the normative principle that people *ought* to act in accordance with this desire. Mill recognizes that an adequate defense of Utilitarianism must show how the transition can be made from an interest in one's own happiness to that of others, and from a psychological theory to a moral theory. He endeavors to bridge the first of these two gaps by recourse to the concept of *sanctions*, the inducements to action that give binding force to moral rules. There is no general agreement that Mill or anyone else has bridged the second gap.

In Mill's system of ethics, sanctions are rooted in the hedonistic motive; that is, moral rules are acknowledged and obeyed by virtue of anticipated pleasures or pains. There are both "external" and "internal" sanctions. External sanctions are those forces of punishment and reward in the universe around us that control people's actions through their fear of pain and propensity for pleasure. For example, in our society, fear of social disapproval and imprisonment are both deterrents to crime. But, Mill cautions, conformity to the letter of the law in the presence of such external sanctions is not to be taken as a sign of a true sense of moral obligation: *The ultimate moral sanction must come from within.*

The force of an internal sanction derives from the feeling of pleasure that is experienced when a moral law is obeyed and the feeling of pain that accompanies a violation of it. That the "greatest happiness principle" can be sanctioned from within is attested to by observation. In some people at least, Mill holds, the feeling of sympathy for others is so well developed that the individual's happiness depends on the well-being of others. Thus, by means of the doctrine of internal sanctions, Mill is able to reconcile the psychological theory that people desire their own happiness with the moral theory that one ought to act to serve the public good.

However, Mill acknowledges that his argument in support of sanctions does not constitute a logical demonstration of the greatest happiness principle. In fact, he argues that *no direct proof of any first principle or ultimate end is possible*, and the problem of proof is in reality reduced to the problem of *rational assent:*

> To be incapable of proof by reasoning is common to all first principles; to the first premises of our knowledge as well as to those of our conduct. But the former, being matters of fact, may be the subject of a direct appeal to the faculties which judge of fact—namely, our senses, and our internal consciousness. . . .
>
> The only proof capable of being given that an object is visible, is that people actually see it. The only proof that a sound is audible, is that people hear it; and so of the other sources of our experience. In like manner, I apprehend, the sole evidence it is possible to produce that anything is desirable, is that people do actually desire it. If the end which the utilitarian doctrine proposes to itself were not, in theory and in practice, acknowledged to be an end, nothing could ever convince any person that it was so. No reason can be given why the general happiness is desirable except that each person, so far as he believes it to be attainable, desires his own happiness.[a,2]

---

**1.** Mill's first objective in defending Utilitarianism is to clarify the doctrine. He attempts this both by exposing misrepresentations and by straightforward exposition of the principle. He begins by opposing those who fail to associate "utility" with pleasure and pain.

A passing remark is all that needs to be given to the ignorant blunder of supposing that those who stand up for utility as the test of right and wrong, use the term in that restricted and merely colloquial sense in which utility is opposed to pleasure. An apology is due to the philosophical opponents of utilitarianism, for even the momentary appearance of confounding them with anyone capable of so absurd a misconception; which is the more extraordinary, inasmuch as the contrary accusation of referring everything to pleasure, and that too in its grossest form, is another of the common charges against utilitarianism: and, as has been pointedly remarked by an able writer, the same sort of persons, and often the very same persons, denounce the theory "as impracticably dry when the word utility precedes the word pleasure, and as too practicably voluptuous when the word pleasure precedes the word utility." Those who know anything about the matter are aware that every writer, from Epicurus to Bentham, who maintained the theory of utility, meant by it, not something to be contradistinguished from pleasure, but pleasure itself, together with exemption from pain; and instead of opposing the useful to the agreeable or the ornamental, have always declared that the useful means these, among other things. Yet the common herd, including the herd of writers, not only in newspapers and periodicals, but in books of weight and pretension, are perpetually falling into this shallow mistake. Having caught up the word "utilitarian," while knowing nothing whatever about it but its sound, they habitually

---

[2]As a formal proof, this would be fallacious: *Visible* is used in the sense of "*can* be seen," whereas *desirable* is used in the sense of "*ought* to be desired"; thus, the analogy is not a legitimate one. In addition, it does not follow from an admission that *each* individual desires *personal* happiness that *all* people desire the happiness of *all* people. Nevertheless, the argument, such as it is, bespeaks Mill's conviction that the evidence for an ethical theory is to be sought in the facts of human experience.

express by it the rejection, or the neglect, of pleasure in some of its forms; of beauty, of ornament, or of amusement. Nor is the term thus ignorantly misapplied solely in disparagement, but occasionally in compliment; as though it implied superiority to frivolity and the mere pleasures of the moment. And this perverted use is the only one in which the word is popularly known, and the one from which the new generation are acquiring their sole notion of its meaning. Those who introduced the word, but who had for many years discontinued it as a distinctive appellation, may well feel themselves called upon to resume it, if by doing so they can hope to contribute anything towards rescuing it from this utter degradation.[b]

**2.** Mill then states concisely the doctrine of utility.

The creed which accepts as the foundation of morals Utility, or the Greatest Happiness Principle, holds that actions are right in proportion as they tend to promote happiness, wrong as they tend to produce the reverse of happiness. By "happiness," is intended pleasure, and the absence of pain; by "unhappiness," pain, and the privation of pleasure. To give a clear view of the moral standard set up by the theory, much more requires to be said; in particular, what things it includes in the ideas of pain and pleasure; and to what extent this is left an open question. But these supplementary explanations do not affect the theory of life on which this theory of morality is grounded—namely, that pleasure, and freedom from pain, are the only things desirable as ends; and that all desirable things (which are as numerous in the utilitarian as in any other scheme) are desirable either for the pleasure inherent in themselves, or as means to the promotion of pleasure and the prevention of pain.[c]

**3.** Even when the principle of utility is clearly understood to be directed to pleasures and pains, however, there remains the charge that it is a "swinish" doctrine. This misconception is due to the failure to recognize that pleasures vary in *kind* as well as in degree.

Now, such a theory of life excites in many minds, and among them in some of the most estimable in feeling and purpose, inveterate dislike. To suppose that life has (as they express it) no higher end than pleasure—no better and nobler object of desire and pursuit—they designate as utterly mean and groveling; as a doctrine worthy only of swine, to whom the followers of Epicurus were, at a very early period, contemptuously likened; and modern holders of the doctrine are occasionally made the subject of equally polite comparisons by its German, French, and English assailants.

When thus attacked, the Epicureans have always answered that it is not they, but their accusers, who represent human nature in a degrading light; since the accusation supposes human beings to be capable of no pleasures except those of which swine are capable. If this supposition were true, the charge could not be gainsaid, but would then be no longer an imputation: for if the sources of pleasure were precisely the same to human beings and to swine, the rule of life which is good enough for the one would be good enough for the other. The comparison of the Epicurean life to that of beasts is felt as degrading, precisely because a beast's pleasures do not satisfy a human being's conceptions of happiness. Human beings have faculties more elevated than the animal appetites, and when once made conscious of them, do not regard anything as happiness which does not include their gratification. I do not, indeed, consider the Epicureans to have been by any means faultless in drawing out their scheme of consequences from the utilitarian principle. To do this in any sufficient manner, many Stoic, as well as Christian elements require to be included. But there is no known Epicurean theory of life which does not assign to the pleasures of the intellect, of the feelings and imagination, and of the moral sentiments, a much higher value as pleasures than to those of mere sensation. It must be admitted, however, that utilitarian writers in general have placed the superiority of mental over bodily pleasures chiefly in the greater permanency, safety, uncostliness, etc., of the former—that is, in their circumstantial advantages rather than in their intrinsic nature. And on all these points utilitarians have fully proved their case; but they might have taken the other, and, as it may be called, higher ground, with entire consistency. It is quite compatible with the principle of utility to recognize the fact, that some *kinds* of pleasure are more desirable and more valuable than others. It would be absurd that while, in estimating all other things, quality is considered as well as quantity, the estimation of pleasures should be supposed to depend on quantity alone.[d]

> **4.** The superiority of one kind of pleasure over another is properly determined by those who have experienced both kinds. Such competent judges, Mill argues, do, in fact, prefer the pleasures of the higher faculties to those of the lower.

If I am asked what I mean by difference of quality in pleasures, or what makes one pleasure more valuable than another, merely as a pleasure, except its being greater in amount, there is but one possible answer. Of two pleasures, if there be one to which all or almost all who have experience of both give a decided preference, irrespective of any feeling of moral obligation to prefer it, that is the more desirable pleasure. If one of the two is, by those who are competently acquainted with both, placed so far above the other that they prefer it, even though knowing it to be attended with a greater amount of discontent, and would not resign it for any quantity of the other pleasure which their nature is capable of, we are justified in ascribing to the preferred enjoyment a superiority in quality, so far outweighing quantity as to render it, in comparison, of small account.

Now it is an unquestionable fact that those who are equally acquainted with, and equally capable of appreciating and enjoying, both, do give a most marked preference to the manner of existence which employs their higher faculties. Few human creatures would consent to be changed into any of the lower animals, for a promise of the fullest allowance of a beast's pleasures; no intelligent human being would consent to be a fool, no instructed person would be an ignoramus, no person of feeling and conscience would be selfish and base, even though they should be persuaded that the fool, the dunce, or the rascal is better satisfied with his lot than they are with theirs. They would not resign what they possess more than he, for the most complete satisfaction of all the desires which they have in common with him. If they ever fancy they would, it is only in cases of unhappiness so extreme, that to escape from it they would exchange their lot for almost any other, however undesirable in their own eyes. A being of higher faculties requires more to make him happy, is capable probably of more acute suffering, and certainly accessible to it at more points, than one of an inferior type; but in spite of these liabilities, he can never really wish to sink into what he feels to be a lower grade of existence. We may give what explanation we please of this unwillingness; we may attribute it to pride, a name which is given indiscriminately to some of the most and to some of the least estimable feelings of which mankind are capable; we may refer to it the love of liberty and personal independence, an appeal to which was with the Stoics one of the most effective means for the inculcation of it; to the love of power, or to the love of excitement, both of which do really enter into and contribute to it: but its most appropriate appellation is a sense of dignity, which all human beings possess in one form or other, and in some, though by no means exact, proportion to their higher faculties, and which is so essential a part of the happiness of those in whom it is strong, that nothing which conflicts with it could be, otherwise than momentarily, an object of desire to them. Whoever supposes that this preference takes place at a sacrifice of happiness—that the superior being, in anything like equal circumstances, is not happier than the inferior—confounds the two very different ideas, of happiness and content. It is indisputable that the being whose capacities of enjoyment are low, has the greatest chance of having them fully satisfied; and a highly endowed being will always feel that any happiness which he can look for, as the world is constituted, is imperfect. But he can learn to bear its imperfections, if they are at all bearable; and they will not make him envy the being who is indeed unconscious of the imperfections, but only because he feels not at all the good which those imperfections qualify. It is better to be a human being dissatisfied than a pig satisfied; better to be Socrates dissatisfied than a fool satisfied. And if the fool, or the pig, is of a different opinion, it is because they only know their own side of the question. The other party to the comparison knows both sides.[e]

**5.** Mill moves to discount the judgments of those who abandon the higher pleasures for the lower by explaining that they are incapable, either inherently or by lack of opportunity, of enjoying the higher kind. The only competent and final judges are those who have tested the entire spectrum of pleasures.

It may be objected, that many who are capable of the higher pleasures, occasionally, under the influence of temptation, postpone them to the lower. But this is quite compatible with a full appreciation of the intrinsic superiority of the higher. Men often, from infirmity of character, make their election for the nearer good, though they know it to be the less valuable; and this no less when the choice is between two bodily pleasures, than when it is between bodily and mental. They pursue sensual indulgences to the injury of health, though perfectly aware that health is the greater good. It may be further objected, that many who begin with youthful enthusiasm for everything noble, as they advance in years sink to indolence and selfishness. But I do not believe that those who undergo this very common change, voluntarily choose the lower description of pleasures in preference to the higher. I believe that before they devote themselves exclusively to the one, they have already become incapable of the other. Capacity for the nobler feelings is in most natures a very tender plant, easily killed, not only by hostile influences, but by mere want of sustenance; and in the majority of young persons it speedily dies away if the occupations to which their position in life has devoted them, and the society into which it has thrown them, are not favorable to keeping that higher capacity in exercise. Men lose their high aspirations as they lose their intellectual tastes, because they have not time or opportunity for indulging them; and they addict themselves to inferior pleasures, not because they deliberately prefer them, but because they are either the only ones to which they have access, or the only ones which they are any longer capable of enjoying. It may be questioned whether anyone who has remained equally susceptible to both classes of pleasures, ever knowingly and calmly preferred the lower; though many, in all ages, have broken down in an ineffectual attempt to combine both.

From this verdict of the only competent judges, I apprehend there can be no appeal. On a question which is the best worth having of two pleasures, or which of two modes of existence is the most grateful to the feelings, apart from its moral attributes and from its consequences, the judgment of those who are qualified by knowledge of both, or, if they differ, that of the majority among them, must be admitted as final. And there needs be the less hesitation to accept this judgment respecting the quality of pleasures, since there is no other tribunal to be referred to even on the question of quantity. What means are there of determining which is the acutest of two pains, or the intensest of two pleasurable sensations, except the general suffrage of those who are familiar with both? Neither pains nor pleasures are homogeneous, and pain is always heterogeneous with pleasure. What is there to decide whether a particular pleasure is worth purchasing at a cost of a particular pain, except the feelings and judgment of the experienced? When, therefore, those feelings and judgment declare the pleasures derived from the higher faculties to be preferable *in kind,* apart from the question of intensity, to those of which the animal nature, disjoined from the higher faculties, is suspectible, they are entitled on this subject to the same regard.[f]

6. The "greatest happiness principle" is restated to include the distinction drawn between the quantitative and qualitative aspects of pleasure.

I have dwelt on this point, as being a necessary part of a perfectly just conception of Utility, or Happiness, considered as the directive rule of human conduct. But it is by no means an indispensable condition to the acceptance of the utilitarian standard; for that standard is not the agent's own greatest happiness, but the greatest amount of happiness altogether; and if it may possibly be doubted whether a noble character is always the happier for its nobleness, there can be no doubt that it makes other people happier, and that the world in general is immensely a gainer by it. Utilitarianism, therefore, could only attain its end by the general cultivation of nobleness of character, even if each individual were only benefited by the nobleness of others, and his own, so far as happiness is concerned, were a sheer deduction from the benefit. But the bare enunciation of such an absurdity as this last, renders refutation superfluous.

According to the Greatest Happiness Principle, as above explained, the ultimate end, with reference to and for the sake of which all other things are desirable (whether we are considering our own good or that of other people), is an existence exempt as far as possible from pain, and as rich as possible in enjoyments, both in point of quantity and quality; the test of quality, and the rule for measuring it against quantity, being the preference felt by those who, in their opportunities of experience, to which must be added their habits of self-consciousness and self-observation, are best furnished with the means of comparison. This, being, according to the utilitarian opinion, the end of human action is necessarily also the standard of morality; which may accordingly be defined, the rules and precepts for human conduct, by the observance of which an existence such as has been described might be, to the greatest extent possible, secured to all mankind; and not to them only, but, so far as the nature of things admits, to the whole sentient creation.[g]

7. The process of clarification is continued through stating various objections to the doctrine and answering them. For example, the argument that Utilitarianism is invalid because happiness cannot be attained is answered by Mill with a realistic description of happiness and a suggestion for the social means of achieving it.

When, however, it is thus positively asserted to be impossible that human life should be happy, the assertion, if not something like a verbal quibble, is at least an exaggeration. If by happiness be meant a continuity of highly pleasurable excitement, it is evident enough that this is impossible. A state of exalted pleasure lasts only moments, or in some cases, and with some intermissions, hours or days, and is the occasional brilliant flash of enjoyment, not its permanent and steady flame. Of this the philosophers who have taught that happiness is the end of life were as fully aware as those who taunt them. The happiness which they meant was not a life of rapture; but moments of such, in an existence made up of few and transitory pains, many and various pleasures, with a decided predominance of the active over the passive, and having as the foundation of the whole, not to expect more from life than it is capable of bestowing. A life thus composed, to those who have been fortunate enough to obtain it, has always appeared worthy of the name of happiness. And such an existence is even now the lot of many, during some considerable portion of their lives. The present wretched education, and wretched social arrangements, are the only real hindrance to its being attainable by almost all.

The objectors perhaps may doubt whether human beings, if taught to consider happiness as the end of life, would be satisfied with such a moderate share of it. But great numbers of mankind have been satisfied with much less. The main constituents of a satisfied life appear to be two, either of which by itself is often found sufficient for the purpose: tranquility and excitement. With much tranquility, many find that they can be content with very little pleasure: with much excitement, many can reconcile themselves to a considerable quantity of pain. There is assuredly no inherent impossibility in enabling even the mass of mankind to unite both; since the two are so far from being incompatible that they are in natural alliance, the prolongation of either being a preparation for, and exciting a wish for, the other. . . . When people who are tolerably fortunate in their outward lot do not find in life sufficient enjoyment to make it valuable to them, the cause generally is, caring for nobody but themselves. To those who have neither public nor private affections, the excitements of life are much curtailed, and in any case dwindle in value as the time approaches when all selfish interests must be terminated by death: while those who leave after them objects of personal affection, and especially those who have also cultivated a fellow feeling with the collective interests of mankind, retain as lively an interest in life on the eve of death as in the vigor of youth and health. Next to selfishness, the principal cause which makes life unsatisfactory is want of mental cultivation. A cultivated mind—I do not mean that of a philosopher, but any mind to which the fountains of knowledge have been opened, and which has been taught, in any tolerable degree, to exercise its faculties—finds sources of inexhaustible interest in all that surrounds it; in the objects of nature, the achievements of art, the imaginations of poetry, the incidents of history, the ways of mankind past and present, and their prospects in the future.[h]

> **8.** Another objection that Mill discounts is the claim that Utilitarian morality is incompatible with the acts of personal sacrifice that are so revered in our Christian culture. On closer analysis, those actions of self-sacrifice that we acknowledge to be good derive their value from their promotion of the general happiness, although they may deny individual happiness. Furthermore, this is not to be misinterpreted to mean that the happiness of one individual is less important than that of another.

Let utilitarians never cease to claim the morality of self-devotion as a possession which belongs by as good a right to them, as either to the Stoic or the Transcendentalist. The utilitarian morality does recognize in human beings the power of sacrificing their own greatest good for the good of others. It only refuses to admit that the sacrifice is itself a good. A sacrifice which does not increase, or tend to increase, the sum total of happiness, it considers as wasted. The only self-renunciation which it applauds, is devotion to the happiness, or to some of the means of happiness, of others; either of mankind collectively, or of individuals within the limits imposed by the collective interests of mankind.

I must again repeat, what the assailants of utilitarianism seldom have the justice to acknowledge, that the happiness which forms the utilitarian standard of what is right in conduct, is not the agent's own happiness, but that of all concerned. As between his own happiness and that of others, utilitarianism requires him to be as strictly impartial as a disinterested and benevolent spectator. In the golden rule of Jesus of Nazareth, we read the complete spirit of the ethics of utility. To do as one would be done by, and to love one's neighbor as oneself, constitute the ideal perfection of utilitarian morality. As the means of making the nearest approach to this ideal, utility would enjoin, first, that laws and social arrangements should place the happiness, or (as speaking practically it may be called) the interest, of every individual, as nearly as possible in harmony with the interest of the whole; and secondly, that education and opinion, which have so vast a power over human character, should so use that power as to establish in the mind of every individual an indissoluble association between his own happiness and the good of the whole; especially between his own happiness and the practice of such modes of conduct, negative and positive, as regard for the universal happiness prescribes: so that not only he may be unable to conceive the possibility of happiness to himself, consistently with conduct opposed to the general good, but also that a direct impulse to promote the general good may be in every individual one of the habitual motives of action, and the sentiments connected therewith may fill a large and prominent place in every human being's sentient existence. If the impugners of the utilitarian morality represented it to their own minds in this its true character, I know not what recommendation possessed by any other morality they could possibly affirm to be wanting to it: what more beautiful or more exalted developments of human nature any other ethical system can be supposed to foster, or what springs of action, not accessible to the utilitarian, such systems rely on for giving effect to their mandates.[i]

**9.** To the objection that people are not so constituted as always to be motivated by social concern, Mill rejoins that this is indeed true but that it in no way invalidates his thesis. The greatest happiness principle is not essential as a motive for conduct, but it is essential as the rule by which conduct is judged and sanctioned. The psychological question of motivation is distinct from the ethical questions of obligation and evaluation. Moral evaluation is directed to actions and to the manner in which they affect the general happiness.

They say it is exacting too much to require that people shall always act from the inducement of promoting the general interests of society. But this is to mistake the very meaning of a standard of morals, and confound the rule of action with the motive of it. It is the business of ethics to tell us what are our duties, or by what test we may know them; but no system of ethics requires that the sole motive of all we do shall be a feeling of duty; on the contrary, ninety-nine hundredths of all our actions are done from other motives, and rightly so done, if the rule of duty does not condemn them. It is the more unjust to utilitarianism that this particular misapprehension should be made a ground of objection to it, inasmuch as utilitarian moralists have gone beyond almost all others in affirming that the motive has nothing to do with the morality of the action, though much with the worth of the agent. He who saves a fellow creature from drowning does what is morally right, whether his motive be duty, or the hope of being paid for his trouble; he who betrays the friend that trusts him, is guilty of a crime, even if his object to be to serve another friend to whom he is under greater obligations. But to speak only of actions done from the motive of duty, and in direct obedience to principle: it is a misapprehension of the utilitarian mode of thought, to conceive it as implying that people should fix their minds upon so wide a generality as the world, or society at large. The great majority of good actions are intended not for the benefit of the world, but for that of individuals, of which the good of the world is made up; and the thoughts of the most virtuous man need not on these occasions travel beyond the particular persons concerned, except so far as is necessary to assure himself that in benefiting them he is not violating the rights—that is, the legitimate and authorized expectations—of anyone else. The multiplication of happiness is, according to the utilitarian ethics, the object of virtue: the occasions on which any person (except one in a thousand) has it in his power to do this on an extended scale, in other words to be a public benefactor, are but exceptional; and on these occasions alone is he called on to consider public utility; in every other case, private utility, the interest or happiness of some few persons, is all he has to attend to. Those alone the influence of whose actions extends to society in general, need concern themselves habitually about so large an object. In the case of abstinences indeed—of things which people forbear to do from moral considerations, though the consequences in the particular case might be beneficial—it would be unworthy of an intelligent agent not to be consciously aware that the action is of a class which, if practiced generally, would be generally injurious, and that this is the ground of the obligation to abstain from it. The amount of regard for the public interest implied in this recognition, is no greater than is demanded by every system of morals; for they all enjoin to abstain from whatever is manifestly pernicious to society.[j]

**10.** Having removed the major misconceptions about the principle of utility, Mill next proposes to investigate its ultimate sanction.

The question is often asked, and properly so, in regard to any supposed moral standard—What is its sanction? what are the motives to obey it? or more specifically, what is the source of its obligation? whence does it derive its binding force? It is a necessary part of moral philosophy to provide the answer to this question; which, though frequently assuming the shape of an objection to the utilitarian morality, as if it had some special applicability to that above others, really arises in regard to all standards. It arises, in fact, whenever a person is called on to *adopt* a standard or refer morality to any basis on which he has not been accustomed to rest it. For the customary morality, that which education and opinion have consecrated, is the only one which presents itself to the mind with the feeling of being *in itself* obligatory; and when a person is asked to believe that this morality *derives* its obligation from some general principle round which custom has not thrown the same halo, the assertion is to him a paradox; the supposed corollaries seem to have a more binding force than the original theorem; the superstructure seems to stand better without, than with, what is represented as its foundation. He says to himself, I feel that I am bound not to rob or murder, betray or deceive; but why am I bound to promote the general happiness? If my own happiness lies in something else, why may I not give that the preference?[k]

**11.** Mill argues that although the external sanctions, social and supernatural, enforce the Utilitarian principle, they do not obligate us to follow it. In and of themselves, they cannot bind us satisfactorily to any moral principle, because people are truly bound only when they feel inwardly that the principle is binding on them. It is our "feeling for humanity" that provides the ultimate sanction of the principle of utility, and this Mill calls the *internal sanction.*

The principle of utility either has, or there is no reason why it might not have, all the sanctions which belong to any other system of morals. Those sanctions are either external or internal. Of the external sanctions it is not necessary to speak at any length. They are, the hope of favor and the fear of displeasure from our fellow creatures or from the Ruler of the Universe, along with whatever we may have of sympathy or affection for them, or of love and awe of Him, inclining us to do His will independently of selfish consequences. There is evidently no reason why all these motives for observance should not attach themselves to the utilitarian morality, as completely and as powerfully as to any other. Indeed, those of them which refer to our fellow creatures are sure to do so, in proportion to the amount of general intelligence; for whether there be any other ground of moral obligation than the general happiness or not, men do desire happiness; and however imperfect may be their own practice, they desire and commend all conduct in others towards themselves, by which they think their happiness is promoted. With regard to the religious motive, if men believe, as most profess to do, in the goodness of God, those who think that conduciveness to the general happiness is the essence, or even only the criterion of good, must necessarily believe that it is also that which God approves. The whole force therefore of external reward and punishment, whether physical or moral, and whether proceeding from God or from our fellow men, together with all that the capacities of human nature admit, of disinterested devotion to either, become available to enforce the utilitarian morality, in proportion as that morality is recognized; and the more powerfully, the more the appliances of education and general cultivation are bent to the purpose.

So far as to external sanctions. The internal sanction of duty, whatever our standard of duty may be, is one and the same—a feeling in our own mind; a pain, more or less intense, attendant on violation of duty, which in properly cultivated moral natures rises, in the more serious cases, into shrinking from it as an impossibility. This feeling, when disinterested, and connecting itself with the pure idea of duty, and not with some particular form of it, or with any of the merely accessory circumstances, is the essence of Conscience; though in that complex phenomenon as it actually exists, the simple fact is in general all encrusted over with collateral associations, derived from sympathy, from love, and still more from fear; from all the forms of religious feeling; from the recollections of childhood and of all our past life;

from self-esteem, desire of the esteem of others, and occasionally even self-abasement. This extreme complication is, I apprehend, the origin of the sort of mystical character which, by a tendency of the human mind of which there are many other examples, is apt to be attributed to the idea of moral obligation, and which leads people to believe that the idea cannot possibly attach itself to any other objects than those which, by a supposed mysterious law, are found in our present experience to excite it. Its binding force, however, consists in the existence of a mass of feeling which must be broken through in order to do what violates our standard of right, and which, if we do nevertheless violate that standard, will probably have to be encountered afterwards in the form of remorse. Whatever theory we have of the nature or origin of conscience, this is what essentially constitutes it.

The ultimate sanction, therefore, of all morality (external motives apart) being a subjective feeling in our own minds, I see nothing embarrassing to those whose standard is utility, in the question, what is the sanction of that particular standard? We may answer, the same as of all other moral standards—the conscientious feelings of mankind. Undoubtedly this sanction has no binding efficacy on those who do not possess the feelings it appeals to; but neither will these persons be more obedient to any other moral principle than to the utilitarian one. On them morality of any kind has no hold but through the external sanctions. Meanwhile the feelings exist, a fact in human nature, the reality of which, and the great power with which they are capable of acting on those in whom they have been duly cultivated, are proved by experience. No reason has ever been shown why they may not be cultivated to as great intensity in connection with the utilitarian, as with any other rule of morals.[1]

> **12.** Regardless of whether this inner feeling for humanity is inborn or acquired, Mill contends that it can be a powerful force and a sound basis for Utilitarian morality.

It is not necessary, for the present purpose, to decide whether the feeling of duty is innate or implanted. Assuming it to be innate, it is an open question to what objects it naturally attaches itself; for the philosophic supporters of that theory are now agreed that the intuitive perception is of principles of morality, and not of the details. If there be anything innate in the matter, I see no reason why the feeling which is innate should not be that of regard to the pleasures and pains of others. If there is any principle of morals which is intuitively obligatory, I should say it must be that. If so, the intuitive ethics would coincide with the utilitarian, and there would be no further quarrel between them. Even as it is, the intuitive moralists, though they believe that there are other intuitive moral obligations, do already believe this to be one; for they unanimously hold that a large *portion* of morality turns upon the consideration due to the interests of our fellow creatures. Therefore, if the belief in the transcendental origin of moral obligation gives any additional efficacy to the internal sanction, it appears to me that the utilitarian principle has already the benefit of it.

On the other hand, if, as is my own belief, the moral feelings are not innate, but acquired, they are not for that reason the less natural. It is natural to man to speak, to reason, to build cities, to cultivate the ground, though these are acquired faculties. The moral feelings are not indeed a part of our nature, in the sense of being in any perceptible degree present in all of us; but this, unhappily, is a fact admitted by those who believe the most strenuously in their transcendental origin. Like the other acquired capacities above referred to, the moral faculty, if not a part of our nature, is a natural outgrowth from it; capable, like them, in a certain small degree, of springing up spontaneously; and susceptible of being brought by cultivation to a high degree of development. Unhappily it is also susceptible, by a sufficient use of the external sanctions and of the force of early impressions, of being cultivated in almost any direction: so that there is hardly anything so absurd or so mischievous that it may not, by means of these influences, be made to act on the human mind with all the authority of conscience. To doubt that the same potency might be given by the same means to the principle of utility, even if it had no foundation in human nature, would be flying in the face of all experience.

But moral associations which are wholly of artificial creation, when intellectual culture goes on, yield by degrees to the dissolving force of analysis: and if the feeling of duty, when associated with utility, would appear equally arbitrary; if there were no leading department of our nature, no powerful class of sentiments, with which that association would harmonize, which would make us feel it congenial, and incline us not only to foster it in others (for which we have abundant interested motives), but also to cherish it in ourselves; if there were not, in short, a natural basis of sentiment for utilitarian morality, it might well happen that this association also, even after it had been implanted by education, might be analyzed away.

But there *is* this basis of powerful natural sentiment; and this it is which, when once the general happiness is recognized as the ethical standard, will constitute the strength of the utilitarian morality. This firm foundation is that of the social feelings of mankind; the desire to be in unity with our fellow creatures, which is already a powerful principle in human nature, and happily one of those which tend to become stronger, even without express inculcation, form the influences of advancing civilization.[m]

**13.** Mill's moving description of the origin and nature of the feeling for humanity may serve as a fitting conclusion to his exposition of the greatest happiness principle.

The deeply rooted conception which every individual even now has of himself as a social being, tends to make him feel it one of his natural wants that there should be harmony between his feeling and aims and those of his fellow creatures. If differences of opinion and of mental culture make it impossible for him to share many of their actual feelings—perhaps make him denounce and defy those feelings—he still needs to be conscious that his real aim and theirs do not conflict; that he is not opposing himself to what they really wish for, namely, their own good, but is, on the contrary, promoting it. This feeling in most individuals is much inferior in strength to their selfish feelings, and is often wanting altogether. But to those who have it, it possesses all the characters of a natural feeling. It does not present itself to their minds as a superstition of education, or a law despotically imposed by the power of society, but as an attribute which it would not be well for them to be without. This conviction is the ultimate sanction of the greatest happiness morality. This it is which makes any mind, of well-developed feelings, work with, and not against, the outward motives to care for others, afforded by what I have called the external sanctions; and when those sanctions are wanting, or act in an opposite direction, constitutes in itself a powerful internal binding force, in proportion to the sensitiveness and thoughtfulness of the character; since few but those whose mind is a moral blank, could bear to lay out their course of life on the plan of paying no regard to others except so far as their own private interest compels.[n]

## QUESTIONS

1. What is the "principle of utility"? Why does Mill feel called on to defend the doctrine in such detail?
2. In what respects is Mill's conception of Utilitarianism different from that of Bentham?
3. What is Mill's reply to the objection that the greatest happiness principle is a "swinish doctrine"?
4. Distinguish between "psychological hedonism" and "ethical hedonism." Is it necessary to maintain both if you subscribe to either? Is it necessary to reject one if you subscribe to the other?
5. Why does Mill distinguish different kinds of pleasure? What criterion does he set up to judge differences in the quality of pleasures?
6. Discuss the role of sanctions in Mill's ethical theory, paying special attention to the "feeling for humanity."
7. Elaborate on Mill's distinction between a *motive for conduct* and a *rule of conduct*. What does he mean by his assertion that the motive has nothing to do with the morality of an action?

8. Looking back at Kant's ethics (Ch. 12), think about the ways in which he would disagree with Mill's theory of determining which action is right. Mill says at one point that he is trying to express what is correct in Kant's ethics. Would Kant accept that statement?
9. Reconstruct Mill's replies to (a) the accusation that the Utilitarian doctrine is incompatible with the Christian ideal of self-sacrifice and (b) the argument that the doctrine is invalid because it is not possible for people to achieve happiness.
10. Do you believe that the Utilitarian doctrine, as Mill presents it, has value for our times?

## KEY TO SELECTIONS

John Stuart Mill, *Utilitarianism*, London, Longmans, Green, 1897.
[a]Ch. IV, pp. 52–53.
[b]Ch. II, pp. 8–9.
[c]Ch. II, pp. 9–10.
[d]Ch. II, pp. 10–12.
[e]Ch. II, pp. 12–14.
[f]Ch. II, pp. 14–16.
[g]Ch. II, pp. 16–17.
[h]Ch. II, pp. 18–20.
[i]Ch. II, pp. 24–25.
[j]Ch. II, pp. 26–28.
[k]Ch. III, pp. 39–40.
[l]Ch. III, pp. 40–43.
[m]Ch. III, pp. 44–46.
[n]Ch. III, pp. 50–51.

## GUIDE TO ADDITIONAL READING


**PRIMARY SOURCES**

Mill, J. S., *Autobiography*, World's Classics (Oxford University Press).

_____, *Two Letters on the Measures of Value* (Johns Hopkins Press).

_____, *Utilitarianism, Liberty and Representative Government*, Everyman's Library (Dutton).

_____, *Utilitarianism*, Great Books Foundation (Regnery).

_____, _____, Little Library of Liberal Arts (Liberal Arts).

_____, "Utilitarianism" and "On Liberty," in *English Philosophers from Bacon to Mill*, Modern Library (Random House).

Bentham, J., *An Introduction to the Principle of Morals and Legislation*, Hafner Library of Classics (Hafner).

**DISCUSSION AND COMMENTARY**

Baumgardt, D., *Bentham and the Ethics of Today*, Princeton University Press, 1952.

Berger, F., *Happiness, Justice and Freedom: The Moral and Political Philosophy of John Stuart Mill*, Berkeley, University of California Press, 1984.

Brandt, R. B., *Facts, Values, and Morality*, Cambridge, Cambridge University Press, 1996.

Broad, C. D., *Five Types of Ethical Theory*, New York, Harcourt, Brace, 1930, Ch. 6.

Gorovitz, S. (ed.), *Utilitarianism with Critical Essays*, New York, Bobbs-Merrill, 1971.

Harrison, R., *Bentham*, London, Routledge and Kegan Paul, 1983.

Lyons, D., *Ethics and the Rule of Law*, Cambridge, Cambridge University Press, 1984, Ch. 5.

McCloskey, H., *John Stuart Mill: A Critical Study*, London, Macmillan, 1971.

Miller, H., and Williams, W. (eds.), *The Limits of Utilitarianism*, Minneapolis, University of Minnesota Press, 1982.

Moore, G. E., *Ethics*, New York, Henry Holt, Home University Library, 1912, Chs. 1 and 2.

Plamenatz, J., *The English Utilitarians*, Oxford, Basil Blackwell and Mott, 1944.

Sidgwick, H., *The Methods of Ethics*, London, Macmillan, 1907, Bks. 2 and 4.

PART TWO

# Modern Continuations and Critiques

CHAPTER FOURTEEN

# The Leap of Faith

© Bettmann/CORBIS

SØREN KIERKEGAARD

ALTHOUGH SØREN KIERKEGAARD (1813–1855) is widely regarded as the father of the philosophical, theological, and literary movement known as existentialism, his recognition as an important thinker was long delayed. It was only after World War II, when the consequent loss in human dignity and individuality was manifest throughout Europe, that intellectuals focused on his writings. Generalized, his century-old message seemed suddenly prophetic: Institutions based on self-serving presumptions about human beings in the abstract tend to transform actual men and women into anonymous conformists.

The youngest member of a Copenhagen family that was both prosperous in business and devoutly Lutheran, Kierkegaard was himself indifferent to financial affairs but intensely concerned with religious ones throughout his relatively brief life. He entered the University of Copenhagen in 1830, a conspicuously intelligent but physically frail young man who was gifted at self-expression. He found himself increasingly out of step with the dominating philosophy of Hegel and its developing variants, because reason, for all its clarity and objectivity, cannot be extended to embrace the concrete reality of human existence. His thesis, *The Concept of Irony*, was finally accepted in 1841. Kierkegaard recounts in his *Journal* that he led a dissolute life in his early student days and that, in doing so, he was rebelling both against his dominating father and against God. That parental and religious reconciliation came before the death of his father was one of the abiding joys of Kierkegaard's largely melancholy life. Another important event of this period that weighed heavily on him was his love affair with Regine Olsen, the daughter of a prominent government official. They met four years before the completion of his thesis. Although he fell in love immediately, Kierkegaard quite properly delayed courting her until she turned seventeen. Then, after having won her affection, he requested that she end the engagement. At one level this amounted to his rejection of a settled, ordinary life in favor of one devoted to study and writing. At quite another level, it was Kierkegaard's decision not to contaminate his loved one with his morbidity and his youthful sins. To avoid scandal, he moved to Berlin for the next six years and began to write voluminously on a variety of subjects.

While living in the withdrawn way of an author, Kierkegaard increasingly felt the need to involve himself in public controversies and to criticize certain Danish institutions and officials. The chief target of his forceful denunciations was the Lutheran State Church of Denmark and its primate: Kierkegaard charged that "Christendom" under this Bishop had lost contact with Christianity. However, it was a lesser target that destroyed him as a public figure. He wrote that the popular Copenhagen journal *The Corsair* had low standards, and his attack stimulated an immediate and continuing response. Kierkegaard was reduced to a caricature and his views were ridiculed as rantings. When he died in the fall of 1855, few Danes recognized their loss.

Among the most important of his works are *Journals* (1839–1843), *Either/Or: A Fragment of Life* (1843), *Fear and Trembling* (1843), *The Concept of Dread* (1843), and *Concluding Unscientific Postscript* (1846).

While admitting the usefulness of objective knowledge, Kierkegaard denies that such knowledge can satisfy our hunger for self-understanding.

> What I really need is to get clear about *what I must do*, not what I must know. . . . The crucial thing is to find a truth which is a truth *for me*, to find *the idea for which I* am willing to live or die.[1]

To understand ourselves we must face up to difficult spiritual questions: How can I find inner peace and significance? How can I avoid being a mere aggregate of chance occurrences? How can I see what God intends for me to do? Whether hesitant or assured, Kierkegaard's responses to such questions testify to the predominance of will over reason, and they underscore the chastening fact that we *are* what we choose to be. He argues that, properly interpreted, the Socratic admonition "Know thyself" directs us to ask and answer inward questions. For him it is a long-term error of philosophy to believe that Socrates recommended making ourselves the primary objects of rational inquiry: We are *subjects*, and thus we cannot be reduced to objects without losing sight of truth.

According to Kierkegaard, the historical turn in human affairs from subjectivity to objectivity—from the primacy of will to the primacy of reason—began with Plato and Aristotle. They assumed that methods of reason alone could disclose truths about human beings and thus obviate the need for subjective truths. For Kierkegaard, this unfortunate dogma has been strengthened over time by the successes of rational methods in mathematics, logic, and natural philosophy (the formal and physical sciences), by the fascination that attends building speculative metaphysical and theological systems, and by the quick results that simple conceptual techniques bring to social and moral philosophy. In his view, much of this intellectual edifice

[1]Søren Kierkegaard, *Journals and Papers*, vol. 5, pt. 1, 1839, ed. and tr. Howard V. Hong and Edna H. Hong (Bloomington, Indiana University Press, 1978), p. 35.

stands condemned. Our inward questions have been forestalled; they have been neglected; they have not been answered.

For Kierkegaard, it is an outright mistake to subsume existent, concrete, unique human beings under a concept or collection of concepts and thereby reduce them to mere *abstract entities.* The fallacy of converting persons into *types* of people is, perhaps, most evident in moral psychology. Thus, for example, the moral psychology on which Aristotle develops his ethical theory assumes that humans are *essentially* rational; Hume's moral psychology assumes that they are *essentially* passional; and Hobbes's that they are *essentially* egoistic. According to Kierkegaard, the resulting ethical theories tend to mask rather than disclose moral truths. He does grant, however, that the treasury of ethical and moral thought of which such theories are a part has a role to play at the level of subjective reality. Thus, for example, Kierkegaard *chose* to guide his actions by Kantian-like principles during much of his life.

At a basic level, Kierkegaard in effect is reversing Descartes' dictum "I think, therefore I am" to "I am, therefore I think," or, more precisely, to "I am, therefore I choose to do." Although my bare existence does not depend on conscious activity, the more I become aware of myself, the more acute the problem of choosing among various courses of action becomes. Furthermore, there is no way to escape to a neutral point of view from which to make my decisions. And finally, there is the pervasive agony of recognizing that to choose one alternative is to preclude pursuit of any others. Thus I arrive at the unadorned, risky condition of being human. Relief from the agony of choosing comes to us only from passionately committing ourselves to the decision being made. But even this relief may turn out to be temporary; Kierkegaard insists that existential commitments that do not derive from unconditional commitment to the Christian God are transient.

Whether Kierkegaard was influenced by the nineteenth-century notion of developmental change or felt the need for an expository device, he proposes three "stages on life's way," three kinds of existence. In ascending order, they are the *aesthetic*, the *ethical*, and the *religious*, and they indicate three sharply contrasting attitudes toward choice. However, many people do not genuinely experience any of the three states during their lives. They are often conformists of one sort or another who choose by default to follow the crowd and thus to sacrifice their freedom. Additionally, some people remain at one level rather than passing through to another; and finally, the succession of stages is not fixed.

In the aesthetic mode of life, choice is not taken seriously. At one extreme are the individuals who just pursue their whims; at another are the hedonists who are tempted by what they believe will provide continuing pleasure. Life at this stage is variously marked by the growing discontent of aimlessness, irresponsibility, or boredom. When such discontent becomes unbearable, the individual has reached the threshold of the ethical stage, the threshold of a qualitative change in one's attitude toward choice.

The ethical stage emerges when we fully acknowledge the authority of virtue and duty. Kierkegaard's account of this stage draws conspicuously from rational components of Kant's ethical theory: We must choose to meet our obligations and responsibilities as determined by universal principles; furthermore, if our actions are mere instances of conforming to the rules, or of serving our own interests by following the rules, then they lack moral worth. In their turn, however, the peace and significance of the ethical phase fade away. Not only do feelings of guilt from our moral failures accumulate, but also—and more basically—the deceit underlying the very ethics to which we adhere becomes clear. In terms of Kant's ethical theory, Kierkegaard's point is this: We can determine a moral rule rationally because, when universalized, its denial involves a contradiction. But unless we have *already decided* that this *is* the criterion for moral truth and have thereby chosen to believe that it is, this test by the "categorical imperative" has no authority. Also, as we become more clearly aware of our limited power to know and do what is right, our passional commitments to moral action are undermined by feelings of inadequacy. The agony of the predicament of choice returns.

What are we to do? We now understand that it is deceptive to regard reason as providing moral truth. Is there an untried, qualitatively different attitude toward choice? Is there an attitude that ensures genuine choice? An attitude that induces passional commitments that provide enduring relief? Kierkegaard finds the answer in the religious mode. Our salvation depends on adopting a conviction of faith in which our choices are under infinite God's control rather than our own. What we do is what God wills us to do. Subjective histories of failed choices, nonenduring passional commitments, and recurring anxiety invite the humility that this leap to faith requires.

Kierkegaard's radical distinction between subjective and objective truth allows him to sidestep many would-be criticisms by theologians. Thus, for example, suppose we ask him how persons in the religious stage resolve their concern about questions like these: Might it be that I am not under God's control but merely think that I am? Might it be that in accepting Christ as both God (eternal) and historic man (temporal), I am accepting a logical absurdity? Kierkegaard could reply that if such questions become important, then we have lost the concreteness and intimacy of our religious experience and are again captives of speculative, abstract thought. Because of the sharpness of his distinction between subjective and objective, Kierkegaard turns to paradigmatic accounts (models of faith) rather than "proofs" to authenticate the religious attitude. Perhaps the most compelling of these models is the Old Testament figure Abraham—an exemplar of religious values—in following God's command that he sacrifice his son. In Kierkegaard's words, the decisive fact is that Abraham "transgressed the ethical altogether and had a higher *telos* [purpose] outside it, in which he suspended it."[2]

---

**1.** Kierkegaard stresses the importance of choice in situations that are critical, as well as in those that are insignificant to the individual, believing that a person's decisions determine his or her quality or character.

What I have said so often to you I say once again, or, more exactly, I shout it to you: Either/Or... There are conditions of life in which it would be ludicrous or a kind of derangement to apply an Either/Or, but there are also people whose souls are too dissolute to comprehend the implications of such a dilemma, whose personalities lack the energy to be able to say with pathos: Either/Or.

These words have always made a great impression on me and still do, especially when I

---

[2]Søren Kierkegaard, *Fear and Trembling,* ed. Howard V. Hong and Edna H. Hong (Princeton: Princeton University Press, 1983), p. 59.

say them this way plainly and by themselves; there lies the possibility of setting in motion the most terrifying contradictions. They act upon me like an incantation formula, and my soul becomes exceedingly earnest, at times is almost in a state of shock. I think of my early youth, when without really comprehending what it is to make a choice in life I listened with childish trust to the talk of my elders, and the moment of choice became a very solemn and momentous matter, although in choosing I only followed someone else's directions. I think of moments later in life when I stood at the crossroads, when my soul was made ripe in the hour of decision. I think of the many less important but for me not trivial incidents in my life when it was a matter of choosing, for even if there is only one situation in which these words have absolute meaning—namely, every time truth, justice, and sanctity appear on one side and lust and natural inclinations, dark passions and perdition on the other side. Nevertheless, even in matters that in and by themselves are innocent, what a person chooses is always important. It is important that he choose properly, test himself, so that eventually he does not have to begin a painful retreat to the point where he started and thank God if he has no more for which to upbraid himself than having wasted his time.[a]

> **2.** The heart of human existence lies in the power of choice (will). Indeed, the manner in which one chooses (intensity and earnestness of choice) is as meaningful as the content of choice (what one chooses). Ethical choices are absolute and strict, constituting the basis for finding oneself; aesthetic choices are not genuine because they have either momentary or indifferent effects on the person's life.

Now, if a person could continually keep himself on the spear tip of the moment of choice, if he could stop being a human being, if in his innermost being he could be nothing more than an ethereal thought, if personality meant nothing more than being a nisse [sprite] who admittedly goes through the motions but nevertheless always remains the same—if that were the situation, it would be foolish to speak of its being too late for a person to choose, since in a deeper sense there could be no question of a choice at all. The choice itself is crucial for the content of the personality: through the choice the personality submerges itself in that which is being chosen, and when it does not choose, it withers away in atrophy. For a moment that between which the choice is to be made lies—for a moment it seems to lie—outside the person who is choosing; he stands in no relation to it, can maintain himself in a state of indifference toward it. This is the moment of deliberation, but, like the Platonic [moment], it actually is not at all, and least of all in the abstract sense in which you wish to hold onto it; and the longer one stares at it, the smaller it is. That which is to be chosen has the deepest relation to the one who is choosing, and when the choice is about an issue of elemental importance to life, the individual must at the same time continue to live, and this is why the longer he puts off the choice, the more easily he comes to alter it, although he goes on pondering and pondering and thereby believes that he is really keeping separate the two alternatives of the choice.

If one views life's Either/Or in this way, one is not easily tempted to trifle with it. One sees that the inner working of the personality has no time for imaginary constructions in thought, so that it continually speeds ahead and in one way or another posits either the one or the other, whereby the choice is made more difficult in the next moment, for that which has been posited will be withdrawn. Imagine a captain of a ship the moment a shift of direction must be made; then he may be able to say: I can do either this or that. But if he is not a mediocre captain he will also be aware that during all this the ship is ploughing ahead with its ordinary velocity, and thus there is but a single moment when it is inconsequential whether he does this or does that. So also with a person—if he forgets to take into account the velocity—there eventually comes a moment where it is no longer a matter of an Either/Or, not because he has chosen, but because he has refrained from it, which also can be expressed by saying: Because others have chosen for him—or because he has lost himself.[b]

> **3.** Genuine choice is an absolute matter of ethics. One's inner personality is involved. The aesthetic mode does not represent choice in a strict sense, because one does not have to operate in terms of good and bad.

On the whole, to choose is an intrinsic and stringent term for the ethical. Wherever in the stricter sense there is a question of an Either/Or, one can always be sure that the ethical has something to do with it. The only absolute Either/Or is the choice between good and evil, but this is also absolutely ethical.

The aesthetic choice is either altogether immediate, and thus no choice, or it loses itself in a great multiplicity. For example, when a young girl follows her heart's choice, this choice, however beautiful it is otherwise, is no choice in the stricter sense, because it is altogether immediate. If a man aesthetically ponders a host of life tasks, then he . . . does not readily have one Either /Or but a great multiplicity, because the self-determining aspect of the choice has not been ethically stressed and because, if one does not choose absolutely, one chooses only for the moment and for that reason can choose something else the next moment.

Therefore, the ethical choice is in a certain sense much easier, much simpler, but in another sense it is infinitely more difficult. The person who wants to decide his life task ethically does not ordinarily have such a wide range; the act of choosing, however, is much more meaningful to him. Now, if you are to understand me properly, I may very well say that what is important in choosing is not so much to choose the right thing as the energy, the earnestness, and the pathos with which one chooses. In the choosing the personality declares itself in its inner infinity and in turn the personality is thereby consolidated. Therefore, even though a person chose the wrong thing, he nevertheless, by virtue of the energy with which he chose, will discover that he chose the wrong thing. In other words, since the choice has been made with all the inwardness of his personality, his inner being is purified and he himself is brought into an immediate relationship with the eternal power that omnipresently pervades all existence. The person who chooses only aesthetically never reaches this transfiguration, this higher dedication. Despite all its passion, the rhythm in his soul is only a *spiritus lenis* [weak aspiration].

Like a Cato, then, I shout my Either/Or to you, and yet not like a Cato, for my soul has not yet attained the resigned coldness that he had. But I know that this adjuration alone, if I have sufficient strength, will be able to arouse you, not to the activity of thinking, for in that you are not deficient, but to earnestness of spirit. Without it, you may succeed in accomplishing a great deal, even in astounding the world (for I am not stingy), and yet you will miss out on the highest, on the only thing that truly gives life meaning; you may win the whole world and lose yourself.

What, then, is that I separate in my Either/Or? Is it good and evil? No, I only want to bring you to the point where this choice truly has meaning for you. It is on this that everything turns. As soon as a person can be brought to stand at the crossroads in such a way that there is no way out for him except to choose, he will choose the right thing. Therefore, if it should so happen that before you finish reading this somewhat lengthy exploration, which again is being sent to you in the form of a letter, you feel that the moment of choice has arrived, then throw away the remainder—do not bother with it; you have lost nothing. But choose, and you will see the validity inherent in so doing; indeed, no young girl can be as happy with her heart's choice as a man who has known how to choose. Consequently, either a person has to live aesthetically or he has to live ethically. Here, as stated, it is still not a matter of a choice in the stricter sense, for the person who lives aesthetically does not choose, and the person who chooses the aesthetic after the ethical has become manifest to him is not living aesthetically, for he is sinning and is subject to ethical qualifications, even if this life must be termed unethical. You see, this is, so to speak, the *character indelebilis* of the ethical, that the ethical, although it modestly places itself on the same level as the aesthetic, nevertheless is essentially that which makes the choice a choice.

And this is what is sad when one contemplates human life, that so many live out their lives in quiet lostness; they outlive themselves, not in the sense that life's content successively unfolds and is now possessed in this unfolding, but they live, as it were, away from themselves and vanish like shadows. Their immortal souls are blown away, and they are not disquieted by the question of its immortality, because they are already disintegrated before they die. They do not live aesthetically, but neither has the ethical become manifest to them in its wholeness; nor have they actually rejected it, and therefore they are not sinning either, except insofar as it is a sin to be neither one thing nor the other. Nor do they doubt their immortality, for the person who deeply and fervently doubts it on his own behalf is sure to find what is right. I say "on his own behalf," and it certainly is high time that someone warns against the magnanimous, gallant objectivity with which many thinkers think on behalf of all others and not on their own. If anyone calls what I am claiming here self-love, then I shall answer: That comes from having no idea of what this "self" is and from the futility of a person's gaining the whole world but losing himself, and also it is bound to be a poor argument that does not first and foremost convince the person who presents it.

Rather than designating the choice between good and evil, my Either/Or designates the choice by which one chooses good and evil or rules them out. Here the question is under what qualifications one will view all existence and personally live. That the person who chooses good and evil chooses the good is indeed true, but only later does this become manifest, for the aesthetic is not evil but the indifferent. And that is why I said that the ethical constitutes the choice. Therefore, it is not so much a matter of choosing between willing good or willing evil as of choosing to will, but that in turn posits good and evil. The person who chooses the ethical chooses the good, but here the good is altogether abstract; its being is thereby merely posited, and this by no means precludes that the one choosing cannot in turn choose evil even though he chose the good. Here you see again how important it is that a choice is made and that it does not depend so much upon deliberation as on the baptism of the will, which assimilates this into the ethical.[c]

**4.** Kierkegaard characterizes the aesthetic way of life as one in which the object of pursuit is pleasure, though the conceptions of pleasure may vary. However, the condition of their enjoyment always is external; that is, it resides in such capabilities as one's business acumen or literary talent rather than one's inner personality.

But what does it mean to live aesthetically, and what does it mean to live ethically? What is the aesthetic in a person, and what is the ethical? To that I would respond: the aesthetic in a person is that by which he spontaneously and immediately is what he is; the ethical is that by which he become what he becomes. That person who lives in and by and from and for the aesthetic that is in him, that person lives aesthetically....

Every human being, no matter how slightly gifted he is, however subordinate his position in life may be, has a natural need to formulate a life-view, a conception of the meaning of life and of its purpose. The person who lives aesthetically also does that, and the popular expression heard in all ages and from various stages is this: One must enjoy life. There are, of course, many variations of this, depending on differences in the conceptions of enjoyment, but all are agreed that we are to enjoy life. *But the person who says that he wants to enjoy life always posits a condition that either lies outside the individual or is within the individual in such a way that it is not there by virtue of the individual himself.* I beg you to keep rather fixed the phrases of this last sentence, for they have been carefully chosen....

We proceed. We encounter life-views that teach that we are to enjoy life but place the condition for it outside the individual. This is the case with every life-view in which wealth, honors, noble birth, etc. are made life's task and its content. Here, again, I would like to mention a certain kind of falling in love. If I imagine a young girl in love with all her soul, whose eyes have no delight except in seeing her beloved, whose soul has no thought except of him, whose heart has no desire except to belong to him, for whom nothing, nothing, neither in heaven nor on earth, has any meaning except him, then this, too, is an aesthetic life-view in which the condition is placed outside the individual. You, of course, think that it is foolish to love this way; you think that it is something that happens only in novels. But it can be imagined, and this much is certain: In the eyes of many people a love such as that would be regarded as something extraordinary. . . .

We proceed. We encounter life-views that teach that we are to enjoy life, but the condition for it lies within the individual himself, yet in such a way that it is not posited by himself. Here the personality is ordinarily defined as talent. It is a talent for practical affairs, a talent for business, a talent for mathematics, a talent for writing, a talent for art, a talent for philosophy. Satisfaction in life, enjoyment, is sought in the unfolding of this talent. Perhaps one does not stop with the talent in its immediacy but refines it in every way, but the condition for satisfaction in life is the talent itself, a condition that is not posited by the individual himself. People with this life-view frequently are among those who are usually the butt of your constant ridicule because of their unflagging activity. You believe that you yourself are living aesthetically and will by no means acknowledge that they are. That you have another view of enjoying life is undeniable, but that is not the essential point; the essential point is that one wants to enjoy life. Your life is much more distinguished than theirs, but theirs is also much more innocent than yours.

Just as all these life-views have their aesthetic nature in common, so they also resemble one another in having a certain unity, a certain coherence, the one particular thing around which everything revolves. What they build their lives upon is something simple, and therefore this life-view is not fragmented as is the life-view of those who build upon something intrinsically multiple.

This is the case with the life-view on which I shall now dwell a bit longer. It teaches "Enjoy life" and interprets it as "Live for your desire." But desire per se is a multiplicity, and thus it is easy to see that this life splits up into a boundless multiplicity except insofar as desire in a particular individual has from childhood been limited to one specific desire, which then might rather be called an inclination, for example, a bent toward fishing or hunting or keeping horses etc.[d]

> **5.** The ethical way of life, according to Kierkegaard, consists in more than mere conformity to duty. It must also include the person's inner passion and earnestness to help others. Otherwise, one simply obeys the letter of the law and ignores the spirit.

In contrast to an aesthetic life-view, which wants to enjoy life, we often hear about another life-view that places the meaning of life in living for the performance of one's duties. This is supposed to signify an ethical view of life. But the formulation falls far short, and one could almost believe that it was devised to discredit the ethical. One thing is sure, that in our day we often see it used in such a way that it almost makes us smile, for example, when Scribe has this thesis recited with a certain farcical solemnity that makes a very disparaging contrast to the joy and mirth of enjoyment. The mistake is that the individual is placed in an external relation to duty. The ethical is defined as duty, and duty in turn as a multiplicity of particular rules, but the individual and duty stand outside each other. Of course, a life of duty such as that is very unlovely and boring, and if the ethical did not have a much deeper connection with the personality it would always be very difficult to champion it against the aesthetic. That there are many people who do not advance beyond this, I shall not deny, but that is not owing to duty but to the people themselves.

It is curious that the word "duty" can prompt one to think of an external relation, since the very derivation of the word suggests an internal one; for that which is incumbent upon me, not as this individual with accidental characteristics but in accordance with my true being, certainly has the most intimate relation with myself. That is, duty is not something laid upon but something that lies upon. When duty is regarded in this way, it is a sign that the individual is oriented within himself. Then duty will not split up for him into a multiplicity of particular stipulations, for this always indicates that he has only an external relation to duty. He has put on duty; for him it is the expression of his innermost being. When he is thus oriented within himself, he has immersed himself in the ethical, and he will not run himself ragged performing his duties. Therefore, the truly ethical person has an inner serenity and sense of security, for he does not have duty outside himself but within himself. The more deeply a man has structured his life ethically, the less he will feel compelled to talk about duty every moment, to worry every moment whether he is performing it, every moment to seek the advice of others about what his duty is. When the ethical is viewed properly, it makes the individual infinitely secure within himself; when it is viewed improperly, it makes the individual utterly insecure, and I cannot imagine an unhappier or more tormented life than when a person has his duty outside himself and yet continually wants to carry it out.

If the ethical is regarded as outside the personality and in an external relation to it, then one has given up everything, then one has despaired. The aesthetic as such is despair; the ethical is the abstract and as such is without the means for accomplishing the least thing. That is why it is both comic and tragic to see at times people with a kind of honest zeal working their fingers to the bone in order to carry out the ethical, which like a shadow continually evades them as soon as they try to grasp it....

The ethical is the universal and thus the abstract. That is why in its perfect abstraction the ethical is always interdictory. Thus the ethical takes the form of law. As soon as the ethical is prescriptive, it already has something of the aesthetic. The Jews were the people of the law. Therefore they understood most of the commandments in the Mosaic law splendidly, but the commandment they did not seem to have understood was the commandment to which Christianity attached itself most of all: You shall love God with all your heart. This commandment is neither negative nor abstract; it is highly positive and highly concrete. When the ethical becomes more concrete, it crosses over into the category of morals....

When a person has felt the intensity of duty with all his energy, then he is ethically matured, and then duty will break forth within him. The fundamental point, therefore, is not whether a person can count on his fingers how many duties he has, but that he has once and for all felt the intensity of duty in such a way that the consciousness of it is for him the assurance of the eternal validity of his being. That is why I by no means praise being a man of duty, no more than I recommend being a bookworm, and yet I am sure that the person for whom the meaning of duty has never become manifest in all its infinitude is just as second-rate a human being as someone is a scholar who *ad modum* [in the fashion of] "the Grenaa-men" thinks he will find wisdom *mir nichts und dir nichts* [without further ado]. Let the casuist immerse himself in finding out the complexity of duty; the primary question, the only salutary thing, is always that a person with respect to his own life is not his uncle but his father.

Let me illustrate what I mean by an example. To that end I select an impression I have preserved from my earliest childhood. When I was five years old, I was sent to school. That such an event always makes an impression on a child is natural, but the question is—what impression? Childish inquisitiveness is fascinated by all the bewildering ideas about what it may really mean. That this was also the case with me was to be expected; however, the main impression I received was entirely different. I arrived at school; I was presented to the teacher and was given my assignment for the next day—the first ten lines in Balle's catechism, which I was to learn by heart. Every other impression was now erased from my soul; only my task stood vividly before it. As a child I had a very good memory. Very soon I had done my homework. My sister had heard me several times and testified that I knew it. I went to bed, and before I fell asleep I recited it again to myself. I fell asleep with the firm intention of reading it over again the next morning. I awoke at five o'clock in the morning, dressed myself, took my catechism, and read it again. It is all as vivid to me this moment as if it happened yesterday. It seemed to me that heaven and earth would tumble down if I did not do my homework, and on the other hand it seemed to me that if heaven and earth did tumble down this upheaval would in no way excuse me from doing what had once been set before me—doing my homework. At that age I knew very little about my duties; I had not yet become acquainted with them in Balle's catechism. I had but one duty, to do my homework, and yet I can derive my whole ethical view of life from this impression.

I can smile at such a little fellow of five years who approaches a matter that passionately, and yet I assure you that I have no higher wish than that at any period of my life I may approach my work with the energy, with the ethical earnestness, I did then.[c]

**6.** For Kierkegaard, a third mode of existence is living by religious faith. It is neither mystical nor irrational but rather is suprarational. That is, one must go beyond reason and make a "leap of faith" because there are no universal rules to provide guidance to a given individual. This is exemplified in the story of Abraham and Isaac. God's demand that Abraham sacrifice Isaac requires a father to ignore the ethical law, the duty to his son. In this moment of decision, Abraham faces despair and the absurdity of suspending what is ethical by obeying God's will instead.

The ethical as such is the universal, and as the universal it applies to everyone, which from another angle means that it applies at all times. It rests immanent in itself, has nothing outside itself that is its τέλος [end, purpose] but is itself the τέλος for everything outside itself, and when the ethical has absorbed this into itself, it goes not further. The single individual, sensately and psychically qualified in immediacy, is the individual who has his τέλος in the universal, and it is his ethical task continually to express himself in this, to annul his singularity in order to become the universal. As soon as the single individual asserts himself in his singularity before the universal, he sins, and only by acknowledging this can he be reconciled again with the universal. Every time the single individual, after having entered the universal, feels an impulse to assert himself as the single individual, he is in a spiritual trial . . . from which he can work himself only by repentantly surrendering as the single individual in the universal. If this is the highest that can be said of man and his existence, then the ethical is of the same nature as a person's eternal salvation, which is his τέλος forevermore and at all times, since it would be a contradiction for this to be capable of being surrendered (that is, teleologically suspended), because as soon as this is suspended it is relinquished, whereas that which is suspended is not relinquished but is preserved in the higher, which is its τέλος.

If this is the case, then Hegel is right in "The Good and Conscience," where he qualifies man only as the individual and considers this qualification as a "moral form of evil" (see especially *The Philosophy of Right*), which must be annulled . . . in the teleology of the moral in such a way that the single individual who remains in that stage either sins or is immersed in spiritual trial. But Hegel is wrong in speaking about faith; he is wrong in not protesting loudly and clearly against Abraham's enjoying honor and glory as a father of faith when he ought to be sent back to a lower court and shown up as a murderer.

Faith is namely this paradox that the single individual is higher than the universal—yet, please note, in such a way that the movement repeats itself, so that after having been in the universal he as the single individual isolates himself as higher than the universal. If this is not faith, then Abraham is lost, then faith has never existed in the world precisely because it has always existed.

For if the ethical—that is, social morality—is the highest and if there is in a person no residual incommensurability in some way such that this incommensurability is not evil (i.e., the single individual, who is to be expressed in the universal), then no categories are needed other than what Greek philosophy had or what can be deduced from them by consistent thought. Hegel should not have concealed this, for, after all, he had studied Greek philosophy. . . .

The story of Abraham contains . . . a teleological suspension of the ethical. There is no dearth of keen minds and careful scholars who have found analogies to it. What their wisdom amounts to is the beautiful proposition that basically everything is the same. If one looks more closely, I doubt very much that anyone in the whole wide world will find one single analogy, except for a later one, which proves nothing if it is certain that Abraham represents faith and that it is manifested normatively in him, whose life not only is the most paradoxical that can be thought but is also so paradoxical that it simply cannot be thought. He acts by virtue of the absurd, for it is precisely the absurd that he as the single individual is higher than the universal. This paradox cannot be mediated, for as soon as Abraham begins to do so, he has to confess that he was in a spiritual trial, and if before it, not as inferior to it but as superior—yet in such a way, please note, that it is the single individual who, after being subordinate as the single individual to the universal, now by means of the universal becomes the single individual who as the single individual is superior, that the single individual as the single individual stands in an absolute relation to the absolute. This position cannot be mediated, for all mediation takes place only by virtue of the universal; it is and remains for all eternity a paradox, impervious to thought. And yet faith is this paradox, or else (and I ask the reader to bear these consequences *in mente* [in mind] even though it would be too prolix for me to write them all down) or else faith has never existed simply because it has always existed, or else Abraham is lost.

It is certainly true that the single individual can easily confuse this paradox with spiritual trial, but it ought not to be concealed for that reason. It is certainly true that many persons may be so constituted that they are repulsed by it, but faith ought not therefore to be made into something else to enable one to have it, but one ought rather to admit to not having it, while those who have faith ought to be prepared to set forth some characteristics whereby the paradox can be distinguished from a spiritual trial. . . .

The difference between the tragic hero and Abraham is very obvious. The tragic hero is still within the ethical. He allows an expression of the ethical to have its τέλος in a higher expression of the ethical; he scales down the ethical relation between father and son or daughter and father to a feeling that has its dialectic in its relation to the idea of moral conduct. Here there can be no question of a teleological suspension of the ethical self.

Abraham's situation is different. By his act he transgressed the ethical altogether and had a higher τέλος outside it, in relation to which he suspended it. For I certainly would like to know how Abraham's act can be related to the universal, whether any point of contact between what Abraham did and the universal can be found other than that Abraham transgressed it. It is not to save a nation, not to uphold the idea of the state that Abraham does it; it is not to appease the angry gods. If it were a matter of the deity's being angry, then he was, after all, angry only with Abraham, and Abraham's act is totally unrelated to the universal, is a purely private endeavor. Therefore, while the tragic hero is great because of his moral virtue, Abraham is great because of a purely personal virtue. There is no higher expression for the ethical in Abraham's life than that the father shall love the son. The ethical in the sense of the moral is entirely beside the point. Insofar as the universal was present, it was cryptically in Isaac, hidden, so to speak, in Isaac's loins, and must cry out with Isaac's mouth: Do not do this, you are destroying everything.

Why, then, does Abraham do it? For God's sake and—the two are wholly identical—for his own sake. He does it for God's sake because

God demands this proof of his faith; he does it for his own sake so that he can prove it.[f]

**7.** Kierkegaard maintains that the ultimate concern of a person is to *become* a Christian. However, Christianity is not a set of doctrines with objective certainty. In brief, no rational theology is available in his view. Religion has its basis in revelations of God. Without the risk involved in faith, one cannot become a Christian. Because there are no objective facts or propositions to be held, one must be passionately or inwardly committed to God.

When subjectivity is the truth, the conceptual determination of the truth must include an expression for the antithesis to objectivity, a memento of the fork in the road where the way swings off; this expression will at the same time serve as an indication of the tension of the subjective inwardness. Here is such a definition of truth: *An objective uncertainty held fast in an appropriation-process of the most passionate inwardness is the truth*, the highest truth attainable for an *existing* individual. At the point where the way swings off (and where this is cannot be specified objectively, since it is matter of subjectivity), there objective knowledge is placed in abeyance. Thus the subject merely has, objectively, the uncertainty; but it is this which precisely increases the tension of that infinite passion which constitutes his inwardness. The truth is precisely the venture which chooses an objective uncertainty with the passion of the infinite. I contemplate the order of nature in the hope of finding God, and I see omnipotence and wisdom; but I also see much else that disturbs my mind and excites anxiety. The sum of all this is an objective uncertainty. But it is for this very reason that the inwardness becomes as intense as it is, for it embraces this objective uncertainty with the entire passion of the infinite. In the case of a mathematical proposition the objectivity is given, but for this reason the truth of such a proposition is also an indifferent truth.

But the above definition of truth is an equivalent expression for faith. Without risk there is no faith. Faith is precisely the contradiction between the infinite passion of the individual's inwardness and the objective uncertainty. If I am capable of grasping God objectively, I do not believe, but precisely because I cannot do this I must believe. If I wish to preserve myself in faith I must constantly be intent upon holding fast the objective uncertainty, so as to remain out upon the deep, over seventy thousand fathoms of water, still preserving my faith.

In the principle that subjectivity, inwardness, is the truth, there is comprehended the Socratic wisdom, whose everlasting merit it was to have become aware of the essential significance of existence, of the fact that the knower is an existing individual. For this reason Socrates was in the truth by virtue of his ignorance, in the highest sense in which this was possible within paganism. To attain to an understanding of this, to comprehend that the misfortunte of speculative philosophy is again and again to have forgotten that the knower is an existing individual, is in our objective age difficult enough.[g]

**8.** Kierkegaard maintains that a Christian believes God has become man. This must, of course, be regarded as paradoxical and absurd by a rational person, because there can be no interchange between an eternal (timeless) being and a temporal (perishable) individual. Kierkegaard is not denying the absurdity of this belief. Indeed, the absurdity tests the individual's faith.

When subjectivity, inwardness, is the truth, the truth becomes objectively a paradox; and the fact that the truth is objectively a paradox shows in its turn that subjectivity is the truth. For the objective situation is repellent; and the expression for the objective repulsion constitutes the tension and the measure of the corresponding inwardness. The paradoxical character of the truth is its objective uncertainty; this uncertainty is an expression for the passionate inwardness, and this passion is precisely the truth. . . .

What now is the absurd? The absurd is—that the eternal truth has come into being in time, that God has come into being, has been born, has grown up, and so forth, precisely like any other individual human being, quite indistinguishable from other individuals. For every assumption of immediate recognizability is pre-Socratic paganism, and from the Jewish point of view, idolatry; and every determination of what really makes an advance beyond the Socratic must essentially bear the stamp of having a relationship to God's having come into being; for faith *sensu strictissimo*, as was developed in the *Fragments*, refers to becoming. When Socrates believed that there was a God, he saw very well that where the way swings off there is also an objective way of approximation, for example by the contemplation of nature and human history, and so forth. His merit was precisely to shun this way, where the quantitative siren song enchants the mind and deceives the existing individual.

In relation to the absurd, the objective approximation-process is like the comedy, *Misunderstanding upon Misunderstanding*, which is generally played by *Privatdocents* and speculative philosophers. The absurd is precisely by its objective repulsion the measure of the intensity of faith in inwardness. Suppose a man who wishes to acquire faith; let the comedy begin. He wishes to have faith, but he wishes also to safeguard himself by means of an objective inquiry and its approximation-process. What happens? With the help of the approximation-process the absurd becomes something different; it becomes probable, it becomes increasingly probable, it becomes extremely and emphatically probable. Now he is ready to believe it, and he ventures to claim for himself that he does not believe as shoemakers and tailors and simple folk believe, but only after long deliberation. Now he is ready to believe it; and lo, now it has become precisely impossible to believe it. Anything that is almost probable, or probable, or extremely and emphatically probable, is something he can almost know, or as good as know, or extremely and emphatically almost *know*—but it is impossible to *believe. For the absurd is the object of faith, and the only object that can be believed* [italics added].[h]

**9.** Christianity's truth lies in the individual's subjectivity and not in something objective.

That is why genuine faith is an individual's passional concern and not an object of study for a society. In sum, as Kierkegaard phrases it, "Christianity is not a doctrine but an existential communication expressing an existential contradiction. If Christianity were a doctrine it would *eo ipse* not be an opposite to speculative thought, but rather a phrase within it. Christianity has to do with existence, with the act of existing; but existence and existing constitute precisely the opposite of speculation" (*Concluding Unscientific Postscript*, p. 339).

Christianity is spirit, spirit is inwardness, inwardness is subjectivity, subjectivity is essentially passion, and in its maximum an infinite, personal, passionate interest in one's eternal happiness.

As soon as subjectivity is eliminated, and passion eliminated from subjectivity, and the infinite interest eliminated from passion, there is in general no decision at all, either in this problem or in any other. All decisiveness, all essential decisiveness, is rooted in subjectivity. A contemplative spirit, and this is what the objective subject is, feels nowhere any infinite need of a decision, and sees no decision anywhere. This is the *falsum* that is inherent in all objectivity. . . .

Christianity proposes to endow the individual with an eternal happiness, a good which is not distributed wholesale, but only to one individual at a time. Though Christianity assumes that there inheres in the subjectivity of the individual, as being the potentiality of the appropriation of this good, the possibility for its acceptance, it does not assume that the subjectivity is immediately ready for such acceptance, or even has, without further ado, a real conception of the significance of such a good. The development or transformation of the individual's subjectivity, its infinite concentration in itself over against the conception of an eternal happiness, that highest good of the infinite—this constitutes the developed potentiality of the primary potentiality which subjectivity as such presents. In this way Christianity protests every form of objectivity; it desires that the subject should be infinitely concerned about himself. It is subjectivity that Christianity is concerned with, and it is only in subjectivity that its truth exists, if it exists at all; objectively, Christianity has absolutely no existence. If its truth happens to be in only a single subject, it exists in him alone; and there is greater Christian joy in heaven over this one individual than over universal history and the System, which as objective entities are incommensurable for that which is Christian.[i]

## QUESTIONS

1. What constitutes an ethical choice for Kierkegaard? Why is it so important?
2. Distinguish among living aesthetically, living ethically, and living religiously.
3. Discuss the biblical story of Abraham and Isaac in terms of its significance for Kierkegaard.
4. What is a "teleological suspension of ethics"? Does it constitute an absurdity?
5. Do you believe that human beings have an "essential nature"? How would you support such a position? How would Kierkegaard respond to your answer?
6. In what sense do Kierkegaard and Kant agree about ethics and in what ways do they differ?
7. Briefly describe a variety of people whom Kierkegaard would consider to be in the aesthetic stage.
8. Give Kierkegaard's account of passional commitments, relating it to the agony of choice and to the three stages.
9. Kierkegaard was critical of the Danish Church for being inauthentic, for relying on formulaic *objective* theology, and for losing sight of both the individual and the real nature of "the leap of faith." Can you draw any contemporary parallels illustrating the difference between authentic faith and pseudofaith?
10. A commentator pointed out that Kierkegaard's response to the Socratic directive, "Know Thyself," is radically different from that of Plato and Aristotle and, indeed, from that of most philosophers. Explain, and use the phrase "the final collapse of intellect issues in the freedom to *be*" in doing so.

## KEY TO SELECTIONS

Søren Kierkegaard, *Either/Or*, vol. II, tr. Howard V. Hong and Edna H. Hong, Princeton, Princeton University Press, 1987. Reprinted with the kind permission of the publisher.

[a]pp. 157–158.
[b]pp. 163–164.
[c]pp. 166–169.
[d]pp. 178–180, pp. 182–183.
[e]pp. 254–255, pp. 266–267.

Søren, Kierkegaard, *Fear and Trembling*, ed. and tr. Howard V. Hong and Edna H. Hong, Princeton, Princeton University Press, 1983. Reprinted with the kind permission of the publisher.

[f]pp. 54–56, pp. 59–60.

Søren Kierkegaard, *Concluding Unscientific Postscript*, tr. David Swanson and Walter Lowrie, Princeton, Princeton University Press, 1941. Reprinted with the kind permission of the publisher.

[g]pp. 182–183.
[h]p. 183, pp. 188–189.
[i]p. 33, p. 116.

## GUIDE TO ADDITIONAL READING

**PRIMARY SOURCES**

Bretall, R. (ed.), *A Kierkegaard Anthology*, New York, The Modern Library, 1948.

**DISCUSSION AND COMMENTARY**

Chamberlain, J., and Ree, J. (eds.), *The Kierkegaard Reader*, Boston, Blackwell, 2000.

Collins, J., *The Mind of Kierkegaard*, Chicago, Regnery, 1953.

Gardner, P., *Kierkegaard*, Oxford, Oxford University Press, 1988.

Gill, J. H. (ed.), *Essays on Kierkegaard*, Minneapolis, Burgess, 1969.

Hall, R. L., "Transcending The Human: A Kierkegaardian Reading of Martha Nussbaum," *International Philosophical Quarterly*, September 1994.

Kleinke, E. D., *Studies in the Philosophy of Kierkegaard*, The Hague, Martin Nijhof, 1976.

Molina, F., *Existentialism as Philosophy*, Englewood Cliffs, Prentice-Hall, 1963.

Sullivan, F. R., *Faith and Reason in Kierkegaard*, Washington, D.C., University Press of America, 1978.

CHAPTER FIFTEEN

# Morality as Ideology

© Bettmann/CORBIS

KARL MARX

THE MOST CONTROVERSIAL social reformer of the past century, Karl Marx (1818–1883), was born in the Prussian city of Trier. Karl was the oldest son in a large family of Jewish lineage, but he was brought up as a Protestant. His parents had converted to Lutheranism shortly after the anti-Jewish laws of 1816 precluded Jews from entering the professions. Consequently, Karl's father was allowed to continue a legal career and to provide modestly for his family.

In his youth Karl Marx was influenced by his future father-in-law, Ludwig von Westphalen, a well-educated Prussian government official. Marx's love of classical literature and intellectual self-confidence can be traced to this person. After a brief study of law at the University of Bonn, he transferred to the University of Berlin, where his interest shifted to philosophy. In 1841, he received his doctorate at the University of Jena. Two years later, against the wishes of many in her family, he married Jenny von Westphalen. In spite of trials and tribulations, their long marriage was one of mutual devotion.

While at the University of Berlin, Marx was influenced by Hegel (1770–1831), whose absolute idealism was the dominant German philosophy. Karl joined a radical Hegelian group that found convincing Hegel's view that *the real is the rational and the rational is the real:* Self-realizing Absolute Spirit or Mind, of which the human being is a unique embodiment, is the essence of reality in all its aspects and temporal configurations (history). The neophyte Marx and others concerned themselves more with applying Hegel's philosophy concretely than with addressing its internal problems.

Shortly after completing his dissertation, Marx became acquainted with and was impressed in part by the work of Louis Feuerbach (1804–1872), a relatively minor philosopher. Feuerbach proposed a "correction" of Hegelianism, which, as laboriously developed by Marx, became a key feature of Marxism. Feuerbach argued that it is the material order that determines the mental order rather than the other way around; furthermore, he held that the idea of Absolute Spirit or God is merely a projection of human feelings or desires, which also are consequences of prevailing material conditions. Marx was convinced that, with adjustments and reinterpretations, the structure and organizing concepts of Hegelian philosophy could withstand this radical shift from a form of idealism to a form of materialism. For example, in Hegel, human history reflects the succession of dialectically related stages in the self-realization of Absolute Spirit, but in Marx, it reflects the succession of dialectically related stages in the evolution of the material (economic) environment.

Marx's reputation as a social and political reformer became an embarrassment to German authorities; as a result, they took steps to suppress his work. He and his wife moved to Paris, a center for artists and intellectuals of all persuasions. There he met Friedrich Engels (1820–1895), who became his friend and colleague for life. After being expelled from Paris, as an accommodation to the Germans, Marx retreated to Brussels, where he and Engels formed the International Communist League. They wrote *The Manifesto of the Communist Party* (1848) as its statement of principles. As a result of his participation in the abortive revolution of Paris in 1849, Marx was barred from all leading centers on the Continent. He found political asylum in England, where he and his family lived the rest of their lives.

Although he did journalistic work, including regular articles on European affairs for the radical *New York Daily Tribune* for ten years, he spent most of his time perfecting his theory of socialism. His initial systematic treatment of economics appeared in 1859, and the first volume of his massive work, *Capital*, appeared in 1867 (the other two volumes, assembled and edited by Engels, were published in 1885 and 1894). By the time of his death at the age of sixty-five, Karl Marx had become a world figure as a consequence of his writings.

Impressed by the ruthless economic aspects of the Industrial Revolution, such as the exploitation of the working classes, and convinced of the historical view that social changes result from class conflicts, Karl Marx and a lifelong collaborator, Friedrich Engels, concluded that a radical reform of society was both inevitable and proper. Understanding the development of Marx's philosophical outlook, in which there are elements of an ethics but no consciously formulated ethical system, requires an analysis of at least four concepts: historical materialism, ideology, alienation, and surplus value.

According to Marx's doctrine of historical materialism, there is an economic basis for all human institutions, thought, and action. An individual's intellectual, political, and social development is conditioned by the mode of production of the material means of existence. Those who control the social economic system in which human beings live and work determine which ideas of history, art, religion, and philosophy prevail in a given era. Moral ideas and standards, though falsely believed by traditional moral philosophers to be products of pure reason, are also conditioned by the "material (economic) conditions of life."

As we have seen, Marx believed that all genuine systems of thought are inextricably connected with the interests of the social class that controls the material means of existence. By contrast, he considered abstract, philosophical systems as deceptions, "forms of ideology." For Marx, ideology represented a false consciousness of the social and economic facts of life. It appears typically in the beliefs of traditional thinkers who are unaware of the motive force (economic realities) underlying their views and who believe, mistakenly, that their systems are pure creations of the mind. Thus one can understand the reason for Marx's criticism of ethical theorists who formulate universal principles of conduct. These moralists fail to see that the claims of morality are merely rationalizations designed by the ruling economic classes and that as these classes change, so does morality. Kant's moral philosophy, based on an abstract, formal principle of reason called the *categorical imperative*, provides a specific form of ideology that Marx holds in contempt. Indeed, when Marx asserts that "communists preach no morality," he is proclaiming that morality *in general* is meaningless.

However, Marx did not hold the same perspective on morality throughout his life. Some contemporary philosophers find that his writings provide a case for moral relativism—that is, the doctrine that what is right (good, obligatory) for one society is not necessarily right (good, obligatory) for another, even if the situations in both groups are similar. On this interpretation, Marx would hold the ethical view that every value judgment (of right and wrong) serves the interests of a particular social class at a given time. For example, he would readily admit that the capitalist's economy can be condemned (critically evaluated) from the working class's viewpoint as failing to serve their interests. Different evaluations might be appropriate for other classes. However, as a consequence, Marx would deny that there could ever be an objective value judgment, completely independent of all classes, for that would constitute the traditional standpoint, typified by Kant, that he condemned. It is, in fact, what he had in mind when he characterized all morality as ideology. But the final word on what is the correct interpretation of Marx's conception of ethics has yet to be written.

Elements of an ethics are clearly present in the treatise *Economic and Philosophical Manuscripts* (1844). Marx adopts Hegel's moral concept of alienation and gives it a materialistic interpretation by contrasting alienated labor with productive activity. In dealing with this topic, he begins with a traditional question of ethics: How do human beings truly fulfill themselves? The answer to the question is to be found in work. For Marx, history provides sufficient evidence that human life not only is sustained but also is shaped by productive activity. The quality of our lives depends on the quality of the work in which we engage. Human beings fulfill themselves (that is, acquire a sense of identity, pride, and direction) through meaningful work. But this can be achieved only under social conditions in which workers are intimately related to their creations, in the sense that the products are the fulfillment of their own ideas and aspirations.[1] Unfortunately, Marx insists, the reverse is the case in a society in which labor is alienated or externalized. It is a dismal condition in which the workers find no satisfaction in their activities because they are not engaging in meaningful work related to their own aims. Rather, they are compelled to turn out products in order to sustain their bodies. The capitalistic system epitomizes alienated labor, because the workers produce commodities for someone else and are given a bare subsistence. Moreover, each worker is alienated from every other worker by being an isolated cog, an "appendage of a machine." Laborers cannot even share socially in common hopes and aspirations. In Marxist terms, the motive

[1]Marx was influenced here by Hegel's philosophical idealism: Thinkers are "internally related" to their thoughts insofar as ideas can be akin only to minds. For Marx, there is the same sort of relationship between human beings as producers and their creations. However, under capitalism, producers are separated from their products. They are regarded as commodities insofar as their activities belong to someone else. The individuals, whose work was once spontaneous and meaningful, are reduced to mere means.

of greed—symbolized by the capitalist's desire for money and private property—is the cause of labor alienation and exploitation. Both of these evils will be overcome only when the workers revolt and take control of the means of production.

Explaining how the workers' (proletarian) revolution comes about is directly connected with Marx's concept of surplus value. In *Capital,* he maintains that value signifies the amount of labor socially needed to produce a commodity, whereas surplus value refers to the percentage of society's work that exceeds what is necessary to keep the working class alive. What capitalists (the bourgeoisie) buy from the workers is their "labor power"—that is, their capacity to work—but not their output. If the finished products did not exceed the cost of the workers' livelihood, the capitalist would not have any motive to hire them. The workers are paid only the value of their labor, but they produce more value than they receive. The excess is the surplus value (profit), which the capitalist keeps. For Marx, this surplus is a measure of the degree of working class exploitation.

Of course, competition among those who control the means of production forces them to utilize the working class as efficiently as possible. This leads to large-scale organization, which constitutes the height of business efficiency. Consolidation and accumulation of capital go hand in hand. The capitalists become richer while the laborers become poorer, thus bringing on the inevitable class struggle and the ultimate victory of the proletariat.[2] According to Marx, the capitalistic system "sows the seeds of its own destruction." This state of affairs is followed by the rise of the proletariat, who take over the instruments of production and distribution and form a "classless society" (that is, a "free association of producers under their conscious and purposive control"). The proletariat, being a majority, will represent the interests of the whole society. Marx concludes that the resulting socialist (communist) society with its new economic structure will be free from all forms of alienation and exploitation. Furthermore, social disruption and conflict will end because the causes of both, class distinction, will no longer exist. Class differences will be seen as relics of capitalism and earlier stages of social development.

---

**1.** In analyzing an individual's nature, Marx focuses on the actual or concrete historical setting for a person rather than characterizing an agent in terms of some vacuous, logical abstractions. Human lives are inextricably bound up with the existing mode of production (that is, the way they organize themselves to produce the goods they need).

The premises from which we begin are not arbitrary ones, not dogmas, but real premises from which abstraction can only be made in the imagination. They are the real individuals, their activity and the material conditions under which they live, both those which they find already existing and those produced by their activity. These premises can thus be verified in a purely empirical way.

[2]Marx and Engels accepted Hegel's logical principle of dialectic—that thought proceeds by a series of contradictions (conflicts) and resolutions in some higher synthesis—but applied it to material social systems. Every society, a product of its economic structure, generates its opposite (its antithesis), thus leading to a new stage in social development. This process, which Marx and Engels term ***dialectical materialism***, is their way of accounting for social changes throughout history.

The first premise of all human history is, of course, the existence of living human individuals. Thus the first fact to be established is the physical organization of these individuals and their consequent relation to the rest of nature. Of course, we cannot here go either into the actual physical nature of man, or into the natural conditions in which man finds himself—geological, orohydrographical, climatic, and so on. The writing of history must always set out from these natural bases and their modification in the course of history through the action of men.

Men can be distinguished from animals by consciousness, by religion, or anything else you like. They themselves begin to distinguish themselves from animals as soon as they begin to produce their means of subsistence, a step which is conditioned by their physical organization. By producing their means of subsistence men are indirectly producing their actual material life.

The way in which men produce their means of subsistence depends first of all on the nature of the actual means of subsistence they find in existence and have to reproduce. This mode of production must not be considered simply as being the production of the physical existence of the individuals. Rather it is a definite form of activity of these individuals, a definite form of expressing their life, a definite mode of life on their part. As individuals express their life, so they are. What they are, therefore, coincides with their production, both with *what* they produce and with *how* they produce. The nature of individuals thus depends on the material conditions determining their production.[a]

**2.** Marx maintains that the more sophisticated forms of human intelligence—morality, religion, politics, and so forth—are determined by the economic conditions of a given society and have no independent status. For example, moral values are ideological in character (that is, they are not products of pure reason but are the effects of material forces that are their source).

The production of ideas, of conceptions, of consciousness, is at first directly interwoven with the material activity and the material intercourse of men, the language of real life. Conceiving, thinking, the mental intercourse of men, appear at this stage as the direct efflux of their material behavior. The same applies to mental production as expressed in the language of politics, laws, morality, religion, metaphysics, etc. of a people. Men are the producers of their conceptions, ideas, etc.—real, active men, as they are conditioned by a definite development of their productive forces and of the intercourse corresponding to these, up to its furthest forms. Consciousness can never be anything else than conscious existence, and the existence of men is their actual life-process. If in all ideology men and their circumstances appear upside-down as in a *camera obscura*, this phenomenon arises just as much from their historical life-process as the inversion of objects on the retina does from their physical life-process.

In direct contrast to German philosophy which descends from heaven to earth, here we ascend from earth to heaven. That is to say, we do not set out from what men say, imagine, conceive, nor from men as narrated, thought of, imagined, conceived, in order to arrive at men in the flesh. We set out from real, active men, and on the basis of their real life-process we demonstrate the development of the ideological reflexes and echoes of this life-process. The phantoms formed in the human brain are also, necessarily, sublimates of their material life-process, which is empirically verifiable and bound to material premises. Morality, religion, metaphysics, all the rest of ideology and their corresponding forms of consciousness, thus no longer retain the semblance of independence. They have no history, no development; but men, developing their material production and their material intercourse, alter, along with this their real existence, their thinking and the products of their thinking. Life is not determined by consciousness, but consciousness by life. In the first method of approach the starting-point is consciousness taken as the living individual; in the second method, which conforms to real life, it is the real living individuals themselves, and consciousness is considered solely as their consciousness.

This method of approach is not devoid of premises. It starts out from the real premises and does not abandon them for a moment. Its premises are men, not in any fantastic isolation and rigidity, but in their actual, empirically perceptible process of development under definite conditions. As soon as this active life-process is described, history ceases to be a collection of dead facts as it is with the empiricists (themselves still abstract), or an imagined activity of imagined subjects, as with the idealists.

Where speculation ends—in real life—there real, positive science begins: the representation of the practical activity, of the practical process of development of men. Empty talk about consciousness ceases, and real knowledge has to take its place. When reality is depicted, philosophy as an independent branch of knowledge loses its medium of existence. At the best its place can only be taken by a summing-up of the most general results, abstractions which arise from the observation of the historical development of men. Viewed apart from real history, these abstractions have in themselves no value whatsoever.[b]

**3.** There are no moral philosophies that hold for all cultures and times. Those who govern (that is, those who control the means of production and distribution) determine which conceptions will prevail in a given society.

The ideas of the ruling class are in every epoch the ruling ideas, i.e., the class which is the ruling material force of society is at the same time its ruling intellectual force. The class which has the means of material production at its disposal, has control at the same time over the means of mental production, so that thereby, generally speaking, the ideas of those who lack the means of mental production are subject to it. The ruling ideas are nothing more than the ideal expression of the dominant material relationships, the dominant material relationships grasped as ideas; hence of the relationships which make the one class the ruling one, therefore, the ideas of its dominance. The individuals composing the ruling class possess among other things consciousness, and therefore think. In so far, therefore, as they rule as a class and determine the extent and compass of an epoch, it is self-evident that they do this in its whole range, hence among other things rule also as thinkers, as producers of ideas, and regulate the production and distribution of the ideas of their age: thus their ideas are the ruling ideas of the epoch. For instance, in an age and in a country where royal power, aristocracy, and bourgeoisie are contending for mastery and where, therefore, mastery is shared, the doctrine of the separation of powers proves to be the dominant idea and is expressed as an "eternal law". . . . Social relations are closely bound up with productive forces. In acquiring new productive forces men change their mode of production; and in changing their mode of production, in changing the way of earning their living, they change all their social relations. The hand-mill gives you society with the feudal lord; the steam-mill, society with the industrial capitalist.

The same men who establish their social relations in conformity with their material productivity, produce also principles, ideas, and categories in conformity with their social relations.

Thus these ideas, these categories, are as little eternal as the relations they express. They are historical and transitory products.

There is a continual movement of growth in productive forces, of destruction in social relations, of formation in ideas; the only immutable thing is the abstraction of movement—mors immortalis.[c]

**4.** The key concept, "alienation," is defined. In capitalist societies, human beings become mere objects when the product of their labor is no longer theirs and when their activities are controlled by others.

We start with a contemporary fact of political economy:

The worker becomes poorer the richer is his production, the more it increases in power and scope. The worker becomes a commodity, that is all the cheaper the more commodities he creates. The depreciation of the human world progresses in direct proportion to the increase in value of the world of things. Labor does not only produce commodities; it produces itself and the laborer as a commodity and that to the extent to which it produces commodities in general.

What this fact expresses is merely this: the object that labor produces, its product, confronts it as an alien being, as a power independent of the producer. The product of labor is labor that has solidified itself into an object, made itself into a thing, the objectification of labor. The realization of labor is its objectification. In political economy this realization of labor appears as a loss of reality for the worker, objectification as a loss of the object or slavery to it, and appropriation as alienation, as externalization.

The realization of labor appears as a loss of reality to an extent that the worker loses his reality by dying of starvation. Objectification appears as a loss of the object to such an extent that the worker is robbed not only of the objects necessary for his life but also of the objects of his work. Indeed, labor itself becomes an object he can only have in his power with the greatest of efforts and at irregular intervals. The appropriation of the object appears as alienation to such an extent that the more objects the worker produces, the less he can possess and the more he falls under the domination of his product, capital.

All these consequences follow from the fact that the worker relates to the product of his labor as to an alien object. For it is evident from this presupposition that the more the worker externalizes himself in his work, the more powerful becomes the alien, objective world that he creates opposite himself, the poorer he becomes himself in his inner life and the less he can call his own. It is just the same in religion. The more man puts into God, the less he retains in himself. The worker puts his life into the object and this means that it no longer belongs to him but to the object. So the greater this activity, the more the worker is without an object. What the product of his labor is, that he is not. So the greater this product the less he is himself. The externalization of the worker in his product implies not only that his labor becomes an object, an exterior existence but also that it exists outside him, independent and alien, and becomes a self-sufficient power opposite him, that the life that he has lent to the object affronts him, hostile and alien.

Let us now deal in more detail with objectification, the production of the worker, and the alienation, the loss of the object, his product, which is involved in it.

The worker can create nothing without nature, the sensuous exterior world. It is the matter in which his labor realizes itself, in which it is active, out of which and through which it produces.

But as nature affords the means of life for labor in the sense that labor cannot live without objects on which it exercises itself, so it affords a means of life in the narrower sense, namely the means for the physical subsistence of the worker himself.[d]

**5.** Marx analyzes in detail the consequences of human alienation: the loss of personal dignity and the reduction of human beings in their functions to the level of lower animals.

What does the externalization of labor consist of then?

Firstly, that labor is exterior to the worker, that is, it does not belong to his essence. Therefore he does not confirm himself in his work, he denies himself, feels miserable instead of happy, deploys no free physical and intellectual energy, but mortifies his body and ruins his mind. Thus the worker only feels a stranger. He is at home when he is not working and when he works he is not at home. His labor is therefore not voluntary but compulsory, forced labor. It is therefore not the satisfaction of a need but only a means to satisfy needs outside itself. How alien it really is is very evident from the fact that when there is no physical or other compulsion, labor is avoided like the plague. External labor, labor in which man externalizes himself, is a labor of self-sacrifice and mortification. Finally, the external character of labor for the worker shows itself in the fact that it is not his own but someone else's, that it does not belong to him, that he does not belong to himself in his labor but to someone else. As in religion the human imagination's own activity, the activity of man's head and his heart, reacts independently on the individual as an alien activity of gods or devils, so the activity of the worker is not his own spontaneous activity. It belongs to another and is the loss of himself.

The result we arrive at then is that man (the worker) only feels himself freely active in his animal functions of eating, drinking, and procreating, at most also in his dwelling and dress, and feels himself an animal in his human functions.

Eating, drinking, procreating, etc., are indeed truly human functions. But in the abstraction that separates them from the other round of human activity and makes them into final and exclusive ends they become animal.

We have treated the act of alienation of practical human activity, labor, from two aspects. (1) The relationship of the worker to the product of his labor as an alien object that has power over him. This relationship is at the same time the relationship to the sensuous exterior world and to natural objects as to an alien and hostile world opposed to him. (2) The relationship of labor to the act of production inside labor. This relationship is the relationship of the worker to his own activity as something that is alien and does not belong to him; it is activity that is passivity, power that is weakness, procreation that is castration, the worker's own physical and intellectual energy, his personal life (for what is life except activity?) as an activity directed against himself, independent of him and not belonging to him. It is self-alienation, as above it was the alienation of the object.[c]

**6.** According to Marx, capitalism creates divisiveness among individuals by creating classes of labor. Self-activity (creative, meaningful productivity) ceases because persons become mere cogs in the industrial complex. This state of affairs will be rectified only when the inevitable proletarian revolution takes place. In brief, true freedom will be expressed when the masses take control of the instruments of production.

Our investigation hitherto started from the instruments of production, and it has already shown that private property was a necessity for certain industrial stages. In *industrie extractive* [raw materials industry] private property still coincides with labor; in small industry and all agriculture up till now property is the necessary consequence of the existing instruments of production; in big industry the contradiction between the instrument of production and private property appears for the first time and is the product of big industry; moreover, big industry must be highly developed to produce this contradiction. And thus only with big industry does the abolition of private property become possible.

In big industry and competition the whole mass of conditions of existence, limitations, biases of individuals, are fused together into the two simplest forms: private property and labor. With money every form of intercourse, and intercourse itself, is considered fortuitous for the individuals. Thus money implies that all previous intercourse was only intercourse of individuals under particular conditions, not of individuals as individuals. These conditions are reduced to two: accumulated labor or private property, and actual labor. If both or one of these ceases, then intercourse comes to a standstill. The modern economists themselves . . . oppose "association of individuals" to "association of capital." On the other hand, the individuals themselves are entirely subordinated to the division of labor and hence are brought into the most complete dependence on one another. Private property, in so far as within labor itself is opposed to labor, evolves out of the necessity of accumulation, and has still, to begin with, rather the form of the communality; but in its further development it approaches more and more the modern form of private property.

The division of labor implies from the outset the division of the conditions of labor, of tools and materials, and thus the splitting-up of accumulated capital among different owners, and thus, also, the division between capital and labor, and the different forms of property itself. The more the division of labor develops and accumulation grows, the sharper are the forms that this process of differentiation assumes. Labor itself can only exist on the premise of this fragmentation.

Thus two facts are here revealed. First the productive forces appear as a world for themselves, quite independent of and divorced from the individuals, alongside the individuals: the reason for this is that the individuals, whose forces they are, exist split up and in opposition to one another, while, on the other hand, these forces are only real forces in the intercourse and association of these individuals. Thus, on the one hand, we have a totality of productive forces, which have, as it were, taken on a material form and are for the individuals no longer the forces of the individuals but of private property, and hence of the individuals only in so far as they are owners of private property themselves. Never, in any earlier period, have the productive forces taken on a form so indifferent to the intercourse of individuals as individuals, because their intercourse itself was formerly a restricted one. On the other hand, standing over against these productive forces, we have the majority of the individuals from whom these forces have been wrested away, and who, robbed thus of all real life-content, have become abstract individuals, but who are, however, only by this fact put into a position to enter into relation with one another as individuals.

The only connection which still links them with the productive forces and with their own existence—labor—has lost all semblance of self-activity and only sustains their life by stunting it. While in the earlier periods self-activity and the production of material life were separated, in that they devolved on different persons, and while, on account of the narrowness of the individuals themselves, the production of material life was considered as a subordinate mode of self-activity, they now diverge to such an extent that altogether material life appears as the end, and what produces this material life, labor (which is now the only possible but, as we see, negative form of self-activity), as the means.

Thus things have now come to such a pass that the individuals must appropriate the existing totality of productive forces, not only to achieve self-activity, but also merely to safeguard their very existence. This appropriation is first determined by the object to the appropriated, the productive forces, which have been developed to a totality and which only exist within a universal intercourse. From this aspect alone, therefore, this appropriation must have a universal character corresponding to the productive forces and the intercourse.

The appropriation of these forces is itself nothing more than the development of the individual capacities corresponding to the material instruments of production. The appropriation of a totality of instruments of production is, for this very reason, the development of a totality of capacities in the individuals themselves.

This appropriation is further determined by the persons appropriating. Only the proletarians of the present day, who are completely shut off from all self-activity, are in a position to achieve a complete and no longer restricted self-activity, which consists in the appropriation of a totality of productive forces and in the thus postulated development of a totality of capacities. All earlier revolutionary appropriations were restricted; individuals, whose self-activity was restricted by a crude instrument of production and a limited intercourse, appropriated this crude instrument of production, and hence merely achieved a new state of limitation. Their instrument of production became their property, but they themselves remained subordinate to the division of labor and their own instrument of production. In all expropriations up to now, a mass of individuals remained subservient to a single instrument of production; in the appropriation by the proletarians, a mass of instruments of production must be made subject to each individual, and property to all. Modern universal intercourse can be controlled by individuals, therefore, only when controlled by all.

This appropriation is further determined by the manner in which it must be effected. It can only be effected through a union, which by the character of the proletariat itself can again only be a universal one, and through a revolution, in which, on the one hand, the power of the earlier mode of production and intercourse and social organization is overthrown, and, on the other hand, there develops the universal character and the energy of the proletariat, without which the revolution cannot be accomplished; and in which, further, the proletariat rids itself of everything that still clings to it from its previous position in society.

Only at this stage does self-activity coincide with material life, which corresponds to the development of individuals into complete individuals and the casting-off of all natural limitations. The transformation of labor into self-activity corresponds to the transformation of the earlier limited intercourse into the intercourse of individuals as such. With the appropriation of the total productive forces through united individuals, private property comes to an end. While previously in history a particular condition always appeared as accidental, now the isolation of individuals and the particular private gain of each man have themselves become accidental.[f]

**7.** Marx points out that when society no longer has a structure of classes, the antagonism and opposition that attend such relationships will disappear. And because moral principles originate in class conflicts, they will no longer be needed or have any authoritative role in society. (There is a parallel here to Kant's view: Kant observes that angels, in contrast to humans, have no need for morality because they have no inclinations that conflict with their rational capacities.)

It follows from all we have been saying up till now that the communal relationship into which the individuals of a class entered, and which was determined by their common interests over against a third party, was always a community to which these individuals belonged only as average individuals, only in so far as they lived within the conditions of existence of their class—a relationship in which they participated not as individuals but as members of a class. With the community of revolutionary proletarians, on the other hand, who take their conditions of existence and those of all members of society under their control, it is just the reverse; it is as individuals that the individuals participate in it. It is just this combination of individuals (assuming the advanced stage of modern productive forces, of course) which puts the conditions of the free development and movement of individuals under their control—conditions which were previously abandoned to chance and had won an independent existence over against the separate individuals just because of their separation as individuals, and because of the necessity of their combination which had been determined by the division of labor, and through their separation had become a bond alien to them. Combination up till now (by no means an arbitrary one, such as is expounded for example in the *Contrat social*, but a necessary one) was an agreement upon these conditions, within which the individuals were free to enjoy the freaks of fortune (compare, e.g., the formation of the North American State and the South American republics). This right to the undisturbed enjoyment, within certain conditions, of fortuity and chance has up till now been called personal freedom. These conditions of existence are, of course, only the productive forces and forms of intercourse at any particular time. . . .

For the proletarians, on the other hand, the condition of their existence, labor, and with it all the conditions of existence governing modern society, have become something accidental, something over which they, as separate individuals, have no control, and over which no social organization can give them control. The contradiction between the individuality of each separate proletarian and labor, the condition of life forced upon him, becomes evident to him himself, for he is sacrificed from youth upwards and, within his own class, has no chance of arriving at the conditions which would place him in the other class.

Thus, while the refugee serfs only wished to be free to develop and assert those conditions of existence which were already there, and hence, in the end, only arrived at free labor, the proletarians, if they are to assert themselves as individuals, will have to abolish the very condition of their existence hitherto (which has, moreover, been that of all society up to the present), namely, labor. Thus they find themselves directly opposed to the form in which, hitherto, the individuals, of which society consists, have given themselves collective expression, that is, the State. In order, therefore, to assert themselves as individuals, they must overthrow the State. . . .

We have already shown above that the abolition of a state of things in which relationships become independent of individuals, in which individuality is subservient to chance and the personal relationships of individuals are subordinated to general class relationships, etc.—the abolition of this state of things is determined in the final analysis by the abolition of division of labor. We have also shown that the abolition of division of labor is determined by the development of intercourse and productive forces to such a degree of universality that private property and division of labor become fetters on them. We have further shown that private property can be abolished only on condition of an all-round development of individuals, because the existing character of intercourse and productive forces is an all-round one, and only individuals that are developing in an all-round fashion can appropriate them, i.e., can turn them into free manifestations of their lives. We have shown that at the present time individuals must abolish private property, because the productive forces and forms of intercourse have developed so far that, under the domination of private property, they have become destructive forces, and because the contradiction between the classes has reached its extreme limit. Finally, we have shown that the abolition of private property and of the division of labor is itself the union of individuals on the basis created by modern productive forces and world intercourse.

Within communist society, the only society in which the original and free development of individuals ceases to be a mere phrase, the development is determined precisely by the connection of individuals, a connection which consists partly in the economic prerequisites and partly in the necessary solidarity of the free development of all, and, finally, in the universal character of the activity of individuals on the basis of the existing productive forces. Here, therefore, the matter concerns individuals at a definite historical stage of development and by no means merely individuals chosen at random, even disregarding the indispensable communist revolution which itself is a general condition of their free development. The individuals' consciousness of their mutual relations will, of course, likewise become something quite different, and, therefore, will no more be the "principle of love" or *dévouement*, than it will be egoism.[g]

**8.** Utilitarianism, a popular moral theory in the nineteenth century, reflects the same form of exploitation found among the bourgeoisie (middle class) in all capitalistic societies, according to Marx.

The apparent stupidity of merging all the manifold relationships of people in the one relation of usefulness, this apparently metaphysical abstraction arises from the fact that, in modern bourgeois society, all relations are subordinated in practice to the one abstract monetary-commercial relation. This theory came to the fore with Hobbes and Locke at the same time as the first and second English revolutions, those first battles by which the bourgeoisie won political power. It is to be found even earlier, of course, among writers on political economy, as a tacit premise. . . .

All this is actually the case with the bourgeois. For him only one relation is valid on its own account—the relation of exploitation; all other relations have validity for him only in so far as he can include them under this one relation, and even where he encounters relations which cannot be directly subordinated to the relation of exploitation, he does at least subordinate them to it in his imagination. The material expression of this use is money, the representative of the value of all things, people, and social relations. Incidentally, one sees at a glance that the category of "utilization" is first of all abstracted from the actual relations of intercourse which I have with other people (but by no means from reflection and mere will) and then these relations are made out to be the reality of the category that has been abstracted from them themselves, a wholly metaphysical method of procedure. . . .

The advances made by the theory of utility and exploitation, its various phases, are closely connected with the various periods of development of the bourgeoisie. In the case of Helvétius and Holbach, the actual content of the theory never went much beyond paraphrasing the mode of expression of the writers at the time of the absolute monarchy. With them it was a different method of expression; it reflected not so much the actual fact but rather the desire to reduce all relations to the relation of exploitation, and to explain the intercourse of people from material needs and the ways of satisfying them. The problem was set. Hobbes and Locke had before their eyes both the earlier development of the Dutch bourgeoisie (both of them had lived for some time in Holland) and the first political actions by which the English bourgeoisie emerged from local and provincial limitations, as well as a comparatively highly developed stage of manufacture, overseas trade, and colonization. This particularly applies to Locke, who wrote during the first period of English economy, at the time of the rise of joint-stock companies, the Bank of England, and England's mastery of the seas. In their case, and particularly in that of Locke, the theory of exploitation was still directly connected with the economic content.

Helvétius and Holbach were confronted not only by English theory and the preceding development of the Dutch and English bourgeoisie, but also by the French bourgeoisie which was still struggling for its free development. The commercial spirit, universal in the eighteenth century, had especially in France taken possession of all classes in the form of speculation. The financial difficulties of the government and the resulting disputes over taxation occupied the attention of all France even at that time. In addition, Paris in the eighteenth century was the only world city, the only city where there was personal intercourse among individuals of all nations. These premises, combined with the more universal character typical of Frenchmen in general, gave the theory of Helvétius and Holbach its peculiar universal coloring, but at the same time deprived it of the positive economic content that was still to be found among the English. The theory which for the English still was simply the registration of a fact becomes for the French a philosophical system. This generality devoid of positive content, such as we find it in Helvétius and Holbach, is essentially different from the substantial comprehensive view which is first found in Bentham and Mill. The former corresponds to the struggling, still undeveloped bourgeoisie, the latter to the ruling, developed bourgeoisie.

. . . The complete subordination of all existing relations to the relation of utility, and its unconditional elevation to be the sole content of all other relations, we find for the first time in Bentham, where, after the French Revolution and the development of large-scale industry, the bourgeoisie no longer appears as a special class, but as the class whose conditions of existence are those of the whole society.

When the sentimental and moral paraphrases, which for the French were the entire content of the utility theory, had been exhausted, all that remained for its further development was the question how individuals and relations were to be used, to be exploited. Meanwhile the reply to this question had already been given in political economy; the only possible step forward was by inclusion of the economic content. Bentham achieved this advance. But the idea had already been stated in political economy that the chief relations of exploitation are determined by production by and large, independently of the will of individuals who find them already in existence. Hence, no other field of speculative thought remained for the utility theory than the attitude of individuals to these important relations, the private exploitation of an already existing world by individuals. On this subject Bentham and his school indulged in lengthy moral reflections. Thereby the whole criticism of the existing world provided by the utility theory also moved within a narrow compass. Prejudiced in favor of the conditions of the bourgeoisie, it could criticize only those relations which had been handed down from a past epoch and were an obstacle to the development of the bourgeoisie. Hence, although the utility theory does expound the connection of all existing relations with economic relations it does so only in a restricted way.

From the outset the utility theory had the aspect of a theory of general utility, yet this aspect only became fraught with meaning when economic relations, especially division of labor and exchange, were included. With division of labor, the private activity of the individual becomes generally useful; Bentham's general utility becomes reduced to the same general utility that is operative in competition. By taking into account the economic relations of rent, profit, and wages, the definite exploitation relations of separate classes were introduced, since the manner of exploitation depends on the position in life of the exploiter. Up to this point the theory of utility was able to base itself on definite social facts; its further account of the manner of exploitation amounts to a mere recital of catechism phrases.

The economic content gradually turned the utility theory into a mere apologia for the existing state of affairs, an attempt to prove that under existing conditions the mutual relations of people today are the most advantageous and generally useful. It has this character among all modern economists.[h]

**9.** Marx blends a dispassionate, scientific analysis of capitalism with a critical, moral evaluation of its economic system. His view represents a neutral indictment of the capitalist system, but it is not clear whether the values expressed by Marx are those of a particular class.

Within the capitalist system all methods for raising the social productiveness of labor are brought about at the cost of the individual laborer; all means for the development of production transform themselves into means of domination over, and exploitation of, the producers; they mutilate the laborer into a fragment of a man, degrade him to the level of an appendage of a machine, destroy every remnant of charm in his work and turn it into a hated toil; they estrange from him the intellectual potentialities of the labor process in the same proportion as science is incorporated in it as an independent power; they distort the conditions under which he works, subject him during the labor process to a despotism the more hateful for its meanness; they transform his lifetime into working-time, and drag his wife and child beneath the wheels of the Juggernaut of capital. But all methods for the production of surplus value are at the same time methods of accumulation; and every extension of accumulation becomes again a means for the development of those methods. It follows therefore that in proportion as capital accumulates, the lot of the laborer, be his payment high or low, must grow worse. The law, finally, that always equilibrates the relative surplus population, or industrial reserve army, to the extent and energy of accumulation, this law rivets the laborer to capital more firmly than the wedges of Vulcan did Prometheus to the rock. It establishes an accumulation of misery, corresponding with accumulation of capital. Accumulation of wealth at one pole is, therefore, at the same time accumulation of misery, agony of toil, slavery, ignorance, brutality, mental degradation, at the opposite pole, i.e., on the side of the class that produces its own product in the form of capital.[i]

## QUESTIONS

1. Discuss the relationship between individuals and the economic conditions of their lives, according to Marx.
2. What does Marx mean when he says that morality is essentially ideology?
3. What is "alienation" and what is its philosophical importance?
4. On what grounds does Marx criticize Bentham's utilitarian principle?

5. According to Marx, how does capitalism "sow the seeds of its own destruction"?
6. What is meant by the theory of "surplus value"?
7. How is it possible for Marx to reconcile an objectively scientific view of capitalism with a moral assessment of its economic structure?
8. Discuss Marx's claim that "the communists preach no morality at all." Is he being consistent?
9. Marx says that "it is not the consciousness of men that determines their being, but, on the contrary, their social being that determines their consciousness." What does this mean? Does it mean, for example, that moral and social theories play no role in the life of societies? Both defend and attack Marx.
10. While Marx acknowledges the moral hunger that brings people to accept Utilitarianism, he argues that this doctrine ultimately reduces to a "mere apologia for the existing state of affairs." Could he argue in some nearly analogous way that Kant's deontological doctrine also reduces to a "mere apologia for the existing state of affairs"? Defend your answer.

## KEY TO SELECTIONS

Karl Marx: *Selected Writings*, David McLellan, ed., Oxford, Oxford University Press, 1977. 

[a]pp. 160–161.
[b]pp. 164–165.
[c]pp. 176, 202.
[d]pp. 78–79.
[e]pp. 80–81.
[f]pp. 176–178.
[g]pp. 181–182, 190–191.
[h]pp. 185–186, 186–187, 188–189.
[i]pp. 482–483.

## GUIDE TO ADDITIONAL READING


### PRIMARY SOURCES

Bottomore, T. B., *Karl Marx, Early Writings*, New York, McGraw-Hill, 1963.

McLellanD., *Karl Marx: Selected Writings*, Oxford, Oxford University Press, 1977.

Tucker, R. C. (ed.), *The Marx-Engels Reader*, New York, W. W. Norton, 1978.

### DISCUSSION AND COMMENTARY

Fromm, E., *Marx's Concept of Man*, New York, Ungar, 1966.

Hook, S., *Towards the Understanding of Karl Marx*, New York, John Day, 1933.

Kamenka, E., *The Ethical Foundations of Marxism*, 2nd ed., London, Routledge and Kegan Paul, 1972.

_____, *Marxism and Ethics*, London, Macmillan, 1969.

Lukes, S., *Marxism and Morality*, New York, Oxford University Press, 1985.

MacIntyre, A. C., *Marxism: An Interpretation*, London, S.C.M. Press, 1953.

Mandel, E., *An Introduction to Marxist Economic Theory*, 2nd ed., New York, Pathfinder Press, 1979.

McLellan, D., *Karl Marx*, New York, Viking Press, 1975.

McMurtry, J., *The Structure of Marx's World-View*, Princeton, Princeton University Press, 1978.

Ollman, B., *Alienation: Marx's Conception of Man in Capitalist Society*, Cambridge, Cambridge University Press, 1971.

Tucker, R., *Philosophy and Myth in Karl Marx*, Cambridge, Cambridge University Press, 1961.

Wolfson, M., *Karl Marx*, New York, Columbia University Press, 1971.

Wood, Allen, "Marx Against Morality," in *A Companion to Ethics*, ed. P. Singer, Cambridge, Blackwell, 1993, pp. 511–524.

CHAPTER SIXTEEN

# Utilitarianism Revised

HENRY SIDGWICK

MEASURED BY HIS INFLUENCE on ethical theorists, Henry Sidgwick (1838–1900) is very important, but measured by his public recognition, he is just another figure in the long history of moral philosophy. His lack of recognition traces to his being a later-day champion of utilitarianism, a dominating view that had already been persuasively promoted by Jeremy Bentham and John Stuart Mill (their "Greatest Happiness for the Greatest Number" was an idiom of the time). His influence on subsequent philosophers can be attributed to his revision of the foundation of utilitarianism and to his meticulous style of inquiry.

Born in Yorkshire, England, Sidgwick was quickly judged to be a brilliant student. This judgment was confirmed at Trinity College, Cambridge, where he successfully attempted a "double" (taking both the classical and mathematical examinations rather than just one). He was first of the firsts in classics and thirty-third of the firsts in mathematics; he was also awarded the Chancellor's Medal and made a fellow.

His academic career successfully launched, Sidgwick nevertheless found himself drifting into personal crisis. Despite deliberate scholarly efforts to the contrary, he was developing serious religious doubts. By 1869 he realized that he no longer accepted the tenets of established Christianity. For him, integrity dictated that he resign his fellowship; acknowledging these tenets was a condition for holding it. Although his college responded by appointing him to a lectureship and his career continued without interruption (his master work, *The Methods of Ethics*, appeared in 1874 and he became the Knightsbridge Professor of Moral Philosophy in 1883), his resignation of his fellowship had ramifications that went far beyond Cambridge. It became a case in point in subsequent decisions by Parliament and Prime Minister

William Gladstone to abolish religious testing once and for all. Matters came full circle when, in 1881, Sidgwick was made an honorary Fellow of Trinity College.

Beginning as an unwitting academic reformer, Sidgwick became a witting one. He and his allies helped to create a second college for women in 1867 at Cambridge, Newnham Hall, and, feeding on success, they became advocates for removing the men-only criterion from the graduate studies policy at Cambridge. They prevailed: Since 1881 women have had the right to "sit examinations."

Sidgwick married Eleanor Mildred Balfour, the sister of the future prime minister, in the year Newnham Hall opened. As fate would have it, she became president of that institution sixteen years later. Sidgwick continued to write—most notably, *Outlines of the History of Ethics* (1886) and the posthumously published *Lectures on the Ethics of Green, Spencer and Martineau* (1902)—and to teach until his death.

According to Sidgwick, the role of technical philosophy is to bring our knowledge of the natural world into a systematic and coherent whole, and, analogously, the role of practical philosophy is to bring our knowledge of the moral world into systematic coherence. In the first instance, the source of items of factual knowledge is the sciences, whereas in the second, the source of items of moral knowledge is common sense. The underlying thesis here is that the methods—the reasoned procedures—of philosophy are *not* those of discovery; they are, rather, those of analyzing and unifying materials otherwise provided.

Sidgwick is not suggesting, however, that the nonphilosophical methods of scientific inquiry and of common-sense revelation are beyond the attention of philosophy. Far from it. What we call the scientific method is the best so-far-achieved effort of technical philosophy to bring the methods of the sciences into systematic coherence. And again, "the method of common morality" is the hoped-for result of practical philosophy as it examines the methods of common sense in a comparable manner.

Sidgwick finds that the evident methods of common sense reduce to three. The first of these reasoned procedures for deciding what we *ought* and what we *ought not* to do in a specific circumstance is "intuitive" and quite direct. The second is "egoistic" and requires relatively simple calculations. The third is "utilitarian" and requires relatively complex calculations. The intuitive method serves a felt need for excellence and provides self-evident principles under which proposals for specific actions can or cannot be subsumed. The egoistic and utilitarian methods serve our desire for personal happiness and for the happiness of all, respectively; each arrives at its specific course-of-action decisions by comparing calculations of prospective happiness.

Practical philosophy is immediately confronted with the reality that when applied, these methods may place us under conflicting demands. We have all confronted the opposed decisions proffered by egoistic and utilitarian calculations—so frequently, in fact, that we experience moral relief when the decisions of these two methods happen to agree, when, as is often said, our decision is one of "enlightened self-interest." But Sidgwick sees the problem of methodological incoherence as running deeper than examples at this level suggest. He is convinced that the explicating theories defending either egoism or utilitarianism at the expense of the other, or, alternatively, defending them as ultimately compatible are based on conceptual confusions. In response, and with hope, Sidgwick undertakes a thorough investigation of the intuitive method.[1]

His claim is that, with careful analysis, we can isolate the self-evident normative principles from among the normative principles that common sense provides. Sidgwick reminds us in the first place that self-evident normative principles must be known intuitively because they cannot be derived from other normative principles. And he reminds us in the second place that genuine self-evident normative principles are responsive to a number of manifestly relevant tests. Thus, for example, such principles must be statable in clearly understandable terms; they cannot be tautologies or result from circular thinking; they cannot be so abstract that they fail to provide practical moral guidance or so specific that they lack scope of moral guidance; they must be consistent with each other; and they must be agreed to by those skilled in inquiry.

The first of Sidgwick's four intuitively known self-evident normative principles, or "axioms," the *justice* principle, declares that "whatever action any of us judges to be right for himself, he implicitly judges to be right for all similar persons in similar circumstances. . . ."[2] That this principle widens the Golden Rule and makes it more precise is obvious. The second, the *prudence* principle, declares that "a smaller present good is not to be preferred to a greater future good. . . ."[3] This theme characterizes most age-old prudential admonitions. The third, the *rational benevolence* principle, declares that "each one is morally bound to regard the good of any other individual as much as his own."[4] This principle captures the underlying requirement of many principles demanding concern for the well-being of others: It is the requirement that we regard others as being on the same plane of moral worth as ourselves.

Taking stock before introducing Sidgwick's fourth principle, note that these principles taken together declare that, with the good of all people affected by our actions regarded as equally important, we ought to act in the ways that produce the most good over time. Note, that is, that what these principles declare is the framework of utilitarianism. It is just the framework, however: Although it spells out how what is good ought to be distributed, it does not declare what it is that is morally good.

Sidgwick's fourth principle fills this need. The *desirable consciousness* principle declares that "Desirable Consciousness . . . must be regarded as the ultimate Good."[5] What it is that is being regarded as the Good is pleasure; but it is "pleasure" taken in the broad, universally applicable sense of the term, the sense underlying all the term's familiar but restricted senses. Thus, for example, it is the sense that underlies but is not limited to pleasures of sense, or to pleasures of virtue, or to pleasures of realized ambition, or to pleasures that can be achieved by directly pursuing them. With the foregoing understood, Sidgwick frequently supplants the awkward term "Desirable Consciousness" with "Universal Pleasure" or "Universal Happiness."

---

[1]Sidgwick acknowledges that he was influenced by the ethical intuitionist Samuel Clarke (1675–1729). More than anyone else, Sidgwick is both the historical and the substantive link between the ethical intuitionism of the eighteenth and twentieth centuries.

[2]Henry Sidgwick, *The Methods of Ethics*, 7th ed. (London: Macmillan, 1907), p. 379.

[3]*Ibid.*, p. 381.

[4]*Ibid.*, p. 382.

[5]*Ibid.*, p. 397.

It is basic for Sidgwick that the fourth principle *not* be regarded as a truth gained by definition. Its truth is the truth of a self-evident proposition and thereby is comparable to the truth of, say, "things equal to the same thing are equal to each other." With respect to its truth, the fourth normative principle is no different from the other three normative principles. Sidgwick is convinced that John Stuart Mill's account of utilitarianism is undermined by his having succumbed to the temptation of linking "Good" and "pleasure" by definition. Sidgwick's criticisms on this point are subtle and far-reaching, but, deeper criticisms aside, Sidgwick would insist that Mill's definition is merely a stipulation.[6] And he would no doubt add, "If it seems correct rather than arbitrary, it is because it appears to be more responsive than other stipulative definitions, e.g., 'Good' defined by 'pain,' to the fourth self-evident principle. Remember, the principles of common sense are affective whether or not we have isolated and assembled them."

In summary, Sidgwick's thesis is this: Practical philosophy ascertains that the intuitive method is the coherent method of common sense. Further, when properly understood, hedonistic utilitarianism is the message of the intuitive method. And finally, the moral advice of the dominant hedonistic utilitarians of the recent past is much sounder than their theory.[7]

---

**1.** Sidgwick discusses his hopes for the method he calls "philosophical intuitionism." He also suggests, in a general way, what the relationship is between this method and common sense.

Is there. . . no possibility of attaining, by a more profound and discriminating examination of our common moral thought, to real ethical axioms—intuitive propositions of real clearness and certainty?

This question leads us to the examination of that third phase of the intuitive method, which was called Philosophical Intuitionism. For we conceive it as the aim of a philosopher, as such, to do somewhat more than define and formulate the common moral opinions of mankind. His function is to tell men what they ought to think, rather than what they do think: he is

---

[6]That Sidgwick set the stage for much of the ethical theory of the first half of the twentieth century and beyond can be suggested this way: He not only begins with the natural and moral worlds sharply distinguished, but he also insists that no normative principles can be logically inferred from factual (descriptive) propositions. Further, he is skeptical about there being *real* definitions that bridge this gap; in particular, he challenged the nineteenth-century enthusiasm for regarding moral psychology as the basic component of moral philosophy. Again, he introduced the idea that at least one ethical term basic for the definitions of others is, in itself, indefinable. G. E. Moore, Sidgwick's most influential student, cast these issues in a more modern form, and the pros and cons about them have marked our century (see Chapters 19, 20, and 21 of this book).

[7]With respect to comparing pleasures, Sidgwick is more Bentham-like than Mill-like. For Bentham, the measure of pleasures is purely quantitative, whereas for Mill, the measure is both quantitative and qualitative. Mill was sensitive to the fact that his predecessor's account was charged with being a "swinish" doctrine. Sidgwick insists that, given the self-evident *desirable consciousness* principle, ". . . consistency requires that pleasures should be sought in proportion to their pleasantness; and therefore the less pleasant consciousness must not be preferred to the more pleasant on the ground of any other qualities that it may possess. The distinctions of *quality* that Mill and others urge may still be admitted as ground of preference, but only in so far as they can be resolved into distinctions of quantity" (*The Methods of Ethics*, p. 121).

expected to transcend Common Sense in his premises, and is allowed a certain divergence from Common Sense in his conclusions. It is true that the limits of this deviation are firmly, though indefinitely, fixed: the truth of a philosopher's premises will always be tested by the acceptability of his conclusions: if in any important point he be found in flagrant conflict with common opinion, his method is likely to be declared invalid. Still, though he is expected to establish and concatenate at least the main part of the commonly accepted moral rules, he is not necessarily bound to take them as the basis on which his own system is constructed. Rather, we should expect that the history of Moral Philosophy—so far at least as those whom we may call orthodox thinkers are concerned—would be a history of attempts to enunciate, in full breadth and clearness, those primary intuitions of Reason, by the scientific application of which the common moral thought of mankind may be at once systematized and corrected.[a]

**2.** Without exercising caution, it is easy to mistake non–self-evident principles for self-evident ones, "sham-axioms" for genuine ones. Most mistakes of this sort are a consequence of failures in identifying tautologies. Sidgwick suggests that all of us have made these mistakes.

But here a word of caution seems required, which has been somewhat anticipated in earlier chapters, but on which it is particularly needful to lay stress at this point of our discussion: against a certain class of sham-axioms, which are very apt to offer themselves to the mind that is earnestly seeking for a philosophical synthesis of practical rules, and to delude the unwary with a tempting aspect of clear self-evidence. These are principles which appear certain and self-evident because they are substantially tautological: because, when examined, they are found to affirm no more than that it is right to do that which is—in a certain department of life, under certain circumstances and conditions—right to be done. One important lesson which the history of moral philosophy teaches is that, in this region, even powerful intellects are liable to acquiesce in tautologies of this kind; sometimes expanded into circular reasonings, sometimes hidden in the recesses of an obscure notion, often lying so near the surface that, when once they have been exposed, it is hard to understand how they could ever have presented themselves as important.

Let us turn, for illustration's sake, to the time-honored Cardinal Virtues. If we are told that the dictates of Wisdom and Temperance may be summed up in clear and certain principles, and that these are, respectively,

1. It is right to act rationally,
2. It is right that the Lower parts of our nature should be governed by the Higher,

we do not at first feel that we are not obtaining valuable information. But when we find . . . that "acting rationally" is merely another phrase for "doing what we see to be right," and, again, that the "higher art" of our nature to which the rest are to submit is explained to be Reason, so that "acting temperately" is only "acting rationally" under the condition of special non-rational impulses needing to be resisted, the tautology of our "principles" is obvious. Similarly when we are asked to accept as the principle of Justice "that we ought to give every man his own," the definition seems plausible—until it appears that we cannot define "his own" except as equivalent to "that which is right he should have."[b]

**3.** Sidgwick points out that a self-evident principle cannot be so abstract that it fails to provide specific moral guidance. The nature of this problem becomes clear as he works to isolate the self-evident *justice* principle.

Can we then, between this Scylla and Charybdis of ethical inquiry, avoiding on the one hand doctrines that merely bring us back to common opinion with all its imperfections, and on the other hand doctrines that lead us round in a circle, find any way of obtaining self-evident moral principles of real significance? It would be disheartening to have to regard as altogether illusory the strong instinct of Common Sense that points to the existence of such principles, and the deliberate convictions of the long line of moralists who have enunciated them. At the same time, the more we extend our knowledge of man and his environment, the more we realize the vast variety of human natures and circumstances that have existed in different ages and countries, the less disposed we are to believe that there is any definite code of absolute rules, applicable to all human beings without exception. And we shall find, I think, that the truth lies between these two conclusions. There are certain absolute practical principles, the truth of which, when they are explicitly stated, is manifest; but they are of too abstract a nature, and too universal in their scope, to enable us to ascertain by immediate application of them what we ought to do in any particular case; particular duties have still to be determined by some other method.

One such principle was given . . . where I pointed out that whatever action any of us judges to be right for himself, he implicitly judges to be right for all similar persons in similar circumstances. Or, as we may otherwise put it, "if a kind of conduct that is right (or wrong) for me is not right (or wrong) for some one else, it must be on the ground of some difference between the two cases, other than the fact that I and he are different persons." A corresponding proposition may be stated with equal truth in respect of what ought to be done *to*—not *by*—different individuals. These principles have been most widely recognized, not in their most abstract and universal form, but in their special application to the situation of two (or more) individuals similarly related to each other: as so applied, they appear in which is popularly known as the Golden Rule, "Do to others as you would have them do to you." This formula is obviously unprecise in statement; for one might wish for another's co-operation in sin, and be willing to reciprocate it. Nor is it even true to say that we ought to do to others only what we think it right for them to do to us; for no one will deny that there may be differences in the circumstances—and even in the natures—of two individuals, *A* and *B*, which would make it wrong for *A* to treat *B* in the way in which it is right for *B* to treat *A*. In short the self-evident principle strictly stated must take some such negative form as this; "it cannot be right for *A* to treat *B* in a manner in which it would be wrong for *B* to treat *A*, merely on the ground that they are two different individuals, and without there being any difference between the natures or circumstances of the two which can be stated as a reasonable ground for difference of treatment." Such a principle manifestly does not give complete guidance—indeed its effect, strictly speaking, is merely to throw a definite *onus probandi* on the man who applies to another a treatment of which he would complain if applied to himself; but Common Sense has amply recognized the practical importance of the maxim: and its truth, so far as it goes, appears to me self-evident.

A somewhat different application of the same fundamental principle that individuals in similar conditions should be treated similarly finds its sphere in the ordinary administration of Law, or (as we say) of "Justice." Accordingly in . . . this Book I drew attention to "impartiality in the application of general rules," as an important element in the common notion of Justice; indeed, there ultimately appeared to be no other element which could be intuitively known with perfect clearness and certainty. Here again it must be plain that this precept of impartiality is insufficient for the complete determination of just conduct, as it does not help us to decide what kind of rules should be thus impartially applied; though all admit the importance of excluding from government, and human conduct generally, all conscious partiality and "respect of persons."

The principle just discussed, which seems to be more or less clearly implied in the common notion of "fairness" or "equity," is obtained by considering the similarity of the individuals that make up a Logical Whole or Genus.[c]

**4.** Sidgwick isolates the self-evident *prudence* principle with little difficulty.

The proposition "that one ought to aim at one's own good" is sometimes given as the maxim of

Rational Self-love or Prudence: but as so stated it does not clearly avoid tautology; since we may define "good" as "what one ought to aim at." If, however, we say "one's good on the whole," the addition suggests a principle which, when explicitly stated, is, at any rate, not tautological. I have already referred to this principle as that "of impartial concern for all parts of our conscious life":—we might express it concisely by saying "that Hereafter *as such* is to be regarded neither less nor more than Now." It is not, of course, meant that the good of the present may not reasonably be preferred to that of the future on account of its greater certainty: or again, that a week ten years hence may not be more important to us than a week now, through an increase in our means or capacities of happiness. All that the principle affirms is that the mere difference of priority and posteriority in time is not a reasonable ground for having more regard to the consciousness of one moment than to that of another. The form in which it practically presents itself to most men is "that a smaller present good is not to be preferred to a greater future good" (allowing for difference of certainty): since Prudence is generally exercised in restraining a present desire (the object or satisfaction of which we commonly regard as *pro tanto* "a good"), on account of the remoter consequences of gratifying it.[d]

**5.** Noting that the first two principles address what is good for the individual who realizes that each event is an integral part of his or her lifetime, Sidgwick turns to isolating the self-evident *rational benevolence* principle that addresses what is good for individuals who realize that they are integral parts of humanity.

So far we have only been considering the "Good on the Whole" of a single individual: but just as this notion is constructed by comparison and integration of the different "goods" that succeed one another in the series of our conscious states, so we have formed the notion of Universal Good by comparison and integration of the goods of all individual human—or sentient—existences. And here again, just as in the former case, by considering the relation of the integrant parts to the whole and to each other, I obtain the self-evident principle that the good of any one individual is of no more importance, from the point of view (if I may say so) of the Universe, than the good of any other; unless, that is, there are special grounds for believing that more good is likely to be realized in the one case than in the other. And it is evident to me that as a rational being I am bound to aim at good generally,—so far as it is attainable by my efforts,—not merely at a particular part of it.

From these two rational intuitions we may deduce, as a necessary inference, the maxim of Benevolence in an abstract form: viz. that each one is morally bound to regard the good of any other individual as much as his own, except in so far as he judges it to be less, when impartially viewed, or less certainly knowable or attainable by him. I before observed that the duty of Benevolence as recognized by common sense seems to fall somewhat short of this. But I think it may be fairly urged in explanation of this that *practically* each man, even with a view to universal Good, ought chiefly to concern himself with promoting the good of a limited number of human beings, and that generally in proportion to the closeness of their connection with him. I think that a "plain man," in a modern civilized society, if his conscience were fairly brought to consider the hypothetical question, whether it would be morally right for him to seek his own happiness on any occasion if it involved a certain sacrifice of the greater happiness of some other human being,—without any counterbalancing gain to any one else,—would answer unhesitatingly in the negative.[e]

**6.** After observing that all three of these principles serve our understanding of utilitarianism and that *rational benevolence* alone among the three sets utilitarianism apart, Sidgwick assesses why John Stuart Mill's attempt to provide a foundation for utilitarianism fails.[8]

---

[8]See Chapter 13 of this book.

Still, when I examine the "proof" of the "principle of Utility" presented by the most persuasive and probably the most influential among English expositors of Utilitarianism,—J. S. Mill,—I find the need of some such procedure to complete the argument very plain and palpable.

Mill begins by explaining that though "questions of ultimate ends are not amenable" to "proof in the ordinary and popular meaning of the term," there is a "larger meaning of the word proof" in which they are amenable to it. "The subject," he says is "within the cognizance of the rational faculty. . . . Considerations may be presented capable of determining the intellect to" accept "the Utilitarian formula." He subsequently makes clear that by "acceptance of the Utilitarian formula" he means the acceptance, not of the agent's own greatest happiness, but of "the greatest amount of happiness altogether" as the ultimate "end of human action" and "standard of morality": to promote which is, in the Utilitarian view, the supreme "directive rule of human conduct." Then when he comes to give the "proof"—in the larger sense before explained—of this rule or formula, he offers the following argument. "The sole evidence it is possible to produce that anything is desirable, is that people do actually desire it. . . . No reason can be given why the general happiness is desirable, except that each person, so far as he believes it to be attainable, desires his own happiness. This, however, being a fact, we have not only all the proof which the case admits of, but all which it is possible to require, that happiness is a good: that each person's happiness is a good to that person, and the general happiness, therefore, a good to the aggregate of persons." He then goes on to argue that pleasure, and pleasure alone, is what all men actually do desire.

Now, as we have seen, it is as a "standard of right and wrong," or "directive rule of conduct," that the utilitarian principle is put forward by Mill: hence, in giving as a statement of this principle that "the general happiness is *desirable*," he must be understood to mean (and his whole treatise shows that he does mean) that it is what each individual *ought* to desire, or at least—in the stricter sense of "ought"—to aim at realizing in action. But this proposition is not established by Mill's reasoning, even if we grant that what is actually desired may be legitimately inferred to be in this sense desirable. For an aggregate of actual desires, each directed toward a different part of the general happiness, does not constitute an actual desire for the general happiness, existing in any individual; and Mill would certainly not contend that a desire which does not exist in any individual can possibly exist in an aggregate of individuals. There being therefore no actual desire—so far as this reasoning goes—for the general happiness, the proposition that the general happiness is desirable cannot be in this way established: so that there is a gap in the expressed argument, which can, I think, only be filled by some such proposition as that which I have above tried to exhibit as the intuition of Rational Benevolence.[f]

> **7.** Sidgwick's efforts to clarify "desirable consciousness" involve extensive analyses. One of these concerns the difference in the relationship to desirability that an activity can have when it is serving as an *end* and when it is serving as a *means.*

[The] fact that particular virtues and talents and gifts are largely valued as means to ulterior good does not necessarily prevent us from regarding their exercise as also an element of ultimate Good: just as the fact that physical action, nutrition, and repose, duly proportioned and combined, are means to the maintenance of our animal life, does not prevent us from regarding them as indispensable elements of such life. Still it seems difficult to conceive any kind of activity or process as both means and end, from precisely the same point of view and in respect of precisely the same quality: and in both the cases above mentioned it is, I think, easy to distinguish the aspect in which the activities or processes in question are to be regarded as means from that in which they are to be regarded as in themselves good or desirable. Let us examine this first in the case of the physical processes. It is in their purely physical aspect, as complex processes of corporeal change, that they are means to the maintenance of life: but so long as we confine our attention to their corporeal aspect,—regarding them merely as complex movements of certain particles of organized matter—it seems impossible to attribute to these movements, considered in themselves, either goodness or badness. I cannot conceive it to be an ultimate end of rational action to secure that these complex movements should be of one kind rather than another, or that they should be continued for a longer rather than a shorter period. In short, if a certain quality of human Life is that which is ultimately desirable, it must belong to human Life regarded on its psychical side, or briefly, Consciousness.

But again: it is not all life regarded on its psychical side which we can judge to be ultimately desirable: since psychical life as known to us includes pain as well as pleasure, and so far as it is painful it is not desirable. I cannot therefore accept a view of the wellbeing or welfare of human beings—as of other living things—which is suggested by current zoological conceptions and apparently maintained with more or less definiteness by influential writers; according to which, when we attribute goodness or badness to the manner of existence of any living organism, we should be understood to attribute to it a tendency either (1) to self-preservation, or (2) to the preservation of the community or race to which it belongs—so that what "Wellbeing" adds to mere "Being" is just promise of future being. It appears to me that this doctrine needs only to be distinctly contemplated in order to be rejected. If all life were as little desirable as some portions of it have been, in my own experience and in that (I believe) of all or most men, I should judge all tendency to the preservation of it to be unmitigatedly bad. Actually, no doubt, as we generally hold that human life, even as now lived, has on the average, a balance of happiness, we regard what is preservative of life as generally good, and what is destructive of life as bad: and I quite admit that a most fundamentally important part of the function of morality consists in maintaining such habits and sentiments as are necessary to the continued existence, in full numbers, of a society of human beings under their actual conditions of life. But this is not because the mere existence of human organisms, even if prolonged to eternity, appears to me in any way desirable; it is only assumed to be so because it is supposed to be accompanied by Consciousness on the whole desirable; it is therefore this Desirable Consciousness which we must regard as ultimate Good.

In the same way, so far as we judge virtuous activity to be a part of Ultimate Good, it is, I conceive, because the consciousness attending it is judged to be in itself desirable for the virtuous agent; though at the same time this consideration does not adequately represent the importance of Virtue to human wellbeing, since we have to consider its value as a means as well as its value as an end. We may make the distinction clearer by considering whether Virtuous life would remain on the whole good for the virtuous agent, if we suppose it combined with extreme pain. The affirmative answer to this question was strongly supported in Greek philosophical discussion: but it is a paradox from which a modern thinker would recoil: he would hardly venture to assert that the portion of life spent by a martyr in tortures was in itself desirable,—though it might be his duty to suffer the pain with a view to the good of others, and even his interest to suffer it with a view to his own ultimate happiness.[g]

**8.** Sidgwick recognizes that our dispositions to realize the various ideals of virtue can make us reluctant to accept the *desirable consciousness* principle. He points out in rebuttal that pleasure is derived not only from attaining an ideal but also, indirectly, from just pursuing it.

But lastly, from the universal point of view no less than from that of the individual, it seems true that Happiness is likely to be better attained if the extent to which we set ourselves consciously to aim at it be carefully restricted. And this not only because action is likely to be more effective if our effort is temporarily concentrated on the realization of more limited ends—though this is no doubt an important reason:—but also because the fullest development of happy life for each individual seems to require that he should have other external objects of interest besides the happiness of other conscious beings. And thus we may conclude that the pursuit of the ideal objects before mentioned, Virtue, Truth, Freedom, Beauty, etc., *for their own sakes*, is indirectly and secondarily, though not primarily and absolutely, rational; on account not only of the happiness that will result from their attainment, but also of that which springs from their disinterested pursuit. While yet if we ask for a final criterion of the comparative value of the different objects of men's enthusiastic pursuit, and of the limits within which each may legitimately engross the attention of mankind, we shall none the less conceive it to depend upon the degree in which they respectively conduce to Happiness.[h]

**9.** Continuing with his defense of pleasure as the final criterion by which we compare our objectives, Sidgwick insists that we can account for our choice to pursue one of our ideals rather than another by comparing the prospective balances of pleasures over pain. Further, he insists that this account must be regarded as decisive because, it would seem after inquiry, no alternative account can be suggested.

If however, this view be rejected, it remains to consider whether we can frame any other coherent account of Ultimate Good. If we are not to systematize human activities by taking Universal Happiness as their common end, on what other principles are we to systematize them? It should be observed that these principles must not only enable us to compare among themselves the values of the different nonhedonistic ends which we have been considering, but must also provide a common standard for comparing these values with that of Happiness; unless we are prepared to adopt the paradoxical position of rejecting happiness as absolutely valueless. For we have a practical need of determining not only whether we should pursue Truth rather than Beauty, or Freedom or some ideal constitution of society rather than either, or perhaps desert all of these for the life of worship and religious contemplation; but also how far we should follow any of these lines of endeavour, when we foresee among its consequences the pains of human or other sentient beings, or even the loss of pleasures that might otherwise have been enjoyed by them.

I have failed to find—and am unable to construct—any systematic answer to this question that appears to me deserving of serious consideration: and hence I am finally led to the conclusion . . . that the Intuitional method rigorously applied yields as its final result the doctrine of pure Universalistic Hedonism—which it is convenient to denote by the single word, Utilitarianism.[i]

## QUESTIONS

1. Sidgwick argues that the Golden Rule— "Do unto others as you would have them do unto you"—lacks precision. Think of a specific case that is not in the spirit of the maxim even though it abides by it when taken literally.
2. Let it be that by exercising the scientific method, we know that smoking is injurious to health. Armed with this knowledge, Mother tells Junior that it is immoral to smoke. Explain her statement in a utilitarian manner. Suppose Junior counters by saying that her father smoked. Does she have to agree that her father too was being immoral?
3. In determining "the method of common morality," Sidgwick appeals to the standard of "systematic coherence." Is this an appeal to people as rational animals? Discuss.
4. Utilitarianism is said by some to fail because it cannot account for self-sacrifice. How does Sidgwick respond? Is he convincing?
5. Explain what Sidgwick means by "desirable consciousness."
6. Are you convinced that Sidgwick's four normative principles are, indeed, self-evident? If not, why not?
7. Sidgwick and other utilitarians stress pleasure and happiness (a sum of pleasures) more than pain. Does this mean that pleasure and happiness have little application for a miserable society? Discuss.

8. While defending his intuitive hedonistic utilitarianism from the charge that it cannot account for moral thinking in past periods, Sidgwick offers this example: "Aristotle sees that the sphere of the Virtue of Courage as recognized by the Common Sense of Greece, is restricted to dangers in war: and we can now explain this limitation by a reference to the utilitarian importance of this kind of courage, at a period of history when the individual's happiness was bound up more completely than it is now with the welfare of the state, while the very existence of the latter was frequently imperilled by hostile invasions . . ." (*The Methods of Ethics*, p. 456.) How closely is this question related to question 2? Elaborate.
9. Be a Sidgwickian and respond to the charge that "utilitarian principles, logically carried out, would result in far more cheating, lying, and unfair action than any good man would tolerate" (A. C. Ewing, *Ethics* [New York: Macmillan, 1935], p. 40).
10. How near and how far do you think Sidgwick is from embracing Kant's categorical imperative?

## KEY TO SELECTIONS

Henry Sidgwick, *The Methods of Ethics*, 7th ed., London, Macmillan, 1907.

[a]pp. 373–374.
[b]pp. 374–375.
[c]pp. 379–380.
[d]p. 381.
[e]p. 382.
[f]pp. 387–388.
[g]pp. 396–397.
[h]pp. 405–406.
[i]pp. 406–407.

## GUIDE TO ADDITIONAL READING


### PRIMARY SOURCES

Sidgwick, H., *Outlines of the History of Ethics*, 4th ed., New York, Macmillan, 1896.

_____, *Practical Ethics*, London, Macmillan, 1898.

Singer, Marcus, (ed.), *Henry Sidgwick: Essays on Ethics and Method*, Oxford, Oxford University Press, 2001.

### DISCUSSION AND COMMENTARY

Broad, C. D., *Five Types of Ethical Theories*, New York, Harcourt, Brace and Co., 1930.

_____, *Ethics and the History of Philosophy*, London, Macmillan, 1952.

Frankena, W. K., "Sidgwick and the Dualism of Practical Reason," *Monist*, 58 (1974), pp. 449–467.

Schneewind, J. B., *Sidgwick's Ethics and Victorian Moral Philosophy*, Oxford, Clarendon Press, 1977.

Schultz, Bart, ed., *Essays on Henry Sidgwick*, Cambridge, Cambridge University Press, 1992.

Smart, J. J. C., "Hedonistic and Ideal Utilitarianism," *Midwest Studies in Philosophy*, Vol. III, 1978, pp. 240–251.

Williams, B. A. O., "What Does Intuitionism Imply?" in *Human Agency: Language, Duty, and Value*, ed. J. Dancy et al., Stanford, Stanford University Press, 1988, pp. 189–198.

CHAPTER SEVENTEEN

# The Transvaluation of Values

Picture Collection, The Branch Libraries, The New York Public Library, Astor, Lenox, and Tilden Foundations

FRIEDRICH NIETZSCHE

ALTHOUGH HE WAS DESCENDED through both his parents from theologians, Friedrich Nietzsche (1844–1900) made his reputation in philosophy through a "campaign against morality." No hint of his widespread influence on European thought is given by the facts of his history. He was born in the Prussian city of Röcken, and his father's premature death left Friedrich to be petted and spoiled as the only male in a household consisting of his mother, a younger sister, and other female relatives. His home life and early education were entirely in keeping with the family tradition of piety, but when he was a student at the universities of Bonn and Leipzig, Nietzsche's thinking underwent a radical transformation. He was much impressed by the vitality of the ancient Greco-Roman civilization and by the grim realism of the contemporary principle of the "survival of the fittest." These influences, together with the pessimistic, antirationalistic philosophy of Arthur Schopenhauer, were the chief external sources of Nietzsche's extreme revulsion at the ideals of his time; to him, European civilization appeared despicably weak and decadent.

Throughout his life, Nietzsche was plagued by physical disability. An injury suffered in military training in 1867 made active duty impossible, but he later interrupted his academic career to seek the stimulation of the military scene as a volunteer in the hospital corps during the Franco-Prussian War (1870). Illness contracted while he was in service—the beginning of a lifetime of increasing physical suffering—forced him to leave the army, and he returned to the academic world. On the strength of his exceptional academic ability, he had been appointed professor of classical philology at the University of Basel in Switzerland at the age of twenty-four. By the time he was thirty-five, poor health obliged him to resign, and for nearly a decade, he traveled through Europe in a vain search for an environment in which he might recover his health.

Despite the wretchedness of protracted sickness and loneliness, Nietzsche produced a succession of brilliant books. His first important work, *The Birth of Tragedy from the Spirit of Music* (1872), was probably influenced by his brief attachment to the famous composer Richard Wagner. Of his major philosophical works, many express in their titles his protest against the accepted ideals of his time: *Thoughts Out of Season* (1876), *Human All-Too-Human* (1880), *Beyond Good and Evil* (1886), *The Genealogy of Morals* (1887), and *The Antichrist* (1889). Nietzsche's more positive and constructive writings include *The Dawn of Day* (1881), *The Joyful Wisdom* (1882), and the dramatic *Thus Spake Zarathustra* (1884). His final work—a collection of fragments—was *The Will to Power* (1889). A violent seizure, early in 1889, followed by insanity, terminated Nietzsche's career; his sister, Elizabeth Foerster-Nietzsche, edited his unfinished works and saw to their publication.

Perhaps more than any other philosopher, Nietzsche stands in need of defense against the tendency to evaluate ideas in terms of the man rather than on their own merits. Against the view sometimes expressed that Nietzsche's extremist theories and emotional style were the expression of a warped mind, there stands the fact that his works are distinguished for brilliance of insight, shrewdness of argument, and soundness of scholarship. Moreover, his radical ideas have been welcomed by many conscientious thinkers in literature, art, pedagogy, politics, religion, and ethics, who, with him, have been alarmed by the decline of individuality and free expression in the "machine age."

Fortified with the conviction that philosophers must serve as "the bad conscience of their age," Nietzsche attacks relentlessly what he sees as the decadence and hypocrisy of traditional European morality—a morality that, he predicts, will inevitably lead to the eclipse of Western civilization. To avert this disaster, Nietzsche proposes a moral countermovement:

> After thousands of years of error and confusion, it is my good fortune to have rediscovered the road which leads to a Yea and to a Nay.
>
> I teach people to say Nay in the face of all that makes for weakness and exhaustion.
>
> I teach people to say Yea in the face of all that makes for strength, that preserves strength, and justifies the feeling of strength.[a]

Nietzsche holds up to ridicule the accepted ideals of the Judeo-Christian religion and Greek rationalism, describing them as *reversals* of the true values. To implement the needed moral revolution, he presents a corrected table of virtues: in place of humility, pride; in place of sympathy and pity, contempt and aloofness; in place of love of one's neighbor, no more than tolerance. However, Nietzsche does not intend this doctrine of the *transvaluation of values* for the "common herd," but for the few "free spirits" of the day who are intellectually fit to receive it.[1]

---

[1]Nietzsche's works are frequently, but erroneously, regarded as philosophical support for the National Socialist (Nazi) movement in Germany. A few themes from his philosophy may support the Nazi doctrines, but there are fundamental differences—for example, in the opposition of Nietzsche's principle of radical creative individualism to the Nazi principle of the priority of the state over the individual.

In a series of pungent aphorisms, replete with invective and wit, Nietzsche addresses himself to the aristocracy of free spirits. He exhorts them to prepare for the highest stage in human development, the Superman. For Nietzsche, the Superman symbolizes the unfettered spirit, reveling in his magnificent strength and his own worth. Although humanity in its present condition may be regarded as the highest form of existence, our dominance over nature is still precarious. Indeed, "Man is something to be surpassed." The Superman represents a higher level of mastery over nature.

Although the conception of evolution is fundamental in Nietzsche's ethical system, his interpretation of it departs from the widely accepted Darwinian hypothesis. In Darwin's theory, evolution is conceived as passive and mechanical adaptation to the environment, but Nietzsche finds the true meaning of evolution in an aggressive "will to power" to dominate the environment: "The strongest and highest Will to Life does not find expression in a miserable struggle for existence, but in a Will to War, a Will to Power, a Will to Overpower!" There is in evolution no progress toward a goal: Each thing in the universe manifests a ceaseless, blind striving for power, shifting back and forth between success and failure in the competition for mastery.

Our struggle for dominance over the environment is hampered by the teachings of false moralities. The true morality, Nietzsche holds, must build from the immediate sense of power that all people can feel within themselves. Like numerous moralists before him, Nietzsche approves as good whatever conforms to nature and condemns as bad whatever is contrary to it. But he dismisses as unrealistic the description of nature as a rational or providential order. Nature is essentially the will to power, a brutal and savage contest of strength, characterized by frightfulness and tragedy, bloodshed, suffering, and cruelty. Affirming the values that enhance the will to power, saying "yea" to life as it actually is, constitutes for Nietzsche the true morality.

From the point of view of the Nietzschean morality, all ethical theories that conceal the hard facts of existence and teach the repression of the will to power are insidious. Nietzsche therefore castigates Christians and Jews, Germans and Englishmen, philosophers and scientists—and women—for preferring life-denying values. The Judeo-Christian ethic is singled out as the most pernicious source of antinatural morality. Its perversion of the will to power is seen in clergymen seeking mastery under cover of hypocritical sermons on meekness, and its repression of the will to power is seen in the "botched and bungled" masses who are taken in by the deceptions of the priests.

The rationalism of traditional philosophy, because it too misrepresents reality, is regarded as reinforcing the debilitating influence of Christianity. In holding up the ideal of a human being as a rational animal, the philosophers mistakenly elevate reason to the preeminent position in human nature. In actuality, the essence of an individual is not reason, but will—the will to power. In the Nietzschean scheme, the role of reason is to facilitate the functioning of the drive for power by organizing efficiently the conditions of action. Nietzsche uses the Greek gods Dionysus and Apollo to dramatize the relationship between the will and the reason. Dionysus, the frenzied and passionate, is revered as the symbol of the undisciplined will to power. Apollo, representing rationality and order, must be the instrument by which the will to power can increase its mastery. With the Apollonian element supporting rather than suppressing the Dionysian, humans can defy God and dominate the universe: The moral person "lives dangerously."[2]

**1.** Drawing on his knowledge of philology and history for evidence, Nietzsche contradicts the main currents of the liberal, democratic thought of his time. The cardinal distinction of his ethical theory is that between the "master-morality" of the noble and free spirits and the "slave-morality" of the common run of people.

In a tour through the many finer and coarser moralities which have hitherto prevailed or still prevail on the earth, I found certain traits recurring regularly together, and connected with one another, until finally two primary types revealed themselves to me, and a radical distinction was brought to light. There is *master-morality* and *slave-morality;*—I would at once add, however, that in all higher and mixed civilizations, there are also attempts at the reconciliation of the two moralities; but one finds still oftener the confusion and mutual misunderstanding of them, indeed, sometimes their close juxtaposition—even in the same man, within one soul. The distinctions of moral values have either originated in a ruling caste, pleasantly conscious of being different from the ruled—or among the ruled class, the slaves and dependents of all sorts....

The noble type of man regards *himself* as a determiner of values; he does not require to be approved of; he passes the judgment: "What is injurious to me is injurious in itself"; he knows that it is he himself only who confers honor on things; he is a *creator of values.* He honors whatever he recognizes in himself: such morality is self-glorification. In the foreground there is the feeling of plenitude, of power, which seeks to overflow, the happiness of high tension, the consciousness of a wealth which would fain give and bestow:—the noble man also helps the unfortunate, but not—or scarcely—out of pity, but rather from an impulse generated by the superabundance of power. The noble man honors in himself the powerful one, him also who has power over himself, who knows how to speak and how to keep silence, who takes pleasure in subjecting himself to severity and hardness, and has reverence for all that is severe and hard....

It is otherwise with the second type of morality, *slave-morality.* Supposing that the abused, the oppressed, the suffering, the unemancipated, the weary, and those uncertain of themselves, should moralize, what will be the common element in their moral estimates? Probably a pessimistic suspicion with regard to the entire situation of man will find expression, perhaps a condemnation of man, together with his situation. The slave has an unfavorable eye for the virtues of the powerful; he has a skepticism and distrust, a *refinement* of distrust of everything "good" that is there honored—he would fain persuade himself that the very happiness there is not genuine. On the other hand, *those* qualities which serve to alleviate the existence of sufferers are brought into prominence and flooded with light; it is here that sympathy, the kind, helping hand, the warm heart, patience, diligence, humility, and friendliness attain to honor; for here these are the most useful qualities, and almost the only means of supporting the burden of existence. Slave-morality is essentially the morality of utility. Here is the seat of the origin of the famous antithesis "good" and "evil":—power and dangerousness are assumed to reside in the evil, a certain dreadfulness, subtlety, and strength, which do not admit of being despised. According to slave-morality, therefore, the "evil" man arouses fear; according to master-morality, it is precisely the

[2]Nietzsche is notoriously difficult to understand. Roughly speaking, there are "tough" and "gentle" interpretations. Ours falls in the former category.

"good" man who arouses fear and seeks to arouse it, while the bad man is regarded as the despicable being.[b]

**2.** There are, then, different ethical terms for the two moralities: the distinction between "good" and "bad" is made by the aristocrat, whereas the opposition of "good" and "evil" is the invention of the slaves. Motivated by resentment, the latter call "evil" those characteristics that the aristocrats most honor in themselves.

The guidepost which first put me on the *right* track was this question—what is the true etymological significance of the various symbols for the idea "good" which have been coined in the various languages? I then found that they all led back to *the same evolution of the same idea*—that everywhere "aristocrat," "noble"(in the social sense), is the root idea, out of which have necessarily developed "good" in the sense of "with aristocratic soul," "noble," in the sense of "with a soul of high calibre," "with a privileged soul"—a development which invariably runs parallel with that other evolution by which "vulgar," "plebeian," "low," are made to change finally into "bad." . . .

The revolt of the slaves in morals begins in the very principle of *resentment* becoming creative and giving birth to values—a resentment experienced by creatures who, deprived as they are of the proper outlet of action, are forced to find their compensation in an imaginary revenge. While every aristocratic morality springs from a triumphant affirmation of its own demands, the slave morality says "no" from the very outset to what is "outside itself," "different from itself," and "not itself": and this "no" is its creative deed. . . .

What respect for his enemies is found, forsooth, in an aristocratic man—and such a reverence is already a bridge to love! He insists on having his enemy to himself as his distinction. He tolerates no other enemy but a man in whose character there is nothing to despise and *much* to honor! On the other hand, imagine the "enemy" as the resentful man conceives him—and it is here exactly that we see his work, his creativeness; he has conceived "the evil enemy," "the evil one," and indeed that is the root idea from which he now evolves as a contrasting and corresponding figure a "good one," himself—his very self!

The method of this man is quite contrary to that of the aristocratic man, who conceives the root idea "good" spontaneously and straight away, that is to say, out of himself, and from that material then creates for himself a concept of "bad"! This "bad" of aristocratic origin and that "evil" out of the cauldron of unsatisfied hatred—the former an imitation, an "extra," an additional nuance; the latter, on the other hand, the original, the beginning, the essential act in the conception of a slave-morality—these two words "bad" and "evil," how great a difference do they mark, in spite of the fact that they have an identical contrary in the idea "good." But the idea "good" is *not* the same: much rather let the question be asked, "Who is really evil according to the meaning of the morality of resentment?" In all sternness let it be answered thus:—*just* the good man of the other morality, just the aristocrat, the powerful one, the one who rules, but who is distorted by the venomous eye of resentfulness, into a new color, a new signification, a new appearance. This particular point we would be the last to deny: the man who learned to know those "good" ones only as enemies, learned at the same time not to know them only as "*evil enemies*," and the same men who *inter pares* [between equals] were kept so rigorously in bounds through convention, respect, custom, and gratitude, though much more through mutual vigilance and jealousy *inter pares,* these men who in their relations with each other find so many new ways of manifesting consideration, self-control, delicacy, loyalty, pride, and friendship, these men are in reference to what is outside their circle (where the foreign element, a *foreign* country, begins), not much better than beasts of prey, which have been let loose. They enjoy their freedom from all social control, they feel that in the wilderness they can give vent with impunity to that tension which is produced by enclosure and imprisonment in the peace of society, they *revert* to the innocence of the beast-of-prey conscience, like jubilant monsters, who perhaps come from a ghostly bout of murder, arson, rape, and torture, with bravado and a moral equanimity, as though merely some wild student's prank had been played, perfectly convinced that the poets have now an ample theme to sing and celebrate. It is impossible not to recognize at the core of all these aristocratic races the beast of prey; the magnificent *blond brute,* avidly rampant for spoil and victory; this hidden core needed an outlet from time to time, the beast must get loose again, must return into the wilderness.[c]

**3.** Nietzsche argues that creativity is the privilege and gift of the aristocratic—that is, the barbarian, ferocious components of society. Only they, he claims, have accomplished improvements in human nature.

Every elevation of the type "man," has hitherto been the work of an aristocratic society and so it will always be—a society believing in a long scale of gradations of rank and differences of worth among human beings, and requiring slavery in some form or other. Without the *pathos of distance,* such as grows out of the incarnated difference of classes, out of the constant outlooking and downlooking of the ruling caste on subordinates and instruments, and out of their equally constant practice of obeying and commanding, of keeping down and keeping at a distance—that other more mysterious pathos could never have arisen, the longing for an ever new widening of distance within the soul itself, the formation of ever higher, rarer, further, more extended, more comprehensive states, in short, just the elevation of the type "man," the continued "self-surmounting of man," to use a moral formula in a supermoral sense. To be sure, one must not resign oneself to any humanitarian illusions about the history of the origin of an aristocratic society (that is to say, of the preliminary condition for the elevation of the type "man"): the truth is hard. Let us acknowledge unprejudicedly how every higher civilization hitherto has *originated!* Men with a still natural nature, barbarians in every terrible sense of the word, men of prey, still in possession of unbroken strength of will and desire for power, threw themselves upon weaker, more moral, more peaceful races (perhaps trading or cattle-rearing communities), or upon old mellow civilizations in which the final vital force was flickering out in brilliant fireworks of wit and depravity. At the commencement, the noble caste was always the barbarian caste: their superiority did not consist first of all in their physical, but in their psychical power—they were more *complete* men (which at every point also implies the same as "more complete beasts").[d]

**4.** The psychical impotence of the "herd" is reflected in the morality it produces. The basic principle of all slave-morality, Nietzsche tells us, is *resentment* of the aristocratic spirit. For example, altruism, a typical slave ideal, denies the value of creative egoism that is central to the master-morality.

The preponderance of an altruistic way of valuing is the result of a consciousness of the fact that one is botched and bungled. Upon examination, this point of view turns out to be: "I am not worth much," simply a psychological valuation; more plainly still: it is the feeling of impotence, of the lack of the great self-asserting impulses of power (in muscles, nerves, and ganglia). This valuation gets translated, according to the particular culture of these classes, into a moral or religious principle (the preeminence of religious or moral precepts is always a sign of low culture): it tries to justify itself in spheres whence, as far as it is concerned, the notion "value" hails. The interpretation by means of which the Christian sinner tries to understand himself, is an attempt at justifying his lack of power and of self-confidence: he prefers to feel himself a sinner rather than feel bad for nothing: it is in itself a symptom of decay when interpretations of this sort are used at all. In some cases the bungled and the botched do not look for the reason of their unfortunate condition in their own guilt (as the Christian does), but in society: when, however, the Socialist, the

Anarchist, and the Nihilist are conscious that their existence is something for which someone must be *guilty,* they are very closely related to the Christian, who also believes that he can more easily endure his ill ease and his wretched constitution when he has found someone whom he can hold *responsible* for it. The instinct of *revenge* and *resentment* appears in both cases here as a means of enduring life, as a self-preservative measure, as is also the favor shown to *altruistic* theory and practice. The *hatred of egoism,* whether it be one's own (as in the case of the Christian), or another's (as in the case of the Socialists), thus appears as a valuation reached under the predominance of revenge; and also as an act of prudence on the part of the preservative instinct of the suffering, in the form of an increase in their feelings of cooperation and unity.... At bottom, as I have already suggested, the discharge of resentment which takes place in the act of judging, rejecting, and punishing egoism (one's own or that of others) is still a self-preservative measure on the part of the bungled and the botched. In short: the cult of altruism is merely a particular form of egoism, which regularly appears under certain definite physiological circumstances.

When the Socialist, with righteous indignation, cries for "justice," "rights," "equal rights," it only shows that he is oppressed by his inadequate culture, and is unable to understand why he suffers: he also finds pleasure in crying;—if he were more at ease he would take jolly good care not to cry in that way: in that case he would seek his pleasure elsewhere. The same holds good of the Christian: he curses, condemns, and slanders the "world"—and does not even except himself. But there is no reason for taking him seriously. In both cases we are in the presence of invalids who feel better for crying, and who find relief in slander.[e]

**5.** Continuing in the same vein, Nietzsche condemns the ideals of peace and universal equality, exposing their life-denying qualities. Exploitation and competition, he argues, characterize all living things, because they are the very essence of the will to power.

To refrain mutually from injury, from violence, from exploitation, and put one's will on a par with that of others: this may result in a certain rough sense in good conduct among individuals when the necessary conditions are given (namely, the actual similarity of the individuals in amount of force and degree of worth, and their co-relation within one organization). As soon, however, as one wished to take this principle more generally, and if possible even as *the fundamental principle of society,* it would immediately disclose what it really is—namely, a Will to the *denial* of life, a principle of dissolution and decay. Here one must think profoundly to the very basis and resist all sentimental weakness: life itself is *essentially* appropriation, injury, conquest of the strange and weak, suppression, severity, obtrusion of peculiar forms, incorporation, and at the least, putting it mildest, exploitation;—but why should one forever use precisely these words on which for ages a disparaging purpose has been stamped? Even the organization within which, as was previously supposed, the individuals treat each other as equal—it takes place in every healthy aristocracy—must itself, if it be a living and not a dying organization, do all that towards other bodies, which the individuals within it refrain from doing to each other: it will have to be the incarnated Will to Power, it will endeavor to grow, to gain ground, attract to itself and acquire ascendency—not owing to any morality or immorality, but because it *lives,* and because life *is* precisely Will to Power. On no point, however, is the ordinary consciousness of Europeans more unwilling to be corrected than on this matter; people now rave everywhere, even under the guise of science, about coming conditions of society in which "the exploiting character" is to be absent:—that sounds to my ears as if they promised to invent a mode of life which should refrain from all organic functions. "Exploitation" does not belong to a depraved, or imperfect and primitive society: it belongs to the *nature* of the living being as a primary organic function; it is a consequence of the intrinsic Will to Power, which is precisely the Will to Life.—Granting that as a theory this is a novelty—as a reality it is the *fundamental fact* of all history: let us be so far honest towards ourselves![f]

**6.** Nietzsche assigns to Judaism and Christianity the primary responsibility for the dishonest morality that is exhausting European civilization.

I regard Christianity as the most fatal and seductive lie that has ever yet existed—as the greatest and most *impious lie:* I can discern the last sprouts and branches of its ideal beneath every form of disguise, I decline to enter into any compromise or false position in reference to it—I urge people to declare open war with it.

The *morality of paltry people* as the measure of all things: this is the most repugnant kind of degeneracy that civilization has ever yet brought into existence. And this *kind of ideal* is hanging still, under the name of "God," over men's heads!!

However modest one's demands may be concerning intellectual cleanliness, when one touches the New Testament one cannot help experiencing a sort of inexpressible feeling of discomfort; for the unbounded cheek with which the least qualified people will have their say in its pages, in regard to the greatest problems of existence, and claim to sit in judgment on such matters, exceeds all limits. The impudent levity with which the most unwieldy problems are spoken of here (life, the world, God, the purpose of life), as if they were not problems at all, but the most simple things which these little bigots *know all about!!!*...

The *law,* which is the fundamentally realistic formula of certain self-preservative measures of a community, forbids certain actions that have a definite tendency to jeopardize the welfare of that community: it does *not* forbid the attitude of mind which gives rise to these actions—for in the pursuit of other ends the community requires these forbidden actions, namely, when it is a matter of opposing its *enemies.* The moral idealist now steps forward and says: "God sees into men's hearts: the action itself counts for nothing; the reprehensible attitude of mind from which it proceeds must be extirpated. . . . " In normal conditions men laugh at such things; it is only in exceptional cases, when a community lives *quite* beyond the need of waging war in order to maintain itself, that an ear is lent to such things. Any attitude of mind is abandoned, the utility of which cannot be conceived.

This was the case, for example, when Buddha appeared among a people that was both peaceable and afflicted with great intellectual weariness.

This was also the case in regard to the first Christian community (as also the Jewish), the primary condition of which was the absolutely *unpolitical* Jewish society. Christianity could grow only upon the soil of Judaism—that is to say, among a people that had already renounced the political life, and which led a sort of parasitic existence within the Roman sphere of government. Christianity goes a step *further:* it allows men to "emasculate" themselves even more; the circumstances actually favor their doing so.—*Nature* is *expelled* from morality when it is said, "Love ye your enemies": for *Nature's* injunction, "Ye shall *love* your neighbor and *hate* your enemy," has now become senseless in the law (in instinct); now, even *the love a man feels for his neighbor* must first be based upon something (*a sort of love of God*). *God* is introduced everywhere, and *utility* is withdrawn; the natural *origin* of morality is denied everywhere: the *veneration of Nature,* which lies in *acknowledging a natural morality,* is *destroyed* to the roots...

What is it I protest against? That people should regard this paltry and peaceful mediocrity, this spiritual equilibrium which knows nothing of the fine impulses of great accumulations of strength, as something high, or possibly as the standard of all things.[g]

**7.** Nietzsche sums up his case against Judaism and Christianity, stressing their unsuitability for the evolutionary struggle.

Among men, as among all other animals, there is a surplus of defective, diseased, degenerating, infirm, and necessarily suffering individuals; the successful cases, among men also, are always the exception; and in view of the fact that man is *the animal not yet properly adapted to his environment,* the rare exception. But worse still. The higher type a man represents, the greater is the improbability that he will *succeed;* the accidental, the law of irrationality in the general constitution of mankind, manifests itself most terribly in its destructive effect on the higher orders of men, the conditions of whose lives are delicate, diverse, and difficult to determine. What, then, is the attitude of the two greatest religions above-mentioned to the *surplus* of failures in life? The endeavor to preserve and keep alive whatever can be preserved; in fact, as the religions for *sufferers,* they take the part of these upon principle; they are always in favor of those who suffer from life as from a disease, and they would fain treat every other experience of life as false and impossible. However, highly we may esteem this indulgent and preservative care (inasmuch as in applying to others, it has applied, and applies also to the highest and usually the most suffering type of man), the hitherto *paramount* religions—to give a general appreciation of them—are among the principal causes which have kept the type of "man" upon a lower level—they have preserved too much *that which should have perished.* One has to thank them for invaluable services; and who is sufficiently rich in gratitude not to feel poor at the contemplation of all that the "spiritual men" of Christianity have done for Europe hitherto! But when they had given comfort to the sufferers, courage to the oppressed and despairing, a staff and support to the helpless, and when they had allured from society into convents and spiritual penitentiaries the broken-hearted and distracted: what else had they to do in order to work systematically in that fashion, and with a good conscience, for the preservation of all the sick and suffering, which means, in deed and in truth, to work for *deterioration of the European race?* To *reverse* all estimates of value—*that* is what they had to do! And to shatter the strong, to spoil great hopes, to cast suspicion on the delight in beauty, to break down everything autonomous, manly, conquering, and imperious—all instincts which are natural to the highest and most successful type of "man"—into uncertainty, distress of conscience, and self-destruction; forsooth, to invert all love of the earthly and of supremacy over the earth, in hatred of the earth and earthly things.[h]

**8.** The moral philosophers, no less than the priests, teach the denial of life, and Nietzsche attacks the "superstitions which heretofore have been fashionable among philosophers." False psychology, faulty logic, and a misunderstanding of the role of reason serve the philosophers in their hatred of life.

In the whole of moral evolution, there is no sign of truth: all the conceptual elements which come into play are fictions; all the psychological tenets are false; all the forms of logic employed in this department of prevarication are sophisms. The chief feature of all moral philosophers is their total lack of intellectual cleanliness and self-control: they regard "fine feelings" as arguments: their heaving breasts seem to them the bellows of godliness.... Moral philosophy is the most suspicious period in the history of the human intellect...

*Why everything resolved itself into mummery.*—Rudimentary psychology, which only considered the *conscious* lapses of men (as causes), which regarded "consciousness" as an attribute of the soul, and which sought a will behind every action (*i.e.*, an intention), could only answer *"Happiness"* to the question: *"What does man desire?"* (it was impossible to answer "Power," because that would have been *immoral*);—consequently behind all men's actions there is the intention of attaining to happiness by means of them. Secondly: if man as a matter of fact does not attain to happiness, why is it? Because he mistakes the means thereto.—*What is the unfailing means of acquiring happiness?* Answer: *virtue*—Why virtue? Because virtue is supreme rationalness, and rationalness makes mistakes in the choice of means impossible: virtue in the form of *reason* is the way to happiness. Dialectics is the constant occupation of virtue, because it does away with passion and intellectual cloudiness.

As a matter of fact, man does *not* desire "happiness." Pleasure is a sensation of power: if the passions are excluded, those states of the mind are also excluded which afford the greatest sensation of power and therefore of pleasure. The highest rationalism is a state of cool clearness, which is very far from being able to bring about that feeling of power which every kind of *exaltation* involves. . . .

[Slave moralists] combat everything that intoxicates and exalts—everything that impairs the perfect coolness and impartiality of the mind. . . . They were consistent with their first false principle: that consciousness was the *highest*, the *supreme* state of mind, the prerequisite of perfection—whereas the reverse is true.

If one should require a proof of how deeply and thoroughly the actually *barbarous* needs of man, even in his present state of tameness and "civilization," still seek gratification, one should contemplate the "leitmotifs" of the whole of the evolution of philosophy:—a sort of revenge upon reality, a surreptitious process of destroying the values by means of which men live, a *dissatisfied* soul to which the condition of discipline is one of torture, and which takes a particular pleasure in morbidly severing all the bonds that bind it to such a condition.

The history of philosophy is the story of a *secret and mad hatred* of the prerequisites of Life, of the feelings which make for the real values of Life, and of all partisanship in favor of Life. Philosophers have never hesitated to affirm a fanciful world, provided it contradicted this world, and furnished them with a weapon wherewith they could calumniate this world. Up to the present, philosophy has been the *grand school of slander:* and its power has been so great, that even today our science, which pretends to be the advocate of Life, has *accepted* the fundamental position of slander. . . . What is the hatred which is active here?

I fear that it is still the *Circe of philosophers*—Morality, which plays them the trick of compelling them to be ever slanderers. . . . They believed in moral "truths," in these they thought they had found the highest values; what alternative had they left, save that of denying existence every more emphatically the more they got to know about it? . . . For this life is *immoral*. . . . And it is based upon immoral first principles: and morality says *nay* to Life.[i]

**9.** The life-seeking values of cruelty and Homeric deception are rediscovered by Nietzsche in the search for values that will stand up alongside the brute facts of existence.

Even obvious truths, as if by the agreement of centuries, have long remained unuttered, because they have the appearance of helping the finally slain wild beast back to life again. I perhaps risk something when I allow such a truth to escape; let others capture it again and give it so much "milk of pious sentiment" to drink, that it will lie down quiet and forgotten, in its old corner.—One ought to learn anew about cruelty, and open one's eyes; one ought at last to learn impatience, in order that such immodest gross errors—as, for instance, have been fostered by ancient and modern philosophers with regard to tragedy—may no longer wander about virtuously and boldly. Almost everything that we call "higher culture" is based upon the spiritualizing and intensifying of *cruelty*—this is my thesis; the "wild beast" has not been slain at all, it lives, it flourishes, it has only been—transfigured. That which constitutes the painful delight of tragedy is cruelty; that which operates agreeably in so-called tragic sympathy, and at the basis even of everything sublime, up to the highest and most delicate thrills of metaphysics, obtains its sweetness solely from the intermingled ingredient of cruelty. What the Roman enjoys in the arena, the Christian in the ecstasies of the cross, the Spaniard at the sight of the faggot and stake, or of the bullfight, the present-day Japanese who presses his way to the tragedy, the workman of the Parisian suburbs who has a homesickness for bloody revolutions, the Wagnerienne who, with unhinged will, "undergoes" the performance of "Tristan and Isolde"—what all these enjoy, and strive with mysterious ardor to drink in, is the philtre of the great Circe "cruelty." . . . Finally, let us consider that even the seeker of knowledge operates as an artist and glorifier of cruelty, in that he compels his spirit to perceive ***against*** its own inclination, and often enough against the wishes of his heart:—he forces it to say Nay, where he would like to affirm, love, and adore; indeed, every instance of taking a thing profoundly and fundamentally, is a violation, an intentional injuring of the fundamental will of the spirit, which instinctively aims at appearance and superficiality,—even in every desire for knowledge there is a drop of cruelty.

In this connection, there is the not unscrupulous readiness of the spirit to deceive other spirits and dissemble before them—the constant pressing and straining of a creating, shaping, changeable power: the spirit enjoys therein its craftiness and its variety of disguises, it enjoys also its feeling of security therein—it is precisely by its Protean arts that it is best protected and concealed!—*Counter to* this propensity for appearance, for simplification, for a disguise, for a cloak, in short, for an outside—for every outside is a cloak—there operates the sublime tendency of the man of knowledge, which takes, and *insists* on taking things profoundly, variously, and thoroughly; as a kind of cruelty of the intellectual conscience and taste, which every courageous thinker will acknowledge in himself, provided, as it ought to be, that he has sharpened and hardened his eye sufficiently long for introspection, and is accustomed to severe discipline and even severe words. He will say: "There is something cruel in the tendency of my spirit": let the virtuous and amiable try to convince him that it is not so! In fact, it would sound nicer, if instead of our cruelty, perhaps our "extravagant honesty" were talked about, whispered about and glorified—we free, *very* free spirits—and some day perhaps *such* will actually be our—posthumous glory![j]

**10.** The ennobling character of suffering can be appreciated only by the aristocrat. Despising as weakness the longing of the "herd" for freedom from pain, free spirits revel in the elevating power of suffering, for it spurs them on to raise the will to life to an "unconditioned Will to Power."

What they would fain attain with all their strength, is the universal, green-meadow happiness of the herd, together with security, safety, comfort, and alleviation of life for everyone; their two most frequently chanted songs and doctrines are called "Equality of Rights" and "Sympathy with all Sufferers"—and suffering itself is looked upon by them as something which must be *done away with.* We opposite ones, however, who have opened our eye and conscience to the question how and where the plant "man" has hitherto grown most vigorously, believe that this has always taken place under the opposite conditions, that for this end the dangerousness of his situation had to be increased enormously, his inventive faculty and dissembling power (his "spirit") had to develop into subtlety and daring under long oppression and compulsion, and his Will to Life had to be increased to the unconditioned Will to Power:—we believe that severity, violence, slavery, danger in the street and in the heart, secrecy, stoicism, tempter's art and devilry of every kind,—that everything wicked, terrible, tyrannical, predatory, and serpentine in man, serves as well for the elevation of the human species as its opposite:—we do not even say enough when we only say *this much;* and in any case we find ourselves here, both with our speech and our science, at the *other* extreme of all modern ideology and gregarious desirability, as their antipodes perhaps? What wonder that we "free spirits" are not exactly the most communicative spirits? that we do not wish to betray in every respect *what* a spirit can free itself from, and *where* perhaps it will then be driven? And as to the import of the dangerous formula, "Beyond Good and Evil," with which we at least avoid confusion, we *are* something else than "*libres-penseurs,*" "*liberi pensatori,*" "free-thinkers," and whatever these honest advocates of "modern ideas" like to call themselves. Having been at home, or at least guests, in many realms of the spirit; having escaped again and again from the gloomy, agreeable nooks in which preferences and prejudices, youth, origin, the accident of men and books, or even the weariness of travel seemed to confine us; full of malice against the seductions of dependency which lie concealed in honors, money, positions, or exaltation of the senses: grateful even for distress and the vicissitudes of illness, because they always free us from some rule, and its "prejudice," grateful to the God, devil, sheep, and worm in us; inquisitive to a fault, investigators to the point of cruelty, with unhesitating fingers for the intangible, with teeth and stomachs for the most indigestible, ready for any business that requires sagacity and acute senses, ready for every adventure, owing to an excess of "free will"; with anterior and posterior souls, into the ultimate intentions of which it is difficult to pry, with foregrounds and backgrounds to the end of which no foot may run; hidden ones under the mantles of light, appropriators, although we resemble heirs and spendthrifts, arrangers and collectors from morning till night, misers of our wealth and our full-crammed drawers, economical in learning and forgetting, inventive in scheming; sometimes proud of tables of categories, sometimes pedants, sometimes night-owls of work even in full day; yea, if necessary, even scarecrows—and it is necessary nowadays, that is to say, inasmuch as we are the born, sworn, jealous friends of *solitude*, of our own profoundest midnight and midday solitude:—such kind of men are we, we free spirits! And perhaps *ye* are also something of the same kind, ye coming ones, ye *new* philosophers?[k]

**11.** The philosophers of the future, understanding the values dictated by the will to power, will stand apart from the masses. They will be aristocrats, not levelers like the philosophers of the present. True freedom, rather than the false freedom sought by slaves, will be their doctrine.

Will they be new friends of "truth," these coming philosophers? Very probably, for all philosophers hitherto have loved their truths. But assuredly they will not be dogmatists. It must be contrary to their pride, and also contrary to their taste, that their truth should still be truth for every-one—that which has hitherto been the secret wish and ultimate purpose of all dogmatic efforts. "My opinion is *my* opinion: another person has not easily a right to it"—such a philosopher of the future will say, perhaps. One must renounce the bad taste of wishing to agree with many people. "Good" is no longer good when one's neighbor takes it into his mouth. And how could there be a "common good"! The expression contradicts itself; that which can be common is always of small value. In the end things must be as they are and have always been—the great things remain for the great, the abysses for the profound, the delicacies and thrills for the refined, and, to sum up shortly, everything rare for the rare.

Need I say expressly after all this that they will be free, *very* free spirits, these philosophers of the future—as certainly also they will not be merely free spirits, but something more, higher, greater, and fundamentally different, which does not wish to be misunderstood and mistaken? But while I say this, I feel under *obligation* almost as much to them as to ourselves (we free spirits who are their heralds and forerunners), to sweep away from ourselves altogether a stupid old prejudice and misunderstanding, which, like a fog, has too long made the conception of "free spirit" obscure. In every country of Europe, and the same in America, there is at present something which makes an abuse of this name: a very narrow, prepossessed, enchained class of spirits, who desire almost the opposite of what our intentions and instincts prompt—not to mention that in respect to the *new* philosophers who are appearing, they must still more be closed windows and bolted doors. Briefly and regrettably, they belong to the *levelers*, these wrongly named "free spirits"—as glib-tongued and scribe-fingered slaves of the democratic taste and its "modern ideas": all of them men without solitude, without personal solitude, blunt, honest fellows to whom neither courage nor honorable conduct ought to be denied; only, they are not free, and are ludicrously superficial, especially in their innate partiality for seeing the cause of almost *all* human misery and failure in the old forms in which society has hitherto existed—a notion which happily inverts the truth entirely.[l]

**12.** The further progress of humanity requires a *transvaluation of values* that will give the will to power its rightful place.

Transvalue values—what does this mean? It implies that all spontaneous motives, all new, future, and stronger motives, are still extant; but that they now appear under false names and false valuations, and have not yet become conscious of themselves.

We ought to have the courage to become conscious, and to affirm all that which has been *attained*—to get rid of the humdrum character of old valuations, which makes us unworthy of the best and strongest things that we have achieved.

Any doctrine would be superfluous for which everything is not already prepared in the way of accumulated forces and explosive material. A transvaluation of values can only be accomplished when there is a tension of new needs, and a new set of needy people who feel all old values as painful,—although they are not conscious of what is wrong.

The standpoint from which my values are determined: is abundance or desire active? . . . Is one a mere spectator, or is one's own shoulder at the wheel—is one looking away or is one turning aside? . . . Is one acting spontaneously, or is one merely reacting to a goad or to a stimulus? . . . Is one simply acting as the result of a paucity of elements, or of such an overwhelming dominion over a host of elements that this power enlists the latter into its service if it requires them? . . . Is one a *problem* one's self or is one a *solution* already? . . . Is one *perfect* through the smallness of the task, or *imperfect* owing to the extraordinary character of the aim? . . . Is one genuine or only an *actor;* is one genuine as an actor, or only the bad copy of an actor? Is one a representative or the creature represented? Is one a personality or merely a rendezvous of personalities? . . . Is one ill from a disease or from surplus health? Does one lead as a shepherd, or as an "exception"(third alternative: as a fugitive)? Is one in need of dignity, or can one play the clown? Is one in search of resistance, or is one evading it? Is one imperfect owing to one's precocity or to one's tardiness? Is it one's nature to say yea, or no, or is one a peacock's tail of garish parts? Is one proud enough not to feel ashamed even of one's vanity? Is one still able to feel a bite of conscience (this species is becoming rare; formerly conscience had to bite too often: it is as if it now no longer had enough teeth to do so)? Is one still capable of a "duty"? (there are some people who would lose the whole joy of their lives if they were *deprived* of their duty—this holds good especially of feminine creatures, who are born subjects). . . .

It is only a question of power: to have all the morbid traits of the century, but to balance them by means of overflowing, plastic, and rejuvenating power. The *strong* man.[m]

**13.** Before the new philosophy of strength can become effective, there is a task that must be performed: The truth must be shown to those who are fit to receive it. This is the task to which Nietzsche devotes himself.

Meanwhile—for there is plenty of time until then—we should be least inclined to deck ourselves out in such florid and fringed moral verbiage; our whole former work has just made us sick of this taste and its sprightly exuberance. They are beautiful, glistening, jingling, festive words: honesty, love of truth, love of wisdom, sacrifice for knowledge, heroism of the truthful—there is something in them that makes one's heart swell with pride. But we anchorites and marmots have long ago persuaded ourselves in all the secrecy of an anchorite's conscience, that this worthy parade of verbiage also belongs to the old false adornment, frippery, and gold dust of unconscious human vanity, and that even under such flattering color and repainting, the terrible original text *homo natura* must again be recognized. In effect, to translate man back again into nature; to master the many vain and visionary interpretations and subordinate meanings which have hitherto been scratched and daubed over the eternal original text, *homo natura;* to bring it about that man shall henceforth stand before man as he now, hardened by the discipline of science, stands before the *other* forms of nature, with fearless Oedipus-eyes, and stopped Ulysses-ears, deaf to the enticements of old metaphysical bird-catchers, who have piped to him far too long: "Thou art more! thou art higher! thou hast a different origin!"—this may be a strange and foolish task, but that it is a *task*, who can deny!"[n]

## QUESTIONS

1. In what sense is Nietzsche the "conscience of his age"?
2. Explain Nietzsche's doctrine of the "transvaluation of values," illustrating his meaning with specific ideals.
3. Contrast the master and slave moralities. What differences in ethical vocabulary are required to express their opposed ethical themes?
4. What are the underlying principles that lead Nietzsche to attack Christianity, pacifism, and democracy?
5. What are Nietzsche's criticisms of traditional moral philosophy? What is his conception of the "true" philosopher?
6. What does "Superman" symbolize in Nietzsche's ethical theory? How does this fit in with his doctrine of "following Nature"?
7. Nietzsche advises us to "live dangerously." What benefits does he anticipate from following this rule of life?
8. Examine critically the Nietzschean theory of the "will to power." Is the conception of nature it involves more or less true to fact than that of such philosophers as Epictetus?
9. What is the relationship between reason and emotion in Nietzsche's ethics? Compare his views with those of the Greek Sophists and of Socrates.
10. Adopting Nietzsche's viewpoint, criticize twentieth-century America.

## KEY TO SELECTIONS

Friedrich Nietzsche, *The Complete Works of Friedrich Nietzsche,* vols. XII, XIII, XVI, O. Levy, ed., New York, Macmillan, 1924. With the kind permission of the publishers.

From *The Will to Power* (tr. A. M. Ludovici)
[a]No. 54.
[e]No. 373.
[g]No. 200–201, No. 204, No. 249.
[i]No. 428, No. 434, No. 461.
[m]No. 1007–1009, No. 1014.

From *The Genealogy of Morals,* First Essay (tr. H. B. Samuel)
[c]No. 4, No. 10–11.

From *Beyond Good and Evil* (tr. H. Zimmern)
[b]No. 260.
[d]No. 257.
[f]No. 259.
[h]No. 62.
[j]No. 229–230.
[k]No. 44.
[l]No. 43–44.
[n]No. 230.

## GUIDE TO ADDITIONAL READING

**PRIMARY SOURCES**

Nietzsche, F., *Beyond Good and Evil,* Great Books Foundation (Regnery).

_____, *Thus Spake Zarathustra,* Everyman's Library (Dutton) and Modern Library (Random House).

———, *The Philosophy of Nietzsche,* Modern Library (Random House).

### DISCUSSION AND COMMENTARY

Copleston, F. C., *Frederick Nietzsche: Philosopher of Culture,* New York, Harper & Brothers, 1942 (2nd ed., 1975).

Danto, A., *Nietzsche as Philosopher,* New York, Columbia University Press, 1980.

Foot, Philippa, "The Brave Immoralist," *New York Review of Books,* Vol. 27, May 1, 1980, pp. 35–37.

Hayman, R., *Nietzsche: A Critical Life,* New York, Penguin Books, 1982.

Kaufmann, W. A., *Nietzsche: Philosopher, Psychologist, Antichrist,* Princeton, Princeton University Press, 1950.

Magnus, Bernd, and Higgins, Kathleen (eds.), *The Cambridge Companion to Nietzsche,* Cambridge, Cambridge University Press, 1996.

Morgan, G. A., *What Nietzsche Means,* Cambridge, Harvard University Press, 1943.

Ridley, Aaron, *Nietzsche's Conscience,* Ithaca, Cornell University Press, 1998.

Solomon, R. (ed.), *Nietzsche: A Collection of Critical Essays,* Notre Dame, University of Notre Dame Press, 1980.

Stern, J., *A Study of Nietzsche,* Cambridge, Cambridge University Press, 1979.

Williams, B., "Nietzsche's Minimalist Moral Psychology," *European Journal of Philosophy,* April 1993.

CHAPTER EIGHTEEN

# Scientific Method in Ethics

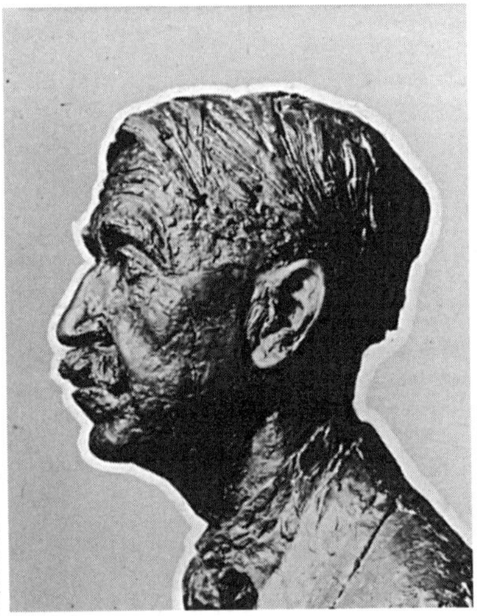



JOHN DEWEY

IN THE NINETY-TWO YEARS of his full and active life, John Dewey (1859–1952) established himself as one of the foremost American philosophers and educators. Born in Burlington, Vermont, he spent his life in an environment in which democracy set the keynote of existence. In his pragmatic philosophy and theory of progressive education, he sought to spell out the idea of democracy not merely as a political belief but also as a way of life, a guiding principle in education, and a moral ideal. To implement this ideal, he undertook to remove philosophy and education from the exclusive possession of "ivory tower" specialists by relating the process of thinking to living social experience.

Each phase of Dewey's academic career provided him with new interests, activities, and concepts. These he fused into a unified system of ideas, in which philosophy, psychology, and educational theory were combined. As an undergraduate at the University of Vermont, and then at Johns Hopkins University, where he received his Ph.D. degree, Dewey was intensely stimulated by the theory of evolution, German idealistic philosophy, and the theories of the "father of sociology," Auguste Comte. These ideas, new and unorthodox in the 1870s and 1880s, began a liberation of American intellectual life that was appreciably advanced by Dewey's contributions to philosophy and pedagogy.

The personal history of John Dewey was as much a part of his intellectual development as the strictly academic phase of his experience, and he conscientiously kept his theories in close rapport with the actual conditions of his life. His wife, Alice Chipman—whom he married in 1886—added to her role as wife and mother of a large family that of a welcome influence on Dewey's thinking, through her active participation in intellectual, social, and political affairs. In the course of his long career as a teacher of philosophy—at the University of Michigan, the University of Minnesota, the University of Chicago, and Columbia University—he formed close associations with many distinguished men and women whose original thinking and vigorous social and political activities enriched his own academic and practical experience. One of his most distinctive achievements was the founding of an experimental elementary school at the University of Chicago. From this venture in the application of modern principles of psychology to teaching methods and the integration of thinking and doing in democratically conducted classrooms, he developed his theory of progressive education. At universities in Japan, China, Turkey, and elsewhere abroad, he taught and at the same time learned the importance of democracy and education in promoting individual and social improvement.

A small sample of Dewey's numerous educational and social projects, lectures, articles, and books provides a sufficient indication of his broad interests and great-energy. His influence in education was carried abroad through the translation of *The School and Society* (1900) into twelve languages and of *Democracy and Education* (1916) into nine. *Reconstruction in Philosophy* (1920), *A Common Faith* (1934), and *Art as Experience* (1934), in their respective branches of philosophy, express essentially the same thesis as the more specialized works in which Dewey places logic and ethics together in the framework of practical experience. Chief among the books devoted to this special concern are *How We Think* (1910), *Human Nature and Conduct* (1922), *Experience and Nature* (1929), *The Quest for Certainty* (1928), and *Logic: The Theory of Inquiry* (1939). Until his death, Dewey continued to write and to take an active interest in philosophy, education, and events in the world about him.

John Dewey attempts to apply the methods of science to the problems of morality. He holds the view that the study of human behavior, especially in regard to moral values, has continued to follow outmoded methods, while the best-developed techniques of inquiry have been limited almost entirely to the investigation of the physical world. The resulting discrepancy between our knowledge of physical nature and our knowledge of human nature defines the problem of contemporary ethics:

> The problem of restoring integration and cooperation between man's beliefs about the world in which he lives and his beliefs about the values and purposes that should direct his conduct is the deepest problem of modern life. It is the problem of any philosophy that is not isolated from that life.[a]

Dewey attributes the lag of morality behind technology to the effect of the traditional conception of human beings as passive spectators in a fixed and unchanging universe where truth is absolute and eternal. To bridge the resultant gap between theory and practice, ideas and actions, ideals and behavior, he advocates a thoroughgoing reconstruction of beliefs.

Dewey's ethical theory is built upon the principles of pragmatism, of which the chief elements are scientific method and the conception of the universe as evolutionary.[1]

---

[1]Pragmatism was first formulated and named by Charles S. Peirce (1839–1914), a physicist and logician who was influenced in his thinking by the biological theory of evolution. His pragmatism was adopted and modified by William James, John Dewey, and others, chiefly in the United States. Dewey's pragmatism is frequently referred to as "instrumentalism," because it centers on the conception that ideas are "instruments" or plans of action for problem solving.

Throughout his writing, he depicts human beings as problem solvers, constantly making adjustments to the changing conditions that confront them. He classifies human responses to the uncertainties of life situations as *impulsive, habitual*, or *reflective*. Evaluated in terms of effectiveness in solving adjustment problems, impulsive behavior fails because it leads to random reactions, and habitual action fails because it is not adaptable to new conditions. However, reflective thinking, which Dewey equates with scientific inquiry, is a satisfactory method of problem solving, because it is guided to a solution by both past experience and creative ideas. It can thereby "transform a situation in which there is experienced obscurity, doubt, conflict, disturbance of some sort, into a situation that is clear, coherent, settled, harmonious. . . ."

The pragmatic criterion of truth is directly related to the outcome of the reflective process. Those ideas that are successful in resolving problematic situations are true, whereas those that do not lead to satisfactory adjustments are false. For the pragmatists, then, truth is relative rather than absolute, changing rather than eternal. The principles of scientific method are readily adapted to the pragmatic position. In science, ideas function as tentative solutions for concrete problems—that is, as hypotheses, which must be tested by experiment. The empirical verification of hypotheses effects a union of theory and practice. Moreover, through the continuous modification of knowledge that results from the application of scientific method to the solution of the steady stream of problems that characterizes the human scene, knowledge can keep pace with the changing conditions of life and continue to guide it.

As a consequence of his preoccupation with the dynamic aspect of the universe, Dewey produces an ethical theory that "involves nothing less than the problem of the directed reconstruction of economic, political and religious institutions." The conception of what is good must undergo change as society changes and as knowledge of the physical environment increases. The discrepancy between stated ideals and actual behavior in contemporary society can be understood as due in part to the persistence of obsolete values. Dewey maintains that only the use of the methods of science in ethics can secure the continuing adaptation of values to changing human needs. This is tantamount to a recommendation to make active use of intelligence and of the facts of experience in the conduct of the moral life.

**1.** Dewey attacks two extremes in ethics: radical empiricism and rationalism. In the former, moral values are identified with subjective experiences of liking and disliking. Dewey regards experiences of this kind as providing only the *possibilities* of values. Values as such emerge only after examination of the *conditions* under which liking and disliking occur, and of the *results* to which they lead. The distinction between an experience as such and a valuable experience is given careful and detailed attention.

The formal statement [of this distinction] may be given concrete content by pointing to the difference between the enjoyed and the enjoyable, the desired and the desirable, the satis*fying* and the satis*factory*. To say that something is enjoyed is to make a statement about a fact, something already in existence; it is not to judge the value of that fact. There is no difference between such a proposition and one which says that something is sweet or sour, red or black. It is just correct and incorrect and that is the end of the matter. But to call an object a value is to assert that it satisfies or fulfills certain conditions. Function and status in meeting conditions is a different matter from bare existence. The fact that something is desired only raises the *question* of its desirability; it does not settle it. Only a child in the degree of his immaturity thinks to settle the question of desirability by reiterated proclamation: "I want it, I want it, I want it." What is objected to in the current empirical theory of values is not connection of them with desire and enjoyment but failure to distinguish between enjoyments of radically different sorts. There are many common expressions in which the difference of the two kinds is clearly recognized. Take for example the difference between the ideas of "satisfying" and "satisfactory." To say that something satisfies is to report something as an isolated finality. To assert that it is satis*factory* is to define it in its connections and interactions. The fact that it pleases or is immediately congenial poses a problem to judgment. How shall the satisfaction be rated? Is it a value or is it not? Is it something to be prized and cherished, *to be* enjoyed? Not stern moralists alone but everyday experience informs us that finding satisfaction in a thing may be a warning, a summons to be on the lookout for consequences. To declare something satis*factory* is to assert that it meets specifiable conditions. It is, in effect, a judgment that the thing "will do." It involves a prediction; it contemplates a future in which the thing will continue to serve; it *will* do. It asserts a consequence the thing will actively institute; it will *do*. That it is satisfying is the content of a proposition of fact; that it is satisfactory is a judgment, an estimate, an appraisal. It denotes an attitude *to be* taken, that of striving to perpetuate and to make secure.[b]

**2.** The bare facts in which preferences are merely stated are, then, no more than the point of departure for the forming of value judgments. Only through examining the consequences of likings and dislikings can it be decided whether they are to be sought after. In other words, the facts function as instruments for the construction of value judgments.

Propositions about what is or has been liked are of instrumental value in reaching judgments of value, in as far as the conditions and consequences of the thing liked are thought about. In themselves they make no claims; they put forth no demand upon subsequent attitudes and acts; they profess no authority to direct. If one likes a thing he likes it; that *is* a point about which there can be no dispute:—although it is not so easy to state just *what* is liked as is frequently assumed. A judgment about what is *to be* desired and enjoyed is, on the other hand, a claim on future action; it possesses *de jure* and not merely *de facto* quality. It is a matter of frequent experience that likings and enjoyments are of all kinds, and that many are such as reflective judgments condemn. By way of self-justification and "rationalization," an enjoyment creates a tendency to assert that the thing enjoyed is a value. This assertion of validity adds authority to the fact. It is a decision that the object has a right to exist and hence a claim upon action to further its existence. . . .

Not even the most devoted adherents of the notion that enjoyment and value are equivalent facts would venture to assert that because we have once liked a thing we should go on liking it; they are compelled to introduce the idea that *some* tastes are to be cultivated. Logically, there is no ground for introducing the idea of cultivation; liking is liking, and one is as good as another. If enjoyments *are* values, the judgment of value cannot regulate the form which liking takes; it cannot regulate its own conditions. Desire and purpose, and hence action, are left without guidance, although the question of regulation of their formation is the supreme problem of practical life. Values (to sum up) may be connected inherently with liking, and yet not with *every* liking but only with those that judgment has approved, after examination of the relation upon which the object liked depends. A casual liking is one that happens without knowledge of how it occurs nor to what effect. The difference between it and one which is sought because of a judgment that it is worth having and is to be striven for, makes just the difference between enjoyments which are accidental and enjoyments that have value and hence a claim upon our attitude and conduct.[c]

**3.** Dewey then turns his attention from extreme empiricism to extreme rationalism. He criticizes it too from the standpoint of scientific standards. Whereas empiricism fails to go beyond the mere facts of preference, rationalism in ethics is too far removed from the facts to be of practical use. Even in those cases where rationalism proposes concrete values, they are tied to the dead past. The penalty for failure to use scientific method in morals, as it is used in the study of the physical world, is the control of changes in values by arbitrary or accidental forces.

In any case, the alternative rationalistic theory does not afford the guidance for the sake of which eternal and immutable norms are appealed to. The scientist finds no help in determining the probable truth of some proposed theory by comparing it with a standard of absolute truth and immutable being. He has to rely upon definite operations undertaken under definite conditions—upon method. We can hardly imagine an architect getting aid in the construction of a building from an ideal at large, though we can understand his framing an ideal on the basis of knowledge of actual conditions and needs. Nor does the ideal of perfect beauty in antecedent Being give direction to a painter in producing a particular work of art. In morals, absolute perfection does not seem to be more than a generalized hypostatization of the recognition that there is a good to be sought, an obligation to be met—both being concrete matters. Nor is the defect in this respect merely negative. An examination of history would reveal, I am confident, that these general and remote schemes of value actually obtain a content definite enough and near enough to concrete situations as to afford guidance in action only by consecrating some institution or dogma already having social currency. Concreteness is gained, but it is by protecting from inquiry some accepted standard which perhaps is outworn and in need of criticism.

When theories of values do not afford intellectual assistance in framing ideas and beliefs about values that are adequate to direct action, the gap must be filled by other means. If intelligent method is lacking, prejudice, the pressure of immediate circumstance, self-interest and class-interest, traditional customs, institutions of accidental historic origin, are *not* lacking, and they tend to take the place of intelligence. Thus we are led to our main proposition: *Judgments about values are judgments about the conditions and the results of experienced objects; judgments about that which should regulate the formation of our desires, affections and enjoyments.* For whatever decides their formation will determine the main course of our conduct, personal and social. . . .

The time will come when it will be found passing strange that we of this age should take such pains to control by every means at command the formation of ideas of physical things, even those most remote from human concern, and yet are content with haphazard beliefs about the qualities of objects that regulate our deepest interests; that we are scrupulous as to methods of forming ideas of natural objects, and either dogmatic or else driven by immediate conditions in framing those about values. There is, by implication, if not explicitly, a prevalent notion that values are already well known and that all which is lacking is the will to cultivate them in the order of their worth. In fact the most profound lack is not the will to act upon goods already known but the will to know what they are.

It is not a dream that it is possible to exercise some degree of regulation of the occurrence of enjoyments which are of value. Realization of the possibility is exemplified, for example, in the technologies and arts of industrial life—that is, up to a definite limit. Men desired heat, light, and speed of transit and of communication beyond what nature provides of itself. These things have been attained not by lauding the enjoyment of these things and preaching their desirability, but by study of the conditions of their manifestation. Knowledge of relations having been obtained, ability to produce followed, and enjoyment ensued as a matter of course.[d]

**4.** In physical science, it is realized that knowledge of an object increases as more of its connections and interactions are understood. However in social science, there is a tendency to ignore the study of *the conditions under which values arise, change, and become obsolete.* This is the result of the traditional view that technological skills are inferior to moral skills and of the erroneous assumption that we already know what is valuable.

With respect to [technological skills] there is no assumption that they can be had and enjoyed with definite operative knowledge. With respect to them it is also clear that the degree in which we value them is measurable by the pains taken to control the conditions of their occurrence. With respect to the latter, it is assumed that no one who is honest can be in doubt what they are; that by revelation, or conscience, or the instruction of others, or immediate feeling, they are clear beyond question. And instead of action in their behalf being taken to be a measure of the extent in which things *are* values to us, it is assumed that the difficulty is to persuade men to act upon what they already know to be good. Knowledge of conditions and consequences is regarded as wholly indifferent to judging what is of serious value, though it is useful in a prudential way in trying to actualize it. In consequence, the existence of values that are by common consent of a secondary and technical sort are under a fair degree of control, while those denominated supreme and imperative are subject to all the winds of impulse, custom and arbitrary authority.

This distinction between higher and lower types of value is itself something to be looked into. Why should there be a sharp division made between some goods as physical and material and others as ideal and "spiritual"? The question touches the whole dualism of the material and the ideal at its root. To denominate anything "matter" or "material" is not in truth to disparage it. It is, if the designation is correctly applied, a way of indicating that the thing in question is a condition or means of the existence of something else. And disparagement of effective means is practically synonymous with disregard of the things that are termed, in eulogistic fashion, ideal and spiritual. For the latter terms if they have any concrete application at all signify something which is a desirable consummation of conditions, a cherished fulfillment of means. The sharp separation between material and ideal good thus deprives the latter of the underpinning of effective support while it opens the way for treating things which should be employed as means as ends in themselves. For since men cannot after all live without some measure of possession of such matters as health and wealth, the latter things will be viewed as values and ends in isolation unless they are treated as integral constituents of the goods that are deemed supreme and final.[e]

**5.** The transfer of the scientific method from the physical sciences to the study of human affairs admittedly involves difficulties. These arise out of the fact that human behavior is more complex than the behavior of physical objects. However, Dewey rejects the view that there is a difference in kind between the physical world and human nature.

But this difference is not a ground for making a sharp division between the two, nor does it account for the fact that we make so little use of the experimental method of forming our ideas and beliefs about the concerns of man in his characteristic social relations. For this separation religions and philosophies must admit some responsibility. They have erected a distinction between a narrower scope of relations and a wider and fuller one into a difference of kind, naming one kind material, and the other mental and moral. They have charged themselves gratuitously with the office of diffusing belief in the necessity of the division, and with instilling contempt for the material as something inferior in kind in its intrinsic nature and worth. Formal philosophies undergo evaporation of their technical solid contents; in a thinner and more viable form they find their way into the minds of those who know nothing of their original forms. When these diffuse and, so to say, airy emanations recrystallize in the popular mind they form a hard deposit of opinion that alters slowly and with great difficulty.

What difference would it actually make in the arts of conduct, personal and social, if the experimental theory were adopted not as a mere theory, but as a part of the working equipment of habitual attitudes on the part of everyone? It would be impossible, even were time given, to answer the question in adequate detail, just as men could not foretell in advance the consequences for knowledge of adopting the experimental method. It is the nature of the method that it has to be tried. But there are generic lines of difference which, within the limits of time at disposal, may be sketched.

Change from forming ideas and judgments of value on the basis of conformity to antecedent objects, to constructing enjoyable objects directed by knowledge of consequences, is a change from looking to the past to looking to the future. I do not for a moment suppose that the experiences of the past, personal and social, are of no importance. For without them we should not be able to frame any ideas whatever of the conditions under which objects are enjoyed nor any estimate of the consequences of esteeming and liking them. But past experiences are significant in giving us intellectual instrumentalities of judging just these points. They are tools, not finalities. Reflection upon what we have liked and have enjoyed is a necessity. But it tells us nothing about the *value* of these things until enjoyments are themselves reflectively controlled, or, until, as they are recalled, we form the best judgment possible about what led us to like this sort of thing and what has issued from the fact that we liked it.[f]

**6.** In presenting the underlying assumptions and general frame of reference of ethical experimentalism, Dewey attempts to clarify his attitude toward customary or traditional values. He is not suggesting the sweeping away of time-honored values. Rather, he is recommending the use of intelligent criticism for the sake of integrating values and behavior in the constantly changing context of human experience.

We are not, then, to get away from enjoyments experienced in the past and from recall of them, but from the notion that they are the arbiters of things to be further enjoyed. At present, the arbiter is found in the past, although there are many ways of interpreting what in the past is authoritative. Nominally, the most influential conception doubtless is that of a revelation once had or a perfect life once lived. Reliance upon precedent, upon institutions created in the past, especially in law, upon rules of morals that have come to us through unexamined customs, upon uncriticized tradition, are other forms of dependence. It is not for a moment suggested that we can get away from customs and established institutions. A mere break would doubtless result simply in chaos. But there is no danger of such a break. Mankind is too inertly conservative both by constitution and by education to give the idea of this danger actuality. What there is genuine danger of is that the force of new conditions will produce disruption externally and mechanically: this is an ever present danger. The prospect is increased, not mitigated, by that conservatism which insists upon the adequacy of old standards to meet new conditions. What is needed is intelligent examination of the consequences that are actually effected by inherited institutions and customs, in order that there may be intelligent consideration of the ways in which they are to be intentionally modified in behalf of generation of different consequences.

This is the significant meaning of transfer of experimental method from the technical field of physical experience to the wider field of human life. We trust the method in forming our beliefs about things are not directly connected with human life. In effect, we distrust it in moral, political and economic affairs. In the fine arts, there are many signs of a change. In the past, such a change has often been an omen and precursor of changes in other human attitudes.

But, generally speaking, the idea of actively adopting experimental method in social affairs, in the matters deemed of most enduring and ultimate worth, strikes most persons as a surrender of all standards and regulative authority. But in principle, experimental method does not signify random and aimless action; it implies direction by ideas and knowledge. The question at issue is a practical one. Are there in existence the ideas and the knowledge that permit experimental method to be effectively used in social interest and affairs?[g]

**7.** We must recognize that we need new ideas and facts to use the experimental method in ethics. If the uncritical acceptance of traditional values is to end, however, a substitute is required that can provide sound moral standards. Dewey again turns to the scientific method for a solution.

Where will regulation come from if we surrender familiar and traditionally prized values as our directive standards? Very largely from the findings of the natural sciences. For one of the effects of the separation drawn between knowledge and action is to deprive scientific knowledge of its proper service as a guide of conduct—except once more in those technological fields which have been degraded to an inferior rank. Of course, the complexity of the conditions upon which objects of human and liberal value depend is a great obstacle, and it would be too optimistic to say that we have as yet enough knowledge of the scientific type to enable us to regulate our judgments of value very extensively. But we have more knowledge than we try to put to use, and until we try more systematically we shall not know what are the important gaps in our sciences judged from the point of view of their moral and humane use.

For moralists usually draw a sharp line between the field of the natural sciences and the conduct that is regarded as moral. But a moral that frames its judgments of value on the basis of consequences must depend in a most intimate manner upon the conclusions of science. For the knowledge of the relations between changes which enable us to connect things as antecedents and consequences *is* science. The narrow scope which moralists often give to morals, their isolation of some conduct as virtuous and vicious from other large ranges of conduct, those having to do with health and vigor, business, education, with all the affairs in which desires and affection are implicated, is perpetuated by this habit of exclusion of the subject-matter of natural science from a role in formation of moral standards and ideals. The same attitude operates in the other direction to keep natural science a technical specialty, and it works unconsciously to encourage its use exclusively in regions where it can be turned to personal and class advantage, as in war and trade.[h]

**8.** The social implications of experimentalism in ethics are developed through a subtle criticism of subjectivism and egoism in ethical theories. Dewey includes in his criticism theories that are not ordinarily classified as subjective—for example, philosophical realism, in which values are regarded as independent of human experience. However, Dewey makes the charge of subjectivism because, in such a view, moral improvement is made to depend solely on changes within individuals; the social context of human activity and its definitive role in modifying values are neglected.

This constant throwing of emphasis back upon a change made in ourselves instead of one made in the world in which we live seems to me the essence of what is objectionable in "subjectivism." Its taint hangs about even Platonic realism with its insistent evangelical dwelling upon the change made within the mind by contemplation of the realm of essence, and its depreciation of action as transient and all but sordid—a concession to the necessities of organic existence. All the theories which put conversion "of the eye of the soul" in the place of a conversion of natural and social objects that modifies goods actually experienced, is a retreat and escape from existence—and this retraction into self is, once more, the heart of subjective egoisms. The typical example is perhaps the otherworldliness found in religions whose chief concern is with the salvation of the personal soul. But otherworldliness is found as well in aestheticism and in all seclusion within ivory towers.

It is not in the least implied that change in personal attitudes, in the disposition of the "subject," is not of great importance. Such change, on the contrary, is involved in any attempt to modify the conditions of the environment. But there is a radical difference between a change in the self that is cultivated and valued as an end, and one that is a means to alteration, through action, of objective conditions. The Aristotelian-medieval conviction that highest bliss is found in contemplative possession of ultimate Being presents an ideal attractive to some types of mind; it sets forth a refined sort of enjoyment. It is a doctrine congenial to minds that despair of the effort involved in creation of a better world of daily experience. It is, apart from theological attachments, a doctrine sure to recur when social conditions are so troubled as to make actual endeavor seem hopeless. But the subjectivism so externally marked in modern thought as compared with ancient is either a development of the old doctrine under new conditions or is of merely technical import. The medieval version of the doctrine at least had the active support of a great social institution by means of which man could be brought into the state of mind that prepared him for ultimate enjoyment of eternal Being. It had a certain solidity and depth which is lacking in modern theories that would attain the result by merely emotional or speculative procedures, or by any means not demanding a change in objective existence so as to render objects of value more empirically secure.

The nature in detail of the revolution that would be wrought by carrying into the region of values the principle now embodied in scientific practice cannot be told; to attempt it would violate the fundamental idea that we know only after we have acted and in consequences of the outcome of action. But it would surely effect a transfer of attention and energy from the subjective to the objective. Men would think of themselves as agents not as ends; ends would be found in experienced enjoyment of the fruits of a transforming activity.[i]

> **9.** Thus far, two of the changes that would result from the application of experimentalism to ethics have been sketched: the change of perspective from past to future and the change of emphasis from the subjective to the objective.

A third significant change that would issue from carrying over experimental method from physics to man concerns the import of standards, principles, rules. With the transfer, these, and all tenets and creeds about good and goods, would be recognized to be hypotheses. Instead of being rigidly fixed, they would be treated as intellectual instruments to be tested and confirmed—and altered—through consequences effected by acting upon them. They would lose all pretense of finality—the ulterior source of dogmatism. It is both astonishing and depressing that so much of the energy of mankind has gone into fighting for (with weapons of the flesh as well as of the spirit) the truth of creeds, religious, moral and political, as distinct from what has gone into effort to try creeds by putting them to the test of acting upon them. The change would do away with the intolerance and fanaticism that attend the notion that beliefs and judgments are capable of inherent truth and authority; inherent in the sense of being independent of what they lead to when used as directive principles. The transformation does not imply merely that men are responsible for acting upon what they profess to believe; that is an old doctrine. It goes much further. Any belief as such is tentative, hypothetical; it is not just to be acted upon, but is to be *framed* with reference to its office as a guide to action. Consequently, it should be the last thing in the world to be picked up casually and then clung to rigidly. When it is apprehended as a tool and only a tool, an instrumentality of direction, the same scrupulous attention will go to its formation as now goes into the making of instruments of precision in technical fields. Men, instead of being proud of accepting and asserting beliefs and "principles" on the ground of loyalty, will be as ashamed of that procedure as they would now be to confess their assent to a scientific theory out of reference for Newton or Helmholtz or whomever, without regard to evidence.

If one stops to consider the matter, is there not something strange in the fact that men should consider loyalty to "laws," principles, standards, ideals to be an inherent virtue, accounted unto them for righteousness? It is as if they were making up for some secret sense of weakness by rigidity and intensity of insistent attachment. A moral law, like a law in physics, is not something to swear by and stick to at all hazards; it is a formula of the way to respond when specified conditions present themselves. Its soundness and pertinence are tested by what happens when it is acted upon. Its claim or authority rests finally upon the imperativeness of the situation that has to be dealt with, not upon its own intrinsic nature—as any tool achieves dignity in the measure of needs served by it. The idea that adherence to standards external to experienced objects is the only alternative to confusion and lawlessness was once held in science. But knowledge became steadily progressive when it was abandoned, and clews and tests found within concrete acts and objects were employed. The test of consequences is more exacting than that afforded by fixed general rules. In addition, it secures constant development, for when new acts are tried new results are experienced, while the lauded immutability of eternal ideals and norms is in itself a denial of the possibility of development and improvement.[j]

**10.** In elaborating the change of attitude toward ideals that would result from regarding them as hypotheses, Dewey deals with the question of the relationship of *means* to *ends*. The observed discrepancies between ideals and actual behavior may be interpreted as a consequence of the persistent separation of means from ends.

The various modifications that would result from adoption in social and humane subjects of the experimental way of thinking are perhaps summed up in saying that it would place *method and means* upon the level of importance that has, in the past, been imputed exclusively to ends. Means have been regarded as menial, and the useful as the servile. Means have been treated as poor relations to be endured, but not inherently welcome. The very meaning of the word "ideals" is significant of the divorce which has obtained between means and ends. "Ideals" are thought to be remote and inaccessible of attainment; they are too high and fine to be sullied by realization. They serve vaguely to arouse "aspiration," but they do not evoke and direct strivings for embodiment in actual existence. They hover in an indefinite way over the actual scene; they are expiring ghosts of a once significant kingdom of divine reality whose rule penetrated to every detail of life.

It is impossible to form a just estimate of the paralysis of effort that has been produced by indifference to means. Logically, it is truistic that lack of consideration for means signifies that so-called ends are not taken seriously. It is as if one professed devotion to painting pictures conjoined with contempt for canvas, brush and paints; or love of music on condition that no instruments, whether the voice or something external, be used to make sounds. The good workman in the arts is known by his respect for his tools and by his interest in perfecting his technique. The glorification in the arts of ends at the expense of means would be taken to be a sign of complete insincerity or even insanity. Ends separated from means are either sentimental indulgences or if they happen to exist are merely accidental. The ineffectiveness in action of "ideals" is due precisely to the supposition that means and ends are not on exactly the same level with respect to the attention and care they demand.

It is however, much easier to point out the formal contradiction implied in ideals that are professed without equal regard for the instruments and techniques of their realization, than it is to appreciate the concrete ways in which belief in their separation has found its way into life and borne corrupt and poisonous fruits. The separation marks the form in which the traditional divorce of theory and practice has expressed itself in actual life. It accounts for the relative impotency of arts concerned with enduring human welfare. Sentimental attachment and subjective eulogy take the place of action. For there is no art without tools and instrumental agencies. But it also explains the fact that in actual behavior, energies devoted to matters nominally thought to be inferior, material and sordid, engross attention and interest. After a polite and pious deference has been paid to "ideals," men feel free to devote themselves to matters which are more immediate and pressing.[k]

**11.** An example of the dangers of separating means from ends is found in the contemporary economic scene. The assumption that the pursuit of high ideals is unrelated to a concern for material welfare is a time-honored but dangerous fallacy, Dewey points out. As a consequence of this view, economic activity is deprived of the guidance of moral values, and moral values are deprived of their indispensable foundation in material welfare.

It is usual to condemn the amount of attention paid by people in general to material ease, comfort, wealth, and success gained by competition, on the ground that they give to mere means the attention that ought to be given to ends, or that they have taken for ends things which in reality are only means. Criticisms of the place which economic interest and action occupy in present life are full of complaints that men allow lower aims to usurp the place that belongs to higher and ideal values. The final source of the trouble is, however, that moral and spiritual "leaders" have propagated the notion that ideal ends may be cultivated in isolation from "material" means, as if means and material were not synonymous. While they condemn men for giving to means the thought and energy that ought to go to ends, the condemnation should go to them. For they have not taught their followers to think of material and economic activities as *really* means. They have been unwilling to frame their conception of the values that should be regulative of human conduct on the basis of the actual conditions and operations by which alone values can be actualized.

Practical needs are imminent; with the mass of mankind they are imperative. Moreover, speaking generally, men are formed to act rather than to theorize. Since the ideal ends are so remotely and accidentally connected with immediate and urgent conditions that need attention, after lip service is given to them, men naturally devote themselves to the latter. If a bird in the hand is worth two in a neighboring bush, an actuality in hand is worth, for the direction of conduct, many ideals that are so remote as to be invisible and inaccessible. Men hoist the banner of the ideal, and then march in the direction that concrete conditions suggest and reward. . . .

The present state of industrial life seems to give a fair index of the existing separation of means and ends. Isolation of economics from ideal ends, whether of morals or of organized social life, was proclaimed by Aristotle. Certain things, he said, are conditions of a worthy life, personal and social, but are not constituents of it. The economic life of man, concerned with satisfaction of wants, is of this nature. Men have wants and they must be satisfied. But they are only prerequisites of a good life, not intrinsic elements in it. Most philosophers have not been so frank nor perhaps so logical. But upon the whole, economics has been treated as on a lower level than either morals or politics. Yet the life which men, women and children actually lead, the opportunities open to them, the values they are capable of enjoying, their education, their share in all the things of art and science, are mainly determined by economic conditions. Hence we can hardly expect a moral system which ignores economic conditions to be other than remote and empty.

Industrial life is correspondingly brutalized by failure to equate it as the means by which social and cultural values are realized. That the economic life, thus exiled from the pale of higher values, takes revenge by declaring that it is the only social reality, and by means of the doctrine of materialistic determinism of institutions and conduct in all fields, denies to deliberate morals and politics any share of causal regulation, is not surprising.

When economists were told that their subject matter was merely material, they naturally thought they could be "scientific" only by excluding all reference to distinctively human values. Material wants, efforts to satisfy them, even the scientifically regulated technologies highly developed in industrial activity, are then taken to form a complete and closed field. If any reference to social ends and values is introduced it is by way of an external addition, mainly hortatory. That economic life largely determines the conditions under which mankind has access to concrete values may be recognized or it may not be. In either case, the notion that it is the means to be utilized in order to secure significant values as the common and shared possession of mankind is alien and inoperative. To many persons, the idea that the ends professed by morals are impotent save as they are connected with the working machinery of economic life seems like deflowering the purity of moral values and obligations.[l]

**12.** The relationship of means to ends raises again the problem of the lack of integration in contemporary moral life. The "split personality" of present-day ethics may be remedied by bringing together means and ends, theory and practice. What is needed is action guided by intelligent thinking, rather than ineffectual appeals to "good intentions."

Deliberate insincerity and hypocrisy are rare. But the notion that action and sentiment are inherently unified in the constitution of human nature has nothing to justify it. Integration is something to be achieved. Division of attitudes and responses, compartmentalizing of interests, is easily acquired. It goes deep just because the acquisition is unconscious, a matter of habitual adaptation to conditions. Theory separated from concrete doing and making is empty and futile; practice then becomes an immediate seizure of opportunities and enjoyments which conditions afford without the direction which theory—knowledge and ideas—has power to supply. The problem of the relation of theory and practice is not a problem of theory alone; it is that, but it is also the most practical problem of life. For it is the question of how intelligence may inform action, and how action may bear the fruit of increased insight into meaning: a clear view of the values that are worthwhile and of the means by which they are to be made secure in experienced objects. Construction of ideals in general and their sentimental glorification are easy; the responsibilities both of studious thought and of action are shirked. Persons having the advantage of positions of leisure and who find pleasure in abstract theorizing—a most delightful indulgence to those to whom it appeals—have a large measure of liability for a cultivated diffusion of ideals and aims that are separated from the conditions which are the means of actualization. Then other persons who find themselves in positions of social power and authority readily claim to be the bearers and defenders of ideal ends in church and state. They then use the prestige and authority their representative capacity as guardians of the highest ends confers on them to cover actions taken in behalf of the harshest and narrowest of material ends.[m]

**13.** In concluding his discussion, Dewey attempts to estimate the responsibility of philosophers and theologians for the lag of ethics behind technology. He looks upon the traditional ethical systems as expressing rather than creating the preference for values that are placed beyond criticism or modification. In any case, Dewey is convinced that the proved effectiveness of the methods of science makes the traditional approach superfluous.

The social and moral effects of the separation of theory and practice have been merely hinted at. They are so manifold and so pervasive that an adequate consideration of them would involve nothing less than a survey of the whole field of morals, economics and politics. It cannot be justly stated that these effects are in fact direct consequences of the quest for certainty by thought and knowledge isolated from action.

For, as we have seen, this quest was itself a reflex product of actual conditions. But it may be truly asserted that this quest, undertaken in religion and philosophy, has had results which have reinforced the conditions which originally brought it about. Moreover, search for safety and consolation amid the perils of life by means other than intelligent action, by feeling and thought alone, began when actual means of control were lacking, when arts were undeveloped. It had then a relative historic justification that is now lacking. The primary problem for thinking which lays claim to be philosophic in its breadth and depth is to assist in bringing about a reconstruction of all beliefs rooted in a basic separation of knowledge and action; to develop a system of operative ideas congruous with present knowledge and with present facilities of control over natural events and energies.[n]

## QUESTIONS

1. What does Dewey regard as the basic moral problem of modern life? What does he propose as a solution to this critical problem?
2. Explain what is meant by a *value* in Dewey's ethics. How are *values* and *facts* related?
3. What are Dewey's criticisms of (a) extreme empiricism and (b) extreme rationalism? Give examples of theories containing these views.
4. Discuss the distinction Dewey draws between the *desired* and the *desirable*. Why does he find it necessary to make this contrast?
5. How does Dewey explain the lag of social science behind physical science? In what ways are traditional philosophies responsible for this situation?
6. What is Dewey's attitude toward customary moral values? How can the scientific method affect the selection of ethical standards?
7. Describe the changes that would result from the introduction of experimentalism into ethics.
8. Discuss Dewey's theory of means and ends. How would he judge the belief that "the end justifies the means"?
9. What advantage does Dewey anticipate from the application of the scientific method to ethics? Do you agree with him that (a) it is possible to have a scientific theory of ethics and that (b) if it is possible, it would be beneficial?
10. What are the implications of Dewey's theory of value for education, society, and political organization?

## KEY TO SELECTIONS

John Dewey, *The Quest for Certainty*, New York, Minton Balch, 1929, Ch. X. With the kind permission of the publishers, G. P. Putnam's.

[a]p. 255.
[b]pp. 260–261.
[c]pp. 262–263.
[d]pp. 264–265, 268–269.
[e]pp. 269–270.
[f]pp. 271–272.
[g]pp. 272–273.
[h]pp. 273–274.
[i]pp. 275–276.
[j]pp. 277–278.
[k]p. 279
[l]pp. 280–281, 282–283.
[m]pp. 281–282.
[n]pp. 283–284.

## GUIDE TO ADDITIONAL READING

### PRIMARY SOURCES

Dewey, J., *Human Nature and Conduct*, Modern Library (Random House).

_____, *Intelligence in the Modern World: John Dewey's Philosophy*, Modern Library (Random House).

_____, *Reconstruction in Philosophy*, Mentor (New American Library).

_____, *Theory of Valuation*, Foundations of the Unity of Science (University of Chicago Press).

_____, "Three Independent Factors in Morals," tr. Jo Ann Boylston, *Educational Theory*, July 1966, pp. 197–209.

Dewey and Tufts, *Ethics*, rev. ed. (1932), Henry Holt.

**DISCUSSION AND COMMENTARY**

Bernstein, R., *John Dewey*, New York, Washington Square Press, 1966.

Gouinlock, J., *John Dewey's Philosophy of Values*, New York, Humanities Press, 1972.

Hook, S., *John Dewey: An Intellectual Portrait*, New York, John Day, 1939.

Misak, C. J. (ed.), *Pragmatism*, Vancouver, University of Calgary Press, 1999.

Noble, C., "A Common Misunderstanding of Dewey on the Nature of Value Judgments," *Journal of Value Inquiry*, Spring 1978, pp. 53–63.

Schilpp, P. A. (Ed.), *The Philosophy of John Dewey*, Evanston and Chicago, Northwestern University, Library of Living Philosophers, 1939.

Stroh, G., *American Ethical Thought*, Chicago, Nelson-Hall, 1979, Ch. 6.

CHAPTER NINETEEN

# The Indefinability of Good

Master and Fellows of Trinity College, Cambridge

G. E. MOORE

GEORGE EDWARD MOORE (1873–1958) was Emeritus Professor of Philosophy at Cambridge University, with which he had been affiliated almost continuously since he entered it as an undergraduate in 1892. His association with his brilliant fellow student, Bertrand Russell, was a decisive factor in Moore's entering the field of philosophy. He studied under such outstanding teachers of philosophy as Henry Sidgwick, James Ward, and J. E. McTaggart. Honored as one of the most influential of contemporary ethical theorists, Moore was invited to lecture in the United States. He was a visiting professor at Smith College in 1940, and, enjoying his new environment, he remained in this country for several years. He taught at Princeton University, Mills College, and Columbia University and lectured at other major American universities. Between 1921 and 1947, Moore served as editor of the distinguished philosophical journal *Mind*. His most important works are *Principia Ethica* (1903), *Ethics* (1912), and *Philosophical Studies* (1922).

In his *Principia Ethica*, G. E. Moore effects a significant reorientation in ethics and sets the pattern for the modern "analytic movement" in philosophy. Instead of constructing a philosophical system in the traditional way, he starts with an *analysis of the fundamental philosophical questions*. Though his conclusions are not shared by all twentieth-century philosophers, there are few who fail to acknowledge the importance of analyzing the basic questions before constructing a philosophical system. As Moore puts it,

> It appears to me that in Ethics, as in all other philosophical studies, the difficulties and disagreements, of which its history is full, are mainly due to a very simple cause: namely to the attempt to answer questions, without first discovering precisely *what*

> question it is which you desire to answer. I do not know how far this source of error would be done away, if philosophers would *try* to discover what question they were asking, before they set about to answer it; for the work of analysis and distinction is often very difficult: we may often fail to make the necessary discovery, even though we make a definite attempt to do so. But I am inclined to think that in many cases a resolute attempt would be sufficient to ensure success; so that, if only this attempt were made, many of the most glaring difficulties and disagreements in philosophy would disappear.[a]

Moore points out that traditionally, ethical theorists have taken as primary the unanalyzed question "What is intrinsically good?"—that is, what is good unconditionally and invariably? By failing to perceive that this is in fact a complex issue, they have given answers that have been for the most part futile and obscure. Moore finds, upon analysis, that the question is in fact two questions: "How is *good* to be defined?" and "What things are good?" He insists that we must deal with the former before we address the latter.

In order to discover whether it is possible to define the term *good*, Moore reviews the principal techniques of definition: (1) definition by example of illustration (for example, a *conifer* is such a tree as a pine, fir, or hemlock); (2) definition by synonym (a *spinster* is an unmarried woman); and (3) definition by description (a *tiger* is a large, Asiatic, carnivorous mammal of the cat family, of a tawny color, transversely striped with black). For the purpose of defining *good*, he finds definitions that point to examples or cite illustrations unsatisfactory, because these deal with *things* that are *good*, not with the *meaning* of the word. Likewise, definitions that present expressions synonymous with *good* evade the real issue, because they merely substitute one set of words for another without *identifying the property* to which they refer. The final alternative, defining *good* through description, also fails, Moore tells us, because it is not possible to discover any collection of different qualities and properties referred to by the term. Then, because no known mode of definition is satisfactory, and yet the term has meaning, he concludes that *good* is *indefinable*. It follows that the term *good* refers to a simple property of things—*it is a primitive and irreducible quality*. Moore insists, however, that although *good* cannot itself be defined, all other ethical terms can be defined through it.[1]

The conception of the indefinability of the good in Moore's ethical theory is augmented by the doctrine of *ethical realism*. According to this doctrine, there are ethical properties that exist independently of human consciousness. For Moore, goodness is such a property. It exists in the real world, apart from the desires and aversions, the pleasures and pains of human beings.

The term *good* refers to a quality that is analogous in some ways to sensory qualities. The philosophical realist maintains that when we speak of a sensory quality, as when we say, "The apple is red," the word *red* is not the name of a particular kind of *experience* but is the name of an *objectively real property* of the apple. The property, though clearly not the experience, is independent of human perception. In Moore's ethical theory, however, the analogy is not carried beyond this point, because goodness, unlike sensory qualities, cannot be imagined "as existing *by itself* in time." The objective reality of goodness consists in its being *intrinsic*—that is, it is *unchanging*

---

[1]Moore credits Henry Sidgwick with alerting him to the possibility that the key ethical term may be indefinable (see Chapter 16, fn. 6 of this book).

and *absolute*, in the sense that "when anything possesses it . . . it would *necessarily* or *must* always, under all circumstances, possess it in exactly the same degree."[2]

Moore regards statements in ethics as essentially of the same kind as any other statements about reality; the certification of their truth or falsity depends on either *self-evidence* or *external evidence*. Such a statement as "Personal affection is good" is regarded by Moore as self-evidently true. By contrast, he believes that the truth of propositions of the form "All men desire happiness" can be established only by external evidence. Asserting that the fundamental propositions of ethics are of the former variety, he attempts to clarify the meaning that he attaches to the notion of "self-evidence" in the following manner:

> The expression "self-evident" means properly that the proposition so called isevident or true, *by itself*, alone; that it is not an inference from some proposition other than *itself*. The expression does *not* mean that the proposition is true, because it is evident to you or me or all mankind, because in other words it appears to us to be true. That a proposition appears to be true can never be a valid argument that true it really is. By saying that a proposition is self-evident, we mean emphatically that its appearing so to us, is *not* the reason why it is true: for we mean that it has absolutely no reason.[b]

In sum, the result of Moore's analysis of the primary ethical question "How is *good* to be defined?" is as follows: The term *good* is meaningful yet indefinable; it refers to an independently existent quality, yet it is unlike the natural qualities of the sensory world; and, finally, certain propositions containing the term *good* are true by self-evidence, even though they may not be known by any individual.

---

> **1.** Moore begins his discussion of ethics by rejecting the conception of ethics as an examination of human conduct. He argues that it is "the general enquiry into what is good."

It is very easy to point out some among our everyday judgments, with the truth of which Ethics is undoubtedly concerned. Whenever we say, "So and so is a good man," or "That fellow is a villain"; whenever we ask, "What ought I to do?" or "Is it wrong for me to do like this?"; whenever we hazard such remarks as "Temperance is a virtue and drunkenness a vice"—it is undoubtedly the business of Ethics to discuss such questions and such statements; to argue what is the true answer when we ask what it is right to do, and to give reasons for thinking that our statements about the character of persons or the morality of actions are true or false. In the vast majority of cases, where we make statements involving any of the terms "virtue," "vice," "duty," "right," "ought," "good," "bad," we are making ethical judgments; and if we wish to discuss their truth, we shall be discussing a point of Ethics.

So much as this is not disputed; but it falls very far short of defining the province of Ethics. That province may indeed be defined as the whole truth about that which is at the same time common to all such judgments and peculiar to them. But we have still to ask the question: What is it that is thus common and peculiar? And this is a question to which very different answers have been given by ethical philosophers of acknowledged reputation, and none of them, perhaps, completely satisfactory.

[2] G. E. Moore, *Philosophical Studies* (London: Kegan Paul, Trench, Trubner, 1922), p. 273.

If we take such examples as those given above, we shall not be far wrong in saying that they are all of them concerned with the question of "conduct"—with the question, what, in the conduct of us, human beings, is good, and what is bad, what is right, and what is wrong. For when we say that a man is good, we commonly mean that he acts rightly; when we say that drunkenness is a vice, we commonly mean that to get drunk is a wrong or wicked action. And this discussion of human conduct is, in fact, that with which the name "Ethics" is most intimately associated. It is so associated by derivation; and conduct is undoubtedly by far the commonest and most generally interesting object of ethical judgments.

Accordingly, we find that many ethical philosophers are disposed to accept as an adequate definition of "Ethics" the statement that it deals with the question what is good or bad in human conduct. They hold that its enquiries are properly confined to "conduct" or to "practice;" they hold that the name "practical philosophy" covers all the matter with which it has to do. Now, without discussing the proper meaning of the word (for verbal questions are properly left to the writers of dictionaries and other persons interested in literature; philosophy, as we shall see, has no concern with them), I may say that I intend to use "Ethics" to cover more than this—a usage, for which there is, I think, quite sufficient authority. I am using it to cover an enquiry for which, at all events, there is no other word: the general enquiry into what is good.

Ethics is undoubtedly concerned with the question what good conduct is; but, being concerned with this, it obviously does not start at the beginning, unless it is prepared to tell us what is good as well as what is conduct. For "good conduct" is a complex notion: all conduct is not good; for some is certainly bad and some may be indifferent. And on the other hand, other things, beside conduct, may be good; and if they are so, then, "good" denotes some property, that is common to them and conduct; and if we examine good conduct alone of all good things, then we shall be in danger of mistaking for this property, some property which is not shared by those other things: and thus we shall have made a mistake about Ethics even in this limited sense; for we shall not know what good conduct really is. This is a mistake which many writers have actually made, from limiting their enquiry to conduct. And hence I shall try to avoid it by considering first what is good in general; hoping, that if we can arrive at any certainty about this, it will be much easier to settle the question of good conduct: for we all know pretty well what "conduct" is. This, then is our first question: What is good? and What is bad? and to the discussion of this question (or these questions) I give the name of Ethics, since that science must, at all events, include it.[c]

**2.** Having stated his task in a general way, Moore finds it necessary to remove any remaining misconceptions about the nature of the analysis in which he is engaging. He begins with an examination of the question "What is good?"

But this is a question which may have many meanings. If, for example, each of us were to say "I am doing good now" or "I had a good dinner yesterday," these statements would each of them be some sort of answer to our question, although perhaps a false one. So, too, when A asks B what school he ought to send his son to, B's answer will certainly be an ethical judgment. And similarly all distribution of praise or blame to any personage or thing that has existed, now exists, or will exist, does give some answer to the question "What is good?" In all such cases some particular thing is judged to be good or bad: the question "what?" is answered by "this." But this is not the sense in which a scientific Ethics asks the question. Not one, of all the many million answers of this kind, which must be true, can form a part of an ethical system; although that science must contain reasons and principles sufficient for deciding on the truth of all of them. There are far too many persons, things and events in the world, past, present, or to come, for a discussion of their individual merits to be embraced in any science. Ethics, therefore, does not deal at all with facts of this nature, facts that are unique, individual, absolutely particular; facts with which such studies as history, geography, astronomy, are compelled, in part at least, to deal. And, for this reason, it is not the business of the ethical philosopher to give personal advice or exhortation.

But there is another meaning which may be given to the question "What is good?" "Books are good" would be an answer to it, though an answer obviously false; for some books are very bad indeed. And ethical judgments of this kind do indeed belong to Ethics; though I shall not deal with many of them. Such is the judgment "Pleasure is good"—a judgment, of which Ethics should discuss the truth, although it is not nearly as important as that other judgment, with which we shall be much occupied presently— "Pleasure *alone* is good." It is judgments of this sort, which are made in such books on Ethics as contain a list of "virtues"—in Aristotle's "Ethics" for example.[d]

**3.** After clarifying the nature of the basic ethical question, Moore emphasizes its primacy for any ethical inquiry.

But our question "What is good?" may have still another meaning. We may . . . mean to ask, not what thing or things are good, but how "good" is to be defined. This is an enquiry which belongs only to Ethics . . . and this is the enquiry which will occupy us first.

It is an enquiry to which most special attention should be directed; since this question, how "good" is to be defined, is the most fundamental question in all Ethics. That which is meant by "good" is, in fact, except its converse "bad," the *only* simple object of thought which is peculiar to Ethics. Its definition, is, therefore, the most essential point in the definition of Ethics; and moreover a mistake with regard to it entails a far larger number of erroneous ethical judgments than any other. Unless this first question be fully understood, and its true answer clearly recognized, the rest of Ethics is as good as useless from the point of view of systematic knowledge.[e]

**4.** Moore discusses the inadequacy of defining good by the techniques on which traditional ethical theorists have relied. He concludes that *there is no way to define* good.

What, then, is good? How is good to be defined? Now, it may be thought that this is a verbal question. A definition does indeed often mean the expressing of one word's meaning in other words. But this is not the sort of definition I am asking for. Such a definition can never be of ultimate importance in any study except lexicography. If I wanted that kind of definition I should have to consider in the first place how people generally used the word "good"; but my business is not with its proper usage, as established by custom. I should, indeed, be foolish, if I tried to use it for something which it did not usually denote; if, for instance, I were to announce that, whenever I used the word "good," I must be understood to be thinking of that object which is usually denoted by the word "table." I shall, therefore, use the word in the sense in which I think it is ordinarily used; but at the same time I am not anxious to discuss whether I am right in thinking that it is so used. My business is solely with that object or idea, which I hold, rightly or wrongly, that the word is generally used to stand for. What I want to discover is the nature of that object or idea, and about this I am extremely anxious to arrive at an agreement.

But, if we understand the question in this sense, my answer to it may seem a very disappointing one. If I am asked "What is good?" my answer is that good is good, and that is the end of the matter. Or if I am asked "How is good to be defined?" my answer is that it cannot be defined, and that is all I have to say about it. But disappointing as these answers may appear, they are of the very last importance. To readers who are familiar with philosophic terminology, I can express their importance by saying that they amount to this: That propositions about the good are all of them synthetic and never analytic; and that is plainly no trivial matter. And the same thing may be expressed more popularly, by saying that, if I am right, then nobody can foist upon us such an axiom as that "Pleasure is the only good" or that "The good is the desired" on the pretense that this is "the very meaning of the word."

Let us, then, consider this position. My point is that "good" is a simple notion, just as "yellow" is a simple notion; that, just as you cannot, by any manner of means, explain to anyone who does not already know it, what yellow is, so you cannot explain what good is. Definitions of the kind that I was asking for, definitions which describe the real nature of the object or notion denoted by a word, and which do not merely tell us what the word is used to mean, are only possible when the object or notion in question is something complex. You can give a definition of a horse, because a horse has many different properties and qualities, all of which you can enumerate. But when you have enumerated them all, when you have reduced a horse to his simplest terms, then you can no longer define those terms. They are simply something which you think of or perceive, and to anyone who cannot think of or perceive them, you can never, by any definition, make their nature known. It may perhaps be objected to this that we are able to describe to others, objects which they have never seen or thought of. We can, for instance, make a man understand what a chimera is, although he has never heard of one or seen one. You can tell him that it is an animal with a lioness's head and body, with a goat's head growing from the middle of its back, and with a snake in place of a tail. But here the object which you are describing is a complex object; it is entirely composed of parts, with which we are all perfectly familiar—a snake, a goat, a lioness; and we know, too, the manner in which those parts are to be put together, because we know what is meant by the middle of a lioness's back, and where her tail is wont to grow. And so it is with all objects, not previously known, which we are able to define: they are all complex; all composed of parts, which may themselves, in the first instance, be capable of similar definition, but which must in the end be reducible to simplest parts, which can no longer be defined. But yellow and good, we say, are not complex: they are notions of that simple kind, out of which definitions are composed and with which the power of further defining ceases.[f]

**5.** The distinction between the *property* designed by the term *good* and things that have this property is reemphasized. Because the term *good* denotes a simple and unanalyzable property, it is indefinable. However, it does not follow from this that objects or activities that "possess" this property cannot be defined. On the contrary, they are complexes, and goodness is one of their specifiable characteristics.

But I am afraid I have still not removed the chief difficulty which may prevent acceptance of the proposition that good is indefinable. I do not mean to say that *the* good, that which is good, is thus indefinable; if I did think so, I should not be writing on Ethics, for my main object is to help towards discovering that definition. It is just because I think there will be less risk of error in our search for a definition of "the good," that I am now insisting that *good* is indefinable. I must try to explain the difference between these two. I suppose it may be granted that "good" is an adjective. Well "the good," "that which is good," must therefore be the substantive to which the adjective "good" will apply: it must be the whole of that to which the adjective will apply, and the adjective must *always* truly apply to it. But if it is that to which the adjective will apply, it must be something different from that adjective itself; and the whole of that something different, whatever it is, will be our definition of *the* good. Now it may be that this something will have other adjectives, beside "good," that will apply to it. It may be full of pleasure, for example; it may be intelligent: and if these two adjectives are really part of its definition, then it will certainly be true, that pleasure and intelligence are good. And many people appear to think that, if we say "Pleasure and intelligence are good," or if we say "Only pleasure and intelligence are good," we are defining "good." Well, I cannot deny that propositions of this nature may sometimes be called definitions; I do not know well enough how the word is generally used to decide upon this point. I only wish it to be understood that this is not what I mean when I say there is no possible definition of good, and that I shall not mean this if I use the word again. I do most fully believe that some true proposition of the form "Intelligence is good and intelligence alone is good" can be found; if none could be found, our definition of *the* good would be impossible. As it is, I believe *the* good to be definable; and yet I still say that good itself is indefinable.[g]

**6.** If, as Moore holds, *good* is indefinable, theories that undertake to define it are subject to criticism. He characterizes as the *naturalistic fallacy* any attempts to define *good,* whether as "the pleasant," "the desirable," "the rational," "that which is approved," or anything else.

"Good," then, if we mean by it that quality which we assert to belong to a thing, when we say that the thing is good, is incapable of any definition, in the most important sense of the word. The most important sense of "definition" is that in which a definition states what are the parts which invariably compose a certain whole; and in this sense "good" has no definition because it is simple and has no parts. It is one of those innumerable objects of thought which are themselves incapable of definition, because they are the ultimate terms by reference to which whatever *is* capable of definition must be defined. That there must be an indefinite number of such terms is obvious, on reflection; since we cannot define anything except by an analysis, which, when carried as far as it will go, refers us to something, which is simply different from anything else, and which by that ultimate difference explains the peculiarity of the whole which we are defining: for every whole contains some parts which are common to other wholes also. There is, therefore, no intrinsic difficulty in the contention that "good" denotes a simple and indefinable quality. There are many other instances of such qualities.

Consider yellow, for example. We may try to define it, by describing its physical equivalent; we may state what kind of light-vibrations must stimulate the normal eye, in order that we may perceive it. But a moment's reflection is sufficient to show that those light-vibrations are not themselves what we mean by yellow. *They* are not what we perceive. Indeed we should never have been able to discover their existence, unless we had first been struck by the patent difference of quality between the different colors. The most we can be entitled to say of those vibrations is that they are what corresponds in space to the yellow which we actually perceive.

Yet a mistake of this simple kind has commonly been made about "good." It may be true that all things which are good are *also* something else, just as it is true that all things which are yellow produce a certain kind of vibration in the light. And it is a fact, that Ethics aims at discovering what are those other properties belonging to all things which are good. But far too many philosophers have thought that when they named those other properties they were actually defining good; that these properties, in fact, were simply not "other," but absolutely and entirely the same with goodness. This view I propose to call the "naturalistic fallacy."[h]

**7.** Because of its great importance, Moore enlarges on his discussion of the naturalistic fallacy through illustration.

I do not care about the name: what I do care about is the fallacy. It does not matter what we call it, provided we recognize it when we meet with it. It is to be met with in almost every book on Ethics; and yet it is not recognized: and that is why it is necessary to multiply illustrations of it, and convenient to give it a name. It is a very simple fallacy indeed. When we say that an orange is yellow, we do not think our statements binds us to hold that "orange" means nothing else than "yellow," or that nothing can be yellow but an orange. Supposing the orange is also sweet! Does that bind us to say that "sweet" is exactly the same thing as "yellow," that "sweet" must be defined as "yellow"? And supposing it be recognized that "yellow" just means "yellow" and nothing else whatever, does that make it any more difficult to hold that oranges are yellow? Most certainly it does not: on the contrary, it would be absolutely meaningless to say that oranges were yellow, unless yellow did in the end mean just "yellow" and nothing else whatever—unless it was absolutely indefinable. We should not get any very clear notion about things, which are yellow—we should not get very far with our science, if we were bound to hold that everything which was yellow, *meant* exactly the same thing as yellow. We should find we had to hold that an orange was exactly the same thing as a stool, a piece of paper, a lemon, anything you like. We could prove any number of absurdities; but should we be the nearer to the truth? Why, then, should it be different with "good"? Why, if good is good and indefinable, should I be held to deny that pleasure is good? Is there any difficulty in holding both to be true at once? On the contrary, there is no meaning in saying that pleasure is good, unless good is something different from pleasure. It is absolutely useless, so far as Ethics is concerned, to prove, as Mr. [Herbert] Spencer tries to do, that increase of pleasure coincides with increase of life, unless good *means* something different from either life or pleasure. He might just as well try to prove that an orange is yellow by showing that it always is wrapped up in paper.[i]

**8.** Moore elaborates on the essential arbitrariness of all definitions of *good* and illustrates the futility of attempting to resolve arguments in ethics through the agency of definitions. Those who engage in definitional polemics, he charges, are dealing in irrelevancies. Moreover, Moore points out that when an ethical theorist defines *good* as "pleasant," he automatically makes a triviality out of such a statement as "those acts which produce pleasure are good,"' because this tells us nothing more than that "those acts which produce pleasure are pleasant."

Let us consider what it is such philosophers say. And first it is to be noticed that they do not agree among themselves. They not only say that they are right as to what good is, but they endeavor to prove that other people who say that it is something else, are wrong. One, for instance, will affirm that good is pleasure, another, perhaps, that good is that which is desired; and each of these will argue eagerly to prove that the other is wrong. But how is that possible? One of them says that good is nothing but the object of desire, and at the same time tries to prove that it is not pleasure. But from his first assertion, that good just means the object of desire, one of two things must follow as regards his proof:

1. He may be trying to prove that the object of desire is not pleasure. But, if this be all, where is his Ethics? The position he is maintaining is merely a psychological one. Desire is something which occurs in our minds, and pleasure is something else which so occurs; and our would-be ethical philosopher is merely holding that the latter is not the object of the former. But what has that to do with the question in dispute? His opponent held the ethical proposition that pleasure was the good, and although he should prove a million times over the psychological proposition that pleasure is not the object of desire, he is no nearer proving his opponent to be wrong. The position is like this. One man says a triangle is a circle: another replies "A triangle is a straight line, and I will prove to you that I am right: *for*" (this is the only argument) "a straight line is not a circle." "That is quite true," the other may reply; "but nevertheless a triangle is a circle, and you have said nothing whatever to prove the contrary. What is proved is that one of us is wrong, for we agree that a triangle cannot be both a straight line and a circle: but which is wrong, there can be no earthly means of proving, since you define triangle as straight line and I define it as circle."—Well, that is one alternative which any naturalistic Ethics has to face; if good is *defined* as something else, it is then impossible either to prove that any other definition is wrong or even to deny such definition.

2. The other alternative will scarcely be more welcome. It is that the discussion is after all a verbal one. When A says "Good means pleasant" and B says "Good means desired," they may merely wish to assert that most people have used the word for what is pleasant and for what is desired respectively. And this is quite an interesting subject for discussion: only it is not a whit more an ethical discussion than the last was. Nor do I think that any exponent of naturalistic Ethics would be willing to allow that this was all he meant. They are all so anxious to persuade us that what they call the good is what we really ought to do. "Do, pray, act so, because the word 'good' is generally used to denote actions of this nature": such, on this view, would be the substance of their teaching. And insofar as they tell us how we ought to act, their teaching is truly ethical, as they mean it to be. But how perfectly absurd is the reason they would give for it! "You are to do this, because most people use a certain word to denote conduct such as this." "You are to say the thing which is not, because most people call it lying." That is an argument just as good!—My dear sirs, what we want to know from you as ethical teachers, is not how people use a word; it is not even, what kind of actions they approve, which the use of this word "good" may certainly imply: what we want to know is simply what *is* good. We may indeed agree that what most people do think good, is actually so; we shall at all events be glad to know their opinions: but when we say their opinions about what *is* good, we do mean what we say; we do not care whether they call that thing which they mean "horse" or "table" or "chair," "gut" or "bon" or "ἀγαθός"; we want to know what it is that they so call. When they say "Pleasure is good," we cannot believe that they merely mean "Pleasure is pleasure" and nothing more than that.[j]

**9.** He points out that if one does not accept the indefinability of *good,* one must regard it either as a complex notion or as having no meaning whatever. Moore insists that neither of these alternatives fits the facts.

If it is not the case that "good" denotes something simple and indefinable, only two alternatives are possible: either it is a complex, a given whole, about the correct analysis of which there may be disagreement; or else it means nothing at all, and there is no such subject as Ethics. In general, however, ethical philosophers have attempted to define good, without recognizing what such an attempt must mean. They actually use arguments which involve one or both of the absurdities considered [in Section 8]. . . . We are, therefore, justified in concluding that the attempt to define good is chiefly due to want of clearness as to the possible nature of definition. There are, in fact, only two serious alternatives to be considered, in order to establish the conclusion that "good" does denote a simple and indefinable notion. It might possibly denote a complex, as "horse" does; or it might have no meaning at all. Neither of these possibilities has, however, been clearly conceived and seriously maintained, as such, by those who presume to define good; and both may be dismissed by a simple appeal to facts.

1. The hypothesis that disagreement about the meaning of good is disagreement with regard to the correct analysis of a given whole, may be most plainly seen to be incorrect by consideration of the fact that, whatever definition be offered, it may be always asked, with significance, of the complex so defined, whether it is itself good. To take, for instance, one of the more plausible, because one of the more complicated, of such proposed definitions, it may easily be thought, at first sight, that to be good may mean to be that which we desire to desire. Thus if we apply this definition to a particular instance and say "When we think that A is good, we are thinking that A is one of the things which we desire to desire," our proposition may seem quite plausible. But, if we carry the investigation further, and ask ourselves "Is it good to desire to desire A?" it is apparent, on a little reflection, that this question is itself as intelligible, as the original question "Is A good?"—that we are, in fact, now asking for exactly the

same information about the desire to desire A, for which we formerly asked with regard to A itself. But it is also apparent that the meaning of this second question cannot be correctly analyzed into "Is the desire to desire A one of the things which we desire to desire?": we have not before our minds anything so complicated as the question "Do we desire to desire to desire to desire A?" Moreover anyone can easily convince himself by inspection that the predicate of this proposition—"good"—is positively different from the notion of "desiring to desire" which enters into its subject: "That we should desire to desire A is good" is *not* merely equivalent to "That A should be good is good." It may indeed be true that what we desire to desire is always also good; perhaps, even the converse may be true: but it is very doubtful whether this is the case, and the mere fact that we understand very well what is meant by doubting it, shows clearly that we have two different notions before our minds.

2. And the same consideration is sufficient to dismiss the hypothesis that "good" has no meaning whatsoever. It is very natural to make the mistake of supposing that what is universally true is of such a nature that its negation would be self-contradictory: the importance which has been assigned to analytic propositions in the history of philosophy shows how easy such a mistake is. And thus it is very easy to conclude that what seems to be a universal ethical principle is in fact an identical proposition; that, if, for example, whatever is called "good" seems to be pleasant, the proposition "Pleasure is the good" does not assert a connection between two different notions, but involves only one, that of pleasure, which is easily recognized as a distinct entity. But whoever will attentively consider with himself what is actually before his mind when he asks the question "Is pleasure (or whatever it may be) after all good?" can easily satisfy himself that he is not merely wondering whether pleasure is pleasant. And if he will try this experiment with each suggested definition in succession, he may become expert enough to recognize that in every case he has before his mind a unique object, with regard to the connection of which with any other object, a distinct question may be asked. Everyone does in fact understand the question "Is this good?" When he thinks of it, his state of mind is different from what it would be, were he asked "Is this pleasant, or desired, or approved?" It has a distinct meaning for him, even though he may not recognize in what respect it is distinct. Whenever he thinks of "intrinsic value," or "intrinsic worth," or says that a thing "ought to exist," he has before his mind the unique object—the unique property of things—which I mean by "good." Everybody is constantly aware of this notion, although he may never become aware at all that it is different from other notions of which he is also aware. But, for correct ethical reasoning, it is extremely important that he should become aware of this fact; and, as soon as the nature of the problem is clearly understood, there should be little difficulty in advancing so far in analysis.[k]

**10.** Moore is now in a position to show the detrimental effect of the naturalistic fallacy upon investigation in ethics: It closes inquiry by defining in advance what things will be recognized as good, without shedding any light on the nature of intrinsic goodness. The avoidance of this fallacy is a necessary part of "prolegomena to any future Ethics that can possibly pretend to be scientific."

If . . . we once recognize that we must start our Ethics without a definition, we shall be much more apt to look about us, before we adopt any ethical principle whatever; and the more we look about us, the less likely are we to adopt a false one. It may be replied to this: Yes, but we shall look about us just as much, before we settle on our definition, and are therefore just as likely to be right. But I will try to show that this is not the case. If we start with the conviction that a definition of good can be found, we start with the conviction that good *can mean* nothing else than some one property of things; and our only business will then be to discover what the property is. But if we recognize that, so far as the meaning of good goes, anything whatever may be good, we start with a much more open mind. Moreover, apart from the fact that, when we think we have a definition, we cannot logically defend our ethical principles in any way whatever, we shall also be much less apt to define them well, even if illogically. For we shall start with the conviction that good must mean so and so, and shall therefore be inclined either to misunderstand our opponent's arguments or to cut them short with the reply, "This is not an open question: the very meaning of the word decides it; no one can think otherwise except through confusion."[l]

## QUESTIONS

1. What new orientation in ethical theory is provided by Moore's *Principia Ethica?* What judgment of traditional ethics would be made if Moore's basic thesis were adopted?
2. Why does Moore maintain that "intrinsic good" is indefinable? Discuss critically his explanation of his position.
3. Give Moore's definition of the "naturalistic fallacy" and cite several illustrations.
4. How does Moore refute the hedonistic doctrine? Do you think his method is an effective one in ethics?
5. Comment on Moore's view of the nature of self-evident propositions. What would happen to his general ethical theory if there were no self-evident ethical statements?
6. What is ethical realism? Would you say that the average person is an ethical realist? Explain your answer, making reference to specific instances of ethical convictions.
7. In what respect can Moore's investigation in ethics be defended as open-minded? Is it logically possible to use his basic method but to reach different conclusions about the nature of ethics?
8. Why is the distinction between "properties of things" and "things having properties" a crucial one for Moore?
9. How would Moore respond to the following assertion of William James: "There is no *status* for good and evil to exist in, in a purely insentient world."
10. Discuss in detail your opinion as to whether two individuals, both convinced of the validity of Moore's ethical theory, could nevertheless have disputes at the level of practical morality.

## KEY TO SELECTIONS

G. E. Moore, *Principia Ethica*, New York, Cambridge University Press, 1948. With the kind permission of the publishers.

[a]Preface, p. vii.
[b]p. 143.
[c]pp. 1–3.
[d]pp. 3–4.
[e]p. 5.
[f]pp. 6–8.
[g]pp. 8–9.
[h]pp. 9–10.
[i]pp. 14–15.
[j]pp. 10–12.
[k]pp. 15–17.
[l]pp. 20–21.

## GUIDE TO ADDITIONAL READING

### PRIMARY SOURCES

Moore, G. E., *Ethics*, Home University Library, New York, Henry Holt, 1912.

_____, *Philosophical Studies*, New York, Harcourt, Brace, 1922, Chs. 8–10.

_____, Joseph, H. W. B., and Taylor, A. E., "Is Goodness a Quality?" *Aristotelian Society*, Supplementary vol. 2, 1932.

**DISCUSSION AND COMMENTARY**

Frankena, W. K., "The Naturalistic Fallacy," *Mind*, 48 (October 1939), pp. 464–467.

Hudson, W., *A Century of Moral Philosophy*, New York, St. Martin's Press, 1980.

Levy, P., *Moore*, New York, Holt, Rinehart, 1979.

Schilpp, P. A. (ed.), *The Philosophy of G. E. Moore*, Evanston and Chicago, Northwestern University, Library of Living Philosophers, 1939.

Starker, S., *Epistemology and Ethics of G. E. Moore, a Critical Evaluation,* Atlantic Highlands, Humanities Press, 1981.

Warnock, M., *Ethics since 1900*, London, Oxford University Press, 1960.

CHAPTER TWENTY

# Prima Facie Duty

W. D. ROSS

SIR WILLIAM DAVID ROSS (1877–1971) was born in Scotland and educated at both Edinburgh University and Balliol College, Oxford. Ross was not only an authority on Aristotle's philosophy but also a splendid example of Aristotle's "ideal man." Beyond Aristotelian scholarship and original contributions to ongoing philosophy, his career included educational leadership at Oxford and roles in public affairs. In short, Ross combined theoretical and practical wisdom. His moral philosophy, found primarily in *The Right and the Good* (1930) and *Foundations of Ethics* (1939), has had lasting influence. He was awarded the Order of the British Empire for his service in the ministry of munitions during World War I, and he was knighted in 1938. During World War II, he performed excellent public service as chairman of three governmental committees. His administrative academic service was also extensive. Ross served as Vice Chancellor of Oriel College, Oxford, for three years and was its provost for eighteen.

The ethical theory of W. D. Ross resembles that of G. E. Moore in important ways. Both theories hold that intrinsic goodness is an indefinable quality of things; moreover, both theories hold that certain statements about objects being intrinsically good are self-evidently true. There is a decisive difference between them, however, concerning the status of our concepts of the obligatory: In Moore's system the meanings of such terms as *right, ought,* and *duty* are linked to maximizing intrinsic goodness; for Ross there is no such linkage. Ross contends that rightness is a distinct, indefinable characteristic of acts, that it is generally independent of whatever good may result from their occurrence, and that certain statements about the acts being morally right are self-evidently true.[1]

In making his case for ethical intuitionism, Ross insists that the distinction between what he terms *prima facie* and *actual* duties makes all the difference. He warns that any ethical theory that neglects drawing this distinction in some effective way is systematically directed toward either too much or too little definiteness in its account of obligation. Such a theory fails to fit the beliefs and actions of ordinary morality, beliefs and actions that seem reasonable despite the persuasive attacks against them by ethical theorists.

Consider: It is self-evidently true that if I make a promise to someone, or if I request and accept assistance from someone, I thereby create a moral claim on myself in that person. I know immediately and without question that I *ought* to keep that promise and that I *ought* to reciprocate in some way. Now Ross terms the kind of act that has the characteristic of generating moral claims as "*prima facie* duty."[2]

As we have just seen, Ross is an intuitionist in his doctrine of *prima facie* duty. But, as it turns out, this doctrine is more an account of the materials from which we must make a selection than it is an account of our actual obligations. In our daily lives, we are more frequently than not confronted with conflicting and competing *prima facie* duties. Furthermore, we do not find it to be self-evidently true that one such duty rather than another necessarily has jurisdiction. I ought, for example, to honor my promise to be home early, but I ought also to stay late and speak encouragingly to a friend in distress. Where does my actual duty lie? Note that we don't deny that there *are* conflicting duties here, but note also that we want fuller knowledge of the context: Is an important purpose being served by my getting home early? How great is my friend's distress? Aren't other *prima facie* duties involved here? Our *prima facie* duties do not arise in a prearranged harmony of ranked priority, nor do they occur singly. Ross contends that we can only bring our imperfect knowledge of a situation to bear in making our decisions, without any guarantee of an objectively correct answer. Our judgments about right action in all but the simplest actual cases are tentative rather than certain. The above-mentioned statement is not intended to deny that, in the abstract, some *prima facie* duties have a greater claim on us than others. As Ross insists in *The Right and the Good*, "a great deal of stringency belongs to the duties of 'perfect obligation'—the duties of keeping our promises, of repairing wrongs we have done, and of returning the equivalent of services we have received" (pp. 41–42).

In the full development of his theory, Ross does deal specifically with the relationship between actual and *prima facie* duty. His answer is what one might expect: The actually right action is the one that "would discharge in the fullest possible

---

[1]Ross was greatly influenced by his teacher H. A. Prichard (1871–1947), who maintained that some types of actions are right by their very nature and that one can apprehend when "something ought to be done" by a simple "act of moral thinking."

[2]Ross remarks, "I should make it plain . . . that I am assuming the correctness of some of our main convictions as to *prima facie* duties, or, more strictly, am claiming that we *know* them to be true. To me it seems as self-evident as anything could be, that to make a promise, for instance, is to create a moral claim on us in someone else. Many readers will perhaps say that they do *not* know this to be true. If so, I certainly cannot prove it to them: I can only ask them to reflect again, in the hope that they will ultimately agree that they know it." *The Right and the Good* (Oxford: Clarendon Press, 1930), pp. 20–21 fn.

measurethe various claims or *prima facie* duties that are involved in the situation."[3] Note, however, that although this answer serves to clarify *what* we seek to realize, it affords little instruction about *how* we are to do so. It remains that the best we can expect from anyone in a moral situation is a morally informed, carefully assessed judgment that is neither certain nor immediate.

Ross is at his most skillful in arguing that some positions about the nature of actual duties involve serious errors. At one extreme he finds infallible conscience theorists who subscribe to the view that we can always have immediate or direct knowledge of our actual duty. At the other, he finds Utilitarians of various sorts who subscribe to the belief that there is only one criterion for determining our actual duty, whatever the circumstances. Ross rejects the position of the former on several related grounds: (1) It fails to take into account the complexity of the concrete situations in which we must act. (2) It fails to face up to the fact that there are honest differences of opinion between people of good faith about what ought to be done in a given context. (3) It simply assumes that there is no problem about selecting one's actual duty from among the variety of moral claims simultaneously incumbent on a person in a particular situation. He rejects the position of the latter on the ground that the single criterion on which an actual obligation is supposed to rest—namely, whatever maximizes good—is both too simple for the diverse circumstances we face and too restricted in its scope.

This insistence that the Utilitarian principle is restricted in its scope is of special importance in understanding his position. To put it positively, Ross thinks that there is, indeed, a *prima facie* duty to be beneficent, but he observes that this *prima facie* duty, no less than others, occurs only in connection with certain concrete situations. Thus there are circumstances in which, just as the Utilitarians insist, beneficence takes precedence over all other considerations. By the same token, however, there are also circumstances in which the general welfare is beside the point, whereas one's honesty or integrity is very much to the point.

Ross's view is a good example of an ethical position that is partly consequentialist and partly anti-consequentialist or deontologist. This can be seen by comparing this selection with the selections from Kant (Ch. 12) and Mill (Ch. 13). According to Ross's view, ethical assessments of an action depend partly on its consequences, and partly on other features of it (such as whether it is a case of telling the truth). In this regard, Ross's view is probably closer to our actual ethical judgments than either pure consequentialist or pure deontologist positions.

---

**1.** Ross is convinced that ethical theories such as Utilitarianism fail to recognize the complex relations involved in circumstances of obligation. Note that he uses the term *prima facie duty* in this analysis to indicate the direction of his own thinking.

When a plain man fulfills a promise because he thinks he ought to do so, it seems clear that he does so with no thought of its total consequences, still less with any opinion that these are likely to be the best possible. He thinks in fact much more of the past than of the future. What makes him think it right to act in a certain

[3]W. D. Ross, *Foundations of Ethics* (Oxford: Clarendon Press, 1939), p. 190.

way is the fact that he has promised to do so—that and, usually, nothing more. That his act will produce the best possible consequences is not his reason for calling it right. What lends color to the theory we are examining, then, is not the actions (which form probably a great majority of our actions) in which some such reflection as "I have promised" is the only reason we give ourselves for thinking a certain action right, but the exceptional cases in which the consequences of fulfilling a promise (for instance) would be so disastrous to others that we judge it right not to do so. It must of course be admitted that such cases exist. If I have promised to meet a friend at a particular time for some trivial purpose, I should certainly think myself justified in breaking my engagement if by doing so I could prevent a serious accident or bring relief to the victims of one. And the supporters of the view we are examining hold that my thinking so is due to my thinking that I shall bring more good into existence by the one action than by the other. A different account may, however, be given of the matter, an account which will, I believe, show itself to be the true one. It may be said that besides the duty of fulfilling promises I have and recognize a duty of relieving distress, and that when I think it right to do the latter at the cost of not doing the former, it is not because I think I shall produce more good thereby but because I think it the duty which is in the circumstances more of a duty. This account surely corresponds much more closely with what we really think in such a situation. If, so far as I can see, I could bring equal amounts of good into being by fulfilling my promise and by helping someone to whom I had made no promise, I should not hesitate to regard the former as my duty. Yet on the view that what is right is right because it is productive of the most good I should not so regard it. . . .

In fact the theory of "ideal utilitarianism" . . . seems to simplify unduly our relations to our fellows. It says, in effect, that the only morally significant relation in which my neighbors stand to me is that of being possible beneficiaries by my action. They do stand in this relation to me, and this relation is morally significant. But they may also stand to me in the relation of promisee to promiser, of creditor to debtor, of wife to husband, of child to parent, of friend to friend, of fellow countryman to fellow countryman, and the like; and each of these relations is the foundation of a *prima facie* duty, which is more or less incumbent on me according to the circumstances of the case. When I am in a situation, as perhaps I always am, in which more than one of these *prima facie* duties is incumbent on me, what I have to do is to study the situation as fully as I can until I form the considered opinion (it is never more) that in the circumstances one of them is more incumbent than any other; then I am bound to think that to do this *prima facie* duty is my duty *sans phrase* in the situation.[a]

**2.** Ross now defines and clarifies his basic concept *prima facie duty.* His clarification includes a catalogue of the many types of duty. (He does not claim that his list is exhaustive.)

I suggest "*prima facie* duty" or "conditional duty" as a brief way of referring to the characteristic (quite distinct from that of being a duty proper) which an act has, in virtue of being of a certain kind (e.g., the keeping of a promise), of being an act which would be a duty proper if it were not at the same time of another kind which is morally significant. Whether an act is a duty proper or actual duty depends on *all* the morally significant kinds it is an instance of. . . .

There is nothing arbitrary about these *prima facie* duties. Each rests on a definite circumstance which cannot seriously be held to be without moral significance. Of *prima facie* duties I suggest, without claiming completeness or finality for it, the following division.

(1) Some duties rest on previous acts of my own. These duties seem to include two kinds, (a) those resting on a promise or what may fairly be called an implicit promise, such as the implicit undertaking not to tell lies which seems to be implied in the act of entering into conversation (at any rate by civilized men), or of writing books that purport to be history and not fiction.

These may be called the duties of fidelity. (b) Those resting on a previous wrongful act. These may be called the duties of reparation. (2) Some rest on previous acts of other men, i.e., services done by them to me. These may be loosely described as the duties of gratitude. (3) Some rest on the fact or possibility of a distribution of pleasure or happiness (or of the means thereto) which is not in accordance with the merit of the persons concerned; in such cases there arises a duty to upset or prevent such a distribution. These are the duties of justice. (4) Some rest on the mere fact that there are other beings in the world whose condition we can make better in respect of virtue, or of intelligence, or of pleasure. These are the duties of beneficence. (5) Some rest on the fact that we can improve our own condition in respect of virtue or of intelligence. These are the duties of self-improvement. (6) I think that we should distinguish from (4) the duties that may be summed up under the title of "not injuring others." No doubt to injure others is incidentally to fail to do them good; but it seems to me clear that nonmaleficence is apprehended as a duty distinct from that of beneficence, and as a duty of a more stringent character. It will be noticed that this alone among the types of duty has been stated in a negative way. An attempt might no doubt be made to state this duty, like the others, in a positive way. It might be said that it is really the duty to prevent ourselves from acting either from an inclination to harm others or from an inclination to seek our own pleasure, in doing which we should incidentally harm them. But on reflection it seems clear that the primary duty here is the duty not to harm others, this being a duty whether or not we have an inclination that if followed would lead to our harming them; and that when we have such an inclination the primary duty not to harm others gives rise to a consequential duty to resist the inclination. The recognition of this duty of nonmaleficence is the first step on the way to the recognition of the duty of beneficence; and that accounts for the prominence of the commands, "thou shalt not kill," "thou shalt not commit adultery," "thou shalt not steal," "thou shalt not bear false witness," in so early a code as the Decalogue. But even when we have come to recognize the duty of beneficence, it appears to me that the duty of nonmaleficence is recognized as a distinct one, as *prima facie* more binding. We should not in general consider it justifiable to kill one person in order to keep another alive, or to steal from one in order to give alms to another.

The essential defect of the "ideal utilitarian" theory is that it ignores, or at least does not do full justice to, the highly personal character of duty. If the only duty is to produce the maximum of good, the question who is to have the good—whether it is myself, or my benefactor, or a person to whom I have made a promise to confer that good on him, or a mere fellow man to whom I stand in no such special relation—should make no difference to my having a duty to produce that good. But we are in fact sure that it makes a vast difference.[b]

**3.** After arguing that it is a mistake to regard every dutiful act as being so for one and the same reason, Ross then turns to the distinction between *prima facie duty* and actual or absolute duty.

I would contend that in principle there is no reason to anticipate that every act that is our duty is so for one and the same reason. Why should two sets of circumstances, or one set of circumstances, *not* possess different characteristics, any one of which makes a certain act our *prima facie* duty? When I ask what it is that makes me in certain cases sure that I have a *prima facie* duty to do so and so, I find that it lies in the fact that I have made a promise; when I ask the same question in another case, I find the answer lies in the fact that I have done a wrong. And if on reflection I find (as I think I do) that neither of these reasons is reducible to the other, I must not on any *a priori* ground assume that such a reduction is possible.

It is necessary to say something by way of clearing up the relation between *prima facie* duties and the actual or absolute duty to do one particular act in particular circumstances. If as almost all moralists except Kant are agreed, and as most plain men think, it is sometimes right to tell a lie or to break a promise, it must be maintained that there is a difference between *prima facie* duty and actual or absolute duty. When we think ourselves justified in breaking, and indeed morally obligated to break, a promise in order to relieve someone's distress, we do not for a moment cease to recognize a *prima facie* duty to keep our promise, and this leads us to feel, not indeed shame or repentance, but certainly compunction, for behaving as we do; we recognize, further, that it is our duty to make up somehow to the promisee for the breaking of the promise. We have to distinguish from the characteristic of being our duty that of tending to be our duty. Any act that we do contains various elements in virtue of which it falls under various categories. In virtue of being the breaking of a promise, for instance, it tends to be wrong; in virtue of being an instance of relieving distress it tends to be right. Tendency to be one's duty may be called a parti-resultant attribute, i.e., one which belongs to an act in virtue of some one component in its nature. *Being* one's duty is a toti-resultant attribute, one which belongs to an act in virtue of its whole nature and of nothing less than this.[c]

**4.** Ross's ethical intuitionism is exhibited in connection with his doctrine of *prima facie duty:* A proposition such as "keeping promises is right" is self-evidently true.

Something should be said of the relation between our apprehension of the *prima facie* rightness of certain types of act and our mental attitude towards particular acts. It is proper to use the word "apprehension" in the former case and not in the latter. That an act, *qua* fulfilling a promise, or *qua* effecting a just distribution of good, or *qua* returning services rendered, or *qua* promoting the good of others, or *qua* promoting the virtue or insight of the agent, is *prima facie* right, is self-evident; not in the sense that it is evident from the beginning of our lives, or as soon as we attend to the proposition for the first time, but in the sense that when we have reached sufficient mental maturity and have given sufficient attention to the proposition it is evident without any need of proof, or of evidence beyond itself. It is self-evident just as a mathematical axiom, or the validity of a form of inference, is evident. The moral order expressed in these propositions is just as much part of the fundamental nature of the universe (and, we may add, of any possible universe in which there were moral agents at all) as is the spatial or numerical structure expressed in the axioms of geometry or arithmetic. In our confidence that these propositions are true there is involved the same trust in our reason that is involved in our confidence in mathematics; and we should have no justification for trusting it in the latter sphere and distrusting it in the former. In both cases we are dealing with propositions that cannot be proved, but that just as certainly need no proof.[d]

**5.** Ross is *not* an intuitionist concerning our actual duties.

Our judgments about our actual duty in concrete situations have none of the certainty that attaches to our recognition of the general principles of duty. A statement is certain, i.e., is an expression of knowledge, only in one or other of two cases: when it is either self-evident, or a valid conclusion from self-evident premises. And our judgments about our particular duties have neither of these characters (1) They are not self-evident. Where a possible act is seen to have two characteristics, in virtue of one of which it is *prima facie* right, and in virtue of the other *prima facie* wrong, we are (I think) well aware that we are not certain whether we ought or ought not to do it; that whether we do it or not, we are taking a moral risk. We come in the long run, after consideration, to think one duty more pressing than the other, but we do not feel certain that it is so. And though we do not always recognize that a possible act has two such characteristics, and though there *may* be cases in which it has not, we are never certain that any particular possible act has not, and therefore never certain that it is right, nor certain that it is wrong. For, to go no further in the analysis, it is enough to point out that any particular act will in all probability in the course of time contribute to the bringing about of good or of evil for many human beings, and thus have a *prima facie* rightness or wrongness of which we know nothing. (2) Again, our judgments about our particular duties are not logical conclusions from self-evident premises. The only possible premises would be the general principles stating their *prima facie* rightness or wrongness *qua* having the different characteristics they do have; and even if we could (as we cannot) apprehend the extent to which an act will tend on the one hand, for example, to bring about advantages for our benefactors and on the other hand to bring about disadvantages for fellow men who are not our benefactors, there is no principle by which we can draw the conclusion that is on the whole right or on the whole wrong. In this respect the judgment as to the rightness of a particular act is just like the judgment as to the beauty of a particular natural object or work of art. A poem is, for instance, in respect of certain qualities beautiful and in respect of certain others not beautiful; and our judgment as to the degree of beauty it possesses on the whole is never reached by logical reasoning from the apprehension of its particular beauties or particular defects. Both in this and in the moral case we have more or less probable opinions which are not logically justified conclusions from the general principles that are recognized as self-evident.[c]

**6.** The most distinctive contribution Ross made to ethical theory is found in his answer to the following question: Can one conclude from the fact that our *prima facie* duties are self-evidently true that our actual duties are also self-evidently true? He answers in the negative. Ross insists that whereas the properties, for example, of a given mathematical object such as a triangle are consistent with one another, the properties of a moral act are not necessarily or usually consistent.

The general principles of duty are obviously not self-evident from the beginning of our lives. How do they come to be so? The answer is, that they come to be self-evident to us just as mathematical axioms do. We find by experience that this couple of matches and that couple makes four matches, that this couple of balls on a wire and that couple make four balls; and by reflection on these and similar discoveries we come to see that it is of the nature of two and two to make four. In a precisely similar way, we see the *prima facie* rightness of an act which would be the fulfillment of a particular promise, and of another which would be the fulfillment of another promise, and when we have reached sufficient maturity to think in general terms, we apprehend *prima facie* rightness to belong to the nature of any fulfillment of promise. What comes first in time is the apprehension of the self-evident *prima facie* rightness of an individual act of a particular type. From this we come by reflection to apprehend the self-evident general principle of *prima facie* duty. From this, too, perhaps along with the apprehension of the self-evident *prima facie* rightness of the same act in virtue of its having another characteristic as well, and perhaps in spite of the apprehension of its *prima facie* wrongness in virtue of its having some third characteristic, we come to believe something not self-evident at all, but an object of probable opinion, viz., that this particular act is (not *prima facie* but) actually right.

In this respect there is an important difference between rightness and mathematical properties. A triangle which is isosceles necessarily has two of its angles equal, whatever other characteristics the triangle may have—whatever, for instance, be its area, or the size of its third angle. The equality of the two angles is a parti-resultant attribute. And the same is true of all mathematical attributes. It is true, I may add, of *prima facie* rightness. But no act is ever, in virtue of falling under some general description, not necessarily actually right; its rightness depends on its whole nature and not on any element in it. The reason is that no mathematical object (no figure, for instance, or angle) ever has two characteristics that tend to give it opposite resultant characteristics, while moral acts often (as everyone knows) and indeed always (as on reflection we must admit) have different characteristics that tend to make them at the same time *prima facie* right and *prima facie* wrong; there is probably no act, for instance, which does good to anyone without doing harm to someone else, and vice versa.[f]

**7.** Ross is confident that no reflective person regards the terms *duty* and *right* as synonymous with "productive of the best possible consequences." Moreover, he argues that we do not apprehend in *a priori* fashion or on an empirical basis an invariant relationship between what is dutiful (*prima facie* or actual) and what is productive of the best consequences.

Supposing it to be agreed, as I think on reflection it must, that no one *means* by "right" just "productive of the best possible consequences," or "optimific," the attributes "right" and "optimific" might stand in either of two kinds of relation to each other. (1) They might be so related that we could apprehend *a priori,* either immediately or deductively, that any act that is optimific is right and any act that is right is optimific, as we can apprehend that any triangle that is equilateral is equiangular and vice versa. Professor [G. E.] Moore's view is, I think, that the coextensiveness of "right" and "optimific" is apprehended immediately. He rejects the possibility of any proof of it. Or (2) the two attributes might be such that the question whether they are invariably connected had to be answered by means of an inductive inquiry. Now at first sight it might seem as if the constant connection of the two attributes could be immediately apprehended. It might seem absurd to suggest that it could be right for anyone to do an act which would produce consequences less good than those which would be produced by some other act in his power. Yet a little thought will convince us that this is not absurd. The type of case in which it is easiest to see that this is so is, perhaps, that in which one has made a promise. In such a case we all think that *prima facie* it is our duty to fulfill the promise irrespective of the precise goodness of the total consequences. And though we do not think it is necessarily our actual or absolute duty to do so, we are far from thinking that any, even the slightest, gain in the value of the total consequences will necessarily justify us in doing something else instead. Suppose, to simplify the case by abstraction, that the fulfillment of a promise to A would produce 1,000 units of good for him, but that by doing some other act I could produce 1,001 units of good for B, to whom I have made no promise, the other consequences of the two acts being of equal value; should we really think it self-evident that it was our duty to do the second act and not the first? I think not. We should, I fancy, hold that only a much greater disparity of value between the total consequences would justify us in failing to discharge our *prima facie* duty to A. After all, a promise is a promise, and is not to be treated so lightly as the theory we are examining would imply. What, exactly, a promise is, is not so easy to determine, but we are surely agreed that it constitutes a serious moral limitation to our freedom of action. To produce the 1,001 units of good for B rather than fulfill our promise to A would be to take, not perhaps our duty as philanthropists too seriously, but certainly our duty as makers of promises too lightly.[g]

**8.** Ross continues his attack on the foregoing views, paying special attention to the inductive basis. He concludes that considerations about duty are generally independent of our calculations regarding the best possible consequences.

The coextensiveness of the right and the optimific is, then, not self-evident. And I can see no way of proving it deductively; nor, so far as I know, has anyone tried to do so. There remains the question whether it can be established inductively. Such an inquiry, to be conclusive, would have to be very thorough and extensive. We should have to take a large variety of the acts which we, to the best of our ability, judge to be right. We should have to trace as far as possible their consequences, not only for the persons directly affected but also for those indirectly affected, and to these no limit can be set. To make our inquiry thoroughly conclusive, we should have to do what we cannot do, viz., trace these consequences into an unending future. And even to make it reasonably conclusive, we should have to trace them far into the future. It is clear that the most we could possibly say is that a large variety of typical acts that are judged right appear, so far as we can trace their consequences, to produce more good than any other acts possible to the agents in the circumstances. And such a result falls far short of proving the constant connection of the two attributes. But it is surely clear that no inductive inquiry justifying even this result has ever been carried through. The advocates of utilitarian systems have been so much persuaded either of the identity or of the self-evident connection of the attributes "right" and "optimific" (or "felicific") that they have not attempted even such an inductive inquiry as is possible. And in view of the enormous complexity of the task and the inevitable inconclusiveness of the result, it is worth no one's while to make the attempt. What, after all, would be gained by it? If, as I have tried to show, for an act to be right and to be optimific are not the same thing, and an act's being optimific is not even the ground of its being right, then if we could ask ourselves (though the question is really unmeaning) which we ought to do, right acts because they are right or optimific acts because they are optimific, our answer must be "the former." If they are optimific as well as right, that is interesting but not morally important; if not, we still ought to do them (which is only another way of saying that they are right acts), and the question whether they are optimific has no importance for moral theory.[h]

> **9.** In offering an ultimate defense of his theory that our obligations do not reduce to a mere production of good consequences, Ross employs a telling example.

There is one direction in which a fairly serious attempt has been made to show the connection of the attributes "right" and "optimific." One of the most evident facts of our moral consciousness is the sense which we have of the sanctity of promises, a sense which does not, on the face of it, involve the thought that one will be bringing more good into existence by fulfilling the promise than by breaking it. It is plain, I think, that in our normal thought we consider that the fact that we have made a promise is in itself sufficient to create a duty of keeping it, the sense of duty resting on remembrance of the past promise and not on thoughts of the future consequences of its fulfillment. Utilitarianism tries to show that this is not so, that the sanctity of promises rests on the good consequences of the fulfillment of them and the bad consequences of their nonfulfillment. It does so in this way: it points out that when you break a promise you not only fail to confer a certain advantage on your promisee but you diminish his confidence, and indirectly the confidence of others, in the fulfillment of promises. . . . It may be suspected . . . that the effect of a single keeping or breaking of a promise in strengthening or weakening the fabric of mutual confidence is greatly exaggerated by the theory we are examining. And if we suppose two men dying together alone, do we think that the duty of one to fulfill before he dies a promise he has made to the other would be extinguished by the fact that neither act would have any effect on the general confidence? Anyone who holds this may be suspected of not having reflected on what a promise is.

I conclude that the attributes "right" and "optimific" are not identical, and that we do not know either by intuition, by deduction, or by induction that they coincide in their application, still less that the latter is the foundation of the former. It must be added, however, that if we are ever under no special obligation such as that of fidelity to a promisee or of gratitude to a benefactor, we ought to do what will produce most good; and that even when we are under a special obligation the tendency of acts to promote general good is one of the main factors in determining whether they are right.[i]

## QUESTIONS

1. What does Ross mean by "*prima facie* duty"?
2. How does Ross, an intuitionist, account for the fact that two people of moral character can disagree about what is actually right in a given situation?
3. How receptive would he be to the Kantian conception of the categorical imperative?
4. Wherein do Ross and Moore agree and wherein do they differ concerning their ethical intuitionism? How important is their disagreement?
5. Give an example that tends to support Ross in his criticism of Utilitarianism. Explain.
6. How would Ross argue against those who claim that one's actual duty in any situation depends entirely on how one feels about it?
7. Do you think that Ross's theory comes close to capturing the moral convictions of the average person? Discuss.
8. Is it self-evidently true that when I make a promise, all things being equal, I ought to keep it? Or is it merely a matter of one's cultural background?
9. Do you agree with Ross's contention that it is false to subsume all duties under the duty of beneficence?
10. In a situation in which there are several claims incumbent on us simultaneously, is Ross's account capable of determining which course of action is right? Does each *prima facie* duty impose as great a claim on us as any other?

## KEY TO SELECTIONS

W. D. Ross, *The Right and the Good*, New York, Oxford University Press, 1930. Reprinted by permission of the publisher.

[a]pp. 17–19.
[b]pp. 19–22.
[c]pp. 24–28.
[d]pp. 29–30.
[e]pp. 30–31.
[f]pp. 32–34.
[g]p. 34.
[h]pp. 36–37.
[i]pp. 37–39.

## GUIDE TO ADDITIONAL READING


### PRIMARY SOURCES

Ross, W. D., *Foundations of Ethics,* Oxford, Clarendon Press, 1939.

_____, *Kant's Ethical Theory,* Oxford, Clarendon Press, 1934.

### DISCUSSION AND COMMENTARY

Blanshard, B., *Reason and Goodness,* London, G. Allen, 1961, Ch. 6.

Dancy, J., "An Ethics of Prima Facie Duties," in *A Companion to Ethics,* ed. P. Singer, Cambridge, Blackwell, 1993, pp. 219–229.

Johnson, A. O., *Rightness and Goodness,* The Hague, Martinus Nijhoff, 1959.

McCloskey, H. J., "Ross and the Concept of Prima Facie Duty," *Australasian Journal of Philosophy,* 41 (1964), pp. 336–345.

Nagel, T., "War and Massacre," in *Mortal Questions,* Cambridge, Cambridge University Press, 1949, pp. 53–74.

Searle, J., "Prima-Facie Obligations," from *Philosophical Subjects,* Oxford, Clarendon Press, 1980, pp. 238–259.

Strawson, P. F., "Ethical Intuitionism," *Philosophy,* 24 (1949), pp. 23–33.

Wheeler, A., "Prima Facie and Actual Duty," *Analysis,* March 1977, pp. 142–144.

CHAPTER TWENTY-ONE

# Ethics as Emotive Expression

Jane Bown/Camera Press/Retna Ltd., NYC

A. J. AYER

Courtesy of Mrs. Nora Stevenson

C. L. STEVENSON

ALFRED J. AYER (1910–1989), Professor of Mind and Logic at the University of London, was a scholar at Eton College and Christ Church, Oxford. He lectured at Christ Church from 1932 to 1935 and from 1935 to 1944 was a research scholar there, receiving his M.A. degree in 1936. Professor Ayer was a Fellow of Wadham College, Oxford, from 1944 to 1946, and was Dean of Wadham during 1945–1946. During World War II, he served in the Welsh Guards and performed intelligence duties. Also, in 1945, he was an attaché to the British Embassy in Paris. His appointment as Grote Professor of Philosophy at the University of London came in 1946; the academic year 1948–1949 Ayer spent as a visiting professor at New York University. One of the clearest expositors of logical positivism, Ayer wrote, besides a number of articles, *Language, Truth and Logic* (1936, revised in 1946), *The Foundations of Empirical Knowledge* (1940), *Logical Positivism* (1959), and *The Origins of Pragmatism* (1968).

Professor Charles L. Stevenson (1908–1979), of the Department of Philosophy of the University of Michigan, received his A.B. degree from Yale University in 1930, his B.A. degree from Cambridge University in 1933, and his Ph.D. degree from Harvard in 1935. From 1934 to 1939, he was at Harvard doing graduate work and teaching, and from 1939 to 1946, he was an assistant professor at Yale; he joined the staff at the University of Michigan in 1946. During the academic year 1945–1946, Professor Stevenson was a Guggenheim Memorial Foundation Fellow. His chief work in ethics, *Ethics and Language*, was published in 1944, and he wrote a number of articles for British and American journals.

The ethical theories of Ayer and Stevenson are understandable only in terms of the narrowed role that philosophy plays for the logical positivists.[1] Looking upon the methods of science and mathematics as the only means by which reliable knowledge can be obtained, they assign to philosophy a subordinate position among the theoretical disciplines. Once esteemed as the "queen of the sciences," philosophy becomes in their view, the "handmaiden of the sciences." It is defined as *logical* or *linguistic analysis*, and its primary function is clarification of the meanings of scientific statements.

Viewed as analysis, philosophy deals with the language used in speaking about actual objects, not with the objects themselves; it operates on the level of language rather than experience. Philosophers have frequently speculated about reality and have made judgments about it that they put forward as factually true. Admittedly, some of these judgments have been found to be true (for example, Democritus' theory, later restated by Newton as the first law of motion, that the motion of a body will persist unless opposed). However, many of them turn out to be false (such as Aristotle's theory that the heavenly bodies are unchanging and indestructible). But the point is that the decision as to which judgments were in keeping with fact and which were false was reached only when the method of science was brought to bear on them. Philosophical speculation, the positivists have concluded, is a vain way to discover facts. However, philosophers have made valuable contributions through their analyses of scientific concepts, judgments, and language. The positivists therefore propose that philosophers leave the discovery of facts to the scientists and devote themselves exclusively to the analysis and improvement of the language used to communicate facts.

In their analysis of language, the positivists maintain that only two kinds of sentences are meaningful and therefore genuine: *empirical* or *synthetic* statements[2] and *analytic* statements. An empirical statement, such as "Some metals expand when heated," is one that can be confirmed to a high degree of probability by *observation and experiment*. An analytic statement, such as "All spinsters are unmarried," and "All circles are squares," is one that can be established as true or false by an examination of the *definitions* of its terms. Utterances that are neither empirical nor analytic are termed "literal nonsense"—that is, even though they may seem to, they do

[1]As a philosophical movement, logical positivism received its initial impetus form the work of Moritz Schlick (1882–1936), Rudolf Carnap (1891–1970), and other members of the "Vienna Circle" in the early 1920s.

[2]Not all philosophers use the terms *synthetic* and *empirical* interchangeably in their classification of statements.

not really assert or deny any confirmable fact, nor are they true or false by definition. They are therefore relegated to the status of pseudostatements or "metaphysical" sentences. Expressions like "Everything has a purpose in the natural order" and "Disease is caused by the presence of evil spirits in the body" are typical of this class of expression. Although the logical positivists maintain that pseudostatements have no literal or logical meaning, they believe that some of them possess *emotive meaning*—that is, they express or evoke feelings.

The distinction between meaningful and literally nonsensical sentences—between genuine statements and pseudostatements—is brought to bear on ethics. Statements that are *descriptive* of moral behavior—those which have literal meaning—are regarded as belonging to the social sciences, even though traditional ethical theorists include them in their theories. Normative sentences—those that say what "ought" to be done—are the special province of ethics. However, being neither confirmable by experience nor true by definition, they must be looked on as literally meaningless expressions; if they have *any* meaning, as they seem to have, it must be an *emotive* meaning.[3]

The positivists are agreed that ethics, because it is normative, cannot be a science. In its extreme form, the positivistic position excludes ethics from the realm of systematic inquiry on the grounds that it has no factual content. A. J. Ayer, however, takes the stand that the ethical theorist has a legitimate function—namely, *the logical analysis of ethical (normative) terms*, such as *good* and *evil*, *right* and *wrong*, as they are actually used in ethical discourse. Through his examination of the symbols of ethical language and their logical relations, he substantiates the positivistic contention that normative terms are different in kind from descriptive terms, because they do not have referents. Ayer concludes that ethical theorists' tasks are completed when they have shown that normative sentences are purely emotive and therefore merely pseudostatements.

The conception of ethics developed by C. L. Stevenson—one that in recent years has gained popularity with many of the positivists—extends the boundaries of the legitimate limits of ethical inquiry. He argues that Ayer, like the extreme positivists who deny that ethics has any place as an intellectual enterprise, fails to take sufficient account of the significant role played by emotive meaning in human behavior. Even though emotive expressions do not themselves convey knowledge, they have great importance in the ethical decisions people must make and should not be ignored:

> It is certainly mandatory that the term "emotive". . . be kept as a tool for use in careful study, not as a device for relegating the nondescriptive aspects of language to limbo.[4]

Consequently, Stevenson carries his analysis beyond ethical statements to include ethical situations, and, in particular, ethical disagreements.

---

[3]Although there is general agreement among the logical positivists that ethical sentences are emotive, different interpretations have arisen regarding the type of emotive meaning involved. For example, the sentence "Cheating is wrong" may be taken to mean: (1) "Don't cheat!" (Imperative); (2) "I wish you wouldn't cheat." (optative); (3) "Cheating!!!" in a tone of disgust (exclamatory); and (4) "I disapprove of cheating—you should disapprove as well!!" (persuasive).

[4]C. L. Stevenson, *Ethics and Language* (New Haven: Yale University Press , 1944), p. 79.

**1.** Ayer develops his position from the assumption that a *strictly philosophical treatment of ethics can be concerned only with definitions of ethical terms.* It cannot deal with moral exhortations, descriptions of moral experiences, or actual value judgments, in the manner of traditional ethical systems. Moreover, the inclusion of pseudostatements in an ethical theory obscures its logical structure, creating needless discussion and controversy.

The ordinary system of ethics, as elaborated in the works of ethical philosophers, is very far from being a homogeneous whole. Not only is it apt to contain pieces of metaphysics, and analyses of nonethical concepts: its actual ethical contents are themselves of very different kinds. We may divide them, indeed, into four main classes. There are, first of all, propositions which express definitions of ethical terms, or judgments about the legitimacy or possibility of certain definitions. Secondly, there are propositions describing the phenomena of moral experience, and their causes. Thirdly, there are exhortations to moral virtue. And, lastly, there are actual ethical judgments. It is unfortunately the case that the distinction between these four classes, plain as it is, is commonly ignored by ethical philosophers; with the result that it is often very difficult to tell from their works what it is that they are seeking to discover or prove.

In fact, it is easy to see that only the first of our four classes, namely that which comprises the propositions relating to the definitions of ethical terms, can be said to constitute ethical philosophy. The propositions which describe the phenomena of moral experience, and their causes, must be assigned to the science of psychology, or sociology. The exhortations to moral virtue are not propositions at all, but ejaculations or commands which are designed to provoke the reader to action of a certain sort. Accordingly, they do not belong to any branch of philosophy or science. As for the expressions of ethical judgments, we have not yet determined how they should be classified. But inasmuch as they are certainly neither definitions nor comments upon definitions, nor quotations, we may say decisively that they do not belong to ethical philosophy. A strictly philosophical treatise on ethics should therefore make no ethical pronouncements. But it should, by giving an analysis of ethical terms, show what is the category to which all such pronouncements belong. And this is what we are now about to do.

A question which is often discussed by ethical philosophers is whether it is possible to find definitions which would reduce all ethical terms to one or two fundamental terms. But this question, though it undeniably belongs to ethical philosophy, is not relevant to our present enquiry. We are not now concerned to discover which term, within the sphere of ethical terms, is to be taken as fundamental; whether, for example, "good" can be defined in terms of "right" or "right" in terms of "good," or both in terms of "value." What we are interested in is the possibility of reducing the whole sphere of ethical terms to nonethical terms. We are enquiring whether statements of ethical value can be translated into statements of empirical fact.[a]

**2.** Ayer is critical of subjectivists and Utilitarians, who define value expressions in terms of such psychological states as "feelings of approval" or "pleasure." Although they can thus convert ethical statements into factual ones, Ayer points out that their definitions of ethical terms do not follow normal linguistic usage. For example, the subjectivist may define "good" as "what is approved." However, our language permits us to say without contradiction, "This act at the same time is really bad but is nevertheless approved." The subjectivist is led to the linguistic absurdity of regarding such a statement as self-contradictory.

That [statements of ethical value can be translated into statements of empirical fact] is the contention of those ethical philosophers who are commonly called subjectivists, and of those who are known as utilitarians. For the utilitarian defines the rightness of actions, and the goodness of ends, in terms of the pleasure, or happiness, or satisfaction, to which they give rise; the subjectivist, in terms of the feelings of approval which a certain person, or group of people, has towards them. Each of these types of definition makes moral judgments into a subclass of psychological or sociological judgments; and for this reason they are very attractive to us. For, if either was correct, it would follow that ethical assertions were not generically different from the factual assertions which are ordinarily contrasted with them. . . .

Nevertheless we shall not adopt either a subjectivist or a utilitarian analysis of ethical terms. We reject the subjectivist view that to call an action right, or a thing good, is to say that it is generally approved of, because it is not self-contradictory to assert that some actions which are generally approved of are not right, or that some things which are generally approved of are not good. And we reject the alternative subjectivist view that a man who asserts that a certain action is right, or that a certain thing is good, is saying that he himself approves of it, on the ground that a man who confessed that he sometimes approved of what was bad or wrong not be contradicting himself. And a similar argument is fatal to utilitarianism. We cannot agree that to call an action right is to say that of all the actions possible in the circumstances it would cause, or be likely to cause, the greatest happiness, or the greatest balance of pleasure over pain, or the greatest balance of satisfied over unsatisfied desire, because we find that it is not self-contradictory to say that it is sometimes wrong to perform the action which would actually or probably cause the greatest happiness, or the greatest balance of pleasure over pain, or of satisfied over unsatisfied desire. And since it is not self-contradictory to say that some pleasant things are not good, or that some bad things are desired, it cannot be the case that the sentence "*x* is good" is equivalent to "*x* is pleasant," or to "*x* is desired." And to every other variant of utilitarianism with which I am acquainted the same objection can be made. And therefore we should, I think, conclude that the validity of ethical judgments is not determined by the felicific tendencies of actions, any more than by the nature of people's feelings; but that it must be regarded as "absolute" or "intrinsic," and not empirically calculable.

If we say this, we are not, of course, denying that it is possible to invent a language in which all ethical symbols are definable in nonethical terms, or even that it is desirable to invent such a language and adopt it in place of our own; what we are denying is that the suggested reduction of ethical to nonethical statements is consistent with the conventions of our actual language. That is, we reject utilitarianism and subjectivism, not as proposals to replace our existing ethical notions by new ones, but as analyses of our existing ethical notions. Our contention is simply that, in our language, sentences which contain normative ethical symbols are not equivalent to sentences which express psychological propositions, or indeed empirical propositions of any kind.[b]

**3.** Having denied that value sentences can be translated into factual statements, Ayer turns his attention to the analysis of normative sentences. He points out that certain terms or symbols may be used either normatively or descriptively. For example, in the sentence "*x* (killing, stealing, and so on) is wrong," the term *wrong* is used descriptively if it refers to an actual attitude found in a particular society. On the other hand, "*x* is wrong" is a normative expression when the term *wrong* is intended to express a value judgment about some type of behavior. Because the same words may be employed in the formation of a normative or a descriptive sentence, it is necessary to exercise caution and single out the normative symbols with which this analysis is concerned.

It is advisable here to make it plain that it is only normative ethical symbols, and not descriptive ethical symbols, that are held by us to be indefinable in factual terms. There is a danger of confusing these two types of symbols, because they are commonly constituted by signs of the same sensible form. Thus a complex sign of the form "*x* is wrong" may constitute a sentence which expresses a moral judgment concerning a certain type of conduct, or it may constitute a sentence which states that a certain type of conduct is repugnant to the moral sense of a particular society. In the latter case, the symbol "wrong" is a descriptive ethical symbol, and the sentence in which it occurs expresses an ordinary sociological proposition; in the former case, the symbol "wrong" is a normative ethical symbol, and the sentence in which it occurs does not, we maintain, express an empirical proposition at all. It is only with normative ethics that we are at present concerned; so that whenever ethical symbols are used in the course of this argument without qualification, they are always to be interpreted as symbols of the normative type.[c]

**4.** Because normative ethical terms cannot be reduced to factual terms, the absolutist in ethics may claim that ethical expressions can be grasped only by intuition. Because he does not accept intuition as a reliable test of truth or falsity, Ayer finds this position untenable. Having already rejected the subjectivist and Utilitarian views, which claim that value statements are genuinely synthetic—in other words, that they are genuine factual statements—he asks what other possibilities exist.

In admitting that normative ethical concepts are irreducible to empirical concepts, we seem to be leaving the way clear for the "absolutist" view of ethics—that is, the view that statements of value are not controlled by observation, as ordinary empirical propositions are, but only by a mysterious "intellectual intuition." A feature of this theory, which is seldom recognized by its advocates, is that it makes statements of value unverifiable. For it is notorious that what seems intuitively certain to one person may seem doubtful, or even false, to another. So that unless it is possible to provide some criterion by which one may decide between conflicting intuitions, a mere appeal to intuition is worthless as a test of a proposition's validity. But in the case of moral judgments, no such criterion can be given. Some moralists claim to settle the matter by saying that they "know" that their own moral judgments are correct. But such an assertion is of purely psychological interest, and has not the slightest tendency to prove the validity of any moral judgment. For dissentient moralists may equally well "know" that their ethical views are correct. And, as far as subjective certainty goes; there will be nothing to choose between them. When such differences of opinion arise in connection with an ordinary empirical proposition, one may attempt to resolve them by referring to, or actually carrying out, some relevant empirical test. But with regard to ethical statements, there is, on the "absolutist" or "intuitionist" theory, no relevant empirical test. We are therefore justified in saying that on this theory ethical statements are held to be unverifiable. They are, of course, also held to be genuine synthetic propositions.

Considering the use which we have made of the principle that a synthetic proposition is significant only if it is empirically verifiable, it is clear that the acceptance of an "absolutist" theory of ethics would undermine the whole of our main argument. And as we have already rejected the "naturalistic" theories which are commonly supposed to provide the only alternative to "absolutism" in ethics, we seem to have reached a difficult position. We shall meet the difficulty by showing that the correct treatment of ethical statements is afforded by a third theory, which is wholly compatible with our radical empiricism.[d]

**5.** The theory by which Ayer intends to establish the status of normative terms starts with the assumption that basic ethical terms are pseudo-symbols that cannot be analyzed into component parts. Consequently, ethical statements made up of such terms are emotive expressions, not genuine propositions that have factual meaning.

We begin by admitting that the fundamental ethical concepts are unanalyzable, inasmuch as there is no criterion by which one can test the validity of the judgments in which they occur. So far we are in agreement with the absolutists. But, unlike the absolutists, we are able to give an explanation of this fact about ethical concepts. We say that the reason why they are unanalyzable is that they are mere pseudoconcepts. The presence of an ethical symbol in a proposition adds nothing to its factual content. Thus if I say to someone, "You acted wrongly in stealing that money," I am not stating anything more than if I had simply said, "You stole that money," In adding that this action is wrong I am not making any further statement about it. I am simply evincing my moral disapproval of it. It is as if I had said, "You stole that money," in a peculiar tone of horror, or written it with the addition of some special exclamation marks. The tone, or the exclamation marks, adds nothing to the literal meaning of the sentence. It merely serves to show that the expression of it is attended by certain feelings in the speaker.

If now I generalize my previous statement and say, "Stealing money is wrong," I produce a sentence which has no factual meaning—that is, expresses no proposition which can be either true or false. It is as if I had written "Stealing money!!"—where the shape and thickness of the exclamation marks show, by a suitable convention, that a special sort of moral disapproval is the feeling which is being expressed. It is clear that there is nothing said here which can be true or false. Another man may disagree with me about the wrongness of stealing, in the sense that he may not have the same feelings about stealing as I have, and he may quarrel with me on account of my moral sentiments. But he cannot, strictly speaking, contradict me. For in saying that a certain type of action is right or wrong, I am not making any factual statement, not even a statement about my own state of mind. I am merely expressing certain moral sentiments. And the man who is ostensibly contradicting me is merely expressing his moral sentiments. So that there is plainly no sense in asking which of us is in the right. For neither of us is asserting a genuine proposition.[e]

**6.** For the further development of this view, several qualifications are made. First, "expression" is reserved for the "emotive," and "assertion" for the "cognitive" elements of language. Second, ethical terms not only may express feelings but also may evoke feelings in others. Third, the distinction between "expression of feeling" and "assertion of feeling" is employed by Ayer in order to distinguish his position from that of orthodox subjectivism.

What we have just been saying about the symbol "wrong" applies to all normative ethical symbols. Sometimes they occur in sentences which record ordinary empirical facts besides expressing ethical feelings about those facts: sometimes they occur in sentences which simply express ethical feeling about a certain type of action, or situation, without making any statement of fact. But in every case in which one would commonly be said to be making an ethical judgment, the function of the relevant ethical word is purely "emotive." It is used to express feeling about certain objects, but not to make any assertion about them.

It is worth mentioning that ethical terms do not serve only to express feeling. They are calculated also to arouse feeling, and so to stimulate action. Indeed some of them are used in such a way as to give the sentences in which they occur the effect of commands. Thus the sentence "It is your duty to tell the truth" may be regarded both as the expression of a certain sort of ethical feeling about truthfulness and as the expression of the command "Tell the truth." The sentence "You ought to tell the truth" also involves the command "Tell the truth," but here the tone of the command is less emphatic. In the sentence "It is good to tell the truth" the command has become little more than a suggestion. And thus the "meaning" of the word "good," in its ethical usage, is differentiated from that of the word "duty" or the word "ought." In fact we may define the meaning of the various ethical words in terms both of the different feelings they are ordinarily taken to express, and also the different responses which they are calculated to provoke.

We can now see why it is impossible to find a criterion for determining the validity of ethical judgments. It is not because they have an "absolute" validity which is mysteriously independent of ordinary sense-experience, but because they have no objective validity whatsoever. If a sentence makes no statement at all, there is obviously no sense in asking whether what it says is true or false. And we have seen that sentences which simply express moral judgments do not say anything. They are pure expressions of feeling and as such do not come under the category of truth and falsehood. They are unverifiable for the same reason as a cry of pain or a word of command is unverifiable—because they do not express genuine propositions.

Thus, although our theory of ethics might fairly be said to be radically subjectivist, it differs in a very important respect from the orthodox subjectivist theory. For the orthodox subjectivist does not deny, as we do, that the sentences of a moralizer express genuine propositions. All he denies is that they express propositions of a unique nonempirical character. His own view is that they express propositions about the speaker's feelings. If this were so, ethical judgments clearly would be capable of being true or false. They would be true if the speaker had the relevant feelings, and false if he had not. And this is a matter which is, in principle, empirically verifiable. Furthermore they could be significantly contradicted. For if I say, "Tolerance is a virtue," and someone answers, "You don't approve of it," he would, on the ordinary subjectivist theory, be contradicting me. On our theory, he would not be contradicting me, because, in saying that tolerance was a virtue, I should not be making any statement about my own feelings or about anything else. I should simply be evincing my feelings, which is not at all the same thing as saying that I have them.[f]

> **7.** Once the distinction between expressing and having an emotion is recognized, Ayer argues, it becomes apparent that a genuine dispute in ethics has to be on a factual level. This is so because value sentences, being expressions of feelings, cannot be true or false: One person's emotions cannot contradict another person's emotions.

The distinction between the expression of feeling and the assertion of feeling is complicated by the fact that the assertion that one has a certain feeling often accompanies the expression of that feeling, and is then, indeed, a factor in the expression of that feeling. Thus I may simultaneously express boredom and say that I am bored, and in that case my utterance of the words, "I am bored," is one of the circumstances which make it true to say that I am expressing or evincing boredom. But I can express boredom without actually saying that I am bored. I can express it by my tone and gestures, while making a statement about something wholly unconnected with it, or by an ejaculation, or without uttering any words at all. So that even if the assertion that one has a certain feeling always involves the expression of that feeling, the expression of a feeling assuredly does not always involve the assertion that one has it. And this is the important point to grasp in considering the distinction between our theory and the ordinary subjectivist theory. For whereas the subjectivist holds that ethical statements actually assert the existence of certain feelings, we hold that ethical statements are expressions and excitants of feeling which do not necessarily involve any assertions.

We have already remarked that the main objection to the ordinary subjectivist theory is that the validity of ethical judgments is not determined by . . . their author's feelings. And this is an objection which our theory escapes. For it does not imply that the existence of any feelings is a necessary and sufficient condition of the validity of an ethical judgment. It implies, on the contrary, that ethical judgments have no validity.

There is, however, a celebrated argument against subjectivist theories which our theory does not escape. It has been pointed out by Moore that if ethical statements were simply statements about the speaker's feelings, it would be impossible to argue about questions of value. To take a typical example: if a man said that thrift was a virtue, and another replied that it was a vice, they would not, on this theory, be disputing with one another. One would be saying that he approved of thrift, and the other that *he* didn't; and there is no reason why both these statements should not be true.

Now Moore held it to be obvious that we do dispute about questions of value, and accordingly concluded that the particular form of subjectivism which he was discussing was false.

It is plain that the conclusion that it is impossible to dispute about questions of value follows from our theory also. For as we hold that such sentences as "Thrift is a virtue" and "Thrift is a vice" do not express propositions at all, we clearly cannot hold that they express incompatible propositions. We must therefore admit that if Moore's argument really refutes the ordinary subjectivist theory, it also refutes ours. But, in fact, we deny that it does refute even the ordinary subjectivist theory. For we hold that one really never does dispute about questions of value.

This may seem, at first sight, to be a very paradoxical assertion. For we certainly do engage in disputes which are ordinarily regarded as disputes about questions of value. But, in all such cases, we find, if we consider the matter closely, that the dispute is not really about a question of value, but about a question of fact. When someone disagrees with us about the moral value of a certain action or type of action, we do admittedly resort to argument in order to win him over to our way of thinking. But we do not attempt to show by our arguments that he has the "wrong" ethical feeling towards a situation whose nature he has correctly apprehended. What we attempt to show is that he is mistaken about the facts of the case. We argue that he has misconceived the agent's motive: or that he has misjudged the effects of the action, or its probable effects in view of the agent's knowledge; or that he has failed to take into account the special circumstances in which the agent was placed. Or else we employ more general arguments about the effects which actions of a certain type tend to produce, or the qualities which are usually manifested in their performance. We do this in the hope that we have only to get our opponent to agree with us about the nature of the empirical facts for him to adopt the same moral attitude towards them as we do. And as the people with whom we argue have generally received the same moral education as ourselves, and live in the same social order, our expectation is usually justified.[g]

> **8.** If two parties to an ethical dispute have similar moral backgrounds, they may resolve their differences once they agree on the facts of the case. However, when the parties to the dispute have different moral standards, their disagreements spring from differences in the disputants' emotional attitudes, even if they agree on matters of fact. As a result, the dispute is only an exchange of derogatory remarks, which express emotions. Because legitimate arguments can occur only on the factual level, Ayer concludes "that ethics, as a branch of knowledge, is nothing more than a department of psychology and sociology."

But if our opponent happens to have undergone a different process of moral "conditioning" from ourselves, so that, even when he acknowledges all the facts, he still disagrees with us about the moral value of the actions under discussion, then we abandon the attempt to convince him by argument. We say that it is impossible to argue with him because he has a distorted or undeveloped moral sense; which signifies merely that he employs a different set of values from our own. We feel that our own system of values is superior, and therefore speak in such derogatory terms of his. But we cannot bring forward any arguments to show that our system is superior. For our judgment that it is so is itself a judgment of value, and accordingly outside the scope of argument. It is because argument fails us when we come to deal with pure questions of value, as distinct from questions of fact, that we finally resort to mere abuse.

In short, we find that argument is possible on moral questions only if some system of values is presupposed. If our opponent concurs with us in expressing moral disapproval of all actions of a given type *t*, then we may get him to condemn a particular action A, by bringing forward arguments to show that A is of type *t*. For the questions whether A does or does not belong to that type is a plain question of fact. Given that a man has certain moral principles, we argue that he must, in order to be consistent, react morally to certain things in a certain way. What we do not and cannot argue about is the validity of these moral principles. We merely praise or condemn them in the light of our own feelings.

If anyone doubts the accuracy of this account of moral disputes, let him try to construct even an imaginary argument on a question of value which does not reduce itself to an argument about a question of logic or about an empirical matter of fact. I am confident that he will not succeed in producing a single example. And if that is the case, he must allow that its involving the impossibility of purely ethical arguments is not, as Moore thought, a ground of objection to our theory, but rather a point in favor of it.

Having upheld our theory against the only criticism which appeared to threaten it, we may now use it to define the nature of all ethical enquiries. We find that ethical philosophy consists simply in saying that ethical concepts are pseudoconcepts and therefore unanalyzable. The further task of describing the different feelings that the different ethical terms are used to express, and the different reactions that they customarily provoke, is a task for the psychologist. There cannot be such a thing as ethical science, if by ethical science one means the elaboration of a "true" system of morals. For we have seen that, as ethical judgments are mere expressions of feeling, there can be no way of determining the validity of any ethical system, and, indeed, no sense in asking whether any such system is true. All that one may legitimately enquire in this connection is, What are the moral habits of a given person or group of people, and what causes them to have precisely those habits and feelings? And this enquiry falls wholly within the scope of the existing social sciences.[h]

**9.** Having transferred all the factual statements of ethics to the social scientists and relegated all the normative expressions of ethics to the limbo of emotive utterances, Ayer regards his task as an analyst completed. Stevenson agrees in general with Ayer's analysis of ethical language. However, in his judgment, ethical inquiry must be extended to include an examination of the role of emotive expressions in ethical disputes. Stevenson begins by pointing out that ethical arguments involve both factual and value elements. Although there is a complex interplay of attitudes and beliefs, ethical disagreement is a matter primarily of *disagreement in attitude* and secondarily of *disagreement in belief.* He approaches the subject of ethical disagreement through a question about the method of resolving disputes.

When people disagree about the value of something—one saying that it is good or right, and another that it is bad or wrong—by what methods of argument or inquiry can their disagreement be resolved? Can it be resolved by the methods of science, or does it require methods of some other kind, or is it open to no rational solution at all?

The question must be clarified before it can be answered. And the word that is particularly in need of clarification, as we shall see, is the word "disagreement."

Let us begin by noting that "disagreement" has two broad senses: In the first sense it refers to what I shall call "disagreement I belief." This occurs when Mr. A believes *p*, when Mr. B. believes *not-p*, or something incompatible with *p*, and when neither is content to let the belief of the other remain unchallenged. Thus doctors may disagree in belief about the causes of an illness; and friends may disagree in belief about the exact date on which they last met.

In the second sense, the word refers to what I shall call "disagreement in attitude." This occurs when Mr. A has a favorable attitude to something, when Mr. B has an unfavorable or less favorable attitude to it, and when neither is content to let the other's attitude remain unchanged. . . . This second sense can be illustrated in this way: Two men are planning to have dinner together. One is particularly anxious to eat at a certain restaurant, but the other doesn't like it. Temporarily, then, the men cannot "agree" on where to dine. Their argument may be trivial and perhaps only half serious; but in any case it represents a disagreement *in attitude.* The men have divergent preferences, and each is trying to redirect the preference of the other. . . .

The difference between the two senses of "disagreement" is essentially this: the first involves an opposition of beliefs, both of which cannot be true, and the second involves an opposition of attitudes, both of which cannot be satisfied.[i]

**10.** The distinction between disagreement in belief and disagreement in attitude is the basis of Stevenson's analysis of ethical disagreements. He is opposed to the doctrine that all genuine ethical disputes are primarily matters of belief; he contends that the distinguishing feature of ethical disagreement is the underlying disagreement in attitude.

Let us apply this distinction to a case that will sharpen it. Mr. A believes that most voters will favor a proposed tax, and Mr. B. disagrees with him. The disagreement concerns attitudes—those of the voters—but note that A and B are *not* disagreeing in attitude. Their disagreement is *in belief about* attitudes. It is simply a special kind of disagreement in belief, differing from disagreement in belief about head colds only with regard to subject matter. It implies not an opposition of the actual attitudes of the speakers, but only of their beliefs about certain attitudes. Disagreement *in* attitude, on the other hand, implies that the very attitudes of the speakers are opposed. A and B may have opposed beliefs about attitudes without having opposed attitudes, just as they may have opposed beliefs about head colds without having opposed head colds. Hence we must not, from the fact that an argument is concerned with attitudes, infer that it necessarily involves disagreement *in* attitude.

We may now turn more directly to disagreement about values, with particular reference to normative ethics. When people argue about what is good, do they disagree in belief, or do they disagree in attitude? A long tradition of ethical theorists strongly suggest, whether they always intend to or not, that the disagreement is one *in belief*. Naturalistic theorists, for instance, identify an ethical judgment with some sort of scientific statement, and so make normative ethics a branch of science. Now a scientific argument typically exemplifies disagreement in belief, and if an ethical argument is simply a scientific one, then it too exemplifies disagreement in belief.... Disagreement about what is good is disagreement *in belief* about attitudes; but we have seen that that is simply one sort of disagreement in belief, and by no means the same as disagreement *in* attitude. Analyses that stress disagreement *in* attitude are extremely rare.

If ethical arguments, as we encounter them in everyday life, involved disagreement in belief exclusively—whether the beliefs were about attitudes or about something else—then I should have no quarrel with the ordinary sort of naturalistic analysis. Normative judgments could be taken as scientific statements, and amenable to the usual scientific proof. But a moment's attention will readily show that disagreement in belief has not the exclusive role that theory has so repeatedly ascribed to it. It must be readily granted that ethical arguments usually involve disagreement in belief; but they *also* involve disagreement in attitude. And the conspicuous role of disagreement in attitude is what we usually take, whether we realize it or not, as the distinguishing feature of ethical arguments. For example:

Suppose that the representative of a union urges that the wage level in a given company ought to be higher—that it is only right that the workers receive more pay. The company representative urges in reply that the workers ought to receive no more than they get. Such an argument clearly represents a disagreement in attitude. The union is *for* higher wages; the company is *against* them, and neither is content to let the other's attitude remain unchanged. *In addition* to this disagreement in attitude, of course, the argument may represent no little disagreement in belief. Perhaps the parties disagree about how much the cost of living has risen, and how much the workers are suffering under the present wage scale. Or perhaps they disagree about the company's earnings, and the extent to which the company could raise wages and still operate at a profit. Like any typical ethical argument, then, this argument involves both disagreement in attitude and disagreement in belief.[j]

**11.** Stevenson enlarges on his thesis that ethical disagreements are chiefly matters of attitude by showing two ways in which they function in actual situations. First, the conflicting attitudes determine what disagreements in belief are relevant to an argument, and second, they determine whether the argument has been settled.

In the first place, disagreement in attitude determines what beliefs are *relevant* to the argument. Suppose that the company affirms that the wage scale of fifty years ago was far lower than it is now. The union will immediately urge that this contention, even though true, is irrelevant. And it is irrelevant simply because information about the wage level of fifty years ago, maintained under totally different circumstances, is not likely to affect the present attitudes of either party. To be relevant, any belief that is introduced into the argument must be one that is likely to lead one side or the other to have a different attitude, and so reconcile disagreement in attitude. Attitudes are often functions of beliefs. We often change our attitudes to something when we change our beliefs about it; just as a child ceases to *want* to touch a live coal when he comes to *believe* that it will burn him. Thus in the present argument, any beliefs that are at all likely to alter attitudes, such as those about the increasing cost of living or the financial state of the company, will be considered by both sides to be relevant to the argument. Agreement in belief on these matters may lead to agreement in attitude toward the wage scale. But beliefs that are likely to alter the attitudes of neither side will be declared irrelevant. They will have no bearing on the disagreement in attitude, with which both parties are primarily concerned.

In the second place, ethical argument usually terminates when disagreement in attitude terminates, even though a certain amount of disagreement in belief remains. Suppose, for instance, that the company and the union continue to disagree in belief about the increasing cost of living, but that the company, even so, ends by favoring the higher wage scale. The union will then be content to end the argument, and will cease to press its point about living costs. It may bring up that point again, in some future argument of the same sort, or in urging therighteousness of its victory to the newspaper columnists; but for the moment the fact that the company has agreed in attitude is sufficient to terminate the argument. On the other hand: suppose that both parties agreed on all beliefs that were introduced into the argument, but even so continued to disagree in attitude. In that case neither party would feel that their dispute had been successfully terminated. They might look for other beliefs that could be introduced into the argument. They might use words to play on each other's emotions. They might agree (in attitude) to submit the case to arbitration, both feeling that a decision, even if strongly adverse to one party or the other, would be preferable to a continued impasse. Or, perhaps, they might abandon hope of settling their dispute by any peaceable means.[k]

**12.** The presuppositions of positivism result necessarily in the conclusion that *normative ethics cannot be a science.* Stevenson, as a positivist, shares this view, but at the same time he recognizes normative ethics as a vital *human activity,* in which science can—in favorable circumstances—contribute materially to the resolution of ethical (attitudinal) disagreements. As a human activity, ethics has its own characteristic functions and methods for the treatment of moral issues—that is, issues involving "personal and social decisions about what is to be approved." To sum up, ethics is not itself a science, though science may be of major importance in the resolution of ethical problems.

It will be obvious that to whatever extent an argument involves disagreement in belief, it is open to the usual methods of the sciences. If these methods are the *only* rational methods for supporting beliefs—as I believe to be so, but cannot now take time to discuss—then scientific methods are the only rational methods for resolving the disagreement in *belief* that arguments about values may include.

But if science is granted an undisputed sway in reconciling beliefs, it does not thereby acquire, without qualification, an undisputed sway in reconciling attitudes. We have seen that arguments about values include disagreement in attitude, no less than disagreement in belief, and that in certain ways the disagreement in attitude predominates. By what methods shall the latter sort of disagreement be resolved?

The methods of science are still available for that purpose, but only in an indirect way. Initially, these methods have only to do with establishing agreement in belief. If they serve further to establish agreement in attitude, that will be due simply to the psychological fact that altered beliefs may cause altered attitudes. Hence scientific methods are conclusive in ending arguments about values only to the extent that their success in obtaining agreement in belief will in turn lead to agreement in attitude.

In other words, the extent to which scientific methods can bring about agreement on values depends on the extent to which a commonly accepted body of scientific beliefs would cause us to have a commonly accepted set of attitudes.

How much is the development of science likely to achieve, then, with regard to values? To what extent *would* common beliefs lead to common attitudes? It is, perhaps, a pardonable enthusiasm to *hope* that science will do everything—to hope that in some rosy future, when all men know the consequences of their acts, they will all have common aspirations, and live peaceably in complete moral accord. But if we speak not from our enthusiastic hopes, but from our present knowledge, the answer must be far less exciting. We usually *do not know*, at the beginning of any argument about values, whether an agreement in belief, scientifically established, will lead to an agreement in attitude or not. It is logically possible, at least, that two men should continue to disagree in attitude even though they had all their beliefs in common, and even though neither had made any logical or inductive error, or omitted any relevant evidence. Differences in temperament, or in early training, or in social status, might make the men retain different attitudes even though both were possessed of the complete scientific truth. Whether this logical possibility is an empirical likelihood I shall not presume to say; but it is unquestionably a possibility that must not be left out of account.

To say that science can always settle arguments about value, we have seen, is to make this assumption: Agreement in attitude will always be consequent upon complete agreement in belief, and science can always bring about the latter. Taken as purely heuristic, this assumption has its usefulness. It leads people to discover the discrepancies in their beliefs, and to prolong enlightening argument that *may* lead, as a matter of fact, from commonly accepted beliefs to commonly accepted attitudes. It leads people to reconcile their attitudes in a rational, permanent way, rather than by rhapsody or exhortation. But the assumption is *nothing more*, for present knowledge, than a heuristic maxim. It is wholly without any proper foundation of probability. I conclude, therefore, that scientific methods cannot be guaranteed the definite role in the so-called normative sciences that they may have in the natural sciences. . . .

Insofar as normative ethics draws from the sciences, in order to change attitudes *via* changing people's beliefs, it *draws* from *all* the sciences; but a moralist's peculiar aim—that of *redirecting* attitudes—is a type of activity, rather than knowledge, and falls within no science. Science may study that activity, and may help indirectly to forward it; but it is not *identical* with that activity.[1]

## QUESTIONS

1. How does Ayer describe the basic task of the ethical theorist?
2. According to Ayer, what is the difference between "normative ethical symbols" and "descriptive ethical symbols?" What function does this distinction have in his theory of ethics?
3. What characteristics does Ayer assign to ethical statements? How does his view of their nature affect the evaluation of traditional ethical theories?
4. Assuming that Ayer's position is correct, is there need for any further work to be done in ethics? If so, whose task is it?

5. What is the difference between "disagreement in belief" and "disagreement in attitude," according to Stevenson's usage?
6. In what respect does Stevenson believe "disagreement in attitude" to be basic to ethics? What relationship is there between disagreement in attitude and disagreement in belief, in ethical disputes?
7. What grounds does Stevenson provide for his conclusion that ethics is not a branch of science? Is his position completely opposed to that of John Dewey, or are there significant areas of agreement between pragmatists and positivists?
8. Compare the positivism of Ayer with that of Stevenson, pointing out the respects in which they are similar and the respects in which they are different.
9. Compare the analytic approach of G. E. Moore with that of the positivists. How can you account for the fact that these two theories reach widely different conclusions, despite the essential similarity of their methods and conceptions of ethical theory?
10. What do you believe are the implications for morality of a positivistic ethical theory?

## KEY TO SELECTIONS

A. J. Ayer, *Language, Truth and Logic*, New York, Dover Publications, 1950. Reprinted with the kind permission of the publishers, Dover Publications, New York, 1950. Canadian circulation by permission of Victor Gollancz, publishers.

[a]pp. 103–144.
[b]pp. 104–105.
[c]pp. 105–106.
[d]pp. 106–107.
[e]pp. 107–108.
[f]pp. 108–109.
[g]pp. 109–111.
[h]pp. 111–112.

C. L. Stevenson, "The Nature of Ethical Disagreement," *Sigma*, vols. 1–2, 1947–1948. With the kind permission of the author and of the *Centro di Metodologia*, Milan, the publishers. (Our pagination conforms to that of C. L. Stevenson's reprint in his *Facts and Values*, New Haven, Yale University Press , 1963.)

[i]pp. 1–2.
[j]pp. 2–4.
[k]pp. 4–5.
[l]pp. 6–8.

## GUIDE TO ADDITIONAL READING


### PRIMARY SOURCES

Ayer, A. J., *Language, Truth and Logic*, Ch. 6, pp. 103–112. Reprinted with the kind permission of the publishers, Dover Publications, New York, 1950. Canadian circulation by permission of Victor Gollancz, publishers.

_____, "On the Analysis of Moral Judgements," *Horizon*, 10 (September 1949), pp. 171–184.

Stevenson, C. L., "The Nature of Ethical Disagreement," *Sigma*, 1–2, nos. 8–9 (1947–1948). With the kind permission of the author and of the *Centro di Metodologia*, Milan, the publishers.

_____, *Ethics and Language*, New Haven, Yale University Press, 1946.

_____, "The Emotive Meaning of Ethical Terms," *Mind*, 46 (January 1937), pp. 14–31.

_____, "Ethical Judgments and Avoidability," *Mind*, 47 (January 1938), pp. 45–57.

_____, "Meaning: Descriptive and Emotive," *Philosophical Review*, 57 (April 1948), pp. 127–144.

_____, "The Emotive Conception of Ethics and Its Cognitive Implications," *Philosophical Review*, 59 (July 1950), pp. 291–304.

Frankena, W. K., *Ethics*, Englewood Cliffs, Prentice-Hall, 1963.

Schlick, M., *Problems of Ethics*, tr. D. Rynin, New York, Prentice-Hall, 1939.

### DISCUSSION AND COMMENTARY

Foster, J., and Honderich, T. (Eds.), *A. J. Ayer*, London, Routledge and Kegan Paul, 1985.

Hudson, W. D., *Modern Moral Philosophy*, New York, Doubleday, 1970.

Satris, S., "The Theory of Value and the Rise of Ethical Emotivism," *Journal of the History of Ideas*, January, 1982, pp. 109–128.

Stevenson, C. L., *Facts and Values: Studies in Ethical Analysis*, New Haven, Yale University Press, 1963.

Urmson, J. O., *The Emotive Theory of Ethics,* London, Hutchinson, 1968.

Warnock, G. J., *Contemporary Moral Philosophy*, London, Macmillan, 1967.

Warnock, M., *Ethics since 1900*, London, Oxford University Press, 1960.

Wellman, C., "Emotivism and Ethical Objectivity," *American Philosophical Quarterly*, April 1968, pp. 90–99.

_____, "Ethical Disagreement and Objective Truth," *American Philosophical Quarterly*, July 1975, pp. 211–221.

CHAPTER TWENTY-TWO

# Radical Freedom

JEAN-PAUL SARTRE

ONE OF THE BEST-KNOWN and most widely discussed intellectuals since World War II, Jean-Paul Sartre (1905–1980), was born in Paris. His mother was a cousin of the renowned Christian and missionary doctor Albert Schweitzer, and his father, who died when Sartre was an infant, was a naval officer. Sartre was brought up in the home of his maternal grandfather and entered the École Normale Supérieure in 1924, concentrating on philosophy and literature. He completed his examinations in 1929 and, after meeting his military obligation, divided his time during the next eight years between teaching philosophy in several *lycées* and studying at the Institut Français in Berlin and the University of Freiburg. In this period he produced the acclaimed philosophical novel *Nausea*.

When the war began in 1939, Sartre returned to the army as a private. He was captured at the infamous Maginot line and remained a prisoner of war for nine months. Upon his release—prompted by ill health—he joined and was active in the Resistance movement and wrote for underground newspapers. He also completed his major philosophical work, *Being and Nothingness,* before the liberation. In this work Sartre lays the psychological and ontological foundations for his distinctive brand of existential philosophy. In the immediate postwar period, Sartre wrote several novels and plays that led to his recognition as a world literary figure. He also joined with his companion Simone de Beauvoir (1908–1986) and his friend Maurice Merleau-Ponty (1908–1961) in founding *Les Temps Modernes,* a critical review that addressed politics and literature from the viewpoint of existentialism.

Sartre became increasingly active politically as his fame grew. As early as 1951 he attempted to unify the noncommunist parties on the left, which brought him into conflict with the French Communist Party. Not long thereafter, however, his political agenda to secure freedom, justice, and equality became difficult to distinguish from the Communists'. At the theoretical level, he strove with great sophistication to explain, in *Critique of Dialectical Reason* (1960), that there is an underlying harmony between Marxism and existentialism. The lasting contribution of Sartre, however, does not reside in his political sagacity; it resides rather in his literary works and in his casting of existential philosophy. In literature, he was awarded the 1964 Nobel Prize (which he declined), and in philosophy, he has joined the select ranks of those who must be studied.

Some of Sartre's most important philosophical works are *The Transcendence of the Ego* (1937), *Being and Nothingness* (1943), *Existentialism Is a Humanism* (1946), and *The Psychology of Imagination* (1948).

The opposition of existentialism to the rationalist tradition can scarcely be exaggerated. From Kierkegaard to Sartre and beyond, existentialists have insisted that the attempt to understand humanity by imposing rational categories is ill-fated. In the first place, as rationalists employ the familiar dichotomies of freedom and responsibility, object and subject, being and nonbeing, existence and essence, they fail to meet their own standard of logical consistency. In the second place, they forever preclude themselves from encountering reality. In the third place, they never encounter the existing individual in his or her totality.

It is the hallmark of existentialism to speak of the human condition as one in which individuals are radically free. But this thesis leads the existentialist immediately into the seeming paradox that freedom is our essential characteristic, that humans are slaves of the concept of freedom; thus human beings are not free to be *un*free. The existentialist counters that the term *freedom,* when properly used, refers to the *condition of human existence* rather than to a *characteristic of human nature.* Our freedom is manifested in our creative endeavors, in spontaneous actions, and most of all in decision making. It falls to individuals alone to commit themselves at every moment to a limitless range of possibilities. Furthermore, according to the existential doctrine of Sartre, neither reason, nor social convention, nor God's will can relieve a person of the burden and responsibility of having to make choices. Even not choosing is a choice. Moreover, none of these factors can ensure the superiority of one decision over another. The human circumstance is agonizing and admits of no palliatives. Sartre summarizes the consequences of facing up to the true state of affairs in this way:

> If existence really does precede essence, there is no explaining things away by reference to a fixed and given human nature. In other words, there is no determinism, man is free, man is freedom. On the other hand, if God does not exist, we find no values or commands to turn to which legitimize our conduct. So in the bright realm of values, we have no excuse behind us, nor justification before us. We are alone, with no excuses.[1]

Existential philosophy holds that *who* people are is a function of the choices they make, not that the choices they make are a function of *who* they are. The ever-present danger for us as individuals in our highly organized society is that we will lose our uniqueness through submitting to external forces. It is difficult, however, to envision

---

[1]Jean-Paul Sartre, *Existentialism* (New York: Philosophical Library, 1947), p. 27. 

anyone choosing freely against the immense number of determinative pressures—social, political, economic, religious, and intellectual—that sanction and demand mere conformity. Is not the pathetic weakness of the individual sufficient in itself to justify moving with the crowd? The existentialist points out that such a plea is nothing more than a pretense for shirking responsibility. The question is not whether, like a hero of one's imagination, a person can overcome tremendous odds, but rather whether that individual has the courage to live *authentically*—to live, that is, according to choices made consciously and responsibly. To claim that one has no choice because of all the external pressures that can be brought to bear is to exchange the human situation for that of an automaton—to sacrifice being a genuine subject in favor of becoming a mere object. Furthermore, even if such an exchange occurs, the choice bringing it about and the responsibility for the resulting renunciation of individuality are still the individual's. In brief, at no time or place can individuals plead that who they are has been shaped by any factor other than themselves in the process of choosing and acting.

According to the existentialist, although our individual decisions may have a profound impact on others, we are still confronted with the dreadful realization that there are no universal principles to guide or sanctify our conduct. Between one person and another, there are no assured bonds. Social order, like natural order, is a fabrication, an avoidance of the fact of our total isolation. The virtue of authentic or genuine people lies in their honest recognition of this fact. They alone have integrity; their reward in an admittedly unique sense of the word is that they do not suffer self-alienation.

Sartre stresses the facticity of the situation wherein we choose. Indeed, he holds that if we were not constantly confronted by an array of brute facts, we could *not* act freely. In the absence of the existence of things, of our memories, of other people, of social institutions, and of other givens, there would be nothing to bring into conformity with our purposes, nothing to invest with significance, nothing to which a policy could pertain. For example, that rock on the ground may go virtually unnoticed until, say, my interest turns to establishing a lawn, or to scientific identification, or to building a retaining wall. Thus the rock can be molded by me and *for me* into an object to be removed, into an item for geological classification, or into a potential component of a structure. The possibilities for choice here seem limitless, but the *responsibility* for that choice and its consequences *is mine alone*. For Sartre, such unmitigated responsibility marks all of my policies, and most emphatically, all policies wherein I bring others into conformity with my ends.

Although classifying existentialists is difficult and risks error, it can be pointed out that some among them show a decided religious orientation, whereas others steadfastly reject religion in any form. Kierkegaard and Paul Tillich (1886–1965) are clearly members of the first group; Sartre and his associate Simone de Beauvoir belong to the second. Kierkegaard does not claim any objective knowledge of God; nevertheless he believes, after the manner of a Christian mystic, that however absurd and paradoxical it seems, the individual can establish rapport with the eternal God by a "leap of faith." Sartre and de Beauvoir, on the other hand, warn that it is as self-deceptive for human beings to escape the burden of responsibility for their actions through an appeal to supernatural belief as it is to avoid responsibility by claiming that one's actions fall under natural laws. From birth to death, Sartrian humans are bound only by the ideals and obligations that, in their freedom, they create for themselves.

---

**1.** According to Sartre, who a person is is a function of what she or he chooses or wills. But he insists that this in fact means "in creating the man we want to be, there is not a single one of our acts which does not at the same time create an image of man as we think he ought to be."

Atheistic existentialism, which I represent . . . states that if God does not exist, there is at least one being in whom existence precedes essence, a being who exists before he can be defined by any concept, and that this being is man, or, as Heidegger says, human reality. What is meant here by saying that existence precedes essence? It means that, first of all, man exists, turns up, appears on the scene, and, only afterwards, defines himself. If man, as the existentialist conceives him, is indefinable, it is because at first he is nothing. Only afterward will he be something, and he himself will have made what he will be. Thus, there is no human nature, since there is no God to conceive it. Not only is man what he conceives himself to be, but he is also only what he wills himself to be after this thrust toward existence.

Man is nothing else but what he makes of himself. Such is the first principle of existentialism. It is also what is called subjectivity, the name we are labeled with when charges are brought against us. But what do we mean by this, if not that man has a greater dignity than a stone or table? For we mean that man first exists, that is, that man first of all is the being who hurls himself toward a future and who is conscious of imagining himself as being in the future. Man is at the start a plan which is aware of itself, rather than a patch of moss, a piece of garbage, or a cauliflower; nothing exists prior to this plan, there is nothing in heaven; man will be what he will have planned to be. Not what he will want to be. Because by the word "will" we generally mean a conscious decision, which is subsequent to what we have already made of ourselves. I may want to belong to a political party, write a book, get married; but all that is only a manifestation of an earlier, more spontaneous choice that is called "will." But if existence really does precede essence, man is responsible for what he is. Thus, existentialism's first move is to make every man aware of what he is and to make the full responsibility of his existence rest on him. And when we say that a man is responsible for himself, we do not only mean that he is responsible for his own individuality, but that he is responsible for all men.

The word subjectivism has two meanings, and our opponents play on the two. Subjectivism means, on the one hand, that an individual chooses and makes himself; and, on the other, that it is impossible for man to transcend human subjectivity. The second of these is the essential meaning of existentialism. When we say that man chooses his own self, we mean that every one of us does likewise; but we also mean by that that in making this choice he also chooses all men. In fact, in creating the man that we want to be, there is not a single one of our acts which does not at the same time create an image of man as we think he ought to be. To choose to be this or that is to affirm at the same time the value of what we choose, because we can never choose evil. We always choose the good, and nothing can be good for us without being good for all.

If, on the other hand, existence precedes essence, and if we grant that we exist and fashion our image at one and the same time, the image is valid for everybody and for our whole age. Thus, our responsibility is much greater than we might have supposed, because it involves all mankind. If I am a workingman and choose to join a Christian trade-union rather than be a communist, and if by being a member I want to show that the best thing for man is resignation, that the kingdom of man is not of this world, I am not only involving my own case—I want to be resigned for everyone. As a result, my action has involved all humanity. To take a more individual matter, if I want to marry, to have children; even if this marriage depends solely on my own circumstances or passion or wish, I am involving all humanity in monogamy and not merely myself. Therefore, I am responsible for myself and for everyone else. I am creating a certain image of man of my own choosing. In choosing myself, I choose man.[a]

**2.** An acute source of anxiety and despair lies in the fact that we choose for humanity rather than for ourselves as isolated beings. What we do must be what others might do as well.

The existentialists say at once that man is anguish. What that means is this: the man who involves himself and who realizes that he is not only the person he chooses to be, but also a lawmaker who is, at the same time, choosing all mankind as well as himself, can not help escape the feeling of his total and deep responsibility. Of course, there are many people who are not anxious; but we claim that they are hiding their anxiety, that they are fleeing from it. Certainly, many people believe that when they do something, they themselves are the only ones involved, and when someone says to them, "What if everyone acted that way?" they shrug their shoulders and answer, "Everyone doesn't act that way." But really, one should always ask himself, "What would happen if everybody looked at things that way?" There is no escaping this disturbing thought except by a kind of double-dealing. A man who lies and makes excuses for himself by saying "not everybody does that," is someone with an uneasy conscience, because the act of lying implies that a universal value is conferred upon the lie.

Anguish is evident even when it conceals itself. This is the anguish that Kierkegaard called the anguish of Abraham. You know the story: an angel has ordered Abraham to sacrifice his son; if it really were an angel who has come and said, "You are Abraham, you shall sacrifice your son," everything would be all right. But everyone might first wonder, "Is it really an angel, and am I really Abraham? What proof do I have?"

There was a madwoman who had hallucinations; someone used to speak to her on the telephone and give her orders. Her doctor asked her, "Who is it who talks to you?" She answered, "He says it's God." What proof did she really have that it was God? If an angel comes to me, what proof is there that it's an angel? And if I hear voices, what proof is there that they come from heaven and not from hell, or from the subconscious, or a pathological condition? What proves that they are addressed to me? What proof is there that I have been appointed to impose my choice and my conception of man on humanity? I'll never find any proof or sign to convince me of that. If a voice addresses me, it is always for me to decide that this is the angel's voice; if I consider that such an act is a good one, it is I who will choose to say that it is good rather than bad.

Now, I'm not being singled out as an Abraham, and yet at every moment I'm obliged to perform exemplary acts. For every man, everything happens as if all mankind had its eyes fixed on him and were guiding itself by what he does. And every man ought to say to himself, "Am I really the kind of man who has the right to act in such a way that humanity might guide itself by my actions?" And if he does not say that to himself, he is masking his anguish.[b]

**3.** For Sartre, human freedom and the denial of God's existence place us in the precarious position of being solely responsible for our actions. There are no *a priori* guidelines to give direction to our lives. This is a brute fact that each of us must face.

When we speak of forlornness, a term Heidegger was fond of, we mean only that God does not exist and that we have to face all the consequences of this. The existentialist is strongly opposed to a certain kind of secular ethics which would like to abolish God with the least possible expense. About 1880, some French teachers tried to set up a secular ethics which went something like this: God is a useless and costly hypothesis; we are discarding it; but, meanwhile, in order for there to be an ethics, a society, a civilization, it is essential that certain values be taken seriously and that they be considered as having an *a priori* existence. It must be obligatory, *a priori,* to be honest, not to lie, not to beat your wife, to have children, etc., etc. So we're going to try a little device which will make it possible to show that values exist all the same, inscribed in a heaven of ideas, though otherwise God does not exist. In other words—and this, I believe, is the tendency of everything called reformism in France—nothing will be changed if God does not exist. We shall find ourselves with the same norms of honesty, progress, and humanism, and we shall have made of God an outdated hypothesis which will peacefully die off by itself.

The existentialist, on the contrary, thinks it very distressing that God does not exist, because all possibility of finding values in a heaven of ideas disappears along with Him; there can no longer be an *a priori* Good, since there is no infinite and perfect consciousness to think it. Nowhere is it written that the Good exists, that we must be honest, that we must not lie; because the fact is we are on a plane where there are only men. Dostoevski said, "If God didn't exist, everything would be possible." That is the very starting point of existentialism. Indeed, everything is permissible if God does not exist, and as a result man is forlorn, because neither within him nor without does he find anything to cling to. He can't start making excuses for himself.

If existence really does precede essence, there is no explaining things away by reference to a fixed and given human nature. In other words, there is no determinism, man is free, man is freedom. On the other hand, if God does not exist, we find no values or commands to turn to which legitimize our conduct. So, in the bright realm of values, we have no excuse behind us, nor justification before us. We are alone, with no excuses.

That is the idea I shall try to convey when I say that man is condemned to be free. Condemned, because he did not create himself, yet, in other respects is free; because, once thrown into the world, he is responsible for everything he does.[c]

**4.** Sartre provides examples and comments about our need to choose an active life, one in which we seek to make decisions rather than to avoid them. Failing to act is tantamount to retreating from the challenge of life.

Actually, things will be as man will have decided they are to be. Does that mean that I should abandon myself to quietism? No. First, I should involve myself; then, act on the old saw, "Nothing ventured, nothing gained." Nor does it mean that I shouldn't belong to a party, but rather that I shall have no illusions and shall do what I can. For example, suppose I ask myself, "Will socialization, as such, ever come about?" I know nothing about it. All I know is that I'm going to do everything in my power to bring it about. Beyond that, I can't count on anything. Quietism is the attitude of people who say, "Let others do what I can't do." The doctrine I am presenting is the very opposite of quietism, since it declares, "There is no reality except in action." Moreover, it goes further, since it adds, "Man is nothing else than his plan; he exists only to the extent that he fulfills himself; he is therefore nothing else than the ensemble of his acts, nothing else than his life."

According to this, we can understand why our doctrine horrifies certain people. Because often the only way they can bear their wretchedness is to think, "Circumstances have been against me. What I've been and done doesn't show my true worth. To be sure, I've had no great love, no great friendship, but that's because I haven't met a man or woman who was worthy. The books I've written haven't been very good because I haven't had the proper leisure. I haven't had children to devote myself to because I didn't find a man with whom I could have spent my life. So there remains within me, unused and quite viable, a host of propensities, inclinations, possibilities, that one wouldn't guess from the mere series of things I've done."

Now, for the existentialist there is really no love other than one which manifests itself in a person's being in love. There is no genius other than one which is expressed in works of art; the genius of Proust is the sum of Proust's works; the genius of Racine is his series of tragedies. Outside of that, there is nothing. Why say that Racine could have written another tragedy, when he didn't write it? A man is involved in life, leaves his impress on it, and outside of that there is nothing. To be sure, this may seem a harsh thought to someone whose life hasn't been a success. But, on the other hand, it prompts people to understand that reality alone is what counts, that dreams, expectations, and hopes warrant no more than to define a man as a disappointed dream, as miscarried hopes, as vain expectations. In other words, to define him negatively and not positively. However, when we say, "You are nothing else than your life," that does not imply that the artist will be judged solely on the basis of his works of art; a thousand other things will contribute toward summing him up. What we mean is that a man is nothing else than a series of undertakings, that he is the sum, the organization, the ensemble of the relationships which make up these undertakings.[d]

**5.** Sartre acknowledges that one given of the human condition is that all persons are born and live in a definite time, place, and culture, but he denies that this implies that they possess an "essential nature."

If it is impossible to find in every man some universal essence which would be human nature, yet there does exist a universal human condition. It's not by chance that today's thinkers speak more readily of man's condition than of his nature. By condition they mean, more or less definitely, the *a priori* limits which outline man's fundamental situation in the universe. Historical situations vary; a man may be born a slave in a pagan society or a feudal lord or a proletarian. What does not vary is the necessity for him to exist in the world, to be at work there, to be there in the midst of other people, and to be mortal there. The limits are neither subjective nor objective, or, rather, they have an objective and a subjective side. Objective because they are to be found everywhere and are recognizable everywhere; subjective because they are *lived* and are nothing if man does not live them, that is, freely determine his existence with reference to them. And though the configurations may differ, at least none of them are completely strange to me, because they all appear as attempts either to pass beyond these limits or recede from them or deny them or adapt to them. Consequently, every configuration, however individual it may be, has a universal value.

Every configuration, even the Chinese, the Indian, or the Negro, can be understood by a Westerner. "Can be understood" means that by virtue of a situation that he can imagine, a European of 1945 can, in like manner, push himself to his limits and reconstitute within himself the configuration of the Chinese, the Indian or the African. Every configuration has universality in the sense that every configuration can be understood by every man. This does not at all mean that this configuration defines man forever, but that it can be met with again. There is always a way to understand the idiot, the child, the savage, the foreigner, provided one has the necessary information.

In this sense we may say that there is a universality of man; but it is not given, it is perpetually being made. I build the universal in choosing myself; I build it in understanding the configuration of every other man, whatever age he might have lived in. This absoluteness of choice does not do away with the relativeness of each epoch. At heart, what existentialism shows is the connection between the absolute character of free involvement, by virtue of which every man realizes himself in realizing a type of mankind, an involvement always comprehensible in any age whatsoever and by any person whosoever, and the relativeness of the cultural ensemble which may result from such a choice.[e]

**6.** Two senses of the term *humanism* must be distinguished. Rejecting that form of it in which we judge the human race by its outstanding accomplishments, Sartre adopts instead that form that is appropriate for existentialism—namely, one in which people are dynamic agents seeking common goals.

Moreover, to say that we invent values means nothing else but this: life has no meaning *a priori*. Before you come alive, life is nothing; it's up to you to give it a meaning, and value is nothing else but the meaning that you choose. In that way, you see, there is a possibility of creating a human community.

I've been reproached for asking whether existentialism is humanistic. It's been said, "But you said in *Nausea* that the humanists were all wrong. You made fun of a certain kind of humanist. Why come back to it now?" Actually, the word humanism has two very different meanings. By humanism one can mean a theory which takes man as an end and as a higher value. Humanism in this sense can be found in Cocteau's tale *Around the World in Eighty Hours* when a character, because he is flying over some mountains in an airplane, declares, "Man is simply amazing." That means that I, who did not build the airplanes, shall personally consider myself responsible for, and honored by, acts of a few particular men. This would imply that we ascribe a value to man on the basis of the highest deeds of certain men. This humanism is absurd, because only the dog or the horse would be able to make such an overall judgment about man, which they are careful not to do, at least to my knowledge.

But it cannot be granted that a man may make a judgment about man. Existentialism spares him from any such judgment. The existentialist will never consider man as an end because he is always in the making. Nor should we believe that there is a mankind to which we might set up a cult in the manner of Auguste Comte. The cult of mankind ends in the self-enclosed humanism of Comte, and, let it be said, of fascism. This kind of humanism we can do without.

But there is another meaning of humanism. Fundamentally it is this: man is constantly outside of himself; in projecting himself, in losing himself outside of himself, he makes for man's existing; and, on the other hand, it is by pursuing transcendent goals that he is able to exist; man, being this state of passing-beyond, and seizing upon things only as they bear upon this passing-beyond is at the heart, at the center of this passing-beyond. There is no universe other than a human universe, the universe of human subjectivity. This connection between transcendency, as a constituent element of man—not in the sense that God is transcendent, but in the sense of passing beyond—and subjectivity, in the sense that man is not closed in on himself but is always present in a human universe, is what we call existentialism humanism. Humanism, because we remind man that there is no lawmaker other than himself, and that in his forlornness he will decide by himself; because we point out that man will fulfill himself as man, not in turning toward himself, but in seeking outside of himself a goal which is just this liberation, just this particular fulfillment.

From these few reflections it is evident that nothing is more unjust than the objections that have been raised against us. Existentialism is nothing else than an attempt to draw all the consequences of a coherent atheistic position. It isn't trying to plunge man into despair at all. But if one calls every attitude of unbelief despair, like the Christians, then the word is not being used in its original sense. Existentialism isn't so atheistic that it wears itself out showing that God doesn't exist. Rather, it declares that even if God did exist, that would change nothing. There you've got our point of view. Not that we believe that God exists, but we think that the problem of His existence is not the issue. In this sense existentialism is optimistic, a doctrine of action, and it is plain dishonesty for Christians to make no distinction between their own despair and ours and then to call us despairing.[f]

**7.** Sartre criticizes all efforts to place human beings on the same level as inanimate objects or things. To shirk one's responsibility in this way is a form of concealment and indicates "bad faith." Even in a war situation, a person cannot claim to be an innocent victim, as psychological determinists maintain.

The essential consequence of our earlier remarks is that man being condemned to be free carries the weight of the whole world on his shoulders; he is responsible for the world and for himself as a way of being. We are taking the word "responsibility" in its ordinary sense as "consciousness (of) being the incontestable author of an event or of an object.". . .

Furthermore this absolute responsibility is not resignation; it is simply the logical requirement of the consequences of our freedom. What happens to me happens through me, and I can neither affect myself with it nor revolt against it nor resign myself to it. Moreover everything which happens to me is *mine*. By this we must understand first of all that I am always equal to what happens to me *qua* man, for what happens to a man through other men and through himself can be only human. The most terrible situations of war, the worst tortures do not create a nonhuman state of things; there is no nonhuman situation. It is only through fear, flight, and recourse to magical types of conduct that I shall decide on the nonhuman, but this decision is human, and I shall carry the entire responsibility for it. But in addition the situation is *mine* because it is the image of my free choice of myself, and everything which it presents to me is *mine* in that this represents me and symbolizes me. . . .

If I am mobilized in a war, this war is *my* war; it is in my image and I deserve it. I deserve it first because I could always get out of it by suicide or by desertion; these ultimate possibles are those which must always be present for us when there is a question of envisaging a situation. For lack of getting out of it, I have *chosen* it. This can be due to inertia, to cowardice in the face of public opinion, or because I prefer certain other values to the value of the refusal to join in the war (the good opinion of my relatives, the honor of my family, *etc.*). Any way you look at it, it is a matter of a choice. This choice will be repeated later on again and again without a break until the end of the war. Therefore we must agree with the statement by J. Romains, "In war there are no innocent victims." If therefore I have preferred war to death or to dishonor, everything takes place as if I bore the entire responsibility for this war. Of course others have declared it, and one might be tempted perhaps to consider me as a simple accomplice. But this notion of complicity has only a juridical sense, and it does not hold here. For it depended on me that for me and by me this war should not exist, and I have decided that it does exist. There was no compulsion here, for the compulsion could have got no hold on a freedom. I did not have any excuse; for as we have said repeatedly in this book, the peculiar character of human-reality is that it is without excuse. Therefore it remains for me only to lay claim to this war.[g]

**8.** In his view, freedom extends to the brute fact of being born, for which one is, of course, not literally responsible.

Yet this responsibility is of a very particular type. Someone will say, "I did not ask to be born." This is a naive way of throwing greater emphasis on our facticity. *I am responsible for everything, in fact, except for my very responsibility, for I am not the foundation of my being* [italics added]. Therefore, everything takes place as if I were compelled to be responsible. I am *abandoned* in the world, not in the sense that I might remain abandoned and passive in a hostile universe like a board floating on the water, but rather in the sense that I find myself suddenly alone and without help, engaged in a world for which I bear the whole responsibility without being able, whatever I do, to tear myself away from this responsibility for an instant. For I am responsible for my very desire of feeling responsibilities. To make myself passive in the world, to refuse to act upon things and upon others is still to choose myself, and suicide is one mode among others of being-in-the-world.

Yet I find an absolute responsibility for the fact that my facticity (here the fact of my birth) is directly inapprehensible and even inconceivable . . . . I am ashamed of being born or I am astonished at it or I rejoice over it, or in attempting to get rid of my life I affirm that I live and I assume this life as bad. Thus in a certain sense I *choose* being born. This choice itself is integrally affected with facticity since I am not able not to choose, but this facticity in turn will appear only in so far as I surpass it toward my ends. Thus facticity is everywhere but is inapprehensible; I never encounter anything except my responsibility. That is why I can not ask, "*Why* was I born?" or curse the day of my birth or declare that I did not ask to be born, for these various attitudes toward my birth—*i.e.*, toward the *fact* that I realize a presence in the world—are absolutely nothing else but ways of assuming this birth in full responsibility and of making it *mine*. Here again I encounter only myself and my projects so that finally my abandonment—*i.e.*, my facticity—consists simply in the fact that I am condemned to be wholly responsible for myself.[h]

## QUESTIONS

1. What are the philosophical consequences of Sartre's view that "existence precedes essence"?
2. Sartre claims that he is an "existentialist humanist." What does he mean?
3. What would be Sartre's defense of nontheistic existentialist ethics against the implications of Dostoevski's maxim "If God does not exist, everything is permitted"?
4. Develop Sartre's thesis that humans are condemned to be free.
5. Kierkegaard and Sartre are both existentialists. What are their points of agreement and difference?
6. What does Sartre mean when he says that "we invent values"?
7. When Sartre speaks of our being responsible for the choices we make, is he using the term *responsible* in an ordinary sense or in a special sense? Discuss.
8. Review Sartre's thesis that in creating the person we want to be, we are at the same time creating "an image of man as we think he ought to be." Is this convincing?
9. What are the chief characteristics of humans as moral beings in Sartre's view?
10. What problems of social morality are posed by the radical subjectivity of existential ethics? Is the solution proposed by Sartre adequate to ensure social order?

## KEY TO SELECTIONS

Jean-Paul Sartre, *Existentialism and Human Emotions*, New York, Philosophical Library, 1957. 

[a]pp. 15–18.
[b]pp. 18–20.
[c]pp. 21–23.
[d]pp. 31–33.
[e]pp. 38–40.
[f]pp. 49–51.
[g]p. 52, pp. 53–54, pp. 54–55.
[h]p. 57, pp. 57–58.

## GUIDE TO ADDITIONAL READING

### PRIMARY SOURCES

Jaspers, K., *Existentialism and Humanism* tr. E. B. Ashton, New York, R. F. Moore, 1952.

Marcel, G., *The Existential Background of Human Dignity*, Cambridge, Harvard University Press, 1963.

Sartre, Jean-Paul, *Notebooks for an Ethics*, tr. D. Pelauer, Chicago, University of Chicago Press, 1992.

## DISCUSSION AND COMMENTARY


Anderson, T. C., *The Foundation and Structure of Sartrean Ethics,* Lawrence, Kansas State Regents Press, 1979.

Barnes, H. E., *Sartre,* Philadelphia, Lippincott, 1973.

Beauvoir, Simone de, *The Ethics of Ambiguity*, tr. B. Freeman, New York, The Citadel Press, 1948.

Dante, A., *Jean-Paul Sartre,* New York, Viking Press, 1975.

Heidegger, Martin, *Being and Time,* tr. J. MacQuarrie and E. Robinson, New York, Harper & Row, 1962.

Stack, G. J., *Sartre's Philosophy of Social Existence,* St. Louis, Warren H. Green, 1977.

# Good Reasons in Ethics

KURT BAIER

KURT BAIER (b. 1917), an Austrian by birth, received his advanced philosophical training at Oxford University, England. He began his professional life in Australia, where he taught at such institutions as the University of Melbourne and Canberra University College. Before coming to the United States in 1962, he served as president of the Australian Association of Philosophy. A fellow of the American Academy of Arts and Sciences, Professor Baier has also been the head of the Department of Philosophy at the University of Pittsburgh and president of the Eastern Division of the American Philosophical Association. In addition to his chief work in ethics, *The Moral Point of View* (1958), he has contributed numerous articles to philosophical journals.

Baier is a prominent member of a group of ethical theorists frequently referred to as "prescriptivists," a group that emphasizes the directive or guiding function of moral judgments in arriving at moral decisions. These philosophers are not primarily concerned with challenging the analyses of ethical language insisted on by Ayer, Stevenson, and others—analyses wherein moral judgments are regarded as essentially emotive in meaning. Rather, they conceive of themselves as embarking on what they consider the more traditional and relevant task of analyzing the role that moral judgments play in our quest for solutions to concrete and vital moral problems.

According to Baier, moral investigation begins with the question "What shall I do?" or, more precisely, "What is the best thing to do?" or, to be more precise still, "What course of action is supported by the best reasons?" When he uses the term *best reasons*, he is thinking of a class of *good reasons*—facts that can play a part in effecting a decision for one course of action rather than another—some of which are superior to others. Baier's evidence that there are good reasons is simply that people actually do believe that certain kinds of facts will guide them in making proper decisions. For most of us, learning that if we do A rather than B, we will be doing something detrimental to society, counts, in and of itself, as a good reason for not doing A; or, again, learning that doing C rather than D will produce pleasure rather than pain for someone constitutes, in and of itself, a good reason for doing C. In brief, he is content to work from the psychosociological fact that people do have "consideration-making beliefs" without attempting to settle the ultimate philosophical status of such beliefs.

As we have indicated, Baier does not regard good reasons as either all of a kind or all on the same level. Just as John Stuart Mill insisted that some pleasures are superior to others, Baier insists that some reasons are superior to others. Again, just as Mill ultimately defends his hierarchy by an appeal to "competent judges," Baier submits the matter to those who can appreciate the entire range of reasons. He declares that, in general, selfish reasons are superior to reasons of immediate pleasure and that moral reasons outweigh selfish reasons.

An examination of the nature of an ethical dispute will illustrate the role of the hierarchy of good reasons. Suppose A struck B in anger, but now both are calm enough to debate the morality of the action. B claims that A broke a rule of courteous behavior. A objects that rules are made to be broken when they fail to serve our private interests. B counters that if the rules of conduct are abandoned, society will degenerate into a human jungle. This interchange of "good reasons" points up the fact that there are various justifications for rules of behavior—we typically offer various kinds of reasons for behavior. After B pointed out that a rule of conduct had been transgressed, A offered a justification or good reason for breaking the rule (promotion of personal interest), whereupon B responded with a justification in terms of social welfare. The question now becomes one of finding a viewpoint from which the disputants can determine fairly and effectively the superiority of one kind of reason over another. Baier holds that there is such a viewpoint: "the moral point of view."

The only standpoint from which we can judge between the kinds of good reasons is one that fulfills two conditions. First, it must, as Kant emphasized, be one in which everyone is regarded as subject to the same rules; second, it must be one that is for the good of everyone alike. The essence of the second condition is simply that a given action be such that an individual would find it acceptable whether he or she was related to it as an active agent or as a passive recipient. Only when we adopt a genuinely impartial viewpoint in which no one is morally exempt, and no one is morally neglected, can we carry out the judicial function of deciding how to rank good reasons. When we avail ourselves of "the moral point of view," we are "looking at the world from the point of view of anyone" and for the good of everyone. In brief, then, Baier offers a theory that assures us that good reasons can be ranked in such a way that they provide us with an effective basis for moral decisions.

**1.** Baier raises a question that has been central to the history of ethics: Is there a distinction between the moral point of view and that of self-interest?

Throughout the history of philosophy, by far the most popular candidate for the position of the moral point of view has been self-interest. There are obvious parallels between these two standpoints. Both aim at the good. Both are rational. Both involve deliberation, the surveying and weighing of reasons. The adoption of either yields statements containing the word "ought." Both involve the notion of self-mastery and control over the desires. It is, moreover, plausible to hold that a person could not have a reason for doing anything whatsoever unless his behavior was designed to promote his own good. Hence, if morality is to have the support of reason, moral reasons must be self-interested, hence the point of view of morality and self-interest must be the same. On the other hand, it seems equally obvious that morality and self-interest are very frequently opposed. Morality often requires us to refrain from doing what self-interest recommends or to do what self-interest forbids. Hence morality and self-interest cannot be the same points of view.[a]

**2.** By drawing a distinction within a distinction, Baier isolates the view of "enlightened self-interest" so that it presents the most plausible case for asserting that morality and egoism coincide. This plausibility is enhanced by the limited support of the notable commentator on ethics Henry Sidgwick. However, Baier points out that far from being "the moral viewpoint," it would substitute chaos for moral order, if universally practiced.

Can we save the doctrine that the moral point of view is that of self-interest? One way of circumventing the difficulty just mentioned is to draw a distinction between two senses of "self-interest," shortsighted and enlightened. The shortsighted egoist always follows his short-range interest without taking into consideration how this will affect others and how their reactions will affect him. The enlightened egoist, on the other hand, knows that he cannot get the most out of life unless he pays attention to the needs of others on whose good will he depends. On this view, the standpoint of (immoral) egoism differs from that of morality in that it fails to consider the interests of others even when this costs little or nothing or when the long-range benefits to oneself are likely to be greater than the short-range sacrifices.

This view can be made more plausible still if we distinguish between those egoists who consider each course of action on its own merits and those who, for convenience, adopt certain rules of thumb which they have found will promote their long-range interest. Slogans such as "Honesty is the best policy," "Give to charity rather than to the Department of Internal Revenue," "Always give a penny to a beggar when you are likely to be watched by your acquaintances," "Treat your servants kindly and they will work for you like slaves," "Never be arrogant to anyone—you may need his services one day," are maxims of this sort. They embody the "wisdom" of a given society. The enlightened long-range egoist may adopt these as rules of thumb, that is as *prima facie* maxims, as rules which he will observe unless he has good evidence that departing from them will pay him better than abiding by them. It is obvious that the rules of behavior adopted by the enlightened egoist will be very similar to those of a man who rigidly follows our own moral code.

Sidgwick appears to believe that egoism is one of the legitimate "methods of ethics," although he himself rejects it on the basis of an "intuition" that it is false. He supports the legitimacy of egoism by the argument that everyone could consistently adopt the egoistic point of view. "I quite admit that when the painful necessity comes for another man to choose between his own happiness and the general happiness, he must as a reasonable being prefer his own, i.e., it is right for him to do this on my principle." The consistent enlightened egoist satisfies the categorical imperative, or at least one version of it, "Act only on that maxim whereby thou canst at the same time will that it should become a universal law."

However, no "intuition" is required to see that this is not the point of view of morality, even though it can be universally adopted without self-contradiction. In the first place, a consistent egoist adopts for all occasions the principle "everyone for himself" which we allow (at most) only in conditions of chaos, when the normal moral order breaks down. Its adoption marks the return to the law of the jungle, the state of nature, in which the "softer," more "chivalrous" ways of morality have no place.[b]

**3.** He further argues that self-interested views, whether short-range or enlightened, are logically self-defeating.

It can be shown that those who adopt consistent egoism cannot make moral judgments. Moral talk is impossible for consistent egoists. But this amounts to a *reductio ad absurdum* of consistent egoism.

Let B and K be candidates for the presidency of a certain country and let it be granted that it is in the interest of either to be elected, but that only one can succeed. It would then be in the interest of B but against the interest of K if B were elected, and vice versa, and therefore in the interest of B but against the interest of K if K were liquidated, and vice versa. But from this it would follow that B ought to liquidate K, that it is wrong for B not to do so, that B has not "done his duty" until he has liquidated K; and vice versa. Similarly K, knowing that his own liquidation is in the interest of B and therefore anticipating B's attempts to secure it, ought to take steps to foil B's endeavors. It would be wrong for him not to do so. He would "not have done his duty" until he had made sure of stopping B. It follows that if K prevents B from liquidating him, his act must be said to be both wrong and not wrong—wrong because it is the prevention of what B ought to do, his duty, and wrong for B not to do it; not wrong because it is what K ought to do, his duty, and wrong for K not to do it. But one and the same act (logically) cannot be both morally wrong and not morally wrong. Hence in cases like these morality does not apply.

This is obviously absurd. For morality is designed to apply in just such cases, namely, those where interests conflict. But if the point of view of morality were that of self-interest, then there could *never* be moral solutions of conflicts of interest. However, when there are conflicts of interest, we always look for a "higher" point of view, one from which such conflicts can be settled. Consistent egoism makes everyone's private interest the "highest court of appeal." But by "the moral point of view" we *mean* a point of view which is a court of appeal for conflicts of interest. Hence it cannot (logically) be identical with the point of view of self-interest.[c]

**4.** Having asserted that ethical disputes are insoluble unless we can show some reasons to be superior to others, Baier turns his attention to the way in which the hierarchy of reasons is established. He begins with a ranking or comparison of self-regarding reasons and other-regarding reasons with respect to pleasure.

How can we establish rules of superiority? It is a *prima facie* reason for me to do something not only that I would enjoy it if *I* did it, but also that *you* would enjoy it if *I* did it. People generally would fare better if this fact were treated as a pro, for if this reason were followed, it would create additional enjoyment all around. But which of the two *prima facie* reasons is superior when they conflict? How would we tell?

At first it would seem that these reasons are equally good, that there is nothing to choose between them, that no case can be made out for saying that people generally would fare better if the one or the other were treated as superior. But this is a mistake.

Suppose I could be spending half an hour in writing a letter to Aunt Agatha who would enjoy receiving one though I would not enjoy writing it, or alternatively in listening to a lecture which

I would enjoy doing. Let us also assume that I cannot do both, that I neither enjoy writing the letter nor dislike it, that Aunt Agatha enjoys receiving the letter as much as I enjoy listening to the lecture, and that there are no extraneous considerations such as that I deserve especially to enjoy myself there and then, or that Aunt Agatha does, or that she has special claims against me, or that I have special responsibilities or obligations toward her.

In order to see which is the better of these two reasons, we must draw a distinction between two different cases: the case in which someone derives pleasure from giving pleasure to others and the case where he does not. Everyone is so related to certain other persons that he derives greater pleasure from doing something together with them than doing it alone because in doing so he is giving them pleasure. He derives pleasure not merely from the game of tennis he is playing but from the fact that in playing he is pleasing his partner. We all enjoy pleasing those we love. Many of us enjoy pleasing even strangers. Some even enjoy pleasing their enemies. Others get very little enjoyment from pleasing their fellow men.

We must therefore distinguish between people with two kinds of natural makeup: on the one hand, those who need not always choose between pleasing themselves and pleasing others, who can please themselves *by* pleasing others, who can please themselves more by not merely pleasing themselves, and, on the other hand, those who always or often have to choose between pleasing themselves and pleasing others, who derive no pleasure from pleasing others, who do not please themselves more by pleasing not merely themselves.

If I belong to the first kind, then I shall derive pleasure from pleasing Aunt Agatha. Although writing her a letter is not enjoyable in itself, as listening to the lecture is, I nevertheless derive enjoyment from writing it because it is a way of pleasing her and I enjoy pleasing people. In choosing between writing the letter and listening to the lecture, I do not therefore have to choose between pleasing her and pleasing myself. I have merely to choose between two different ways of pleasing myself. If I am a man of the second kind, then I must choose between pleasing myself and pleasing her. When we have eliminated all possible moral reasons, such as standing in a special relationship to the person, then it would be strange for someone to prefer pleasing someone else to pleasing himself. How strange this is can be seen if we substitute for Aunt Agatha a complete stranger.

I conclude from this that the fact that I would enjoy it if *I* did $x$ is a better reason for doing $x$ than the fact that you would enjoy it if *I* did $x$. Similarly in the fact that I would enjoy doing $x$ if I did it I have a reason for doing $x$ which is better than the reason for doing $y$ which I have in the fact that you would enjoy doing $y$ as much as I would enjoy doing $x$. More generally speaking, we can say that self-regarding reasons are better than other-regarding ones. Rationally speaking, the old quip is true that everyone is his own nearest neighbor.[d]

> **5.** Again and quite surprisingly, Baier suggests that generally speaking, when self-interested reasons and altruistic reasons are pitted against each other, the former properly takes precedence.

This is more obvious still when we consider the case of self-interest. Both the fact that doing $x$ would be in my interest and the fact that it would in someone else's interest are excellent *prima facie* reasons for me to do $x$. But the self-interested reason is better than the altruistic one. Of course, interests need not conflict, and then I need not choose. I can do what is in both our interests. But sometimes interests conflict, and then it is in accordance with reason (*prima facie*) to prefer my own interest to someone else's. That my making an application for a job is in *my* interest is a reason for me to apply, which is better than the reason against applying, which I have in the fact that my not applying is in *your* interest.

There is no doubt that this conviction is correct for all cases. It is obviously better that everyone should look after his own interest than that everyone should neglect it in favor of someone else's. For whose interest should have precedence?

It must be remembered that we are considering a case in which there are no special reasons for preferring a particular person's interests to one's own, as when there are no special moral obligations or emotional ties. Surely, in the absence of any *special* reasons for preferring someone else's interest, *everyone's* interests are best served if *everyone* puts his own interests first. For, by and large, everyone is himself the best judge of what is in his own best interest, since everyone usually knows best what his plans, aims, ambitions, or aspirations are. Moreover, everyone is more diligent in the promotion of his own interests than that of others. Enlightened egoism is a possible, rational, orderly system of running things, enlightened altruism is not. Everyone can look after himself, no one can look after everyone else. Even if everyone had to look after only two others, he could not do it as well as looking after himself alone. And if he has to look after only one person, there is no advantage in making that person someone other than himself. On the contrary, he is less likely to know as well what that person's interest is or to be as zealous in its promotion as in that of his own interest.[e]

**6.** Baier is unwilling to concede, however, that reasons of self-interest are the highest. He then presents a case for the superiority of moral reasons.

Are moral reasons really superior to reasons of self-interest as we all believe? Do we really have reason on our side when we follow moral reasons against self-interest? What reasons could there be for being moral? Can we really give an answer to "Why should we be moral?" It is obvious that all these questions come to the same thing. When we ask, "Should we be moral?" or "Why should we be moral?" or "Are moral reasons superior to all others?" we ask to be shown the reasons for being moral. What is this reason?

Let us begin with a state of affairs in which reasons of self-interest are supreme. In such a state everyone keeps his impulses and inclinations in check when and only when they would lead him into behavior detrimental to his own interest. Everyone who follows reason will discipline himself to rise early, to do his exercises, to refrain from excessive drinking and smoking, to keep good company, to marry the right sort of girl, to work and study hard in order to get on, and so on. However, it will often happen that peoples' interests conflict. In such a case, they will have to resort to ruses or force to get their own way. As this becomes known, men will become suspicious, for they will regard one another as scheming competitors for the good things in life. The universal supremacy of the rules of self-interest must lead to what Hobbes called the state of nature. At the same time, it will be clear to everyone that universal obedience to certain rules overriding self-interest would produce a state of affairs which serves everyone's interest much better than his unaided pursuit of it in a state where everyone does the same. Moral rules are universal rules designed to override those of self-interest when following the latter is harmful to others. "Thou shalt not kill," "Thou shalt not lie," "Thou shalt not steal" are rules which forbid the inflicting of harm on someone else even when this might be in one's interest.

The very *raison d'être* of a morality is to yield reasons which overrule the reasons of self-interest in those cases when everyone's following self-interest would be harmful to everyone. Hence moral reasons are superior to all others.[f]

**7.** But can we convince a defender of enlightened self-interest that moral reasons are superior? Baier responds to this challenge by pointing out that in the first place, the typical argument for self-interest is circular and therefore fallacious and that in the second place, although moral theorists may be tempted to respond with an equally circular counterargument, they need not do so: They can propose a viewpoint from which a decision about the two types of reasons can be rendered—a decision that favors moral reasons.

"But what does this mean?" it might be objected. "If it merely means that we do so regard them, then you are of course right, but your contention is useless, a mere point of usage. And how could it mean any more? If it means that we not only do so regard them, but *ought* so to regard them, then there must be *reasons* for saying this. But there could not be any reasons for it. If you offer reasons of self-interest, you are arguing in a circle. Moreover, it cannot be true that it is always in my interest to treat moral reasons as superior to reasons of self-interest. If it were, self-interest and morality could never conflict, but they notoriously do. It is equally circular to argue that there are moral reasons for saying that one ought to treat moral reasons as superior to reasons of self-interest. And what other reasons are there?"

The answer is that we are not looking at the world from the point of view of *anyone*. We are not examining particular alternative courses of action before this or that person; we are examining two alternative worlds, one in which moral reasons are always treated by everyone as superior to reasons of self-interest and one in which the reverse is the practice. And we can see that the first world is the better world, because we can see that the second world would be the sort which Hobbes describes as the state of nature.

This shows that I ought to be moral, for when I ask the question "What ought I to do?" I am asking, "Which is the course of action supported by the best reasons?" But since it has just been shown that moral reasons are superior to reasons of self-interest, I have been given a reason for being moral, for following moral reasons rather than any other, namely, they are better reasons than any other.[g]

**8.** Through an analysis of Hobbesian political and ethical theory, Baier both clarifies a portion of his own position and provides an answer to the question "Do we have a reason for being moral, whatever the conditions we find ourselves in?"

Could there not be situations in which it is not true that we have reasons for being moral, that, on the contrary, we have reasons for ignoring the demands of morality? Is not Hobbes right in saying that in a state of nature the laws of nature, that is, the rules of morality, bind only *in foro interno* [before the inner tribunal]?

Hobbes argues as follows.

1. To live in a state of nature is to live outside society. It is to live in conditions in which there are no common ways of life and, therefore, no reliable expectations about other people's behavior other than that they will follow their inclination or their interest.

2. In such a state reason will be the enemy of cooperation and mutual trust. For it is too risky to hope that other people will refrain from protecting their own interests by the preventive elimination of probable or even possible dangers to them. Hence reason will counsel everyone to avoid these risks by preventive action. But this leads to war.

3. It is obvious that everyone's following self-interest leads to a state of affairs which is desirable from no one's point of view. It is, on the contrary, desirable that everybody should follow rules overriding self-interest whenever that is to the detriment of others. In other words, it is desirable to bring about a state of affairs in which all obey the rules of morality.

4. However, Hobbes claims that in the state of nature it helps nobody if a single person or a small group of persons begins to follow the rules of morality, for this could only lead to the extinction of such individuals or groups. In such a state, it is therefore contrary to reason to be moral.

5. The situation can change, reason can support morality, only when the presumption about other people's behavior is reversed. Hobbes thought that this could be achieved only by the creation of an absolute ruler with absolute power to enforce his laws. We have already seen that this is not true and that it is quite different if people live in a society, that is, if they have common ways of life, which are taught to all members and somehow enforced by the group. Its members have reason to expect their fellows generally to obey its rules, that is, its religion, morality, customs, and law, even when doing so is not, on

certain occasions, in their interest. Hence they too have reason to follow these rules.

Is this argument sound? One might, of course, object to step (1) on the grounds that this is an empirical proposition for which there is little or no evidence. For how can we know whether it is true that people in a state of nature would follow only their inclinations or, at best, reasons of self-interest, when nobody now lives in that state or has ever lived in it?

However, there is some empirical evidence to support this claim. For in the family of nations, individual states are placed very much like individual persons in a state of nature. The doctrine of the sovereignty of nations and the absence of an effective international law and police force are a guarantee that nations live in a state of nature, without commonly accepted rules that are somehow enforced. Hence it must be granted that living in a state of nature leads to living in a state in which individuals act either on impulse or as they think their interest dictates. For states pay only lip service to morality. They attack their hated neighbors when the opportunity arises. They start preventive wars in order to destroy the enemy before he can deliver his knockout blow. Where interests conflict, the stronger party usually has his way, whether his claims are justified or not. And where the relative strength of the parties is not obvious, they usually resort to arms in order to determine "whose side God is on." Treaties are frequently concluded but, morally speaking, they are not worth the paper they are written on. Nor do the partners regard them as contracts binding in the ordinary way, but rather as public expressions of the belief of the governments concerned that for the time being their alliance is in the interest of the allies. It is well understood that such treaties may be canceled before they reach their predetermined end or simply broken when it suits one partner.In international affairs, there are very few examples of *Nibelungentreue* [absolute fidelity], although statesmen whose countries have profited from keeping their treaties usually make such high moral claims.[h]

**9.** The implications for international affairs are further examined, and considerations are uncovered to indicate the hierarchy of good reasons on a moral rather than a self-interested basis.

It is, moreover, difficult to justify morality in international affairs. For suppose a highly moral statesman were to demand that his country adhere to a treaty obligation even though this meant its ruin or possibly its extinction. Suppose he were to say that treaty obligations are sacred and must be kept whatever the consequences. How could he defend such a policy? Perhaps one might argue that someone has to make a start in order to create mutual confidence in international affairs. Or one might say that setting a good example is the best way of inducing others to follow suit. But such a defense would hardly be sound. The less skeptical one is about the genuineness of the cases in which nations have adhered to their treaties from a sense of moral obligation, the more skeptical one must be about the effectiveness of such examples of virtue in effecting a change of international practice. Power politics still govern in international affairs.

We must, therefore, grant Hobbes the first step in his argument and admit that in a state of nature people, as a matter of psychological fact, would not follow the dictates of morality. But we might object to the next step that knowing this psychological fact about other people's behavior constitutes a reason for behaving in the same way. Would it not still be immoral for anyone to ignore the demands of morality even though he knows that others are likely or certain to do so, too? Can we offer as a justification for morality the fact that no one is entitled to do wrong just because someone else is doing wrong? This argument begs the question whether it *is* wrong for anyone in this state to disregard the demands of morality. It cannot be wrong to break a treaty or make preventive war if we have no reason to obey the moral rules. For to say that it is wrong to do so is to say that we ought not to do so. But if we have no reason for obeying the moral rule, then we have no reason for overruling self-interest, hence no reason for keeping the treaty when keeping it is not in our interest, hence it is not true that we have a reason for keeping it, hence not true that we ought to keep it, hence not true that it is wrong not to keep it.

I conclude that Hobbes's argument is sound. Moralities are systems of principles whose acceptance by everyone as overruling the dictates of self-interest is in the interest of everyone alike, though following the rules of a morality is not of course identical with following self-interest. If it were, there could be no conflict between a morality and self-interest and no point in having moral rules overriding self-interest. Hobbes is also right in saying that the application of this system of rules is in accordance with reason only in social conditions, that is, when there are well established ways of behavior.

The answer to our question "Why should we be moral?" is therefore as follows. We should be moral because being moral is following rules designed to overrule self-interest whenever it is in the interest of everyone alike that everyone should set aside his interest. It is not self-contradictory to say this, because it may be in one's interest *not* to follow one's interest at times. We have already seen that enlightened self-interest acknowledges this point. But while enlightened self-interest does not require any genuine sacrifice from anyone, morality does. In the interest of the possibility of the good life for everyone, voluntary sacrifices are sometimes required from everybody. Thus, a person might do better for himself by following enlightened self-interest rather than morality. It is not possible, however, that *everyone* should do better for himself by following enlightened self-interest rather than morality. The best possible life *for everyone* is possible only by everyone's following the rules of morality, that is, rules which quite frequently may require individuals to make genuine sacrifices.

It must be added to this, however, that such a system of rules has the support of reason only where people live in societies, that is, in conditions in which there are established common ways of behavior. Outside society, people have no reason for following such rules, that is, for being moral. In other words, outside society, the very distinction between right and wrong vanishes.[i]

**10.** Even if we admit that some types of reasons are qualitatively superior to others, it can still be asked why we should follow reason at all. Baier approaches this question by first clarifying what it means to act "contrary to reason."

What is it to follow reason? . . . It involves two tasks, the theoretical, finding out what it would be in accordance with reason to do in a certain situation, what contrary to reason, and the practical task, to act accordingly. . . . We must remind ourselves that there are many different ways in which what we do or believe or feel can be contrary to reason. It may be *irrational*, as when, for no reason at all, we set our hand on fire or cut off our toes one by one, or when, in the face of conclusive evidence to the contrary, someone *believes* that her son killed in the war is still alive, or when someone is *seized by fears* as a gun is pointed at him although he knows for certain that it is not loaded. What we do, believe, or feel is called irrational if it is the case not only that there are conclusive or overwhelming reasons against doing, believing, or feeling these things, but also that we must know there are such reasons and we still persist in our action, belief, or feeling.

Or it may be *unreasonable*, as when we make demands which are excessive or refuse without reason to comply with requests which are reasonable. We say of demands or requests that they are excessive if, though we are entitled to make them, the party against whom we make them has good reasons for not complying, as when the landlord demands the immediate vacation of the premises in the face of well-supported pleas of hardship by the tenant.

Being unreasonable is a much weaker form of going counter to reason than being irrational. The former applies in cases where there is a conflict of reasons and where one party does not acknowledge the obvious force of the case of the other or, while acknowledging it, will not modify his behavior accordingly. A person is irrational only if he flies in the face of reason, if, that is, all reasons are on one side and he acts contrary to it when he either acknowledges that this is so or, while refusing to acknowledge it, has no excuse for failing to do so.

Again, someone may be *inconsistent*, as when he refuses a Jew admission to a club although he has always professed strong positive views on racial equality. Behavior or remarks are inconsistent if the agent or author professes principles adherence to which would require him to say or do the opposite of what he says or does.

Or a person may be *illogical*, as when he does something which, as anyone can see, cannot or is not at all likely to lead to success. Thus when I cannot find my glasses or my fountain pen, the logical thing to do is to look for them where I can remember I had them last or where I usually have them. It would be illogical of me to look under the bed or in the oven unless I have special reason to think they might be there. To say of a person that he is a logical type is to say that he always does what, on reflection, anyone would agree is most likely to lead to success. Scatterbrains, people who act rashly, without thinking, are the opposite of logical.[j]

**11.** With some understanding of what it would mean to reject reason as a guide, Baier indicates that, in one sense at least, the question "Why follow reason?" is a trivial exercise in rhetoric.

When we speak of following reason, we usually mean "doing what is supported by the best reasons because it is so supported," or perhaps "doing what we think (rightly or wrongly) is supported by the best reasons because we think it is so supported." It might, then occur to someone to ask, "Why should I follow reason?" During the last hundred years or so, reason has had a very bad press. Many thinkers have sneered at it and have recommended other guides, such as the instincts, the unconscious, the voice of the blood, inspiration, charisma, and the like. They have advocated that one should not follow reason but be guided by these other forces.

However, in the most obvious sense of the question "Should I follow reason?" this is a tautological question like "Is a circle a circle?"; hence the advice "You should not follow reason" is as nonsensical as the claim "A circle is not a circle." Hence the question "Why should I follow reason?" is as silly as "Why is a circle a circle?" We need not, therefore, take much notice of the advocates of unreason. They show by their advocacy that they are not too clear on what they are talking about.

How is it that "Should I follow reason?" is a tautological question like "Is a circle a circle?" Questions of the form "Shall I do this?" or "Should I do this?" or "Ought I to do this?" are . . . requests to someone (possibly oneself) to deliberate on one's behalf. That is to say, they are requests to survey the facts and weigh the reasons for and against this course of action. These questions could therefore be paraphrased as follows. "I wish to do what is supported by the best reasons. Tell me whether this is so supported." As already mentioned, "following reason" means "doing what is supported by the best reasons." Hence the question "Shall (should, ought) I follow reason?" must be paraphrased as "I wish to do what is supported by the best reasons. Tell me whether doing what is supported by the best reasons is doing what is supported by the best reasons." It is, therefore, not worth asking.

The question "*Why* should I follow reason?" simply does not make sense. Asking it shows complete lack of understanding of the meaning of "why questions." "Why should I do this?" is a request to be given the reasons for saying that I should do this. It is normally asked when someone has already said, "You should do this" and answered by giving the reason. But since "Should I follow reason?" means "Tell me whether doing what is supported by the best reasons is doing what is supported by the best reasons," there is simply no possibility of adding "Why?" For the question now comes to this, "Tell me the reason why doing what is supported by the best reasons is doing what is supported by the best reasons." It is exactly like asking, "Why is a circle a circle?"[k]

**12.** Baier does acknowledge that the question "Why follow reason?" is meaningful, but only in the sense in which it pertains to reason in its theoretical rather than its practical role. In an argument somewhat reminiscent of Epictetus nineteen centuries earlier, Baier points out that any effort to displace the authority of reason depends on the very authority of that which it would displace.[1]

However, it must be admitted that there is another possible interpretation to our question according to which it makes sense and can even be answered. "Why should I follow reason?" may not be a request for a reason in support of a tautological remark, but a request for a reason why one should enter on the theoretical task of deliberation. . . . Following reason involves the completion of two tasks, the theoretical and the practical. The point of the theoretical is to give guidance in the practical task. We perform the theoretical only because we wish to complete the practical task in accordance with the outcome of the theoretical. On our first interpretation, "Should I follow reason?" means "Is the practical task completed when it is completed in accordance with the outcome of the theoretical task?" And the answer to this is obviously "Yes," for that is what we mean by "completion of the practical task." On our second interpretation, "Should I follow reason?" is not a question about the practical but about the theoretical task. It is not a question about whether, given that one is prepared to perform both these tasks, they are properly completed in the way indicated. It is a question about whether one should enter on the whole performance at all, whether the "game" is worth playing. And this is a meaningful question. It might be better to "follow inspiration" than to "follow reason," in this sense: better to close one's eyes and wait for an answer to flash across the mind.

But while, so interpreted, "Should I follow reason?" makes sense, it seems to me obvious that the answer to it is "Yes, because it pays." Deliberation is the only reliable method. Even if there were other reliable methods, we could only tell whether they were reliable by checking them against this method. Suppose some charismatic leader counsels, "Don't follow reason, follow me. My leadership is better than that of reason"; we would still have to check his claim against the ordinary methods of reason. We would have to ascertain whether in following his advice we were doing the best thing. And this we can do only by examining whether he has advised us to do what is supported by the best reasons. His claim to be better than reason can in turn only be supported by the fact that he tells us precisely the same as reason does.

Is there any sense, then, in his claim that his guidance is preferable to that of reason? There may be, for working out what is supported by the best reasons takes a long time. Frequently, the best thing to do is to do something quickly now rather than the most appropriate thing later. A leader may have the ability to "see," to "intuit," what is the best thing to do more quickly than it is possible to work this out by the laborious methods of deliberation. In evaluating the qualities leadership of such a person, we are evaluating *his ability to perform correctly the practical task of following reason* without having to go through the lengthy operations of the theoretical. Reason is required to tell us whether anyone has qualities of leadership better than ordinary, in the same way that pencil and paper multiplications are required to tell us whether a mathematical prodigy is genuine or a fraud.[1]

## QUESTIONS

1. What types of "good reasons" does Baier distinguish, and how does he arrange them in hierarchical order? Can you think of any types of good reasons that might be added?
2. In what ways is Baier's ethical theory dependent on the moral philosophy of John Stuart Mill? On that of Immanuel Kant? Include consideration of the purposes of moral philosophy.

---

[1]See p. 3 of this book.

3. What distinctions does Baier make among types of self-interest? What value is assigned to self-interest among good reasons?
4. Outline Baier's demonstration of the illogical character of egoistic theories.
5. Apply Baier's method of moral decision making to the problem of cheating on examinations and to one or more actual moral problems in your own experience.
6. What is Baier's evaluation of altruistic reasons? Do you agree or disagree and why?
7. What does Baier mean by "moral reasons"? How does he explain their superiority to other good reasons?
8. What is the function of Baier's detailed examination of Hobbes' theory?
9. Discuss Baier's analysis of international morality. Does he provide adequate support for the analogy between individual and international morality?
10. (a) Discuss and evaluate Baier's distinctions among "irrational," "unreasonable," and "inconsistent." Do these contrasts hold for the positive forms? (b) What answers does Baier give to the question "Why follow reason?" Of what importance is the answer in his ethical theory?

## KEY TO SELECTIONS

Kurt Baier, *The Moral Point of View*, Ithaca, N.Y., Cornell University Press, 1958. © 1958 by Cornell University. Used by permission of Cornell University Press.

[a]pp. 187–188.
[b]pp. 188–189.
[c]pp. 189–190.
[d]pp. 304–306.
[e]pp. 306–307.
[f]pp. 308–309.
[g]pp. 309–310.
[h]pp. 310–313.
[i]pp. 313–315.
[j]pp. 315–317.
[k]pp. 317–318.
[l]pp. 318–320.

## GUIDE TO ADDITIONAL READING

**PRIMARY SOURCES**

Baier, K., *The Rational and the Moral Order*, Chicago, Open Court, 1995.

Hare, R. M., *The Language of Morals*, New York, Oxford University Press, 1964.

Noel-Smith, P. H., *Ethics*, Baltimore, Penguin Books, 1954.

Toulmin, S., *Reason in Ethics*, Cambridge, Cambridge University Press, 1960.

**DISCUSSION AND COMMENTARY**

Baier, K., "Defining Morality without Prejudice," *Monist*, June 1981, pp. 325–341.

_____, "Good Reasons," *Philosophical Studies*, 4(1953), pp. 1–15.

_____, "Moral Reasons," *Midwest Studies in Philosophy*, 1978, pp. 62–74.

_____, "Proving a Moral Judgement," *Philosophical Studies*, 4(1953), pp. 33–44.

_____, "Rationality and Morality," *Erkenntnis*, August 1977, pp. 197–223.

Frankena, W. K., *Ethics*, Englewood Cliffs, Prentice-Hall, 1963.

Kerner, G., *The Revolution in Ethical Theory*, New York, Oxford University Press, 1966.

# CHAPTER TWENTY-FOUR

# Ethics and Social Justice

Harvard University Archives, call # HUP Rawls, John (2)

JOHN RAWLS

PROFESSOR JOHN RAWLS (1921–2002) received his Ph.D. degree in philosophy from Princeton University in 1950. After being a Fulbright scholar at Oxford in 1952–1953, he taught at Cornell University until 1959. While there, Rawls served as co-editor of the journal *Philosophical Review* for a brief period. From 1960 to 1962, he was Professor of Philosophy at Massachusetts Institute of Technology, and from 1962 on he taught at Harvard University where, in 1976, he was appointed to the John Cowles Chair of Philosophy. Chief among his ethical writings is *A Theory of Justice*, published in 1971.

John Rawls's *A Theory of Justice* has received widespread public attention. This is an unusual reception for a lengthy, fully argued philosophical treatise, and it is, perhaps, indicative of a view that may become the mark of our historical period: Sociopolitical institutions are themselves proper subjects for moral assessment. With the resolution of a Plato, Rawls insists that social morality is not a matter merely of personal morality or of institutional efficiency. Rawls is not Platonistic, however, in his approach to social and normative problems. In this regard, he belongs to the tradition of Hobbes, Locke, Rousseau, and (in some interpretations) Kant—the tradition of social-contract theorists.

Adopting the thesis that the ultimate basis of society is a set of tacit agreements, Rawls identifies his initial problem to be that of discovering the conditions that such agreements must satisfy. To the end of indicating his conclusions about this, an examination of accounts that he would judge unsuccessful becomes instructive. Thus he would argue that Hobbes's explication of the social contract cannot be basic. Hobbes insists that it is solely because of our self-serving desire for security that we agree to subordinate ourselves completely to an absolute sovereign power.

But this having been done, and the benefit of a measure of security achieved through the power of the sovereign, would we remain bound by the agreements made? It does not seem likely. On the Hobbesian account, for example, if a citizen in a relatively secure state desires to commit an illegal act and is confident that he can avoid detection, there is no reason in theory or practice for him to feel morally constrained from acting on that desire. If there is no fear, there is no obligation. Rawls is led by considerations of this sort to recognize that *basic social* agreements must be such that they are acceptable in perpetuity—that is, they must not be conditional on the happenstance of one's position in a society at a given time.

Consider another account of a social principle. In presenting an ideal state (the *Republic*), Plato invokes the notion that, on occasions, the leaders must manipulate some citizens through the device of a "Noble Lie" in order to achieve a well-ordered state. Rawls would contend that no people, of their own volition, will agree to a social principle that reduces them to mere means. An example of this sort isolates an additional criterion that social agreements must satisfy: Compacts must be such that if they were made public, everyone would continue to support them. In Plato's case, publicity would surely work toward the disaffection of those being lied to. Strangely enough, this would be so even if such individuals acknowledged their inferior abilities.

Rawls therefore isolates what he takes to be two important conditions for anyone entering into social agreements. Put negatively, the first is that the commitment to them does not depend on the vagaries of an individual's circumstances; the second is that the commitment to them does not depend on the individual's ignorance of their precise nature. Put positively, the first requirement is that everyone can make this commitment in perpetuity; the second is that everyone's commitment to the social principles involved increases as his or her understanding of them grows.

In line with the foregoing analysis, Rawls introduces the notion of an *ideal observer*. Such an observer would systematically ignore the happenstance of participants' special talents and inclinations, relative social status, political ideology, and all other accidental features of their lives. Furthermore, viewed from this vantage point, all participants ought properly to operate under a "veil of ignorance"—that is, to operate as free and rational persons with all factors of inequality eliminated in their thinking. With this background, we can understand Rawls's "original position" in which the principles of social justice are set forth. These are the principles "agreed to in an initial situation that is fair": (1) Each person in a society has an equal right to the maximum liberty compatible with the same amount of liberty for everyone else, and (2) inequality is permissible to the extent that it serves everyone's advantage and arises under conditions of equal opportunity.[1] These two principles—the equal liberty principle and the difference principle—are not correlative for Rawls. Although people under desperate economic and human circumstances would agree to a great loss of personal liberty in order to survive at a minimal level, they would not do so under less stringent conditions.

---

[1] In the full development of his viewpoint, which appears in *A Theory of Justice* (Cambridge: Harvard University Press, 1971), p. 302, Rawls gives a more technical formulation of the principles:

> *First Principle.* Each person is to have an equal right to the most extensive total system of equal basic liberties compatible with a similar system of liberty for all. *Second Principle.* Social and economic inequalities are to be arranged so that they are both: (a) to the greatest benefit of the least advantage, consistent with the just savings principle, and (b) attached to offices and positions open to all under conditions of fair equality of opportunity.

Since Rawls's second principle is reminiscent of the Utilitarian ideal of promoting "the greatest happiness for the greatest number," it is appropriate to ask whether his view is merely classical Utilitarianism in modern, sophisticated form.[2] Rawls's answer to this question would be that their divergence is much greater than a Utilitarian suspects. As has just been pointed out, if the difference principle conflicts with the equal liberty principle, the latter takes priority unless we are faced with a condition of stark survival. On the other hand, according to the Utilitarian or neo-Benthamite, Rawls's concern about the liberty of individuals is taken care of by the second principle. For experience shows that in the long run, gains in equal liberty have indeed been a fundamental and significant means for the promotion of social well-being. Rawls' objection to this prudential appeal is categorical: The ultimate justification of equal liberty in society is not that of a mere means to an end; rather, the principle of equal liberty is logically prior to the difference principle. Unfortunately, the Utilitarian perceives the relationship between liberty and social well-being as a mere matter of contingency. This position leaves open unjust possibilities, such as a benign slavery. No basis is provided for objecting to the loss of personal dignity in a conceivable context in which animal wants and needs are amply met.

The point Rawls is making is that any principle that allows for the possibility of such a case is unacceptable once it is understood. His message is clear: "Each person possesses an inviolability founded on justice that even the welfare of society as a whole cannot override. . . . Therefore . . . the rights secured by justice are not subject to political bargaining or to the calculus of social interests."[3]

The selections that follow are drawn from Rawls's article "Justice as Reciprocity," which constitutes a brief survey of some salient points contained in *A Theory of Justice*.

---

**1.** Rawls sets for himself the task of analyzing that virtue of social institutions termed *justice*. He supplies the distinctions between justice and fairness that are required for bringing the concepts into focus.

It might seem at first sight that the concepts of justice and fairness are the same, and that there is no reason to distinguish between them. To be sure, there may be occasions in ordinary speech when the phrases expressing these notions are not readily interchangeable, but it may appear that this is a matter of style and not a sign of important conceptual differences. I think that this impression is mistaken, yet there is, at the same time, some foundation for it. Justice and fairness are, indeed, different concepts, but they share a fundamental element in common, which I shall call the concept of reciprocity. They represent this concept as applied to two distinct cases: very roughly, justice to a practice in which there is no option whether to engage in it or not, and one must play; fairness to a practice in which there is such an option, and one may decline the invitation. In this paper I shall present an analytic construction of the concept of justice from this point of view, and I shall refer to this analysis as the analysis of justice as reciprocity.

Throughout I consider justice as a virtue of social institutions only, or of what I have called practices. Justice as a virtue of particular actions

[2]See Chapter 13 of this book, especially with respect to Bentham.
[3]Rawls, *A Theory of Justice*, p. 4.

or of persons comes in at but one place, where I discuss the *prima facie* duty of fair play. . . . Further, the concept of justice is to be understood in its customary way as representing but one of the many virtues of social institutes; for these institutions may be antiquated, inefficient, or degrading, or any number of other things, without being unjust. Justice is not to be confused with an all-inclusive vision of a good society, or thought of as identical with the concept of right. It is only one part of any such conception, and it is but one species of right. I shall focus attention, then, on the usual sense of justice in which it means essentially the elimination of arbitrary distinctions and the establishment within the structure of a practice of a proper share, balance, or equilibrium between competing claims. The principles of justice serve to specify the application of "arbitrary" and "proper," and they do this by formulating restrictions as to how practices may define positions and offices, and assign thereto powers and liabilities, rights and duties. While the definition of the sense of justice is sufficient to distinguish justice as a virtue of institutions from other such virtues as efficiency and humanity, it does not provide a complete conception of justice. For this the associated principles are needed. The major problem in the analysis of the concept of justice is how these principles are derived and connected with this moral concept, and what is their logical basis; and further, what principles, if any, have a special place and may properly be called the principles of justice. The argument is designed to lay the groundwork of answering these questions.[a]

**2.** Rawls introduces the two basic principles associated with the concept of justice. According to his reasoning, they apply to the *practices* of *persons*. By *persons* he means either particular human beings or collective agencies, and by *practices* he means "any form of activity specified by a system of rules which defines offices and roles, rights and duties."

The conception of justice which I want to consider has two principles associated with it. Both of them, and so the conception itself, are extremely familiar; and indeed, this is as it should be, since one would hope eventually to make a case for regarding them as the principles of justice. It is unlikely that novel principles could be candidates for this position. It may be possible, however, by using the concept of reciprocity as a framework, to assemble these principles against a different background and to look at them in a new way. I shall now state them and then provide a brief commentary to clarify their meaning.

First, each person participating in a practice, or affected by it, has an equal right to the most extensive liberty compatible with a like liberty for all; and second, inequalities are arbitrary unless it is reasonable to expect that they will work out to everyone's advantage, and provided that the positions and offices to which they attach, or from which they may be gained, are open to all. These principles express justice as a complex of three ideas: liberty, equality, and reward for services contributing to the common good.

A word about the term "person." This expression is to be construed variously depending on the circumstances. On some occasions it will mean human individuals, but in others it may refer to nations, provinces, business firms, churches, teams, and so on. The principles of justice apply to conflicting claims made by persons of all of these separate kinds. There is, perhaps, a certain logical priority to the case of human individuals: it may be possible to analyze the actions of so-called artificial persons as logical constructions of the actions of human persons, and it is plausible to maintain that the worth of institutions is derived solely from the benefits they bring to human individuals. Nevertheless an analysis of justice should not begin by making either of these assumptions, or by restricting itself to the case of human persons; and it can gain considerably from not doing so. As I shall use the term "person," then, it will be ambiguous in the manner indicated.[b]

**3.** Rawls clarifies and qualifies *equal liberty,* the first principle of justice.

The first principle holds, of course, only if other things are equal: that is, while there must always be a justification for departing from the initial position of equal liberty (liberty being defined by reference to the pattern of rights and duties, powers and liabilities, established by a practice), and the burden of proof is placed on him who would depart from it, nevertheless, there can be, and often there is, a justification for doing so. Now, that similar particular cases, as defined by a practice, should be treated similarly as they arise, is part of the very concept of a practice; in accordance with the analysis of justice as regularity, it is involved in the notion of an activity in accordance with rules, and expresses the concept of equality in one of its forms: that is equality as the impartial and equitable administration and application of the rules whatever they are, which define a practice. The first principle expresses the concept of equality in another form, namely, as applied to the definition and initial specification of the structure of practices themselves. It holds, for example, that there is a presumption against the distinctions and classifications made by legal systems and other practices to the extent that they infringe on the original and equal liberty of the persons participating in them, or affected by them. The second principle defines how this presumption may be rebutted.

It might be argued at this point that justice requires only that there be an equal liberty. If, however, a more extensive liberty were possible for all without loss or conflict, then it would be irrational to settle upon a lesser liberty. There is no reason for circumscribing rights unless their exercise would be incompatible, or would render the practice defining them less effective. Where such a limitation of liberty seems to have occurred, there must be some special explanation. It may have arisen from a mistake or misapprehension; or perhaps it persists from a time past when it had a rational basis, but does so no longer. Otherwise, such a limitation would be inexplicable; the acceptance of it would conflict with the premise that the persons engaged in the practice want the things which a more extensive liberty would make possible. Therefore no serious distortion of the concept of justice is likely to follow from associating with it a principle requiring the greatest equal liberty. This association is necessary once it is supposed, as I shall suppose, that the persons engaged in the practices to which the principles of justice apply are rational.[c]

**4.** Rawls continues with the clarification and qualification of the *difference principle.*

The second principle defines what sorts of inequalities are permissible; it specifies how the presumption laid down by the first principle may be put aside. Now by inequalities it is best to understand not any differences between offices and positions, but differences in the benefits and burdens attached to them either directly or indirectly, such as prestige and wealth, or liability to taxation and compulsory services. Players in a game do not protest against there being different positions, such as that of batter, pitcher, catcher, and the like, nor to there being various privileges and powers specified by the rules. Nor do citizens of a country object to there being the different offices of government such as that of president, senator, governor, judge, and soon, each with its special rights and duties. It is not differences of this kind that are normally thought of as inequalities, but differences in the resulting distribution established by a practice, or made possible by it, of the things men strive to attain or to avoid. Thus they may complain about the pattern of honors and rewards set up by a practice (e.g., the privileges and salaries of government officials) or they may object to the distribution of power and wealth which results from the various ways in which men avail themselves of the opportunities allowed by it (e.g., the concentration of wealth which may develop in a free price system allowing large entrepreneurial or speculative gains).

It should be noted that the second principle holds an inequality is allowed only if there is a reason to believe that the practice with the inequality, or resulting in it, will work for the advantage of *every* person engaging in it. Here it is important to stress that every person must gain from the inequality. Since the principle applies to practices, it implies then that the representative man in every office or position defined by a practice, when he views it as a going concern, must find it reasonable to prefer his condition and prospects with the inequality to what they would be under the practice without it. The principles exclude, therefore, the justification of inequalities on the grounds that the disadvantages of those in one position are outweighed by the greater advantages of those in another position. This rather simple restriction is the main modification I wish to make in the utilitarian principle as usually understood. When coupled with the notion of a practice, it is a restriction of consequence, and one which some utilitarians, notably Hume and Mill, have used in their discussions of justice without realizing apparently its significance, or at least without calling attention to it.

Further, it is also necessary that the various offices to which special benefits or burdens attach are open to all. It may be, for example, to the common advantage, as just defined, to attach special benefits to certain offices. Perhaps by doing so the requisite talent can be attracted to them and encouraged to give its best efforts. But any offices having special benefits must be won in a fair competition in which contestants are judged on their merits. If some offices were not open, those excluded would normally be justified in feeling unjustly treated, even if they benefited from the greater efforts of those who were allowed to compete for them. Moreover, they would be justified in their complaint not only because they were excluded from certain external emoluments of office, but because they were barred from attaining the great intrinsic goods which the skillful and devoted exercise of some offices represents, and so they would be deprived, from the start, of one of the leading ways to achieve a full human life.[d]

**5.** Having presented the principles of justice, Rawls next considers how they are derived. Although he does not dismiss the possibility that the equal liberty principle is self-evident, he offers instead a set of assumptions from which both principles seem to follow: He assumes that people are mutually self-interested, rational, and similar in needs, interests, and capacities.

I want to bring out how they [the principles of justice] are generated by imposing the constraints of having a morality upon persons who confront one another on those occasions when questions of justice arise.

In order to do this, it seems simplest to present a conjectural account of the derivation of these principles as follows. Imagine a societyof persons amongst whom a certain system of practices is already well established. Now suppose that by and large they are mutually self-interested; their allegiance to their established practices is normally founded on the prospect of their own advantage. One need not, and indeed ought not, to assume that, in all senses of the term "person," the persons in this society are mutually self-interested. If this characterization holds when the line of division is the family, it is nevertheless likely to be true that members of families are bound by ties of sentiment and affection and willingly acknowledge duties in contradiction to self-interest. Mutual self-interestedness in the relations between families, nations, churches, and the like, is commonly associated with loyalty and devotion on the part of individual members. If this were not so the conflicts between these forms of association would not be pursued with such intensity and would not have such tragic consequences. If Hobbes's description of relations between persons seems unreal as applied to human individuals, it is often true enough of the relations between artificial persons; and these relations may assume their Hobbesian character largely in consequence of that element which that description professedly leaves out, the loyalty and devotion of individuals. Therefore, one can form a more realistic conception of this society if one thinks of it as consisting of mutually self-interested families, or some other association. Taking the term "person" widely from the start prepares one for doing this. It is not necessary to suppose, however, that these persons are mutually self-interested under all circumstances, but only in the usual situations in which they participate in their common practices concerning which the question of justice arises.

Now suppose further that these persons are rational: they know their own interests more or less accurately; they realize that the several ends they pursue may conflict with each other, and they are able to decide what level of attainment of one they are willing to sacrifice for a given level of attainment of another; they are capable of tracing out the likely consequences of adopting one practice rather than another, and of adhering to a course of action once they have decided upon it; they can resist present temptations and the enticements of immediate gain; and the bare knowledge or perception of the difference between their condition and that of others is not, within certain limits and in itself, a source of great dissatisfaction. Only the very last point adds anything to the standard definition of rationality as it appears say in the theory of price; and there is no need to question the propriety of this definition given the purposes for which it is customarily used. But the notion of rationality, if it is to play a part in the analysis of justice should allow, I think, that a rational man will resent or will be dejected by differences of condition between himself and others only where there is an accompanying explanation: that is, if they are thought to derive from injustice, or from some other fault of institutions, or to be the consequence of letting chance work itself out for no useful common purpose. At any rate, I shall include this trait of character in the notion of rationality for the purpose of analyzing the concept of justice. The legitimacy of doing so will, I think, become clear as the analysis proceeds. So if these persons strike us as unpleasantly egoistic in their relations with one another, they are at least free in some degree from the fault of envy.

Finally, assume that these persons have roughly similar needs, interests, and capacities, or needs, interests, and capacities in various ways complementary, so that fruitful cooperation amongst them is possible; and suppose that they are sufficiently equal in power and the instruments thereof to guarantee that in normal circumstances none is able to dominate the others. This condition (as well as the other conditions) may seem excessively vague; but in view of the conception of justice to which the argument leads, there seems to be no reason for making it more exact at this point.

Since these persons are conceived as engaging in their common practices, which are already established, there is no question of our supposing them to come together to deliberate as to how they will set up these practices for the first time. Yet we can imagine that from time to time they discuss with one another whether any of them has a legitimate complaint against their established institutions. This is only natural in any normal society. Now suppose that they have settled on doing this in the following way. They first try to arrive at the principles by which complaints and so practices themselves are to be judged. That is, they do not begin by complaining; they begin instead by establishing the criteria by which a complaint is to be counted legitimate. Their procedure for this is to let each person propose the principles upon which he wishes his complaints to be tried with the understanding that, if acknowledged, the complaints of others will be similarly tried; and moreover, that no complaints will be heard at all until everyone is roughly of one mind as to how complaints are to be judged. Thus while each person has a chance to propose the standards he wishes, these standards must prove acceptable to the others before his charges can be given a hearing. They all understand further that the principles proposed and acknowledged on this occasion are binding on future occasions. So each will be wary of proposing a principle which would give him a peculiar advantage in his present circumstances, supposing it to be accepted (which is, perhaps, in most cases unlikely). Each person knows that he will be bound by it in future circumstances the peculiarities of which cannot be known, and which might well be such that the principle is then to his disadvantage. The basic idea in this procedure is that everyone should be required to make in advance a firm commitment to acknowledge certain principles as applying to his own case and such that others also may reasonably be expected to acknowledge them; and that no one be given the opportunity to tailor the canons of a legitimate complaint to fit his own special conditions, and then to discard them when they no longer suit his purpose. Hence each person will propose principles of a general kind which will, to a large degree, gain their sense from the various applications to be made of them, the particular circumstances of these applications being as yet unknown. These principles will express the conditions in accordance with which each person is the least unwilling to have his interests limited in the design of practices, given the competing interests of the others, on the supposition that the interests of others will be limited likewise. The restriction[s] which would so arise might be thought of as those a person would keep in mind if he were designing a practice in which his enemy were to assign him his place.[e]

**6.** When people are impartial—that is, when they operate under a Rawlsian "veil of ignorance"—the appropriateness of the two principles of justice is manifest.

Given all the conditions as described in the conjectural account, it would be natural if the two principles of justice were to be jointly acknowledged. Since there is no way for anyone to win special advantages for himself, each would consider it reasonable to acknowledge equality as an initial principle. There is, however, no reason why they should regard this position as final. If there are inequalities which satisfy the conditions of the second principle, the immediate gain which equality would allow can be considered as intelligently invested in view of its future return. If, as is quite likely, these inequalities work as incentives to draw out better efforts, the members of this society may look upon them as concessions to human nature: they, like us, may think that people ideally should want to serve one another. But as they are mutually self-interested, their acceptance of these inequalities is merely the acceptance of the relations in which they actually stand, and a recognition of the motives which lead them to engage in their common practices. Being themselves self-interested, they have no title to complain of one another. And so provided the conditions of the principle are met, there is no reason why they should not allow such inequalities. Indeed, it would be shortsighted of them not to do so, and could result, in most cases, only from their being dejected by the bare knowledge, or perception, that others are better situated. Each person will, however, insist on an advantage to himself, and so on a common advantage, for none is willing to sacrifice anything for the others.

These remarks are not offered as a rigorous proof that persons conceived and situated as the conjectural account supposes, and required to adopt the procedure described, would settle on the two principles of justice stated and commented upon. . . . For this a much more elaborate and formal argument would have to be given. I shall not undertake a proof in this sense. In a weaker sense, however, the argument may be considered a proof, or as a sketch of a proof, although there still remain certain details to be filled in, and various alternatives to be ruled out.[f]

**7.** As developed earlier by Rawls, the concepts of fairness and justice are distinguishable. Fairness applies to "practices where persons are cooperating with or competing against one another and which allow a choice whether or not to do so." Justice applies to those "practices in which there is no such choice whether or not to participate." It is to be recalled as well, however, that both concepts have "a fundamental element in common"—namely, the concept of reciprocity. Turning his attention to the importance of reciprocity for his social thesis, Rawls argues that unless justice is founded on the "mutual acknowledgment of principles by free and equal persons," it becomes subject to the contingencies of "force and circumstance."

That the principles of justice may be regarded as associated with the sense of justice in the manner described illustrates some important facts about them. For one thing it suggests the thought that justice is the first moral virtue in the sense that it arises once the concept of morality is imposed on mutually self-interested persons who are similarly situated; it is the first moral concept to be generated when one steps outside the bounds of rational self-interest. More relevant at the moment, the conjectural derivation emphasizes that fundamental to both justice and fairness is the concept of reciprocity. In the sense in which I shall use this concept, the question of reciprocity arises when free persons, who have no moral authority over one another and who are engaging in or who find themselves participating in a joint activity, are amongst themselves settling upon or acknowledging the rules which define it and which determine their respective shares in its benefits and burdens. The principle of reciprocity requires of a practice that it satisfy those principles which the persons who participate in it could reasonably propose for mutual acceptance under the circumstances and conditions of the hypothetical account. Persons engaged in a practice meeting this principle can then face one another openly and support their respective positions, should they appear questionable, by reference to principles which it is reasonable to expect each to accept. A practice will strike the parties as conforming to the notion of reciprocity if none feels that, by participating in it, he or any of the others are taken advantage of or forced to give in to claims which they do not accept as legitimate. But if they are prepared to complain this implies that each has a conception of legitimate claims which he thinks it reasonable for all to acknowledge. If one thinks of the principles of justice as arising in the manner described, then they specify just this sort of conception.

It is this requirement of the possibility of mutual acknowledgment of principles by free and equal persons who have not authority over one another which makes the concept of reciprocity fundamental to both justice and fairness. Only if such acknowledgment is possible can there be true community between persons in their common practices; otherwise their relations will appear to them as founded to some degree on force and circumstance.[g]

**8.** Additional clarification of the concept of justice as reciprocity is achieved by contrasting its principles with those of classical Utilitarianism on the issue of slavery.

One may begin by noticing that classical utilitarianism permits one to argue that slavery is unjust on the grounds that the advantages to the slaveholder as slaveholder do not counterbalance the disadvantages to the slave and to society at large, burdened by a comparatively inefficient system of labor. Now the conception of justice as reciprocity, when applied to the practice of slavery with its offices of slaveholder and slave, would not allow one to consider the advantages of the slaveholder in the first place. As that office is not in accordance with principles which could be mutually acknowledged, the gains accruing to the slaveholder, assuming them to exist, cannot be counted as in any way mitigating the injustice of the practice. The question whether these gains outweigh the disadvantages to the slaves and to society cannot arise, since in considering the justice of slavery these gains have no weight at all which requires that they be overridden. Where the conception of justice as reciprocity applies, slavery is always unjust.

I am not, of course, suggesting the absurdity that the classical utilitarians approved of slavery.[4] I am only rejecting a type of argument which their view allows them to use in support of their disapproval of it. The conception of justice as derivative from efficiency implies that judging the justice of a practice is always, in principle at least, a matter of weighing up advantages and disadvantages, each having an intrinsic value or disvalue as the satisfaction of interests, irrespective of whether or not these interests necessarily involve acquiescence in principles which could not mutu-

[4]To the contrary, Bentham argued very powerfully against it. See *A Fragment of Government*, ch. 2, par. 34, fn. 2; *The Principles of Morals and Legislation*, ch. 16, par. 44, fn.; ch. 17, par. 4, fn.; *The Theory of Legislation*, pt. 3, ch.2.

ally be acknowledged. Utilitarianism cannot account for the fact that slavery is always unjust, nor for the fact that it would be recognized as irrelevant in defeating the accusation of injustice for one person to say to another, engaged with him in a common practice and debating its merits, that nevertheless it allowed of the greatest satisfaction of desire. The charge of injustice cannot be rebutted in this way. If justice were derivative from a higher order executive efficiency, this would not be so.

But now, even if it is taken as established that, so far as the ordinary conception of justice goes, slavery is always unjust (that is, slavery by definition violates commonly recognized principles of justice), the classical utilitarian would surely reply that these principles, like other moral principles subordinate to that of utility, are only generally correct. It is simply for the most part true that slavery is less efficient than other institutions; and while common sense may define the concept of justice in such a way that slavery is proved unjust, nevertheless, where slavery would lead to the greatest satisfaction of desire, it is not wrong. Indeed, it is then right, and for the very same reason that justice, as ordinarily understood, is usually right. If, as ordinarily understood, slavery is always unjust, to this extent the utilitarian conception of justice might be admitted to differ from that of moral opinion. Still the utilitarian would want to hold that, as a matter of moral principle, his view is correct in giving no special weight to considerations of justice beyond that allowed for by the general presumption of effectiveness. And this, he claims, is as it should be. The everyday opinion is morally in error, although, indeed, it is a useful error, since it protects rules of generally high utility.

The question, then, relates not simply to the analysis of the concept of justice as common sense defines it, but the analysis of it in the wider sense as to how much weight considerations of justice, as defined, are to have when laid against other kinds of moral considerations. Here again I wish to argue that reasons of justice have a special weight for which only the conception of justice as reciprocity can account. Moreover, it belongs to the concept of justice that they do have this special weight. While Mill recognized that this was so, he thought that it could be accounted for by the special urgency of the moral feelings which naturally support principles of such high utility. But it is a mistake to resort to the urgency of feeling; as with the appeal to intuition, it manifests a failure to pursue the question far enough. The special weight of considerations of justice can be explained from the conception of justice as reciprocity. It is only necessary to elaborate a bit what has already been said, as follows.

If one examines the circumstances in which a certain tolerance of slavery is justified, or perhaps better, excused, it turns out that these are of a rather special sort. Perhaps slavery exists as an inheritance from the past and it proves necessary to dismantle it piece by piece; at times slavery may conceivably be an advance on previous institutions. Now while there may be some excuse for slavery in special conditions, it is never an excuse for it that it is sufficiently advantageous to the slaveholder to outweigh the disadvantages to the slave and to society. A person who argues in this way is not perhaps making a wildly irrelevant remark; but he is guilty of a moral fallacy. There is disorder in this conception of the ranking of moral principles. For the slaveholder, by his own admission, has no moral title to the advantages which he receives as a slaveholder. He is no more prepared than the slave to acknowledge the principle upon which is founded the respective positions in which they both stand. Since slavery does not accord with principles which they could mutually acknowledge, they each may be supposed to agree that it is unjust: it grants claims which it ought not to grant and in doing so denies claims which it ought not to deny. Amongst persons in a general position who are debating the form of their common practices, it cannot, therefore, be offered as a reason for a practice that, in conceding these very claims that ought to be denied, it nevertheless meets existing interests more effectively. By their very nature the satisfaction of these claims is without weight and cannot enter into any tabulation of advantages and disadvantages.

Furthermore, it follows from the concept of morality that, to the extent that the slaveholder recognizes his position vis-à-vis the slave to be unjust, he would not choose to press his claims. His not wanting to receive his special advantages is one of the ways in which he shows that he thinks slavery is unjust. It would be fallacious for the legislator to suppose, then, that it is a ground for having a practice that it brings advantages greater than disadvantages, if those for whom the practice is designed and to whom the advantages flow, acknowledge that they have no moral title to them and do not wish to receive them.

For these reasons the principles of justice have a special weight; and with respect to the principle of the greatest satisfaction of desire, as cited in the general position amongst those discussing the merits of their common practices, the principles of justice have an absolute weight. In this sense they are not contingent; and this is why their force is greater than can be accounted for by the general presumption (assuming that there is one) of the effectiveness, in the utilitarian sense, of practices which in fact satisfy them.[h]

**9.** Drawing his accounts together, Rawls sums up, in a positive way, his concept of justice in terms of the social contract.

If, however, the argument above regarding slavery is correct, granting these assumptions as moral and political principles make no difference. To view individuals as equally fruitful lines for the allocation of benefits, even as a matter of moral principle, still leaves the mistaken notion that the satisfaction of desire has value in itself irrespective of the relations between persons as members of a common practice, and irrespective of the claims upon one another which the satisfaction of interests represents. To see the error of this idea one must give up the conception of justice as an executive decision altogether and refer to the notion of justice as fairness: that participants in a common practice be regarded as having an original and equal liberty and that their common practices be considered unjust unless they accord with principles which persons so circumstanced and related could freely acknowledge before one another, and so could accept as fair. Once the emphasis is put upon the concept of the mutual recognition of principles by participants in a common practice the rules of which are to define their several relations and give form to their claims on one another, then it is clear that the granting of a claim the principle of which could not be acknowledged by each in the general position (that is, in the position in which the parties propose and acknowledge principles before one another) is not a reason for adopting a practice. Viewed in this way, the background of the claim is seen to exclude it from consideration; that it can represent a value in itself arises from the conception of individuals as separate lines for the assignment of benefits, as isolated persons who stand as claimants on an administrative or benevolent largesse. Occasionally persons do so stand to one another; but this is not the general case, nor, more importantly, is it the case when it is a matter of the justice of practices themselves in which participants stand in various relations to be appraised in accordance with standards which they may be expected to acknowledge before one another. Thus, however mistaken the notion of the social contract may be as history, and however far it may overreach itself as a general theory of social and political obligation, it does express, suitably interpreted, an essential part of the concept of justice.[i]

## QUESTIONS

1. How sharp a distinction does Rawls draw between the concepts of justice and fairness? Can you suggest some circumstances in which the terms *justice* and *fairness* might be used interchangeably and some circumstances in which they could not? How is the concept of reciprocity related to these concepts?
2. What is the principle of equal liberty? Illustrate its meaning by providing a situation to which it might apply.

3. What is the principle of difference? Illustrate it by providing a circumstance to which it might apply.
4. Sometimes Rawls emphasizes the priority of the equal liberty principle to the difference principle. Why is this order of priority important?
5. Would Rawls's contract theory be undermined if one assumed that people were *not* mutually self-interested, rational, and similar in needs, interests, and capacities? Discuss the theoretical significance of the assumption that humans have these traits.
6. Must Rawls deny Hobbes's depiction of the state of nature as "a time of war, where every man is enemy to every man"? Discuss.
7. What meaning does Rawls's metaphor "veil of ignorance" convey? In your dealings with others, are you ever willing to place yourself under the veil of ignorance?
8. Rawls charges that Utilitarianism does not necessarily preclude slavery as a theoretical possibility. Does his discussion unduly emphasize the difference between theory and practice? Develop.
9. According to Rawls, it is a mistaken notion that "the satisfaction of desire has value in itself irrespective of the relations between persons as members of a common practice." By insisting on this point, does Rawls ally himself more nearly with Kant than with Mill? Defend your answer.
10. Suppose that one fully accepts the Rawlsian social theory. Would such a person be free to adopt an individual morality such as Epicurus proposes? Or Epictetus? Or Nietzsche?

## KEY TO SELECTIONS

John Rawls, "Justice as Reciprocity," from John Stuart Mill, *Utilitarianism,* S. Gorovitz, ed., Bobbs-Merrill, New York, 1971. Reprinted with the kind permission of the publisher.

[a]pp. 242–243.
[b]pp. 144–245.
[c]p. 145.
[d]pp. 245–247.
[e]pp. 248-250.
[f]pp. 251–252.
[g]pp. 255–256.
[h]pp. 264–265.
[i]pp. 266–267.

## GUIDE TO ADDITIONAL READING

**PRIMARY SOURCES**

Rawls, J., "Justice as Fairness," *Philosophical Review*, 67 (1958), pp. 164–194.

_____, "Two Concepts of Rules," *Philosophical Review*, 64 (1955), pp. 3–32.

_____, *A Theory of Justice*, Cambridge, Harvard University Press, 1971.

**DISCUSSION AND COMMENTARY**

Arrow, K., "Some Ordinalist-Utilitarian Notes on Rawls' Theory of Justice," *Journal of Philosophy*, 70 (1973), pp. 245–263.

Barry, B., *The Liberal Theory of Justice*, Oxford, Clarendon Press, 1973.

Blocker, H., and Smith, E. (eds.), *John Rawls' Theory of Social Justice,* Athens, Ohio University Press, 1980.

Feinberg, J., "Duty and Obligation in the Non-Ideal World," *Journal of Philosophy*, 70 (1973), pp. 263–275.

Gordon, S., "John Rawls' Difference Principle, Utilitarianism, and the Optimum Degree of Inequality," *Journal of Philosophy*, 70 (1973), pp. 275–280.

Kymlicka, W., "The Social Contract Tradition," in *A Companion to Ethics,* ed. P. Singer, Cambridge, Blackwell,1993, pp. 186–198.

Martin, R., *Rawls and Rights*, Lawrence, University of Kansas Press, 1985.

O'Neal, P., "A Refutation of John Rawls' 'A Theory of Justice,'" *Dialogue*, April 1977, pp. 40–48.

CHAPTER TWENTY-FIVE

# Moral Virtue and Human Interest

PHILIPPA FOOT (b. 1920), English by birth, received degrees from Oxford in 1942 and 1946. She was a lecturer in philosophy (1947–1949) and tutor and fellow (1949–1969). Currently she divides her time between Oxford University, where she is a senior research fellow at Somerville College, and the University of California at Los Angeles, where she is a professor of philosophy. Foot has been president of the Pacific Division of the American Philosophical Association and has lectured in various countries. In addition to her major work in ethics, *Virtues and Vices* (1978), she has edited *Theories of Ethics* (1967) and has contributed numerous articles and reviews to philosophical journals.

Theories of ethical naturalism—theories claiming that value judgments can be reduced to, assimilated by, or at least justified by statements of fact alone—were popular in the last century, but they have been widely criticized in this one. The first of three distinguishable forms of attack was by ethical intuitionists,[1] the second by emotivists, and the third by prescriptivists. Despite this array of criticism, however, the number of able theorists arguing for a cautious return to naturalism is on the rise. Philippa Foot is a good representative. She is convinced that one can bridge the gap between fact and value and that certain factual statements provide "good reasons" for value judgments. Her view can be introduced by noting her critical responses to the emotivist C. L. Stevenson and the prescriptivist R. M. Hare (b. 1919).

Although Foot would admit that Stevenson has attempted to supply a role for "reasons" in regard to ethical judgments, she would deny that his so-called reasons constitute a *logical* justification. Stevenson admits that to the extent that beliefs (factual data) alter attitudes (the basic source of value judgments), they constitute some form of support for these attitudes. But for him, the relationship between the factual matters and value expressions is a *causal* one. That is, insofar as a set of factual beliefs can change attitudes, they will be regarded as reasons. However, according to Stevenson, value judgments are essentially rooted in attitudes, and because factual beliefs do not always succeed in producing attitudinal changes, they do not constitute an ultimate justification for value judgments.

[1]The initial and most influential criticism was made by G. E. Moore (see Chapter 19, particularly secs. 8 and 9).

What Foot finds puzzling and peculiar in Stevenson's position is this: If Stevenson's view is adopted, two people may use the *same* set of facts (beliefs) to arrive at opposite moral judgments and claim that their respective positions are equally well founded. Thus Foot suggests that Stevenson is employing "reasons" in a specious and arbitrary way. Facts become mere means to altering attitudes but cease to provide objective reasons for a given position. According to Foot, this represents a breakdown in moral arguments and weakens the case for genuine moral disputes.

Hare provides a more complicated view for Foot to deal with. He, like G. E. Moore, believes that one cannot reduce value judgments to empirical (factual) statements. He rejects Moore's intuitionism as well as Moore's view that the basic value term *good* describes some (nonnatural, simple) property. Rather, Hare thinks that values and value judgments function as action guiding, as commendations. For example, to say "X is courageous" is to commend X for exhibiting courage. But Hare denies that you can discover a set of natural properties that describe every good thing or that such a list related to a good thing constitutes its meaning. For example, in stating "X is a good strawberry," we may assert that "X is sweet, juicy, red, and so forth," but the list of properties (criteria for judging the goodness of an object) is not identical with the meaning of *good strawberry*. The meaning of *good* is its commendatory force, which all good things have in common. It has the same meaning in every context, though the criteria (descriptive characteristics) vary with the context. Thus the criteria for judging a good strawberry would obviously differ from those for judging a good lawyer or good tennis player.

Foot does not accept Hare's thesis that in making a value judgment such as "X is courageous" we must be commending X, for one may commend another person for courage and yet not prescribe it for anyone else or even for oneself. Furthermore, Foot would question Hare's thesis that one can be arbitrary as to what constitutes evidence ("good reason") for a value judgment. As she puts it, if one takes Hare's prescriptivism seriously, then

> One man may say that a thing is good because of some fact about it, and another may refuse to take that fact as any evidence at all, for nothing is laid down in the meaning of "good" [its being commendatory] which connects it with one piece of "evidence" rather than another. It follows that a moral eccentric could argue to moral conclusions from quite idiosyncratic premises; he could say, for instance, that a man was a good man because he clasped and unclasped his hands, and never turned N.N.E. after turning S.S.W.[2]

Foot makes an interesting and strong case for ethical naturalism. She contends that only those beliefs that are necessarily connected with human welfare (benefit or need) are moral beliefs. Thus, for instance, it would be as absurd for a person to maintain that wisdom, courage, and temperance were not moral virtues as it would be to believe that losing one's hands and losing one's eyes were not injuries, for if one's physical organs do not operate as they should (exhibiting injury), one cannot take care of one's basic needs. An injury is a defect that human beings have good reason to avoid. The same sort of reasoning applies to moral qualities such as Plato's cardinal virtues. Without them, individuals cannot act effectively in the face of dangers, temptations, and so forth. Therefore, human beings have good

---

[2] P. Foot, "Moral Beliefs," *Proceedings of the Aristotelian Society*, 59, 1958–1959, p. 83.

reasons to display these qualities (dispositions). The connection between the virtues of courage, wisdom, and temperance and their benefit to an individual is fairly clear. In brief, these qualities are as necessary for the health of the human psyche as good organs are for that of the body.

Foot acknowledges that justice differs from the other three virtues insofar as it is a social virtue involving an obligation to others. Also, as Thrasymachus suggests, it would appear that an individual might not benefit from being just. However, Foot holds that Thrasymachus would be right only if that person were isolated from society or could remain undetected by others (as described in the Gyges Ring Story). But she regards these conditions as unrealistic because a person is bound to interact with others. Besides, it would take such a gigantic vigilance to practice injustice as a way of life that it would not be worth the price. Of course, Foot does admit that there are occasions in which justice is not beneficial to a given individual, but she insists that because one *generally* has good reason to practice justice, one should not act unjustly even in those exceptional situations. More recently she has admitted—reluctantly—that there is no necessary, invariable relationship between justice and human benefit. Indeed, she has begun to have some doubts about whether justice is really a virtue.[3] As she puts it, "It seems obvious that a man who acts justly must on occasion be ready to go against his own interests, but so determined was I to think that every man must have reason to act morally that I was prepared to doubt that justice is a virtue rather than give up that idea."[4]

It is noteworthy in the selections that Foot blends and balances a modern metaethical concern—justifying value judgments on the basis of factual statements—with a traditional concern for "virtue ethics." For the past twenty-five years, many other ethical theorists have also revived classical interests by concentrating on the nature of the good life, on human character (moral psychology), and on specific virtues of moral agents. This is in sharp contrast to metaethical issues, which have been dominant since the turn of the century. The latter orientation, which still prevails, has come to be regarded by some moral philosophers as sterile, empty, and too detached from the moral problems with which ordinary persons struggle. The detached neutrality of metaethics is best captured by the prefatory remarks of C. D. Broad (1887–1971) in *Five Types of Ethical Theory:*

> I find it difficult to excite myself very much over right and wrong, in practice. I have no clear idea of what people have in mind when they say they labor under a sense of sin. . . . A healthy appetite for righteousness, kept in due control by good manners, is an excellent thing; but to "hunger and thirst after" it is often merely a symptom of spiritual diabetes. And a white-heat of moral enthusiasm is not perhaps the most

---

[3]Despite Foot's admission that in logical strictness, there is no necessary connection between morality and human interest, she rejects the neo-Kantian view that moral judgments can be justified independent of human concerns. Kant, for example, believed that one does not possess the moral virtue of honesty if one is honest only because of its benefits. This represents to Kantians an ulterior, tainted motive rather than the pure motive of duty. In contrast, Foot claims that there are many times when some of our interests (desires, needs, and so forth) represent reasons for being morally virtuous. As she puts it, "But what reason could there be for refusing to call a man a just man if he acted justly because he loved truth and liberty, and wanted every man to be treated with a certain respect? And why should the truly honest man not follow honesty for the sake of the good that honest dealing brings to man?" (*Virtues and Vices,* p. 165). Thus, for Foot, moral judgments can be hypothetical (rather than categorical) imperatives, because she sees a definite relationship between what is moral and its good-producing tendency.

[4]P. Foot, *Virtues and Vices* (Berkeley: University of California Press, 1978), p. xiii.

favorable condition in which to conduct the analysis of ethical concepts or the criticisms of ethical theories.[5]

Both Alasdair MacIntyre (b. 1929) in his book *After Virtue* and Philippa Foot in *Virtues and Vices* have given added impetus to "virtue ethics." MacIntyre has argued in the Aristotelian tradition that the modern morality of rules (Utilitarian or Kantian) must be rejected unless it fits into a larger scheme in which the virtues are central. In similar fashion, Foot has criticized moralists within the "school of analytic philosophy" who have neglected altogether the subject of virtues and vices.

**1.** According to Foot, a person is generally better off with a virtue than without it, although some virtues, such as justice, benefit others.

First of all it seems clear that virtues are, in some general way, beneficial. Human beings do not get on well without them. Nobody can get on well if he lacks courage, and does not have some measure of temperance and wisdom, while communities where justice and charity are lacking are apt to be wretched places to live, as Russia was under the Stalinist terror, or Sicily under the Mafia. But now we must ask to whom the benefit goes, whether to the man who has the virtue or rather to those who have to do with him? In the case of some of the virtues the answer seems clear. Courage, temperance, and wisdom benefit both the man who has these dispositions and other people as well; and moral failings such as pride, vanity, worldliness, and avarice harm both their possessor and others, though chiefly perhaps the former. But what about the virtues of charity and justice? These are directly concerned with the welfare of others, and with what is owed to them; and since each may require sacrifice of interest on the part of the virtuous man both may seem to be deleterious to their possessor and beneficial to others. Whether in fact it is so has, of course, been a matter of controversy since Plato's time or earlier. It is a reasonable opinion that on the whole a man is better off for being charitable and just, but this is not to say that circumstances may not arise in which he will have to sacrifice everything for charity or justice.[a]

**2.** In attempting to define virtue, she notes that one's intentions will play a key role.

Let us say then, leaving unsolved problems behind us, that virtues are in general beneficial characteristics, and indeed ones that a human being needs to have, for his own sake and that of his fellows. This will not, however, take us far towards a definition of a virtue, since there are many other qualities of a man that may be similarly beneficial, as for instance bodily characteristics such as health and physical strength, and mental powers such as those of memory and concentration. What is it, we must ask, that differentiates virtues from such things?

As a first approximation to an answer we might say that while health and strength are excellences of the body, and memory and concentration of the mind, it is the will that is good in a man of virtue. But this suggestion is worth only as much as the explanation that follows it. What might we mean by saying that virtue belongs to the will?

In the first place we observe that it is primarily by his intentions that a man's moral dispositions are judged. If he does something unintentionally this is usually irrelevant to our estimate of his virtue. But of course this thesis

[5] C. D. Broad, *Five Types of Ethical Theory* (London: Routledge and Kegen Paul, 1930), pp. xxiv–xxv.

must be qualified, because failures in performance rather than intention may show a lack of virtue. This will be so when, for instance, one man brings harm to another without realizing he is doing it, but where his ignorance is itself culpable. Sometimes in such cases there will be a previous act or omission to which we can point as the source of the ignorance. Charity requires that we take care to find out how to render assistance where we are likely to be called on to do so, and thus, for example, it is contrary to charity to fail to find out about elementary first aid. But in an interesting class of cases in which it seems again to be performance rather than intention that counts in judging a man's virtue there is no possibility of shifting the judgment to previous intentions. For sometimes one man succeeds where another fails not because there is some specific difference in their previous conduct but rather because his heart lies in a different place; and the disposition of the heart is part of virtue.[b]

**3.** The relationship between moral virtue and will requires some qualification, especially in dealing with wisdom. It involves consideration of general, good ends as well as an ability to distinguish what is trivial or superficial from what is genuine.

A different set of considerations will, however, force us to give up any simple statement about the relation between virtue and will, and these considerations have to do with the virtue of wisdom. Practical wisdom, we said, was counted by Aristotle among the intellectual virtues, and while our *wisdom* is not quite the same as *phronesis* or *prudentia* it too might seem to belong to the intellect rather than the will. Is not wisdom a matter of knowledge, and how can knowledge be a matter of intention or desire? The answer is that it isn't, so that there is good reason for thinking of wisdom as an intellectual virtue. But on the other hand wisdom has special connections with the will, meeting it at more than one point.

In order to get this rather complex picture in focus we must pause for a little and ask what it is that we ourselves understand by wisdom: what the wise man knows and what he does. Wisdom, as I see it, has two parts. In the first place the wise man knows the means to certain good ends; and secondly he knows how much particular ends are worth. Wisdom in its first part is relatively easy to understand. It seems that there are some ends belonging to human life in general rather than to particular skills such as medicine or boatbuilding, ends having to do with such matters as friendship, marriage, the bringing up of children, or the choice of ways of life; and it seems that knowledge of how to act well in these matters belongs to some people but not to others. We call those who have this knowledge wise, while those who do not have it are seen as lacking wisdom. So, as both Aristotle and Aquinas insisted, wisdom is to be contrasted with cleverness because cleverness is the ability to take the right steps to any end, whereas wisdom is related only to good ends, and to human life in general rather than to the ends of particular arts.

In short wisdom, in what we called its first part, is connected with the will in the following ways. To begin with it presupposes good ends: the man who is wise does not merely know *how* to do good things such as looking after his children well, or strengthening someone in trouble, but must also want to do them. And then wisdom, in so far as it consists of knowledge which anyone can gain in the course of an ordinary life, is available to anyone who really wants it. As Aquinas put it, it belongs "to a power under the direction of the will."

The second part of wisdom, which has to do with values, is much harder to describe, because here we meet ideas which are curiously elusive, such as the thought that some pursuits are more worthwhile than others, and some matters trivial and some important in human life. Since it makes good sense to say that most men waste a lot of their lives in ardent pursuit of what is trivial and unimportant it is not possible to explain the important and the trivial in terms of the amount of attention given to different subjects by the average man. But I have never seen, or been able to think out, a true account of this matter, and I believe that a complete account of wisdom, and of certain other virtues and vices must wait until this gap can be filled. What we can see is that one of the things a wise man knows and a foolish man does not is that such things as social position, and wealth, and the good opinion of the world, are too dearly bought at the cost of health or friendship or family ties. So we may say that a man who lacks wisdom "has false values," and that vices such as vanity and worldliness and avarice are contrary to wisdom in a special way. There is always an element of false judgment about these vices, since the man who is vain for instance sees admiration as more important than it is, while the worldly man is apt to see the good life as one of wealth and power. Adapting Aristotle's distinction between the weak-willed man (the akratēs) who follows pleasure though he knows, in some sense, that he should not, and the licentious man (the akolastos) who sees the life of pleasure as the good life, we may say that moral failings such as these are never purely "akratic." It is true that a man may criticise himself for his worldliness or vanity or love of money, but then it is his values that are the subject of his criticism.[c]

> **4.** The virtues also require correctives or curbs. For instance, out of fear or temptation of pleasure, one might be led astray. Control of such passions must be acquired if the appropriate dispositions of courage and temperance are to be attained.

I shall now turn to another thesis about the virtues, which I might express by saying that they are *corrective,* each one standing at a point at which there is some temptation to be resisted or deficiency of motivation to be made good. As Aristotle put it, virtues are about what is difficult for men, and I want to see in what sense this is true, and then to consider a problem in Kant's moral philosophy in the light of what has been said.

Let us first think about courage and temperance. Aristotle and Aquinas contrasted these virtues with justice in the following respect. Justice was concerned with operations and courage and temperance with passions. What they meant by this seems to have been, primarily, that the man of courage does not fear immoderately nor the man of temperance have immoderate desires for pleasure, and that there was no corresponding moderation of a passion implied in the idea of justice. This particular account of courage and temperance might be disputed on the ground that a man's courage is measured by his action and not by anything as uncontrollable as fear; and similarly that the temperate man who must on occasion refuse pleasures need not *desire* them any less than the intemperate man. Be that as it may (and something will be said about it later) it is obviously true that courage and temperance have to do with particular springs of action as justice does not. Almost any desire can lead a man to act unjustly, not even excluding the desire to help a friend or to save a life, whereas a cowardly act must be motivated by fear or a desire for safety, and an act of intemperance by a desire for pleasure, perhaps even for a particular range of pleasures such as those of eating or drinking or sex. And now, going back to the idea of virtues as correctives one may say that it is only because fear and the desire for pleasure often operate as temptations that courage and temperance exist as virtues at all. As things are we often want to run away not only where that is the right thing to do but also where we should stand firm; and we want pleasure not only where we should seek pleasure but also where we should not. If human nature had been different there would have been no need of a corrective disposition in either place, as fear and pleasure would have been good guides to conduct throughout life. So Aquinas says, about the passions:

> They may incite us to something against reason, and so we need a curb, which we name temperance. Or they may make us shirk a course of action dictated by reason, through fear of dangers or hardships. Then a person needs to be steadfast and not run away from what is right; and for this courage is named.

As with courage and temperance so with many other virtues: there is, for instance, a virtue of industriousness only because idleness is a temptation; and of humility only because men tend to think too well of themselves. Hope is a virtue because despair too is a temptation; it might have been that no one cried that all was lost except where he could really see it to be so, and in this case there would have been no virtue of hope.

With virtues such as justice and charity it is a little different, because they correspond not to any particular desire or tendency that has to be kept in check but rather to a deficiency of motivation; and it is this that they must make good. If people were as much attached to the goods of others as they are to their own good there would no more be a general virtue of benevolence than there is a general virtue of self-love. And if people cared about the rights of others as they care about their own rights no virtue of justice would be needed to look after the matter, and rules about such things as contracts and promises would only need to be made public, like the rules of a game that everyone was eager to play.

On this view of the virtues and vices everything is seen to depend on what human nature is like, and the traditional catalogue of the two kinds of dispositions is not hard to understand. Nevertheless it may be defective, and anyone who accepts the thesis that I am putting forward will feel free to ask himself where the temptations and deficiencies that need correcting are really to be found. It is possible, for example, that the theory of human nature lying behind the traditional list of the virtues and vices puts too much emphasis on hedonistic and sensual impulses, and does not sufficiently take account of less straightforward inclinations such as the desire to be put upon and dissatisfied, or the unwillingness to accept good things as they come along.[d]

> **5.** Foot discusses the following knotty issue: Who is more genuinely virtuous—the person who desires to flee in the face of danger or the one who is not tempted at all to escape in that situation?

It should now be clear why I said that virtues should be seen as correctives; and part of what is meant by saying that virtue is about things that are difficult for men should also have appeared. The further application of this idea is, however, controversial, and the following difficulty presents itself: that we both are and are not inclined to think that the harder a man finds it to act virtuously the more virtue he shows if he does act well. For on the one hand great virtue is needed where it is particularly hard to act virtuously; yet on the other it could be argued that difficulty in acting virtuously shows that the agent is imperfect in virtue: according to Aristotle, to take pleasure in virtuous action is the mark of true virtue, with the self-mastery of the one who finds virtue difficult only a second best. How then is this conflict to be decided? Who shows most courage, the one who wants to run away but does not, or the one who does not even want to run away? Who shows most charity, the one who finds it easy to make the good of others his object, or the one who finds it hard?

What is certain is that the thought that virtues are corrective does not constrain us to relate virtue to difficulty in each individual man. Since men in general find it hard to face great dangers or evils, and even small ones, we may count as courageous those few who without blindness or indifference are nevertheless fearless even in terrible circumstances. And when someone has a natural charity or generosity it is, at least part of the virtue that he has; if natural virtue cannot be the whole of virtue this is because a kindly or fearless disposition could be disastrous without justice and wisdom, and these virtues have to be learned, not because natural virtue is too easily acquired. I have argued that the virtues can be seen as correctives in relation to human nature in general but not that each virtue must present a difficulty to each and every man.

Nevertheless many people feel strongly inclined to say that it is for moral effort that moral praise is to be bestowed, and that in proportion as a man finds it easy to be virtuous so much the less is he to be morally admired for his good actions. The dilemma can be resolved only when we stop talking about difficulties standing in the way of virtuous action as if they were of only one kind. The fact is that some kinds of difficulties do indeed provide an occasion for much virtue, but that others rather show that virtue is incomplete.

To illustrate this point I shall first consider an example of honest action. We may suppose for instance that a man has an opportunity to steal, in circumstances where stealing is not morally permissible, but that he refrains. And now let us ask our old question. For one man it is hard to refrain from stealing and for another man it is not: which shows the greater virtue in acting as he should? It is not difficult to see in this case that it makes all the difference whether the difficulty comes from circumstances, as that a man is poor, or that his theft is unlikely to be detected, or whether it comes from something that belongs to his own character. The fact that a man is *tempted* to steal is something about him that shows a certain lack of honesty: of the thoroughly honest man we say that it "never entered his head," meaning that it was never a real possibility for him. But the fact that he is poor is something that makes the occasion more *tempting*, and difficulties of this kind make honest action all the more virtuous.[e]

**6.** A critical analysis of Kant's view on "moral worth" is assessed in terms of acts of self-preservation. Foot attempts to demonstrate that preserving one's life sometimes has moral import even though people are naturally inclined to remain alive.

In spite of problems such as these, which have certainly not all been solved, both the distinction between different kinds of obstacles to virtuous action, and the general idea that virtues are correctives, will be useful in resolving a difficulty in Kant's moral philosophy closely related to the issues discussed in the preceding paragraphs. In a passage in the first section of the *Groundwork of the Metaphysics of Morals* Kant notoriously tied himself into a knot in trying to give an account of those actions which have as he put it "positive moral worth." Arguing that only actions done out of a sense of duty have this worth he contrasts a philanthropist who "takes pleasure in spreading happiness around him" with one who acts out of respect for duty, saying that the actions of the latter but not the former have moral worth. Much scorn has been poured on Kant for this curious doctrine, and indeed it does seem that something has gone wrong, but perhaps we are not in a position to scoff unless we can give our own account of the idea on which Kant is working. After all it does seem that he is right in saying that some actions are in accordance with duty, and even required by duty, without being the subjects of moral praise, like those of the honest trader who deals honestly in a situation in which it is in his interest to do so.

It was this kind of example that drove Kant to his strange conclusion. He added another example, however, in discussing acts of self-preservation; these he said, while they normally have no positive moral worth, may have it when a man preserves his life not from inclination but without inclination and from a sense of duty. Is he not right in saying that acts of self-preservation normally have no moral significance but that they may have it, and how do we ourselves explain this fact?

To anyone who approaches this topic from a consideration of the virtues the solution readily suggests itself. Some actions are in accordance with virtue without requiring virtue for their performance, whereas others are both in accordance with virtue and such as to show possession of a virtue. So Kant's trader was dealing honestly in a situation in which the virtue of honesty is not required for honest dealing, and it is for this reason that his action did not have "positive moral worth." Similarly, the care that one ordinarily takes for one's life, as for instance on some ordinary morning in eating one's breakfast and keeping out of the way of a car on the road, is something for which no virtue is required. As we said earlier there is no general virtue of self-love as there is a virtue of benevolence or charity, because men are generally attached sufficiently to their own good. Nevertheless in special circumstances virtues such as temperance, courage, fortitude, and hope may be needed if someone is to preserve his life. Are these circumstances in which the preservation of one's own life is a duty? Sometimes it is so, for sometimes it is what is owed to others that should keep a man from destroying himself, and then he may act out of a sense of duty. But not all cases in which acts of self-preservation show virtue are like this. For a man may display each of the virtues just listed even where he does not do any harm to others if he kills himself or fails to preserve his life. And it is this that explains why there may be a moral aspect to suicide which does not depend on possible injury to other people. It is not that suicide is "always wrong," whatever that would mean, but that suicide is *sometimes* contrary to virtues such as courage and hope.

Let us now return to Kant's philanthropists, with the thought that it is action that is in accordance with virtue and also displays a virtue that has moral worth. We see at once that Kant's difficulties are avoided, and the happy philanthropist reinstated in the position which belongs to him. For charity is, as we said, a virtue of attachment as well as action, and the sympathy that makes it easier to act with charity is part of the virtue. The man who acts charitably out of a sense of duty is not to be undervalued, but it is the other who most shows virtue and therefore to the other that most moral worth is attributed. Only a detail of Kant's presentation of the case of the dutiful philanthropist tells on the other side. For what he actually said was that this man felt no sympathy and took no pleasure in the good of others because "his mind was clouded by some sorrow of his own," and this is the kind of circumstance that increases the virtue that is needed if a man is to act well.[f]

> **7.** Other complexities connected with the moral virtues are considered. Although Aquinas thought that an individual with a virtuous disposition can perform only good deeds, some contemporaries believe that moral virtues can be employed for diabolical purposes. On the basis of certain distinctions, Foot adopts a form of compromise between the two extremes.

Aquinas, in his definition of virtue, said that virtues can produce only good actions, and that they are dispositions "of which no one can make bad use," except when they are treated as objects, as in being the subject of hatred or pride. The common opinion nowadays is, however, quite different. With the notable exception of Peter Geach hardly anyone sees any difficulty in the thought that virtues may sometimes be displayed in bad actions. Von Wright, for instance, speaks of the courage of the villain as if this were a quite unproblematic idea, and most people take it for granted that the virtues of courage and temperance may aid a bad man in his evil work. It is also supposed that charity may lead a man to act badly, as when someone does what he has no right to do, but does it for the sake of a friend.

There are, however, reasons for thinking that the matter is not as simple as this. If a man who is willing to do an act of injustice to help a friend, or for the common good, is supposed to act out of charity, and he so acts where a just man will not, it should be said that the unjust man has more charity than the just man. But do we not think that someone not ready to act unjustly may yet be perfect in charity, the virtue having done its whole work in prompting a man to do the acts that are permissible? And is there not more difficulty than might appear in the idea of an act of injustice which is nevertheless an act of courage? Suppose for instance that a sordid murder were in question, say a murder done for gain or to get an inconvenient person out of the way, but that this murder had to be done in alarming circumstances or in the face of real danger; should we be happy to say that such an action was an act of courage or a courageous act? Did the murderer, who certainly acted boldly, or with intrepidity, if he did the murder, also act courageously? Some people insist that they are ready to say this, but I have noticed that they like to move over to a murder for the sake of conscience, or to some other act done in the course of a villainous enterprise but whose immediate end is innocent or positively good. On their hypothesis, which is that bad acts can easily be seen as courageous acts or acts of courage, my original example should be just as good.

What are we to say about this difficult matter? There is no doubt that the murderer who murdered for gain was *not a coward:* he did not have a second moral defect which another villain might have had. There is no difficulty about this because it is clear that one defect may neutralize another. As Aquinas remarked, it is better for a blind horse if it is slow. It does not follow, however, that an act of villainy can be courageous; we are inclined to say that it "took courage," and yet it seems wrong to think of courage as equally connected with good actions and bad.

One way out of this difficulty might be to say that the man who is ready to pursue bad ends does indeed have courage, and shows courage in his action, but that in him courage is not a virtue. Later I shall consider some cases in which this might be the right thing to say, but in this instance it does not seem to be. For unless the murderer consistently pursues bad ends his courage will often result in good; it may enable him to do many innocent or positively good things for himself or for his family and friends. On the strength of an individual bad action we can hardly say that in him courage is not a virtue. Nevertheless there is something to be said even about the individual action to distinguish it from one that would readily be called an act of courage or a courageous act. Perhaps the following analogy may help us to see what it is. We might think of words such as "courage" as naming characteristics of human beings in respect of a certain power, as words such as "poison" and "solvent" and "corrosive" so name the properties of physical things. The power to which virtue-words are so related is the power of producing good action, and good desires. But just as poisons, solvents, and corrosives do not always operate characteristically, so it could be with virtues. If P (say arsenic) is a poison it does not follow that P acts as a poison wherever it is found. It is quite natural to say on occasion "P does not act as a poison here" though P is a poison and it is P that is acting here. Similarly courage is not operating as a virtue when the murderer turns his courage, which is a virtue to bad ends. Not surprisingly the resistance that some of us registered was not to the expression "the courage of the murderer" or to the assertion that what he did "took courage" but rather to the description of that action as an act of courage or a courageous act. It is not that the action *could* not be so described, but that the fact that courage does not here have its characteristic operation is a reason for finding the description strange.

In this example we were considering an action in which courage was not operating as a virtue, without suggesting that in that agent it generally failed to do so. But the latter is also a possibility. If someone is both wicked and foolhardy this may be the case with courage, and it is even easier to find examples of a general connection with evil rather than good in the case of some other virtues. Suppose, for instance, that we think of someone who is over-industrious, or too ready to refuse pleasure, and this is characteristic of him rather than something we find on one particular occasion. In this case the virtue of industry, or the virtue of temperance, has a systematic connection with defective action rather than good action; and it might be said in either case that the virtue did not operate as a virtue in this man. Just as we might say in a certain setting "P is not a poison here" though P is a poison and P is here, so we might say that industriousness, or temperance, is not a virtue in some. Similarly in a man habitually given to wishful thinking, who clings to false hopes, hope does not operate as a virtue and we may say that it is not a virtue in him.[g]

## QUESTIONS

1. Which characteristics does Foot consider basic to moral virtue? Show why they are important.
2. In what ways does her analysis of moral virtue differ from those of Aristotle and Aquinas?
3. How does justice differ from other virtues, according to Foot?
4. Contrast her view of "moral worth" with that of Kant.

5. Thrasymachus claims that it is better (more profitable) to be unjust than to be just. How does Foot refute this thesis?
6. Aquinas maintains that a morally virtuous person can do only good deeds, and some contemporaries hold that such an individual can behave immorally. What is Foot's position on this issue and why?
7. According to Foot, who is more genuinely virtuous—the person who is easily tempted to stray from the proper course of action but overcomes the temptation or the individual who is "naturally disposed" to act properly? How does she develop her thesis?
8. In what ways does wisdom differ from cleverness?
9. Discuss Foot's criticisms of emotivism and prescriptivism.
10. As an ethical naturalist, Foot insists that there is a genuine analogy between losing one's hand and lacking a moral disposition of courage. Is there any way an opponent of ethical naturalism can respond? Discuss.

## KEY TO SELECTIONS

Philippa Foot, *Virtues and Vices and Other Essays in Moral Philosophy*, Berkeley, University of California Press, 1978. 

[a]pp. 2–3.
[b]pp. 3–4.
[c]pp. 5–7.
[d]pp. 8–10.
[e]pp. 10–11.
[f]pp. 12–14.
[g]pp. 14–17.

## GUIDE TO ADDITIONAL READING

### PRIMARY SOURCES

Hare, R. M., *The Language of Morals*, New York, Oxford University Press, 1964.

Stevenson, C. L., *Ethics and Language*, New Haven, Yale University Press, 1944.

Von Wright, G. H., *The Varieties of Goodness*, London, Routledge and Kegan Paul, 1963.

Warnock, G. J., *The Object of Morality*, London, Methuen, 1971.

### DISCUSSION AND COMMENTARY

Foot, P., "Moral Arguments," *Mind*, October 1958, pp. 502–513.

Foot, P., "Moral Beliefs," in *Theories of Ethics*, ed. P. Foot, London, Oxford University Press, 1967.

Frankena, W. K., "The Philosopher's Attack on Morality," *Philosophy*, October 1974, pp. 345–356.

Louden, R. B., "On Some Vices of Virtue Ethics," *American Philosophical Quarterly*, July 1984, pp. 227–236.

Phillips, D. Z., "Does It Pay to Be Good?" *Proceedings of the Aristotelian Society*, 1964–1965, vol. 65, pp. 45–60.

Phillips, D. Z., and Mounce, H. O., "On Morality Having a Point," *Philosophy*, October 1965, pp. 308–319.

Pincoffs, E., *Virtues and Quandries*, Lawrence, University of Kansas Press, 1986.

Tanner, M., "Examples in Moral Philosophy," *Proceedings of the Aristotelian Society*, 1964–1965, vol. 65, pp. 61–76.

Thornton, J. C., "Can the Moral Point of View Be Justified?" in *Readings in Contemporary Ethical Theory*, ed. K. Pahel and M. Schiller, Englewood Cliffs, Prentice-Hall, 1970.

CHAPTER TWENTY-SIX

# Ethics as Trusting in Trust

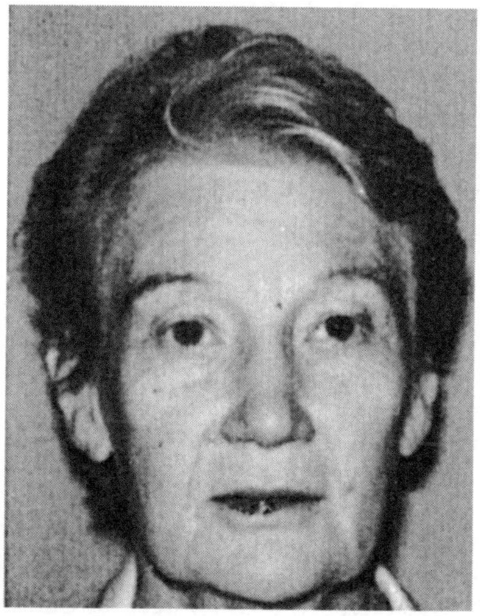

Courtesy of Annette Baier

ANNETTE BAIER

ANNETTE BAIER WAS BORN in New Zealand in 1929. She received her bachelor's and master's degrees in philosophy at the University of Otago and her bachelor of philosophy at Oxford University. After teaching at the Universities of Aberdeen, Auckland, and Sydney and at Carnegie-Mellon, she was appointed Professor of Philosophy at the University of Pittsburgh. In addition to her chief work in philosophy, *Postures of the Mind* (1985), she has contributed numerous articles to philosophical journals. She is currently regarded as a major figure in the feminist ethics movement.

No assessment of the current literature about the theory and practice of morality can ignore the ever-increasing body of work loosely collected under the term *feminist ethics.* At one extreme, these works represent sweeping historical indictments of human institutions and systems of value as biased instruments of men to subordinate women.[1] At the other extreme, they provide specific inquiries into neglected areas of vital concern wherein women are the directly involved moral agents. However, a double claim unites most of these papers and books: There are *moral insights to which women are more open than men*, and these insights have been ignored throughout the history of ethical reflection. In pursuing this claim, feminists are enriching moral discourse. Thus, for example, they are stimulating applied ethics and widening its scope to include such topics as marital relations

[1] ". . . Our society, like all other historical organizations, is a patriarchy. The fact is evident . . . that . . . every avenue of power . . . is in male hands. . . . What lingers of supernatural authority . . . together with the ethics and values, the philosophy and art of our culture . . . is of male manufacture." Kate Millet, *Sexual Politics* (New York: Doubleday, 1969), p. 25.

and maternal practices, and they are contributing substantially to moral psychology on topics such as the female basis for decision making and the importance of a morality of care. Despite these accomplishments, however, the work of feminist thinkers frequently reflects a schism that has its origin in the broader feminist movement itself:

> Feminist theory today appears to be caught between the seemingly mutually exclusive and exhaustive alternatives of seeking "equality" with men, on the one hand, and seeking respect and space for "difference" from men, on the other. Each alternative poses its characteristic difficulties. . . . In practice, the equality view calls upon women to become more like men . . . [whereas] the difference perspective . . . encourages women to opt out of activities that challenge men's domination.[2]

As feminist ethics comes of age, the expectation of capturing its message in a comprehensive theory grows apace. This expectation is shared by apologists and critics alike. The former want the resolution of inconsistencies as well as the conceptual focus that such a theory can bring. The latter want an "official" target for their objections. The work under way by the philosopher Annette Baier to produce such a comprehensive theory is noteworthy. Baier suggests that it was only after reading Carol Gilligan's *In a Different Voice*, with its account of what is distinctive about the moral attitudes and the moral development of women, that she fully realized the importance of the philosophical challenge.[3] Baier concluded that the historic absence of women in the formulation of the classical ethical theories has worked against their sufficiency. Put positively, she concluded that a proper theory

> . . . must accommodate both the insights men have more easily than women, and those women have more easily than men. It should swallow up its predecessor theories. Women moral theorists, if any, will have this very great advantage . . . they can stand on the shoulders of men moral theorists. . . . So women theorists will need to connect their ethics of love with what has been the men theorists' preoccupation, namely, obligation.[4]

Annette Baier and feminists in ethics generally believe there is little prospect for connecting their position with Kant's moral rationalism, which stresses abstract rules. Indeed, opposition to Kant's view that moral worth attaches only to an act that issues from duty as prescribed by reason serves as a feminist rallying point.[5] They argue that the price Kant pays for denying moral relevance to actions that proceed from mere inclinations and self-interest is too great: It includes withholding moral relevance from actions motivated by love and compassion. Thus, for example, Kant is forced to conclude that although it is praiseworthy for us to visit injured John Smith

---

[2]Elizabeth S. Anderson, "Women and Contracts: No Deal," *Michigan Law Review*, 88(6), 1990, pp. 1792–1793.

[3]From her empirical and psychological investigations, Gilligan concludes that whereas men tend to hold a morality of justice, emphasizing fairness and equality, women frequently lean toward a morality of care, seeking security from danger and harm.

[4]"What Do Women Want in a Moral Theory?" *Nous*, 19, March 1985, p. 56.

[5]"[Kant's moral rationalism] is a philosophy which reflects a male-dominated society, and implicitly sanctions male superiority. . . . My use of 'male' and 'female' is meant to reflect a certain social reality—that in our society women are in general more likely (than men) to possess the qualities I call 'female' and men those I call 'male'. " Lawrence Blum, "Kant's and Hegel's Moral Rationalism: A Feminist Perspective," *Canadian Journal of Philosophy*, 12, 1982, p. 294.

because we care for him and blameworthy for us to visit him out of contempt, it is, nevertheless, morally irrelevant in either case.

Annette Baier's response to Kant—and that of a growing number of feminists—is a reinforced interest in the ethical theory of Hume as providing a foundation that can accommodate their insights. She is well aware that it was Hume's view that Kant sought to correct, that Hume's arguments against reason and for sentiment as the source of morality are substantial, that Hume's ethical theory is undogmatic, and that there is no principled basis in it for precluding the vital moral insights of women. In short, Humean ethical theory is compatible with feminist views.

Although Baier is quick to concede that she is far from realizing the goal of a comprehensive theory of feminist ethics, she believes that she is on the track of its keystone concept. This concept—let us call it "appropriate trust in trust"—is to mediate between and supplement the moral insights of men and women. The concept is being shaped to endorse the following scheme of things: Trust relationships permeate human life, and our awareness of them is a basic source of moral precepts. It is our nature to be doubly responsive to these data. In the first place, we assess some trusts as moral and others as immoral; in the second, we feel obligated to trust those who are moral and to distrust those who are immoral.[6] Many trusts are, of course, inherently amoral.

In "Trust and Antitrust," Annette Baier both considers the conditions of human trust in general and investigates a variety of trust relationships in the interest of finding those that have morally relevant traits. Reflection reveals, for instance, that merely abiding by a trust relationship does not ensure that we are morally good. In entering into a trust relationship, we are relying "on others' competence and willingness to look after, rather than harm, things one cares about which are entrusted to their care,"[7] but this is as true for a mutually trusting pair of criminals as for a mutually trusting pair of trapeze performers. Clearly, the more pronounced the climate of trust is for the criminal pair, the greater their ability is to exploit other people. Their mutual trust promotes deplorable actions.

Recognizing that many trust relationships are asymmetrical rather than symmetrical in the weight (and kind) of responsibility borne by their participants is an important step in arriving at Baier's viewpoint. Neglecting refinements, we see that the trust relationship binding doctor and patient is asymmetrical. At its core, the relationship involves (1) advice derived from properly applied medical knowledge, and (2) acceptance of this advice. The patient entrusts the doctor to provide the former, whereas the doctor entrusts the patient to alter his or her behavior on the basis of the latter. That the relationship is asymmetrical becomes clear when we notice the consequences of breeching the trust. To take a serious case, suppose that the doctor advises in haste or from ignorance. He risks far less than the patient: At most, the doctor may lose the license to practice, but the patient may die. In terms of the ability to affect each other's well-being, the doctor's power exceeds the patient's. And, because power translates into responsibility in relationships of trust, this means that the doctor bears the greater burden of responsibility.

---

[6]"I need to show or begin to show how [the appropriate trust in trust] would include obligation, indeed shed light on obligations and shed light on their justification, as well as include love. . . ." Baier, "What Do Women Want in a Moral Theory?" *ibid.*, p. 57.

[7]Annette Baier, "Trust and Antitrust," *Ethics*, 96, January 1986, p. 259.

According to Annette Baier,

> modern moral philosophy has concentrated [on moral symmetrical relationships,] on the morality of fairly cool relationships between those who are deemed to be roughly equal in power to determine the rules and to instigate sanctions against rule breakers. It is not surprising, then, that the main form of trust that any attention has been given to is trust in governments and in parties to voluntary agreements to do what they have agreed to do.[8]

She admits that, viewed historically, this exclusive intellectual focus on symmetrical trust relationships was responsive to the repressive asymmetrical relationships—monarch to subjects, master to slaves, feudal lord to serfs—that had for so long prevailed. But, Baier insists, by emphasizing reason-guided, volitionally accepted symmetrical trusts that are thought to be moral, we have neglected primal moral trusts that are, in part or whole, asymmetrical in form; moreover, as it happens, women tend to be more aware of trusts of the latter sort than are men.

Having stated her general thesis, Annette Baier turns to the inescapable question: How do we determine whether a given trust is moral? The question is particularly demanding for her because she acknowledges that there has been very little difficulty answering it with regard to symmetrical trusts. Baier selects for analysis the intimate trust between husband and wife in caring for their children. The parents-to-children trust relationship is not only natural to the species but also, she believes, not fully reducible to the symmetrical form.[9] Consider the case in which one parent is entrusted by the other to care for one of their children. The trust is morally good *only* if it would not be weakened by exposure to, or awareness of, the other's reliance on certain qualities for continued trustworthiness.[10] Baier is claiming that if either parent relies on the other's love of the child along with the capacity for and commitment to bringing about all aspects of the child's proper development, then *knowing* that the other person relies on such qualities would tend to strengthen the trust; conversely, she is claiming that if, say, either relies on concealed selfishness or greed or uncontrolled emotional responses, then *exposing* what the other relies on would undermine the trust.

---

**1.** Human beings can prosper only in a climate of trust. However, trust relationships themselves are morally neutral, even though they possess morally relevant features.

Whether or not everything which matters to us is the sort of thing that can thrive or languish (I may care most about my stamp collection) or even whether all the possibly thriving things we care about need trust in order to thrive (does my rubber tree?), there surely is something basically right

---

[8]Ibid., pp. 255–256.
[9]Because it is irreducible, this trust cannot, for example, be shown to be moral through demonstrating it as a form of promise keeping. Demonstrations of the promise-keeping sort are frequently used in establishing symmetrical moral trusts.
[10]She is not denying that there may be other requirements.

about Bok's claim.[11] Given that I cannot myself guard my stamp collection at all times, nor take my rubber tree with me on my travels, the custody of these things that matter to me must often be transferred to others, presumably to others I trust. Without trust, what matters to me would be unsafe, unless like the Stoic I attach myself only to what can thrive, or be safe from harm, *however* others act. The starry heavens above and the moral law within had better be about the only things that matter to me, if there is no one I can trust in any way. Even my own Stoic virtue will surely thrive better if it evokes some trust from others, inspires some trustworthiness in them, or is approved and imitated by them.

To Bok's statement, however, we should add another, that not all the things that thrive when there is trust between people, and which matter, are things that should be encouraged to thrive. Exploitation and conspiracy, as much as justice and fellowship, thrive better in an atmosphere of trust. There are immoral as well as moral trust relationships, and trust-busting can be a morally proper goal. If we are to tell when morality requires the preservation of trust, when it requires the destruction of trust, we obviously need to distinguish different forms of trust, and to look for some morally relevant features they may possess. In this paper I make a start on this large task.

It is a start, not a continuation, because there has been a strange silence on the topic in the tradition of moral philosophy with which I am familiar. Psychologists and sociologists have discussed it, lawyers have worked out the requirements of equity on legal trusts, political philosophers have discussed trust in governments, and there has been some discussion of trust when philosophers address the assurance problem in Prisoner's Dilemma contexts. But we, or at least I, search in vain for any general account of the morality of trust relationships. The question, Who should I trust in what way, and why? has not been the central question in moral philosophy as we know it. Yet if I am right in claiming that morality, as anything more than a law within, itself requires trust in order to thrive, and that immorality too thrives on some forms of trust, it seems pretty obvious that we ought, as moral philosophers, to look into the question of what forms of trust are needed for the thriving of the version of morality we endorse, and into the morality of that and other forms of trust. A minimal condition of adequacy for any version of the true morality, if truth has anything to do with reality, is that it not have to condemn the conditions needed for its own thriving. Yet we will be in no position to apply that test to the trust in which morality thrives until we have worked out, at least in a provisional way, how to judge trust relationships from a moral point of view.[a]

**2.** The philosophical tradition is more notable for its omission of, than for its explicit treatment of, the concept of trust.

Moral philosophers have always been interested in cooperation between people, and so it is surprising that they have not said more than they have about trust. It seems fairly obvious that any form of cooperative activity, including the division of labor, requires the cooperators to trust one another to do their bit, or at the very least to trust the overseer with his whip to do his bit, where coercion is relied on. One would expect contractarians to investigate the forms of trust and distrust parties to a contract exhibit. Utilitarians too should be concerned with the contribution to the general happiness of various climates of trust, so be concerned to understand the nature, roots, and varieties of trust. One might also have expected those with a moral theory of the virtues to have looked at trustworthiness, or at willingness to give trust. But when we turn to the great moral philosophers, in our tradition, what we find can scarcely be said to be even a sketch of a moral theory of trust. At most we get a few hints of directions in which we might go.

[11]"Whatever matters to human beings, trust is the atmosphere in which it thrives." Sissela Bok, *Lying* (New York: Pantheon Bodes, 1978), p. 31n.

Plato in the *Republic* presumably expects the majority of citizens to trust the philosopher kings to rule wisely and expects that elite to trust their underlings not to poison their wine, nor set fire to their libraries, but neither proper trust nor proper trustworthiness are among the virtues he dwells on as necessary in the cooperating parties in his good society. His version of justice and of the "friendship" supposed to exist between ruler and ruled seems to *imply* such virtues of trust, but he does not himself draw out the implications. In the *Laws* he mentions distrust as an evil produced by association with seafaring traders, but it is only a mention. The same sort of claim can also be made about Aristotle—his virtuous person, like Plato's, must place his trust in that hypothetical wise person who will teach him just how much anger and pride and fear to feel with what reasons, when, and toward which objects. Such a wise man presumably also knows just how much trust in whom, on what matters, and how much trustworthiness, should be cultivated, as well as who should show trust toward whom, but such crucial wisdom and such central virtues are not discussed by Aristotle, as far as I am aware. (He does, in the *Politics*, condemn tyrants for sowing seeds of distrust, and his discussion of friendship might be cited as one place where he implicitly recognizes the importance of trust; could someone one distrusted be a second self to one? But that is implicit only, and in any case would cover only trust between friends.) Nor do later moral philosophers do much better on this count.

There are some forms of trust to which the great philosophers *have* given explicit attention. Saint Thomas Aquinas, and other Christian moralists, have extolled the virtue of faith and, more relevantly, of hope, and so have said something about trust in God. And in the modern period some of the great moral and political philosophers, in particular John Locke, looked at trust in governments and officials, and some have shown what might be called an obsessive trust in contracts and contractors, even if not, after Hobbes's good example here, an equal obsession with the grounds for such trust. It is selective attention then, rather than total inattention, which is the philosophical phenomenon on which I wish to remark, tentatively to explain, and try to terminate or at least to interrupt.[b]

> **3.** Annette Baier notes that relying on others is not the same as trusting them. Reliance depends on the psychological assessment of the other person's attitudes, habits, and so on, whereas trust requires recognition of another individual's good will.

What is the difference between trusting others and merely relying on them? It seems to be reliance on their good will toward one, as distinct from their dependable habits, or only on their dependably exhibited fear, anger, or other motives compatible with ill will toward one, or on motives not directed on one at all. We may rely on our fellows' fear of the newly appointed security guards in shops to deter them from injecting poison into the food on the shelves, once we have ceased to trust them. We may rely on the shopkeeper's concern for his profits to motivate him to take effective precautions against poisoners and also trust him to *want* his customers not to be harmed by his products, at least as long as this want can be satisfied without frustrating his wish to increase his profits. Trust is often mixed with other species of reliance on persons. Trust which is reliance on another's good will, perhaps minimal good will, contrasts with the forms of reliance on others' reactions and attitudes which are shown by the comedian, the advertiser, the blackmailer, the kidnapper-extortioner, and the terrorist, who all depend on particular attitudes and reactions of others for the success of their actions. We all depend on one anothers' psychology in countless ways, but this is not yet to trust them. The trusting can be betrayed, or at least let down, and not just disappointed. Kant's neighbors who counted on his regular habits as a clock for their own less automatically regular ones might be disappointed with him if he slept in one day, but not let down by him, let alone had their trust betrayed. When I trust another, I depend on her good will toward me. I need not either acknowledge this reliance nor believe that she has either invited or acknowledged such trust since there is such a thing as unconscious trust, as unwanted trust, as forced receipt of trust, and as trust which the trusted is unaware of. (Plausible conditions for proper trust will be that it survives consciousness, by both parties, and that the trusted has had some opportunity to signify acceptance or rejection, to warn the trusting if their trust is unacceptable.)

Where one depends on another's good will, one is necessarily vulnerable to the limits of that good will. One leaves others an opportunity to harm one when one trusts, and also shows one's confidence that they will not take it. Reasonable trust will require good grounds for such confidence in another's good will, or at least the absence of good grounds for expecting their ill will or indifference. Trust then, on this first approximation, is accepted vulnerability to another's possible but not expected ill will (or lack of good will) toward one.[c]

**4.** Because human beings are obviously not self-sufficient, trust relationships are basic to our existence. Thus it is inevitable that those we trust will have discretionary power in various circumstances and use it wisely.

The next thing to attend to is why we typically do leave things that we value close enough to others for them to harm them. The answer, simply, is that we need their help in creating, and then in not merely guarding but looking after the things we most value, so we have no choice but to allow some others to be in a position to harm them. The one in the best position to harm something is its creator or its nurse-cum-caretaker. Since the things we typically do value include such things as we cannot singlehandedly either create or sustain (our own life, health, reputation, our offspring and their well-being, as well as intrinsically shared goods such as conversation, its written equivalent, theater and other forms of play, chamber music, market exchange, political life, and so on) we must allow many other people to get into positions where they can, if they choose, injure what we care about, since those are the same positions that they must be in in order to help us take care of what we care about. The simple Socratic truth that no person is self-sufficient gets elaborated, once we add the equally Socratic truth that the human soul's activity is *caring* for things into the richer truth that no one is able by herself to look after everything she wants to have looked after, nor even alone to look after her own "private" goods, such as health and bodily safety. If we try to distinguish different forms of trust by the different valued goods we confidently allow another to have some control over, we are following Locke in analyzing trusting on the model of *en*trusting. Thus, there will be an answer not just to the question, Whom do you trust? but to the question, *What* do you trust to them?—what good is it that they are in a position to take from you, or to injure? Accepting such an analysis, taking trust to be a three-place predicate(A trusts B with valued thing C) will involve some distortion and regimentation of some cases, where we may have to strain to discern any definite candidate for C, but I think it will prove more of a help than a hindrance.

One way in which trusted persons can fail to act as they were trusted to is by taking on the care of more than they were entrusted with—the babysitter who decides that the nursery would be improved if painted purple and sets to work to transform it, will have acted, as a babysitter, in an untrustworthy way, however great his good will. When we are trusted, we are relied upon to realize *what* it is for whose care we have some discretionary responsibility, and normal people can pick up the cues that indicate the limits of what is entrusted. For example, if I confide my troubles to a friend, I trust her to listen, more or less sympathetically, and to preserve confidentiality, but usually not, or not without consulting me, to take steps to remove the source of my worry. That could be interfering impertinence, not trustworthiness as a confidante. She will, nevertheless, within the restricted scope of what is trusted to her (knowledge of my affairs, not their management) have some discretion both as to how to receive the confidence and, unless I swear her to absolute secrecy, as to when to share it. The relativization of trust to particular things cared about by the truster goes along with the discretion the trusted usually has in judging just what should be done to "look after" the particular good entrusted to her care. This discretionary power will of course be limited by the limits of what is entrusted and usually by some other constraints.

It is plausible to construe all cases of being trusted not merely as cases of being trusted by someone with access to what matters to the truster, but as some control over that, expected to be used to take care of it, and involving some discretionary powers in so doing.[d]

> **5.** According to Baier, trust relationships often come into being without conscious effort by either party. She also reminds us that trust relationships involve factors admitting of degrees, most notably in the discretionary powers of the parties concerned.

Trust, on the analysis I have proposed, is letting other persons (natural or artificial, such as firms, nations, etc.) take care of something the truster cares about, where such "caring for" involves some exercise of discretionary powers. But not all the variables involved in trust are yet in view. One which the entrusting model obscures rather than highlights is the degree of explicitness. To entrust is intentionally and usually formally to hand over the care of something to someone, but trusting is rarely begun by making up one's mind to trust, and often it has no definite initiation of any sort but grows up slowly and imperceptibly. What I have tried to take from the notion of entrusting is not its voluntarist and formalist character but rather the possible specificity and restrictedness of *what* is entrusted, along with the discretion the trustee has in looking after that thing. Trust can come with no beginnings, with gradual as well as sudden beginnings, and with various degrees of self-consciousness, voluntariness, and expressness. My earlier discussion of the delicacy and tact needed by the truster in judging the performance of the trusted applied only to cases where the truster not merely realizes that she trusts but has some conscious control over the continuation of the trust relationship. The discussion of abuses of discretionary power applied only to cases where the trusted realizes that she is trusted and trusted with discretionary powers. But trust relationships need not be so expressed, and some important forms of them cannot be verbally acknowledged by the persons involved. Trust between infant and parent is such a case, and it is one which also reminds us of another crucial variable in trust relations to which so far I have only indirectly alluded. This is the relative power of the truster and the trusted, and the relative costs to each of a breakdown of their trust relationship. In emphasizing the toleration of vulnerability by the truster I have made attitudes to relative power and powerlessness the essence of trust and distrust; I have not yet looked at the varieties of trust we discern when we vary the power of the truster in relation to the power of the trusted, both while the trust endures and in its absence. Trust alters power positions, and both the position one is in without a given form of trust and the position one has within a relation of trust need to be considered before one can judge whether that form of trust is sensible and morally decent. Infant trust reminds us not just of inarticulate and uncritical or blind trust, but of trust by those who are maximally vulnerable, whether or not they give trust.[e]

> **6.** Although it is instructive to note a resemblance between an infant's trust in its mother and human faith in God, an evident difference must also be recognized. The trust relationship between God and humans is invariant, whereas the mother-infant relationship is altered as the infant matures.

Infant trust is like one form of non-contract-based trust to which some attention has been given in our philosophical tradition, namely, trust in God. Trust in God is total, in that whatever one cares about, it will not thrive if God wills that it not thrive. A young child too is totally dependent on the good will of the parent, totally incapable of looking after anything he cares about without parental help or against parental will. Such total dependence does not, in itself, necessarily elicit trust—some theists curse God, display futile distrust or despair rather than trust. Infants too can make suspicious, futile, self-protective moves against the powerful adults in their world or retreat into autism. But surviving infants will usually have shown some trust, enough to accept offered nourishment, enough not to attempt to prevent such close approach. The ultra-Hobbist child who fears or rejects the mother's breast, as if fearing poison from that source, can be taken as displaying innate distrust, and such newborns must be the exception in a surviving species. Hobbes tells us that, in the state of nature, "seeing the infant is in the power of the Mother, and is therefore obliged to obey her, so she may either nourish or expose it; if she nourish it, it oweth its life to the Mother and is therefore obliged to obey her rather than any other" (*Leviathan*, chap. 20). Even he, born a twin to fear, is apparently willing to take mother's milk on trust. Some degree of innate, if selective, trust seems a necessary element in any surviving creature whose first nourishment (if it is not exposed) comes from another, and this innate but fragile trust could serve as the explanation both of the possibility of other forms of trust and of their fragility.

Infant trust that normally does not need to be won but is there unless and until it is destroyed is important for an understanding of the possibility of trust. Trust is much easier to maintain than it is to get started and is never hard to destroy. Unless some form of it were innate, and unless that form could pave the way for new forms, it would appear a miracle that trust ever occurs. The postponement of the onset of distrust is a lot more explicable than hypothetical Hobbesian conversions from total distrust to limited trust. The persistent human adult tendency to profess trust in a creator-God can also be seen as an infantile residue of this crucial innate readiness of infants to initially impute goodwill to the powerful persons on whom they depend. So we should perhaps welcome, or at least tolerate, religious trust, if we value any form of trust. Nevertheless the theological literature on trust in God is of very limited help to us if we want to understand trust in human persons, even that trust in parents of which it can be seen as a nostalgic fantasy-memory. For the child soon learns that the parent is not, like God, invulnerable, nor even, like some versions of God, subject to offense or insult but not injury. Infant trust, although extreme in the discrepancy of power between the truster and the trusted, is to some extent a matter of mutual trust and mutual if unequal vulnerability. The parents' enormous power to harm the child and disappoint the child's trust is the power of ones also vulnerable to the child's at first insignificant but ever-increasing power, including power as one trusted by the parent. So not very much can be milked from the theological literature on the virtues of trust, faith, and hope in God and returned to the human context, even to the case of infant and parent. Indeed we might cite the theological contamination of the concept of trust as part of the explanation for the general avoidance of the topic in modern moral philosophy. If trust is seen as a variant of the suspect virtue of faith in the competence of the powers that be, then readiness to trust will be seen not just as a virtue of the weak but itself as a moral weakness, better replaced by vigilance and self-assertion, by self-reliance or by cautious, minimal, and carefully monitored trust. The psychology of adolescents, not infants, then gets glorified as the moral ideal. Such a reaction against a religious version of the ethics of trust is as healthy, understandable, and, it is hoped, as passing a phenomenon as is adolescent self-assertive individualism in the life of a normal person.[f]

**7.** Though Baier agrees with Hume that promises are an important form of trust, she warns that they cannot serve as models for trust relationships in general. She argues that Hume was insufficiently aware of the social preconditions for trust making that promissory trusts require.

In his famous account of what a promise (and a contract) involves, Hume strongly implies that it is an artificially contrived and secured case of mutual trust. The penalty to which a promisor subjects himself in promising, he says, is that of "never being trusted again in case of failure." The problem which the artifice of promise solves is a generally disadvantageous "want of mutual confidence and security." It is plausible to construe the offer whose acceptance counts as acceptance of a contract or a promise as at least implicitly including an invitation to trust. Part of what makes promises the special thing they are, and the philosophically intriguing thing they are, is that we *can* at will accept *this* sort of invitation to trust, whereas in general we cannot trust at will. Promises are puzzling because they seem to have the power, by verbal magic, to initiate real voluntary short-term trusting. They do not merely create obligations apparently at the will of the obligated, but they create trust at the will of the truster. They present a very fascinating case of trust and trustworthiness, but one which, because of those very intriguing features, is ill suited to the role of paradigm. Yet in as far as modern moral philosophers have attended at all to the morality of trust, it is trust in parties to an agreement that they have concentrated on, and it is into this very special and artificial mold that they have tried to force other cases of trust, when they notice them at all.

Trust of any particular form is made more likely, in adults, if there is a climate of trust of that sort. Awareness of what is customary, as well as past experience of one's own, affects one's ability to trust. We take it for granted that people will perform their role-related duties and trust any individual worker to look after whatever her job requires her to. The very existence of that job, as a standard occupation, creates a climate of some trust in those with that job. Social artifices such as property, which allocate rights and duties as a standard job does, more generally also create a climate of trust, a presumption of a sort of trustworthiness. On the Humean account of promises and contracts which I find more or less correct, their establishment as a customary procedure also reverses a presumption concerning trustworthiness, but only in limited conditions. Among these is a special voluntary act by the promisor, giving it to be understood that what he offers is a promise, and another voluntary act by the promisee, acceptance of that promise. Promises are "a bond or security," and "the sanction of the interested commerce of mankind." To understand them is to see what sort of sanction is involved, what sort of security they provide, and the social preconditions of each. Then one understands how the presumption about the trustworthiness of self-interested strangers can be reversed, and how the ability to trust them (for a limited time, on a limited matter) can become a voluntary ability. To adapt Hume's words, "Hence I learn to count on a service from another, although he bears me no real kindness." Promises are a most ingenious social invention, and trust in those who have given us promises is a complex and sophisticated moral achievement. Once the social conditions are right for it, once the requisite climate of trust in promisors is there, it is easy to take it for a simpler matter than it is and to ignore its background conditions. They include not merely the variable social conventions and punitive customs Hume emphasizes, but the prior existence of less artificial and less voluntary forms of trust, such as trust in friends and family, and enough trust in fellows to engage with them in agreed exchanges of a more or less simultaneous nature, exchanges such as barter or handshakes, which do not require one to rely on strangers over a period of time, as exchange of promises typically does.[g]

> **8.** According to Annette Baier, the failure of traditional ethical theorists to recognize the full range and variety of trust relationships and their moral reference is correlated with the virtual absence of women from the field.

The great moral theorists in our tradition not only are all men, they are mostly men who had minimal adult dealings with (and so were then minimally influenced by) women. With a few significant exceptions (Hume, Hegel, J. S. Mill, Sidgwick, maybe Bradley) they are a collection of gays, clerics, misogynists, and puritan bachelors. It should not surprise us, then, that particularly in the modern period they managed to relegate to the mental background the web of trust tying most moral agents to one another, and to focus their philosophical attention so single-mindedly on cool, distanced relations between more or less free and equal adult strangers, say, the members of an all male club, with membership rules and rules for dealing with rule breakers and where the form of cooperation was restricted to ensuring that each member could read his *Times* in peace and have no one step on his gouty toes. Explicitly assumed or recognized obligations toward others with the same obligations and the same power to see justice done to rule breakers then are seen as the moral norm.

Relations between equals and nonintimates will *be* the moral norm for adult males whose dealings with others are mainly business or restrained social dealings with similarly placed males. But for lovers, husbands, fathers, the ill, the very young, and the elderly, other relationships with their moral potential and perils will loom larger. For Hume, who had several strong-willed and manipulative women to cooperate or contend with in his adult life, for Mill, who had Harriet Taylor on his hands, for Hegel, whose domestic life was of normal complication, the rights and duties of equals to equals in a civil society which recognized only a male electorate could only be *part* of the moral story. They could not ignore the virtues and vices of family relationships, male-female relationships, master-slave, and employer-employee relationships as easily as could Hobbes, Butler, Bentham, or Kant. Nor could they as easily adopt the usual compensatory strategies of the moral philosophers who confine their attention to the rights and duties of free and equal adults to one another—the strategy of claiming, if pressed, that these rights are the *core* of all moral relationships and maybe also claiming that any other relationships, engendering additional or different rights and duties, come about only by an exercise of one of the core rights, the right to promise. Philosophers who remember what it was like to be a dependent child, or know what it is like to be a parent, or to have a dependent parent, an old or handicapped relative, friend, or neighbor will find it implausible to treat such relations as simply cases of comembership in a kingdom of ends, in the given temporary conditions of one-sided dependence.

To the extent that these claims are correct (and I am aware that they need more defense that I have given them here) it becomes fairly easy to see one likely explanation of the neglect in Western moral philosophy of the full range of sorts of trust. Both before the rise of a society which needed contract as a commercial device, and after it, women were counted on to serve their men, to raise their children to fill the roles they were expected to fill and not deceive their men about the paternity of these children. What men counted on one another for, in work and war, presupposed this background domestic trust, trust in women not merely not to poison their men (Nietzsche derides them for learning less than they might have in the kitchen), but to turn out sons who could trust and be trusted in traditional men's roles and daughters who would reduplicate their own capacities for trust and trustworthiness. Since the women's role did not include the writing of moral treatises, any thoughts they had about trust, based on their experience of it, did not get into our tradition (or did Diotima teach Socrates something about trust as well as love?). And the more powerful men, including those who did write the moral treatises, were in the morally awkward position of being, collectively, oppressors of women, exploiters of women's capacity for trustworthiness in unequal, nonvoluntary, and non-contract-based relationships. Understandably, they did not focus their attention on forms of trust and demands for trustworthiness which it takes a Nietzsche to recognize without shame. Humankind can bear only so much reality.[h]

**9.** Carol Gilligan's psychological research discloses the reason why contractual trusts have dominated modern ethical thought: Male moral tendencies have not been modified by female reflection.

The recent research of Carol Gilligan has shown us how intelligent and reflective twentieth-century women see morality, and how different their picture of it is from that of men, particularly the men who eagerly assent to the claims of currently orthodox contractarian-Kantian moral theories. Women cannot now, any more than they could when oppressed, ignore that part of morality and those forms of trust which cannot easily be forced into the liberal and particularly the contractarian mold. Men may but women cannot see morality as essentially a matter of keeping to the minimal moral traffic rules, designed to restrict close encounters between autonomous persons to self-chosen ones. Such a conception presupposes both an equality of power and a natural separateness from others, which is alien to women's experience of life and morality. For those most of whose daily dealings are with the less powerful or the more powerful, a moral code designed for those equal in power will be at best nonfunctional, at worst an offensive pretense of equality as a substitute for its actuality. But equality is not even a desirable ideal in all relationships—children not only are not but should not be equal in power to adults, and we need a morality to guide us in our dealings with those who either cannot or should not achieve equality of power (animals, the ill, the dying, children while still young) with those with whom they have unavoidable and often intimate relationships.

Modern moral philosophy has concentrated on the morality of fairly cool relationships between those who are deemed to be roughly equal in power to determine the rules and to instigate sanctions against the rule breakers. It is not surprising, then, that the main form of trust that any attention has been given to is trust in governments, and in parties to voluntary agreements to do what they have agreed to do. As much as possible is absorbed into the latter category, so that we suppose that paying for what one takes from a shop, doing what one is employed to do, returning what one has borrowed, supporting one's spouse, are all cases of being faithful to binding voluntary agreements, to contracts of some sort. (For Hume, none of these would count as duties arising from contract or promise.) Yet if I think of the trust I show, say, in the plumber who comes from the municipal drainage authority when I report that my drains are clogged, it is not plausibly seen as trust that he will fulfill his contractual obligations to me or to his employer. When I trust him to do whatever is necessary and safe to clear my drains, I take his expertise and his lack of ill will for granted. Should he plant explosives to satisfy some unsuspected private or social grudge against me, what I might try to sue him for (if I escaped alive) would not be damages for breach of contract. His wrong, if wrong it were, is not breach of contract, and the trust he would have disappointed would not have been that particular form of trust.

Contract enables us to make explicit just what we count on another person to do, in return for what, and should they not do just that, what damages can be extracted from them. The beauty of promise and contract is its explicitness. But we can only make explicit provisions for such contingencies as we imagine arising. Until I become a victim of a terrorist plumber I am unlikely, even if I should insist on a contract before giving plumbers access to my drains, to extract a solemn agreement that they not blow me up. Nor am I likely to specify the alternative means they *may* use to clear my drains, since if I knew enough to compile such a list I would myself have to be a competent plumber. Any such detailed instructions must come from their plumbing superiors; I know nothing or little about it when I confidently welcome the plumber into the bowels of my basement. I trust him to do a nonsubversive plumbing job, as he counts on me to do a nonsubversive teaching job, should he send his son to my course in the history of ethics. Neither of us relies on a contract with the other, and neither of us need know of any contract (or much about its contents) the other may have with a third coordinating party.[i]

**10.** Insofar as the parents rely on each other to promote the proper development of the child, their trust relationship is potentially moral. The test for its morality that Baier emphasizes is this: When each parent reflects carefully about the other's motives and human traits, each finds his or her confidence in the trust strengthened rather than weakened.

I now turn to the question of when a given form of trust is morally decent, so properly preserved by trustfulness and trustworthiness, and when it fails in moral decency. What I say about this will be sketchy and oversimplified. I shall take as the form of trust to test for moral decency the trust which one spouse has in the other, in particular as concerns their children's care.

Earlier in discussing infant trust I said that the child has reason to trust the parents when both child and parents care about the same good—the child's happiness, although the child may not see eye to eye with those trusted parents about how that is best taken care of. When one parent, say the old-style father, entrusts the main care of his young child's needs to the old-style mother, there, too, there can be agreement on the good they both want cared for but disagreement about how best it is cared for. The lord and master who entrusts such care to his good wife, the mother, and so gives her discretionary power in making moment-by-moment decisions about what is to be done, will have done so sensibly if these disagreements are not major ones, or if he has reason to think that she knows better than he does about such matters. He should defer to her judgment, as the child is encouraged to do to the parents', and as I do to my plumber's. He sensibly trusts if he has reason to think that the discretionary powers given, even when used in ways he does not fully understand or approve of, are still used to care for the goods he wants cared for. He would be foolish to trust if he had evidence that she has other ends in view in her treatment of the child, or had a radically different version of what, say, the child's healthy development and proper relation to his father consisted in. Once he suspects that she, the trusted nurse of his sons and daughters, is deliberately rearing the daughters to be patriarch-toppling Amazons, the sons to be subverters of the father's values, he will sensibly withdraw his trust and dispatch his children to suitably chosen female relatives or boarding schools. What would properly undermine his trust would be beliefs he came to hold about the formerly trusted person's motives and purposes in her care of what was entrusted to her. The disturbing and trust-undermining suspicion is not necessarily that she doesn't care about the children's good, or cares only about her own—it is the suspicion that what she cares about conflicts with rather than harmonizes with what he cares about and that she is willing to sacrifice his concerns to what she sees as the children's and her own. Trusting is rational, then, in the absence of any reason to suspect in the trusted strong and operative motives which conflict with the demands of trustworthiness as the truster sees them. . . .

Meanwhile, my account of what it is to trust, and my partial account of when it is immoral to expect or meet trust, will have to be treated as merely a beginning (or, for some, a resumption, since there doubtless are other attempts at this topic which have escaped my notice). Trust, I have claimed, is reliance on others' competence and willingness to look after, rather than harm, things one cares about which are entrusted to their care. The moral test of such trust relationships which I have proposed is that they be able to survive awareness by each party to the relationship of *what* the other relies on in the first to ensure their continued trustworthiness or trustingness. This test elevates to a special place one form of trust, namely, trusting others with knowledge of what it is about them which enables one to trust them as one does, or expect them to be trustworthy. The test could be restated this way: trust is morally decent only if, in addition to whatever else is entrusted, knowledge of each party's reasons for confident reliance on the other to continue the relationship could in principle also be entrusted—since such mutual knowledge would be itself a good, not a threat to others' goods. To the extent that mutual reliance can be accompanied by mutual knowledge of the conditions for that reliance, trust is above suspicion, and trustworthiness a nonsuspect virtue.[j]

## QUESTIONS

1. What are the identifying characteristics of a trust, according to Baier? Can there be a master-dog trust in this sense? A cab driver–passenger trust? An author-literary critic trust?
2. Compare and contrast an infant's trust in its mother and human faith in God.
3. Give some examples of symmetrical trusts and some examples of asymmetrical trusts. In each case, assess the extent to which the trust is overtly volitional.
4. Because most social contract theories—forms of contractualism—deny that power and responsibility ought to be based on gender differences, it would seem that feminists would be attracted to them. Explain why many feminists are not.
5. Amplify the thesis that Hume's ethical theory is more compatible with feminist views than is Kant's. Are feminists being fair to Kant in their criticisms?
6. Is Baier open to the charge that the trust relationship of a gang of bank robbers can meet her test for moral goodness? Discuss.
7. Annette Baier says that "a trust relationship is morally bad to the extent that either party relies on qualities in the other which would be weakened by the knowledge that the other relies on them." Suggest how an employer-employee trust relationship might be morally bad.
8. Baier regards promising as a "very special and artificial" form of trust. Explain. Does her own test for morally good trusts have application for trusts of this sort?
9. "Men may but women cannot see morality as essentially a matter of keeping to the minimal moral traffic rules, designed to restrict close encounters between autonomous persons to self-chosen ones." Does this statement by Baier imply that there is a fundamental gender-based difference with respect to morality? Or does it imply that the social conditioning of men and women is typically quite different? Or does it imply neither? Discuss.
10. Annette Baier acknowledges that the research of Carol Gilligan shows that "intelligent and reflective twentieth-century women" are more attracted to certain instances of moral theorizing than are their male counterparts. Baier's theorizing about trust may be taken as an example of this psychological fact. Does it follow from the foregoing that there is a fundamental distinction between male and female moral theorizing? Discuss.

## KEY TO SELECTIONS

Annette Baier, "Trust and Antitrust," *Ethics*, 96, January, 1986. Reprinted by permission of the University of Chicago Press and Annette Baier.

[a]pp. 231–232.
[b]pp. 232–233.
[c]pp. 234–235.
[d]pp. 236–237.
[e]pp. 240–241.
[f]pp. 241–242.
[g]pp. 245–246.
[h]pp. 247–249.
[i]pp. 249–250.
[j]pp. 253–254, pp. 259–260.

## GUIDE TO ADDITIONAL READINGS


### PRIMARY SOURCES

Baier, A., *Moral Prejudices*, Cambridge, Harvard University Press, 1994.

Held, V., *Rights and Goods*, New York and London, Free Press, 1983. Ch. 5.

Thomas, D. O., "The Duty to Trust," *Proceedings of the Aristotelian Society*, 1970, pp. 89–101.

### DISCUSSION AND COMMENTARY

Baier, A., *Postures of the Mind*, Minneapolis, University of Minnesota Press, 1985.

Bok, S., *Lying*, New York, Pantheon Books, 1978.

Gatens, Moira J. (ed.), *Feminist Ethics*, Brookfield, Vt., Ashgate, 1998.

Grimshaw, Jean, "The Idea of a Female Ethic," in *A Companion to Ethics*, ed. P. Singer, Cambridge, Blackwell, 1993, pp. 491–499.

Jaggar, A., *Feminist Politics and Human Nature*, Ohio, University of Cincinnati Press, 1990.

Kittay, E. and Meyers, D. (eds.), *Women and Moral Theory*, Totowa, N. J., Rowman & Littlefield, 1987.

CHAPTER TWENTY-SEVEN

# Inventing Right and Wrong

BORN IN 1917 in Sydney, Australia, John Mackie was educated there and, from 1938 to 1940, in Oxford. After serving in the army in World War II, he was a lecturer in Moral and Political Philosophy at the University of Sydney from 1946 to 1954. From 1955 to 1959, he was Professor at Otago University in New Zealand, and then Professor at Sydney (1959–1963). In 1963, he moved to England, first to the University of York (1963–1967) and then to University College, Oxford, until his death in 1981. He was named a Fellow of the British Academy in 1974.

Mackie published widely in philosophy, in ethics, and in other areas. His book *Ethics: Inventing Right and Wrong* (1977) is still widely read and discussed. He also wrote a study of the concept of causation, *The Cement of the Universe* (1974) and *Problems from Locke* (1976), among other books.

The ethical views of John Mackie are a part of the great twentieth-century debate about the nature of ethical judgments and beliefs. This debate revolves chiefly around the question of whether an ethical judgment is a judgment about "objective facts in the world," or, on the other hand, something more "subjective" like emotion or attitude. To a great extent this debate is given force by the feeling, which many philosophers and nonphilosophers share, that if ethical judgments cannot be claimed to be about "objective facts," then they lose their claim to be taken seriously.

The most striking thing about Mackie's position is the fact that he combines two contentions. The first is that ethical judgments are not about objective facts and that we make an error when we think that they do. The second is that even though ethical judgments are not objective, nevertheless there is every reason for a person to take them seriously.

Of the other philosophers included in this book, those who come closest in a vague and general way to Mackie's concerns are Ayer and Stevenson (Ch. 21) and also Bernard Williams (Ch. 28). All of these philosophers have something to say against the idea, represented most forcefully by Plato (Ch. 2), that ethical beliefs can be objectively correct or incorrect. Nevertheless, Mackie's views about ethical beliefs are significantly different from those of Ayer, Stevenson, and Williams. These differences are reflected beyond the area of abstract discourse about ethical belief in the character of the ethical concerns that Mackie expresses.

Ayer and Stevenson are concerned as much as anything with the meanings of ethical statements, with trying to say what we mean when we say something like "Lying is wrong" or "Kindness is good." In an important sense, their views are focused on analyzing ethical language. Mackie's real focus is on his view that we are just plain wrong, in "error," when we think that ethics has to do with objective facts. There are no such "facts," Mackie believes. We should not regard whether an ethical judgment is objectively true or false as the relevant thing about it.

Ethical judgments, according to Mackie, are *never* objectively true or "valid," because there are no objective facts to back them up. Here Mackie criticizes the theory of Kant (Ch. 12). What we should look for in ethical judgments—and also in other evaluative judgments such as those in aesthetics or art as well as in the special area of "morality"—is not whether they are true but rather whether they serve a certain sort of purpose or fulfill a certain function.

The primary function of ethical judgments, says Mackie, is to help human beings in a world in which things are, unfortunately, often "liable to go badly." In particular, the function of morality is to counteract the limitedness of the "sympathies" that people have for one another. This limitedness of our sympathies often causes us to harm each other and prevents us from aiding each other as much as we could. Morality has the function of increasing our mutual sympathies to some significant extent.

If the point of morality and thus of much of ethics is to increase our sympathies for each other, then someone is likely to ask, "What if I'm strong and independent enough not to need the sympathies of others? What if I don't need to care about having the help and sympathies of others? Why should I pay any attention to morality if I can get away without being hurt by ignoring it?" This is the kind of question that the Sophist Thrasymachus posed early in Plato's *Republic* (Ch. 2). (Plato tried to answer it in the rest of that work, resting his answer largely on the idea that morality and especially justice are objectively good.)

Mackie does not try to do what Plato had attempted. Mackie does not try to appeal to an "objective" goodness of morality. Rather, he assumes that most people will regard human sympathies favorably and will incline to try to further them. Those who do not so regard them—people like Thrasymachus—can, Mackie thinks, be to some extent persuaded to conform to moral standards at least most of the time, because most of the time they will be harmed if they do not. Nevertheless, we cannot argue against such a person that he will always lose by disobeying moral standards. Sometimes that may unfortunately not be true. (We say "unfortunately," of course, from our own standpoint as people who favor sympathies and morality.) Mackie thinks that we simply have to accept that fact.

If ethics is not a description of "objective facts," then where does it come from? Mackie holds that the large majority of ethical judgments arise from human "institutions." People interact in such a way as to create institutions. Some of these are abstract practices, like promises and the keeping of them. Others are in some ways more concrete and more complicated, like governments or charitable organizations or opera companies.

Associated with any such institutions are tendencies to make judgments about what is to be done. We tend to think that these judgments describe facts. That is an error. Actually the judgments are in some way created by the institutions and are felt to bind the people who participate in them. These institutions and the judgments that they give rise to should serve the practical purpose of enlarging people's sympathies. Mackie criticizes Mill's Utilitarian theory of ethics (Ch. 13) as hopelessly impractical and impossible to live by or put into effect in a society.

What if a person is not a participant in an institution that gives rise to moral standards? What if a person is too weak or debilitated, too isolated? Or what if two institutions are so far apart that their members have no common membership in any institution that gives rise to moral standards? Mackie admits that this is a difficult problem for his view. He thinks that obligations in such cases are not strictly a part of morality, but rather are extensions of morality that a person would want to take seriously, even if those obligations do not belong to morality in the strict sense.

---

**1.** Mackie announces his main thesis: There are no values that are objective, or objectively valid. Values—ethical, moral, aesthetic—are not part of the facts in the world.

There are no objective values. This is a bald statement . . . but before arguing for it I shall try to clarify and restrict it in ways that may meet some objections and prevent some misunderstanding. . . .

The claim that values are not objective, are not part of the fabric of the world, is meant to include not only moral goodness, which might be most naturally equated with moral value, but also other things that could be more loosely called moral values or disvalues—rightness and wrongness, duty, obligation, an action's being rotten and contemptible, and so on. It also includes non-moral values, notably aesthetic ones, beauty and various kinds of artistic merit.[a]

**2.** But this thesis does not imply that ethical judgments and beliefs, and specifically moral ones, do not need to be taken seriously. They do. But it does not require that they be about objective facts.

With [a certain] sort of misunderstanding moral scepticism would seem not so much pernicious as absurd. How could anyone deny that there is a difference between a kind action and a cruel one, or that a coward and a brave man behave differently in the face of danger? Of course, this is undeniable; but it is not to the point. The kinds of behaviour to which moral values and disvalues are ascribed are indeed part of the furniture of the world, and so are the natural, descriptive, differences between them; but not, perhaps, their differences is value. It is a hard fact that cruel actions differ from kind ones, and hence that we can learn, as in fact we all do, to distinguish them fairly well in practice, and to use the words "cruel" and "kind" with fairly clear descriptive meanings; but is it an equally hard fact that actions which are cruel in such a descriptive sense are to be condemned? The present issue is with regard to the objectivity specifically of value, not with regard to the objectivity of those natural, factual differences on the basis of which differing values are assigned.[b]

**3.** Whether a person or action actually measures up to a given standard is an objective fact. So is whether a given sheepdog fits the standard required for entering dog shows, or whether a particular thing satisfies a given desire. But these facts do not make the standard or the desire an objectively valid value.

In one important sense of the word it is a paradigm case of injustice if a court declares someone to be guilty of an offence of which it knows him to be innocent. More generally, a finding is unjust if it is at variance with what the relevant law and the facts together require, and particularly if it is known by the court to be so. More generally still, any award of marks, prizes, or the like is unjust if it is at variance with the agreed standards for the contest in question: if one diver's performance in fact measures up better to the accepted standards for diving than another's, it will be unjust if the latter is awarded higher marks or the prize. In this way the justice or injustice of decisions relative to standards can be a thoroughly objective matter, though there may still be a subjective element in the interpretation or application of standards. But the statement that a certain decision is thus just or unjust will not be objectively prescriptive: in so far as it can be simply true it leaves open the question whether there is any objective requirement to do what is just and to refrain from what is unjust, and equally leaves open the practical decision to act in either way.

The standards used in sheepdog trials clearly bear some relation to the work that sheepdogs are kept to do, the standards for grading apples bear some relation to what people generally want in or like about apples, and so on. On the other hand, standards are not as a rule strictly validated by such purposes. The appropriateness of standards is neither fully determinate nor totally indeterminate in relation to independently specifiable aims or desires. But however determinate it is, the objective appropriateness of standards in relation to aims or desires is no more of a threat to the denial of objective values than is the objectivity of evaluation relative to standards. In fact, it is logically no different from the objectivity of goodness relative to desires. Something may be called good simply in so far as it satisfies or is such as to satisfy a certain desire; but the objectivity of such relations of satisfaction does not constitute in our sense an objective value.[c]

> **4.** Kant was mistaken, Mackie maintains, in claiming that the categorical imperatives given by morality are objectively valid.

A categorical imperative . . . would express a reason for acting which was unconditional in the sense of not being contingent upon any present desire of the agent to whose satisfaction the recommended action would contribute as a means—or more directly: "You ought to dance," if the implied reason is just that you want to dance or like dancing, is still a hypothetical imperative. Now, Kant himself held that moral judgements are categorical imperatives, or perhaps are all applications of one categorical imperative, and it can plausibly be maintained at least that many moral judgements contain a categorically imperative element. So far as ethics is concerned, my thesis that there are no objective values is specifically the denial that any such categorically imperative element is objectively valid. The objective values which I am denying would be action-directing absolutely, not contingently (in the way indicated), upon the agent's desires and inclinations.[d]

> **5.** Morality is not to be discovered, but to be made. The task of moral philosophy is not to determine what is true, but what to do and support, and what principles to use to guide one's action.

I have argued . . . that there are no objective values, and that no substantive moral conclusions or serious constraints on moral views can be derived from either the meanings of moral terms or the logic of moral discourse. What tasks, then, remain for moral philosophy?

We can look at the matter in another way. Morality is not to be discovered but to be made: we have to decide what moral views to adopt, what moral stands to take. No doubt the conclusions we reach will reflect and reveal our sense of justice, our moral consciousness—that is, our moral consciousness as it is at the end of the discussion, not necessarily as it was at the beginning. But that is not the object of the exercise: the object is rather to decide what to do, what to support and what to condemn, what principles of conduct to accept and foster as guiding or controlling our own choices and perhaps those of other people as well.[e]

**6.** To determine such things, we need to determine the object or function of morality. Human happiness is limited by a number of factors, but especially by the limited sympathies and concern that people have for each other. The function of morality is to enlarge those sympathies.

We shall understand [morality better] if we ask what it is for, what is the object of morality. Morality is a species of evaluation, a kind of appraisal of human conduct; this must have some distinctive point, there must be something that is supposed to bring about this in terms of certain general and persistent features of the human predicament, which is "inherently such that, things are liable to go very badly"—badly in the natural, non-moral sense that human wants, needs, and interests are likely to be frustrated in large measure. Among the factors which contribute to make things go badly in the natural course of events are various limitations—limited resources, limited information, limited intelligence, limited rationality, but above all limited sympathies. Men sometimes display active malevolence to one another, but even apart from that they are almost always concerned more with their selfish ends than with helping one another. The function of morality is primarily to counteract this limitation of men's sympathies. We can decide what the content of morality must be by inquiring how this can best be done.[f]

**7.** Morality is an institution, and is made up of and generated by institutions, such as promising and promise keeping. Institutions are matters of interacting with other people in certain ways. They encourage people to guide their actions by principles and concepts.

There is a fatal objection to, say, a resulting act utilitarian system. It would be wholly impracticable. The system can, indeed, be looked at in several different ways, but this charge can be sustained against each interpretation in turn. Suppose, first, that it is considered as a morality in the broad sense, as an all-inclusive theory of conduct. Then, when utility or the general happiness is proposed as the immediate criterion of right action, is it intended that each agent should take the happiness of all as his goal? This, surely, is too much to expect. Mill himself conceded this, and replied to this objection by saying that it confuses the rule of action with the motive of it. "The great majority of good actions," he said, "are intended not for the benefit of the world, but for that of individuals . . . and the thoughts of the most virtuous man need not . . . travel beyond the particular persons concerned, except so far as is necessary to assure himself that in benefiting them he is not violating the rights, that is, the legitimate and authorized expectations, of any one else." But even if we accept this clarification, and take utilitarianism to be supplying not the motive but only a test of right actions, the charge of impracticality still stands. We cannot require that the actions of people generally should even pass the test of being such as to maximize the happiness of all, whether or not this is their motive. Even within a small village or commune it is too much to expect that the efforts of all members should be wholly directed towards the promoting of the well-being of all. And such total cooperation is out of the question on the scale of a nation state, let alone where the "all" are to be the whole human race, including its future or possible future members, and perhaps all other sentient beings as well.[g]

**8.** Promising, for instance, is created by being embedded in a system of social practices and attitudes. It is one of the institutions that goes to make up morality and encourage the attitudes that are associated with it, among the people who participate in the institution.

Act utilitarianism is by no means the only moral theory that displays this extreme of impracticality. The biblical commandment "Thou shalt love thy neighbour as thyself," though it has its roots in a mistranslation of a much more realistic rule, is often taken as prescribing a universal and equal concern for all men. So interpreted, it is, as Mill says, effectively equivalent to the utilitarian principle. And it is similarly impracticable. People simply are not going to put the interests of all their "neighbours" on an equal footing with their own interests and specific purposes and with the interests of those who are literally near to them. Such universal concern will not be the actual motive of their choices, nor will they act as if it were.

Any institution is constituted by many people behaving in fairly regular ways, with relations between them which transmit and encourage and perhaps enforce those ways of behaving. An institution will have rules or principles of action, or both, which the participants in the institution will formulate fairly explicitly, allow to guide their own actions, and infringements of which they will discourage and condemn. They will use concepts closely associated with these rules and principles which cannot be fully explained without reference to these rules and principles; and the rules and principles in turn will usually be formulated partly in terms of those concepts. An institution can be fairly adequately described in an abstract, formal, way simply by stating and explaining the rules and principles and concepts—the game of chess, for example, could be fully described in this way. But the concrete reality is more than this: it is chess-playing as a persisting social practice, not merely the abstract game.[h]

**9.** "Why should I be moral?" This question may seem to pose a difficulty for the present view. We cannot pretend that each and every person's interest is always furthered by abiding by moral standards. Therefore we cannot completely resolve the tension that people see between morality and self-interest. Nevertheless, people mostly benefit from morality, and it is essential to the well-being of virtually everyone.

It is easy to brush aside the question "Why should I be moral?" by pointing out that if the "should" is a moral one, "You should be moral" is tautological, and if it is anything else, say a prudential one, this statement is sometimes false, so that our question either answers itself or, having a false presupposition, admits of no answer. But this reply is superficial and evasive. The real question is whether there is, as Sidgwick, for example, thought, an unresolvable tension between moral reason and the rationality of self-interest, between any recommendations that we could defend as moral and the advice that anyone could be given about his own well-being.

What I have already said does much to reduce this tension. I have argued that egoism is not immoral, but forms a considerable part of any viable moral system. I have also given abundant reasons why almost everyone should, in his own interest, welcome the fact that there is, and hope that there will continue to be, some system of morality, and why, even if the existing system does not suit him, his aim should be to modify it, at least locally, rather than to destroy it. But this does not completely resolve the tension. It leaves unanswered the question "Why should I not at the same time profit from the moral system but evade it? Why should I not encourage others to be moral and take advantage of the fact that they are, but myself avoid fulfilling moral requirements if I can in so far as they go beyond rational egoism and conflict with it?" It is not an adequate answer to this question to point out that one is not likely to be able to get away with such evasions for long. There will be at least some occasions when one can do so with impunity and even without detection. Then why not? To this no complete answer of the kind that is wanted can be given. In the choice of actions moral reasons and prudential ones will not always coincide. Rather, the point of morality, and particularly of that branch of it which I have called morality in the narrow sense, is that it is necessary for the well-being of people in general that they should act to some extent in ways that they cannot see to be (egoistically) prudential and also in ways that in fact are not prudential. Morality has the function of checking what would be the natural result of prudence alone.[i]

**10.** Another difficulty for the theory might seem to be this. If moral judgments are always generated by some institution or other, what would make one hold judgments about how to treat animals or people who do not belong to the same institutions that one belongs to oneself? We have to accept that our sympathies for such beings, and our judgments about how we should treat them, are an extension of morality, not part of morality itself in the strict sense.

The difficult question is the more restricted one about the moral claims, first of human beings who through mental or physical defect are never, at any time in their lives, independent active participants in the cooperation, competition, and conflict of normal life, and secondly of non-human animals. We could afford to ill-treat members of both these classes: they are never in anything even analogous to a position where we should need to bargain with them. Consequently a moral system which ignored their well-being could still achieve what I have said to be the object of morality.

The claims of these classes, then, lie outside what I must regard as the core of morality. It is only extensions of morality that cover them. Moreover, these are gratuitous extensions of morality. They are different from the sort of extension by which morality has been applied more and more widely, not just between members of some small closed social group such as a clan or tribe, but also between members of neighbouring tribes, and foreigners, and people of different races and different religions. Actual contacts, wider intercourse that brings with it possibilities of mutual help and mutual harm, make it necessary that some moral considerations at least should be applied throughout these larger circles. But no such practical need explains the extension of moral consideration to those who are never in a position deliberately to help or to harm us.

It is the role of dispositions in morality that explains these gratuitous extensions. A humane disposition is a vital part of the core of morality; it would surely have been an element in the *aidōs* that the gods, in Protagoras's myth, gave to men. Such a disposition, if it exists, naturally manifests itself in hostility to and disgust at cruelty and in sympathy with pain and suffering wherever they occur. If we are people of the sort that we need to be, and that—no doubt in consequence, but spontaneously and uncalculatingly—we want to be, we cannot be callous and indifferent, let alone actively cruel, either towards permanently defective human beings or towards non-human animals.[j]

## QUESTIONS

1. According to Mackie, our ethical judgments and beliefs need to be taken seriously even though the skeptics do not do so. What accounts for their mistake?
2. Mackie's use of the term *institution* is important for his account of morality. Explain.
3. Mackie's use of the term *sympathies* is important for his account of morality. Explain.
4. Mackie points out that moral theories, even including Act Utilitarianism (an act is morally correct only if it brings about as much good as any available alternative would), lack practicality. Why is practicality such an important criterion?
5. What is it that morality is for? How can it serve us? Can morality ease the human predicament? Discuss.
6. How does Mackie dismiss the Kantian defense of moral objectivity? Do you find this dismissal convincing?
7. Is Mackie's answer to the question "Why should I be moral?" less promising than Mackie might have hoped? Discuss.
8. Mackie's notable philosophic move is to assert that "morality is not to be discovered, but made." Do you know some people who would deem this good news and some who would deem it bad news? Elaborate a little bit, pro and con.
9. Mackie acknowledges that intersubjective agreements often occur in ethical discussions. The ethical naturalist would claim that, say, "Almost all people want to live under the rule of law" provides evidence of moral objectivity. But Mackie would dismiss this claim by insisting that "Almost all people want to eat ice cream occasionally" comes with equal credentials. Discuss.

10. Although Mackie agrees with ethical naturalists that moral judgments make claims that are either true or false, he insists that all such claims are false. How can this contradiction be accounted for?

## KEY TO SELECTIONS

J. L. Mackie, *Ethics: Inventing Right and Wrong* (Harmondsworth, UK: Penguin Books, 1977), 

[a]p. 15.
[b]pp. 16–17.
[c]pp. 26–27.
[d]p. 29.
[e]pp. 105–106.
[f]pp. 107–108.
[g]pp. 129–130.
[h]p. 130.
[i]pp. 189–190.
[j]p. 194.

## GUIDE TO ADDITIONAL READING


### PRIMARY SOURCES

Mackie, J. L., *Ethics: Inventing Right and Wrong*, Harmondsworth, Penguin, 1977.

——— "For Right-Based Morality," in *Studies in Ethical Theory*, ed. P. French, T. Uehling, and H. Wellstein (Midwest Studies in Philosophy, vol. 3), Minneapolis, University of Minnesota Press, 1978.

### DISCUSSION AND COMMENTARY

Cooper, N., *The Diversity of Moral Thinking*, Oxford, Clarendon Press, 1981.

Warnock, G. J., *The Object of Morality*, London, Methuen, 1971.

CHAPTER TWENTY-EIGHT

# Ethical Skepticism

BERNARD WILLIAMS (1929–2003) was closely associated with both Oxford and Cambridge Universities and, more recently, with the University of California at Berkeley. He graduated from Oxford, became a fellow at Oxford's Corpus Christi College, and, late in his career, returned to Oxford as its White's Professor of Moral Philosophy. In 1967, while teaching at Bedford College, London, he accepted the Knightbridge professorship at Cambridge. He resigned this chair after a decade in order to serve as Provost of Cambridge's King's College. Williams's appointment at the University of California was as Deutsch Professor of Philosophy.

Professor Williams wrote numerous essays and books. Among his published collections of essays, *Utilitarianism, For and Against* (1973, with J. J. C. Smart), *Moral Luck* (1981), and *Making Sense of Humanity* (1995) are critical assessments of ethical theorizing. He also wrote three books on ethics: *Morality: An Introduction to Ethics* (1972), *Ethics and the Limits of Philosophy* (1985)—from which our selections are drawn—and *Shame and Necessity* (1993). His widely discussed *Ethics and the Limits of Philosophy* affirms that, as some of his earlier work suggests, there is no way open to us to escape from ethical skepticism.

Williams's main themes are *morality* and, more broadly, the possibility of a *philosophical* grounding of moral norms and conceptions. On both of these fronts Williams is, to put it mildly, skeptical. He questions the value of morality and also the intelligibility of the concepts involved in it; and he doubts that an overall philosophical (or, for that matter, religious) justification of ethical norms is possible.[1] Williams is especially unconvinced by philosophical attempts to "ground" or "justify" morality against the immoralist, the amoralist, or the person whom he also calls the "ethical skeptic."

This does not mean that Williams himself *is* an "immoralist" or even an "amoralist".[2] He does not oppose the kinds of actions that are normally taken to be recommended by morality in the ordinary sense, and he is in favor of many political institutions that advance them. What he opposes is the idea that *philosophy* can, in

[1]Williams does not discuss religion explicitly in the present selection, but he makes it clear that he does not think that religion can succeed where, in his view, philosophy fails.
[2]See Chapter 1 of this book.

a general way, provide a justification of such things by means of the notion of morality as philosophers have typically developed and explicated it.

Like some earlier philosophers (Joseph Butler is a partial example, and so is Philippa Foot, both discussed in previous chapters),[3] Williams thinks that the motivation to abide by ethical standards is simply a fact of nature, a fact about what most human beings want to do. If someone does not have such wants, Williams thinks, there is nothing that a philosophical argument can do to plant them in him or show him that he *must* have them. The best that philosophical arguments can do is to explain, to those who *already* have those wants, what they involve and imply.

The same point can be put in another way. Williams cites Callicles, who appears in Plato's *Gorgias* as someone who scoffs at morality.[4] Williams questions the possibility of providing a philosophical argument that will actually move Callicles, and people like him, to cease their scoffing. But that does not mean that Williams himself adopts the attitudes of such people. It means, rather, that he denies that philosophical arguments such as Plato's can convince them.

Not only does Williams contend that philosophical arguments are on the whole *ineffective* in achieving their goal of convincing the immoralist or the amoralist; he also at the same time denies that there is any *need* for such argument, that is, for philosophical arguments that might convince the immoralist or amoralist to abide by moral norms. Either we can by other, nonphilosophical arguments bring people to behavior that is acceptable to most of us, Williams thinks, or else we can simply rely on the fact that most people will abide by those norms without arguments, because they regard it as acceptable to act morally or ethically.

One type of traditionally philosophical argument whose force Williams especially questions is the Kantian type. That is, he questions whether it is possible to demonstrate that anyone who rejects morality must therefore be *irrational* or *unreasonable*. Williams seems to agree that a society could not maintain itself if it did not have something like morality. However, he thinks that fact leaves room for an individual to reject the practice and language of morality, without thereby being shown to be irrational. It is not, Williams thinks, that such a person would necessarily be incapable of doing mathematics, thinking logically in many areas of life, planning for his or her future, and so on. He might, that is, exhibit virtually all of the characteristics and activities that we normally associate with rationality or reasonableness or common sense. Such a person might also, Williams thinks, *understand* moral language; however, such a person would reject the idea that moral language, and the ideas supposedly expressed by it, should play any role or have any *force* in helping determine what he would choose to do.

Williams is also known not only for his opposition to Kantian arguments, but also for his rejection of the Utilitarianism of thinkers like John Stuart Mill—a topic that he discussed in writings other than the one quoted here. But the core of Williams's thinking is less his rejection of particular moral theories like Kant's and Mill's than his general rejection of the grounding of morality in general philosophical arguments.

One particular respect in which Williams claims not to side with Callicles is this: Williams does not advocate necessarily adopting an attitude or lifestyle that might be

---

[3]See Chapters 10 and 25 of this book.
[4]See Chapter 2 of this book.

characterized as "egoist" or "selfish." Whereas some thinkers maintain—as Callicles seems to have done—that someone who rejects morality must be selfish in behavior and emotion and feeling, Williams thinks this is not so. According to him, the rejection of morality, and of philosophical argument attempting to support it, does not require or cause one to be callous or uncaring toward other people. If people feel sympathetic to others, Williams contends, and wish for their happiness, then that fact is not affected, and certainly is not *necessarily* affected, by whether or not they accept the project of philosophically defending morality.[5]

At the end of this selection, Williams expresses the "hope" that humane attitudes can be produced in people, if not by philosophical justifications, then by three things that he calls "truth," "truthfulness," and "the meaning of life."[6]

In recent years Williams's arguments have been influential (as part, some would say, of a general tendency in modern times to be skeptical about ethical standards). His ideas have certainly not received universal agreement, but they have led to a terminological shift. Earlier, the words *ethical* and *moral* had been used interchangeably. These days, however, many philosophers draw a distinction between "morality" and "ethics," and this is largely because of Williams's own usage of the terms. Williams tends to use "morality" to designate the kind of philosophical grounding that he thinks cannot, and need not, be supplied for norms and standards. He often (though not always) employs the word "ethics," on the other hand, for standards that are not so supported, and for the intellectual project of developing and thinking about such norms.

---

**1.** Williams addresses the question "How should one live?" which he takes Socrates to have posted, and says that philosophy from Plato onward has tried to answer it in a distinctive way.

It is not a trivial question, Socrates said: what we are talking about is how one should live. Or so Plato reports him, in one of the first books written about this subject. Plato thought that philosophy could answer the question. Like Socrates, he hoped that one could direct one's life, if necessary redirect it, through an understanding that was distinctively philosophical—that is to say, general and abstract, rationally reflective, and concerned with what can be known through different kinds of inquiry.[a]

**2.** Williams turns to the philosophical project of attempting to justify morality. He notes that Callicles was unmoved by Plato's attempt. Why, Williams asks, should an amoralist or a skeptic be moved by such arguments?

A note of urgency can sometimes be heard, even in otherwise unhurried writers, when they ask for

---

[5]It is true that one part of Williams's view seems egoistic. He sometimes defends the importance of an individual's own "projects"—such things, e.g., as the attempt to produce great works of art—which sometimes conflict with moral aims. Williams' point, however, is not that a person ought to try to further his own happiness or pleasure, but rather that some projects can be more important to a person's life than certain ethical aims. See his contribution to *Utilitarianism, For and Against.*

[6]Williams's critics object that these ideas are neither more nor less effective than the philosophical justifications that Williams rejects.

a justification of morality. Unless the ethical life, or (more narrowly) morality, can be justified by philosophy, we shall be open to relativism, amoralism, and disorder. As they often put it: when an amoralist calls ethical considerations in doubt, and suggests that there is no reason to follow the requirements of morality, *what can we say to him?*

But what can we say to him if there is a justification of morality? Well, we can put the justification before him. But why should he be expected to stay where we have put it? Why should he listen? The amoralist, or even his more theoretical associate the relativist, is represented in these writings as an alarming figure, a threat. Why should it make any difference to such a person whether there is a philosophical justification of the ethical life?

Once at least in the history of philosophy the amoralist has been concretely represented as an alarming figure, in the character of Callicles who appears in Plato's dialogue the *Gorgias*. Callicles, indeed, under the conventions of Platonic dialogue, engages in rational conversation and stays to be humbled by Socrates' argument (an argument so unconvincing, in fact, that Plato later had to write the *Republic* to improve on it). What is unnerving about him, however, is something that Plato displays and that is also the subject of the dialogue: he has a glistening contempt for philosophy itself, and it is only by condescension or to amuse himself that he stays to listen to its arguments at all.

—That is not the point. The question is not whether he will be convinced, but whether he ought to be convinced.

—But is it? The writers' note of urgency suggests something else, that what will happen could turn on the outcome of these arguments, that the justification of the ethical life could be a *force*. If we are to take this seriously, then it is a real question, who is supposed to be listening. Why are they supposed to be listening? What will the professor's justification do, when they break down the door, smash his spectacles, take him away?

In any case, even if there is something that the rest of us would count as a justification of morality or the ethical life, is it true that the amoralist, call him Callicles, *ought* to be convinced? Is it meant only that it would be a good thing if he were convinced? It would no doubt be a good thing for us, but that is hardly the point. Is it meant to be a good thing for him? Is he being imprudent, for instance, acting against his own best interests? Or is he irrational in a more abstract sense, contradicting himself or going against the rules of logic?[b]

**3.** Skepticism about some particular sorts of knowledge claims might lead to the rejection of those claims by everyone. Ethical skepticism could not lead a whole society to reject ethics, but it could lead an individual to reject an ethical life.

Ethical skepticism, in these respects, is at the opposite end of a line from skepticism about the external world. It is not, on the other hand, like skepticism about psychical research or psychoanalysis, where a real doubt is raised that might come eventually to be accepted, with the result that these activities would meet the same fate as phrenology: we would come to reject them altogether, finding that their claims to knowledge or even reasoned belief were baseless. It is not possible for ethical considerations to meet a collective rejection of that sort. For the individual, however, there does seem to be an alternative to accepting ethical considerations. It lies in a life that is not an ethical life.[c]

**4.** A skeptic about ethics is different from a skeptic about the possibility of scientific knowledge, in that the former may admit a kind of ethical knowledge, but denies that it has any *force* in determining a person's choices of what to do.

The traditional skeptic was basically a skeptic about *knowledge*, but an ethical skeptic is not necessarily the same as someone who doubts whether there is any ethical knowledge. In my sense, to be skeptical about ethics is to be skeptical about the force of ethical considerations; someone may grant them force, and so not be a skeptic, but still not think that they constitute knowledge because he does not think that the point lies in their being knowledge. . . . But, even when ethical skepticism is taken in this way, we should not assume that the skeptic must be someone who leads a life that goes against ethical considerations. Perhaps we should rather say that he leaves room for such a life.[d]

> **5.** The ethical skeptic might simply walk away from all moral discussions; but he could still live his life.

Moreover, the skeptic has to act, and if he includes himself in the world of ethical discourse at all, then what he does must be taken as expressing thoughts he has within that world. If he speaks in terms of actions being ethically all right or not, and he cheerfully does a certain action, then we must take him to regard it as all right. So this is not an option for ethical skepticism. But there is another, which is to opt out of using ethical discourse altogether, except perhaps to deceive. While it is not an easy thing to do, the skeptic might be able to establish himself as one who is not at all concerned with ethical considerations. One can then see the force of the point that there are alternatives. He is not left with nothing to do.[e]

> **6.** On the other hand, Williams says, there is no reason to assume that anyone who wants an explanation of the ethical life must want to live a *non*ethical life. The question is not what to say *to the skeptic*. Rather, we might want to explain ethics to people who already live within it; and we may provide them with political institutions to support it.

This returns us to the question of "to whom?" When the philosopher raised the question of what we shall have to say to the skeptic or amoralist, he should rather have asked what we shall have to say about him. The justification he is looking for is in fact designed for the people who are largely within the ethical world, and the aim of the discourse is not to deal with someone who probably will not listen to it, but to reassure, strengthen, and give insight to those who will. This puts into a different perspective the idea we saw rather optimistically deployed in the case of the amoralist, that a justification of the ethical would be a force. Plato, who saw more deeply than any other philosopher into the questions raised by the possibility of a life outside the ethical, did not himself take it for granted that a justification of the ethical life would be a force. He thought that the power of the ethical was the power of reason, and that it had to be *made* into a force. He saw it as a problem of politics, and so it is. But he believed that the justification was intellectual and very difficult and, further, that everyone had some natural inclination to break out of the ethical order and destroy it. This inclination was a constant presence in most people, who lacked the capacity to master the justification and hence themselves. For Plato, the political problem of making the ethical into a force was the problem of making society embody the rational justification, and that problem could only have an authoritarian solution. If, by contrast, the justification is addressed to a community that is already an ethical one, then the politics of ethical discourse, including moral philosophy, are significantly different. The aim is not to control the enemies of the community or its shirkers but, by giving reason to people already disposed to hear it, to help in continually creating a community held together by that same disposition.[f]

> **7.** Is there, Williams asks, an "Archimedean point"? That is, is there a firm basis that philosophy can use to justify morality in a way that everyone simply *must* accept, and that *forces* everyone to accept ethical standards? Kant thought that it is the idea of "rational" action; Aristotle thought that it is the idea of a "specifically human life."

In another well-worn image, where is there an Archimedean point? That question is not only worn, but profoundly discouraging for any inquiry it is taken to represent. In the case of some inquiries, we are so familiar with the discouragement that we find it hard to imagine what could count as success. If we were now to set the task of finding some position outside all our knowledge and belief from which we could validate them, we might not understand the idea enough even to recognize it as a task. In the ethical case, however, we do have a better idea of what the task would look like. We would need to find a point of leverage in the idea of rational action. That idea in itself, as we have seen, does not immediately display a commitment to the ethical. That is why Socrates' question is not already an ethical one, and also why the amoralist or skeptic seems to hold out the possibility of a rational life outside ethical considerations. Still, perhaps that is merely how it seems before one has reflected enough. The question itself did not use any specifically ethical terms, and that remains a fact. Nonetheless, it might turn out that when we properly think about it, we shall find that we are committed to an ethical life, merely because we are rational agents. Some philosophers believe that this is true. If they are right, then there is what I have called an Archimedean point: something to which even the amoralist or the skeptic is committed but which, properly thought through, will show us that he is irrational, or unreasonable, or at any rate mistaken.

There are two basic types of philosophical venture that fit this pattern. One of them works from the minimal and most abstract possible conception of rational agency.... The other, which we shall turn to immediately, assumes a richer and more determinate view of what rational agency is, taking it to be expressed in living a specifically human life. Both sets of ideas are rooted in past philosophies, the richer and more determinate conception in Aristotle, the more abstract in Kant. Neither of those philosophers, however, thinks that Socrates' question can be taken simply as it stands, as a question, so to speak, waiting to be answered. Each of them redefines the search for an Archimedean point. They do so in different ways—but they have something important in common, which connects them with Socrates' original questioning, as contrasted with other and less fruitful lines in the history of moral philosophy. Each of them yields an argument in practical reason. Neither aims in the first instance to prove the truth of some ethical proposition, which we are then asked to accept in virtue of our interest in believing the truth. Each of them rather commends certain action to us because of our interest in acting rationally or leading a satisfying human life. For both Aristotle and Kant, the justification of ethical propositions will come only from this, that they will be propositions accepted by one who acts rationally or leads such a life.[g]

> **8.** After arguing (in the rest of the book) that there is no such Archimedean point, Williams expresses hope for another kind of thinking that might encourage people to adopt humane norms: "truth," "truthfulness," and "the meaning of an individual life."

This has been a book about what is rather than about what might be, and the hopes I have expressed are, for now, hopes. They rest on assumptions that some people will think optimistic. They can be compressed into a belief in three things: in truth, in truthfulness, and in the meaning of an individual life. I shall end by saying something briefly about each.[h]

> **9.** Although Williams insists that modern natural science is capable of providing us with objective truths, he acknowledges that such truths are nonnormative. He insists as well, however, that such truths do facilitate our developing a reflective social understanding, an understanding, for example, of the histories of societies, of their institutional structures, and of their techniques for inducing group and individual assent.

I have claimed that the natural sciences, at least, are capable of objective truth.... What matters... is how far notions of objective truth can be extended to social understanding....

We need to have some reflective social knowledge, including history, that can command unprejudiced assent if the better hopes for our self-understanding are to be realized. We shall need it if we are to carry out the kind of critique that gives ethical insight into institutions through explanations of how they work and, in particular, of how they generate belief in themselves. It is worth repeating here something that has come out at various points in the discussion of positive ethical theory: it should not suppose that it can do without such social understanding, or that by a pure moralistic stand it can detach itself from these issues. It needs this understanding in order to answer questions about itself that it cannot ultimately avoid, about its relations to social life, its social or psychological connections with practice, and the ways in which it might hope to turn its supposed rational authority into power.[i]

**10.** Williams gives a rough sketch of how "truthfulness" might bring people to accept norms.

The hope for truthfulness, next, is essentially that ethical thought should stand up to reflection, and that its institutions and practices should be capable of becoming transparent. I have tried to say why ethical thought has no chance of being everything it seems. Even if ethical thought had a foundation in determinate conceptions of well-being, the consequences of that could lie only in justifying a *disposition to accept* certain ethical statements, rather than in showing, directly, the truth of those statements.

How truthfulness to an existing self or society is to be combined with reflection, self-understanding, and criticism is a question that philosophy, itself, cannot answer. It is the kind of question that has to be answered through reflective living. The answer has to be discovered, or established, as the result of a process, personal and social, which essentially cannot formulate the answer in advance, except in an unspecific way. Philosophy can play a part in the process, as it plays a part in identifying the question, but it cannot be a substitute for it.[j]

**11.** The third of Williams's optimistic beliefs is in effect a warning against a reductionism whereby ethically relevant dispositions to act are regarded as fully determined by social factors. In contrast, Williams's belief is that the basic dispositions of an individual remain his or hers in particular even though they are subject to social manifestations and modifications.

The picture I give as the background to these various hopes does require, last, that there be individuals with dispositions of character and a life of their own to lead. . . . In one sense, the primacy of the individual and of personal dispositions is a necessary truth—necessary, at least, up to drastic technological changes such as cloning, pooling of brainstores, and so on. This is the sense in which even radical structuralist descriptions of society, whatever they may say, suppose there to be individuals who acquire certain dispositions and aims and express them in action. If the structuralists are right, then these dispositions will be more thoroughly determined by social factors such as class, more uniform in content, and less understood by the individuals than has been traditionally supposed; but those claims cannot deny the existence and causal role of dispositions. No set of social structures can drive youths into violence at football games except by being represented, however confusedly or obscurely, in those youths' desires and habits of life. In this sense, social or ethical life must exist in people's dispositions. It is the content of the dispositions, their intelligibility and their degree of particularity, that differs between societies and is at issue between different interpretations of modern society.

Yet an individualism rather less formal than that is surely necessary if distinctively ethical thought is to be possible, as opposed to social planning or communal ritual; and with regard to the hopes I am expressing here, it will be obvious that a more substantial individualism is in question. It has been so in other parts of the book, in the account I have given of obligation as one ethical consideration among others, for instance, and in some of the things said about practical necessity. My third optimistic belief is in the continuing possibility of a meaningful individual life, one that does not reject society, and indeed shares its perceptions with other people to a considerable depth, but is enough unlike others, in its opacities and disorder as well as in its reasoned intentions, to make it *somebody's*.[k]

## QUESTIONS

1. Williams distinguishes between ethical skepticism and skepticism about the external world. What is the importance of this distinction for his account of ethics?
2. Williams tells us that even if Callicles becomes convinced about the correctness of Socrates' ethics it does not follow that he (Callicles) is no longer an ethical skeptic. Why?
3. Suppose we observe that, typically, X's behavior is ethically scrupulous. Can we conclude with confidence that X is *not* an ethical skeptic? Discuss.
4. The term *force* is decisively important in Williams's account of ethical skepticism. Explain what the term seems to mean as he uses it.
5. Is Williams's critique of ethical theories so thoroughgoing that it denies that an ethical theory can play a socially constructive role? Discuss.
6. Isn't Williams just providing a covering account for the fact that most of us not only typically act in self-serving ways but also reject any ethical theory that condemns our egoism?
7. When denying that neither Aristotle nor Kant have found an Archimedean point, is Williams denying that there are senses of being a rational agent that commit us to rational actions? Explain.
8. Does Williams believe that to be an amoralist is to be a pessimist about the possibility of one's society being humane? Explain your answer.
9. What, in general terms, is the role of the three "optimistic beliefs," truth, truthfulness, and the meaning of an individual life?
10. Explain as specifically as you can what Williams's hope for the meaning of an individual life is. Are you convinced?

## KEY TO SELECTIONS

Bernard Williams, *Ethics and the Limits of Philosophy*, Cambridge, Harvard University Press, 1985. 

[a]p. 1.
[b]pp. 22–23.
[c]p. 24.
[d]p. 25.
[e]p. 26.
[f]pp. 26–27.
[g]pp. 28–29.
[h]p. 198.
[i]pp. 198–199.
[j]pp. 199–200.
[k]pp. 201–202.

## GUIDE TO ADDITIONAL READING


### PRIMARY SOURCES

Williams, Bernard, *Moral Luck*, New York, Cambridge University Press, 1981.

______, "Egoism and Altruism," in *The Problem of the Self*, ed. Amarty Sen and B. Williams, New York, Cambridge University Press, 1973.

______, *Morality: An Introduction to Ethics*, New York, Harper & Row, 1972.

______, "A Critique of Utilitarianism," in *Utilitarianism: For and Against*, ed. B. Williams and J. J. C. Smart, Cambridge, Cambridge University Press, 1973.

______, *Shame and Necessity*, Berkeley, University of California Press, 1993.

### DISCUSSION AND COMMENTARY

Brandt, Richard, *Facts, Values, and Morality*, Cambridge, Cambridge University Press, 1996.

Butchvarov, Panayot, *Skepticism in Ethics*, Bloomington, Indiana University Press, 1989.

Jameison, Dale, "Method and Moral Theory," in *A Companion to Ethics*, ed. Peter Singer, Oxford, Blackwell, 1991.

APPENDIX

# Traditions and Applications

ONE OF THE MOST prominent features of the recent university landscape in the United States and elsewhere is courses in applied ethics. "Applied ethics" means two things. One is the treatment of pressing practical problems that raise ethical concerns. In this sense, *applied ethics* means direct discussion of practical problems.

But applied ethics also commonly means the "application of" traditional ethical ideas, theories, and outlooks to those problems. That means trying to cope with a practical ethical problem by taking a traditional ethical theory and showing what it would mean for dealing with the problem. That's the kind of applied ethics for which the material in this book is adapted.

Not everyone practices this latter kind of applied ethics, and not everyone agrees with it. Some people take an *anti-theoretical* approach to ethics. They think that practical ethical thinking should be done without traditional ethical theorizing. They believe in taking each ethical problem in daily life as it comes, not worrying too much about how different problems interact with each other.

Anti-theoretical ethicists can go so far as to believe that practical problems should be approached without any traditional theory, or even any general theory or general outlook at all. I've heard university teachers of applied ethics say, "I don't really use much ethical theory in my applied ethics course at all; I don't think it's useful." That's a different kind of applied ethics from what you'd most naturally use this book to develop. But it's not an unusual approach to practical ethics.

On the other hand, applied ethics is nothing new. Most of the traditional ethical theories and doctrines that philosophers have developed were meant to be applicable to everyday problems. They were supposed to be applicable to pressing individual and social decisions. Plato's *Republic* was intended to provide an ideal blueprint for a political constitution. Stoics ethics was designed to help people with their everyday lives. Augustine's view was part of an overall view of the place of a human being in the world. The same is true of Spinoza's. The list goes on and on.

If you wanted to take one of the traditional ethical views presented in this book and apply it, what sort of thing would you do? A response to that question is best conveyed by some examples. One major example comes from the Utilitarianism of

Jeremy Bentham and John Stuart Mill (Ch. 13). Mill's ethical theory is one of the traditional views most often applied to particular problems.

Roughly, what Mill tells you to do when you need to make a decision is (1) survey the various actions or policies open to you, (2) figure out how much net happiness (the amount of happiness, minus the amount of unhappiness) would be produced in the whole world by each, and (3) choose the action or policy that would produce the greatest net happiness. Mill's view is actually a bit more complicated, but this is the essence of how it would be applied.

Mill certainly intended his view to be practically useful and applicable in this way. He wrote about many problems of public policy, including freedom of speech and of the press, women's rights, prison reform, general economics, and many other issues as well. But Mill also thought that Utilitarianism could be applied to the private decisions of an individual, such as how much you should spend on a birthday present for your mother or father. In principle, Mill's answer is consistently the same. Just determine how much happiness or unhappiness your spending might produce, with everyone taken into account.

Mill thought that Utilitarianism offered a precise way of settling—finally!—ethical debates that had raged for centuries and even millennia before his time. Many philosophers have agreed with him. Many others have remained unconvinced.

Utilitarianism has had adherents or sympathizers in disciplines outside philosophy. Many economists and political scientists, for instance, think of their discipline as the inheritor of at least some of Mill's Utilitarian theory. Many think of economics as a discipline that can measure happiness or something close to it, and can on that Utilitarian or quasi-Utilitarian basis make predictions, and policy recommendations, about how to bring about the greatest happiness possible. Others are skeptical about whether economics can do this.

Why would someone be skeptical about the capacity of Utilitarianism—whether through economics or not—to settle ethical questions? Some of the reasons are more or less technical. For instance, you might doubt whether it's feasible to predict the various consequences of each action or policy that's open to you at a given juncture. The prediction of all of the innumerable effects of a policy is a staggeringly complex task. This becomes especially hard if one tries to look into the far future and take into account—as Utilitarianism says you should—all very-long-run consequences.

Take the seemingly simple question, "paper or plastic?" Well, paper requires cutting down trees; plastic doesn't. But plastic requires using oil-derived chemicals, and doesn't decay as quickly in landfills. How does that add up, in terms of happiness or unhappiness produced? Here Utilitarianism has a hard time settling on any decision. Supermarkets have declined to make a decision, and pass the question on to the shopper.

You might doubt that it's possible to measure or quantify the happiness that a given action produces, even in a simple case, or to compare two such amounts with each other (see Ch. *). "Chocolate or vanilla?" Not always easy to say for an individual, let alone a large group of children.

Debate about whether Utilitarianism can supply complete answers to these questions continues. But one thing seems certain to most people (though as usual some philosophers disagree). Sometimes the happiness and unhappiness that our actions and policies produce are so great and so important that our ethical thoughts and decisions simply have to take some account of the quantities involved. Sometimes we'd better try to say—even if it's very difficult—which action or policy would produce more happiness or misery.

But let's turn now to other traditional ethical theories, and the ways in which some of them might be applied to ethical issues.

Kant's ethical view (Ch. 12) is another traditional doctrine that people, and especially philosophers, often try to bring to bear on practical decisions about which actions to perform or policies to pursue.

Kant's theory seems easier to apply to the decisions that an individual makes about his or her private actions than to the kind of broad decisions about policy that Utilitarianism has often claimed to be able to make. It's harder to see just how Kant's theory should be applied to large-scale actions undertaken by a government, a country, or a society.

One central part of Kant's view, the usual form of the so-called *categorical imperative*, might offer a way of tackling practical problems. This part of Kant's view encourages an individual to decide what action is right by focusing on a *maxim*—roughly, a rule or fixed policy—under which he does it, and deciding whether that maxim can be *universalized*, whether it could be willed to be a universal moral rule for everyone. It's a kind of philosophical elaboration of the question, "What if everyone did that?", which people often use for moral argument in everyday situations.

Thus Kant's categorical imperative is used as a kind of test. It's a test for determining whether a maxim, and through the maxim a chosen action, can be considered morally and rationally acceptable. If the maxim cannot or could not be taken as a universal rule, then it cannot be used to support the action, and (it's inferred) the action shouldn't be done (Ch. 12, secs. 10–11). In this way Kant argues, for instance, that one should keep promises, on the ground that a maxim or rule prescribing promise-breaking couldn't be willed to be a universally valid rule.

Now let us consider how this aspect of Kant's view might be applied to large-scale actions by societies, countries, and the like. A straightforward way to make this application would be to think of the actions of a country or a society as resulting from the decisions of an individual leader. For example, we could think of an action by a country as the decision of an Empress.

This application of Kantian thinking would seem to be pretty direct, at least when we are dealing with actions such as promises. It seems clear that heads of state, legislatures, and other governmental bodies do make promises, for example, when they sign treaties. The rightness of keeping these promises arguably could be based on the kind of argument that Kant gives. The student may be able to think of other cases of this sort.

On the other hand it is not evident that all social actions can be treated in this way. For one thing, many things that societies do—and it seems normal to say that a society does this or that, taking the society to be a kind of agent—appear not to be things about which you could ask, "What if everyone did that?" or even "What if every society did that?" One difficulty is that, at least according to a widespread view, it's good for societies to be different, and not good for them all to do the same thing, or to adhere to the same rule. This can be argued to create problems for the application of the categorical imperative test to social action.

Whether or not Kantian thinking can find a way around this problem, and turn into a widely applied ethics, the fact is that most applied Kantian philosophizing does not focus on the idea of universalization contained in the categorical imperative.

Rather, it uses a different Kantian idea, which Kant viewed as a formulation of the categorical imperative. This is a requirement to "treat all human beings as ends in themselves and never as merely means to ends" (Ch. 12, sec. 12).

One implication of this idea—that human beings are "ends in themselves"—is that according to Kantian thinking, the rightness or wrongness of an action is not determined by its consequences. Kant's view is thus anti-consequentialist or deontologist, opposing John Stuart Mill's Utilitarian view. According to Utilitarianism, when we choose what to do we should take account simply of what the results of our action should be; that is, we should simply try to maximize the amount of happiness that would result.

Consider the question of who should be put into prison, and when. It is often claimed that, according to Utilitarianism, it would be permissible or even obligatory, at least in certain circumstances, to put people in jail who have not committed a crime or even done anything wrong. This might be recommended if one knew that the person almost certainly would, or very well might, harm many people. Many philosophers and others would consider this a strong argument against Utilitarianism. They would say that people should not be imprisoned unless they have actually done something to deserve it.

Notice that the foregoing issue is not just a question about a particular situation, but partly one about general policy. The general question is whether a society should institute a practice or policy of (as it is called) "preventive detention": imprisonment to prevent harm and unhappiness. This would mean having laws requiring imprisonment of people who are adjudged dangerous, even if they have not actually done anything.

Most of those holding a typical Kantian view would on the whole agree with this criticism of Utilitarianism, and would oppose preventive detention. Their main point as anti-consequentialists would be that whether to imprison someone should not be determined simply by the consequences of doing so. Rather, the rightness or wrongness of the action depends on other considerations. This is the main idea that emerges from Kantian thinking concerning its application to large-scale practical issues.

Kant is not alone in rejecting the application of a purely consequentialist view such as Utilitarianism. Other ethical views are deontologist and anti-consequentialist as well. One such view is that of W. D. Ross (Ch. 20). He maintains that there is a plurality of *prima facie* duties. We have a prima facie duty of beneficence, that is, a duty to bring about happiness, he says. That coincides with Utilitarianism. But other prima facie duties, such as a duty to tell the truth, duty to keep promises, and so on, don't accord so well. These various duties can conflict with each other.

The duties that conflict with the duty of beneficence always have to be taken account of, according to this position. Thus the fact that an act of telling the truth might diminish the amount of happiness produced does not, according to Ross, make it necessary to ignore the duty of truth-telling. Rather, we have to weigh the two prima facie duties, beneficence and truth-telling, against each other and determine which duty overrides the other.

Because Ross gives no method for accomplishing this weighing, his view does not provide a mechanical decision procedure for policy makers. Those who expect such a decision procedure are accordingly often disappointed by Ross's view. On the other hand, Ross will argue that his view fits our actual ethical thinking far better than any view that tries to offer an algorithm for deliberation. Moreover, Ross's view does have one clear non-consequentialist implication for action. His recognition of a plurality of duties provides a check on any decision that advocates judging an action only by the happiness that results from it, or simply by its consequences.

Another deonotologist view is enunciated by John Rawls (Ch. 24). Rawls is very often cited nowadays in discussions of public issues. Although Rawls may not have intended to be taken in this way, many of his readers think that he provides a method of testing whether a given social arrangement or institution is justly established or not.

One idea derived from Rawls says roughly that a social arrangement or institution is just only if it would be accepted by someone considering it from behind the "veil of ignorance" (Ch. 24, sec. 6). Another Rawls-inspired contention is that an institution is just only if it conforms to what Rawls calls the "difference principle." That is, very roughly, an inequality should be accepted only if it would contribute to the well-being of the least well-off (Ch. 24, sec. 4).

This latter suggestion has been much discussed and is the source of vigorous controversy. Some people find this Rawlsian idea attractive, or even obviously correct, when applied to problems such as world hunger, for instance. Others reject this idea. They say that a social arrangement, even an inequality, can cause so much happiness that it would be ethically imperative even if the worst-off aren't affected by it, or are affected to some degree adversely. Others who reject a Rawlsian outlook hold that some other ethical considerations—for example, truth-telling—can be overriding quite apart from whether they affect the worst-off or not.

Yet another way of applying a traditional ethical doctrine—the last example to be given here—can be seen by considering Aristotle, and somewhat similarly the Stoics. Although the positions of Aristotle and the Stoics are different from each other, they offer comparable ways of dealing with some problems.

A central notion for Aristotle is that of *function* (Ch. 3, sec. 6). He maintains that a human being has a function or characteristic activity, much as an eye or a foot seems to. (Many object at this point, however, that the function of a thing is not natural at all, but only the accidental result of what a person happens to use it for under particular circumstances.)

According to Aristotle, the human good is an excellent activity in accordance with this function. The notion of *nature* plays an analogous role in Stoic ethics. Human beings are to act in accordance with rationality because, the Stoics say, that is their nature. In addition, the Stoics also rely on the idea of acting in a way that fits with the cosmos or nature as a whole (Ch. 5, sec. 3–4).

Within the sphere of practical ethics, the ideas of function and nature are extremely popular. Most people have a tendency to identify the natural as good. This tendency is probably somewhat uncritical—there are, after all, many things that seem natural but are not welcomed as good (bacteria, earthquakes, and so on). Nevertheless, the identification is in many minds still a powerful one.

Environmental ethics is an obvious place to try to apply these two notions. Most people think of environmental pollution and various other results of human activity as working against nature. Thus there can be debates about whether a waste dump works for or against nature—the assumption often being that it is good if it does the former and bad if it does the latter. The effort to identify and promote what is characterizable as natural is one leading idea in this sector of applied ethics. So is the effort to identify the function, or the natural function, of a particular phenomenon.

A difficulty with this line of thinking is that much of what human beings do is just as natural as what is done by parts of nature that are not the result of human activity. It is arguable that a contrast between what human beings do and what occurs without human intervention is not, after all, a contrast between the non-natural and the natural, but rather simply a contrast between two different parts of nature, the human part and the non-human part. Nevertheless, the concept of nature in applied ethics has been extremely influential.

These are only some of the ways in which ethical theories can be applied to concrete problems, and only some of the ethical theories that can be applied. The variety of applications of ethical theories is very great.

One of the complexities that has to be remembered here is that there is usually more than one way to apply a given ethical theory to a particular problem. You can't just find *the* Kantian view of euthanasia, or world hunger, or pollution. There are different Kantian views about each problem (not to mention the various components of each problem). One should not think of an ethical theory as a mechanical recipe for addressing each issue.

That is the reason we often find advocates of one and the same ethical theory espousing different views on a particular issue. Take Utilitarianism again. There are Utilitarian arguments for vigorously protecting endangered species, and there are Utilitarian arguments against such a policy. So there are Utilitarians on both sides of such policy issues. That is because starting from Utilitarian theory as an assumption normally does not force you to a particular conclusion about this issue. This is equally true of other ethical doctrines.

An ethical theory aims to tell you which considerations to take into account. It tries to show you how to reach a practical conclusion. But there are usually many different paths from a starting point, and they don't all arrive at the same conclusion. Engineering does not necessarily tell you what vehicle to use, or even what the best or most efficient design is for a particular type of vehicle, all things taken into account. Ethics is in many ways in a similar position.

What is the use of an ethical theory if it does not provide such a recipe? Why engage in ethical theorizing? Isn't the whole point of it to produce practical decisions, in the way in which the point of theories of nutrition is to produce nourishing food?

The parallel does not seem quite appropriate. Rather than talking about theories of nutrition, we ought to consider theories of biology, or for that matter physics. Many people study these for more detached theoretical reasons. These people are partly interested in thinking about the workings of things for their own sake, or for a mixture of reasons that includes practical applications, detached theoretical interest, and just plain curiosity. This combination of practical and non-practical motivations is probably the driving force behind most work in ethics, whether done by philosophers or non-philosophers.

## QUESTIONS

1. Do individuals arrive at their ethical decisions by applying a general theory to the situation that faces them? Can you think of examples in which a person does this? Or does not do it?
2. Should individuals arrive at their ethical decisions by applying a general theory to the situation that faces them?
3. Do businesses or other large organizations, such as governments, make ethical decisions in this way? Give an example.

4. Should businesses or other large organizations, such as governments, make ethical decisions by applying a general theory?
5. Is the application of Utilitarianism to concrete problems faced by policy makers feasible? Give reasons for or against an affirmative answer.
6. "It would not be good if everyone did that." Can this idea be used as a test for social policies, suggestions for legislation, or the like? Why or why not?
7. Take one of the traditional theories discussed in a previous chapter and explain how it would best be applied to an ethical issue that is currently under discussion.

# Appendix

## Selected Readings from

# Contemporary Moral Problems

*Selected Readings*

# An Argument That Abortion Is Wrong

DON MARQUIS

Don Marquis is professor of philosophy at the University of Kansas. His published articles deal with problems in medical ethics.

Marquis wants to show why abortion is seriously wrong, but he begins by granting some exceptions, including cases of rape, of abortion during the first fourteen days after conception, of threat to the woman's life, and an anencephalic fetus. After showing why the standard arguments fail to resolve the debate about abortion, he proceeds to his own argument: that abortion is wrong for the same reason that killing us is wrong. It is wrong because it deprives the fetus of a "future like ours," a future containing valuable experiences, activities, projects, and enjoyments.

The purpose of this essay is to set out an argument for the claim that abortion, except perhaps in rare instances, is seriously wrong.[1] One reason for these exceptions is to eliminate from consideration cases whose ethical analysis should be controversial and detailed for clear-headed opponents of abortion. Such cases include abortion after rape and abortion during the first fourteen days after conception when there is an argument that the fetus is not definitely an individual. Another reason for making these exceptions is to allow for those cases in which the permissibility of abortion is compatible with the argument of this essay. Such cases include abortion when continuation of a pregnancy endangers a woman's life and abortion when the fetus is anencephalic. When I speak of the wrongness of abortion in this essay, a reader should presume the above qualifications. I mean by an abortion an action intended to bring about the death of a fetus for the sake of the woman who carries it. (Thus, as is standard on the literature on this subject, I eliminate spontaneous abortions from consideration.) I mean by a fetus a developing human being from the time of conception to the time of birth. (Thus, as is standard, I call embryos and zygotes, fetuses.)

[1]This essay is an updated version of a view that first appeared in the *Journal of Philosophy* (1989). This essay incorporates attempts to deal with the objections of McInerney (1990), Norcross (1990), Shirley (1995), Steinbock (1992), and Paske (1994) to the original version of the view.

*Source:* Don Marquis, "An Argument That Abortion Is Wrong," from *Ethics in Practice*, ed. Hugh LaFollette, pp. 91–102. 

The argument of this essay will establish that abortion is wrong for the same reason as killing a reader of this essay is wrong. I shall just assume, rather than establish, that killing you is seriously wrong. I shall make no attempt to offer a complete ethics of killing. Finally, I shall make no attempt to resolve some very fundamental and difficult general philosophical issues into which this analysis of the ethics of abortion might lead.

## WHY THE DEBATE OVER ABORTION SEEMS INTRACTABLE

Symmetries that emerge from the analysis of the major arguments on either side of the abortion debate may explain why the abortion debate seems intractable. Consider the following standard antiabortion argument: Fetuses are both human and alive. Humans have the right to life. Therefore, fetuses have the right to life. Of course, women have the right to control their own bodies, but the right to life overrides the right of a woman to control her own body. Therefore, abortion is wrong.

### Thomson's View

Judith Thomson (1971) has argued that even if one grants (for the sake of argument only) that fetuses have the right to life, this argument fails. Thomson invites you to imagine that you have been connected while sleeping, bloodstream to bloodstream, to a famous violinist. The violinist, who suffers from a rare blood disease, will die if disconnected. Thomson argues that you surely have the right to disconnect yourself. She appeals to our intuition that having to be in bed with a violinist for an indefinite period is too much for morality to demand. She supports this claim by noting that the body being used is *your* body, not the violinist's body. She distinguishes the right to life, which the violinist clearly has, from the right to use someone else's body when necessary to preserve one's life, which it is not at all obvious the violinist has. Because the case of pregnancy is like the case of the violinist, one is no more morally obligated to remain attached to a fetus than to remain attached to the violinist.

It is widely conceded that one can generate from Thomson's vivid case the conclusion that abortion is morally permissible when a pregnancy is due to rape (Warren, 1973, p. 49; and Steinbock, 1992, p. 79). But this is hardly a general right to abortion. Do Thomson's more general theses generate a more general right to an abortion? Thomson draws our attention to the fact that in a pregnancy, although a fetus uses a woman's body as a life-support system, a pregnant woman does not use a fetus's body as a life-support system. However, an opponent of abortion might draw our attention to the fact that in an abortion the life that is lost is the fetus's, not the woman's. This symmetry seems to leave us with a stand-off.

Thomson points out that a fetus's right to life does not entail its right to use someone else's body to preserve its life. However, an opponent of abortion might point out that a woman's right to use her own body does not entail her right to end someone else's life in order to do what she wants with her body. In reply, one might argue that a pregnant woman's right to control her own body doesn't come to much if it is wrong for her to take any action that ends the life of the fetus within her. However, an opponent of abortion can argue that the fetus's right to life doesn't come to much if a pregnant woman can end it when she chooses. The consequence of all of these symmetries seems to be a stand-off. But if we have the stand-off, then one might argue that we are left with a conflict of rights: a fetal right to life versus the right of a woman to control her own body. One might then argue that the right to life seems to be a stronger right than the right to control one's own body in the case of abortion because the loss of one's life is a greater loss than the loss of the right to control one's own body in one respect for nine months. Therefore, the right to life overrides the right to control one's own body and abortion is wrong. Considerations like these have suggested to both opponents of abortion and supporters of choice that a Thomsonian strategy for defending a general right to abortion will not succeed (Tooley, 1972; Warren, 1973; and Steinbock, 1992). In fairness, one must note that Thomson did not intend her strategy to generate a general moral permissibility of abortion.

## Do Fetuses Have the Right to Life?

The above considerations suggest that whether abortion is morally permissible boils down to the question of whether fetuses have the right to life. An argument that fetuses either have or lack the right to life must be based upon some general criterion for having or lacking the right to life. Opponents of abortion, on the one hand, look around for the broadest possible plausible criterion, so that fetuses will fall under it. This explains why classic arguments against abortion appeal to the criterion of being human (Noonan, 1970; Beckwith, 1993). This criterion appears plausible: The claim that all humans, whatever their race, gender, religion or *age*, have the right to life seems evident enough. In addition, because the fetuses we are concerned with do not, after all, belong to another species, they are clearly human. Thus, the syllogism that generates the conclusion that fetuses have the right to life is apparently sound.

On the other hand, those who believe abortion is morally permissible wish to find a narrow, but plausible, criterion for possession of the right to life so that fetuses will fall outside of it. This explains, in part, why the standard prochoice arguments in the philosophical literature appeal to the criterion of being a person (Feinberg, 1986; Tooley, 1972; Warren, 1973; Benn, 1973; Engelhardt, 1986). This criterion appears plausible: The claim that only persons have the right to life seems evident enough. Furthermore, because fetuses neither are rational nor possess the capacity to communicate in complex ways nor possess a concept of self that continues through time, no fetus is a person. Thus, the syllogism needed to generate the conclusion that no fetus possesses the right to life is apparently sound. Given that no fetus possesses the right to life, a woman's right to control her own body easily generates the general right to abortion. The existence of two apparently defensible syllogisms which support contrary conclusions helps to explain why partisans on both sides of the abortion dispute often regard their opponents as either morally depraved or mentally deficient.

Which syllogism should we reject? The anti-abortion syllogism is usually attacked by attacking its major premise: the claim that whatever is biologically human has the right to life. This premise is subject to scope problems because the class of the biologically human includes too much: Human cancer-cell cultures are biologically human, but they do not have the right to life. Moreover, this premise also is subject to moral-relevance problems: The connection of the biological and the moral is merely assumed. It is hard to think of a good *argument* for such a connection. If one wishes to consider the category of "human" a moral category, as some people find it plausible to do in other contexts, then one is left with no way of showing that the fetus is fully human without begging the question. Thus, the classic anti-abortion argument appears subject to fatal difficulties.

These difficulties with the classic anti-abortion argument are well known and thought by many to be conclusive. The symmetrical difficulties with the classic pro-choice syllogism are not as well recognized. The pro-choice syllogism can be attacked by attacking its major premise: Only persons have the right to life. This premise is subject to scope problems because the class of persons includes too little: Infants, the severely retarded, and some of the mentally ill seem to fall outside the class of persons as the supporter of choice understands the concept. The premise is also subject to moral-relevance problems: Being a person is understood by the pro-choicer as having certain psychological attributes. If the pro-choicer questions the connection between the biological and the moral, the opponent of abortion can question the connection between the psychological and the moral. If one wishes to consider "person" a moral category, as is often done, then one is left with no way of showing that the fetus is not a person without begging the question.

Pro-choicers appear to have resources for dealing with their difficulties that opponents of abortion lack. Consider their moral-relevance problem. A pro-choicer might argue that morality rests on contractual foundations and that only those who have the psychological attributes of persons are capable of entering into the moral contract and, as a consequence, being a member of the moral community. [This is essentially Engelhardt's (1986) view.] The great advantage of this contractarian approach to morality is that it seems far more plausible than any approach the anti-abortionist can provide. The great disadvantage of this contractarian approach to morality is that it adds to our earlier scope problems by leaving it unclear how we can have the duty not to inflict pain and suffering on animals.

Contractarians have tried to deal with their scope problems by arguing that duties to some individuals who are not persons can be justified even though those individuals are not contracting members of the moral community. For example, Kant argued that, although we do not have direct duties to animals, we "must practice kindness towards animals, for he who is cruel to animals becomes hard also in his dealings with men" (Kant, 1963, p. 240). Feinberg argues that infanticide is wrong, not because infants have the right to life, but because our society's protection of infants has social utility. If we do not treat infants with tenderness and consideration, then when they are persons they will be worse off and we will be worse off also (Feinberg, 1986, p. 271).

These moves only stave off the difficulties with the pro-choice view; they do not resolve them. Consider Kant's account of our obligations to animals. Kantians certainly know the difference between persons and animals. Therefore, no true Kantian would treat persons as she would treat animals. Thus, Kant's defense of our duties to animals fails to show that Kantians have a duty not to be cruel to animals. Consider Feinberg's attempt to show that infanticide is wrong even though no infant is a person. All Feinberg really shows is that it is a good idea to treat with care and consideration the infants we intend to keep. That is quite compatible with killing the infants we intend to discard. This point can be supported by an analogy with which any pro-choicer will agree. There are plainly good reasons to treat with care and consideration the fetuses we intend to keep. This is quite compatible with aborting those fetuses we intend to discard. Thus, Feinberg's account of the wrongness of infanticide is inadequate.

Accordingly, we can see that a contractarian defense of the pro-choice personhood syllogism fails. The problem arises because the contractarian cannot account for our duties to individuals who are not persons, whether these individuals are animals or infants. Because the pro-choicer wishes to adopt a narrow criterion for the right to life so that fetuses will not be included, the scope of her major premise is too narrow. Her problem is the opposite of the problem the classic opponent of abortion faces.

The argument of this section has attempted to establish, albeit briefly, that the classic anti-abortion argument and the pro-choice argument favored by most philosophers both face problems that are mirror images of one another. A standoff results. The abortion debate requires a different strategy.

## THE "FUTURE LIKE OURS" ACCOUNT OF THE WRONGNESS OF KILLING

Why do the standard arguments in the abortion debate fail to resolve the issue? The general principles to which partisans in the debate appeal are either truisms most persons would affirm in the absence of much reflection, or very general moral theories. All are subject to major problems. A different approach is needed.

Opponents of abortion claim that abortion is wrong because abortion involves killing someone like us, a human being who just happens to be very young. Supporters of choice claim that ending the life of a fetus is not in the same moral category as ending the life of an adult human being. Surely this controversy cannot be resolved in the absence of an account of what it is about killing us that makes killing us wrong. On the one hand, if we know what property we possess that makes killing us wrong, then we can ask whether fetuses have the same property. On the other hand, suppose that we do not know what it is about us that makes killing us wrong. If this is so, we do not understand even easy cases in which killing is wrong. Surely, we will not understand the ethics of killing fetuses, for if we do not understand easy cases, then we will not understand hard cases. Both pro-choicer and anti-abortionist agree that it is obvious that it is wrong to kill us. Thus, a discussion of what it is about us that makes killing us not only wrong, but seriously wrong, seems to be the right place to begin a discussion of the abortion issue.

Who is primarily wronged by a killing? The wrong of killing is not primarily explained in terms of the loss to the family and friends of the victim. Perhaps the victim is a hermit. Perhaps one's friends find it easy to make new friends. The wrong of killing is not primarily explained in terms of the brutalization of the killer. The great wrong to the victim explains the brutalization, not the other way around. The wrongness of killing us is understood in terms of what killing does to us. Killing us imposes on us the misfortune of premature death. That misfortune underlies the wrongness.

Premature death is a misfortune because when one is dead, one has been deprived of life. This misfortune can be more precisely specified. Premature death cannot deprive me of my past life. That part of my life is already gone. If I die tomorrow or if I live thirty more years my past life will be no different. It has occurred on either alternative. Rather than my past, my death deprives me of my future, of the life that I would have lived if I had lived out my natural life span.

The loss of a future biological life does not explain the misfortune of death. Compare two scenarios: In the former I now fall into a coma from which I do not recover until my death in thirty years. In the latter I die now. The latter scenario does not seem to describe a greater misfortune than the former.

The loss of our future conscious life is what underlies the misfortune of premature death. Not any future conscious life qualifies, however. Suppose that I am terminally ill with cancer. Suppose also that pain and suffering would dominate my future conscious life. If so, then death would not be a misfortune for me.

Thus, the misfortune of premature death consists of the loss to us of the future goods of consciousness. What are these goods? Much can be said about this issue, but a simple answer will do for the purposes of this essay. The goods of life are whatever we get out of life. The goods of life are those items toward which we take a "pro" attitude. They are completed projects of which we are proud, the pursuit of our goals, aesthetic enjoyments, friendships, intellectual pursuits, and physical pleasures of various sorts. The goods of life are what make life worth living. In general, what makes life worth living for one person will not be the same as what makes life worth living for another. Nevertheless, the list of goods in each of our lives will overlap. The lists are usually different in different stages of our lives.

What makes the goods of my future good for me? One possible, but wrong, answer is my desire for those goods now. This answer does not account for those aspects of my future life that I now believe I will later value, but about which I am wrong. Neither does it account for those aspects of my future that I will come to value, but which I don't value now. What is valuable to the young may not be valuable to the middle-aged. What is valuable to the middle-aged may not be valuable to the old. Some of life's values for the elderly are best appreciated by the elderly. Thus it is wrong to say that the value of my future to me is just what I value now. What makes my future valuable to me are those aspects of my future that I will (or would) value when I will (or would) experience them, whether I value them now or not.

It follows that a person can believe that she will have a valuable future and be wrong. Furthermore, a person can believe that he will not have a valuable future and also be wrong. This is confirmed by our attitude toward many of the suicidal. We attempt to save the lives of the suicidal and to convince them that they have made an error in judgment. This does not mean that the future of an individual obtains value from the value that others confer on it. It means that, in some cases, others can make a clearer judgment of the value of a person's future to *that person* than the person herself. This often happens when one's judgment concerning the value of one's own future is clouded by personal tragedy. (Compare the views of McInerney, 1990, and Shirley, 1995.)

Thus, what is sufficient to make killing us wrong, in general, is that it causes premature death. Premature death is a misfortune. Premature death is a misfortune, in general, because it deprives an individual of a future of value. An individual's future will be valuable to that individual if that individual will come, or would come, to value it. We know that killing us is wrong. What makes killing us wrong, in general, is that it deprives us of a future of value. Thus, killing someone is wrong, in general, when it deprives her of a future like ours. I shall call this "an FLO."

## Arguments in Favor of the FLO Theory

At least four arguments support this FLO account of the wrongness of killing.

### The Considered Judgment Argument

The FLO account of the wrongness of killing is correct because it fits with our considered judgment concerning the nature of the misfortune of death. The analysis of the previous section is an exposition of the nature of this considered judgment. This judgment can be confirmed. If one were to ask individuals with AIDS or with incurable cancer about the nature of their misfortune, I believe that they would say or imply that their impending loss of an FLO makes their premature death a misfortune. If they would not, then the FLO account would plainly be wrong.

### The Worst of Crimes Argument

The FLO account of the wrongness of killing is correct because it explains why we believe that killing is one of the worst of crimes. My being killed deprives me of more than does my being robbed or beaten or harmed in some other way because my being killed deprives me of all of the value of my future, not merely part of it. This explains why we make the penalty for murder greater than the penalty for other crimes.

As a corollary[,] the FLO account of the wrongness of killing also explains why killing an adult human being is justified only in the most extreme circumstances, only in circumstances in which the loss of life to an individual is outweighed by a worse outcome if that life is not taken. Thus, we are willing to justify killing in self-defense, killing in order to save one's own life, because one's loss if one does not kill in that situation is so very great. We justify killing in a just war for similar reasons. We believe that capital punishment would be justified if, by having such an institution, fewer premature deaths would occur. The FLO account of the wrongness of killing does not entail that killing is always wrong. Nevertheless, the FLO account explains both why killing is one of the worst of crimes and, as a corollary, why the exceptions to the wrongness of killing are so very rare. A correct theory of the wrongness of killing should have these features.

### The Appeal to Cases Argument

The FLO account of the wrongness of killing is correct because it yields the correct answers in many life-and-death cases that arise in medicine and have interested philosophers.

Consider medicine first. Most people believe that it is not wrong deliberately to end the life of a person who is permanently unconscious. Thus we believe that it is not wrong to remove a feeding tube or a ventilator from a permanently comatose patient, knowing that such a removal will cause death. The FLO account of the wrongness of killing explains why this is so. A patient who is permanently unconscious cannot have a future that she would come to value, whatever her values. Therefore, according to the FLO theory of the wrongness of killing, death could not, *ceteris paribus*, be a misfortune to her. Therefore, removing the feeding tube or ventilator does not wrong her.

By contrast, almost all people believe that it is wrong, *ceteris paribus*, to withdraw medical treatment from patients who are temporarily unconscious. The FLO account of the wrongness of killing also explains why this is so. Furthermore, these two unconsciousness cases explain why the FLO account of the wrongness of killing does not include present consciousness as a necessary condition for the wrongness of killing.

Consider now the issue of the morality of legalizing active euthanasia. Proponents of active euthanasia argue that if a patient faces a future of intractable pain and wants to die, then, *ceteris paribus*, it would not be wrong for a physician to give him medicine that she knows would result in his death. This view is so universally accepted that even the strongest *opponents* of active euthanasia hold it. The official Vatican view (Sacred Congregation, 1980) is that it is permissible for a physician to administer to a patient morphine sufficient (although no more than sufficient) to control his pain even if she foresees that the morphine will result in his death. Notice how nicely the FLO account of the wrongness of killing explains this unanimity of opinion. A patient known to be in severe intractable pain is presumed to have a future without positive value. Accordingly, death would not be a misfortune for him and an action that would (foreseeably) end his life would not be wrong.

Contrast this with the standard emergency medical treatment of the suicidal. Even though the suicidal have indicated that they want to die, medical personnel will act to save their lives. This supports the view that it is not the mere *desire* to enjoy an FLO which is crucial to our understanding of the wrongness of killing. *Having* an FLO is what is crucial to the account, although one would, of course, want to make an exception in the case of fully autonomous people who refuse life-saving medical treatment. Opponents of abortion can, of course, be willing to make an exception for fully autonomous fetuses who refuse life support.

The FLO theory of the wrongness of killing also deals correctly with issues that have concerned philosophers. It implies that it would be wrong to kill (peaceful) persons from outer space who come to visit our planet even though they are biologically utterly unlike us. Presumably, if they are persons, then they will have futures that are sufficiently like ours so that it would be wrong to kill them. The FLO account of the wrongness of killing shares this feature with the personhood views of the supporters of choice. Classical opponents of abortion who locate the wrongness of abortion somehow in the biological humanity of a fetus cannot explain this.

The FLO account does not entail that there is another species of animals whose members ought not to be killed. Neither does it entail that it is permissible to kill any non-human animal. On the one hand, a supporter of animals' rights might argue that since some non-human animals have a future of value, it is wrong to kill them also, or at least it is wrong to kill them without a far better reason than we usually have for killing non-human animals. On the other hand, one might argue that the futures of non-human animals are not sufficiently like ours for the FLO account to entail that it is wrong to kill them. Since the FLO account does not specify which properties a future of another individual must possess so that killing that individual is wrong, the FLO account is indeterminate with respect to this issue. The fact that the FLO account of the wrongness of killing does not give a determinate answer to this question is not a flaw in the theory. A sound ethical account should yield the right answers in the obvious cases; it should not be required to resolve every disputed question.

A major respect in which the FLO account is superior to accounts that appeal to the concept of person is the explanation the FLO account provides of the wrongness of killing infants. There was a class of infants who had futures that included a class of events that were identical to the futures of the readers of this essay. Thus, reader, the FLO account explains why it was as wrong to kill you when you were an infant as it is to kill you now. This account can be generalized to almost all infants. Notice that the wrongness of killing infants can be explained in the absence of an account of what makes the future of an individual sufficiently valuable so that it is wrong to kill that individual. The absence of such an account explains why the FLO account is indeterminate with respect to the wrongness of killing non-human animals.

If the FLO account is the correct theory of the wrongness of killing, then because abortion involves killing fetuses and fetuses have FLOs for exactly the same reasons that infants have FLOs, abortion is presumptively seriously immoral. This inference lays the necessary groundwork for a fourth argument in favor of the FLO account that shows that abortion is wrong.

### The Analogy with Animals Argument

Why do we believe it is wrong to cause animals suffering? We believe that, in our own case and in the case of other adults and children, suffering is a misfortune. It would be as morally arbitrary to refuse to acknowledge that animal suffering is wrong as it would be to refuse to acknowledge that the suffering of persons of another race is wrong. It is, on reflection, suffering that is a misfortune, not the suffering of white males or the suffering of humans. Therefore, infliction of suffering is presumptively wrong no matter on whom it is inflicted and whether it is inflicted on persons or nonpersons. Arbitrary restrictions on the wrongness of suffering count as racism or speciesism. Not only is this argument convincing on its own, but it is the only way of justifying the wrongness of animal cruelty. Cruelty toward animals is clearly wrong. (This famous argument is due to Singer, 1979.)

The FLO account of the wrongness of abortion is analogous. We believe that, in our own case and the cases of other adults and children, the loss of a future of value is a misfortune. It would be as morally arbitrary to refuse to acknowledge that the loss of a future of value to a fetus is wrong as to refuse to acknowledge that the loss of a future of value to Jews (to take a relevant twentieth-century example) is wrong. It is, on reflection, the loss of a future of value that is a misfortune; not the loss of a future of value to adults or loss of a future of value to non-Jews. To deprive someone of a future of value is wrong no matter on whom the deprivation is inflicted and no matter whether the deprivation is inflicted on persons or nonpersons. Arbitrary restrictions on the wrongness of this deprivation count as racism, genocide or ageism. Therefore, abortion is wrong. This argument that abortion is wrong should be convincing because it has the same form as the argument for the claim that causing pain and suffering to non-human animals is wrong. Since the latter argument is convincing, the former argument should be also. Thus, an analogy with animals supports the thesis that abortion is wrong.

## REPLIES TO OBJECTIONS

The four arguments in the previous section establish that abortion is, except in rare cases, seriously immoral. Not surprisingly, there are objections to this view. There are replies to the four most important objections to the FLO argument for the immorality of abortion.

### The Potentiality Objection

The FLO account of the wrongness of abortion is a potentiality argument. To claim that a fetus *has* an FLO is to claim that a fetus now has the potential to be in a state of a certain kind in the future. It is not to claim that all ordinary fetuses *will* have FLOs. Fetuses who are aborted, of course, will not. To say that a standard fetus has an FLO is to say that a standard fetus either will have or would have a life it will or would value. To say that a standard fetus would have a life it would value is to say that it will have a life it will value if it does not die prematurely. The truth of this conditional is based upon the nature of fetuses (including the fact that they naturally age) and this nature concerns their potential.

Some appeals to potentiality in the abortion debate rest on unsound inferences. For example, one may try to generate an argument against abortion by arguing that because persons have the right to life, potential persons also have the right to life. Such an argument is plainly invalid as it stands. The premise one needs to add to make it valid would have to be something like: "If Xs have the right to Y, then potential Xs have the right to Y." This premise is plainly false. Potential presidents don't have the rights of the presidency; potential voters don't have the right to vote.

In the FLO argument potentiality is not used in order to bridge the gap between adults and fetuses as is done in the argument in the above paragraph. The FLO theory of the wrongness of killing adults is based upon the adult's potentiality to have a future of value. Potentiality is in the argument from the very beginning. Thus, the plainly false premise is not required. Accordingly, the use of potentiality in the FLO theory is not a sign of an illegitimate inference.

### The Argument from Interests

A second objection to the FLO account of the immorality of abortion involves arguing that even though fetuses have FLOs, nonsentient fetuses do not meet the minimum conditions for having any moral standing at all because they lack interests. Steinbock (1992, p. 5) has presented this argument clearly:

> Beings that have moral status must be capable of caring about what is done to them. They must be capable of being made, if only in a rudimentary sense, happy or miserable, comfortable or distressed. Whatever reasons we may have for preserving or protecting nonsentient beings, these reasons do not refer to their own interests. For without conscious awareness, beings cannot have interests. Without interests, they cannot have a welfare of their own. Without a welfare of their own, nothing can be done for their sake. Hence, they lack moral standing or status.

Medical researchers have argued that fetuses do not become sentient until after 22 weeks of gestation (Steinbock, 1992, p. 50). If they are correct, and if Steinbock's argument is sound, then we have both an objection to the FLO account of the wrongness of abortion and a basis for a view on abortion minimally acceptable to most supporters of choice.

Steinbock's conclusion conflicts with our settled moral beliefs. Temporarily unconscious human beings are nonsentient, yet no one believes that they lack either interests or moral standing. Accordingly, neither conscious awareness nor the capacity for conscious awareness is a necessary condition for having interests.

The counter-example of the temporarily unconscious human being shows that there is something internally wrong with Steinbock's argument. The difficulty stems from an ambiguity. One cannot *take* an interest in something without being capable of caring about what is done to it. However, something can be *in* someone's interest without that individual being capable of caring about it, or about anything. Thus, life support can be in the interests of a temporarily unconscious patient even though the temporarily unconscious patient is incapable of *taking* an interest in that life support. If this can be so for the temporarily unconscious patient, then it is hard to see why it cannot be so for the temporarily unconscious (that is, nonsentient) fetus who requires placental life support. Thus the objection based on interests fails.

## The Problem of Equality

The FLO account of the wrongness of killing seems to imply that the degree of wrongness associated with each killing varies inversely with the victim's age. Thus, the FLO account of the wrongness of killing seems to suggest that it is far worse to kill a five-year-old than an 89-year-old because the former is deprived of far more than the latter. However, we believe that all persons have an equal right to life. Thus, it appears that the FLO account of the wrongness of killing entails an obviously false view (Paske, 1994).

However, the FLO account of the wrongness of killing does not, strictly speaking, imply that it is worse to kill younger people than older people. The FLO account provides an explanation of the wrongness of killing that is sufficient to account for the serious presumptive wrongness of killing. It does not follow that killings cannot be wrong in other ways. For example, one might hold, as does Feldman (1992, p. 184), that in addition to the wrongness of killing that has its basis in the future life of which the victim is deprived, killing an individual is also made wrong by the admirability of an individual's past behavior. Now the amount of admirability will presumably vary directly with age, whereas the amount of deprivation will vary inversely with age. This tends to equalize the wrongness of murder.

However, even if, *ceteris paribus*, it is worse to kill younger persons than older persons, there are good reasons for adopting a doctrine of the legal equality of murder. Suppose that we tried to estimate the seriousness of a crime of murder by appraising the value of the FLO of which the victim had been deprived. How would one go about doing this? In the first place, one would be confronted by the old problem of interpersonal comparisons of utility. In the second place, estimation of the value of a future would involve putting oneself, not into the shoes of the victim at the time she was killed, but rather into the shoes the victim would have worn had the victim survived, and then estimating from that perspective the worth of that person's future. This task seems difficult, if not impossible. Accordingly, there are reasons to adopt a convention that murders are equally wrong.

Furthermore, the FLO theory, in a way, explains why we do adopt the doctrine of the legal equality of murder. The FLO theory explains why we regard murder as one of the worst of crimes, since depriving someone of a future like ours deprives her of more than depriving her of anything else. This gives us a reason for making the punishment for murder very harsh, as harsh as is compatible with civilized society. One should not make the punishment for younger victims harsher than that. Thus, the doctrine of the equal legal right to life does not seem to be incompatible with the FLO theory.

## The Contraception Objection

The strongest objection to the FLO argument for the immorality of abortion is based on the claim that, because contraception results in one less FLO, the FLO argument entails that contraception, indeed, abstention from sex when conception is possible, is immoral. Because neither contraception nor abstention from sex when conception is possible is immoral, the FLO account is flawed.

There is a cogent reply to this objection. If the argument of the early part of this essay is correct, then the central issue concerning the morality of abortion is the problem of whether fetuses are individuals who are members of the class of individuals whom it is seriously presumptively wrong to kill. The properties of being human and alive, of being a person, and of having an FLO are criteria that participants in the abortion debate have offered to mark off the relevant class of individuals. The central claim of this essay is that having an FLO marks off the relevant class of individuals. A defender of the FLO view could, therefore, reply that since, at the time of contraception, there is no individual to have an FLO, the FLO account does not entail that contraception is wrong. The wrong of killing is primarily a wrong to the individual who is killed; at the time of contraception there is no individual to be wronged.

However, someone who presses the contraception objection might have an answer to this reply. She might say that the sperm and egg are the individuals deprived of an FLO at the time of contraception. Thus, there are individuals whom contraception deprives of an FLO and if depriving an individual of an FLO is what makes killing wrong, then the FLO theory entails that contraception is wrong.

There is also a reply to this move. In the case of abortion, an objectively determinate individual is the subject of harm caused by the loss of an FLO. This individual is a fetus. In the case of contraception, there are far more candidates (see Norcross, 1990). Let us consider some possible candidates in order of the increasing number of individuals harmed: (1) The single harmed individual might be the combination of the particular sperm and the particular egg that would have united to form a zygote if contraception had not been used. (2) The two harmed individuals might be the particular sperm itself, and, in addition, the ovum itself that would have physically combined to form the zygote. (This is modeled on the double homicide of two persons who would otherwise in a short time fuse. (1) is modeled on harm to a single entity some of whose parts are not physically contiguous, such as a university.) (3) The many harmed individuals might be the millions of *combinations* of sperm and the released ovum whose (small) chances of having an FLO were reduced by the successful contraception. (4) The even larger class of harmed individuals (larger by one) might be the class consisting of all of the individual sperm in an ejaculate and, in addition, the individual ovum released at the time of the successful contraception. (1) through (4) are all candidates for being the subject(s) of harm in the case of successful contraception or abstinence from sex. Which should be chosen? Should we hold a lottery? There seems to be no non-arbitrarily determinate subject of harm in the case of successful contraception. But if there is no such subject of harm, then no determinate thing was harmed. If no determinate thing was harmed, then (in the case of contraception) no wrong has been done. Thus, the FLO account of the wrongness of abortion does not entail that contraception is wrong.

## CONCLUSION

This essay contains an argument for the view that, except in unusual circumstances, abortion is seriously wrong. Deprivation of an FLO explains why killing adults and children is wrong. Abortion deprives fetuses of FLOs. Therefore, abortion is wrong. This argument is based on an account of the wrongness of killing that is a result of our considered judgment of the nature of the misfortune of premature death. It accounts for why we regard killing as one of the worst of crimes. It is superior to alternative accounts of the wrongness of killing that are intended to provide insight into the ethics of abortion. This account of the wrongness of killing is supported by the way it handles cases in which our moral judgments are settled. This account has an analogue in the most plausible account of the wrongness of causing animals to suffer. This account makes no appeal to religion. Therefore, the FLO account shows that abortion, except in rare instances, is seriously wrong.

## REFERENCES


Beckwith, F. J., *Politically Correct Death: Answering Arguments for Abortion Rights* (Grand Rapids, Michigan: Baker Books, 1993).

Benn, S. I., "Abortion, infanticide, and respect for persons," *The Problem of Abortion*, ed. J. Feinberg (Belmont, California: Wadsworth, 1973), pp. 92–104.

Engelhardt, Jr., H. T., *The Foundations of Bioethics* (New York: Oxford University Press, 1986).

Feinberg, J., "Abortion," *Matters of Life and Death: New Introductory Essays in Moral Philosophy*, ed. T. Regan (New York: Random House, 1986).

Feldman, F., *Confrontations with the Reaper: A Philosophical Study of the Nature and Value of Death* (New York: Oxford University Press, 1992).

Kant, I., *Lectures on Ethics*, tr. L. Infeld (New York: Harper, 1963).

Marquis, D. B., "A future like ours and the concept of person: A reply to McInerney and Paske," *The Abortion Controversy: A Reader*, ed. L. P. Pojman and F. J. Beckwith (Boston: Jones and Bartlett, 1994), pp. 354–68.

———, "Fetuses, futures and values: A reply to Shirley," *Southwest Philosophy Review*, 11 (1995): 263–5.

———, "Why abortion is immoral," *Journal of Philosophy*, 86 (1989): 183–202.

McInerney, P., "Does a fetus already have a future like ours?," *Journal of Philosophy*, 87 (1990): 264–8.

Noonan, J., "An almost absolute value in history," in *The Morality of Abortion*, ed. J. Noonan (Cambridge, Massachusetts: Harvard University Press).

Norcross, A., "Killing, abortion, and contraception: A reply to Marquis," *Journal of Philosophy*, 87 (1990): 268–77.

Paske, G., "Abortion and the neo-natal right to life: A critique of Marquis's futurist argument," *The Abortion Controversy: A Reader*, ed. L. P. Pojman and F. J. Beckwith (Boston: Jones and Bartlett, 1994), pp. 343–53.

Sacred Congregation for the Propagation of the Faith, *Declaration on Euthanasia* (Vatican City, 1980).

Shirley, E. S., "Marquis' argument against abortion: A critique," *Southwest Philosophy Review*, 11 (1995): 79–89.

Singer, P., "Not for humans only: The place of nonhumans in environmental issues," *Ethics and Problems of the 21st Century*, ed. K. E. Goodpaster and K. M. Sayre (South Bend: Notre Dame University Press, 1979).

Steinbock, B., *Life Before Birth: The Moral and Legal Status of Embryos and Fetuses* (New York: Oxford University Press, 1992).

Thomson, J. J., "A defense of abortion," *Philosophy and Public Affairs*, 1 (1971): 47–66.

Tooley, M., "Abortion and infanticide," *Philosophy and Public Affairs*, 2 (1972): 37–65.

Warren, M. A., "On the moral and legal status of abortion," *Monist*, 57 (1973): 43–61.

## REVIEW QUESTIONS

1. What exceptions does Marquis allow to his claim that abortion is seriously wrong? Why does he make these exceptions?
2. What "symmetries" does Marquis find in the abortion debate? Why do these make the debate seem intractable?
3. Why is killing a person wrong, according to Marquis?
4. State and explain the four arguments Marquis uses to support his account of the wrongness of killing.
5. What is the potentiality objection, and how does Marquis respond to it?
6. State and explain Steinbock's argument from interests. How does Marquis reply?
7. What is the problem of equality? How does Marquis deal with it?
8. Explain the contraception objection and Marquis's reply.

## DISCUSSION QUESTIONS

1. There seem to be a number of cases in which the fetus does not have a "future like ours" besides the case of the anencephalic fetus that Marquis mentions. For example, the fetus can be deformed in other ways or have a genetic disease. Or perhaps the child will have abusive parents and a life full of suffering. Does Marquis have to grant that abortion is not wrong in all these cases where the fetus does not have a "future like ours"? Explain your answer.
2. Is the wrongness of killing a matter of degree, such that killing a person at the end of her life is not as wrong as killing a young person? Or is killing the old and the young equally wrong? What is Marquis's position on this? What do you think?
3. Is it wrong to kill nonhuman animals? Why doesn't Marquis take a position on this? What is your view?
4. In his reply to the contraception objection, Marquis assumes that the fetus is one individual. But when the zygote divides into twins there are two individuals, not one. Does twinning pose a problem for Marquis? Why or why not?

# The Egg and I: Conception, Identity, and Abortion

EUGENE MILLS

Eugene Mills is associate professor of philosophy at Virginia Commonwealth University. He has published articles on a wide variety of topics, including analytic philosophy, the liar's paradox, personal identity, mental causation, and justification.

Mills challenges the pro-life assumption, made by Noonan and others, that a human being comes into existence at conception. He argues that humans begin either before or after conception, but not *at* conception. (Although his argument is formulated in the first person, he intends it to apply to all human beings.) His argument for this conclusion takes the form of a dilemma. An adult human being is either identical with the zygote in the mother's womb (so that the adult and the zygote are different stages of development of the same ongoing thing) or else the adult is not identical with the zygote but developed out of it. If the adult is not identical with the zygote, but came into existence later (when the fetus is conscious, which is one

---

*Source:* "The Egg and I: Conception, Identity, and Abortion Problem Cases" by Eugene Mills from *Philosophical Review*, Vol 117, No 3.

*Editor's Note: The footnotes have been deleted.

standard view), then the adult was never a zygote and did not begin at conception. If the adult is identical with the zygote, then the adult existed earlier than the zygote as an unfertilized egg (an oocyte), which became a zygote when it was fertilized by the sperm. Again, the adult's existence did not begin at conception. So, whether or not the adult was once a zygote, the adult did not originate at conception.

Mills goes on to argue that this metaphysical conclusion about origination raises problems for Marquis and Noonan. Marquis argues that no determinate being is harmed by contraception or abstinence. Mills claims that Marquis is simply mistaken. There is a single determinate subject of harm in cases of contraception or abstinence: namely, the oocyte that would or could have been fertilized. If contraception or abstinence is not seriously wrong, as Marquis maintains, then he should agree that an early abortion is not seriously wrong either. As for Noonan, Mills rejects Noonan's claim that a new being comes into existence at conception. The unfertilized egg is already on the scene. Furthermore, Noonan gives no reason for holding that at conception the zygote becomes a member of the genus *Homo*, as distinguished from being human in the sense in which a liver cell is human.

## I. THE METAPHYSICS AND MORALITY OF ORIGINATION

When did I come into existence, and why should you care? Take the second question first. You should care because what goes for me goes for all human persons: we aren't all the same age, but we all came into existence at the same stage of biological development. This fact bears on the morality of abortion. I assume—without argument but for its sake—that you care about *this*.

The answer to the first question may hinge partly on the answer to a different question: what kind of thing am I? I'll suppose for the sake of argument, except where explicitly stated otherwise, that the true, relevant, and known answer is that I'm a "human being" in the sense of a human *animal*, a member of the genus *Homo*. Given this supposition, I'll argue first and foremost that I originated not at the moment of my biological conception, but either before or after. This metaphysical point carries moral freight. I'll argue secondarily that if any familiar "pro-life" moral principle raises moral qualms about the permissibility of zygotic abortion, these qualms apply equally (or at least almost equally) to the permissibility of contraception and abstinence.

Although I think my primary, metaphysical argument is strong, a related but weaker argument will serve for most of my moral purposes. I hope that even if I don't convince you that I originated either before or after conception, I'll at least convince you that it's at least reasonably doubtful that I originated at conception. And if you're convinced of even this much, I'll argue, my primary moral arguments should convince you as well.

Regardless of your moral attitude toward abortion, you probably hold that human biological conception—the fertilization of the egg—creates a new being. You probably hold that this being is at least a candidate for being or becoming a living human being. If you lean one way on abortion's moral status, you probably deny that this being is a person or a "human being" in a moral sense while allowing that it may eventually become one. You may deny that it has moral standing, while allowing that it may eventually gain it. Still, you probably affirm that conception results in *a new being* (even if you think this being a constituent part of the pregnant woman). If you lean the other way on abortion, you're more likely to insist that this new being has moral standing; you may, though you needn't, hold that it's a person right from the start. Whichever way you lean, you probably hold that from conception on, but not before, a being exists that probably will, absent abortion or mishap, become a normal adult human being.

From the retrospective first-person perspective, this shared assumption amounts to the view that I—the human animal that I'm assuming is me—originated with the fertilization of an egg. I'll argue that this assumption is mistaken. "Conception" has an ontological sense on which it's analytic that conception is origination. It's not analytic, though, that *biological* conception is origination. I'll argue that it's not even true; biological conception creates no new being.

I'll then draw out some consequences for abortion. Pro-life arguments typically involve two main premises. The first assigns to the human organism *in utero* some salient metaphysical status. Candidates for this status include: person, potential person, being with the potential for a valuable future, sentient being, and living human being. The second premise is a moral principle to the effect that (at least generally, at least presumptively) it's wrong to kill beings with the metaphysical status in question. I focus here on the metaphysical rather than the moral premise and mainly on the question *at what stage of development* is the salient metaphysical status attained? I argue that there's no good reason to think, for any standard candidate, that biological conception—hereafter, just "conception"—is the point of attainment.

I don't debate whether any sound principle leads from the metaphysical status of beings who could survive to normal adulthood to the presumptive wrongness of abortion. I argue that any such principle of familiar stripe, if true, either renders contraception and sexual abstinence presumptively wrong, or else does *not* rule presumptively wrong zygotic abortion.

"Morning-after pills" destroy zygotes. Though my argument renders no categorical verdict on the permissibility of such destruction, it does show that no familiar basis for condemning morning-after pills while condoning contraception and abstinence can succeed. Given the current public debate over the moral status of morning-after pills, my argument thus has a practical upshot of contemporary relevance.

Here's a sketch of the coming argument. Common sense holds, and I assume for convenience, that an organism existing at one time may be numerically identical to an organism existing at another time, though it grows and otherwise changes in the interim. When I say truly that "I existed ten years ago," I say that I (now) am identical with an organism that existed ten years ago. I argue in section 2 that, given this view, I didn't come into existence at conception. I consider objections in section 3. In sections 5 and 6, I trace some consequences of my metaphysical argument for the morality of abortion.

## II. THE EGG AND I

Suppose, again, that I'm a human animal—a member of the genus *Homo*. When did I originate?

I'm intimately related to a zygote that inhabited my mother's womb when she was pregnant with me. Either the intimate relation connecting me with the zygote is identity, or it isn't. If it's identity, then I (now) and the zygote (then) are the same being at different stages of development. If it isn't identity, then our intimate relation consists in my having "developed out of" the zygote in a distinctive way. In either case, I'll argue, I didn't originate at conception.

Suppose I'm not identical with the zygote from which I developed. Now, temporally gappy existence may be possible. (Dismantle a car, scatter its parts, and then recover and reassemble them. Perhaps the car has gappy existence.) Whether or not existence *can* be gappy, though, my actual existence clearly isn't. So if I was never a zygote, then I didn't exist before or during the existence of the zygote to which I'm intimately related. Conception occurred either before or during the existence of that zygote. Hence if I was never a zygote, then I existed neither before conception nor for some time after. Thus I originated some time after conception. So if I was never a zygote, I didn't originate at conception.

Suppose on the other hand that I once was a zygote. A zygote is a fertilized egg. A fertilized egg doesn't pop into existence upon fertilization; it exists, unfertilized, before its encounter with the fertilizing sperm. So if I was once a fertilized egg, then I was once an unfertilized egg. The fertilization of the egg is (biological) conception. Hence if I was once an unfertilized egg, then I existed before conception. So if I was once a fertilized egg—a zygote—then I did not originate at conception.

In sum: whether or not I was once a zygote, I did not originate at conception.

## III. SOME OBJECTIONS CONSIDERED

I expect that the first horn of my dilemma—that if I was never a zygote, then my conception wasn't my origination—will raise no eyebrows. I expect that the crucial claim of the second horn—that if I was once a zygote, then I was once an unfertilized egg—will inspire incredulity. I now consider some objections to it.

One objection to my argument for the second horn is as follows. A fertilized egg is not, contrary to my suggestion, an egg—just as a crowned prince is not a prince, a victorious candidate not a candidate. So I wrongly claim that a zygote is an egg that was once unfertilized and then became fertilized.

I note that despite my forthcoming concession of this point for argument's sake, it's utterly implausible. You can buy fertilized hen's eggs in grocery stores. I see no license in common sense, biology, ontology or agribusiness for the claim that they aren't really eggs.

The main point, though, is that my argument doesn't require that a fertilized human egg be an *egg*; it's enough that it's an organism (or, in fact, a *thing*). It would indeed be a mistake to say that a crowned prince is a prince who was once uncrowned and then became crowned. It would be no mistake, though, to say that a crowned prince is a thing that was once uncrowned and then became crowned. What matters is that the crowned prince is identical with—the very same being as—the uncrowned prince, not that this being is a prince at both times under consideration. Similarly, it suffices for my argument that a fertilized egg—a zygote—is a thing that existed before fertilization and then became fertilized.

Let me reinforce this claim. If I was once a fertilized egg but never an unfertilized one, then the organism that's the fertilized egg didn't exist before its union with a sperm. More accurately, it didn't exist before its predecessor's union with a sperm: the organism that is the fertilized egg never joined with a sperm, on the suggestion I now consider, since on that suggestion the joining precedes the existence of that organism. If this is true, then eggs can't survive fertilization. Eggs never *become fertilized;* nothing is at one time an unfertilized egg and later a zygote. Fertilization annihilates one organism and creates another.

The problem with this suggestion is that it seems plainly false, notwithstanding its wide uncritical acceptance. Review some sex education materials; watch, via microscope, the fertilization of an egg. You see an unfertilized oocyte—the one-celled human egg. A sperm approaches and, after traversing the corona radiata and zona pellucida, contacts the egg's cell wall. The sperm breaches that wall, enters, and dissolves, discharging its contents. The breach in the cell wall is immediately sealed. The most natural description of these events is that you've watched one egg *become fertilized*, not the annihilation of one organism and the creation of another.

To repeat: the sperm breaches the egg's cell wall, enters, and *dissolves*. Its dissolution is its death. The sperm "lives on" as we live on in our children, our works, and the compost our bodies eventually become: that is, figuratively. The sperm doesn't literally exist after conception. The oocyte does. Life is unfair.

You might just insist that fertilization is different from all other processes involving the absorption of extracellular material or the internal rearrangement of parts. One way or another, fertilization *must* mark the beginning of a new being.

This insistence is as ad hoc and unjustified as it is common and unquestioned. Its wide acceptance gives it no support but does call for diagnostic explanation, and I offer one speculative but plausible such explanation. (Whether it's the correct explanation is an empirical matter that exceeds my expertise.) Long before the biology of human reproduction was understood, the clear sign that a new being had been brought into being was a baby. Sex was the salient recognizable link in the causal chain leading to babies: abstinence prevents them, indulgence produces them. (I ignore in-vitro fertilization and the like because these technologies can't be responsible for the common attitudes that predate their existence.) Given their background knowledge, our ancestors had no reason to think that any human beings existed except those that either had been born or were growing inside pregnant women. So it's easy to understand why our ancestors would believe that sex initiated a causal process that resulted in the creation of a new being, and it's easy to understand how such a belief might become entrenched. Biological conception was later found to be the salient concomitant of sex: babies result only when conception occurs, and conception, when it occurs, is an effect of sex. (Again, I ignore alternatives only recently rendered medically possible.) These simple facts are enough to account for the prevailing belief that conception marks the beginning of existence: that belief would result from combining two independently reasonable beliefs. That the resulting conjunctive belief contradicts another, far more reasonable, belief concerning identity over time is something easily and understandably overlooked. The relevant beliefs of biologists need no diagnostic explanation, for biologists don't *have* the false belief in question. (They don't have it, at least, when wearing their biologist-hats. They can change headgear as well as anyone else.) You'll look in vain in the embryology literature for any hint that conception is anything other than an important event punctuating—not originating—the life of a single being.

## V. ORIGINATION AND THE MORALITY OF ABORTION

I didn't originate, then, at conception. This fact makes trouble of various kinds for some standard pro-life positions. The trouble may be surmountable, but it must be and hasn't been surmounted.

Perhaps the most philosophically prominent pro-life position is that of Don Marquis. Marquis argues that it's seriously wrong to deprive any being of the potential for certain kinds of valuable future experiences—of a "future like ours" (FLO). (By "seriously wrong," Marquis means "seriously presumptively wrong." I'll follow his lead.) Since abortion typically deprives the fetus of an FLO, Marquis says, it is typically seriously wrong.

Marquis considers the objection that on his account, contraception and abstinence are seriously wrong because they deprive a being of an FLO. To take this as an *objection* is to presuppose, as Marquis seems to do, that contraception and abstinence aren't seriously wrong. It's worth noting that even if contraception and abstinence *do* deprive a being of an FLO, they needn't be equally wrong even by Marquis's lights. If you plump for a morally relevant distinction between acts and omissions, you might well see abstinence as less wrong than contraception and both, perhaps, as less wrong than abortion. For abstinence looks like a (mere?) failure to rescue—though the rescue is in most cases an easy and pleasant one—whereas contraception looks like a more odious active interference with a rescue. You might even think that active interference with a rescue is not, unlike abortion, a matter of active killing, and so you might think it less odious than abortion. I don't endorse this hypothetical parsing of moral gravity, but if you do, no matter. What I'm concerned with is the question whether, given Marquis's assumptions, there's something seriously wrong with abstinence or contraception, not with whether they must be equally wrong or *as* wrong as abortion. If actively depriving something of an FLO is seriously wrong, then surely failing to prevent such deprivation, when prevention is easy, is at least very significantly wrong.

You might pin your hopes on the gap, if there is one, between very significant wrongs and serious ones. You might say, that is, that while actively killing a being with an FLO is seriously wrong, failure to perform an easy rescue of such a being isn't. This surely isn't Marquis's view; if it were, he would have said so in response to the objection at issue. In any case, the view looks desperate and ad hoc on its face. (This isn't to deny, of course, that some serious wrongs are worse than others.) I'll take for granted that if abstinence and contraception deprive a being of an FLO, then they are seriously wrong by Marquis's lights. If you want to insist that they are only very significantly but not seriously wrong, go right ahead.

The question for Marquis is this: which being is deprived of an FLO by contraception or abstinence? Marquis surveys the candidates in order of the increasing number of individuals harmed: (1) The single harmed individual might be the combination of the particular sperm and the particular egg that would have united to form a zygote if contraception had not been used. (2) The two harmed individuals might be the particular sperm itself, and, in addition, the ovum itself that would have physically combined to form the zygote. . . . (3) The many harmed individuals might be the millions of *combinations* of sperm and the released ovum whose (small) chances of having an FLO were reduced by the successful contraception. (4) The even larger class of harmed individuals (larger by one) might be the class consisting of all of the individual sperm in an ejaculate and, in addition, the individual ovum released at the time of the successful contraception. (1) through (4) are all candidates for being the subject(s) of harm in the case of successful contraception or abstinence from sex. Which should be chosen? Should we hold a lottery? There seems to be no non-arbitrarily determinate subject of harm in the case of successful contraception. But if there is no such subject of harm, then no determinate thing was harmed.

Marquis is mistaken. There is a single, nonarbitrarily determinate subject of harm in a case of contraception or abstinence: the unique oocyte that would (or could) otherwise have been fertilized. When a woman ovulates, only one oocyte is (typically) ripe for fertilization. If it's fertilized, *it* survives to become a zygote, and nothing else does. Deprive it of fertilization, and you deprive it of an FLO—if, that is, the zygote is identical with the fetus that it becomes. If I was once a zygote, then, Marquis has no adequate defense against the objection that abstinence and contraception are (by his lights) seriously wrong.

Marquis might allow, in light of this point, that I was never a zygote. Suppose I wasn't. Then the zygote from which I developed didn't survive to fetushood, and its failure to survive is a matter of at least nomological necessity. So that zygote lacked the potential for an FLO. It was hardly unique in this respect: if I was never a zygote, then no human zygote has the potential for an FLO. So killing a zygote doesn't deprive it of an FLO. Hence Marquis's argument, even if otherwise sound, does nothing to show the serious wrongness of killing a zygote.

This point might not ruffle Marquis. He allows that "during the first fourteen days after conception . . . there is an argument that the fetus is not definitely an individual," and so he allows that perhaps abortion isn't seriously wrong during those two weeks. (Marquis uses "fetus" to encompass zygote, embryo, and fetus proper.) I don't know what argument Marquis has in mind, but this allowance is confused on its face since if there's anything that is *the fetus*, then that thing is ipso facto an individual. The view that Marquis might more plausibly mean to countenance is that during the first two weeks, there's nothing that would be identical with the later fetus were the pregnancy to progress normally. Hence there's no individual during the first fourteen days that abortion would deprive of an FLO.

It may seem, then, that my argument should resolve Marquis's apparent indecision about whether his argument applies from the moment of conception. He ought, by his own lights and absent some other argument, to view early abortion as no worse than contraception and abstinence, and he seems to view these as not seriously (or even significantly) wrong.

If all of this is right, it's a substantial result. For Marquis leaves it open whether his argument applies to zygotes, whereas the foregoing considerations clinch the case that it doesn't, at least if contraception and abstinence aren't seriously wrong.

## VI. ACQUIRING HUMANITY AND THE MORALITY OF ABORTION

Consider next the claim that what matters is *being a living human being*.

It may seem platitudinous that every living biological organism belongs to some species or other. It's nevertheless false if "belonging" is a matter of *membership*. Some living organisms are members of no species. Consider a particular living cell that's now a constituent of my liver—call it 'Liv'. A living cell is paradigmatically a living organism, and Liv is a living cell. Yet Liv is not a member of the genus *Homo*; Liv is not a "human being" on the usual meaning of that term. Liv isn't a *member* of any genus at all.

Liv is, however, a *human* liver cell, distinct in biological kind from (say) a canine liver cell. Since Liv is a being, and Liv is human, there's a sense in which Liv is a "human being."

We can, then, distinguish two purely biological senses of "human being," in addition to the sense that includes psychological personhood. Let's say that something is a "human-being-1" if and only if it's a *member* of the genus *Homo.* (This is, I think, the normal biological sense of "human being.") Let's say that something is "human-being-2" if and only if it's an organism that is a (not necessarily proper) part of a human-being-1. Liv is a human-being-2 but not a human-being-1.

The unfertilized egg is, it seems, a human-being-2, but not a human-being-1. A baby is a human-being-1. The suggestion I'm now considering is that biological conception marks the acquisition of the property of *being a human-being-1.*

John Noonan Jr. argues that conception marks the point at which there is a new "human being," and he seems to mean that it is the point at which something *becomes* a human-being-1. In some respects his argument echoes, and shares the fate of, Marquis's defense against the contraception-objection that I've already discussed. Noonan also says something new.

The positive argument for conception as the decisive moment of humanization is that at conception the new being receives the genetic code. It is this genetic information which determines his characteristics, which is the biological carrier of the possibility of human wisdom, which makes him a self-evolving being.

Unfortunately, this argument collapses under scrutiny. Leave aside for a moment the bald claim that at conception a *new being* receives a genetic code. It's false that the genetic information encoded in a (male) fertilized egg determines "his characteristics" if this means that it determines *all* the traits he'll have at maturity. (I suppose temporarily for argument's sake, as Noonan supposes in fact, that the fertilized egg is identical with the human adult into which it develops.) A zygote's genetic endowment determines some of the adult's traits (ceteris paribus) and not others; some are determined by later genetic alteration, parenting, education, nutrition, and so on. The same goes for the genetic endowment of the unfertilized oocyte: it determines some adult traits (ceteris paribus) and not others. The only truth in the neighborhood is an impotent truism: the diploid genetic information bestowed by conception determines some of a being's characteristics—namely those determined by that diploid genetic information. These aren't all of the being's characteristics, though, and it's an equally impotent truism that the haploid genetic information contained in the unfertilized oocyte determines some of a being's characteristics—namely those determined by that haploid genetic information.

Noonan suggests that a zygote's having a distinctively human diploid genetic endowment is a biologically necessary condition for the eventual development of human wisdom. Suppose this is right. It's equally true that an unfertilized egg's having a distinctively human haploid genetic endowment is a biologically necessary condition for the eventual development of human wisdom. In both cases, we have a biologically necessary condition for the possibility of human wisdom. In neither case do we have a sufficient one. Again, there's no basis here for the view that conception marks the acquisition of being a human-being-1.

What lies behind Noonan's fallacious argument concerning the acquisition of "humanness" seems pretty clearly to be the explicit, unargued, and untenable assumption that biological conception is in fact *ontological* conception. It may not be silly to think—though it's also far from obvious—that whenever a new being appears that will someday be an uncontroversial human-being-1, it's a human-being-1 from the beginning. You argue in a tight, vicious circle, however, if you invoke the thesis that conception confers genus-membership to support the conception-as-origination thesis, and then offer that very thesis as the sole reason for thinking that conception confers genus-membership. As I've shown, there's no good reason to think that a new being appears at conception. It doesn't follow that conception *doesn't* mark the first moment of something's being a human-being-1. I claim merely that no plausible reason for thinking that it *does* has been articulated.

## REVIEW QUESTIONS

1. According to Mills, pro-life arguments typically involve two premises. What are these premises? Which one is the focus of Mills attention?
2. What are the implications of Mills's argument for contraception, sexual abstinence, the morning-after pill, and zygotic abortion?
3. State and explain Mills's argument for the conclusion that he did not begin at conception.
4. How does Mills reply to the objection that a fertilized egg is not an egg?
5. What is Mills's explanation for the common and unquestioned belief that conception marks the beginning of a new being?
6. How does Mills attack Marquis's FLO argument?
7. Explain Mills's criticism of Noonan.

## DISCUSSION QUESTIONS

1. Mills claims that no biologist wearing a "biologist-hat" believes that conception creates a new being. Is this true?
2. If an early abortion is wrong, then is contraception or sexual abstinence wrong too? Why or why not?
3. Does Mills convince you that a human being does not begin at conception? Why or why not?
4. How would Marquis and Noonan reply to Mills's objections?

# All Animals Are Equal

## PETER SINGER

Peter Singer is the Ira W. DeCamp Professor of Bioethics at the University Center for Human Values, Princeton University, and Laureate Professor, Centre for Applied Philosophy and Public Ethics, University of Melbourne. He has authored, coauthored, and edited forty books, and published more than a hundred articles in professional journals. A recent book is *The Life You Can Save: Acting Now to End World Poverty* (2009).

Singer defines *speciesism* as a prejudice toward the interests of members of one's own species and against those of members of other species. He argues that speciesism is analogous to racism and sexism. If it is unjust to discriminate against women and blacks by not considering their interests, it is also unfair to ignore the interests of animals, particularly their interest in not suffering.

"Animal liberation" may sound more like a parody of other liberation movements than a serious objective. The idea of "The Rights of Animals" actually was once used to parody the case for women's rights. When Mary Wollstonecraft, a forerunner of today's feminists, published her *Vindication of the Rights of Women* in 1792, her views were widely regarded as absurd, and before long an anonymous publication appeared entitled *A Vindication of the Rights of Brutes*. The author of this satirical work (now known to have been Thomas Taylor, a distinguished Cambridge philosopher) tried to refute Mary Wollstonecraft's arguments by showing that they could be carried one stage further. If the argument for equality was sound when applied to women, why should it not be applied to dogs, cats, and horses? The reasoning seemed to hold for these "brutes" too, yet to hold that brutes had rights was manifestly absurd; therefore the reasoning by which this conclusion had been reached must be unsound, and if unsound when applied to brutes, it must also be unsound when applied to women, since the very same arguments had been used in each case.

In order to explain the basis of the case for the equality of animals, it will be helpful to start with an examination of the case for the equality of women. Let us assume that we wish to defend the case for women's rights against the attack by Thomas Taylor. How should we reply?

One way in which we might reply is by saying that the case for equality between men and women cannot validly be extended to nonhuman animals. Women have a right to vote, for instance, because they are just as capable of making rational decisions about the future as men are; dogs, on the other hand, are incapable of understanding the significance of voting, so they cannot have the right to vote. There are many other obvious ways in which men and women resemble each other closely, while humans and animals differ greatly. So, it might be said, men and women are similar beings and should have similar rights, while humans and nonhumans are different and should not have equal rights.

The reasoning behind this reply to Taylor's analogy is correct up to a point, but it does not go far enough. There *are* important differences between humans and other animals, and these differences must give rise to *some* differences in the rights that each have. Recognizing this obvious fact, however, is no barrier to the case for extending the basic principle of equality to

*Source:* Peter Singer, "All Animals Are Equal" from *Animal Liberation* (New York: New York Review of Books, 1975), pp. 1–22. Used by permission of the author.

nonhuman animals. The differences that exist between men and women are equally undeniable, and the supporters of Women's Liberation are aware that these differences may give rise to different rights. Many feminists hold that women have the right to an abortion on request. It does not follow that since these same feminists are campaigning for equality between men and women they must support the right of men to have abortions too. Since a man cannot have an abortion, it is meaningless to talk of his right to have one. Since a dog can't vote, it is meaningless to talk of its right to vote. There is no reason why either Women's Liberation or Animal Liberation should get involved in such nonsense. The extension of the basic principle of equality from one group to another does not imply that we must treat both groups in exactly the same way, or grant exactly the same rights to both groups. Whether we should do so will depend on the nature of the members of the two groups. The basic principle of equality does not require equal or identical *treatment*; it requires equal *consideration*. Equal consideration for different beings may lead to different treatment and different rights.

So there is a different way of replying to Taylor's attempt to parody the case for women's rights, a way that does not deny the obvious differences between humans and nonhumans but goes more deeply into the question of equality and concludes by finding nothing absurd in the idea that the basic principle of equality applies to so-called brutes. At this point such a conclusion may appear odd; but if we examine more deeply the basis on which our opposition to discrimination on grounds of race or sex ultimately rests, we will see that we would be on shaky ground if we were to demand equality for blacks, women, and other groups of oppressed humans while denying equal consideration to nonhumans. To make this clear we need to see first, exactly why racism and sexism are wrong.

When we say that all human beings, whatever their race, creed, or sex, are equal, what is it that we are asserting? Those who wish to defend hierarchical, inegalitarian societies have often pointed out that by whatever test we choose it simply is not true that all humans are equal. Like it or not we must face the fact that humans come in different shapes and sizes; they come with different moral capacities, different intellectual abilities, different amounts of benevolent feeling and sensitivity to the needs of others, different abilities to communicate effectively, and different capacities to experience pleasure and pain. In short, if the demand for equality were based on the actual equality of all human beings, we would have to stop demanding equality.

Still, one might cling to the view that the demand for equality among human beings is based on the actual equality of the different races and sexes. Although, it may be said, humans differ as individuals there are no differences between the races and sexes *as such*. From the mere fact that a person is black or a woman we cannot infer anything about that person's intellectual or moral capacities. This, it may be said, is why racism and sexism are wrong. The white racist claims that whites are superior to blacks, but this is false—although there are differences among individuals, some blacks are superior to some whites in all of the capacities and abilities that could conceivably be relevant. The opponent of sexism would say the same: a person's sex is no guide to his or her abilities, and this is why it is unjustifiable to discriminate on the basis of sex.

The existence of individual variations that cut across the lines of race or sex, however, provides us with no defense at all against a more sophisticated opponent of equality, one who proposes that, say, the interests of all those with IQ scores below 100 be given less consideration than the interests of those with ratings over 100. Perhaps those scoring below the mark, would, in this society, be made the slaves of those scoring higher. Would a hierarchical society of this sort really be so much better than one based on race or sex? I think not. But if we tie the moral principle of equality to the factual equality of the different races or sexes, taken as a whole, our opposition to racism and sexism does not provide us with any basis for objecting to this kind of inegalitarianism.

There is a second important reason why we ought not to base our opposition to racism and sexism on any kind of actual equality, even the limited kind that asserts that variations in capacities and abilities are spread evenly between the different races and sexes: we can have no absolute guarantee that these capacities and abilities really are distributed evenly, without regard to race or sex, among human beings. So far as actual abilities are concerned there do seem to be certain measurable differences between both races and sexes. These differences do not, of course, appear in each case, but only when averages are taken. More important still, we do not yet know how much of these differences is really due to the different genetic endowments of the different races and sexes, and how much is due to poor schools, poor housing, and other factors that are the result of past and continuing discrimination. Perhaps all of the important differences will eventually prove to be environmental rather than genetic. Anyone opposed to racism and sexism will certainly hope that this will be so, for it will make the task of ending discrimination a lot easier; nevertheless it would be dangerous to rest the case against racism and sexism on the belief that all significant differences are environmental in origin. The opponent of, say, racism who takes this line will be unable to avoid conceding that *if* differences in ability do after all prove to have some genetic connection with race, racism would in some way be defensible.

Fortunately there is no need to pin the case for equality to one particular outcome of a scientific investigation. The appropriate response to those who claim to have found evidence of genetically based differences in ability between the races or sexes is not to stick to the belief that the genetic explanation must be wrong, whatever evidence to the contrary may turn up: instead we should make it quite clear that the claim to equality does not depend on intelligence, moral capacity, physical strength, or similar matters of fact. Equality is a moral idea, not an assertion of fact. There is no logically compelling reason for assuming that a factual difference in ability between two people justifies any difference in the amount of consideration we give to their needs and interests. *The principle of the equality of human beings is not a description of an alleged actual equality among humans; it is a prescription of how we should treat humans.*

Jeremy Bentham, the founder of the reforming utilitarian school of moral philosophy, incorporated the essential basis of moral equality into his system of ethics by means of the formula: "Each to count for one and none for more than one." In other words, the interests of every being affected by an action are to be taken into account and given the same weight as the like interests of any other being. A later utilitarian, Henry Sidgwick, put the point in this way: "The good of any one individual is of no more importance, from the point of view (if I may say so) of the Universe, than the good of any other." More recently the leading figures in contemporary moral philosophy have shown a great deal of agreement in specifying as a fundamental presupposition of their moral theories some similar requirement that operates so as to give everyone's interests equal consideration—although these writers generally cannot agree on how this requirement is best formulated.[1]

It is an implication of this principle of equality that our concern for others and our readiness to consider their interests ought not to depend on what they are like or on what abilities they may possess. Precisely what this concern or consideration requires us to do may vary according to the characteristics of those affected by what we do: concern for the well-being of a child growing up in America would require that we teach him to read; concern for the well-being of a pig may require no more than that we leave him alone with other pigs in a place where there is adequate food and room to run freely. But the basic element—the taking into account of the interests of the being, whatever those interests may be—must,

[1]For Bentham's moral philosophy, see his *Introduction to the Principles of Morals and Legislation*, and for Sidgwick's see *The Methods of Ethics* (the passage quoted is from the seventh edition, pp. 382). As examples of leading contemporary moral philosophers who incorporate a requirement of equal consideration of interests, see R. M. Hare, *Freedom and Reason* (New York, Oxford University Press, 1963) and John Rawls, *A Theory of Justice* (Cambridge: Harvard University Press, Belknap Press, 1972). For a brief account of the essential agreement on this issue between these and other positions, see R. M. Hare, "Rules of War and Moral Reasoning," *Philosophy and Public Affairs* 1 (1972).

according to the principle of equality, be extended to all beings, black or white, masculine or feminine, human or nonhuman.

Thomas Jefferson, who was responsible for writing the principle of the equality of men into the American Declaration of Independence, saw this point. It led him to oppose slavery even though he was unable to free himself fully from his slaveholding background. He wrote in a letter to the author of a book that emphasized the notable intellectual achievements of Negroes in order to refute the then common view that they had limited intellectual capacities:

> Be assured that no person living wishes more sincerely than I do, to see a complete refutation of the doubts I have myself entertained and expressed on the grade of understanding allotted to them by nature, and to find that they are on a par with ourselves . . . but whatever be their degree of talent it is no measure of their rights. Because Sir Isaac Newton was superior to others in understanding, he was not therefore lord of the property or person of others.[2]

Similarly when in the 1850s the call for women's rights was raised in the United States a remarkable black feminist named Sojourner Truth made the same point in more robust terms at a feminist convention:

> . . . they talk about this thing in the head; what do they call it? ["Intellect," whispered someone near by.] That's it. What's that got to do with women's rights or Negroes' rights? If my cup won't hold but a pint and yours holds a quart, wouldn't you be mean not to let me have my little half-measure full?[3]

It is on this basis that the case against racism and the case against sexism must both ultimately rest; and it is in accordance with this principle that the attitude that we may call "speciesism," by analogy with racism, must also be condemned. Speciesism—the word is not an attractive one, but I can think of no better term—is a prejudice or attitude of bias toward the interests of members of one's own species and against those members of other species. It should be obvious that the fundamental objections to racism and sexism made by Thomas Jefferson and Sojourner Truth apply equally to speciesism. If possessing a higher degree of intelligence does not entitle one human to use another for his own ends, how can it entitle humans to exploit nonhumans for the same purpose?[4]

Many philosophers and other writers have proposed the principle of equal consideration of interests, in some form or other, as a basic moral principle, but not many of them have recognized that this principle applies to members of other species as well as to our own. Jeremy Bentham was one of the few who did realize this. In a forward-looking passage written at a time when black slaves had been freed by the French but the British dominions were still being treated in the way we now treat animals, Bentham wrote:

> The day may come when the rest of the animal creation may acquire those rights which never could have been withholden from them but by the hand of tyranny. The French have already discovered that the blackness of the skin is no reason why a human being should be abandoned without redress to the caprice of a tormentor. It may one day come to be recognized that the number of the legs, the villosity of the skin, or the termination of the *os sacrum* are reasons equally insufficient for abandoning a sensitive being to the same fate. What else is it that should trace the insuperable line? Is it the faculty of reason, or perhaps the faculty of discourse? But a full-grown horse or dog is beyond comparison a more rational, as well as a more conversable animal, than an infant of a day or a week or even a month old. But suppose they were otherwise, what would it avail? The question is not, Can they reason? nor Can they talk? but, Can they suffer?[5]

In this passage Bentham points to the capacity for suffering as the vital characteristic that gives a being the right to equal consideration. The capacity for suffering—or more strictly, for suffering and/or enjoyment or happiness—is not

---

[2]Letter to Henri Gregoire, February 25, 1809.

[3]Reminiscences by Francis D. Gage, from Susan B. Anthony, *The History of Woman Suffrage*, vol. 1; the passage is to be found in the extract in Leslie Tanner, ed., *Voices from Women's Liberation* (New York: Signet, 1970).

[4]I owe the term "speciesism" to Richard Ryder.

[5]*Introduction to the Principles of Morals and Legislation*, chapter 17.

just another characteristic like the capacity for language or higher mathematics. Bentham is not saying that those who try to mark "the insuperable line" that determines whether the interests of a being should be considered happen to have chosen the wrong characteristic. By saying that we must consider the interests of all beings with the capacity for suffering or enjoyment Bentham does not arbitrarily exclude from consideration any interests at all—as those who draw the line with reference to the possession of reason or language do. The capacity for suffering and enjoyment is a *prerequisite for having interests at all*, a condition that must be satisfied before we can speak of interests in a meaningful way. It would be nonsense to say that it was not in the interests of a stone to be kicked along the road by a schoolboy. A stone does not have interests because it cannot suffer. Nothing that we can do to it could possibly make any difference to its welfare. A mouse, on the other hand, does have an interest in not being kicked along the road, because it will suffer if it is.

If a being suffers there can be no moral justification for refusing to take that suffering into consideration. No matter what the nature of the being, the principle of equality requires that its suffering be counted equally with the like suffering—in so far as rough comparisons can be made—of any other being. If a being is not capable of suffering, or of experiencing enjoyment or happiness, there is nothing to be taken into account. So the limit of sentience (using the term as a convenient if not strictly accurate shorthand for the capacity to suffer and/or experience enjoyment) is the only defensible boundary of concern for the interests of others. To mark this boundary by some other characteristic like intelligence or rationality would be to mark it in an arbitrary manner. Why not choose some other characteristic, like skin color?

The racist violates the principle of equality by giving greater weight to the interests of members of his own race when there is a clash between their interests and the interests of those of another race. The sexist violates the principle of equality by favoring the interests of his own sex. Similarly the speciesist allows the interests of his own species to override the greater interests of members of other species. The pattern is identical in each case.

Most human beings are speciesists. Ordinary human beings—not a few exceptionally cruel or heartless humans, but the overwhelming majority of humans—take an active part in, acquiesce in, and allow their taxes to pay for practices that require the sacrifice of the most important interests of members of other species in order to promote the most trivial interests of our own species. . . .

Animals can feel pain. As we saw earlier, there can be no moral justification for regarding the pain (or pleasure) that animals feel as less important than the same amount of pain (or pleasure) felt by humans. But what exactly does this mean, in practical terms? To prevent misunderstanding I shall spell out what I mean a little more fully.

If I give a horse a hard slap across its rump with my open hand, the horse may start, but it presumably feels little pain. Its skin is thick enough to protect it against a mere slap. If I slap a baby in the same way, however, the baby will cry and presumably does feel pain, for its skin is more sensitive. So it is worse to slap a baby than a horse, if both slaps are administered with equal force. But there must be some kind of blow—I don't know exactly what it would be, but perhaps a blow with a heavy stick—that would cause the horse as much pain as we cause a baby by slapping it with our hand. That is what I mean by "the same amount of pain" and if we consider it wrong to inflict that much pain on a baby for no good reason then we must, unless we are speciesists, consider it equally wrong to inflict the same amount of pain on a horse for no good reason.

There are other differences between humans and animals that cause other complications. Normal adult human beings have mental capacities which will, in certain circumstances, lead them to suffer more than animals would in the same circumstances. If, for instance, we decided to perform extremely painful or lethal scientific experiments on normal adult humans, kidnapped at random from public parks for this purpose, every adult who entered a park would become fearful that he would be kidnapped. The resultant terror would be a form of suffering additional to the pain of the experiment. The same experiments performed on nonhuman animals would cause less suffering since the animals would not have the anticipatory dread of being kidnapped and experimented upon. This does not mean, of course, that it would be right to perform the experiment on animals, but only that there is a reason, which is *not* speciesist, for preferring to use animals rather than normal adult humans, if the experiment is to be done at all. It should be noted, however, that this same argument gives us a reason for preferring to use human infants—orphans perhaps—or retarded humans for experiments, rather than adults, since infants and retarded humans would also have no idea of what was going to happen to them. So far as this argument is concerned nonhuman animals and infants and retarded humans are in the same category; and if we use this argument to justify experiments on nonhuman animals we have to ask ourselves whether we are also prepared to allow experiments on humans, on what basis can we do it, other than a barefaced—and morally indefensible—preference for members of our own species?

There are many areas in which the superior mental powers of normal adult humans make a difference: anticipation, more detailed memory, greater knowledge of what is happening, and so on. Yet these differences do not all point to greater suffering on the part of the normal human being. Sometimes an animal may suffer more because of his more limited understanding. If, for instance, we are taking prisoners in wartime we can explain to them that while they must submit to capture, search, and confinement they will not otherwise be harmed and will be set free at the conclusion of hostilities. If we capture a wild animal, however, we cannot explain that we are not threatening its life. A wild animal cannot distinguish an attempt to overpower and confine from an attempt to kill; the one causes as much terror as the other.

It may be objected that comparisons of the sufferings of different species are impossible to make, and that for this reason when the interests of animals and humans clash the principle of equality gives no guidance. It is probably true that comparisons of suffering between members of different species cannot be made precisely, but precision is not essential. Even if we were to prevent the infliction of suffering on animals only when it is quite certain that the interests of humans will not be affected to anything like the extent that animals are affected, we would be forced to make radical changes in our treatment of animals that would involve our diet, the farming methods we use, experimental procedures in many fields of science, our approach to wildlife and to hunting, trapping and the wearing of furs, and areas of entertainment like circuses, rodeos, and zoos. As a result, a vast amount of suffering would be avoided.

So far I have said a lot about the infliction of suffering on animals, but nothing about killing them. This omission has been deliberate. The application of the principle of equality to the infliction of suffering is, in theory at least, fairly straightforward. Pain and suffering are bad and should be prevented or minimized, irrespective of the race, sex, or species of the being that suffers. How bad a pain is depends on how intense it is and how long it lasts, but pains of the same intensity and duration are equally bad, whether felt by humans or animals.

The wrongness of killing a being is more complicated. I have kept, and shall continue to keep, the question of killing in the background because in the present state of human tyranny over other species the more simple, straightforward principle of equal consideration of pain or pleasure is a sufficient basis for identifying and protesting against all the major abuses of animals that humans practice. Nevertheless, it is necessary to say something about killing.

Just as most humans are speciesists in their readiness to cause pain to animals when they would not cause a similar pain to humans for the same reason, so most humans are speciesists in their readiness to kill other animals when they would not kill humans. We need to proceed more cautiously here, however, because people hold widely differing views about when it is legitimate to kill humans, as the continuing debates over abortion and euthanasia attest. Nor have moral philosophers been able to agree on exactly what it is that makes it wrong to kill humans, and under what circumstances killing a human being may be justifiable.

Let us consider first the view that it is always wrong to take an innocent human life. We may call this the "sanctity of life" view. People who take this view oppose abortion and euthanasia. They do not usually, however, oppose the killing of nonhumans—so perhaps it would be more accurate to describe this view as the "sanctity of *human* life" view.

The belief that human life, and only human life, is sacrosanct is a form of speciesism. To see this, consider the following example.

Assume that, as sometimes happens, an infant has been born with massive and irreparable brain damage. The damage is so severe that the infant can never be any more than a "human vegetable," unable to talk, recognize other people, act independently of others, or develop a sense of self-awareness. The parents of the infant, realizing that they cannot hope for any improvement in their child's condition and being in any case unwilling to spend, or ask the state to spend, the thousands of dollars that would be needed annually for proper care of the infant, ask the doctor to kill the infant painlessly.

Should the doctor do what the parents ask? Legally, he should not, and in this respect the law reflects the sanctity of life view. The life of every human being is sacred. Yet people who would say this about the infant do not object to the killing of nonhuman animals. How can they justify their different judgments? Adult chimpanzees, dogs, pigs, and many other species far surpass the brain-damaged infant in their ability to relate to others, act independently, be self-aware, and any other capacity that could reasonably be said to give value to life. With the most intensive care possible, there are retarded infants who can never achieve the intelligence level of a dog. Nor can we appeal to the concern of the infant's parents, since they themselves, in this imaginary example (and in some actual cases) do not want the infant kept alive.

The only thing that distinguishes the infant from the animal, in the eyes of those who claim it has a "right to life," is that it is, biologically, a member of the species *Homo sapiens*, whereas chimpanzees, dogs, and pigs are not. But to use *this* difference as the basis for granting a right to life to the infant and not to the other animals is, of course, pure speciesism.[6] It is exactly the kind of arbitrary difference that the most crude and overt kind of racist uses in attempting to justify racial discrimination.

This does not mean that to avoid speciesism we must hold that it is as wrong to kill a dog as it is to kill a normal human being. The only position that is irredeemably speciesist is the one that tries to make the boundary of the right to life run exactly parallel to the boundary of our own species. Those who hold the sanctity of life view do this because while distinguishing sharply between humans and other animals they allow no distinctions to be made within our own species, objecting to the killing of the severely retarded and the hopelessly senile as strongly as they object to the killing of normal adults.

To avoid speciesism we must allow that beings which are similar in all relevant respects have a similar right to life—and mere membership in our own biological species cannot be a morally relevant criterion for this right. Within these limits we could still hold that, for instance, it is worse to kill a normal adult human, with a capacity for self-awareness, and the ability to plan for the future and have meaningful relations with others, than it is to kill a mouse, which presumably does not share all of these characteristics; or we might appeal to the close family and other personal ties which humans have but mice do not have to the same degree; or we might think that it is the consequences for other humans, who will be put in fear of their own lives, that makes the crucial difference; or we might think it is some combination of these factors, or other factors altogether.

---

[6]I am here putting aside religious views, for example the doctrine that all and only humans have immortal souls, or are made in the image of God. Historically these views have been very important, and no doubt are partly responsible for the idea that human life has a special sanctity. Logically, however, these religious views are unsatisfactory, since a reasoned explanation of why it should be that all humans and no nonhumans have immortal souls is not offered. This belief too, therefore, comes under suspicion as a form of speciesism. In any case, defenders of the "sanctity of life" view are generally reluctant to base their position on purely religious doctrines, since these doctrines are no longer as widely accepted as they once were.

Whatever criteria we choose, however, we will have to admit that they do not follow precisely the boundary of our own species. We may legitimately hold that there are some features of certain beings which make their lives more valuable than those of other beings; but there will surely be some nonhuman animals whose lives, by any standards, are more valuable than the lives of some humans. A chimpanzee, dog, or pig, for instance, will have a higher degree of self-awareness and a greater capacity for meaningful relations with others than a severely retarded infant or someone in a state of advanced senility. So if we base the right to life on these characteristics we must grant these animals a right to life as good as, or better than, such retarded or senile humans.

Now this argument cuts both ways. It could be taken as showing that chimpanzees, dogs, and pigs, along with some other species, have a right to life and we commit a grave moral offense whenever we kill them, even when they are old and suffering and our intention is to put them out of their misery. Alternatively one could take the argument as showing that the severely retarded and hopelessly senile have no right to life and may be killed for quite trivial reasons, as we now kill animals.

Since the focus here is on ethical questions concerning animals and not on the morality of euthanasia I shall not attempt to settle this issue finally. I think it is reasonably clear, though, that while both of the positions just described avoid speciesism, neither is entirely satisfactory. What we need is some middle position that would avoid speciesism but would not make the lives of the retarded and senile as cheap as the lives of pigs and dogs now are, nor make the lives of pigs and dogs so sacrosanct that we think it wrong to put them out of hopeless misery. What we must do is bring nonhuman animals within our sphere of moral concern and cease to treat their lives as expendable for whatever trivial purposes we may have. At the same time, once we realize that the fact that a being is a member of our own species is not in itself enough to make it always wrong to kill that being, we may come to reconsider our policy of preserving human lives at all costs, even when there is no prospect of a meaningful life or of existence without terrible pain.

I conclude, then, that a rejection of speciesism does not imply that all lives are of equal worth. While self-awareness, intelligence, the capacity for meaningful relations with others, and so on are not relevant to the question of inflicting pain—since pain is pain, whatever other capacities, beyond the capacity to feel pain, the being may have—these capacities may be relevant to the question of taking life. It is not arbitrary to hold that the life of a self-aware being, capable of abstract thought, of planning for the future, of complex acts of communication, and so on, is more valuable than the life of a being without these capacities. To see the difference between the issues of inflicting pain and taking life, consider how we would choose within our own species. If we had to choose to save the life of a normal human or a mentally defective human, we would probably choose to save the life of the normal human; but if we had to choose between preventing pain in the normal human or the mental defective—imagine that both have received painful but superficial injuries, and we only have enough painkiller for one of them—it is not nearly so clear how we ought to choose. The same is true when we consider other species. The evil of pain is, in itself, unaffected by the other characteristics of the being that feels the pain; the value of life is affected by these other characteristics.

Normally this will mean that if we have to choose between the life of a human being and the life of another animal we would choose to save the life of the human, but there may be special cases in which the reverse holds true, because the human being in question does not have the capacities of a normal human being. So this view is not speciesist, although it may appear to be at first glance. The preference, in normal cases, for saving a human life over the life of an animal when a choice *has* to be made is a preference based on the characteristics that normal humans have, and not on the mere fact that they are members of our own species. This is why when we consider members of our own species who lack the characteristics of normal humans we can no longer say that their lives are always to be preferred to those of other animals.

In general, the question of when it is wrong to kill (painlessly) an animal is one to which we need give no precise answer. As long as we remember that we should give the same respect to the lives of animals as we give to the lives of those humans at a similar mental level, we shall not go far wrong.

In any case, the conclusions that are argued for here flow from the principle of minimizing suffering alone. The idea that it is also wrong to kill animals painlessly gives some of these conclusions additional support which is welcome, but strictly unnecessary. Interestingly enough, this is true even of the conclusion that we ought to become vegetarians, a conclusion that in the popular mind is generally based on some kind of absolute prohibition on killing.

## REVIEW QUESTIONS

1. Explain the principle of equality that Singer adopts.
2. How does Singer define *speciesism*?
3. What is the sanctity of life view? Why does Singer reject this view?

## DISCUSSION QUESTIONS

1. Is speciesism analogous to racism and sexism? Why or why not?
2. Is there anything wrong with killing animals painlessly? Defend your view.
3. Do human interests outweigh animal interests? Explain your position.

# Speciesism and the Idea of Equality

BONNIE STEINBOCK

For biographical information on Steinbock, see her reading in Chapter 3.

Steinbock presents a defense of speciesism, the practice of weighing human interests more heavily than those of nonhuman animals. While she agrees with Singer that nonhuman pain and suffering deserve some moral consideration, she denies that this consideration should be equal to that given to humans. She claims that humans have morally relevant capacities that nonhuman animals do not have, and this entitles humans to greater moral consideration. These capacities include the ability to be morally responsible, to reciprocate in ways that animals cannot, and to desire self-respect.

Most of us believe that we are entitled to treat members of other species in ways which would be considered wrong if inflicted on members of our own species. We kill them for food, keep them confined, use them in painful experiments. The moral philosopher has to ask what relevant difference justifies this difference in treatment. A look at this question will lead us to re-examine the distinctions which we have assumed make a moral difference.

It has been suggested by Peter Singer[1] that our current attitudes are "speciesist," a word

*Source:* Speciesism and the Idea of Equality by Bonnie Steinbock from *Philosophy*, Vol. 53, No. 24, 1978, pp. 247–256. NY: Cambridge University Press.

intended to make one think of "racist" or "sexist." The idea is that membership in a species is in itself not relevant to moral treatment, and that much of our behavior and attitudes towards nonhuman animals is based simply on this irrelevant fact.

There is, however, an important difference between racism or sexism and "speciesism." We do not subject animals to different moral treatment simply because they have fur and feathers, but because they are in fact different from human beings in ways that could be morally relevant. It is false that women are incapable of being benefited by education, and therefore that claim cannot serve to justify preventing them from attending school. But this is not false of cows and dogs, even chimpanzees. Intelligence is thought to be a morally relevant capacity because of its relation to the capacity for moral responsibility.

What is Singer's response? He agrees that nonhuman animals lack certain capacities that human animals possess, and that this may justify different treatment. But it does not justify giving less consideration to their needs and interests. According to Singer, the moral mistake which the racist or sexist makes is not essentially the factual error of thinking that blacks or women are inferior to white men. For even if there were no factual error, even if it were true that blacks and women are less intelligent and responsible than whites and men, this would not justify giving less consideration to their needs and interests. It is important to note that the term "speciesism" is in one way like, and in another way unlike, the terms "racism" and "sexism." What the term "speciesism" has in common with these terms is the reference to focusing on a characteristic which is, in itself, irrelevant to moral treatment. And it is worth reminding us of this. But Singer's real aim is to bring us to a new understanding of the idea of equality. The question is, on what do claims to equality rest? The demand for human equality is a demand that the interests of all human beings be considered equally, unless there is a moral justification for not doing so. But why should the interests of all human beings be considered equally? In order to answer this question, we have to give some sense to the phrase, "All men (human beings) are created equal." Human beings are manifestly not equal, differing greatly in intelligence, virtue and capacities. In virtue of what can the claim to equality be made?

It is Singer's contention that claims to equality do not rest on factual equality. Not only do human beings differ in their capacities, but it might even turn out that intelligence, the capacity for virtue, etc., are not distributed evenly among the races and sexes:

> The appropriate response to those who claim to have found evidence of genetically based differences in ability between the races or sexes is not to stick to the belief that the genetic explanation must be wrong, whatever evidence to the contrary may turn up; instead we should make it quite clear that the claim to equality does not depend on intelligence, moral capacity, physical strength, or similar matters of fact. Equality is a moral ideal, not a simple assertion of fact. There is no logically compelling reason for assuming that a factual difference in ability between two people justifies any difference in the amount of consideration we give to satisfying their needs and interests. The principle of equality of human beings is not a description of an alleged actual equality among humans: it is a prescription of how we should treat humans.[2]

Insofar as the subject is human equality, Singer's view is supported by other philosophers. Bernard Williams, for example, is concerned to show that demands for equality cannot rest on factual equality among people, for no such equality exists.[3] The only respect in which all men are equal, according to Williams, is that they are all equally men. This seems to be a platitude, but Williams denies that it is trivial. Membership in the species *Homo sapiens* in itself has no special moral significance, but rather the fact that all men are human serves as a reminder that being human involves the possession of characteristics that are morally relevant. But on what characteristics does Williams focus? Aside from the desire for self-respect (which I will discuss later), Williams is not concerned with uniquely human capacities. Rather, he focuses on the capacity to feel pain and the capacity to feel affection. It is in virtue of these capacities, it seems, that he idea of equality is to be justified.

Apparently Richard Wasserstrom has the same idea as he sets out the racist's "logical and moral mistakes" in "Rights, Human Rights and Racial Discrimination."[4] The racist fails to acknowledge that the black person is as capable of suffering as the white person. According to Wasserstrom, the reason why a person is said to have a right not to be made to suffer acute physical pain is that we all do in fact value freedom from such pain. Therefore, if anyone has a right to be free from suffering acute physical pain everyone has this right, for there is no possible basis of discrimination. Wasserstrom says, "For, if all persons do have equal capacities of these sorts and if the existence of these capacities is the reason for ascribing these rights to anyone, then all persons ought to have the right to claim equality of treatment in respect to the possession and exercise of these rights."[5] The basis of equality, for Wasserstrom as for Williams, lies not in some uniquely human capacity, but rather in the fact that all human beings are alike in their capacity to suffer. Writers on equality have focused on this capacity, I think, because it functions as some sort of lowest common denominator, so that whatever the other capacities of a human being, he is entitled to equal consideration because, like everyone else, he is capable of suffering.

If the capacity to suffer is the reason for ascribing a right to freedom from acute pain, or a right to well-being, then it certainly looks as though these rights must be extended to animals as well. This is the conclusion Singer arrives at. The demand for human equality rests on the equal capacity of all human beings to suffer and to enjoy well-being. But if this is the basis of the demand for equality, then this demand must include all beings which have an equal capacity to suffer and enjoy well-being. That is why Singer places at the basis of the demand for equality, not intelligence or reason, but sentience. And equality will mean, not equality of treatment, but "equal consideration of interests." The equal consideration of interests will often mean quite different treatment, depending on the nature of the entity being considered. (It would be as absurd to talk of a dog's right to vote, Singer says, as to talk of a man's right to have an abortion.)

It might be thought that the issue of equality depends on a discussion of rights. According to this line of thought, animals do not merit equal consideration of interests because, unlike human beings they do not, or cannot, have rights. But I am not going to discuss rights, important as the issue is. The fact that an entity does not have rights does not necessarily imply that its interests are going to count for less than the interests of entities which are right-bearers. According to the view of rights held by H. L. A. Hart and S. I. Benn, infants do not have rights, nor do the mentally defective, nor do the insane, in so far as they all lack certain minimal conceptual capabilities for having rights.[6] Yet it certainly does not seem that either Hart or Benn would agree that therefore their interests are to be counted for less, or that it is morally permissible to treat them in ways in which it would not be permissible to treat right-bearers. It seems to mean only that we must give different sorts of reasons for our obligations to take into consideration the interests of those who do not have rights.

We have reasons concerning the treatment of other people which are clearly independent of the notion of rights. We would say that it is wrong to punch someone because doing that infringes his rights. But we could also say that it is wrong because doing that hurts him, and that is, ordinarily, enough of a reason not to do it. Now this particular reason extends not only to human beings, but to all sentient creatures. One has a prima facie reason not to pull the cat's tail (whether or not the cat has rights) because it hurts the cat. And this is the only thing, normally, which is relevant in this case. The fact that the cat is not a "rational being," that it is not capable of moral responsibility, that it cannot make free choices or shape its life—all of these differences from us have nothing to do with the justifiability of pulling its tail. Does this show that rationality and the rest of it are irrelevant to moral treatment?

I hope to show that this is not the case. But first I want to point out that the issue is not one of cruelty to animals. We all agree that cruelty is wrong, whether perpetrated on a moral or nonmoral, rational or nonrational agent. Cruelty is defined as the infliction of unnecessary pain or suffering. What is to count as necessary or unnecessary is determined, in part, by the nature of the end pursued. Torturing an animal is cruel, because although the pain is logically necessary for the action to be torture, the end (deriving enjoyment from seeing the animal suffer) is monstrous. Allowing animals to suffer from neglect or for the sake of large profits may also be thought to be unnecessary and therefore cruel. But there may be some ends, which are very good (such as the advancement of medical knowledge), which can be accomplished by subjecting animals to pain in experiments. Although most people would agree that the pain inflicted on animals used in medical research ought to be kept to a minimum, they would consider pain that cannot be eliminated "necessary" and therefore not cruel. It would probably not be so regarded if the subjects were nonvoluntary human beings. Necessity, then, is defined in terms of human benefit, but this is just what is being called into question. The topic of cruelty to animals, while important from a practical viewpoint, because much of our present treatment of animals involves the infliction of suffering for no good reason, is not very interesting philosophically. What is philosophically interesting is whether we are justified in having different standards of necessity for human suffering and for animal suffering. Singer says, quite rightly I think, "If a being suffers, there can be no moral justification for refusing to take that suffering into consideration."[7] But he thinks that the principle of equality requires that, no matter what the nature of the being, its suffering be counted equally with the like suffering of any other being. In other words sentience does not simply provide us with reasons for acting; it is the only relevant consideration for equal consideration of interests. It is this view that I wish to challenge.

I want to challenge it partly because it has such counter-intuitive results. It means, for example, that feeding starving children before feeding starving dogs is just like a Catholic charity's feeding hungry Catholics before feeding hungry non-Catholics. It is simply a matter of taking care of one's own, something which is usually morally permissible. But whereas we would admire the Catholic agency which did not discriminate, but fed all children, first come, first served, we would feel quite differently about someone who has this policy for dogs and children. Nor is this, it seems to me, simply a matter of sentimental preference for our own species. I might feel much more love for my dog than for a strange child—and yet I might feel morally obliged to feed the child before I fed my dog. If I gave in to the feelings of love and fed my dog and let the child go hungry, I would probably feel guilty. This is not to say that we can simply rely on such feelings. Huck Finn felt guilty at helping Jim escape, which he viewed as stealing from a woman who had never done him any harm. But while the existence of such feelings does not settle the morality of an issue, it is not clear to me that they can be explained away. In any event, their existence can serve as a motivation for trying to find a rational justification for considering human interests above nonhuman ones.

However, it does seem to me that this requires a justification. Until now, common sense (and academic philosophy) have seen no such need. Benn says, "No one claims equal consideration for all mammals—human beings count, mice do not, though it would not be easy to say why not. . . . Although we hesitate to inflict unnecessary pain on sentient creatures, such as mice or dogs, we are quite sure that we do not need to show good reasons for putting human interests before theirs."[8]

I think we do have to justify counting our interests more heavily than those of animals. But how? Singer is right, I think, to point out that it will not do to refer vaguely to the greater value of human life, to human worth and dignity:

> Faced with a situation in which they see a need for some basis for the moral gulf that is commonly thought to separate humans and animals, but can find no concrete difference that will do this without undermining the equality of humans, philosophers tend to waffle. They resort to high-sounding phrases like 'the intrinsic dignity of the human individual.' They talk of 'the intrinsic worth of all men' as if men had some worth that other beings do not have or they say that human beings, and only human beings, are 'ends in themselves,' while 'everything other than a person can only have value for a person.' . . .

Why should we not attribute 'intrinsic dignity' or 'intrinsic worth' to ourselves? Why should we not say that we are the only things in the universe that have intrinsic value? Our fellow human beings are unlikely to reject the accolades we so generously bestow upon them, and those to whom we deny the honor are unable to object.[9]

Singer is right to be skeptical of terms like "intrinsic dignity" and "intrinsic worth." These phrases are no substitute for a moral argument. But they may point to one. In trying to understand what is meant by these phrases, we may find a difference or differences between human beings and nonhuman animals that will justify different treatment while not undermining claims for human equality. While we are not compelled to discriminate among people because of different capacities, if we can find a significant difference in capacities between human and nonhuman animals, this could serve to justify regarding human interests as primary. It is not arbitrary or smug, I think, to maintain that human beings have a different moral status from members of other species because of certain capacities which are characteristic of being human. We may not all be equal in these capacities but all human beings possess them to some measure and nonhuman animals do not. For example, human beings are normally held to be responsible for what they do. In recognizing that someone is responsible for his or her actions, you accord that person a respect which is reserved for those possessed of moral autonomy, or capable of achieving such autonomy. Secondly, human beings can be expected to reciprocate in a way that nonhuman animals cannot. Nonhuman animals cannot be motivated by altruistic or moral reasons; they cannot treat you fairly or unfairly. This does not rule out the possibility of an animal being motivated by sympathy or pity. It does rule out altruistic motivation in the sense of motivation due to the recognition that the needs and interests of others provide one with certain reasons for acting.[10] Human beings are capable of altruistic motivation in this sense. We are sometimes motivated simply by the recognition that someone else is in pain, and that pain is a bad thing, no matter who suffers it. It is this sort of reason that I claim cannot motivate an animal or any entity not possessed of fairly abstract concepts. (If some nonhuman animals do possess the requisite concepts—perhaps chimpanzees who have learned a language—they might well be capable of altruistic motivation.) This means that our moral dealings with animals are necessarily much more limited than our dealings with other human beings. If rats invade our houses, carrying disease and biting our children, we cannot reason with them, hoping to persuade them of the injustice they do us. We can only attempt to get rid of them. And it is this that makes it reasonable for us to accord them a separate and not equal moral status, even though their capacity to suffer provides us with some reason to kill them painlessly, if this can be done without too much sacrifice of human interests. Thirdly, as Williams points out, there is the "desire for self-respect": "a certain human desire to be identified with what one is doing, to be able to realize purposes of one's own, and not to be the instrument of another's will unless one has willingly accepted such a role."[11] Some animals may have some form of this desire, and to the extent that they do, we ought to consider their interest in freedom and self-determination. (Such considerations might affect our attitudes toward zoos and circuses.) But the desire for self-respect per se requires the intellectual capacities of human beings, and this desire provides us with special reasons not to treat human beings in certain ways. It is an affront to the dignity of a human being to be a slave (even if a well-treated one); this cannot be true for a horse or a cow. To point this out is of course only to say that the justification for the treatment of an entity will depend on the sort of entity in question. In our treatment of other entities, we must consider the desire for autonomy, dignity and respect, but only where such a desire exists. Recognition of different desires and interests will often require different treatment, a point Singer himself makes.

But is the issue simply one of different desires and interests justifying and requiring different treatment? I would like to make a stronger claim, namely, that certain capacities, which seem to be unique to human beings, entitle their possessors to a privileged position in the moral community. Both rats and human beings dislike pain, and so we have a prima facie reason not to inflict pain on either. But if we can free human beings from crippling diseases, pain and death through experimentation which involves making animals suffer, and if this is the only way to achieve such results, then I think that such experimentation is justified because human lives are more valuable than animals' lives. And this is because of certain capacities and abilities that normal human beings have which animals apparently do not, and which human beings cannot exercise if they are devastated by pain or disease.

My point is not that the lack of the sorts of capacities I have been discussing gives us a justification for treating animals just as we like, but rather that it is these differences between human beings and nonhuman animals which provide a rational basis for different moral treatment and consideration. Singer focuses on sentience alone as the basis of equality, but we can justify the belief that human beings have a moral worth that nonhuman animals do not, in virtue of specific capacities, and without resorting to "high-sounding phrases."

Singer thinks that intelligence, the capacity for moral responsibility, for virtue, etc., are irrelevant to equality, because we would not accept a hierarchy based on intelligence any more than one based on race. We do not think that those with greater capacities ought to have their interests weighed more heavily than those with lesser capacities, and this, he thinks, shows that differences in such capacities are irrelevant to equality. But it does not show this at all. Kevin Donaghy argues (rightly, I think) that what entitles us human beings to a privileged position in the moral community is a certain minimal level of intelligence, which is a prerequisite for morally relevant capacities.[12] The fact that we would reject a hierarchical society based on degree of intelligence does not show that a minimal level of intelligence cannot be used as a cut-off point, justifying giving greater consideration to the interests of those entities which meet this standard.

Interestingly enough, Singer concedes the rationality of valuing the lives of normal human beings over the lives of nonhuman animals.[13] We are not required to value equally the life of a normal human being and the life of an animal, he thinks, but only their suffering. But I doubt that the value of an entity's life can be separated from the value of its suffering in this way. If we value the lives of human beings more than the lives of animals, this is because we value certain capacities that human beings have and animals do not. But freedom from suffering is, in general, a minimal condition for exercising these capacities, for living a fully human life. So, valuing human life more involves regarding human interests as counting for more. That is why we regard human suffering as more deplorable than comparable animal suffering.

But there is one point of Singer's which I have not yet met. Some human beings (if only a very few) are less intelligent than some nonhuman animals. Some have less capacity for moral choice and responsibility What status in the moral community are these members of our species to occupy? Are their interests to be considered equally with ours? Is experimenting on them permissible where such experiments are painful or injurious, but somehow necessary for human well-being? If it is certain of our capacities which entitle us to a privileged position, it looks as if those lacking those capacities are not entitled to a privileged position. To think it is justifiable to experiment on an adult chimpanzee but not on a severely mentally incapacitated human being seems to be focusing on membership in a species where that has no moral relevance. (It is being "speciesist" in a perfectly reasonable use of the word.) How are we to meet this challenge?

Donaghy is untroubled by this objection. He says that it is fully in accord with his intuitions, that he regards the killing of a normally intelligent human being as far more serious than the killing of a person so severely limited that he lacked the intellectual capacities of an adult pig. But this parry really misses the point. The question is whether Donaghy thinks that the killing of a human being so severely limited that he lacked the intellectual capacities of an adult pig would be less serious than the killing of that pig. If superior intelligence is what justifies privileged status in the moral community, then the pig who is smarter than a human being ought to have superior moral status. And I doubt that this is fully in accord with Donaghy's intuitions.

I doubt that anyone will be able to come up with a concrete and morally relevant difference that would justify, say, using a chimpanzee in an experiment rather than a human being with less capacity for reasoning, moral responsibility, etc. Should we then experiment on the severely retarded? Utilitarian considerations aside (the difficulty of comparing intelligence between species, for example), we feel a special obligation to care for the handicapped members of our own species, who cannot survive in this world without such care. Nonhuman animals manage very well, despite their "lower intelligence" and lesser capacities; most of them do not require special care from us. This does not, of course, justify experimenting on them. However, to subject to experimentation those people who depend on us seems even worse than subjecting members of other species to it. In addition, when we consider the severely retarded, we think, "That could be me." It makes sense to think that one might have been born retarded, but not to think that one might have been born a monkey. And so, although one can imagine oneself in the monkey's place, one feels a closer identification with the severely retarded human being. Here we are getting away from such things as "morally relevant differences" and are talking about something much more difficult to articulate, namely, the role of feelings and sentiment in moral thinking. We would be horrified by the use of the retarded in medical research. But what are we to make of this horror? Has it moral significance or is it "mere" sentiment, of no more import than the sentiment of whites against blacks? It is terribly difficult to know how to evaluate such feelings.[14] 1 am not going to say more about this, because I think that the treatment of severely incapacitated human beings does not pose an insurmountable objection to the privileged status principle. I am willing to admit that my horror at the thought of experiments being performed on severely mentally incapacitated human beings in cases in which I would find it justifiable and preferable to perform the same experiments on nonhuman animals (capable of similar suffering) may not be a moral emotion. But it is certainly not wrong of us to extend special care to members of our own species, motivated by feelings of sympathy, protectiveness, etc. If this is speciesism, it is stripped of its tone of moral condemnation. It is not racist to provide special care to members of your own race; it is racist to fall below your moral obligation to a person because of his or her race. I have been arguing that we are morally obliged to consider the interests of all sentient creatures, but not to consider those interests equally with human interests. Nevertheless, even this recognition will mean some radical changes in our attitude toward and treatment of other species.[15]

## NOTES

1. Peter Singer, *Animal Liberation* (A New York Review Book, 1975).
2. Singer, 5.
3. Bernard Williams, "The Idea of Equality," *Philosophy, Politics and Society* (Second Series), Laslett and Runciman (Eds.) (Blackwell, 1962), 110–131, reprinted in *Moral Concepts*, Feinberg (Ed.) (Oxford, 1970), 15S 171.
4. Richard Wasserstrom, "Rights, Human Rights, and Racial Discrimination," *Journal of Philosophy 61*, No. 20 (1964), reprinted in *Human Rights*, A. 1. Melden (Ed.) (Wadsworth, 1970), 96–110.
5. Ibid., 106.
6. H. L. A. Hart, "Are There Any Natural Rights?," *Philosophical Review 64* (1955), and S. I. Benn, "Abortion, Infanticide, and Respect for Persons," *The Problem of Abortion*, Feinberg (Ed.) (Wadsworth, 1973), 92–104.
7. Singer, 9.
8. Benn, "Equality, Moral and Social," *The Encyclopedia of Philosophy* 3, 40.
9. Singer, 266–267.
10. This conception of altruistic motivation comes from Thomas Nagel's *The Possibility of Altruism* (Oxford, 1970).
11. Williams, op. cit., 157.
12. Kevin Donaghy, "Singer on Speciesism," *Philosophic Exchange* (Summer 1974).
13. Singer, 22.
14. We run into the same problem when discussing abortion. Of what significance are our feelings toward the unborn when discussing its status? Is it relevant or irrelevant that it looks like a human being?
15. I would like to acknowledge the help of, and offer thanks to, Professor Richard Arneson of the University.

## REVIEW QUESTIONS

1. According to Steinbock, what is the important difference between racism or sexism and speciesism?
2. What is the basis for equality, according to Singer, Williams, Wasserstrom, and Steinbock?
3. Steinbock claims that Singer's view has counterintuitive results. What are they?
4. According to Steinbock, why are we justified in counting human interests more heavily than those of animals?

## DISCUSSION QUESTIONS

1. Steinbock maintains that we should give greater moral consideration to severely mentally incapacitated humans than to animals that may have a greater mental capacity. Does she give a good reason for this? How would Singer reply?
2. Suppose alien beings invade the earth. They are superior to humans in intelligence, moral virtue, the desire for self-respect, and so on. What is their moral status? Are they equal to humans, or do they have a higher moral status than humans, just as humans have a higher moral status than animals? If they have a higher moral status than humans, are they morally permitted to perform experiments on humans and eat them? What would Steinbock say? What do you think?

# World Poverty and Human Rights

THOMAS POGGE

Thomas Pogge is the Leitner Professor of Philosophy and International Affairs at Yale University. He is the author or editor of more than twenty books and numerous publications on global justice and justice in health care. He also writes on Rawls and Kant. His most recent books are *Politics as Usual: What Lies behind the Pro-Poor Rhetoric* (2010) and *World Poverty and Human Rights: Cosmopolitan Responsibilities and Reforms* (2nd ed., 2008).

Pogge argues that rich, developed countries are actively harming poor countries by producing and supporting severe poverty. This radical inequality in wealth cannot be justified historically because it came about by horrendous crimes. It cannot be justified by an appeal to a fictional history such as that described by John Locke. It cannot be justified by consequences because the global economic order has resulted in massive deprivations. Pogge goes on to distinguish between three ways in which the rich harm the poor. Poor people are worse off because of the effects of historical crimes, they are prevented from a fair use of natural resources, and they are harmed by the imposition of an unjust global institutional order. This unjust order includes protectionism by affluent countries, the enforcement of intellectual property rights, and the support of corrupt rulers of resource-rich countries.

Despite a high and growing global average income, billions of human beings are still condemned to life-long severe poverty, with all its attendant evils of low life expectancy, social exclusion, ill health, illiteracy, dependency, and effective enslavement. The annual death toll from poverty-related causes is around 18 million, or one-third of all human deaths, which adds up to approximately 270 million deaths since the end of the Cold War.[1]

This problem is hardly unsolvable, in spite of its magnitude. Though constituting 44 percent of the world's population, the 2,735 million people the World Bank counts as living below its more generous $2 per day international poverty line consume only 1.3 percent of the global product, and would need just 1 percent more to escape poverty so defined.[2] The high-income countries, with 955 million citizens, by contrast, have about

[1]World Health Organization, *World Health Report 2004* (Geneva: WHO, 2004), Annex Table 2; available at www.who.int/whr/2004.

[2]For detailed income poverty figures, see Shaohua Chen and Martin Ravallion, "How Have the World's Poorest Fared since the Early 1980s?" *World Bank Research Observer* 19, no. 2 (2004), p. 153; also available at wbro.oupjournals.org/cgi/content/abstract/19/2/141 (reporting 2001 data). Ravallion and Chen have managed the World Bank's income poverty assessments for well over a decade. My estimate of the poor's share of the global product is justified in Thomas W. Pogge, "The First UN Millennium Development Goal: A Cause for Celebration?" *Journal of Human Development* 5, no. 3 (2004), p. 387. For a methodological critique of the World Bank's poverty statistics, see "The First UN Millennium Development Goal," pp. 381–85, based on my joint work with Sanjay G. Reddy, "How *Not* to Count the Poor"; available at www.socialanalysis.org.

*Source:* World Poverty and Human Rights by Thomas Pogge from *Ethics & International Affairs*, Vol. 19, No. 1, 2005. Oxford, UK: Wiley-Blackwell. Reprinted by permission.

81 percent of the global product.[3] With our average per capita income nearly 180 times greater than that of the poor (at market exchange rates), we could eradicate severe poverty worldwide if we chose to try—in fact, we could have eradicated it decades ago.

Citizens of the rich countries are, however, conditioned to downplay the severity and persistence of world poverty and to think of it as an occasion for minor charitable assistance. Thanks in part to the rationalizations dispensed by our economists, most of us believe that severe poverty and its persistence are due exclusively to local causes. Few realize that severe poverty is an ongoing harm we inflict upon the global poor. If more of us understood the true magnitude of the problem of poverty and our causal involvement in it, we might do what is necessary to eradicate it.

That world poverty is an ongoing harm *we* inflict seems completely incredible to most citizens of the affluent countries. We call it tragic that the basic human rights of so many remain unfulfilled, and are willing to admit that we should do more to help. But it is unthinkable to us that we are actively responsible for this catastrophe. If we were, then we, civilized and sophisticated denizens of the developed countries, would be guilty of the largest crime against humanity ever committed, the death toll of which exceeds, every week, that of the recent tsunami and, every three years, that of World War II, the concentration camps and gulags included. What could be more preposterous?

But think about the unthinkable for a moment. Are there steps the affluent countries could take to reduce severe poverty abroad? It seems very likely that there are, given the enormous inequalities in income and wealth already mentioned. The common assumption, however, is that reducing severe poverty abroad at the expense of our own affluence would be generous on our part, not something we owe, and that our failure to do this is thus at most a lack of generosity that does not make us morally responsible for the continued deprivation of the poor.

I deny this popular assumption. I deny that the 955 million citizens of the affluent countries are morally entitled to their 81 percent of the global product in the face of three times as many people mired in severe poverty. Is this denial really so preposterous that one need not consider the arguments in its support? Does not the radical inequality between our wealth and their dire need at least put the burden on us to show why we should be morally entitled to so much while they have so little? In *World Poverty and Human Rights*,[4] I dispute the popular assumption by showing that the usual ways of justifying our great advantage fail. My argument poses three mutually independent challenges.

## ACTUAL HISTORY

Many believe that the radical inequality we face can be justified by reference to how it evolved, for example through differences in diligence, culture, and social institutions, soil, climate, or fortune. I challenge this sort of justification by invoking the common and very violent history through which the present radical inequality accumulated. Much of it was built up in the colonial era, when today's affluent countries ruled today's poor regions of the world: trading their people like cattle, destroying their political institutions and cultures, taking their lands and natural resources, and forcing products and customs upon them. I recount these historical facts specifically for readers who believe that even the most radical inequality is morally justifiable if it evolved in a benign way. Such readers disagree about the conditions a historical process must meet for it to justify such vast inequalities in life chances. But I can bypass these disagreements because the actual historical crimes were so horrendous, diverse, and consequential that no historical entitlement conception could credibly support the view that our common history was sufficiently benign to justify today's huge inequality in starting places.

Challenges such as this are often dismissed with the lazy response that we cannot be held

[3]World Bank, *World Development Report 2003* (New York: Oxford University Press, 2003), p. 235 (giving data for 2001).

[4]Thomas W. Pogge, *World Poverty and Human Rights: Cosmopolitan Responsibilities and Reforms* (Cambridge: Polity Press, 2002). All in-text citation references are to this book.

responsible for what others did long ago. This response is true but irrelevant. We indeed cannot inherit responsibility for our forefathers' sins. But how then can we plausibly claim the *fruits* of their sins? How can we have been entitled to the great head start our countries enjoyed going into the postcolonial period, which has allowed us to dominate and shape the world? And how can we be entitled to the huge advantages over the global poor we consequently enjoy from birth? The historical path from which our exceptional affluence arose greatly weakens our moral claim to it—certainly in the face of those whom the same historical process has delivered into conditions of acute deprivation. They, the global poor, have a much stronger moral claim to that 1 percent of the global product they need to meet their basic needs than we affluent have to take 81 rather than 80 percent for ourselves. Thus, I write, "A morally deeply tarnished history must not be allowed to result in *radical* inequality" (p. 203).

## FICTIONAL HISTORIES

Since my first challenge addressed adherents of historical entitlement conceptions of justice, it may leave others unmoved. These others may believe that it is permissible to uphold any economic distribution, no matter how skewed, if merely it *could* have come about on a morally acceptable path. They insist that we are entitled to keep and defend what we possess, even at the cost of millions of deaths each year, unless there is conclusive proof that, without the horrors of the European conquests, severe poverty world-wide would be substantially less today.

Now, *any* distribution, however unequal, *could* be the outcome of a sequence of voluntary bets or gambles. Appeal to such a fictional history would "justify" anything and would thus be wholly implausible. John Locke does much better, holding that a fictional history can justify the status quo only if the changes in holdings and social rules it involves are ones that all participants could have rationally agreed to. He also holds that in a state of nature persons would be entitled to a proportional share of the world's natural resources. Whoever deprives others of "enough and as good"—either through unilateral appropriations or through institutional arrangements, such as a radically inegalitarian property regime—harms them in violation of a *negative* duty. For Locke, the justice of any institutional order thus depends on whether the worst-off under it are at least as well off as people would be in a state of nature with a proportional resource share.[5] This baseline is imprecise, to be sure, but it suffices for my second challenge: however one may want to imagine a state of nature among human beings on this planet, one could not realistically conceive it as involving suffering and early deaths on the scale we are witnessing today. Only a thoroughly organized state of civilization can produce such horrendous misery and sustain an enduring poverty death toll of 18 million annually. The existing distribution is then morally unacceptable on Lockean grounds insofar as, I point out, "the better-off enjoy significant advantages in the use of a single natural resource base from whose benefits the worse-off are largely, and without compensation, excluded" (p. 202).

The attempt to justify today's coercively upheld radical inequality by appeal to some morally acceptable *fictional* historical process that *might* have led to it thus fails as well. On Locke's permissive account, a small elite may appropriate all of the huge cooperative surplus produced by modern social organization. But this elite must not enlarge its share even further by reducing the poor *below* the state-of-nature baseline to capture *more* than the entire cooperative surplus. The citizens and governments of the affluent states are violating this negative duty when we, in collaboration with the ruling cliques of many poor countries, coercively exclude the global poor from a proportional resource share and any equivalent substitute.

## PRESENT GLOBAL INSTITUTIONAL ARRANGEMENTS

A third way of thinking about the justice of a radical inequality involves reflection on the institutional rules that give rise to it. Using this

[5]For a fuller reading of Locke's argument, see Pogge, *World Poverty and Human Rights*, ch. 5.

approach, one can justify an economic order and the distribution it produces (irrespective of historical considerations) by comparing them to feasible alternative institutional schemes and the distributional profiles they would produce. Many broadly consequentialist and contractualist conceptions of justice exemplify this approach. They differ in how they characterize the relevant affected parties (groups, persons, time slices of persons, and so on), in the metric they employ for measuring how well off such parties are (in terms of social primary goods, capabilities, welfare, and so forth), and in how they aggregate such information about well-being into an overall assessment (for example, by averaging, or in some egalitarian, prioritarian, or sufficientarian way). These conceptions consequently disagree about how economic institutions should be best shaped under modern conditions. But I can bypass such disagreements insofar as these conceptions agree that an economic order is unjust when it—like the systems of serfdom and forced labor prevailing in feudal Russia or France—foreseeably and avoidably gives rise to massive and severe human rights deficits. My third challenge, addressed to adherents of broadly consequentialist and contractualist conceptions of justice, is that we are preserving our great economic advantages by imposing a global economic order that is unjust in view of the massive and avoidable deprivations it foreseeably reproduces: "There is a shared institutional order that is shaped by the better-off and imposed on the worse-off," I contend. "This institutional order is implicated in the reproduction of radical inequality in that there is a feasible institutional alternative under which such severe and extensive poverty would not persist. The radical inequality cannot be traced to extra-social factors (such as genetic handicaps or natural disasters) which, as such, affect different human beings differentially" (p. 199).

## THREE NOTIONS OF HARM

These three challenges converge on the conclusion that the global poor have a compelling moral claim to some of our affluence and that we, by denying them what they are morally entitled to and urgently need, are actively contributing to their deprivations. Still, these challenges are addressed to different audiences and thus appeal to diverse and mutually inconsistent moral conceptions.

They also deploy different notions of harm. In most ordinary contexts, the word "harm" is understood in a historical sense, either diachronically or subjunctively: someone is harmed when she is rendered worse off than she was at some earlier time, or than she would have been had some earlier arrangements continued undisturbed. My first two challenges conceive harm in this ordinary way, and then conceive justice, at least partly, in terms of harm: we are behaving unjustly toward the global poor by imposing on them the lasting effects of historical crimes, or by holding them below any credible state-of-nature baseline. But my third challenge does not conceive justice and injustice in terms of an independently specified notion of harm. Rather, it relates the concepts of *harm* and *justice* in the opposite way, conceiving harm in terms of an independently specified conception of social justice: we are *harming* the global poor if and insofar as we collaborate in imposing an *unjust* global institutional order upon them. And this institutional order is definitely unjust if and insofar as it foreseeably perpetuates large-scale human rights deficits that would be reasonably avoidable through feasible institutional modifications.[6]

The third challenge is empirically more demanding than the other two. It requires me to substantiate three claims: Global institutional arrangements are causally implicated in the reproduction of massive severe poverty. Governments of our affluent countries bear primary responsibility for these global institutional arrangements and

[6]One might say that the existing global order is not unjust if the only feasible institutional modifications that could substantially reduce the offensive deprivations would be extremely costly in terms of culture, say, or the natural environment. I preempt such objections by inserting the word "reasonably." Broadly consequentialist and contractualist conceptions of justice agree that an institutional order that foreseeably gives rise to massive severe deprivations is unjust if there are feasible institutional modifications that foreseeably would greatly reduce these deprivations without adding other harms of comparable magnitude.

can foresee their detrimental effects. And many citizens of these affluent countries bear responsibility for the global institutional arrangements their governments have negotiated in their names.

## TWO MAIN INNOVATIONS

In defending these three claims, my view on these more empirical matters is as oddly perpendicular to the usual empirical debates as my diagnosis of our moral relation to the problem of world poverty is to the usual moral debates.

The usual *moral* debates concern the stringency of our moral duties to help the poor abroad. Most of us believe that these duties are rather feeble, meaning that it isn't very wrong of us to give no help at all. Against this popular view, some (Peter Singer, Henry Shue, Peter Unger) have argued that our positive duties are quite stringent and quite demanding; and others (such as Liam Murphy) have defended an intermediate view according to which our positive duties, insofar as they are quite stringent, are not very demanding. Leaving this whole debate to one side, I focus on what it ignores: our moral duties not to harm. We do, of course, have positive duties to rescue people from life-threatening poverty. But it can be misleading to focus on them when more stringent negative duties are also in play: duties not to expose people to life-threatening poverty and duties to shield them from harms for which we would be actively responsible.

The usual *empirical* debates concern how developing countries should design their economic institutions and policies in order to reduce severe poverty within their borders. The received wisdom (often pointing to Hong Kong and, lately, China) is that they should opt for free and open markets with a minimum in taxes and regulations so as to attract investment and to stimulate growth. But some influential economists call for extensive government investment in education, health care, and infrastructure (as illustrated by the example of the Indian state of Kerala), or for some protectionist measures to "incubate" fledgling niche industries until they become internationally competitive (as illustrated by the example of South Korea). Leaving these debates to one side, I focus once more on what is typically ignored: the role that the design of the *global* institutional order plays in the persistence of severe poverty.

Thanks to the inattention of our economists, many believe that the existing global institutional order plays no role in the persistence of severe poverty, but rather that national differences are the key factors. Such "explanatory nationalism" (p. 139ff.) appears justified by the dramatic performance differentials among developing countries, with poverty rapidly disappearing in some and increasing in others. Cases of the latter kind usually display plenty of incompetence, corruption, and oppression by ruling elites, which seem to give us all the explanation we need to understand why severe poverty persists there.

But consider this analogy. Suppose there are great performance differentials among the students in a class, with some improving greatly while many others learn little or nothing. And suppose the latter students do not do their readings and skip many classes. This case surely shows that local, student-specific factors play a role in explaining academic success. But it decidedly *fails* to show that global factors (the quality of teaching, textbooks, classroom, and so forth) play no such role. A better teacher might well greatly improve the performance of the class by eliciting stronger student interest in the subject and hence better attendance and preparation.

Once we break free from explanatory nationalism, global factors relevant to the persistence of severe poverty are easy to find. In the WTO negotiations, the affluent countries insisted on continued and asymmetrical protections of their markets through tariffs, quotas, anti-dumping duties, export credits, and huge subsidies to domestic producers. Such protectionism provides a compelling illustration of the hypocrisy of the rich states that insist and command that their own exports be received with open markets (pp. 15–20). And it greatly impairs export opportunities for the very poorest countries and regions. If the rich countries scrapped their protectionist barriers against imports from poor countries, the populations of the latter would benefit greatly: hundreds of millions would escape unemployment, wage levels would rise substantially, and incoming export revenues would be higher by hundreds of billions of dollars each year.

The same rich states also insist that their intellectual property rights—ever-expanding in scope and duration—must be vigorously enforced in the poor countries. Music and software, production processes, words, seeds, biological species, and drugs—for all these, and more, rents must be paid to the corporations of the rich countries as a condition for (still multiply restricted) access to their markets. Millions would be saved from diseases and death if generic producers could freely manufacture and market life-saving drugs in the poor countries.[7]

While charging billions for their intellectual property, the rich countries pay nothing for the externalities they impose through their vastly disproportional contributions to global pollution and resource depletion. The global poor benefit least, if at all, from polluting activities, and also are least able to protect themselves from the impact such pollution has on their health and on their natural environment (such as flooding due to rising sea levels). It is true, of course, that we pay for the vast quantities of natural resources we import. But such payments cannot make up for the price effects of our inordinate consumption, which restrict the consumption possibilities of the global poor as well as the development possibilities of the poorer countries and regions (in comparison to the opportunities our countries could take advantage of at a comparable stage of economic development).

More important, the payments we make for resource imports go to the rulers of the resource-rich countries, with no concern about whether they are democratically elected or at least minimally attentive to the needs of the people they rule. It is on the basis of effective power alone that we recognize any such ruler as entitled to sell us the resources of "his" country and to borrow, undertake treaty commitments, and buy arms in its name. These international resource, borrowing, treaty, and arms privileges we extend to such rulers are quite advantageous to them, providing them with the money and arms they need to stay in power—often with great brutality and negligible popular support. These privileges are also quite convenient to us, securing our resource imports from poor countries irrespective of who may rule them and how badly. But these privileges have devastating effects on the global poor by enabling corrupt rulers to oppress them, to exclude them from the benefits of their countries' natural resources, and to saddle them with huge debts and onerous treaty obligations. By substantially augmenting the perks of governmental power, these same privileges also greatly strengthen the incentives to attempt to take power by force, thereby fostering coups, civil wars, and interstate wars in the poor countries and regions—especially in Africa, which has many desperately poor but resource-rich countries, where the resource sector constitutes a large part of the gross domestic product.

Reflection on the popular view that severe poverty persists in many poor countries because they govern themselves so poorly shows, then, that it is evidence not for but against explanatory nationalism. The populations of most of the countries in which severe poverty persists or increases do not "govern themselves" poorly, but *are* very poorly governed, and much against their will. They are helplessly exposed to such "government" because the rich states recognize their rulers as entitled to rule on the basis of effective power alone. We pay these rulers for their people's resources, often advancing them large sums against the collateral of future exports, and we eagerly sell them the advanced weaponry on which their continued rule all too often depends. Yes, severe poverty is fueled by local misrule. But such local misrule is fueled, in turn, by global rules that we impose and from which we benefit greatly.

Once this causal nexus between our global institutional order and the persistence of severe poverty is understood, the injustice of that order, and of our imposition of it, becomes visible: "What entitles a small global elite—the citizens of the rich countries *and* the holders of political

[7]See Thomas W. Pogge, "Human Rights and Global Health," *Metaphilosophy* 36, nos. 1–2 (2005), pp. 182–209.

and economic power in the resource-rich developing countries—to enforce a global property scheme under which we may claim the world's natural resources for ourselves and can distribute these among ourselves on mutually agreeable terms?" I ask. "How, for instance, can our ever so free and fair agreements with tyrants give us property rights in crude oil, thereby dispossessing the local population and the rest of humankind?" (p. 142).

## REVIEW QUESTIONS

1. Why does Pogge think that world poverty is an ongoing harm inflicted on the poor?
2. According to Pogge, how was the radical inequality in wealth historically caused? How does this show that the inequality is not morally justified?
3. How does Locke try to justify unequal economic distribution? Why does Pogge believe the present unequal distribution is morally unacceptable on Lockean grounds?
4. How does Pogge explain the current global economic order?
5. In what three ways are the rich harming the poor, according to Pogge?
6. Why does Pogge object to explanatory nationalism?
7. According to Pogge, what global practices are relevant to the explanation of severe poverty?

## DISCUSSION QUESTIONS

1. Do you agree that rich countries are actively harming poor people? If so, is there a negative duty not to harm them?
2. Are we entitled to our wealth while others live in poverty? What is Pogge's view? What do you think?
3. Do rich countries have a positive duty to help poor people?
4. Should rich countries eliminate protectionist barriers against imports from poor countries? Should they abandon intellectual property rights for music, software, drugs, and so on? What is your view?
5. Pogge claims that rich countries support corrupt rulers. Can you give examples of this?

# Living on a Lifeboat

GARRETT HARDIN

Garrett Hardin (1915–2003) was professor of biology at the University of California at Santa Barbara. He was the author of nine books and more than fifteen articles. His books include *The Limits of Altruism: An Ecologist's View of Survival* (1977); *Living within Limits: Ecology, Economics, and Population Taboos* (1993); and most recently, *The Ostrich Factor: Our Population Myopia* (1999).

Hardin uses the metaphor of a lifeboat to argue that rich nations such as the United States do not have any moral obligation to help poor nations with needy people. He claims that aid to the poor in the form of food just makes matters worse; it results in more population growth, which in turn leads to a tragedy of the commons, that is, a destruction of natural resources caused by overuse.

Susanne Langer (1942) has shown that it is probably impossible to approach an unsolved problem save through the door of metaphor. Later, attempting to meet the demands of rigor, we may achieve some success in cleansing theory of metaphor, though our success is limited if we are unable to avoid using common language, which is shot through and through with fossil metaphors. (I count no less than five in the preceding two sentences.)

Since metaphorical thinking is inescapable it is pointless merely to weep about our human limitations. We must learn to live with them, to understand them, and to control them. "All of us," said George Eliot in *Middlemarch*, "get our thoughts entangled in metaphors, and act fatally on the strength of them." To avoid unconscious suicide we are well advised to pit one metaphor against another. From the interplay of competitive metaphors, thoroughly developed, we may come closer to metaphor-free solutions to our problems.

No generation has viewed the problem of the survival of the human species as seriously as we have. Inevitably, we have entered this world of concern through the door of metaphor. Environmentalists have emphasized the image of the earth as a spaceship—Spaceship Earth. Kenneth Boulding (1966) is the principal architect of this metaphor. It is time, he says, that we replace the wasteful "cowboy economy" of the past with the frugal "spaceship economy" required for

*Source:* "Living on a Lifeboat" by Garrett Hardin from *Bioscience*, Vol. 24, 1974, pp. 561–568. Washington, DC: American Institute of Biological Sciences.

continued survival in the limited world we now see ours to be. The metaphor is notably useful in justifying pollution control measures.

Unfortunately, the image of a spaceship is also used to promote measures that are suicidal. One of these is a generous immigration policy, which is only a particular instance of a class of policies that are in error because they lead to the tragedy of the commons (Hardin 1968). These suicidal policies are attractive because they mesh with what we unthinkingly take to be the ideals of "the best people." What is missing in the idealistic view is an insistence that rights and responsibilities must go together. The "generous" attitude of all too many people results in asserting inalienable rights while ignoring or denying matching responsibilities.

For the metaphor of a spaceship to be correct, the aggregate of people on board would have to be under unitary sovereign control (Ophuls 1974). A true ship always has a captain. It is conceivable that a ship could be run by a committee. But it could not possibly survive if its course were determined by bickering tribes that claimed rights without responsibilities.

What about Spaceship Earth? It certainly has no captain, and no executive committee. The United Nations is a toothless tiger, because the signatories of its charter wanted it that way. The spaceship metaphor is used only to justify spaceship demands on common resources without acknowledging corresponding spaceship responsibilities.

An understandable fear of decisive action leads people to embrace "incrementalism"—moving toward reform by tiny stages. As we shall see, this strategy is counterproductive in the area discussed here if it means accepting rights before responsibilities. Where human survival is at stake, the acceptance of responsibilities is a precondition to the acceptance of rights, if the two cannot be introduced simultaneously.

## LIFEBOAT ETHICS

Before taking up certain substantive issues let us look at an alternative metaphor, that of a lifeboat. In developing some relevant examples the following numerical values are assumed. Approximately two-thirds of the world is desperately poor, and only one-third is comparatively rich. The people in poor countries have an average per capita GNP (Gross National Product) of about $200 per year, the rich, of about $3,000. (For the United States it is nearly $5,000 per year.) Metaphorically, each rich nation amounts to a lifeboat full of comparatively rich people. The poor of the world are in other, much more crowded, lifeboats. Continuously, so to speak, the poor fall out of their lifeboats and swim for a while in the water outside, hoping to be admitted to a rich lifeboat, or in some other way to benefit from the "goodies" on board. What should the passengers on a rich lifeboat do? This is the central problem of "the ethics of a lifeboat."

First we must acknowledge that each lifeboat is effectively limited in capacity. The land of every nation has a limited carrying capacity. The exact limit is a matter for argument, but the energy crunch is convincing more people every day that we have already exceeded the carrying capacity of the land. We have been living on "capital"—stored petroleum and coal—and soon we must live on income alone.

Let us look at only one lifeboat: ours. The ethical problem is the same for all, and is as follows. Here we sit, say 50 people in a lifeboat. To be generous, let us assume our boat has a capacity of 10 more, making 60. (This, however, is to violate the engineering principle of the "safety factor." A new plant disease or a bad change in the weather may decimate our population if we don't preserve some excess capacity as a safety factor.)

The 50 of us in the lifeboat see 100 others swimming in the water outside, asking for admission to the boat, or for handouts. How shall we respond to their calls?

There are several possibilities.

One. We may be tempted to try to live by the Christian ideal of being "our brother's keeper," or by the Marxian ideal (Marx 1875) of "from each according to his abilities, to each according to his needs." Since the needs of all are the same, we take all the needy into our boat, making a total of 150 in a boat with a capacity of 60. The boat is swamped, and everyone drowns. Complete justice, complete catastrophe.

Two. Since the boat has an unused excess capacity of 10, we admit just 10 more to it. This has the disadvantage of getting rid of the safety factor, for which action we will sooner or later pay dearly. Moreover, which 10 do we let in? "First come, first served?" The best 10? The neediest 10? How do we *discriminate*? And what do we say to the 90 who are excluded?

Three. Admit no more to the boat and preserve the small safety factor. Survival of the people in the lifeboat is then possible (though we shall have to be on our guard against boarding parties).

The last solution is abhorrent to many people. It is unjust, they say. Let us grant that it is.

"I feel guilty about my good luck," say some. The reply to this is simple: *Get out and yield your place to others.* Such a selfless action might satisfy the conscience of those who are addicted to guilt but it would not change the ethics of the lifeboat. The needy person to whom a guilt-addict yields his place will not himself feel guilty about his sudden good luck. (If he did he would not climb aboard.) The net result of conscience-stricken people relinquishing their unjustly held positions is the elimination of their kind of conscience from the lifeboat. The lifeboat, as it were, purifies itself of guilt. The ethics of the lifeboat persist, unchanged by such momentary aberrations.

This then is the basic metaphor within which we must work out our solutions. Let us enrich the image step by step with substantive additions from the real world.

## REPRODUCTION

The harsh characteristics of lifeboat ethics are heightened by reproduction, particularly by reproductive differences. The people inside the lifeboats of the wealthy nations are doubling in numbers every 87 years; those outside are doubling every 35 years, on the average. And the relative difference in prosperity is becoming greater.

Let us, for a while, think primarily of the U.S. lifeboat. As of 1973, the United States had a population of 210 million people who were increasing by 0.8% per year, that is, doubling in number every 87 years.

Although the citizens of rich nations are outnumbered two to one by the poor, let us imagine an equal number of poor people outside our lifeboat—a mere 210 million poor people reproducing at a quite different rate. If we imagine these to be the combined populations of Colombia, Venezuela, Ecuador, Morocco, Thailand, Pakistan, and the Philippines, the average rate of increase of the people "outside" is a 3.3% per year. The doubling time of this population is 21 years.

Suppose that all these countries, and the United States, agreed to live by the Marxian ideal, "to each according to his needs," the ideal of most Christians as well. Needs, of course, are determined by population size, which is affected by reproduction. Every nation regards its rate of reproduction as a sovereign right. If our lifeboat were big enough in the beginning it might be possible to live *for a while* by Christian-Marxian ideals. *Might.*

Initially, in the model given, the ratio of non-Americans to Americans would be one to one. But consider what the ratio would be 87 years later. By this time Americans would have doubled to a population of 420 million. The other group (doubling every 21 years) would now have swollen to 3,540 million. Each American would have more than eight people to share with. How could the lifeboat possibly keep afloat?

All this involves extrapolation of current trends into the future and is consequently suspect. Trends may change. Granted, but the change will not necessarily be favorable. If,—as seems likely—the rate of population increase falls faster in the ethnic group presently inside the lifeboat than it does among those now outside, the future will turn out to be even worse than mathematics predicts, and sharing will be even more suicidal.

## RUIN IN THE COMMONS

The fundamental error of the sharing ethics is that it leads to the tragedy of the commons. Under a system of private property the man (or group of men) who own property recognize their responsibility to care for it, for if they don't they will eventually suffer. A farmer, for instance, if he is intelligent, will allow no more cattle in a pasture than its carrying capacity justifies. If he overloads the pasture, weeds take over, erosion sets in, and the owner loses in the long run.

But if a pasture is run as a commons open to all, the right of each to use it is not matched by an operational responsibility to take care of it. It is no use asking independent herdsmen in a commons to act responsibly, for they dare not. The considerate herdsman who refrains from overloading the commons suffers more than a selfish one who says his needs are greater. (As Leo Durocher says, "Nice guys finish last.") Christian-Marxian idealism is counterproductive. That it *sounds* nice is no excuse. With distribution systems, as with individual morality, good intentions are no substitute for good performance.

A social system is stable only if it is insensitive to errors. To the Christian-Marxian idealist a selfish person is a sort of "error." Prosperity in the system of the commons cannot survive errors. If *everyone* would only restrain himself, all would be well; but it takes *only one less than everyone* to ruin a system of voluntary restraint. In a crowded world of less than perfect human beings—and we will never know any other—mutual ruin is inevitable in the commons. This is the core of the tragedy of the commons.

One of the major tasks of education today is to create such an awareness of the dangers of the commons that people will be able to recognize its many varieties, however disguised. There is pollution of the air and water because these media are treated as commons. Further growth of population and growth in the per capita conversion of natural resources into pollutants require that the system of the commons be modified or abandoned in the disposal of "externalities."

The fish populations of the oceans are exploited as commons, and ruin lies ahead. No technological invention can prevent this fate: in fact, all improvements in the art of fishing merely hasten the day of complete ruin. Only the replacement of the system of the commons with a responsible system can save oceanic fisheries.

The management of western rangelands, though nominally rational, is in fact (under the steady pressure of cattle ranchers) often merely a government-sanctioned system of the commons, drifting toward ultimate ruin for both the rangelands and the residual enterprisers.

## WORLD FOOD BANKS

In the international arena we have recently heard a proposal to create a new commons, namely an international depository of food reserves to which nations will contribute according to their abilities, and from which nations may draw according to their needs. Nobel laureate Norman Borlaug has lent the prestige of his name to this proposal.

A world food bank appeals powerfully to our humanitarian impulses. We remember John Donne's celebrated line, "Any man's death diminishes me." But before we rush out to see for whom the bell tolls, let us recognize where the greatest political push for international granaries comes from, lest we be disillusioned later. Our experience with Public Law 480 clearly reveals the answer. This was the law that moved billions of dollars worth of U.S. grain to food-short, population-long countries during the past two decades. When P. L. 480 first came into being, a headline in the business magazine *Forbes* (Paddock and Paddock 1970) revealed the power behind it: "Feeding the World's Hungry Millions: How It Will Mean Billions for U.S. Business."

And indeed it did. In the years 1960 to 1970 a total of $7.9 billion was spent on the "Food for Peace" program, as P. L. 480 was called. During the years 1948 to 1970 an additional $49.9 billion were extracted from American taxpayers to pay for other economic aid programs, some of which went for food and food-producing machinery. (This figure does not include military aid.) That P. L. 480 was a give-away program was concealed. Recipient countries went through the motions of paying for P. L. 480 food—with IOUs. In December 1973 the charade was brought to an end as far as India was concerned when the United States "forgave" India's $3.2 billion debt (Anonymous 1974). Public announcement of the cancellation of the debt was delayed for two months; one wonders why.

"Famine—1974!" (Paddock and Paddock 1970) is one of the few publications that points out the commercial roots of this humanitarian attempt. Though all U.S. taxpayers lost by P. L. 480, special interest groups gained handsomely. Farmers benefited because they were not asked to contribute the grain—it was bought from them by the taxpayers. Besides the direct benefit there was the indirect effect of increasing demand and thus raising prices of farm products generally. The manufacturers of farm machinery, fertilizers, and pesticides benefited by the farmers' extra efforts to grow more food. Grain elevators profited from storing the grain for varying lengths of time. Railroads made money hauling it to port, and shipping lines by carrying it overseas. Moreover, once the machinery for P. L. 480 was established, an immense bureaucracy had a vested interest in its continuance regardless of its merits.

Very little was ever heard of these selfish interests when P. L. 480 was defended in public. The emphasis was always on its humanitarian effects. The combination of multiple and relatively silent selfish interests with highly vocal humanitarian apologists constitutes a powerful lobby for extracting money from taxpayers. Foreign aid has become a habit that can apparently survive in the absence of any known justification. A news commentator in a weekly magazine (Lansner 1974), after exhaustively going over all the conventional arguments for foreign aid—self-interest, social justice, political advantage, and charity—and concluding that none of the known arguments really held water, concluded: "So the search continues for some logically compelling reasons for giving aid. . . ." In other words, Act now, Justify later—if ever. (Apparently a quarter of a century is too short a time to find the justification for expending several billion dollars yearly.)

The search for a rational justification can be short-circuited by interjecting the word "emergency." Borlaug uses this word. We need to look sharply at it. What is an "emergency"? It is surely something like an accident, which is correctly defined as *an event that is certain to happen, though with a low frequency* (Hardin 1972a). A well-run organization prepares for everything that is certain, including accidents and emergencies. It budgets for them. It saves for them. It expects them—and mature decision-makers do not waste time complaining about accidents when they occur.

What happens if some organizations budget for emergencies and other do not? If each organization is solely responsible for its own well-being, poorly managed ones will suffer. But they should be able to learn from experience. They have a chance to mend their ways and learn to budget for infrequent but certain emergencies. The weather, for instance, always varies and periodic crop failures are certain. A wise and competent government saves out of the production of the good years in anticipation of bad years that are sure to come. This is not a new idea. The Bible tells us that Joseph taught this policy to Pharaoh in Egypt more than two thousand years ago. Yet it is literally true that the vast majority of the governments of the world today have no such policy. They lack either the wisdom or the competence, or both. Far more difficult than the transfer of wealth from one country to another is the transfer of wisdom between sovereign powers or between generations.

"But it isn't their fault! How can we blame the poor people who are caught in an emergency? Why must we punish them?" The concepts of blame and punishment are irrelevant. The question is, what are the operational consequences of establishing a world food bank? If it is open to every country every time a need develops, slovenly rulers will not be motivated to take Joseph's advice. Why should they? Others will bail them out whenever they are in trouble.

Some countries will make deposits in the world food bank and others will withdraw from it: There will be almost no overlap. Calling such a depository-transfer unit a "bank" is stretching the metaphor of bank beyond its elastic limits. The proposers, of course, never call attention to the metaphorical nature of the word they use.

## THE RATCHET EFFECT

An "international food bank" is really, then, not a true bank but a disguised one-way transfer device for moving wealth from rich countries to poor. In the absence of such a bank, in a world inhabited by individually responsible sovereign nations, the population of each nation would repeatedly go through a cycle of the sort shown in Figure 1. $P_2$ is greater than $P_1$, either in absolute numbers or because a deterioration of the food supply has removed the safety factor and produced a dangerously low ratio of resources to population. $P_2$ may be said to represent a state of overpopulation, which becomes obvious upon the appearance of an "accident," e.g., a crop failure. If the "emergency" is not met by outside help, the population drops back to the "normal" level—the "carrying capacity" of the environment or even below. In the absence of population control by a sovereign, sooner or later the population grows to $P_2$ again and the cycle repeats. The long-term population curve (Hardin 1966) is an irregularly fluctuating one, equilibrating more or less about the carrying capacity.

A demographic cycle of this sort obviously involves great suffering in the restrictive phase, but such a cycle is normal to any independent country with inadequate population control. The third century theologian Tertullian (Hardin 1969a) expressed what must have been the recognition of many wise men when he wrote: *"The scourges of pestilence, famine, wars, and earthquakes have come to be regarded as a blessing to overcrowded nations, since they serve to prune away the luxuriant growth of the human race."*

Only under a strong and farsighted sovereign—which theoretically could be the people themselves, democratically organized—can a population equilibrate at some set point below the carrying capacity, thus avoiding the pains normally caused by periodic and unavoidable disasters. For this happy state to be achieved it is necessary that those in power be able to contemplate with equanimity the "waste" of surplus food in times of bountiful harvests. It is essential that those in power resist the temptation to convert extra food into extra babies. On the public relations level it is necessary that the phrase "surplus food" be replaced by "safety factor."

But wise sovereigns seem not to exist in the poor world today.

The most anguishing problems are created by poor countries that are governed by rulers insufficiently wise and powerful. If such countries can draw on a world food bank in times of "emergency," the population *cycle* of Figure 1 will be replaced by the population escalator of Figure 2. The input of food from a food bank acts as the pawl of a ratchet, preventing the population from retracing its steps to a lower level. Reproduction pushes the population upward, inputs from the World Food Bank prevent its moving downward. Population size escalates, as does the absolute magnitude of "accidents" and "emergencies." The process is brought to an end only by the total collapse of the whole system, producing a catastrophe of scarcely imaginable proportions.

Such are the implications of the well-meant sharing of food in a world of irresponsible reproduction.

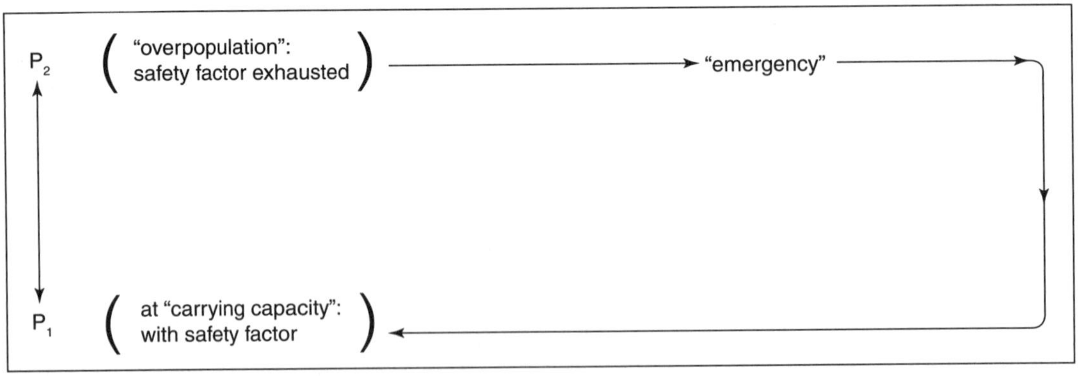


**FIGURE 1.** The population cycle of a nation that has no effective, conscious population control, and which receives no aid from the outside. $P_2$ is greater than $P_1$.

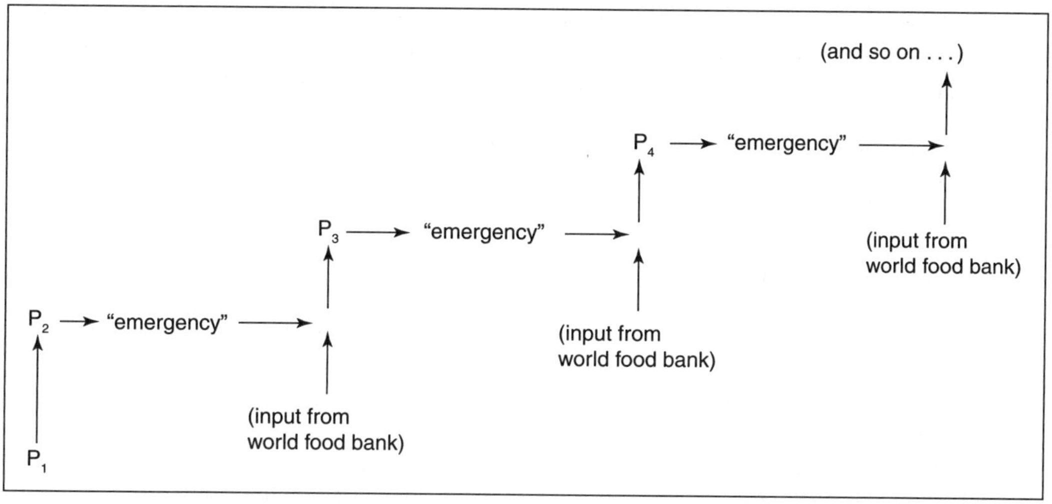


**FIGURE 2.** The population escalator. Note that input from a world food bank acts like the pawl of a ratchet, preserving the normal population cycle shown in Figure 1 from being completed. $P_{n+1}$ is greater than $P_n$, and the absolute magnitude of the "emergencies" escalates. Ultimately the entire system crashes. The crash is not shown, and few can imagine it.

I think we need a new word for systems like this. The adjective "melioristic" is applied to systems that produce continual improvement; the English word is derived from the Latin *meliorare*, to become or make better. Parallel with this it would be useful to bring in the word *pejoristic* (from the Latin *pejorare*, to become or make worse). This word can be applied to those systems which, by their very nature, can be relied upon to make matters worse. A world food bank coupled with sovereign state irresponsibility in reproduction is an example of a pejoristic system.

This pejoristic system creates an unacknowledged commons. People have more motivation to draw from than to add to the common store. The license to make such withdrawals diminishes whatever motivation poor countries might otherwise have to control their populations. Under the guidance of this ratchet, wealth can be steadily moved in one direction only, from the slowly-breeding rich to the rapidly-breeding poor, the process finally coming to a halt only when all countries are equally and miserably poor.

All this is terribly obvious once we are acutely aware of the pervasiveness and danger of the commons. But many people still lack this awareness and the euphoria of the "benign demographic transition" (Hardin 1973) interferes with the realistic appraisal of pejoristic mechanisms. As concerns public policy, the deductions drawn from the benign demographic transition are these:

1. If the per capita GNP rises the birth rate will fall; hence, the rate of population increase will fall, ultimately producing ZPG (Zero Population Growth).

2. The long-term trend all over the world (including the poor countries) is of a rising per capita GNP (for which no limit is seen).

3. Therefore, all political interference in population matters is unnecessary; all we need to do is foster economic "development"—note the metaphor—and population problems will solve themselves.

Those who believe in the benign demographic transition dismiss the pejoristic mechanism of Figure 2 in the belief that each input of food from the world outside fosters development within a poor country thus resulting in a drop in the rate of population increase. Foreign aid has proceeded on this assumption for more than two decades. Unfortunately, it has produced no indubitable instance of the asserted effect. It has, however, produced a library of excuses. The air is filled with plaintive calls for more massive foreign aid appropriations so that the hypothetical melioristic process can get started.

The doctrine of demographic laissez-faire implicit in the hypothesis of the benign demographic transition is immensely attractive. Unfortunately there is more evidence against the melioristic system than there is for it (Davis 1963). On the historical side there are many counterexamples. The rise in per capita GNP in France and Ireland during the past century has been accompanied by a rise in population growth. In the 20 years following the Second World War the same positive correlation was noted almost everywhere in the world. Never in world history before 1950 did the worldwide population growth reach 1% per annum. Now the average population growth is over 2% and shows no signs of slackening.

On the theoretical side, the denial of the pejoristic scheme of Figure 2 probably springs from the hidden acceptance of the "cowboy economy" that Boulding castigated. Those who recognize the limitations of a spaceship, if they are unable to achieve population control at a safe and comfortable level, accept the necessity of the corrective feedback of the population cycle shown in Figure 1. No one who knew in his bones that he was living on a true spaceship would countenance political support of the population escalator shown in Figure 2.

## ECO-DESTRUCTION VIA THE GREEN REVOLUTION

The demoralizing effect of charity on the recipient has long been known. "Give a man a fish and he will eat for a day; teach him how to fish and he will eat for the rest of his days." So runs an ancient Chinese proverb. Acting on this advice the Rockefeller and Ford Foundations have financed a multipronged program for improving agriculture in the hungry nations. The result, known as the "Green Revolution," has been quite remarkable. "Miracle wheat" and "miracle rice" are splendid technological achievements in the realm of plant genetics.

Observant critics have shown how much harm we wealthy nations have already done to poor nations through our well-intentioned but misguided attempts to help them.

Whether or not the Green Revolution can increase food production is doubtful (Harris 1972, Paddock 1970, Wilkes 1972), but in any event not particularly important. What is missing in this great and well-meaning humanitarian effort is a firm grasp of fundamentals. Considering the importance of the Rockefeller Foundation in this effort it is ironic that the late Alan Gregg, a much-respected vice-president of the Foundation, strongly expressed his doubts of the wisdom of all attempts to increase food production some two decades ago. (This was before Borlaug's work—supported by Rockefeller—had resulted in the development of "miracle wheat.") Gregg (1955) likened the growth and spreading of humanity over the surface of the earth to the metastasis of cancer in the human body, wryly remarking that "Cancerous growths demand food; but, as far as I know, they have never been cured by getting it."

"Man does not live by bread alone"—the scriptural statement has a rich meaning even in the material realm. Every human being born constitutes a draft on all aspects of the environment—food, air, water, unspoiled scenery, occasional and optional solitude, beaches, contact with wild animals, fishing, hunting—the list is long and incompletely known. Food can, perhaps, be significantly increased: but what about clean beaches, unspoiled forests, and solitude? If we satisfy the need for food in a growing population we necessarily decrease the supply of other goods, and thereby increase the difficulty of equitably allocating scarce goods (Hardin 1969b, 1972b).

The present population of India is 600 million, and it is increasing by 15 million per year. The environmental load of this population is already great. The forests of India are only a small fraction of what they were three centuries ago. Soil erosion, floods, and the psychological costs of crowding are serious. Every one of the net 15 million lives added each year stresses the Indian environment more severely. *Every life saved this year in a poor country diminishes the quality of life for subsequent generations.*

Observant critics have shown how much harm we wealthy nations have already done to poor nations through our well-intentioned but misguided attempts to help them (Paddock and Paddock 1973). Particularly reprehensible is our failure to carry out post-audits of these attempts (Farvar and Milton 1972). Thus have we shielded our tender consciences from knowledge of the harm we have done. Must we Americans continue to fail to monitor the consequences of our external "do-gooding"? If, for instance, we thoughtlessly make it possible for the present 600 million Indians to swell to 1,200 million by the year 2001—as their present growth rate promises—will posterity in India thank us for facilitating an even greater destruction of their Environment? Are good intentions ever a sufficient excuse for bad consequences?

## IMMIGRATION CREATES A COMMONS

I come now to the final example of a commons in action, one for which the public is least prepared for rational discussion. The topic is at present enveloped by a great silence which reminds me of a comment made by Sherlock Holmes in A. Conan Doyle's story "Silver Blaze." Inspector Gregory had asked, "Is there any point to which you would wish to draw my attention?" To this Holmes responded:

> "To the curious incident of the dog in the nighttime."
> "The dog did nothing in the nighttime," said the Inspector.
> "That was the curious incident," remarked Sherlock Holmes.

By asking himself what would repress the normal barking instinct of a watchdog, Holmes realized that it must be the dog's recognition of his master as the criminal trespasser. In a similar way we should ask ourselves what repression keeps us from discussing something as important as immigration.

It cannot be that immigration is numerically of no consequence. Our government acknowledges a net inflow of 400,000 a year. Hard data are understandably lacking on the extent of illegal entries, but a not implausible figure is 600,000 per year (Buchanan 1973). The natural increase of the resident population is now about 1.7 million per year. This means that the yearly gain from immigration is at least 19%, and may be 37%, of the total increase. It is quite conceivable that educational campaigns like that of Zero Population Growth, Inc., coupled with adverse social and economic factors—inflation, housing shortage, depression, and loss of confidence in national leaders—may lower the fertility of American women to a point at which all of the yearly increase in population would be accounted for by immigration. Should we not at least ask if that is what we want? How curious it is that we so seldom discuss immigration these days!

Curious, but understandable—as one finds out the moment he publicly questions the wisdom of the status quo in immigration. He who does so is promptly charged with *isolationism, bigotry, prejudice, ethnocentrism, chauvinism*, and *selfishness*. These are hard accusations to bear. It is pleasanter to talk about other matters, leaving immigration policy to wallow in the cross-currents of special interests that take no account of the good of the whole—*or of the interests of posterity.*

We Americans have a bad conscience because of things we said in the past about immigrants. Two generations ago the popular press was rife with references to *Dagos, Wops, Polacks, Japs, Chinks, and Krauts*—all pejorative terms which failed to acknowledge our indebtedness to Goya, Leonardo, Copernicus, Hiroshige, Confucius, and Bach. Because the implied inferiority of foreigners was *then* the justification for keeping them out, it is now thoughtlessly assumed that restrictive policies can only be based on the assumption of immigrant inferiority. *This is not so.*

Existing immigration laws exclude idiots and known criminals; future laws will almost certainly continue this policy. But should we also consider the quality of the average immigrant, as compared with the quality of the average resident? Perhaps we should, perhaps we shouldn't. (What is "quality" anyway?) But the quality issue is not our concern here.

From this point on, it will be assumed that *immigrants and native-born citizens are of exactly equal quality*, however quality may be defined. The focus is only on quantity. The conclusions reached depend on nothing else, so all charges of ethnocentrism are irrelevant.

World food banks move food to the people, thus facilitating the exhaustion of the environment of the poor. By contrast, unrestricted immigration moves people to the food, thus speeding up the destruction of the environment in rich countries. Why poor people should want to make this transfer is no mystery; but why should rich hosts encourage it? This transfer, like the reverse one, is supported by both selfish interests and humanitarian impulses.

The principal selfish interest in unimpeded immigration is easy to identify: It is the interest of the employers of cheap labor, particularly that needed for degrading jobs. We have been deceived about the forces of history by the lines of Emma Lazarus inscribed [inside the entrance to] the Statue of Liberty:

> *Give me your tired, your poor*
> *Your huddled masses yearning to breathe free,*
> *The wretched refuse of your teeming shore,*
> *Send these, the homeless, tempest-tossed, to me:*
> *I lift my lamp beside the golden door.*

The image is one of an infinitely generous earth-mother, passively opening her arms to hordes of immigrants who come here on their own initiative. Such an image may have been adequate for the early days of colonization, but by the time these lines were written (1886) the force for immigration was largely manufactured inside our own borders by factory and mine owners who sought cheap labor not to be found among laborers already here. One group of foreigners after another was thus enticed into the United States to work at wretched jobs for wretched wages.

At present, it is largely the Mexicans who are being so exploited. It is particularly to the advantage of certain employers that there be many illegal immigrants. Illegal immigrant workers dare not complain about their working conditions for fear of being repatriated. Their presence reduces the bargaining power of all Mexican-American laborers. Cesar Chavez has repeatedly pleaded with congressional committees to close the doors to more Mexicans so that those here can negotiate effectively for higher wages and decent working conditions. Chavez understands the ethics of a lifeboat.

The interests of the employers of cheap labor are well served by the silence of the intelligentsia of the country. WASPS—White Anglo-Saxon Protestants—are particularly reluctant to call for a closing of the doors to immigration for fear of being called ethnocentric bigots. It was, therefore, an occasion of pure delight for this particular WASP to be present at a meeting when the points he would like to have made were made better by a non-WASP, speaking to other non-WASPS. It was in Hawaii, and most of the people in the room were second-level Hawaiian officials of Japanese ancestry. All Hawaiians are keenly aware of the limits of their environment, and the speaker had asked how it might be practically and constitutionally possible to close the doors to more immigrants to the islands. (To Hawaiians, immigrants from the other 49 states are as much of a threat as those from other nations. There is only so much room in the islands, and the islanders know it. Sophistical arguments that imply otherwise do not impress them.)

Yet the Japanese-Americans of Hawaii have active ties with the land of their origin. This point was raised by a Japanese-American member of the audience who asked the Japanese-American speaker: "But how can we shut the doors now? We have many friends and relations in Japan that we'd like to bring to Hawaii some day so that they can enjoy this land."

The speaker smiled sympathetically and responded slowly: "Yes, but we have children now and someday we'll have grandchildren. We can bring more people here from Japan only by giving away some of the land that we hope to pass on to our grandchildren some day. What right do we have to do that?"

To be generous with one's own possessions is one thing; to be generous with posterity's is quite another. This, I think, is the point that must be gotten across to those who would, from a commendable love of distributive justice, institute a ruinous system of the commons, either in the form of a world food bank or that of unrestricted immigration. Since every speaker is a member of some ethnic group it is always possible to charge him with ethnocentrism. But even after purging an argument of ethnocentrism the rejection of the commons is still valid and necessary if we are to save at least some parts of the world from environmental ruin. Is it not desirable that at least some of the grandchildren of people now living should have a decent place in which to live?

## THE ASYMMETRY OF DOOR-SHUTTING

We must now answer this telling point: "How can you justify slamming the door once you're inside?" You say that immigrants should be kept out. But aren't we all immigrants, or the descendants of immigrants? Since we refuse to leave, must we not, as a matter of justice and symmetry, admit all others?"

It is literally true that we Americans of non-Indian ancestry are the descendants of thieves. Should we not, then, "give back" the land to the Indians; that is, give it to the now-living Americans of Indian ancestry? As an exercise in pure logic I see no way to reject this proposal. Yet I am unwilling to live by it; and I know no one who is. Our reluctance to embrace pure justice may spring from pure selfishness. On the other hand, it may arise from an unspoken recognition of consequences that have not yet been clearly spelled out.

Suppose, becoming intoxicated with pure justice, we "Anglos" should decide to turn our land over to the Indians. Since all our other wealth has also been derived from the land, we would have to give that to the Indians, too. Then what would we non-Indians do? Where would we go? There is no open land in the world on which men without capital can make their living (and not much unoccupied land on which men with capital can, either). Where would 209 million putatively justice-loving, non-Indian, Americans go? Most of them—in the persons of their ancestors—came from Europe, but they wouldn't be welcomed back there. Anyway, Europeans have no better title to their land than we to ours. They also would have to give up their homes. But to whom? And where would *they* go?

Clearly, the concept of pure justice produces an infinite regress. The law long ago invented statutes of limitations to justify the rejection of pure justice, in the interest of preventing massive disorder. The law zealously defends property rights—but only *recent* property rights. It is as though the physical principle of exponential decay applies to property rights. Drawing a line in time may be unjust, but any other action is practically worse.

We are all the descendants of thieves, and the world's resources are inequitably distributed, but we must begin the journey to tomorrow from the point where we are today. We cannot remake the past. We cannot, without violent disorder and suffering, give land and resources back to the "original" owners—who are dead anyway.

We cannot safely divide the wealth equitably among all present peoples, so long as people reproduce at different rates, because to do so would guarantee that our grandchildren—everyone's grandchildren—would have only a ruined world to inhabit.

## MUST EXCLUSION BE ABSOLUTE?

To show the logical structure of the immigration problem I have ignored many factors that would enter into real decisions made in a real world. No matter how convincing the logic may be it is probable that we would want, from time to time, to admit a few people from the outside to our lifeboat. Political refugees in particular are likely to cause us to make exceptions: We remember the Jewish refugees from Germany after 1933, and the Hungarian refugees after 1956. Moreover, the interests of national defense, broadly conceived, could justify admitting many men and women of unusual talents, whether refugees or not. (This raises the quality issue, which is not the subject of this essay.)

Such exceptions threaten to create runaway population growth inside the lifeboat, i.e., the receiving country. However, the threat can be neutralized by a population policy that includes immigration. An effective policy is one of flexible control.

Suppose, for example, that the nation has achieved a stable condition of ZPG, which (say) permits 1.5 million births yearly. We must suppose that an acceptable system of allocating birthrights to potential parents is in effect. Now suppose that an inhumane regime in some other part of the world creates a horde of refugees, and that there is a widespread desire to admit some to our country. At the same time, we do not want to sabotage our population control system. Clearly, the rational path to pursue is the following: If we decide to admit 100,000 refugees this year we should compensate for this by reducing the allocation of birth rights in the following year by a similar amount,—that is, downward to a total of 1.4 million. In that way we could achieve both humanitarian and population control goals. (And the refugees would have to accept the population controls of the society that admits them. It is not inconceivable that they might be given proportionately fewer rights than the native population.)

In a democracy, the admission of immigrants should properly be voted on. But, by whom? It is not obvious. The usual rule of a democracy is votes for all. But it can be questioned whether a universal franchise is the most just one in a case of this sort. Whatever benefits there are in the admission of immigrants presumably accrue to everyone. But the costs would be seen as falling most heavily on potential parents, some of who would have to postpone or forego having their (next) child because of the influx of immigrants. The double question *Who benefits? Who pays?* suggests that a restriction of the usual democratic franchise would be appropriate and just in this case. Would our particular quasi-democratic form of government be flexible enough to institute such a novelty? If not, the majority might, out of humanitarian motives, impose an unacceptable burden (the foregoing of parenthood) on a minority, thus producing political instability. Plainly many new problems will arise when we consciously face the immigration question and seek rational answers. No workable answers can be found if we ignore population problems. And—if the argument of this essay is correct—so long as there is no true world government to control reproduction everywhere it is impossible to survive in dignity if we are to be guided by spaceship ethics. Without a world government that is sovereign in reproductive matters mankind lives, in fact, on a number of sovereign lifeboats.

For the foreseeable future survival demands that we govern our actions by the ethics of a lifeboat. Posterity will be ill served if we do not.

## REFERENCES


Anonymous. 1974. Wall Street Journal, 19 Feb.

Borlaug, N. "Civilization's Future: A Call for International Granaries." *Bull. At. Sci.* 29:7–15, 1973.

Boulding, K. 1966. "The Economics of the Coming Spaceship Earth." In H. Jarrett, ed., *Environmental Quality in a Growing Economy.* Johns Hopkins Press, Baltimore.

Buchanan, W. 1973. "Immigration Statistics." *Equilibrium* 1(3):16–19.

Davis, K. 1963. "Population." *Sci. Amer.* 209(3): 62–71.

Farvar, M. T., and J. P. Milton. 1972. *The Careless Technology.* Natural History Press, Garden City, N.Y.

Gregg, A. 1955. "A Medical Aspect of the Population Problem." *Science* 121:681–682.

Hardin, G. 1966. Chapter 9 in *Biology: Its Principles and Implications*, 2nd ed. Freeman, San Francisco.

———— 1968. "The Tragedy of the Commons," *Science* 162: 1243–1248.

———— 1969a. Page 18 in *Population, Evolution and Birth Control*, 2nd ed. Freeman, San Francisco.

———— 1969b. "The Economics of Wilderness." *Nat. Hist.* 78(6):20–27.

———— 1972a. Pages 81–82 in *Exploring New Ethics for Survival: The Voyage of the Spaceship Beagle.* Viking, N.Y.

———— 1972b. "Preserving Quality on Spaceship Earth." In J. B. Trefethen, ed. *Transactions of the Thirty-Seventh North American Wildlife and Natural Resources Conference*, Wildlife Management Institute, Washington, DC.

———— 1973. Chapter 23 in *Stalking the Wild Taboo*. Kaufmann, Los Altos, CA.

Harris, M. 1972. "How Green the Revolution?" *Nat. Hist.* 81(3):28-30.

Langer, S. K. 1942. *Philosophy in a New Key*. Harvard University Press, Cambridge.

Lansner, K. 1974. "Should Foreign Aid Begin at Home?" *Newsweek*, 11 Feb., p.32.

Marx, K. 1875. "Critique of the Gotha Program." Page 388 in R. C. Tucker, ed. *The Marx-Engels Reader*. Norton, N.Y., 1972.

Ophuls, W. 1974. "The Scarcity Society." *Harpers* 243(1487):47–52.

Paddock, W. C. 1970. "How Green Is the Green Revolution?" *BioScience* 20:897–902.

Paddock, W., and E. Paddock. 1973. *We Don't Know How*. Iowa State University Press, Ames, Iowa.

Paddock, W., and P. Paddock. 1967. *Famine—1975!* Little, Brown, Boston.

Wilkes, H. G. 1972. "The Green Revolution." *Environment* 14(8):32–39.

## REVIEW QUESTIONS

1. What is wrong with the spaceship metaphor, according to Hardin?
2. Explain Hardin's lifeboat metaphor. How does it apply to rich and poor countries?
3. According to Hardin, why can't we live by the Christian or Marxist ideal of helping others and meeting their needs?
4. Explain what Hardin calls the tragedy of the commons. How is this supposed to apply to rich and poor nations?
5. Explain the ratchet effect and a pejoristic system.
6. Why isn't a benign demographic transition possible, according to Hardin?
7. Why does Hardin think that the Green Revolution will not solve the problem of world hunger?
8. Why is Hardin opposed to unrestricted immigration?

## DISCUSSION QUESTIONS

1. Is the lifeboat metaphor accurate? Are there any respects in which the United States is not a lifeboat?
2. Is there a solution to the problem of overpopulation in poor countries that does not involve letting people die from hunger and disease? If so, what is it?
3. Is there any way of avoiding the tragedy of the commons that does not involve private ownership? What is your view?
4. Can the ratchet effect be avoided? How?
5. Should the United States allow more people to immigrate from Mexico and other countries? Why or why not?

# The Terrorist's Tacit Message*

LAURIE CALHOUN

Laurie Calhoun is the author of *Philosophy Unmasked: A Skeptic's Critique* (1997) and many essays on ethics, rhetoric, and war.

Calhoun applies just war theory to terrorism. Terrorism is condemned by the governments of democratic nations, who continue to engage in "just wars." But when the assumptions involved in the "just war" approach to group conflict are examined, it emerges that terrorists merely follow these assumptions to their logical conclusion. They see themselves fighting "just wars," as "warriors for justice." That is their tacit message. Accordingly, unless the stance toward war embraced by most governments of the world transforms radically, terrorism can be expected to continue over time. As groups proliferate, so will conflicts, and some groups will resort to deadly force, reasoning along "just war" lines. Because terrorists are innovative strategists, it is doubtful that measures based upon conventional military operations will effectively counter terrorism.

---

*Source:* Reprinted from *The Peace Review*, vol. 14, no. 1 (2002). Reprinted with permission from Taylor & Francis Ltd.

* Editor's Note: This article was written before 9/11.

The refusal to "negotiate with terrorists" is a common refrain in political parlance. It is often accepted as self-evident that terrorists are so far beyond the pale that it would be morally reprehensible even to engage in discourse with them. But the term "terrorist" remains elusive, defined in various ways by various parties, albeit always derogatorily. Judging from the use of the term by the government officials of disparate nations, it would seem to be analytically true that, whoever the speakers may be, they are not terrorists. "Terrorists" refers exclusively to *them*, a lesser or greater set of political actors, depending ultimately upon the sympathies of the speaker.

Government leaders often speak as though terrorists are beyond the reach of reason, but particular terrorists in particular places believe that they are transmitting to the populace a message with concrete content. The message invariably takes the following general form: *There is something seriously wrong with the world in which we live, and this must be changed.* Terrorists sometimes claim to have as their aim to rouse the populace to consciousness so that they might at last see what the terrorists take themselves to have seen. However, the members of various terrorist groups together transmit (unwittingly) a more global message. The lesson that we ought to glean from terrorists is not the specific, context-dependent message that they hope through their use of violence to convey. Terrorists are right that there is something seriously wrong with the world in which we and they live, but they are no less a party to the problem than are the governments against which they inveigh.

That the annihilation of human life is sometimes morally permissible or even obligatory is embodied in two social practices: the execution of criminals and the maintenance of military institutions. This suggests that there are two distinct ways of understanding terrorists' interpretations of their own actions. Either they are attempting to effect "vigilante justice," or else they are fighting "just wars." Because their victims are typically non-combatants, terrorist actions more closely resemble acts of war than vigilante killings. There are of course killers who do not conceive of their own crimes along these lines, having themselves no political agenda or moral mission. Unfortunately, the tendency of governments to conflate terrorists with ordinary murderers (without political agendas) shrouds the similarity between the violent activities of factional groups and those of formal nations.

Attempts to identify "terrorists" by appeal to what these people do give rise to what some might find to be embarrassing implications. For example, to specify "terrorism" as necessarily *illegal* leads to problems in interpreting the reign of terror imposed by the Third Reich in Nazi Germany and other governmental regimes of ill repute. One might, then, propose a moral rather than a legal basis, for example, by delineating "terrorists" as *ideologically or politically motivated actors who kill or threaten to kill innocent people bearing no responsibility for the grievances of the killers.* This would imply that every nation that has engaged in bombing campaigns resulting in the deaths of innocent children has committed acts of terrorism. Faced with this proposed assimilation of nations and factions that deploy deadly force, most people will simply back away, insisting that, though a precise definition is not possible, certain obvious examples of terrorists can be enumerated, and so "terrorist" can be defined by ostension.

The governments of democratic nations harshly condemn "terrorists," but when the assumptions involved in any view according to which war is sometimes just are carefully examined, it emerges that terrorists merely follow these assumptions to their logical conclusion, given the situations in which they find themselves. While nations prohibit the use of deadly force by individuals and sub-national factions, in fact, violent attacks upon strategic targets can be understood straightforwardly as permitted by "just war" rationales, at least as interpreted by the killers. Small terrorist groups could not, with any chance of success, attack a formal military institution, so instead they select targets for their shock appeal.

While secrecy is often thought to be of the very essence of terrorism, the covert practices of terrorist groups are due in part to their illegality. The members of such groups often hide their identities (or at least their own involvement in particular acts of terrorism), not because they believe that their actions are wrong, but because it would be imprudent to expose themselves. Clearly, if one is subject to arrest for publicly committing an act, then one's efficacy as a soldier for the cause in question will be short-lived. Committing illegal acts in the open renders an actor immediately vulnerable to arrest and incarceration, but it is precisely because factional groups reject the legitimacy of the reigning regime that they undertake secretive initiatives best understood as militarily strategic. "Intelligence agencies" are an important part of modern military institutions, and secrecy has long been regarded as integral to martial excellence. Sun Tzu, author of the ancient Chinese classic *The Art of War*, observed nearly three thousand years ago that "All warfare is based on deception."

It is perhaps often simply terrorists' fervent commitment to their cause that leads them to maximize the efficacy of their campaigns by sheltering themselves from vulnerability to the laws of the land, as any prudent transgressor of the law would do. At the other extreme, suicide missions, in which agents openly act in ways that lead to their personal demise, are undertaken only when such martyrdom appears to be the most effective means of drawing attention to the cause. Far from being beyond rational comprehension, the actions of terrorists are dictated by military strategy deployed in the name of what the actors believe to be justice. The extreme lengths to which terrorists are willing to go, the sacrifices that they will make in their efforts to effect a change in the *status quo*, evidence their ardent commitment to their cause.

The common construal of war as a sometimes "necessary evil" implies that war may be waged when the alternative (not waging war) would be worse. If the military could have achieved its objectives without killing innocent people, then it would have done so. Military spokesmen have often maintained that unintended civilian deaths, even when foreseen, are permissible, provided the situation is sufficiently grave. In the just war tradition, what matters, morally speaking, is whether such "collateral damage" is intended by the actors. Equally integral to defenses of the moral permissibility of collateral damage is the principle of last resort, according to which nonbelligerent means must have been attempted and failed. If war is not a last resort, then collateral damage is avoidable and therefore morally impermissible. Few would deny that, if there exist ways to resolve a conflict without destroying innocent persons in the process, then those methods must, morally speaking, be pursued. But disputes arise, in specific contexts, regarding whether in fact nonbelligerent means to conflict resolution exist. To say that during wartime people *resort* to deadly force is to say that they have a reason, for it is of the very nature of justification to advert to reasons. Defenders of the recourse by nations to deadly force as a means of conflict resolution are willing to condone the killing of innocent people under certain circumstances. The question becomes: When have nonbelligerent means been exhausted?

Perhaps the most important (though seldom acknowledged) problem with just war theory is its inextricable dependence upon the interpretation of the very people considering recourse to deadly force. Human fallibility is a given, so in owning that war is justified in some cases, one must acknowledge that the "facts" upon which a given interpretation is based may prove to be false. And anyone who affirms the right (or obligation) to wage war when *they believe* the tenets of just war theory to be satisfied, must, in consistency, also affirm this right (or obligation) for all those who find themselves in analogous situations. But throughout human history wars have been characterized by their instigators as "just," including those retrospectively denounced as grossly unjust, for example, Hitler's campaign. People tend to ascribe good intentions to their own leaders and comrades while ascribing evil intentions to those stigmatized by officials as "the enemy."

The simplicity of its intuitive principles accounts for the widespread appeal of the "just war" paradigm. Throughout human history appeals to principles of "just cause" and "last resort" have been made by both sides to virtually every violent conflict. "Just war" rationalizations are available to everyone, Hussein as well as Bush, Milosevic as well as Clinton. To take a recent example, we find Timothy McVeigh characterizing the deaths of innocent people in the Oklahoma City bombing as "collateral damage." The public response to McVeigh's "preposterous" appropriation of just war theory suggests how difficult it is for military supporters to admit that they are not so very different from the political killers whose actions they condemn.

The received view is that the intention of planting bombs in public places such as the Federal Building in Oklahoma City or the World Trade Center in New York City is to terrorize, and the people who do such things are terrorists. According to the received view, though some innocent people may have been traumatized and killed during the Vietnam War, the Gulf War, and NATO's 1999 bombing campaign in Kosovo, whatever the intentions behind those actions may have been, they certainly were not to *terrorize* people. Nations excuse as regrettable though unavoidable the deaths of children such as occurred during the Gulf War, the Vietnam War, and in Kosovo during NATO's bombing campaign against the regime of Slobodan Milosevic. "Terrorists" are the people who threaten or deploy deadly force for causes of which we do not approve.

Political organizations have often engaged in actions intended to instill fear in the populace and thus draw attention to their cause. But the groups that engage in what is typically labeled "terrorism" are motivated by grievances no less than are nations engaged in war. Were their grievances somehow alleviated, dissenting political groups would no longer feel the need to engage in what they interpret to be "just wars." In appropriating military rationales and tactics, terrorists underscore the obvious, that nations are conventionally assembled groups of people who appoint their leaders just as do sub-national factions. The problem with the received view is that it exercises maximal interpretive charity when it comes to nations (most often, the interpreter's own), while minimal interpretive charity when it comes to sub-national groups. The intention of a terrorist act, *as understood by the terrorist*, is not the immediate act of terrorism, but to air some grave concern, which the terrorist is attempting to bring to the public's attention. In reality, the requirement of "last resort" seems far simpler to fulfill in the cases of smaller, informal factional groups than in those involving a first-world super power such as the United States, the economic policies of which can, with only minor modifications, spell catastrophe for an offending regime. According to the just war tradition, the permissible use of deadly force is a last resort, deployed only after all pacific means have proven infeasible, and the terrorist most likely reasons along precisely these lines. Indeed, the urgency of the terrorist's situation (to his own mind) makes his own claims regarding last resort all the more compelling. A terrorist, no less than the military spokesmen of established nations, may regret the deaths of the innocent people to which his activities give rise. But, applying the "just war" approach to "collateral damage," terrorists may emerge beyond moral reproach, since were their claims adequately addressed by the powers that be, they would presumably cease their violent activities. It is because they believe that their rights have been denied that groups engage in the activities identified as "terrorism" and thought by most people to be morally distinct from the military actions of states.

Once one grants the possibility of a "just war," it seems to follow straightforwardly that political dissidents convinced of the unjust practices of the government in power ought to engage in violent acts of subversion. Factions lack the advantage of currently enshrined institutions that naturally perpetuate the very *status quo* claimed by dissidents to be unjust. Accordingly, so long as nations continue to wage wars in the name of "justice," it seems plausible that smaller groups and factions will do so as well. Many terrorist groups insist that their claims have been squelched or ignored by the regime in power. But if formal nations may wage war to defend their own integrity and sovereignty, then why not separatist groups? And if such a group lacks a nationally funded and sanctioned army, then must not the group assemble its own?

The terrorist is not a peculiar type of creature who nefariously resorts to deadly force in opposition to the demands of morality upheld by all civilized nations. Rather, the terrorist merely embraces the widely held view that deadly military action is morally permissible, while delimiting "nations" differently than do those who uncritically accept the conventions which they have been raised to believe. The nations in existence are historically contingent, not a part of the very essence of things. The terrorist recognizes that current nations came into being and transformed as a result of warfare. Accordingly, agents who, in the name of justice, wield deadly force against the society in which they live conceive of themselves as civil warriors. Terrorist groups are smaller armies than those of established nations funded by taxpayers and sanctioned by the law, but for this very reason they may feel compelled to avail themselves of particularly drastic methods. No less than the military leaders of most countries throughout history, terrorists maintain that the situations which call for war are so desperate as to require the extremest of measures.

That a terrorist is not *sui generis* can be illustrated as follows: Imagine the commander-in-chief of any established nation being, instead, the leader of a group dissenting from the currently reigning regime. The very same person's acts of deadly violence (or his ordering his comrades to commit such acts) do not differ in his own mind merely because he has been formally designated the commander-in-chief in one case but not in the other. Both parties to every conflict maintain that they are right and their adversaries wrong, and terrorist factions are not exceptional in this respect. When we look carefully at the situation of terrorists, it becomes difficult to identify any morally significant distinction between what they do and what formal nations do in flying planes over enemy nations and dropping bombs, knowing full well that innocent people will die as a result of their actions.

Most advanced nations with standing armies not only produce but also export the types of deadly weapons used by factions in terrorist actions. If we restrict the use of the term "terrorist" to those groups that deploy deadly violence "beyond the pale" of any established legal system, then it follows that terrorists derive their weapons from more formal (and legal) military institutions and industries. The conventional weapons trade has proven all but impossible to control, given the ease with which stockpiled arms are transferred from regime to regime and provided by some countries to smaller groups that they deem to be politically correct. And even when scandals such as Iran-Contra are brought to light, seldom are the culpable agents held more than nominally accountable for their actions. Leniency toward military personnel and political leaders who engage in or facilitate patriotic though illegal weapons commerce results from the basic assumption on the part of most people, that they and their comrades are good, while those who disagree are not.

In some cases, terrorists develop innovative weapons through the use of materials with nonmilitary applications, for example, sulfuric acid or ammonium nitrate. Given the possibility for innovative destruction by terrorist groups, it would seem that even more instrumental to the perpetuation of terrorism than the ongoing exportation of deadly weapons is the support by national leaders of *the idea* that killing human beings can be a mandate of justice. Bombing campaigns serve as graphic illustrations of the approbation by governments of the use of deadly force. It is simple indeed to understand what must be a common refrain among members of dissenting groups who adopt violent means: "If they can do it, then why cannot we?"

Political groups have agendas, and some of these groups deploy violence strategically in attempting to effect their aims. Terrorists are not "beyond the pale," intellectually and morally speaking, for their actions are best understood through appeal to the very just war theory invoked by nations in defending their own military campaigns. Terrorists interpret their own wars as just, while holding culpable all those who benefit from the policies of the government with which they disagree. The groups commonly identified as "terrorists" disagree with governments about not whether there can be a just war, nor whether morality is of such paramount importance as sometimes to require the killing of innocent people. Terrorist groups and the military institutions of nations embrace the very same "just war" schema, disagreeing only about facts.

Thus we find that the terrorist conveys two distinct messages. First, and this is usually the only claim to truth recognized by outsiders, the terrorist alleges injustices within the framework of society. In many cases there may be some truth to the specific charges made by terrorist groups, and this would be enough to turn against them all those who benefit from the regime in power. But a second and more important type of truth is highlighted by the very conduct of the terrorist. Perhaps there is something profoundly misguided about not only some of the specific policies within our societies, but also the manner in which we conceptualize the institutionalized use of deadly force, the activity of war, as an acceptable route to dispute resolution.

The connotations associated with "terrorist" are strongly pejorative and, although terrorists clearly operate from within what they take to be a moral framework, they are often subject to much more powerful condemnation than nonpolitical killers. But murderers who reject the very idea of morality would seem to be worse enemies of society than are political terrorists, who are motivated primarily by moral considerations. Why is it, then, that people fear and loathe terrorists so intensely? Perhaps they recognize, on some level, that terrorists are operating along lines that society in fact implicitly condones and even encourages. Perhaps people see shadows of themselves and their own activities in those of terrorists.

If it is true that terrorists view themselves as warriors for justice, then unless the stance toward war embraced by most governments of the world transforms radically, terrorism should be expected to continue over time. To the extent to which groups proliferate, conflicts will as well, and some subset of the parties to conflict will resort to deadly force, buoyed by what they, along with most of the populace, take to be the respectability of "just war." Military solutions are no longer used even by stable nations merely as "last resorts." Tragically, the ready availability of deadly weapons and the widespread assumption that the use of such weapons is often morally acceptable, if not obligatory, has brought about a world in which leaders often think first, not last, of military solutions to conflict. This readiness to deploy deadly means has arguably contributed to the escalation of violence in the contemporary world on many different levels, the most frightening of which being to many people those involving the unpredictable actions of factional groups, "the terrorists." But the leaders of established nations delude themselves in thinking that they will quell terrorism through threats and weapons proliferation. Terrorists "innovate" by re-defining what are commonly thought of as non-military targets as military. There is no reason for believing that terrorists' capacity for innovation will be frustrated by the construction of an anti-ballistic missile system or the implementation of other initiatives premised upon conventional military practices and strategies.

## RECOMMENDED READINGS

Arendt, Hannah. 1979. *The Origins of Totalitarianism.* New York: Harcourt Brace.

Calhoun, Laurie. 2002. "How Violence Breeds Violence: Some Utilitarian Considerations," *Politics*, vol. 22, no. 2, pp. 95–108.

Calhoun, Laurie. 2001. "Killing, Letting Die, and the Alleged Necessity of Military Intervention," *Peace and Conflict Studies*, vol. 8, no. 2, pp. 5–22.

Calhoun, Laurie. 2001. "The Metaethical Paradox of Just War Theory," *Ethical Theory and Moral Practice*, vol. 4, no. 1, pp. 41–58.

Calhoun, Laurie. 2002. "The Phenomenology of Paid Killing," *International Journal of Human Rights*, vol. 6, no. 1, pp. 1–18.

Calhoun, Laurie. 2001. "Violence and Hypocrisy," and "Laurie Calhoun replies [to Michael Walzer]," *Dissent*, (winter) vol. 48, no. 1, pp. 79–87. Reprinted in *Just War: A Casebook in Argumentation*, eds. Walsh & Asch, Heinle/Thomson, 2004.

Cerovic, Stanko. 2001. *Dans les griffes des humanistes*, trans. Mireille Robin. Paris: Éditions Climats.

Colson, Bruno. 1999. *L'art de la guerre de Machiavel à Clausewitz*. Namur: Bibliothèque Universitaire Moretus Plantin.

Cooper, H. H. A. 2001. "Terrorism: The Problem of Definition Revisited," *American Behavioral Scientist*, vol. 44, no. 6, pp. 881–893.

Gibbs, Jack P. 1989. "Conceptualization of Terrorism," *American Sociological Review*, vol. 54, no. 3, pp. 329–340.

Grossman, Lt. Colonel Dave. 1995. *On Killing: The Psychological Cost of Learning to Kill in War and Society*. Boston: Little Brown.

Harman, Gilbert. 2000. *Explaining Value*. Oxford: Oxford University Press.

Harman, Gilbert. 1977. *The Nature of Morality*. New York: Oxford University Press.

Holmes, Robert L. 1989. *On War and Morality*. Princeton: Princeton University Press.

Le Borgne, Claude. 1986. *La Guerre est Morte . . . mais on ne le sait pas encore*. Paris: Bernard Grasset.

Rapoport, David C. 1984. "Fear and Trembling: Terrorism in Three Religious Traditions," *The American Political Science Review*, vol. 78, no. 3, pp.

## REVIEW QUESTIONS

1. According to Calhoun, what is the concrete message of terrorists? What is the more global message, the "tacit message"?
2. What problems does Calhoun see with the legal and moral definitions of the term *terrorists*?
3. How do terrorists view their actions, according to Calhoun?
4. How do military justify "collateral damage," or the killing of innocent people, according to Calhoun?
5. What role does interpretation play in just war theory, in Calhoun's view? Why does she think that "just war" rationalizations are available to everyone, from Hussein to Bush?
6. According to Calhoun, what is the intention of the terrorist act, as understood by the terrorist?
7. Why does Calhoun believe that terrorism is best understood by appealing to the very just war theory invoked by nations defending their wars?

## DISCUSSION QUESTIONS

1. Calhoun argues that anyone can rationalize war or terrorism by appealing to just war theory. Is this true? Why or why not?
2. Calhoun says, "Terrorists are people who threaten or deploy deadly force for causes of which we do not approve." Do you agree? Why or why not?
3. Calhoun claims that there is hardly any moral difference between what the terrorists do and what nations such as the United States do when they drop bombs on enemy nations knowing full well that innocent people will die. Do you agree? Why or why not?

# What Is Wrong with Terrorism?

THOMAS NAGEL

Thomas Nagel is university professor, professor of law, and professor of philosophy at New York University. He is the author of *The Possibility of Altruism* (1970), *Mortal Questions* (1979), *The View from Nowhere* (1986), *What Does It All Mean* (1987), *Equality and Partiality* (1991), *Other Minds* (1995), *The Last Word* (1997), *The Myth of Ownership: Taxes and Justice* (with Liam Murphy, 2002), and *Concealment and Exposure* (2002).

To explain what is wrong with terrorism, Nagel makes a distinction between means and ends. It is not the ends or goals of the terrorist that make terrorism wrong, but the means used, namely the deliberate killing of harmless persons. This violates the basic moral principle that aiming at the death of a harmless person is morally wrong. In his view, killing in self-defense does not violate this moral prohibition. Also, killing harmless persons in warfare is morally allowed as long this occurs as an unintended side effect of an attack on a legitimate military target.

People all over the world react with visceral horror to attacks on civilians by Al Qaeda, by Palestinian suicide bombers, by Basque or Chechen separatists, or by IRA militants. As there now seems to be a pause in the spate of suicide bombings and other terrorist acts—if only momentary—perhaps now is a moment to grapple with a fundamental question: What makes *terrorist* killings any more worthy of condemnation than other forms of murder?

The special opprobrium associated with the word "terrorism" must be understood as a condemnation of means, not ends. Of course, those who condemn terrorist attacks on civilians often also reject the ends that the attackers are trying to achieve. They think that a separate Basque state, or the withdrawal of US forces from the Middle East, for example, are not aims that anyone should be pursuing, let alone by violent means.

But the condemnation does not depend on rejecting the aims of the terrorists. The reaction to the attacks of September 11, 2001 on New York and Washington and their like underscores that such means are outrageous whatever the end; they should not be used to achieve even a good end—indeed, even if there is no other way to achieve it. The normal balancing of costs against benefits is not allowable here.

This claim is not as simple as it appears because it does not depend on a general moral principle forbidding all killing of non-combatants. Similarly, those who condemn terrorism as beyond the pale are usually not pacifists. They believe not only that it is all right to kill soldiers and bomb munitions depots in times of war, but that inflicting "collateral damage" on non-combatants is sometimes unavoidable—and morally permissible.

But if that is permissible, why is it wrong to aim *directly* at non-combatants if killing them will have a good chance of inducing the enemy to cease hostilities, withdraw from occupied territory, or grant independence? Dying is bad, however one is killed. So why should a civilian death be acceptable if it occurs as a side effect of combat that serves a worthy end, whereas a civilian death that is inflicted deliberately as a means to the *same* end is a terrorist outrage?

The distinction is not universally accepted—certainly not by the major belligerents in World

*Source:* What's Wrong with Terrorism by Thomas Nagel from Project-Syndicate.org, 2002.

War II. Hiroshima is the most famous example of terror bombing, but the Germans, the Japanese, and the British as well as the Americans deliberately slaughtered civilian non-combatants in large numbers. Today, however, terrorism inspires widespread revulsion, which in turn helps to justify military action against it. So it is essential that the reason for that revulsion become better understood.

The core moral idea is a prohibition against *aiming* at the death of a harmless person. Everyone is presumed to be inviolable in this way until he himself becomes a danger to others; so we are permitted to kill in self-defense, and to attack enemy combatants in war. But this is an exception to a general and strict requirement of respect for human life. So long as we are not doing any harm, no one may kill us just because it would be useful to do so. This minimal basic respect is owed to *every* individual, and it may not be violated even to achieve valuable long-term goals.

However, there are some activities, including legitimate self-defense or warfare, that create an unavoidable risk of harm to innocent parties. This is true not only of violent military or police actions but also of peaceful projects like major construction in densely populated cities. In those cases, if the aim is important enough, the activity is not morally prohibited provided due care is taken to minimize the risk of harm to innocent parties, consistent with the achievement of the aim.

The moral point is that we are obliged to do our best to avoid or minimize civilian casualties in warfare, even if we know that we cannot avoid them completely. Those deaths do not violate the strictest protection of human life—that we may not *aim* to kill a harmless person. On the contrary, our aim is if possible to avoid such collateral deaths.

Of course, the victim ends up dead whether killed deliberately by a terrorist or regrettably as the side effect of an attack on a legitimate military target. But in our sense of what we are owed morally by our fellow human beings, there is a huge difference between these two acts, and the attitudes they express toward human life.

So long as it remains an effective means for weak parties to exert pressure on their more powerful enemies, terrorism cannot be expected to disappear. But we should hope nonetheless that the recognition of its special form of contempt for humanity will spread, rather than being lost as a result of its recent successes.

## REVIEW QUESTIONS

1. What is it about terrorist killing that makes it worse than other forms of murder, according to Nagel?
2. What exactly makes terrorism wrong in Nagel's view?

## DISCUSSION QUESTIONS

1. Is terrorism always wrong? What if it produces a good result such as the elimination of apartheid in South Africa or the overthrow of an oppressive government?
2. Nagel says that the atomic bombing of Hiroshima is an example of morally prohibited "terror bombing" rather than an attack on a legitimate military target. Do you agree? Why or why not?
3. Nagel thinks there is a "huge difference" between being deliberately killed by a terrorist and being killed as the side effect of an attack on a military target. But in both cases a harmless person is killed. Is there really such a huge difference? What is your view?

# The War on Terrorism and the End of Human Rights

DAVID LUBAN

David Luban is the Frederick J. Hass Professor of Law and Philosophy at the Georgetown University Law Center. He is the author of *Lawyers and Justice* (1988), *Legal Modernism* (1994), *Legal Ethics and Human Dignity* (2007), and numerous journal articles and book chapters.

Luban argues that the current War on Terrorism combines a war model with a law model to produce a new model of state action, a hybrid war-law model. This hybrid model selectively picks out elements of the war and law models to maximize the use of lethal force while eliminating the rights of both adversaries and innocent bystanders. The result is that the War on Terrorism means the end of human rights.

In the immediate aftermath of September 11, President Bush stated that the perpetrators of the deed would be brought to justice. Soon afterwards, the President announced that the United States would engage in a war on terrorism. The first of these statements adopts the familiar language of criminal law and criminal justice. It treats the September 11 attacks as horrific crimes—mass murders—and the government's mission as apprehending and punishing the surviving planners and conspirators for their roles in the crimes. The War on Terrorism is a different proposition, however, and a different model of governmental action—not law but war. Most obviously, it dramatically broadens the scope of action, because now terrorists who knew nothing about September 11 have been earmarked as enemies. But that is only the beginning.

## THE HYBRID WAR-LAW APPROACH

The model of war offers much freer rein than that of law, and therein lies its appeal in the wake of 9/11. First, in war but not in law it is permissible to use lethal force on enemy troops regardless of their degree of personal involvement with the adversary. The conscripted cook is as legitimate a target as the enemy general. Second, in war but not in law "collateral damage," that is, foreseen but unintended killing of noncombatants, is permissible. (Police cannot blow up an apartment building full of people because a murderer is inside, but an air force can bomb the building if it contains a military target.) Third, the requirements of evidence and proof are drastically weaker in war than in criminal justice. Soldiers do not need proof beyond a reasonable doubt, or even proof by a preponderance of evidence, that someone is an enemy soldier before firing on him or capturing and imprisoning him. They don't need proof at all, merely plausible intelligence. Thus, the U.S. military remains regretful but unapologetic about its January 2002 attack on the Afghani town of Uruzgan, in which 21 innocent civilians were killed, based on faulty intelligence that they were al Qaeda fighters. Fourth, in war one can attack an enemy without concern over whether he has done anything. Legitimate targets are those who in the course of combat *might* harm us, not those who *have* harmed us. No doubt there are other significant differences as well. But the basic point should be clear: Given Washington's mandate to eliminate the danger of future 9/11s, so far as humanly possible, the model of war offers important advantages over the model of law.

There are disadvantages as well. Most obviously, in war but not in law, fighting back is a *legitimate* response of the enemy. Second, when nations fight a war, other nations may opt for neutrality. Third, because fighting back is legitimate, in war the enemy soldier deserves special regard once he is rendered harmless through injury or surrender. It is impermissible to punish him for his role in fighting the war. Nor can he be harshly interrogated after he is captured. The Third Geneva Convention provides: "Prisoners of war who refuse to answer [questions] may not be threatened, insulted, or exposed to unpleasant or disadvantageous treatment of any kind." And, when the war concludes, the enemy soldier must be repatriated.

Here, however, Washington has different ideas, designed to eliminate these tactical disadvantages in the traditional war model. Washington regards international terrorism not only as a military adversary, but also as a criminal activity and criminal conspiracy. In the law model, criminals don't get to shoot back, and their acts of violence subject them to legitimate punishment. That is what we see in Washington's prosecution of the War on Terrorism. Captured terrorists may be tried before military or civilian tribunals, and shooting back at Americans, including American troops, is a federal crime (for a statute under which John Walker Lindh was indicted criminalizes anyone regardless of nationality, who "outside the United States attempts to kill, or engages in a conspiracy to kill, a national of the United States" or "engages in physical violence with intent to cause serious bodily injury to a national of the United States; or with the result that serious bodily injury is caused to a national of the United States"). Furthermore, the U.S. may rightly demand that other countries not be neutral about murder and terrorism. Unlike the war model, a nation may insist that those who are not with us in fighting murder and terror are against us, because by not joining our operations they are providing a safe haven for terrorists or their bank accounts. By selectively combining elements of the war model and elements of the law model, Washington is able to maximize its own ability to mobilize lethal force against terrorists while eliminating most traditional rights of a military adversary, as well as the rights of innocent bystanders caught in the crossfire.

## A LIMBO OF RIGHTLESSNESS

The legal status of al Qaeda suspects imprisoned at the Guantanamo Bay Naval Base in Cuba is emblematic of this hybrid war-law approach to the threat of terrorism. In line with the war model, they lack the usual rights of criminal suspects—the presumption of innocence, the right to a hearing to determine guilt, the opportunity to prove that the authorities have grabbed the wrong man. But, in line with the law model, they are considered *unlawful* combatants. Because they are not uniformed forces, they lack the rights of prisoners of war and are liable to criminal punishment. Initially, the American government declared that the Guantanamo Bay prisoners have no rights under the Geneva Conventions. In the face of international protests, Washington quickly backpedaled and announced that the Guantanamo Bay prisoners would indeed be treated as decently as POWs—but it also made clear that the prisoners have no right to such treatment. Neither criminal suspects nor POWs, neither fish nor fowl, they inhabit a limbo of rightlessness. Secretary of Defense Rumsfeld's assertion that the U.S. may continue to detain them even if they are acquitted by a military tribunal dramatizes the point.

To understand how extraordinary their status is, consider an analogy. Suppose that Washington declares a War on Organized Crime. Troops are dispatched to Sicily, and a number of Mafiosi are seized, brought to Guantanamo Bay, and imprisoned without a hearing for the indefinite future, maybe the rest of their lives. They are accused of no crimes, because their capture is based not on what they have done but on what they might do. After all, to become "made" they took oaths of obedience to the bad guys. Seizing them accords with the war model: they are enemy foot soldiers. But they are foot soldiers out of uniform; they lack a "fixed distinctive emblem," in the words of The Hague Convention. That makes them unlawful combatants, so they lack the rights of POWs. They may object that it is only a unilateral declaration by the American President that has turned them into combatants in the first place—he called it a war, they didn't—and that, since they do not regard themselves as literal foot soldiers it never occurred to them to wear a fixed distinctive emblem. They have a point. It seems too easy for the President to divest anyone in the world of rights and liberty simply by announcing that the U.S. is at war with them and then declaring them unlawful combatants if they resist. But, in the hybrid war-law model, they protest in vain.

Consider another example. In January 2002, U.S. forces in Bosnia seized five Algerians and a Yemeni suspected of al Qaeda connections and took them to Guantanamo Bay. The six had been jailed in Bosnia, but a Bosnian court released them for lack of evidence, and the Bosnian Human Rights Chamber issued an injunction that four of them be allowed to remain in the country pending further legal proceedings. The Human Rights Chamber, ironically, was created under U.S. auspices in the Dayton peace accords, and it was designed specifically to protect against treatment like this. Ruth Wedgwood, a well-known international law scholar at Yale and a member of the Council on Foreign Relations, defended the Bosnian seizure in war-model terms. "I think we would simply argue this was a matter of self-defense. One of the fundamental rules of military law is that you have a right ultimately to act in self-defense. And if these folks were actively plotting to blow up the U.S. embassy, they should be considered combatants and captured as combatants in a war." Notice that Professor Wedgwood argues in terms of what the men seized in Bosnia were *planning to do*, not what they *did*; notice as well that the decision of the Bosnian court that there was insufficient evidence does not matter. These are characteristics of the war model.

More recently, two American citizens alleged to be al Qaeda operatives (Jose Padilla, a.k.a. Abdullah al Muhajir, and Yasser Esam Hamdi) have been held in American military prisons, with no crimes charged, no opportunity to consult counsel, and no hearing. The President described Padilla as "a bad man" who aimed to build a nuclear "dirty" bomb and use it against America; and the Justice Department has classified both men as "enemy combatants" who may be held indefinitely. Yet, as military law expert Gary Solis points out, "Until now, as used by the attorney general, the term 'enemy combatant' appeared nowhere in U.S. criminal law, international law or in the law of war." The phrase comes from the 1942 Supreme Court case *Ex parte Quirin*, but all the Court says there is that "an enemy combatant who without uniform comes secretly through the lines for the purpose of waging war by destruction of life or property" would "not . . . be entitled to the status of prisoner of war, but . . . [they would] be offenders against the law of war subject to trial and punishment by military tribunals." For the Court, in other words, the status of a person as a non-uniformed enemy combatant makes him a criminal rather than a warrior, and determines *where* he is tried (in a military, rather than a civilian, tribunal) but not *whether* he is tried. Far from authorizing open-ended confinement, *Ex parte Quirin* presupposes that criminals are entitled to hearings: without a hearing how can suspects prove that the government made a mistake? *Quirin* embeds the concept of "enemy combatant" firmly in the law model. In the war model, by contrast, POWs may be detained without a hearing until hostilities are over. But POWs were captured in uniform, and only their undoubted identity as enemy soldiers justifies such openended custody. Apparently, Hamdi and Padilla will get the worst of both models—open-ended custody with no trial, like POWs, but no certainty beyond the U.S. government's say-so that they really are "bad men." This is the hybrid war-law model. It combines the *Quirin* category of "enemy combatant without uniform," used in the law model to justify a military trial, with the war model's practice of indefinite confinement with no trial at all.

## THE CASE FOR THE HYBRID APPROACH

Is there any justification for the hybrid war-law model, which so drastically diminishes the rights of the enemy? An argument can be offered along the following lines. In ordinary cases of war among states, enemy soldiers may well be morally and politically innocent. Many of them are conscripts, and those who aren't do not necessarily endorse the state policies they are fighting to defend. But enemy soldiers in the War on Terrorism are, by definition, those who have embarked on a path of terrorism. They are neither morally nor politically innocent. Their sworn aim—"Death to America!"—is to create more 9/11s. In this respect, they are much more akin to criminal conspirators than to conscript soldiers. Terrorists will fight as soldiers when they must, and metamorphose into mass murderers when they can.

Furthermore, suicide terrorists pose a special, unique danger. Ordinary criminals do not target innocent bystanders. They may be willing to kill them if necessary, but bystanders enjoy at least some measure of security because they are not primary targets. Not so with terrorists, who aim to kill as many innocent people as possible. Likewise, innocent bystanders are protected from ordinary criminals by whatever deterrent force the threat of punishment and the risk of getting killed in the act of committing a crime offer. For a suicide bomber, neither of these threats is a deterrent at all—after all, for the suicide bomber one of the hallmarks of a *successful* operation is that he winds up dead at day's end. Given the unique and heightened danger that suicide terrorists pose, a stronger response that grants potential terrorists fewer rights may be justified. Add to this the danger that terrorists may come to possess weapons of mass destruction, including nuclear devices in suitcases. Under circumstances of such dire menace, it is appropriate to treat terrorists as though they embody the most dangerous aspects of both warriors and criminals. That is the basis of the hybrid war-law model.

## THE CASE AGAINST EXPEDIENCY

The argument against the hybrid war-law model is equally clear. The U.S. has simply chosen the bits of the law model and the bits of the war model that are most convenient for American interests, and ignored the rest. The model abolishes the rights of potential enemies (and their innocent shields) by fiat—not for reasons of moral or legal principle, but solely because the U.S. does not want them to have rights. The more rights they have, the more risk they pose. But Americans' urgent desire to minimize our risks doesn't make other people's rights disappear. Calling our policy a War on Terrorism obscures this point.

The theoretical basis of the objection is that the law model and the war model each comes as a package, with a kind of intellectual integrity. The law model grows out of relationships within states, while the war model arises from relationships between states. The law model imputes a ground-level community of values to those subject to the law—paradigmatically, citizens of a state, but also visitors and foreigners who choose to engage in conduct that affects a state. Only because law imputes shared basic values to the community can a state condemn the conduct of criminals and inflict punishment on them. Criminals deserve condemnation and punishment because their conduct violates norms that we are entitled to count on their sharing. But, for the same reason—the imputed community of values—those subject to the law ordinarily enjoy a presumption of innocence and an expectation of safety. The government cannot simply grab them and confine them without making sure they have broken the law, nor can it condemn them without due process for ensuring that it has the right person, nor can it knowingly place bystanders in mortal peril in the course of fighting crime. They are our fellows, and the community should protect them just as it protects us. The same imputed community of values that justifies condemnation and punishment creates rights to due care and due process.

War is different. War is the ultimate acknowledgment that human beings do not live in a single community with shared norms. If their norms conflict enough, communities pose a physical danger to each other, and nothing can safeguard a community against its enemies except force of arms. That makes enemy soldiers legitimate targets; but it makes our soldiers legitimate targets as well, and, once the enemy no longer poses a danger, he should be immune from punishment, because if he has fought cleanly he has violated no norms that we are entitled to presume he honors. Our norms are, after all, our norms, not his.

Because the law model and war model come as conceptual packages, it is unprincipled to wrench them apart and recombine them simply because it is in America's interest to do so. To declare that Americans can fight enemies with the latitude of warriors, but if the enemies fight back they are not warriors but criminals, amounts to a kind of heads-I-win-tails-you-lose international morality in which whatever it takes to reduce American risk, no matter what the cost to others, turns out to be justified. This, in brief, is the criticism of the hybrid war-law model.

To be sure, the law model could be made to incorporate the war model merely by rewriting a handful of statutes. Congress could enact laws permitting imprisonment or execution of persons who pose a significant threat of terrorism whether or not they have already done anything wrong. The standard of evidence could be set low and the requirement of a hearing eliminated. Finally, Congress could authorize the use of lethal force against terrorists regardless of the danger to innocent bystanders, and it could immunize officials from lawsuits or prosecution by victims of collateral damage. Such statutes would violate the Constitution, but the Constitution could be amended to incorporate antiterrorist exceptions to the Fourth, Fifth, and Sixth Amendments. In the end, we would have a system of law that includes all the essential features of the war model.

It would, however, be a system that imprisons people for their intentions rather than their actions, and that offers the innocent few protections against mistaken detention or inadvertent death through collateral damage. Gone are the principles that people should never be punished for their thoughts, only for their deeds, and that innocent people must be protected rather than injured by their own government. In that sense, at any rate, repackaging war as law seems merely cosmetic, because it replaces the ideal of law as a protector of rights with the more problematic goal of protecting some innocent people by sacrificing others. The hypothetical legislation incorporates war into law only by making law as partisan and ruthless as war. It no longer resembles law as Americans generally understand it.

## THE THREAT TO INTERNATIONAL HUMAN RIGHTS

In the War on Terrorism, what becomes of international human rights? It seems beyond dispute that the war model poses a threat to international human rights, because honoring human rights is neither practically possible nor theoretically required during war. Combatants are legitimate targets; noncombatants maimed by accident or mistake are regarded as collateral damage rather than victims of atrocities; cases of mistaken identity get killed or confined without a hearing because combat conditions preclude due process. To be sure, the laws of war specify minimum human rights, but these are far less robust than rights in peacetime—and the hybrid war-law model reduces this schedule of rights even further by classifying the enemy as unlawful combatants.

One striking example of the erosion of human rights is tolerance of torture. It should be recalled that a 1995 al Qaeda plot to bomb eleven U.S. airliners was thwarted by information tortured out of a Pakistani suspect by the Philippine police—an eerie real-life version of the familiar philosophical thought-experiment. The *Washington Post* reports that since September 11 the U.S. has engaged in the summary transfer of dozens of terrorism suspects to countries where they will be interrogated under torture. But it isn't just the

United States that has proven willing to tolerate torture for security reasons. Last December, the Swedish government snatched a suspected Islamic extremist to whom it had previously granted political asylum, and the same day had him transferred to Egypt, where Amnesty International reports that he has been tortured to the point where he walks only with difficulty. Sweden is not, to say the least, a traditionally hard-line nation on human rights issues. None of this international transportation is lawful—indeed, it violates international treaty obligations under the Convention against Torture that in the U.S. have constitutional status as "supreme Law of the Land"—but that may not matter under the war model, in which even constitutional rights may be abrogated.

It is natural to suggest that this suspension of human rights is an exceptional emergency measure to deal with an unprecedented threat. This raises the question of how long human rights will remain suspended. When will the war be over?

Here, the chief problem is that the War on Terrorism is not like any other kind of war. The enemy, Terrorism, is not a territorial state or nation or government. There is no opposite number to negotiate with. There is no one on the other side to call a truce or declare a ceasefire, no one among the enemy authorized to surrender. In traditional wars among states, the war aim is, as Clausewitz argued, to impose one state's political will on another's. The *aim* of the war is not to kill the enemy—killing the enemy is the *means* used to achieve the real end, which is to force capitulation. In the War on Terrorism, no capitulation is possible. That means that the real aim of the war is, quite simply, to kill or capture all of the terrorists—to keep on killing and killing, capturing and capturing, until they are all gone.

Of course, no one expects that terrorism will ever disappear completely. Everyone understands that new anti-American extremists, new terrorists, will always arise and always be available for recruitment and deployment. Everyone understands that even if al Qaeda is destroyed or decapitated, other groups, with other leaders, will arise in its place. It follows, then, that the War on Terrorism will be a war that can only be abandoned, never concluded. The War has no natural resting point, no moment of victory or finality. It requires a mission of killing and capturing, in territories all over the globe, that will go on in perpetuity. It follows as well that the suspension of human rights implicit in the hybrid war-law model is not temporary but permanent.

Perhaps with this fear in mind, Congressional authorization of President Bush's military campaign limits its scope to those responsible for September 11 and their sponsors. But the War on Terrorism has taken on a life of its own that makes the Congressional authorization little more than a technicality. Because of the threat of nuclear terror, the American leadership actively debates a war on Iraq regardless of whether Iraq was implicated in September 11; and the President's yoking of Iraq, Iran, and North Korea into a single axis of evil because they back terror suggests that the War on Terrorism might eventually encompass all these nations. If the U.S. ever unearths tangible evidence that any of these countries is harboring or abetting terrorists with weapons of mass destruction, there can be little doubt that Congress will support military action. So too, Russia invokes the American War on Terrorism to justify its attacks on Chechen rebels, China uses it to deflect criticisms of its campaign against Uighur separatists, and Israeli Prime Minister Sharon explicitly links military actions against Palestinian insurgents to the American War on Terrorism. No doubt there is political opportunism at work in some or all of these efforts to piggy-back onto America's campaign, but the opportunity would not exist if "War on Terrorism" were merely the codename of a discrete, neatly-boxed American operation. Instead, the War on Terrorism has become a model of politics, a world-view with its own distinctive premises and consequences. As I have argued, it includes a new model of state action, the hybrid war-law model, which depresses human rights from their peace-time standard to the war-time standard, and indeed even further. So long as it continues, the War on Terrorism means the end of human rights, at least for those near enough to be touched by the fire of battle.

---

Sources: On the January 2002 attack on the Afghani town of Uruzgan, see: John Ward Anderson, "Afghans Falsely Held by U.S. Tried to Explain; Fighters Recount Unanswered Pleas, Beatings—and an Apology on Their Release," *Washington Post* (March 26, 2002); see also Susan B. Glasser, "Afghans Live and Die With U.S. Mistakes; Villagers Tell of Over 100 Casualties," *Washington Post* (Feb. 20, 2002). On the Third Geneva Convention, see: Geneva Convention (III) Relative to the Treatment of Prisoners of War, 6 U.S.T. 3317, signed on August 12, 1949, at Geneva, Article 17. Although the U.S. has not ratified the Geneva Convention, it has become part of customary international law, and certainly belongs to the war model. Count One of the Lindh indictment charges him with violating 18 U.S.C. 2332(b), "Whoever outside the United States attempts to kill, or engages in a conspiracy to kill, a national of the United States" may be sentenced to 20 years (for attempts) or life imprisonment (for conspiracies). Subsection (c) likewise criminalizes "engag[ing] in physical violence with intent to cause serious bodily injury to a national of the United States; or with the result that serious bodily injury is caused to a national of the United States." Lawful combatants are defined in the Hague Convention (IV) Respecting the Laws and Customs of War on Land, Annex to the Convention, 1 Bevans 631, signed on October 18, 1907, at The Hague, Article 1. The definition requires that combatants "have a fixed distinctive emblem recognizable at a distance." Protocol I Additional to the Geneva Conventions of 1949, 1125 U.N.T.S. 3, adopted on June 8, 1977, at Geneva, Article 44(3) makes an important change in the Hague Convention, expanding the definition of combatants to include non-uniformed irregulars. However, the United States has not agreed to Protocol I. The source of Ruth Wedgwood's remarks: Interview with Melissa Block, National Public Radio program, "All Things Considered" (January 18, 2002); Gary Solis, "Even a 'Bad Man' Has Rights," *Washington Post* (June 25, 2002); *Ex parte Quirin*, 317 U.S. 1, 31 (1942). On the torture of the Pakistani militant by Philippine police: Doug Struck et al., "Borderless Network of Terror; Bin Laden Followers Reach Across Globe," *Washington Post* (September 23, 2001): "'For weeks, agents hit him with a chair and a long piece of wood, forced water into his mouth, and crushed lighted cigarettes into his private parts,' wrote journalists Marites Vitug and Glenda Gloria in 'Under the Crescent Moon,' an acclaimed book on Abu Sayyaf. 'His ribs were almost totally broken and his captors were surprised he survived.'" On U.S. and Swedish transfers of Isamic militants to countries employing torture: Rajiv Chandrasakaran and Peter Finn, "U.S. Behind Secret Transfer of Terror Suspects," *Washington Post* (March 11, 2002); Peter Finn, "Europeans Tossing Terror Suspects Out the Door," *Washington Post* (January 29, 2002); Anthony Shadid, "Fighting Terror/Atmosphere in Europe, Military Campaign/Asylum Bids; in Shift, Sweden Extradites Militants to Egypt," *Boston Globe* (December 31, 2001). Article 3(1) of the Convention against Torture provides that "No State Party shall expel, return ('*refouler*') or extradite a person to another State where there are substantial grounds for believing that he would be in danger of being subjected to torture." Article 2(2) cautions that "No exceptional circumstances whatsoever, whether a state of war or a threat of war, internal political instability or any other public emergency, may be invoked as a justification of torture." But no parallel caution is incorporated into Article 3(1)'s non-*refoulement* rule, and a lawyer might well argue that its absence implies that the rule may be abrogated during war or similar public emergency. *Convention against Torture and Other Cruel, Inhuman or Degrading Treatment or Punishment*, 1465 U.N.T.S. 85. Ratified by the United States, Oct. 2, 1994. Entered into force for the United States, Nov. 20, 1994. (Article VI of the U.S. Constitution provides that treaties are the "supreme Law of the Land.")

## REVIEW QUESTIONS

1. According to Luban, what is the traditional model of war? What are its four main features? What are its disadvantages?
2. How does Luban describe the law model? How is it combined with the war model to produce a hybrid war-law approach to terrorism?
3. In Luban's view, what is the legal status of al-Qaeda suspects? Do they have any rights?
4. Describe the case of the al-Qaeda suspects seized in Bosnia.
5. How does Luban explain the concept of enemy combatant? How is this concept applied to Jose Padilla and Yasser Esam Harudi?
6. According to Luban, what is the case for the hybrid war-law model? What is the case against it?
7. In Luban's view, what becomes of human rights in the War on Terrorism?

## DISCUSSION QUESTIONS

1. In January 2002, the U.S. military killed twenty-one innocent civilians in an attack on the Afghani town of Uruzgan. Was this attack justified? Why or why not?
2. Should the Guantánamo prisoners have rights? If so, what are they? If not, why not?
3. Is it acceptable to confine suspected terrorists indefinitely with no trial?
4. Is the hybrid war-law model of the War on Terrorism acceptable? Why or why not?
5. Should torture be used to fight terrorism? Why or why not?